S0-BAM-201

EDUCATING
THE
DISADVANTAGED

EDUCATING
THE
DISADVANTAGED

1971-1972

AN AMS ANTHOLOGY

edited, with an Introduction, by

Erwin Flaxman
Associate Director
The ERIC Retrieval Center on the Disadvantaged
Columbia University

AMS Press, Inc.
New York

371.96
E23
v. 4

149880

Copyright © 1973 AMS Press, Inc.

All rights reserved. Published in the United States by AMS Press, Inc., 56 East 13th Street, New York, New York 10003.

Library of Congress Catalogue Number: 73-9242

International Standard Book Number:

Buckram-bound   0-404-10104-6
Paperbound   0-404-10156-9

Manufactured in the United States of America.

TABLE OF CONTENTS

IV. SCHOOL DESEGREGATION, ACADEMIC ACHIEVEMENT, AND RACIAL ATTITUDES

ACKNOWLEDGEMENTS

Acknowledgement is made to the authors and publishers below who have granted permission to reprint material and who reserve all rights in the articles appearing in this anthology.

Armor, David J., "The Evidence on Busing," *The Public Interest*, No. 28, Summer, 1972, pp. 90-126. Copyright 1972 National Affairs, Inc.

Backman, Margaret E. "Patterns of Mental Abilities," *American Educational Research Journal*, Volume 9, No. 1, pp. 1-12.

Bane, Mary Jo and Chirstopher Jencks, "The Schools and Equal Opportunity," *Saturday Review of Education*, Volume 55, No. 38, October, 1972, pp. 37-42. Copyright 1972 Saturday Review Company.

Birch, Herbert. "Malnutrition, Learning, and Intelligence," *American Journal of Public Health*, Volume 62, No. 6, June, 1972, pp. 773-784.

Chesler, Mark A. "Teacher Training Designs for Improving Instruction in Interracial Classrooms," *Journal of Applied Behavioral Science*, Volume 7, No. 5, pp. 612-641.

Cole, Michael, and Jerome S. Bruner, "Cultural Differences and Inferences about Psychological Processes, *American Psychologist*, Volume 26, No. 10, October, 1971, pp. 867-876.

Ervin-Tripp, Susan, "Children's Sociolinguistic Competence and Dialect Diversity," *Early Childhood Education*, Part II. Chicago: The National Society for the Study of Education, 1972, pp. 123-160.

Goldberg, Gertrude, "Deschooling and the Disadvantaged," *IRCD Bulletin*, Volume 7, No. 5, pp. 2-10.

Guttentag, Marcia, "Children in Harlem's Community-Controlled Schools," *Journal of Social Issues*, Volume 28, No. 4, Fall, 1972, pp. 1-20.

Karabel, Jerome, "Community Colleges and Social Stratification," *Harvard Educational Review*, Volume 42, No. 4, November, 1972, pp. 521-562. Copyright 1972 President and Fellows of Harvard College.

Kurokawa, Minako, "Mutual Perceptions of Racial Images," *Journal of Social Issues*, Volume 27, No. 4, pp. 213-235.

Mills, Nicolaus, "Free Versus Directed Schools," *IRCD Bulletin*, Volume 7, No. 4, pp. 2-10.

Owen, John D., "The Distribution of Educational Resources in Large American Cities," *Journal of Human Resources*, Volume 7, No. 1, pp. 26-38.

Pettigrew, Thomas F., Elizabeth L. Useem, Clarence Normand, and Marshall S. Smith., "Busing," *The Public Interest*, No. 30, Winter, 1973, pp. 88-118. Copyright 1973 National Affairs, Inc.

Rist, Ray C., "Social Distance and Social Inequality in a Ghetto Kindergarten Classroom," *Urban Education*, Volume 7, No. 3, pp. 241-260. Reprinted by permission of the publisher, Sage Publications, Inc.

Robinson, Halbert B., and Nancy M. Robinson. "Longitudinal Development of Very Young Children in a Comprehensive Day Care Program," *Child Development*, Volume 42, No. 6, pp. 1673-1683.

St. John, Nancy. "Thirty-Six Teachers," *American Educational Research Journal*, Volume 8, No. 4, pp. 635-647.

Salinas, Guadalupe. "Mexican-Americans and the Desegregation of Schools in the Southwest," *Houston Law Review*, Volume 8, pp. 929-951.

Salinas, Guadalupe. "Mexican-Americans and the Desegregation of Schools in the Southwest—A Supplement," *El Grito*, Volume IV, No. 4, Summer, 1971, pp. 59-69. Copyright 1971 Quinto Sol Publications, Inc.

Scarr-Salapatek, Sandra. "Race, Social Class, and I.Q.," *Science*, Volume 174, December 24, 1971, pp. 1285-1295. Copyright 1971 American Association for the Advancement of Science.

Schaefer, Earl S., "Parents as Educators," *Young Children*, Volume XXVII, No. 4, pp. 227-239. Copyright 1972 National Association for the Education of Young Children, 1834 Connecticut Ave., N.W., Washington, D.C. 20009.

Sewell, William H. "Inequality of Opportunity for Higher Education," *American Sociological Review*, Volume 36, No. 5, pp. 793-809.

Thomas, Alexander, Margaret E. Hertzig, Irving Dryman, and Paulina Fernandez, "Examiner Effect in I.Q. Testing of Puerto Rican Working-Class Children," *American Journal of Orthopsychiatry*, Volume 41, No. 5, pp. 809-821.

Wessman, Alden E. "Scholastic and Psychological Effects of a Compensatory Education Program for Disadvantaged High School Students," *American Educational Research Journal*, Volume 9, No. 3, pp. 361-372.

Williams, Frederick, Jack L. Whitehead, and Leslie Miller. "Relations between Language Attitudes and Teacher Expectancy," *American Educational Research Journal*, Volume 9, No. 2, pp. 263-277.

Wilson, Thomasyne Lightfoot, "Notes toward a Process of Afro-American Education," *Harvard Educational Review*, Volume 42, No. 3, pp. 374-389. Copyright 1972 President and Fellows of Harvard College.

The articles in this collection were published during a time when many citizens and government officials began to retreat from the social and economic commitment to equality for poor and minority groups. For educators and social scientists the evaluations of many educational interventions into the lives of the children of these groups were sobering. Neither the national compensatory education efforts, like Head Start and the Elementary and Secondary Education programs, nor the various school desegregation efforts accomplished what many of them hoped they would: to raise the academic achievement level of poor and minority children and make them better able to compete for the resources of the society. Although much of this research is imperfect—the methodology of evaluation research is yet to be worked out—the promise of these programs seems not to have been fulfilled. Many people now question the social and economic investment of these interventions, especially school desegregation, which inevitably causes social conflict. Some of this disillusionment, however, is unfounded. Small-scale, intense compensatory education programs have been able to improve the achievement of disadvantaged students, or at least prevent the cumulation of the learning deficit that they bring to school—something the schools had never been able to do earlier. In addition, learning in desegregated schools has raised the intelligence and achievement levels of many minority children, although not significantly. More important, perhaps, the students graduating from desegregated schools have a greater opportunity to enter college than they had in the past coming from minority schools, and thus now find themselves in better position to obtain the necessary credentials for careers and jobs in our labor market. Opportunities for higher education, which presently is the most useful route to social mobility, had in the past been unavailable to many of these ₋tudents. Yet despite the evidence of the failures or limited successes of these interventions, their effectiveness will be clear only in the future, as young children advance in school, or when they are adults and have children of their own. We must consider the social and psychological benefits for the disadvantaged and minority child living in a society committed to improving his life, and the disastrous consequences for all citizens—children and adults, minority and non-minority—if equality of opportunity is *not* a social goal.

The authors of the articles in this book examine the ways in which this goal can best be reached. In the first section John D. Owen documents the disparity in the distribution of educational resources in the large urban areas where many poor and minority children are educated, and William H. Sewell points to the educational experiences of working class and poor children and the policy of most colleges and universities in the past that have institutionalized unequal opportunities for higher education. But even with greater opportunities, in the community college Jerome Karabel finds that there is tracking according to social class: lower class students are either "pushed out" or invited to enroll in vocational education programs, and thus the community college perpetuates social stratification rather than fostering social mobility. In summarizing their comprehensive analysis of a large body of secondary data on the outcomes of schooling, Mary Jo Bane and Christopher Jencks question whether schooling, for any group, has a significant effect on social mobility and income. Gertrude Goldberg, however, points out that deschooling and free schooling, which many social critics of education advocate, although Bane and Jencks do not, would differentially affect disadvantaged and middle-class and upper-class children; before disestablishing the schools or radically "freeing up" education, we must look at the special needs of the disadvantaged and the goals of the society at large.

The second section brings together research on the developmental status and ability of disadvantaged children on which school programs must be based if they are to be successful. After reviewing a large body of research, Herbert Birch concludes that nutritional factors at a number of different levels contribute significantly to the depressed intellectual level and learning failure of many disadvantaged children, and suggests that we must recognize the effect of nutrition along with social, cultural, and psychological factors in the educational lives of these children. Sandra Scarr-Salapatek outlines ways of studying individual and group variations to better determine the relationship of race, IQ, and social class. In her study of twelfth graders five years after graduation, Margaret E. Backman found that, unlike an earlier study using first graders, sex accounted for differences in mental abilities rather than ethnic background or socioeconomic status. Susan Ervin-Tripp reviews a large body of sociolinguistic research and shows that speakers of nonstandard dialects are linguistically competent. They are bilingual at the comprehension level and thus understand more of the standard dialect than they are able to produce, and they speak dialects that are as semantically and syntactically complex as standard dialects. Michael Cole and Jerome S. Bruner, like Ervin-Tripp, argue that those ordinarily diagnosed as "culturally deprived" have the same underlying competence as those in the dominant culture, "the difference in performance being accounted for by the situations and context in which the competence is expressed." This is an argument for research in which the stimulus must be situationally appropriate to the ethnic or social class under study. Halbert and Nancy Robinson report on their intervention in the early lives of disadvantaged children to show how the development of these children can be enhanced. They found that high quality stimulation in a day care program can foster the development of verbal abilities in infants and young children which can better prepare them intellectually for later schooling.

The nature of schooling for this group is the concern of the articles in the third section. Thomasyne Lightfoot Wilson feels that a goal of the education of black children must be to specify and make legitimate learning tasks that help to clarify the role of the black community in the lives of these children. The community of the Nairobi Day School in East Palo Alto, California, which she describes, is a learning resource for the school, and the children are taught the ways in which their education can maintain the community. In looking at the positive results of the demonstration community-contolled I.S. 201 school in New York City, Marcia Guttentag argues that decentralized smaller educational units controlled by groups that share a social and educational ideology will be more responsive to the needs of educational consumers than large bureaucratic school systems. Looking at more mainstream education, Nicolaus Mills compares a number of free and directed learning programs for the disadvantaged and cautions that the issue is not the educational ideology of the program but how direction and freedom are used, although it is clear that disadvantaged students profit from directedness and a structured learning environment. Alden E. Wessman reports the results of a longitudinal study of a compensatory education program for able disadvantaged boys and explains how they were both intellectually and emotionally affected by the program. Earl S. Schaefer reviews the research on the effectiveness of parents as educators, and suggests that formal educational institutions should develop ways of supporting parents in this role.

Despite the nature of the instructional program, Ray C. Rist insists that we must know more about the ecology of the classroom that creates the social-cultural gap between lower class students and others, so that we can train teachers to overcome it in their behavior. Clearly, the influence of the teacher critically affects the child's performance. Frederick Williams and his associates found a close association between teachers' attitudes toward dialects and pupils' performance in particular subject areas, and recommend that the study of language variations, and an understanding of how they affect a teacher's attitude, should be made part of the teacher education curriculum. In her study of the influence of teachers in a sixth-grade classroom on pupils' academic growth, self-concept, and interracial friendship behavior, Nancy St. John found that child orientation and interpersonal competence, fairness, and task orientation or subject competence contributed to the adjustment of the children. Like many others now, St. John argues that we must use anthropological observation methods to obtain information about the student-teacher interaction, as it yields more information than "objective" quantitative data on teaching quality. Recognizing the importance of teacher behavior in interracial classrooms, Mark A. Chesler describes some practical means of retaining teachers for better instruction. The influence of the adult figure is manifest in the testing situation as well; Alexander Thomas and his colleagues show how Puerto Rican working class children performed better when they were encouraged than when they were not.

Since the Supreme Court *Brown* decision of 1964, desegregated schooling has been seen by many as the most potent way to achieve educational and social equality. In the last section, Guadalupe Salinas takes a long look at the progress of the desegregation of schools in which Mexican Americans are educated. Minako Kurokawa reports research on the ways adults, college students, and children of various ethnic groups (white, black, and Japanese-Americans) view each other and themselves in an interracial society in which contacts with other groups, it has been argued, would reduce stereotyping and raise self-esteem. Two essays review the outcomes of busing programs, which are likely the only way that schools will be effectively desegregated, short of housing integration. David J. Armor maintains that there is little reason to believe that these programs significantly affected the academic achievement or the aspirations and attitudes of black children, as many have felt they could. In rebuttal, Thomas F. Pettigrew and his associates argue that there are methodological shortcomings to the Armor study and some successful programs were overlooked. This argument, like many others among educators, is now no longer a matter of professional disagreement; it affects national and local policies and thus the social commitment to providing equal educational opportunities. Given their influence, educators and social scientists must neither zealously over-dramatize nor underestimate the results of educational interventions if they are to meet their twin responsibilities of the pursuit of scientific truth and the contribution to the improvement of our society.

The large collection of the ERIC Information Retrieval Center on the Disadvantaged allowed me to choose the works reprinted in this book with confidence, although some works could not be included because of necessary space limitations. I tried to choose works representative of significant issues in the education of the disadvantaged, but obviously some worthy articles had to be omitted. Mrs. Betty Rose D. Rios of the ERIC Clearinghouse on Rural Education and Small Schools graciously helped me identify works on American Indians and Mexican Americans. I am grateful for her aid.

—Erwin Flaxman

I.
EQUAL
EDUCATIONAL
OPPORTUNITY

INEQUALITY OF OPPORTUNITY
FOR HIGHER EDUCATION

William H. Sewell

Higher education in American society gains only a part of its significance from the personal satisfactions and self-realization that come from general learning and the mastery of high level skills. More importantly, higher education confers increased chances for income, power, and prestige on people who are fortunate enough to obtain it.(1) In modern technological societies the allocation of social position is increasingly dependent on higher education. Entrance into an ever enlarging range of valued occupations is restricted to those whose educational attainments beyond secondary school are presumed to have given them the habits of thought, attitudes, and special skills that these occupations require (Sorokin, 1927:169-172, 187-193; Lenski, 1966:389-395; Blau and Duncan, 1967: 401-441; Miller and Roby, 1970:119-141; Hauser, 1970).

It has long been accepted that training for the higher professions should be an almost exclusive monopoly of colleges and universities. More recently this near monopoly has been extended to include many subprofessional and technical occupations as well. Even the training required for the skilled blue-collar and lower level white-collar occupations—which formerly was acquired on the job, through apprenticeships, or in vocational curricula in high schools—has increasingly been shifted to post-secondary institutions.

Recently there has been a good deal of criticism of the overemphasis on credentialism and the certification role that colleges and other educational institutions perform (Miller and Reissman, 1969; Berg, 1970; Newman *et al.*, 1971:38-43). This criticism is particularly persuasive whenever it can be shown that the educational requirements for entry into an occupation have little bearing on the activities of that occupation. It is especially unfortunate that when such requirements are artificially high, many otherwise qualified persons from disadvantaged backgrounds are excluded from desirable occupations. However, with high school graduation becoming almost universal in the United States and with the level of technology increasing, it seems quite likely that the trend will be toward more, not less, dependence on post-secondary institutions to select, train, and certify people for an enlarging variety of occupations.(2) Those who fail to obtain this training, for whatever reasons, will be severely disadvantaged in the competition for jobs and in many other areas of social life as well.

With occupational selection, training, and certification carried out mainly through the schools, and particularly in post-secondary institutions, life chances will not be equal until opportunities for advanced education are equal. The extent to which opportunities for higher education are contingent on characteristics of social origin that are not relevant to learning—most notably sex, socio-economic origins, race and ethnic background—is a matter of great importance to the study of social stratification and a pressing problem to a society that stresses equality of opportunity as a national goal.(3)

The purpose of this paper is to review the research my associates and I have been doing on this subject,(4) and to suggest some of its implications for public policy. First, I will summarize briefly our findings, then discuss some of the results of our efforts to elucidate the complex relationships between socioeconomic background and educational attainment, and finally I will consider their policy implications.

Our research has been based on a longitudinal study of approximately 9,000 randomly selected Wisconsin high school students who have been successfully followed since they were high school seniors in 1957.(5) Our data provide information not only on socioeconomic origins, sex, academic ability, and post-high school educational and occupational attainments, but also on such matters as the student's performance in high school, the expectations of parents and teachers and peers, and the student's educational and occupational aspirations. With these data we have examined in detail inequalities in opportunities for higher education and have also devised explanatory models for the educational attainment process.

INEQUALITIES IN HIGHER EDUCATION

Using such measures of socioeconomic status as parental income, father's and mother's educational attainment, and father's occupation—either singly or in combination—we have found enormous differences in educational opportunities among the various socioeconomic groups and between the sexes. These differences are great regardless of what socioeconomic indices are used and regardless of how restrictively or broadly opportunity for higher education is defined—whether it is taken to mean college entry, college graduation, professional or graduate study, or simply continuation in any kind of formal education beyond high school.(6)

To illustrate. When we divide our cohort into quarters ranging from low to high on an index based on a weighted combination of our indicators of socioeconomic status, we estimate that a high SES student has almost a 2.5 times as much chance as a low SES student of continuing in some kind of post-high school education. He has an almost 4 to 1 advantage in access to college, a 6 to 1 advantage in college graduation, and a 9 to 1 advantage in graduate or professional education. In the middle SES categories the rates are consistently between these extremes: the lower the SES group, the more limited the opportunities at each higher level of education.

These socioeconomic differentials in educational attainment hold for both sexes. However, the educational chances of males are uniformly greater than those of females at every SES level. For example, in the bottom SES category males have a 26% advantage over females in obtaining any further schooling, a 58% advantage in attending college, an 86% advantage in completing college, and a 250% advantage in attending graduate or professional school. Likewise, in the top SES category males have an 8% advantage over females in obtaining any further schooling, a 20% advantage in attending college, a 28% advantage in completing college, and a 129% better chance of attending graduate or professional school. Thus, the advantage of males is greatest in the lower SES categories and least in the top SES category.

Even when we control for academic ability by dividing our sample into fourths according to the students' scores on standardized tests,(7) we find that higher SES students have substantially greater post-high school educational attainment than lower SES students. For example, among students in the lowest fourth of the ability distribution, those in the highest SES category have a 2.5 times advantage over those in the lowest SES category in their chances to go on to some form of post-high school education. For students in the highest ability fourth, the chances of continuing their schooling are 1.5 times greater if they are from the highest rather than the lowest SES category. Similarly, in the lowest ability fourth the rate of college attendance is 4 times greater for the highest SES group than for the lowest SES group. Among the top quarter of students in ability, a student from the lowest SES category is only about half as likely to attend college as a student from the highest SES category. A similar pattern holds for the chances of graduating from college, where corresponding ratios range from 9 to 1 among low ability students to 2 to 1 among high ability students. At the level of graduate or professional school entry, where we would expect ability considerations to be determinant, the odds are 3.5 to 1 in favor of high SES over low SES students, even in the high ability category.

The patterns we have described hold for both women and men. When SES and ability are both controlled, women have lower probabilities of obtaining any further schooling, of attending college, of graduating from college, and of entering graduate or professional school. The differences in rates of attainment between the sexes tend to be lower at the higher levels of attainment and in the higher SES groups, but are still marked at all educational levels and in all SES categories.

Our findings lead inexorably to the conclusion that in their opportunities for higher education the members of this sample cohort seldom escape the influence of their social origins. The selective influences of socioeconomic background and sex operate independently of academic ability at every stage in the process of educational attainment. Social selection is most vividly apparent in the transition from high school to college, but it is operative at every other transition point as well. Those who overcome the handicap of origin status or of sex at one level of the system find themselves again disadvantaged in moving on to the next level.

The results presented thus far do not fully indicate the numerical magnitude of the educational inequalities suffered by women and low socioeconomic status members of this cohort, consisting of approximately 36,000 persons. For this purpose we present an estimate obtained by assuming that the members of each SES and ability category, regardless of sex, should have had the same educational opportunities as high SES males of equal ability. Had this goal been realized, there would have been an increase of 8,800 or 32% more students continuing their schooling beyond high school graduation; 10,089 or 43% more students entering college; and 5,770 or 47% more students graduating from college.

Socioeconomic origin contributes more than sex to the failure of all students to enjoy the same educational opportunities, but even so the result of equalizing women's opportunities would have been to increase by 1,176 or 28% the number of women who would have obtained some further schooling beyond high school; by 2,157 or 52% the number who would have attended college; and by 1,455 or 68% the number who would have graduated from college.

Despite Wisconsin's proud record of providing public and private scholarships and low tuition rates in its diverse system of public higher education, by any standard these figures represent a massive failure to provide equality of opportunity for higher education to qualified students of all SES levels and both sexes. The results are that the state and the nation suffer a great loss in potential, high level manpower and the young people involved pay through reduced life chances.

Our study reveals still other inequities suffered by students from low SES groups in their quest for higher education. Holding academic ability constant, low SES persons are less likely to go to college immediately after high school graduation, much less likely to attend or to be graduated from high quality colleges, more likely to drop out of college if they enter, less likely to return if they drop out, and more likely to have their college careers interrupted by military service. On all of these dimensions except military service, women fare worse than men.

It is indeed regrettable that generally comparable and adequate data on equality of opportunity for higher education are not available for large and representative samples for the nation as a whole.(8) The data that exist on national samples, particularly the badly flawed data from Project Talent,(9) remarkably parallel the trends in our data whenever similar analysis has been undertaken (Folger *et al.*, 1970:305-324). We have no basis for making estimates of national parameters, but to the extent that our data are representative they furnish solid documentation for the claim that there is substantially reduced opportunity for higher education in America for those of lower socioeconomic origins and for women, and that this inequality cannot be explained by differences in academic ability. Despite the spectacular increase in the numbers attending college during the past decade, there is no good reason to believe that socioeconomic differentials in opportunity for higher education have altered appreciably.(10)

It is also unfortunate that no comparable date or analyses exist for blacks, Chicanos, Puerto Ricans, or American Indians. These groups are overrepresented in the lower socioeconomic levels of our society, and they suffer disadvantages due to racial and ethnic discrimination over and above those that characaterize the poor in the overwhelmingly white population of Wisconsin (Duncan and Duncan, 1968; Duncan, 1968). We do know that in 1970 only 65% of blacks aged 20-24 had graduated from high school, in contrast to 83% of whites. Only 23% of blacks in the same age cohort had ever completed a year of college, in contrast to 39% of the whites. In the cohort aged 25-29, only 7% of all blacks had college degrees, in contrast to 17% of whites. And only slightly over 1% of the blacks in this same age cohort had completed as much as one year of professional or graduate education, compared with 6% of the whites.(11) The current enrollment situation at the undergraduate and the graduate and professional levels is still heavily unbalanced. In 1970 only 7% of the students enrolled in colleges and universities in the United States were black, and blacks made up only 2% of current graduate school enrollments and less than 2.5% of the enrollments in medical schools, although blacks were approximately 12% of the affected age cohorts (Wright, 1970). The situation of Puerto Rican, Mexican, and Indian Americans is less well known, but may be as bad. We believe that if data comparable with those for our study were available on black and other disadvantaged minorities, the relationships would be even more marked.

THE EDUCATIONAL ATTAINMENT PROCESS

In addition to the descriptive analysis reported thus far, we have attempted to understand more fully the process of higher educational attainment. We have identified a number of experiences that young people undergo in their formative years which have an important bearing on post-high school educational outcomes. These include level of performance in high school, whether significant others encourage or discourage aspirations for higher education, and whether one actually develops high educational and occupational aspirations. All of these experiences intervene between the social origins, academic ability, and sex characteristics of the individual and become the mechanism through which these background characteristics transmit their influence. In addition, these same experiences have direct and indirect effects of their own, quite independent of the background characteristics.

This complex multivariate process has been the focus of much of our recent research, and we have been developing and testing linear causal models to further explicate the process of attainment. Building on the work of Blau and Duncan (1967:163-205), we have devised and published a linear recursive model that attempts to elaborate and explain the effects of socioeconomic origins and academic ability on educational achievements and occupational attainments as these influences are mediated by social psychological processes (Sewell *et al.*, 1969; Sewell *et al.*, 1970).

Recently we have further elaborated our model by disaggregating socioeconomic status into its component parts—parents' income, mother's education, father's education, and father's occupation—and by decomposition of "significant others' influence" into parental encouragement, teachers' encouragement, and peers' plans.(12) This enables us to obtain estimates of the individual role of each of these variables in the educational attainment process.(13)

Because this analysis is quite complicated, we shall present only the major findings for the total sample, making references to sex differences where they are especially large or interesting.

We begin the analysis with a very simple model that includes only the four socioeconomic background variables. We find that these four socioeconomic background variables taken together account for 18% of the total variance in years of post-high school educational attainment. Whether we look at linear or nonlinear effects, each of the four has an approximately equal, direct influence on educational attainment and on all other intervening variables in the model. This approximate equality of effects of such stratification variables as parental education, occupation, or income suggests that there may be little merit in the efforts of some social scientists to interpret all social inequalities in terms of any particular stratification variable.

What is impressive is not so much the extent to which socioeconomic status governs the life chances of any particular individual, but rather the extent to which it reduces the aggregate or average educational achievements of those from the lower strata. For example, each year of parental education, father's or mother's, was worth one-tenth of a year of higher education for their child—after the effects of father's occupational status and family income were taken into account. Thus, the children of parents with only grade school education obtained on the average one and one-half years less education than the children of parents who were both college graduates—even if their fathers had similar jobs and their families had similar incomes.

Likewise, a thousand dollar increase in the annual income of a family on the average yielded an increase of .08 of a year in the educational attainment of their child—slightly less than an additional year of education of either parent. Thus, a shift in income from the poverty level of $3,000—below which 18% of those in the Wisconsin sample fell—to the median income at that time, $6,000, increased the average years of schooling by a quarter of a year when the effects of parental education and occupation were taken into account. A shift from the poverty line to $10,000—which was exceeded by only 11% of the families in the Wisconsin sample—led to an increase of more than half an additional year of post-secondary schooling.

When we add academic ability to the model, the explained variance in higher educational attainment is increased from 18 to 30%. The additional 12% represents a large component of the variance in educational attainment that is completely independent of socioeconomic origins. An important component, varying between 20 and 30%, of the effects of each of the socioeconomic status variables is mediated by academic ability. At the same time the influence of ability on attainment is clearly not spurious. Only one-fifth of the association of academic ability with educational attainment may be attributed to its association with socioeconomic background. Whether one thinks of measured ability as a valid psychological trait or as an administratively convenient basis for social selection, it seems apparent that the effects of ability on schooling are not merely a reflection of one's SES background. We think this is particularly germane to current discussions of the social role of testing.(14)

Next, in order to explain more completely the ways in which socioeconomic status origins influence post-high school attainment, we further complicate the model by adding three sets of social psychological intervening variables: 1. high school performance, 2. significant others' influence, and 3. educational and occupational aspirations. We believe that these variables intervene in the order indicated to mediate the effects of socioeconomic status and academic ability on higher educational attainment. Taken as a whole, these intervening variables account for a large part of the effects of each socioeconomic status variable on post-high school educational attainment. Some 85 to 90% of the total association of each socioeconomic status variable with attainment is mediated by the variables in the model, of which about 75% is mediated by the social psychological variables, leaving only 10 to 15% to be explained by other variables not in the model, by measurement error, and by socioeconomic discrimination. Still, even with this powerful model which explains over 55% of the variance in higher educational attainment, socioeconomic origins continue to influence directly one's chances for educational attainment.

The extent to which our model explains the effects of socioeconomic origin on ultimate educational attainment is remarkable in light of the fact that none of our intervening variables pertains to the post-secondary experience of the cohort. Even for young persons who succeed in graduating from high school, the effect of social background on later educational achievement is largely explicable in terms of events which took place during the high school years.

Again, with this more complex model it is noteworthy that the interpretations for total associations are very similar for each of the SES variables. About 12% of the influence of each SES variable on higher educational attainment is direct. About 16% is due to the association with the other SES variables, about 11% is ultimately mediated by academic ability and high school performance, about 23% is eventually mediated by significant others' influence, and about 38% is ultimately mediated by educational and occupational aspirations.

Not only does the model interpret the various ways in which SES variables influence higher educational attainment, but also it interprets the effects of academic ability. Of the total association between academic ability and educational attainment, 18% is due to the unmediated effect of ability, 21% is due to the relationship between academic ability and socioeconomic background, and the remaining 61% is mediated by the social psychological variables in our model. This indicates that the influence of academic ability can only in a minor way be attributed to SES considerations, but rests more solidly on its direct and pertinent influence on academic performance, and its direct and indirect influences on significant others and on educational and occupational aspirations. In this context it is also pertinent that the model indicates that SES has no effect on performance in high school independent of academic ability.

Next, in the analysis of our full model, we introduce the effects of parental encouragement, teachers' encouragement, and the educational plans of friends. In looking at the effects of these significant others on educational attainment, we are struck by the evidence that parental encouragement and friends' plans depend heavily on the student's socioeconomic origin. Teachers' encouragement, on the other hand, depends much more heavily on ability and academic performance. Indeed, teachers are not perceived to engage in direct socioeconomic status discrimination as parents and peers apparently do, but rather depend mainly on judgments of student academic ability, particularly as it is validated by school performance.

We find that the influence of parents on educational and occupational aspirations and ultimately on attainment of higher education is about twice that of teachers, and the influence of friends only slightly less than that of parents. Holding constant all of the other factors we have included in the model up to this point (SES, academic ability, school performance, parental encouragement, and friends' plans), we find that teachers' encouragement is worth an additional 0.3 of a year of schooling—whereas the net values of parental encouragement and friends' plans are 0.9 of a year and 0.7 of a year, respectively. While all three variables have important effects on students' educational attainments, we are led to conclude that teachers' expectations of students are not a powerful mediating factor in the process of educational stratification. But far from reflecting overt or covert status discrimination, on the whole teachers' expectations seem to be based on academic ability and performance, and as such they make a fundamental though modest contribution to the equalization of opportunities.

Although our model is quite successful in accounting for socioeconomic differentials in educational attainment, it is less successful in accounting for sex differences—which favor men by approximately one-half year of educational attainment on the average. Our analysis indicates that women are most seriously disadvantaged relative to men in levels of teachers' and parents' encouragement and in their own levels of educational aspirations. They enjoy some advantage over men in that they get higher grades in high school and have slightly higher perceptions of their friends' plans and somewhat higher occupational aspirations. Our model tends to predict higher average educational attainments for women than they actually achieve. This may be due to its failure to represent crucial aspects of women's high school experiences, or it may be that the primary sources of the lower attainments of women must be sought in the months and years immediately following the completion of high school. We are inclined toward the latter view, for the effects of socialization in the family and in the school are already manifest in women's levels of school performance, of significant others' influence, and of aspiration.

POLICY IMPLICATIONS

What bearings do our findings have for policies designed to reduce inequality in higher education? Certainly, in this large cohort there is striking evidence of its pervasiveness. Although socioeconomic origin plays an important part in equality in higher education, our analysis indicates that its role is far from simple and direct. Its effects tend to be mediated largely by social psychological factors, which in turn also have independent influences on the processes of educational attainment. Moreover, when we look at the components of socioeconomic status—father's and mother's education, father's occupation, and family income—we find that not one of them plays any unique part in the causal system explaining attainment in higher education. This is unfortunate from the standpoint of policy considerations. One would have wished that family income might have had a larger and a more special set of effects because it is the aspect of socioeconomic background most readily amenable to change.(15) But our evidence raises doubt that programs based on family income supplementation alone will result in any rapid and marked reduction in inequality in higher education. This is not to deny the importance of income in obtaining access to higher education, but it is to warn that family income programs, however desirable they may be for reducing other social inequalities, will not bring quick or dramatic results in overcoming inequality in higher education.(16) Certainly we should not rely on this means alone to bring about equalization of opportunity for higher education.

Rather, I would argue for a more targeted economic approach.(17) I believe that programs specifically limited to financing post-secondary educational costs based strictly on student need would be the most effective and equitable approach to the problem. Besides making it possible for needy students to continue their education, such a grants program might have desirable indirect effects on the educational aspirations and achievements of the disadvantaged. For example, if students and parents became aware that it was national policy to make grants to cover the full cost of post-secondary schooling for qualified students whose families had incomes too low to bear these costs themselves, it is entirely conceivable that this knowledge would lead to better performance in school because now performance would have a greater likelihood of being rewarded. Parents and teachers might then give more attention to the student's academic growth, with consequent favorable effects on the development of the student's self-conceptions, ambitions, and aspirations. All of this might lead to a greater likelihood that the student would continue education beyond high school and be more successful in post-high school studies.

I advocate that all new subsidy programs be limited to those who need the subsidy. There is mounting evidence that existing subsidy programs for higher education do not go primarily to needy students. Not only do federal moneys for training and research go mainly to institutions that are attended primarily by middle- and high-income students, but also most other forms of institutional aid go to high prestige colleges and universities. Even student-aid moneys are not primarily concentrated in the community colleges, city colleges, and less prestigious colleges that serve the poor (Rivlin, 1970:9). Moreover, in their recent analysis of the distribution of subsidy for public higher education in California, Hansen and Weisbrod (1969a; 1969b) argue that because higher income students are more likely to go to college, to attend the most expensive public institutions, and to stay in college longer, their families are in effect receiving a much greater educational subsidy from the state than are low income families.(18) Probably the same trend would be revealed and possibly accentuated in states with less availability of public higher education. Consequently, new programs for the subsidy of higher educational opportunity should be limited to students who need the subsidy in order to continue their education beyond high school.

Most of the funds should go directly to students rather than to institutions.(19) Nor should subsidy programs be limited to those who go to four-year colleges, but rather should include also those whose interests and aptitudes lead them to select community colleges and vocational training schools. Neither would I argue that funds should go only to students of proven academic ability and achievement. Motivated students with qualities that make them admissible to various types of institutions should be given equal opportunity to pursue their education in other appropriate ways. For this group there must be institutions located in all larger communities with open admission policies, programs to remedy prior academic deficiencies, flexible scheduling, pacing and credit loads, and special tutoring and counseling programs (Willingham, 1970:217-223; Gordon, 1971). The grants given should be sufficient to enable the student to attend any post-secondary institution—public or private—to which he could gain admission. In the case of the poor, the grants should cover full costs—tuition, books, board, lodging, travel, and even a modest amount for incidental personal expenses—and should be in effect as long as the student makes satisfactory progress in school.

The low propensity of the families in our sample to trade family income for education leads me to believe that other funding schemes such as the education opportunity bank, various other loan schemes, and tax credit plans are likely to be much less effective in encouraging low-income students to continue their education. Their families are already burdened with debt, and they fear long-time loans—even at low interest or no interest rates—that are likely to run into thousands of dollars before the student has completed his education. Tax credit schemes are likely to appeal greatly to the middle classes who pay heavy income taxes, but not to the poor. In fact, if our goal is to equalize opportunity for post-high school education, it may be necessary, in order to release funds for direct help to students from lower income groups, to reduce current subsidies to students whose parents can afford to pay for their education.

This should not be interpreted as an endorsement for schemes that call for the support of public higher education on the basis of full-cost tuition fees so that all public subsidies for higher education would go only to those who can demonstrate need.(20) I believe that tuitions should be kept as low as possible to encourage all motivated students—especially women—to continue their education beyond high school. But even if there were no tuition fees charged for higher education, access to it would, I think, still be painfully inequitable. Consequently, new resources need to be directed at special and extraordinary steps to attract and serve those groups now least well represented in our colleges and universities.(21) I believe that a grants program along the lines outlined is administratively feasible and could be put into operation rapidly so that its effects would be apparent in the immediate future.

For those not now in the educational pipeline there must be increased opportunities for recurrent education, including part-time study, work-study programs, education on the job, and various other types of continuing education of both general and technical character (Organization for Economic Cooperation and Development, 1971; Newman, 1971; Carnegie Commission on Higher Education, 1971). These will also require special financing and will be expensive, but our evidence suggests that there are millions of disadvantaged youth and adults now in the labor force who dropped out of the educational process early and who have the capacity to profit from such programs. Both as a matter of equity and of intelligent manpower policy, they should be given the opportunity to continue their education.

I do not believe that economic programs alone will be sufficient to overcome inequality in opportunities for higher education. Our analysis also indicates that we must give a good deal of attention to such social psychological factors as the development of cognitive skills, academic performance, the influence of significant others, and the stimulation of educational and occupational aspirations. All of these variables have direct and indirect influences on educational achievement that are quite independent of socioeconomic background. Consequently, any strategies that can be suggested for increasing their strength should be investigated, developed, and given intensive trials in the hope that ways can be found to overcome the deficits in these areas from which so many disadvantaged children suffer.

Particular attention must be given to programs designed to increase the academic ability and performance of lower SES children. Evidence from the Coleman report and other research suggests that many children from disadvantaged homes enter school with a deficit in learning skills that tends to increase steadily throughout the school years, with the consequence that by twelfth grade many lower class children are well behind higher status children in academic skills and achievement (Coleman *et al.*, 1966:20-21). The fact that these academic deficits seem to increase over the years of schooling suggests that special programs designed to develop cognitive and affective skills, beginning in the preschool period and continuing throughout the grades, will be necessary to enlarge the personal and academic potential of socioeconomically disadvantaged children so that they can compete successfully with higher status children.

Unfortunately, current large-scale attempts to improve the cognitive development of socially disadvantaged children have not thus far had promising results (Gordon and Wilkerson, 1966:156-189; Williams and Evans, 1969), despite a good deal of evidence from more restricted laboratory and field studies indicating the possibility of rather large and lasting gains.(22) However, the stakes are so great that rather than give up this line of attack a great deal more ingenuity and effort must be devoted to devising more effective programs, including interventions which involve the family and peers, as well as the school. This will require much research, experimental programming, and structural changes in schools. All of this will be expensive and it may take much more time than we once optimistically thought, but our research suggests that the potential payoffs are very significant, are likely to be largely above and beyond those resulting from economic programs, and are essential if we do not want the early handicap of disadvantaged children to prevent them from realizing their potential for later academic achievement (Carnegie Commission on Higher Education, 1970a).

Our analysis suggests, also, that programs designed to influence the significant others of disadvantaged students would have important effects on the student's educational aspirations and achievements. One immediately thinks of the possible role that teachers and counsellors might play in programs of this kind. If socioeconomically disadvantaged students with good academic potential were discovered early and high school teachers and counsellors were alerted to the students' potential for development so that they might provide special guidance and encouragement, modest gains might accrue in the students' educational aspiration and attainment levels. On the basis of our data, we would not expect gains of great magnitude because our model does not show teachers' influence to be a very powerful determinant of educational attainment. Still other ways should be sought to involve teachers more actively in the academic and career plans of disadvantaged students. This is important because teachers, unlike parents and peers, are relatively free from socioeconomic bias in stimulating and encouraging promising students.

At the same time there must be programs to acquaint parents with the academic potential of their child, to get them interested in his educational development, to make them aware of the importance of academic achievement to later educational and occupational opportunities, and to make sure that they know about scholarship and grants programs that would enable their child to continue in post-high school education. I am not optimistic that such programs could effectively provide the encouragement for educational aspirations and achievements that higher status families give their children in the normal course of their socialization. But, again, our research shows that parental influences are so crucial that every effort must be made to utilize this avenue to reduce educational inequalities.

I have no innovative ideas about how peers could be used to stimulate the educational aspirations and achievements of lower status children, but I do believe that their peer culture might be shifted toward educational achievement through programs designed to make school a more interesting and challenging place—by emphasizing competent and sensitive teaching, by restructuring the school around students' interests, by changing the authority patterns in the schools, by elimination of socioeconomic and racial segregation, and by similar innovations. More direct interventions are also possible. Coleman (1965: 72-87) has emphasized the use of adolescent peer structures to stimulate intellectual values and performance through intergroup competition. Others have stressed monetary rewards to motivate academic achievement (Effrat *et al.*, 1969). Spilerman (1971) has recently suggested a combination of material inducements with a reward structure emphasizing peer group attainment as a strategy for motivating lower class adolescents. As yet these suggestions have not been tested in large-scale practical programs. However, possible programs along these lines and further research should be encouraged because of the important role that peers play in the educational attainment process.

What does our research tell us about the special problem of equality of opportunity for higher education for women? Our analysis indicates that women make better grades in high school than men. Yet, they are disadvantaged at every level of higher education. Our data do not bear directly on all of the sources of these disadvantages, but they do suggest that parents are less likely to encourage high educational aspirations among their daughters than their sons, and that whenever family funds are short parents are more likely to spend them on the sons' education. We also know that women have lower educational aspirations than men. This is no doubt in part due to their uncertainty about career and marriage opportunities and plans. But these factors do not fully account for the lower educational attainments of women. We suspect that a narrow sex-role training that stresses household and family roles for women over educational and occupational opportunities—and which becomes most salient when young women for the first time face the realities of discrimination in higher education and the job market—plays a major part in depressing the women's post-secondary educational attainments.

I endorse the policy recommendations which women have frequently suggested for achieving equality of opportunity for women in higher education, such as requirements that all scholarships, fellowships, part-time jobs, assistantships, and admission to all types of training must be equally open to women and men. Existing rules covering residency, full-time enrollment, and credit transfers should be revised to accommodate the needs of women, and child care centers should be established at all institutions. Also there should be courses in the schools to broaden the conceptions of male and female roles, to reduce prejudice toward women's full participation in all institutional areas, and, particularly, to further encourage women to form (and men to accept) a life-long commitment to educational and occupational achievement. Educational institutions should also lead the way in equal employment programs. All positions, including top administrative jobs, must be equally open to women and men. Women should receive equal pay for equal rank and be considered for faculty tenure on the same standards as men. Also, educational institutions and other organizations must show greater imagination and flexibility in facilitating part-time professional involvement and rewarding careers for women who choose to combine occupational careers with child rearing. Programs to change public attitudes, and particularly those of parents toward female children, doubtless will be necessary, too, if women are not to be discriminated against in higher education and in most other areas of American life.

Finally, special programs will need to be undertaken to increase the participation of blacks, Chicanos, Puerto Ricans, and American Indians in higher education. The measures designed for the poor, if applied without discrimination, would go a long way to reduce the problems of minorities because these minorities are disproportionately represented among low-income families. But we also know that these minorities suffer added disadvantages of discrimination in housing, employment, health care, and in most other areas of American life, and in their personal relations with whites. Discrimination has left many of them not only disadvantaged educationally, but with a well-merited distrust of American institutions and promises of equality in the future. They are likely to distrust educational programs that are planned and carried out by the white majority, and they may also question the relevance of many existing programs of higher education for their personal and community needs. Much joint effort will have to be devoted to revision of existing programs and the establishment of more relevant programs for special needs of minorities. These programs must include ways of making the adjustment to academic life less difficult and should provide opportunities for minority group students to maintain contacts with their communities. Also, much more effort will have to be devoted to recruitment programs designed for the early discovery of potentially talented persons from minority groups and to maximize the development of their abilities and their opportunities. Special efforts must be made to increase the representation of disadvantaged minorities in such professional training programs as law, medicine, and dentistry, and in all graduate training areas. Institutions of higher education must also actively recruit minority staff, faculty, and administrators. And certainly, if increased opportunity for higher education is not to be a sham and a delusion for minority people, it must be accompanied by equal opportunity to participate fully in every aspect of American life.

I would have liked to end this discussion on a note of optimism regarding the immediate prospects for equality of opportunity in higher education. I cannot do so. Our research has shown that the process of higher educational attainment is an exceedingly complex one, and that there are no simple and easy prescriptions for attaining equality of opportunity. Many avenues must be tried, but our knowledge of how to mount successful programs, even in the areas we know are important, is far from perfect. Moreover, political problems abound, and national, state, and local priorities do not currently favor increased expenditures for higher education—and particularly not for novel programs. Many colleges and universities are in severe financial difficulties (Cheit, 1971) and may find it necessary to cut their current inadequate levels of expenditure for opportunity programs of all kinds. In the current emergency many of them are increasing tuition without providing additional scholarship opportunities for needy students. Most experts agree that it will take added annual expenditures running into the billions to provide equality of opportunity for higher education, and that the federal government must provide an increasing proportion of the necessary funds.(23)

On the other hand, pressures are mounting, especially from disadvantaged minorities and from many educators and other citizens. The Carnegie Commission on Higher Education, composed of a number of distinguished citizens and educators, recently announced the following goals: "That (by 1976) the economic barriers to higher education be removed" and "That (by 2000) all remaining barriers to equality of opportunity which are subject to public policy be removed so that ability, motivation, and choice are the only determinants of college attendance" (Carnegie Commission on Higher Education, 1968, 1970a, 1970b). That these are financially feasible goals is documented in their reports, but the pace of the action must be stepped up considerably if either goal is to be achieved. To date, the Congress and the Administration have fallen far short on legislation and appropriations to equalize educational opportunities.

It is a sociological truism that great gaps often exist between stated goals and their implementation. Americans of all political persuasions have expressed the view that equality of educational opportunity is an essential prerequisite for a well-functioning, democratic society. The programs I have discussed detail some measures necessary to begin to implement this essential need. I urge you as citizens to join me in working for their implementation and as sociologists to join me in pursuing further research which will more clearly specify the most effective alternative programs.

NOTES

(1) There is a vast literature on the economic benefits of education which shows that those with advanced education enjoy much higher annual and lifetime earnings than those with lesser education. See especially Schultz (1963), Morgan and David (1963), Becker (1964), Innes *et al.* (1965), Weisbrod and Karpoff (1968), and Bowman (1971). Our own unpublished results indicate that, even when we control for ability, average annual earnings of college graduates are considerably higher than the earnings of those who obtained less post-high school education. These results are based on 1967 data, and these

earning differentials doubtless will increase over the years as those in the professions and business enter the more productive phases of their careers.

(2) We find it difficult to come up with a better alternative to heavy reliance on the educational system for the training and certification function. We agree that other ways to qualify for jobs must remain open and should be expanded, but we would question seriously the equity and efficiency of relying heavily on the selection and training procedures of the many thousands of employers in the job market. Incidentally, some of the criticism of credentialism, insofar as it deals with racial minorities, seems to be misplaced because our best evidence indicates that a large fraction of the disadvantage of these minorities in occupation and income accrues to those who have obtained the right educational credentials but are still discriminated against in the job market (Duncan, 1968).

(3) Recent concern with inequality of opportunity in higher education has resulted in a number of reports and recommendations for national policy. Among the most prominent of these are the Reports of the Carnegie Commission on Higher Education (see especially 1968, 1970a, 1970b) and the Report of the U.S. Department of Health, Education, and Welfare (1969). Other references are given in later footnotes. For a provocative discussion of the evolution of the concept inequality of educational opportunity, see Coleman (1968). For an outstanding statement on inequality and opportunity, see Duncan (1969).

(4) The most directly pertinent publications from our research are: Sewell (1964); Sewell and Haller (1965); Sewell and Armer (1966a and 1966b); Sewell and Shah (1967, 1968a and 1968b); Sewell et al. (1969); Wegner and Sewell (1970); and Sewell et al. (1970).

(5) The original 1957 sample consisted of 10,321 students who were followed up in 1964 by means of mailed questionnaires and telephone interviews. Follow-up data were obtained for 9,007 or 87.2% of those in the original sample. Since that time additional information on the earnings of the students has been obtained periodically, but these data are used only incidentally in this paper. Extensive comparisions of the characteristics of the original and follow-up sample show little if any bias in the follow-up sample. For a description of the original survey, see Little (1958:1–6). A brief description of the follow-up survey is given in Sewell and Shah (1967:6-8). Much more complete information on the data and procedures used in the analysis reported in this paper will be available in a book currently in preparation (Sewell et al., forthcoming).

(6) The detailed tables on which the conclusions in this section of the paper are based are given in Sewell et al. (unpublished). They have also been presented in somewhat different form in Sewell and Shah (1967:9-16).

(7) Academic ability—its definition, its dimensions, its causes, and its measurement—presents vexing questions to social scientists. There is a long history of debate on these issues which has not led to universal agreement on any of them (Goslin, 1963:123-151; Bloom, 1964:52-94; Jensen, 1969). We take the position that by the end of high school the widely used tests of academic ability yield essentially valid measures of individual potential for

success in the system of higher education (Lavia, 1965:42-63; Eckland, 1967). In this study we have used a single standardized measure of academic ability, the Henmon-Nelson Test of Mental Maturity, obtained in the junior year of high school (Henmon-Nelson, 1954). This test, like similar tests, has been said to be culture-bound and, therefore, unfair to lower class respondents (Eells *et al.*, 1950; Lefever, 1959). Whatever the merits of that argument, any class bias in the test will lead us to underestimate the independent influence of socioeconomic background on educational attainments. Since our interest lies in demonstrating that socioeconomic background has an effect independent of academic ability on the completion of every stage of post-high school education, the test bias, if any, will have a conservative effect on our conclusions. If significant social class differences in educational attainment are still in evidence when measured ability is controlled, there will be no doubt about the existence of unequal opportunities in higher education.

(8) Among the national studies in which some attempt has been made to follow up high school students are: the Educational Testing Service (1957) study of college plans and enrollment; Project Talent (Flanagan *et al.*, 1962a, 1962b; Flanagan *et al.*, 1964, 1966; Shaycoft *et al.*, 1963; Shaycoft, 1967); the Trent and Medsker (1968) study of 10,000 high school graduates; the Nam and Cowhig (1962) study of factors related to college attendance of high school graduates; the Bureau of the Census and Bureau of Applied Social Research study of factors related to high school graduation and college attendance (U.S. Bureau of Census, 1969); and study of educational and occupational experiences of male youth by Parnes *et al.* (1970) and Zeller *et al.* (1970). Another national study—The Institute for Social Research study of adolescent boys—which will have follow-up data eventually, is "Youth in Transition," by Bachman *et al.* (1969). Unfortunately, there is little uniformity in the sampling, variables, follow-up procedures, or data analysis in these studies, thus making impossible anything but gross comparison of results. Also it is unfortunate that the design of the Equality of Educational Opportunity Study (Coleman *et al.*, 1966) will not permit any follow-up of the over 600,000 students included in that national survey.

(9) The most glaring defects of the Project Talent Study were its very low response rate (32%) in the five-year follow-up study and high rates of nonresponse to items on the questionnaire. A small nonrandom subsample of nonrespondents to the mailed questionnaire was interviewed, and weighting procedures based on this subsample were employed to make estimates for the larger sample and eventually for the population studied (Folger *et al.*, 1970: Appendix B). We believe that this technique was not adequate to compensate for bias due to nonresponse, e.g., computations we have made using Project Talent data for the 1965 panel (Folger *et al.*, 1970: Appendix B, Table B2) indicate that 36% of the males in their sample graduated from college, whereas the census of 1970 data shows that only 26% of U.S. males in the age cohort 25-29 (the age cohort most comparable with their sample) had completed four or more years of college (U.S. Bureau of Census, 1970).

(10) The booming college enrollments of the Sixties have led many to believe that opportunities for higher education must have become much more widespread during the decade. This is in part true but, from computations we have made using information on the college experiences of persons 20-24 years old in 1960 and 1970 (U.S. Bureau of Census, 1960, 1970), we found that 34% of the increased college experience in the decade was due to the growth in the size of the age cohort, 30% due to the increased rate of high school graduation, and 36% due to increase in the rate of college entry. Unfortunately, we know of no evidence that would permit us to draw a firm conclusion as to whether the increased rate of college enrollment has resulted in a higher rate of collge going among high school graduates from the lower SES groups. One calculation we have made, using data from a U.S. sample, indicates that the proportion of students of manual and service origins enrolled in college increased by 7% during the decade, while the proportion of white-collar students increased by less than 2% (U.S. Bureau of Census, 1961, Current Population Reports, P–20, No. 110, Table 5, and 1971, P–20, No. 222, Table 7). This is a notable increase, but is not likely to have had any marked effect on the validity of the general pattern of socioeconomic differentials in educational opportunity revealed by the Wisconsin data. The fact that the pattern we have described has been quite stable over the years is indicated by Spady's analysis of the data from the 1962 current population supplement, "Occupational Changes in a Generation," showing that SES differences in college attendance had increased over the decades covered in that study (Spady, 1967).

(11) These figures are based on computations from data included in Current Population Reports (U.S. Bureau of the Census, 1970 and 1971).

(12) The operational definitions of the variables used in the models discussed in this section of the paper are basically the same as given in Sewell et al. (1970:1017) except that educational attainment for parents and students has been recorded into approximate years of schooling rather than the four broad categories used in that report. For further details, see Sewell et al. (unpublished).

(13) The tables and formulae for the computations summarized in this section would require several printed pages to reproduce. Consequently they are not presented here but will be given in full in Sewell et al. (unpublished).

(14) Critics of the use of tests for selection for higher education have often overlooked the fact that many poor children of all races score well on the tests and (through family sacrifices and their own efforts and often) with the help of student-aid programs are freed from the handicaps of their social origins. We would not wish to see any reorganization of testing in our society that would overlook this valuable function in efforts to eliminate any undesirable side effects of testing. An interesting result of recent criticisms of testing has been a broadened conception of the responsibility of the major testing services to seek other valid methods of discovering the potential of disadvantaged students and to help disadvantaged students find appropriate educational instutitions in which to develop their talents.

(15) For a provocative discussion of the use of policy variables, see Cain and

Watts (1970) and replies by Coleman (1970) and Aigner (1970).

(16) Rainwater (1970:398-425) has presented a strong case for a national policy of income redistribution as the most effective way of reducing social inequality. In this connection he argues that it is unlikely that educational outcomes for poor children can be greatly improved without increasing the incomes of their families. Masters (1969) presents evidence that although the short-run effects of income transfer programs on educational retardation and dropout may be small, the long-run effects may be quite important.

(17) Financial programs have been stressed by many economists. For a comprehensive review of the various plans, see the papers by Roger E. Bolton, W. Lee Hansen and Burton A. Weisbrod, Alice Rivlin and Jeffrey H. Weiss, Andre Daniere, Clark Kerr, Howard R. Bowen, Jerrold R. Zacharias, and Roger Freeman in a report on financing higher education submitted to the Joint Economic Committee of the Congress of the United States (1969). See also the papers by Theodore W. Schultz, Mary Jean Bowman, W. Lee Hansen and Burton A. Weisbrod, Howard R. Bowen, Robert W. Hartman, Roger A. Freeman, Robert L. Farrell and Charles J. Andersen, John P. Mallan, and M. E. Orwig in Orwig (1971a).

(18) Hansen and Weisbrod's analysis (1969a, 1969c) has drawn critical substantive and methodological comment from Pechman (1970), which in turn has been answered by Hartman (1970). Pechman (1971) has recently made further comments and has been replied to by Hansen and Weisbrod (1971a).

(19) We would agree with the Kerr and Rivlin reports that there should be a cost-of-education allowance to help institutions meet the costs of special services that federally aided students might require and for new facilities necessary to accommodate the additional students (Carnegie Commission on Higher Education, 1968; U.S. Department of Health, Education, and Welfare, 1969). For a full discussion of the debate now going on between those who advocate fuller funding of existing institutional programs and those favoring direct payments to students, see Mallan (1971) and Orwig (1971b:331-360).

(20) Hansen and Weisbrod (1971b) have proposed such a plan for Wisconsin.

(21) The basic political issues in federal funding of the various aid-to-higher-education proposals are well covered in Mallan (1971).

(22) For comprehensive reviews of research and theory in this area, see especially Deutsch and Associates (1967) and Hess and Bear (1968).

(23) The Kerr Commission estimates that expenditures for higher education must be increased from 17.2 billions in 1967-68 to 41 billions in 1976-77 if equality of opportunity for higher education is to be broadly extended and quality is to be maintained. This would require an increase in federal expenditures from 3.5 to 13.0 billions. The Commission estimates that this would be less than one-seventh of the projected increase in federal revenues in the next several years (Carnegie Commission on Higher Education, 1968, 1970b).

REFERENCES

Aigner, D.J., 1970, "A comment on problems in making inferences from the Coleman Report." American Sociological Review 35 (March):249-252.

Bachman, Jerald G., Robert L. Kahn, Martha T. Mednick, *et al.*, 1969, Youth In Transition, Volume 1. Ann Arbor: Institute for Social Research, The University of Michigan.

Becker, Gary S., 1946, Human Capital. New York: Columbia University Press.

Berg, I. 1970, Education and Jobs: The Great Training Robbery. New York: Praeger.

Blau, Peter M. and Otis Dudley Duncan, 1967, The American Occupational Structure. New York: John Wiley.

Bloom, Benjamin S., 1964, Stability and Change in Human Characteristics. New York: John Wiley.

Bowman, Mary Jean, 1971, "Economics of education." Pp. 37-70 in Orwig (ed.), Financing Higher Education: Alternatives for the Federal Government. Iowa City: American College Testing Program.

Cain, Glen G. and Harold W. Watts, 1970, "Problems in making policy inferences from the Coleman Report." American Sociological Review 35 (April):228-242.

Carnegie Commission on Higher Education, 1968, Quality and Equality: New Levels of Federal Responsibility for Higher Education. New York: McGraw-Hill; 1970a, A Chance to Learn: An Action Agenda for Equal Opportunity in Higher Education. New York: McGraw-Hill; 1970b, Quality and Equality: Revised Recommendations, New Levels of Federal Responsibility for Higher Education. New York: McGraw-Hill; 1971, Less Time, More Options: Education Beyond the High School. New York: McGraw-Hill.

Cheit, Earl F., 1971, The New Depression in Higher Education: A Study of Financial Conditions at 41 Colleges and Universities. New York: McGraw-Hill.

Coleman, J.S., 1965, Adolescents and the Schools. New York: Basic Books; 1968, "The concept of equality of educational opportunity." Harvard Educational Review 38 (Winter):7-22; 1970, "Equality of educational opportunity: Reply to Cain and Watts." American Sociological Review 35 (April):242-249.

Coleman, J.S., Ernest Q. Campbell, Carl F. Hobson, *et al.*, 1966, Equality of Educational Opportunity. Washington: U.S. Office of Education.

Deutsch, Martin and Associates, 1967, The Disadvantaged Child. New York: Basic Books.

Duncan, Beverly and Otis Dudley Duncan, 1968, "Minorities and the process of stratification." American Sociological Review 33 (June):356-364.

Duncan, Otis Dudley, 1968, "Inheritance of poverty or inheritance of race?" Pp. 85-110 in Daniel P. Moynihan (ed.), On Understanding Poverty. New York: Basic Books; 1969, "Inequality and opportunity." Population Index

35 (October-December):361-366.

Eckland, Bruce, 1967, "Genetics and sociology: A reconsideration." American Sociological Review 32 (April):173-194.

Educational Testing Service, 1957, Background Factors Relating to College Plans and College Enrollment Among Public High School Students. Princeton, New Jersey: Educational Testing Service.

Eells, Kenneth, Allison Davis, Robert Havighurst, *et al.*, 1950, Intelligence and Cultural Differences. Chicago: University of Chicago Press.

Effrat, Andrew, Roy Feldman, and Harvey M. Sapolsky, 1969, "Inducing poor children to learn." The Public Interest 15 (Spring):106-112.

Flanagan, J.C., W.W. Cooley, P.R. Lohnes, *et al.*, 1966, Project Talent One-Year Follow-up Studies. Final report to the U.S. Office of Education, Cooperative Research Project No. 2333. Pittsburgh: Project Talent Office, University of Pittsburgh.

Flanagan, J.C., J.T. Dailey, Marion F. Shaycoft, *et al.* 1962a The Talents of American Youth, Volume I. Design for a Study of American Youth. Boston: Houghton Mifflin. 1962b Studies of the American High School. Final Report to the U.S. Office of Education, Cooperative Research Project No. 226. Washington: Project Talent Office, University of Pittsburgh.

Flanagan, J.C., F.B. Davis, J.T. Dailey, *et al.* 1964 The American High School Student. Final report to the U.S. Office of Education, Cooperative Research Project No. 635. Pittsburgh: Project Talent Office, University of Pittsburgh.

Folger, John K., Helen S. Astin, and Alan Bayer. 1970 Human Resources and Higher Education. New York: Russell Sage Foundation.

Gordon, Edmund W. 1971, "Programs and practices for minority group youth in higher education." Pp. 109-126 in Stephen W. Wright (ed.), Barriers to Higher Education. New York: College Entrance Examination Board.

Gordon, Edmund W. and Doxey A. Wilkerson, 1966, Compensatory Education for the Disadvantaged. New York: College Entrance Examination Board.

Goslin, David A., 1963, The Search for Ability. New York: Russell Sage Foundation.

Hansen, W. Lee and Burton A. Weisbrod, 1969a, "The distribution of costs and direct benefits of public higher education: The case of California." Journal of Human Resources 4 (Spring):176-191; 1969b "The search for equality in the provision and finance of higher education." Pp. 107-123 in The Economics and Financing of Higher Education in the United States. Washington: U.S. Government Printing Office; 1969c, Benefits, Costs, and Finance of Higher Education. Chicago: Markham; 1971a "On the distribution of costs and benefits of public higher education: Reply." Journal of Human Resources 6 (Summer):363-374; 1971b "A new approach to higher education finance." p. 117-142 in Orwig (ed.), Financing Higher Education: Alternatives for the Federal Government. Iowa City: American College Testing Program.

Hartman, Robert W. 1970, "A comment on Pechman-Hansen-Weisbrod controversy." Journal of Human Resources 5 (Fall):519-523.

Hauser, Robert M. 1970, "Educational stratification in the United States." Sociological Inquiry 40 (Spring): 102-109.

Henmon, V.A.C. and M.J. Nelson, 1954, The Henmon-Nelson Test of Mental Ability: Manual for Administration. Chicago: Houghton-Miflin.

Hess, Robert D. and Roberta Meyer Bear (eds.) 1968, Early Education. Chicago: Aldine.

Innes, J.T., P.B. Jacobson and R.J. Pellegrin, 1965, The Economic Returns to Higher Education: A Survey of Findings. Eugene: The Center for Advanced Study of Educational Administration, University of Oregon.

Jensen, Arthur R. 1969, "How much can we boost IQ and school achievement?" Harvard Educational Review 39 (Winter):1-123.

Joint Economic Committee, Congress of the United States, 1969, The Economics and Financing of Higher Education in the United States. Washington: U.S. Government Printing Office.

Lavin, David E., 1965 The Prediction of Academic Performance. New York: Russell Sage Foundation.

Lefever, D. Welty, 1959, "Review of Henmon-Nelson test of mental ability." Pp. 470-472 in Oscar Krisen Buros (ed.), The Fifth Mental Measurement Year Book. Highland Park, New Jersey: Gryphom Press.

Lenski, Gerhard, 1966, Power and Privilege: A Theory of Social Stratification. New York: McGraw-Hill.

Little, J. Kenneth, 1958, A Statewide Inquiry into Decisions of Youth About Education Beyond High School. Madison: School of Education, University of Wisconsin.

Mallan, John P., 1971, "Current proposals for federal aid to higher education: Some political implications." Pp. 303-330 in Orwig (ed.), Financing Higher Education: Alternatives for the Federal Government. Iowa City: American College Testing Program.

Masters, Stanley H., 1969, "The effects of family income on children's education: Some findings on inequality of oportunity." Journal of Human Resources 4 (Spring):158-175.

Miller, S. M. and F. Reissman, 1969, "The credentials trap." Pp. 69-78 in S.M. Miller and F. Reissman (eds.), Social Class and Social Policy. New York: Basic Books.

Miller, S.M. and Pamela Roby, 1970, The Future of Inequality. New York: Basic Books.

Morgan, James N. and Martin H. David, 1963, "Education and Income." Quarterly Journal of Economics (August):423-437.

Nam, Charles B. and James D. Cowhig, 1962, "Factors related to college attendance of farm and nonfarm high school graduates: 1960." U.S. Department of Commerce, U.S. Department of Agriculture, Farm Population, Series Census-ERS (P-27) 32 (June). Washington: U.S. Government Printing Office.

Newman, Frank (ed.), 1971, Report on Higher Education. Washington: U.S. Government Printing Office.

Organization for Economic Cooperation and Development, 1971, Equal Educational Opportunity. Paris: OECD, Center for Educational Research and Innovation.

Orwig, M.D. (ed.), 1971a, Financing Higher Education: Alternatives for the Federal Government. Iowa City: American College Testing Program; 1971b, "The federal government and the finance of higher education." Pp. 331-360 in Orwig (ed.), Financing Higher Education: Alternatives for the Federal Government. Iowa City: American College Testing Program.

Parnes, Herbert S., Robert C. Miljus, Ruth S. Spitz and Associates, 1970, Career Thresholds: A Longitudinal Study of the Educational and Labor Market Experience of Male Youth, Volume 1. Washington: U.S. Department of Labor, Manpower Administration.

Pechman, Joseph A., 1970, "The distributional effects of public higher education in California." Journal of Human Resources 5 (Summer):361-370; 1971, "The distribution of costs and benefits of public higher education." Journal of Human Resources 6 (Summer):375-376.

Rainwater, Lee, 1970, Behind Ghetto Walls: Black Family Life in a Federal Slum. Chicago: Aldine.

Rivlin, Alice M., 1970, "Equality of Opportunity and Public Policy." Pp. 6-11 in College Entrance Examination Board, Financing Equal Opportunity in Higher Education. New York: College Entrance Examination Board.

Schultz, Theodore W., 1963, The Economic Value of Education. New York: Columbia University Press.

Sewell, William H., 1964, "Community of residence and college plans." American Sociological Review 29 (February):24-38

Sewell, William H. and J. Michael Armer, 1966a, "Neighborhood context and college plans." American Sociological Review 31 (April): 159-168; 1966b, "Response to Turner, Michael and Boyle." American Sociological Review 31 (October):707-712.

Sewell, William H. and Archibald O. Haller, 1965, "Educational and occupational perspectives of farm and rural youth." Pp. 149-169 in Lee G. Burchinal (ed.), Rural Youth in Crisis: Facts, Myths, and Social Change. Washington: U.S. Government Printing Office.

Sewell, William H., Archibald O. Haller, and George W. Ohlendorf, 1970, "The educational and early occupational status achievement process: Replication and revision." American Sociological Review 35 (December):1014-1027.

Sewell, William H., Archibald O. Haller, and Alejandro Portes, 1969, "The educational and early occupational attainment process." American Sociological Review 34 (February):82-92.

Sewell, William H., Robert M. Hauser, and Vimal P. Shah, n.d., Social Status and Higher Education. Unpublished.

Sewell, William H. and Vimal P. Shah, 1967, "Socioeconomic status, intelligence, and the attainment of higher education." Sociology of Education 40 (Winter):1-23; 1968a, "Social class, parental encouragement, and educational aspirations." American Journal of Sociology 73 (March):559-572; 1968b, "Parents' education and children's educational aspirations and achievements." American Sociological Review 33 (April): 191-209.

Shaycoft, Marion F., 1967, The High School Years: Growth in Cognitive Skills. Interim Report 3 to the U.S. Office of Education, Cooperative Research Project No. 3051. Pittsburgh: Project Talent Office, American Institutes for Research and University of Pittsburgh.

Shaycoft, Marion F., J.T. Dailey, D.B. Orr, *et al.*, 1963, Studies of a Complete Age Group—Age 15. Final report to the U.S. Office of Education, Cooperative Research Project No. 635. Pittsburgh: Project Talent Office, University of Pittsburgh.

Sorokin, Pitirim, 1927, Social Mobility. New York: Harper & Brothers.

Spady, William G., 1967, "Educational mobility and access: Growth and paradoxes." American Journal of Sociology 73 (November):273-279.

Spilerman, Seymour, 1971, "Raising academic motivation in lower class adolescents: A convergence of two research traditions." Sociology of Education 44 (Winter):103-118.

Trent, James W. and Leland L. Medsker, 1968, Beyond High School. San Francisco: Jossey-Bass.

U.S. Bureau of the Census, 1960, Census of Population 1960. Volume 1. Characteristics of the Population, Part I. U.S. Summary, Table 173 and Current Population Reports, Population Characteristics, Series P-20, No. 207, Table 1. Washington: U.S. Government Printing Office; 1961, "School enrollment, and education of young adults and their fathers: October 1960." Current Population Reports, P-20, 110 (July). Washington: U.S. Government Printing Office; 1969, "Factors related to high school graduation and college attendance: 1967." Current Population Reports, Series P-20, 185 (July). Washington: U.S. Government Printing Office; 1970, "Educational Attainment: March 1970." Current Population Reports, Series P-20, 207 (November)' Washington: U.S. Government Printing Office; 1971, "School Enrollment: October 1970." Current Population Reports. Series P-20, 222 (June). Washington: U.S. Government Printing Office.

U.S. Department of Health, Education, and Welfare, Office of Assistant Secretary for Planning and Education, 1969, Toward a Long Range Plan for Federal Support for Higher Education (A Report to the President). Washington: U.S. Government Printing Office.

Wegner, Eldon and William H. Sewell, 1970, "Selection and context as factors affecting the probability of graduation from college." American Journal of Sociology 75 (January):665-679.

Weisbrod, Burton A. and Peter Karpoff, 1968, "Monetary returns to college education, student ability, and college quality." Review of Economics and Statistics (November):491-497.

Williams, Walter and John W. Evans, 1969, "The political evaluation: The case of Head Start." The Annals 385 (September): 118-132.

Willingham, Warren (ed.), 1970, Free Access Higher Education. New York: College Entrance Examination Board.

Wright, Stephen J., 1970, "The financing of equal opportunity in higher education: The problem and the urgency." Pp. 1-5 in College Entrance Examination Board, Financing Equality of Educational Opportunity in Higher Education. New York: College Entrance Examination Board.

Zeller, Frederick A., John R. Shea, Andrew I. Kohen, Jack A. Meyer, 1970, Career Thresholds: A Longitudinal Study of the Educational and Labor Market Experience of Male Youth, Volume 2. Columbus, Ohio: The Ohio State University Center for Human Resource Research. Washington: U.S. Department of Labor, Manpower Administration.

COMMUNITY COLLEGES AND
SOCIAL STRATIFICATION

Jerome Karabel

In recent years a remarkable transformation has occurred in American higher education, a change as far-ranging in its consequences as the earlier transformation of the American high school from an elite to a mass institution. At the forefront of this development has been the burgeoning two-year community college movement. Enrolling 153,970 students in 1948, two-year public colleges increased their enrollment by one million over the next twenty years to 1,169,635 in 1968 (Department of Health, Education, and Welfare, 1970, p. 75). This growth in enrollment has been accompanied by an increase in the number of institutions; during the 1960's, the number of community colleges increased from 656 to 1,100. Nationally, one-third of all students who enter higher education today start in a community college. In California, the state with the most intricate network of community colleges, students who begin in a community college represent 80 percent of all entering students (Medsker & Tillery, 1971, 16-17). In the future, the role of community colleges in the system of higher education promises to become even larger.

A complex set of forces underlies this extraordinary change in the structure of American higher education. One critical factor in the expansion and differentiation of the system of colleges and universities has been a change in the structure of the economy. Between 1950 and 1970, the proportion of technical and professional workers in the labor force rose from 7.1 percent to 14.5 percent (Bureau of the Census, 1971a, p. 225). Some of this increase took place among traditional professions, such as law and medicine, but much of it occurred among growth fields such as data processing and the health semi-professions which frequently require more than a high school education but less than a bachelor's degree. Community colleges have been important in providing the manpower for this growing middle-level stratum and, if current projections of occupational trends are correct, they are likely to become indispensable in filling labor force needs during the next few years. Openings for library technicians and dental hygienists, for example, jobs for which community colleges provide much of the training, will number 9,000 and 2,400 respectively per year for the next decade. Overall, the largest growth area until 1980 will be the technical and professional category with a projected increase of 50 percent. (Bushnell and Zagaris, 1972, p. 135). Without these major changes in the American economy, it is extremely unlikely that the community college movement would have attained its present dimensions.

Although a change in the nature of the labor force laid the groundwork for a system of two-year public colleges, the magnitude and shape of the community college movement owe much to American ideology about equal opportunity through education. Observers, both foreign and domestic, have long noted that Americans take pride in their country's openness—in its apparent capacity to let each person advance as far as his abilities can take him, regardless of social origins. This perceived freedom from caste and class is often contrasted to the aristocratic character of many European societies.(1) America, according to the ideology, is the land of opportunity, and the capstone of its open opportunity structure is its system of public education.

TABLE 1

Percentage of U.S. Younger Employed Males in Professional and Managerial Occupations, by Level of Educational Attainment, Latter 1960's

Level of Educational Attainment	Percentage, Professional and Managerial
High school graduation only	7
One or two terms of college	13
Three of four terms of college	28
Five to seven terms of college	32
Eight or more terms of college	82

Source: Unpublished tabulations of the October 1967, 1968, and 1969 Current Population Surveys of the Bureau of the Census, in which the occupations of younger persons, and the imputed earnings for the various occupations were related to levels of educational attainment. (Jaffe and Adams, 1972, p. 249)

Americans have not only believed in the possibility of upward mobility through education, but have also become convinced that, in a society which places considerable emphasis on credentials, the lack of the proper degrees may well be fatal to the realization of their aspirations. In recent years higher education has obtained a virtual monopoly on entrance to middle and upper level positions in the class structure. Table I shows that the probability of holding a high status job, in this case defined as a professional or managerial position, increases sharply with the possession of a bachelor's degree. This stress on diplomas has led to a clamor for access to higher education, regardless of social background or past achievements. The American educational system keeps the mobility "contest"(2) open for as long as possible and has been willing and able to accommodate the demands of the populace for universal access to college.

Response to the pressure for entrance led to greater hierarchical differentiation within higher education.(3) Existing four-year colleges did not, for the most part, open up to the masses of students demanding higher education (indeed, selectivity at many of these institutions has increased in recent years); instead, separate two-year institutions stressing their open and democratic character were created for these new students. Herein lies the genius of the community college movement: it seemingly fulfills the traditional American quest for *equality of opportunity* without sacrificing the principle of *achievement*. On the one hand, the openness of the community college(4) gives testimony to the American commitment to equality of opportunity through education; an empirical study of Medsker and Trent (1965) shows that, among students of high ability and low social status, the rate of college attendance varies from 22 percent in a community with no colleges to 53 percent in a community with a junior college. On the other hand, the community colleges leave the principle of achievement intact by enabling the state colleges and universities to deny access to those citizens who do not meet their qualifications. The latent ideology of the community college movement thus suggests that everyone should have an opportunity to attain elite status, but that once they have had a chance to prove themselves, an unequal distribution of rewards is acceptable. By their ideology, by their position in the implicit tracking system of higher education—indeed, by their very relationship to the larger class structure—the community colleges lend affirmation to the merit principle which, while facilitating individual upward mobility, diverts attention from underlying questions of distributive justice.

The community college movement is part of a larger historical process of educational expansion. In the early twentieth century, the key point of expansion was at the secondary level as the high school underwent a transition from an elite to a mass institution. Then, as now, access to education was markedly influenced by socioeconomic status.(5)

As the high school became a mass institution, it underwent an internal transformation (Trow, 1966). Formerly providing uniform training to a small group of relatively homogeneous students in order to enable them to fill new white-collar jobs, the high school responded to the massive influx of students by developing a differentiated curriculum. The main thrust of this new curriculum was to provide terminal rather than college preparatory education.

Martin Trow places this "first transformation of American secondary education" between 1910 and 1940. During this period, the proportion of the 14 to 17 age group attending rose from about 15 percent to over 70 percent.

Since World War II, a similar transformation has been taking place in American higher education: in 1945, 16.3 percent of the 18 to 21 age group was enrolled in college; by 1968, the proportion had grown to 40.8 percent (Department of Health, Education and Welfare, 1970, p. 67). This growth has been accompanied by increasing differentiation in higher education, with the community colleges playing a pivotal role in this new division of labor. In short, educational expansion seems to lead to some form of tracking which, in turn, distributes people in a manner which is roughly commensurate with both their class origins and their occupational destination.

The process by which the educational system expands without narrowing relative differences between groups or changing the underlying opportunity structure may be referred to as "educational inflation" (cf. Milner, 1972). Like economic inflation, educational inflation means that what used to be quite valuable (e.g., a high school diploma) is worth less than it once was. As lower socioeconomic groups attain access to a specific level of education, educational escalation is pushed one step higher. When the high school was democratized, sorting continued to take place through the mechanism of tracking, with higher status children taking college preparatory programs and lower status children enrolling in terminal vocational courses; similarly as access to college was universalized, the allocative function continued to occur through the provision of separate schools, two-year community colleges, which would provide an education for most students that would not only be different from a bachelor's degree program, but also shorter. The net effect of educational inflation is thus to vitiate the social impact of extending educational opportunity to a higher level.

If the theory of educational inflation is correct, we would expect that the tremendous expansion of the educational system in the twentieth century has been accompanied by minimal changes in the system of social stratification. Indeed, various studies indicate that the rate of social mobility has remained fairly constant in the last half-century (Lipset and Bendix, 1959; Blau and Duncan, 1967) as has the distribution of wealth and income (Kolko, 1962; Miller, 1971; Jencks, 1972). Apparently, the extension of educational opportunity, however much it may have contributed to other spheres such as economic productivity and the general cultural level of the society, has resulted in little or no change in the overall extent of social mobility and economic inequality.

To observe that educational expansion has not resulted in fundamental changes in the American class structure is in no way to deny that it *has* been critical in providing upward mobility for many individuals. Nor is the assertion that patterns of mobility and inequality have been fairly stable over time meant to reflect upon the intentions of those who were instrumental in changing the shape of the educational system; at work have been underlying social processes, particularly economic and ideological ones, which have helped give shape to the community college.

The thesis of this paper is that the community college, generally viewed as the leading edge of an open and egalitarian system of higher education, is in reality a prime contemporary expression of the dual historical patterns of class-based tracking and of educational inflation. The paper will examine data on the social composition of the community college student body, the flow of community college students through the system of higher education, and the distributive effects of public higher education. Throughout, the emphasis will be on social class and tracking. An analysis of existing evidence will show that the community college is itself the bottom track of the system of higher education both in class origins and occupational destinations of its students. Further, tracking takes place *within* the community college in the form of vocational education. The existence of submerged class conflicts, inherent in a class-based tracking system, will receive considerable attention, with special emphasis on the processes which contribute to these conflicts remaining latent. The paper will conclude with a discussion of the implications of its findings on class and the community college.

THE COMPOSITION OF THE COMMUNITY COLLEGE STUDENT BODY

If community colleges occupy the bottom of a tracking system within higher education that is closely linked to the external class structure, the social composition of the two-year public college should be proportionately lower in status than that of more prestigious four-year institutions. Christopher Jencks and David Riesman, in *The Academic Revolution* (1968, p. 485), however, citing 1966 American Council on Education data, suggest that the "parents of students who enroll at community colleges are slightly *richer* than the parents of students at four-year institutions." This conclusion is derived from the small income superiority students at two-year public colleges had over students at four-year public colleges in 1966; it ignores public universities and all private institutions. Several other studies, most of them more recent, show that community college students *do* come from lower class backgrounds, as measured by income, occupation, and education, than do their counterparts at four-year colleges and universities (Medsker and Trent, 1965; Schoenfeldt, 1968; American Council on Education, 1971; Medsker and Tillery, 1971; Bureau of the Census, 1972).

Table 2 presents data showing the distribution of fathers' occupations at various types of colleges. Community colleges are lowest in terms of social class; they have the fewest children of professionals and managers (16 percent) and the most of blue-collar workers (55 percent). Private universities, the most prestigious of the categories and the one linked most closely to graduate and professional schools, have the highest social composition: 49 percent professional and managerial and only 20 percent blue-collar. Interestingly, the proportion of middle-level occupations shows little variation among the various types of colleges.

Having demonstrated the lower-middle and working-class character of community colleges, it would seem to follow that college type is also related to family income. Table 3, based on nationally representative American Council on

Education data for 1971, reveals systematic income differences among the student bodies at various types of colleges. Over one-quarter of all community college students are from relatively low income families (under $8000) compared with about 11 percent at private universities. Affluent students (over $20,000) comprise 12 percent of the student body at community colleges but over 40 percent at private institutions. The four-year public colleges show income distributions between community colleges and private universities.

TABLE 2

Father's Occupational Classification by Type of College Entered (percentages)

| | Father's Occupational Classification | | | |
Type of College	Skilled, Semi-skilled Unskilled	Semi-professional, Small Business, Sales and Clerical	Professional and Managerial	Total
Public two-year	55	29	16	100
Public four-year	49	32	19	100
Private four-year	38	30	32	100
Public university	32	33	35	100
Private university	20	31	49	100

Source: Medsker and Trent (1965)

TABLE 3

Family Income by Type of College Entered (percentages)

| | Family Income | | | | |
Type of College	Under $8,000	$8,000– 12,499	$12,500– 20,000	Over $20,000	Total
Public two-year	27.2	34.8	26.4	11.5	100
Public four-year	25.4	31.7	28.3	14.7	100
Public university	15.1	29.7	32.8	22.3	100
Private university	10.6	20.4	27.3	41.8	100

Source: American Council on Education (1971, p. 39)

Prestige differences among colleges also correspond to differences in fathers' educational attainment. In Table 4, American Council on Education data for 1966 show that the proportion of students whose fathers graduated from college ranges from 15 percent at community colleges to 72.6 percent at elite institutions (colleges with average Scholastic Aptitude Tests over 650). Over one third of public two-year college students have fathers who did not graduate from high school compared with less than 5 percent at elite colleges.

TABLE 4
Father's Education by Type of College Entered (percentages)

	Father's Education						
Type of College	Grammar School or Less	Some High School	High School Graduate	Some College	College Graduate	Post-graduate Degree	Total
Public-two year	12.7	21.3	31.7	19.1	11.5	3.8	100
Public four-year	12.1	19.4	34.7	17.9	11.1	4.8	100
Public university	8.0	13.9	29.0	20.3	19.0	9.8	100
Private university	4.6	9.6	21.9	18.9	24.4	20.5	100
Elite*	1.2	3.5	10.6	13.1	31.3	40.5	100

Source: American Council on Education (1967, p. 22)
*Elite colleges are defined as institutions having average freshman SAT's over 650. For more data on elite colleges see Karabel and Astin (forthcoming).

The data on occupation, income, and education all run in the same direction and testify to an increase in social class position as one ascends the prestige hierarchy of colleges and universities. Community colleges, at the bottom of the tracking system in higher education, are also lowest in student body class composition. That college prestige is a rough indicator of factors leading to adult occupational attainment and of adult socioeconomic status itself is borne out by a number of studies (Havemann and West, 1952; Reed and Miller, 1970; Wolfle, 1971; Pierson, 1969; Collins, 1971; Spaeth, 1968; Sharp, 1970; Folger *et al.*, 1970). Thus, the current tracking system in higher education may help transmit inequality intergenerationally. Lower class students disproportionately attend community colleges which, in turn, channel them into relatively low status jobs.

However related attendance at a community college may be to social origins, students are not explicitly sorted into the hierarchically differentiated system of higher education on the basis of social class. More important than class background in predicting where one goes to college is measured academic ability (Folger *et al.*, 1970, pp. 166-167; Karabel and Astin, forthcoming). Schoenfeldt (1968), using Project TALENT data, reports that junior college students are more like non-college students in terms of academic ability and more like four-year college students in terms of socioeconomic status. A review of research on the ability of junior college students by Cross (1968) concludes that they show substantially less measured academic ability than their four-year counterparts although there is a great diversity in academic ability *among* junior college students. In a sample of 1966 high school graduates in four states who entered community colleges, 19 percent were in the highest quartile of academic ability (Medsker & Tillery, 1971, p. 38). As is common with aggregate data, generalizations obscure important variations among individuals. In California, where admission to the state colleges and university are limited to the top 33-1/3 and 12-1/2 percent in ability respectively, approximately 26 and 6 percent of students who choose a junior college would have been eligible for a state college or university (Coordinating Council, 1969, p. 79).

There is evidence that many high ability students who attend community colleges are of modest social origins. In California, for example, the proportion of eligible students who choose to attend the state colleges or university varies from 22.5 percent among students from families with incomes of under $4,000 to over 50 percent in the $20,000-25,000 category (Hansen and Weisbrod, 1969, p. 74). It is assumed that many of these low-income students attend a nearby two-year college. Table 5 estimates the probability of a male student entering a junior college (public and private). The likeliest entrant at a two-year college is the person of high academic ability and low social status followed by the high status student of less than average ability. These data, however, cannot be construed as providing the relative proportion of intelligent, poor students as opposed to mediocre, rich students in the community college; instead, they merely show the probability of attending a two-year college *if* someone falls into a particular category. Table 5 also illustrates that there is a diversity of both social class and academic ability in the community college. Internal diversity notwithstanding, the community college does indeed stand at the bottom of the tracking system in higher education not only from the perspective of social class, but also from that of academic ability.

TABLE 5
Probability of a Male Entering a Two-Year College

Socioeconomic Quarter	Ability Quarter			
	Low 1	2	3	High 4
Low 1	.04	.07	.06	.16
2	.03	.07	.10	.08
3	.07	.11	.10	.08
High 4	.11	.12	.11	.05

Source: Schoenfeldt (1968, p. 357)

COMMUNITY COLLEGE STUDENTS IN THE EDUCATIONAL SYSTEM

A substantial body of research links the presence of a community college to increased utilization of higher education (Medsker & Trent, 1965; Cross, 1968; Willingham, 1970). The Medsker-Trent study, for example, shows that the existence of a community college increases the percentage of people who enter the system of higher education, especially among low status youth of high ability. This extension of the opportunity to attend college to persons of modest social origins or past achievements is unique to this nation and ranks as one of the community college movement's greatest accomplishments. Widely hailed as the "democratization of higher education" (Cross, 1968, p. 21; Fields, 1962, p. 55), the expansion of educational opportunity provided by two-year public colleges seemingly marks a giant stride toward the realization of the American ideal of upward mobility through education.

Increased access, however, does not automatically lead to a genuine expansion of educational opportunity. The critical question is not who gains access to higher education, but rather what happens to people once they get there. The distinction parallels the distinction between equal access (which is what many people mean by equal opportunity) and equal outcomes or results. For community college students, this interest in both access and outcomes leads naturally into an examination of patterns of aspirations, attrition, and transfer to four-year colleges.

PATTERNS OF ATTENDANCE

Despite the fact that community colleges offer no degrees or certificates higher than an associate of arts degree (A.A.), over 70 percent of their students aspire to a bachelor's degree with more than 20 percent aspiring to a degree beyond the B.A. Occupational aspirations are also high among these students with 64 percent hoping to enter managerial and professional occupations (Cross, 1968, pp. 41-46). Students at two-year colleges, though generally of low to moderate economic and educational backgrounds, desire upward mobility in both education and career.(6) Indeed, high aspirations among community college students, at least upon entrance, is one of the most consistent findings in research on the topic.

In view of the community college's position within the tracking system of higher education, one would expect that unrealized aspirations through attrition would be quite high. Bruce Eckland (1964), in a seminal study of the college dropout, proposed a "diversity hypothesis" which suggested a link between social class and college graduation. The hypothesis is that "the rate of dropout at a college or university varies inversely with the class composition of its student population." Community colleges, with the lowest class composition among American institutions of higher education, are expected to show the highest dropout rate. Indeed, attrition among community college students is commonplace. In California, where the junior college movement is most advanced, the ratio of sophomores to freshmen among full-time students at community colleges is .36 (Jaffe & Adams, 1972, p. 229). While some of these students may transfer to a four-year college and others may later return to higher education, it remains true that there are almost three freshmen for every sophomore in California community colleges. Nationally, 38.4 percent of two-year college students had received an A.A. degree in four years with only an additional 2 percent still enrolled.(7) Among four-year college students, 46.7 percent received a B.A. degree after four years with 11.8 percent still enrolled. Noting that nearly 90 percent of all junior college students expected to obtain at least an A.A. upon entrance to college, Astin (1972, p. 13) concludes that "it may certainly be said that unfilled expectations are the rule rather than the exception among two-year college students." For many community college students the "open door" turns out to be nothing more than a "revolving door."

With less than half of community college students receiving any kind of a degree at all, it is not surprising that few of them transfer to a four-year college and that even fewer obtain a bachelor's degree. The proportion of community college students who actually transfer to a four-year institution is difficult to determine, but estimates seem to range from 25 to 35 percent. Clark (1960, p. 65) in a study of San Jose City College, found that one student in four transferred. Trent and Medsker (1968, p. 79), in a four-year follow-up of students who entered community colleges, found that 11 percent had obtained a B.A., 22 percent were still enrolled and 67 percent were no longer in college. Whatever the precise figures, we can surely say that no more than half of the over 70 percent of community college students who aspire to a bachelor's degree upon entrance transfer to a four-year institution.

The number of community college entrants who obtain a B.A., is, of course, smaller than the number of transfers. Folger et al. (1970, p. 174) report that 22 percent of junior college entrants obtain a B.A. within five years. Trent and Medsker (1968) find that slightly more than one junior college entrant in ten has a bachelor's degree four years after high school graduation. In comparision, 49 percent of students who entered private colleges and universities have a B.A., with an additional 21 percent still enrolled. Knoell and Medsker (1964), in the best study of students who do transfer from community colleges to four-year institutions, show that 62 percent of these transfer students get a B.A. after three years and 9 percent remain enrolled. For those community college entrants who succeed in transferring to a four-year college there is apparently a good chance that, despite a somewhat lower grade point average than native students, they will obtain a diploma.

Some indirect evidence suggests that the community college students who go on to a bachelor's degree are from higher socioeconomic backgrounds than students who never graduate. One indication of this is the finding that students enrolled in the transfer curriculum are from more affluent backgrounds than those in non-transfer programs (Cross, 1970, p. 191; Cohen, 1971, p. 72; Bushnell & Zagaris, 1972, p. 28). Unpublished ACE data from a 1969 follow-up of the entering class of 1966 show that the estimated probability of transferring from a junior college (public or private) to a four-year institution increases in linear fashion as father's educational attainment rises from less than high school (45 percent transfers to a four-year college) to college graduate or higher (58 percent). While the data relating social class at the community college to the attainment of a bachelor's degree are inadequate, they do suggest that the community college serves the middle class at least as well as it serves the working class. Christopher Jencks, in a personal communication, however, has suggested an alternative interpretation: "one of the primary functions of the two-year colleges is not to 'cool out' (see pp. 536-540) the upwardly mobile working class, but to cool out the downwardly mobile middle class who are not so smart." This is a central question for students of higher education and stratification. It is one that is susceptible to empirical investigation, but existing research simply cannot settle the matter.

One of the most interesting findings to emerge from the research on community college attrition is that the sheer fact of attending a community college, *controlling for other variables*, seems to increase the likelihood of dropping out. Astin's recent longitudinal study, which controlled a myriad of variables (including aspirations, SES, and ability) applied the regression formula developed to predict returning for a second year at four-year college to two-year colleges and found that the expected rate of persistence exceeded the actual rate at 14 of 23 institutions. When he applied the formula for two-year colleges at four-year institutions, the actual persistence rates exceeded the expected ones in 151 out of 189 cases. Persistence, as measured by returning for a second year, seems negatively affected by attending a community college.(8)

The finding that community colleges have a negative impact on persistence, taking differential student characteristics at entrance into account, fits in with the repeated finding of a general positive relationship between institutional selectivity and the probability of staying in school. In a four-year national longitudinal study, Astin and Panos (1969) found that college selectivity is positively related to student persistence even when student inputs, including ability and SES are controlled. Wegner and Sewell (1970), using Wisconsin data, have shown that type of college attended accounts for 3.1 percent of the variance in graduation *beyond* the effects of academic ability, occupational aspiration, and SES. It is thus not surprising that community colleges, which are among the least selective institutions of higher education, have a negative impact on student persistence.

Since college selectivity negatively affects grades (Astin, 1971), the finding that attendance at a selective institution, even when controlling for student characteristics at entrance, increases the likelihood of remaining in college is somewhat surprising. Perhaps the greater the selectivity of the college the more likely the institution is to expect its students to graduate. Conversely, less selective colleges may exaggerate the differences between those who are "college material" and those who are not—flunking out students who might otherwise have skimmed by. The community colleges were designed, in part, to provide a limited number of transfer students to four-year colleges. Aware that its reputation as a transfer instution depends on the success of its students who attend four-year colleges and universities, the community college may "cool out" (see the next section) students who might have survived elsewhere. In short, low selectivity coupled with a built-in awareness of a sorting function may contribute to high rates of attrition.

The data presented in Table 6 show dramatically the negative impact of attending a community college, controlling separately for academic ability and socioeconomic status, on the probability of obtaining a bachelor's degree in five years. These data, though lacking a simultaneous control for SES and ability, provide evidence for massive differentials between junior and senior college entrants in rates of college completion within the same categories of class and intelligence. Among high aptitude men, for example, more than two-thirds of senior college entrants obtain a B.A. in five years compared with less than one-third among two-year college entrants. One could argue that these differentials will decrease over time as community college students have a chance to complete their degrees, but Eckland's (1964) study suggests that this may be dubious. Offering a "persistence hypothesis" which proposes that class differentials in rates of college completion increase over time, Eckland verifies this theory with empirical evidence. Since community colleges have a disproportionately large share of lower-class students. the persistence hypothesis suggests that the gap between two- and four-year college entrants in obtaining a four-year diploma may well increase over the years.

TABLE 6

Proportion of Students Receiving Bachelor's Degrees Among Senior and Junior College Entrants with Similar Academic Aptitude, by Sex

Academic Aptitude and SES by Type of College	Percent Graduating from College	Percent Graduating from College
	Men	Women
Academic aptitude		
High		
Senior College	70	74
Junior College	31	40
High-Medium		
Senior College	55	60
Junior College	19	20
Socioeconomic Status		
High		
Senior College	67	70
Junior College	21	26
High-Medium		
Senior College	57	63
Junior College	23	21

Source: Folger, *et al.* (1970, p. 176)

Another notable finding which emerges from studies of the progress of community college students through the educational system is the failure of massive systems of public two-year colleges to increase the number of people obtaining bachelor's degrees. This finding is contrary to what we might expect; community colleges were supposed to increase the number of four-year degrees by increasing the number of low SES and high ability students who received bachelor's degrees. Jaffe and Adams (1972, pp. 230-231), using Census Bureau data from the late 1960's, find that the Pacific division (California accounts for 75 percent of the young population) shows the second lowest proportion of the *age cohort* completing four years of college among the nine census divisions.

California, with the largest system of community colleges in the nation, apparently provides four or more years of college to an unusually small proportion of its population (Knoell and Medsker, 1964, p. 3; Coordinating Council, 1969, p. 28; Jencks and Riesman, 1968, p. 489). The Rocky Mountain region, which also has a highly developed system of two-year colleges (but without the cultural milieu of the Pacific Coast states which, one could argue, might lead to high attrition) is the *lowest* of the nine regions in the proportion of the age group receiving bachelor's degrees.

The implications of the failure of the community college movement to expand opportunity for the attainment of the B.A., the credential which is critical for admission into the professional and managerial upper-middle class, are far-ranging. The Folger Commission, reflecting on their findings regarding socioeconomic status and educational progress, expresses concern:

> Paradoxically, the community colleges appear to have increased college opportunity for low-status youth, and at the same time to have increased socio-economic differentials in college completion. They have been successful in getting low-income youth into college, but have not increased their chances of getting a degree nearly as much. (Folger *et al.*, 1970, p. 319)

The complexity of the relationships among social class, attrition, and the community college should not be allowed to obscure their importance for an understanding of the stratification function of two-year public colleges. Eckland's "diversity hypothesis," stated at the beginning of this section, led us to expect high attrition among community college students. The fact of attending a two-year college, even controlling for ability, social class, and other variables, has a negative impact on persistence. Hence, the high attrition rate at the community college is not merely an outgrowth of the low status social composition of its student body. Tracking in higher education leads to disproportionately high attendance of low status students at community colleges which, in turn, decreases the likelihood that they will stay in school. Further, once a student is in a community college, both Eckland's persistence hypothesis and fragmentary evidence from transfer programs suggest that the high status student is more likely to remain in school, to transfer, and to obtain a bachelor's degree. This process does not contribute to equal educational opportunity, though it may contribute something to explaining the failure of community colleges to increase the proportion of college graduates. Writing in 1964, Eckland warned that "social-class differences will increasingly determine who graduates among the college entrants of the next few decades, since it is apparently among the less qualified students that class origins have the greatest impact" (p. 50). If current trends continue, his analysis will have been prophetic.

The preceding section on patterns of attendance among community college students showed large discrepancies between aspirations and their realization. Unrealized educational aspirations, almost always linked to a desire for upward mobility, reach genuinely massive proportions among community college students. Clearly, the social process which enables those who entered the junior college with high hopes never to be realized to adjust to their situation bears close investigation.

The key to this process is what Burton Clark (1960), in a classic case study of San Jose City College (a two-year institution), referred to as "cooling out." The community college, according to Clark, has three types of students; pure terminal (usually occupational), pure transfer, and latent terminal. The latent terminal student, the one who would like to transfer but who is not likely to meet the qualifications, poses a serious problem for the junior college. The crux of the dilemma is how to gently convince the latent terminal student that a transfer program is inappropriate for him without seeming to deny him the equal educational opportunity that Americans value so highly. Clark does not specify the class origins of these students, but since the modal community college student is of relatively low social status (Cross, 1971) and since SES is itself related to both academic ability and to the probability of dropping out of college, it seems fair to assume that many of them are working class or lower middle class. A great deal is thus at stake here: failure to give these students a "fair shake" would undermine American confidence in the democratic character of the educational system and, very possibly, of the larger society.

"Cooling out," the process described by Clark (pp. 71-76) of handling latent terminal students, begins even before the student arrives as a freshman. A battery of pre-entrance tests are given, and low scores lead to remedial classes which not only cast doubt on the student's promise, but which also slow his movement toward courses for credit. The second step is a meeting with a counselor to arrange the student's class schedule. In view of test scores, high school record, and the student's objectives, the counselor tries to assist the student in choosing a realistic program.(9)

The next step of the process Clark describes in his case study of San Jose is a specially devised course called "Psychology 5, Orientation to College." A one-unit mandatory course, it is designed to assist the student in selecting a program and places special emphasis on the problem of "unrealistic aspirations." Counselors report that the course provides an ideal opportunity "to talk tough" in an impersonal way to latent terminal students.

The cooling out process has, until this point, been gentle, and the latent-terminal student can refuse to heed the subtle and not-so-subtle hints he has been given. The fourth step of the process, however—dissemination of "need for improvement notices," given to students in courses where they are getting low grades—is impossible to ignore. If the student does not seek guidance, the counselor, with the authority of the disciplinary apparatus behind him requests to see the student. All of this goes into the student's permanent record.

The fifth and possibly most decisive step of the process is the placing of a student on probation. This is to pressure him into a realistic program. "The real meaning of probation," says Clark, "lies in its killing off the hope of some of the latent terminal students" (p. 75).

The purpose of the drawn-out counseling procedure is not to bludgeon the student into dropping out, but rather to have the student himself decide to switch out of the transfer program. If the student can be persuaded to take himself out of the competition without being forced out of it (though being flunked out), he is much more likely to retain a benign view of the sorting process.

The opaqueness of the cooling out function is indispensable to its successful performance. In a revealing passage, Clark describes the nature of the problem:

> A dilemma of this role, however, is that it needs to remain reasonably latent, not clearly perceived and understood by prospective clientele. Should the function become obvious, the ability of the junior college to perform it would be impaired. The realization that the junior college is a place where students reach undesired destinations would turn the pressure for college admission back on the "protected" colleges. The widespread identification of the junior college as principally a transfer station, aided by the ambiguity of the "community college" label, helps keep this role reasonably opaque to public scrutiny (p. 165).

The implication of this passage, of course, is that the community college would be unable to perform its task of allowing high aspirations to gently subside if its social function were understood by those most directly affected by it. Clark considers "the student who filters out of education while in the junior college . . . to be very much what such a college is about" (p. 84), and refers to the "transforming of transfer students into terminal students" as the community college's "operational specialty" (p. 146).

One problem with Clark's analysis of the community college is that he perceives the "situation of structured failure" to emerge out of a conflict between the rigorous academic standards of higher education and the non-selective open door. What Clark has failed to do here is to take his analysis a step further to analyze the social function of standards. Rothbart (1970) notes that "objective" academic standards also serve to exclude the poor and minorities from the university. The even-handed application of these standards to all groups gives each individual the feeling that he "had his chance." Academic standards, far from being the quintessential expression of an objective ivory tower concept, justify the university as a means of distributing privilege and of legitimating inequality. This is not to deny that academic standards have important intellectual substance, but it is to say that standards do have a class function. Indeed, what appears to Clark to be a conflict between professors committed to standards and students who do not "measure up" is, in a wider sense, a conflict between low-status students demanding upward mobility and a system unable to fully respond to their aspirations because it is too narrow at the top. Academic standards are located in the midst of this conflict and serve as a "covert mechanism" which, according to Rothbart, enables the university to "do the dirty work for the rest of the society" (p. 174). The cooling out process, the opaqueness of which Clark himself stresses, is thus the expression not only of an academic conflict, but also of a submerged class conflict.

Community colleges, which are located at the very point in the structure of educational and social stratification where cultural aspirations clash head on with the realities of the class system, developed cooling out as a means not only of allocating people to slots in the occupational structure, but also of legitimating the process by which people are sorted. One of its main features is that it causes people to blame themselves rather than the system for their "failure." This process was an organic rather than a conscious one; cooling out was not designed by anyone but rather grew out of the conflict between cultural aspirations and economic reality. Commitment to standards, sincerely held by many academics, may have played a small part in this process, but professorial devotion to academic rigor could disappear and the underlying cultural and structural conflict would remain. Cooling out, or something very much like it, was and is inevitable given this conflict.

The cooling out process not only allows the junior college to perform its sorting and legitimation functions; given the class composition of the community college and the data on attrition, it also enables the two-year college to contribute to the intergenerational transmission of privilege (Bowles, 1971a and 1971b). At the bottom of an increasingly formalized tracking system in higher education, community colleges channel working-class students away from four-year colleges and into middle-level technical occupations. Having gained access to higher education, the low status student is often cooled out and made to internalize his structurally induced failure. The tremendous disjunction between aspirations and their realization, a potentially troublesome political problem, is thus mitigated and the ideology of equal opportunity is sustained. That community colleges have a *negative* impact on persistence, that they do *not* increase the number of bachelor's degrees, that they seem to provide the greatest opportunity for transfer (and hence mobility) to *middle* class students—these are all facts which are unknown to their clientele. The community college movement, seemingly a promising extension of equal educational opportunity, in reality marks the extension of a class-based tracking system into higher education and the continuation of a long historical process of educational escalation without real change.

TRACKING WITHIN THE COMMUNITY COLLEGE

The subordinate position of the community college within the tracking system of higher education has often been noted. What has been less frequently noted is that tracking also takes place *within* the community college. Two-year public colleges are almost always open door institutions, but admission to programs within them is often on a selective basis. What this generally means in practice is that students who are not "transfer material" are either tracked into vocational programs or cooled out altogether.

Class-based tracking, whether between schools, within schools, or both, is not

new in American education. This pattern extends back into the early twentieth
century, the period during which the American high school became a mass
institution.(10) If the theory of class-based hierarchical differentiation in
education is applied to the question of tracking within the community college, it
would lead us to expect a relatively low class composition among students in
vocational programs.

TABLE 7
*Selected Characteristics of Students Enrolled in Three Curriculums in 63
Comprehensive Community Colleges (percentages)*

Characteristics	College Parallel	Technical	Vocational
Father's occupation			
Unskilled or semiskilled	18	26	35
White collar	46	35	25
Parental income			
Less than $6,000	14	14	24
More than $10,000	36	28	21
Father's formal education			
Less than high school graduation	27	34	50
Some college or more	31	20	14
Race			
Caucasian	91	79	70
Negro	5	7	14
Oriental	1	7	7
Other	1	4	6

Source: Comparative Guidance and Placement Program, 1969. (Cross, 1970, p.
191)

Data presented in Table 7 show a pronounced class bias in the composition of
community college students enrolled in vocational programs. Compared with
students in transfer programs, vocational students are markedly lower in family
income, father's education, and father's occupation. While almost half of
community college-students in the transfer curriculum are from white-collar
families, only one-fourth of the students in vocational programs are from such
backgrounds. Students enrolled in technical programs fall in between vocational
and transfer students along various measures of socioeconomic status. Black
students show themselves to be considerably more likely than white students to
enroll in community college vocational programs.(11)

The relatively low social origins of vocational and technical students are likely
to be reflected in their adult occupations. Community college occupational
programs are broadly designed to prepare people for entrance into the growing
technical and semi-professional stratum. Estimates as to the size of this

expanding class suggest that it may comprise one-third of the labor force by 1975 (Harris, 1971:254). This stratum occupies the lower-middle levels of the system of social stratification, but it creates a sensation of upward mobility among its members because it is representative of the change from a blue-collar (or secondary) to a white-collar (or tertiary) economy. Since many members of this "new working class" originate from blue-collar backgrounds, their movement into this stratum does in fact represent mobility. Yet it may be conjectured that this perception of mobility is only temporary; as more and more people move into these jobs, the prestige of a white-collar position may undergo a corresponding decline in status.(12)

TABLE 8

Yearly Income of U.S. Younger Employed Males, by Level of Educational Attainment, Late 1960s (Base: High school graduation income = 100)

Level of Educational Attainment	Income	Percentage of All College Dropouts
High school graduation	100	–
One or two terms of college	110	40
Three or four terms of college	119	37
Five to seven terms of college	121	23
Eight or more terms of college	150	–

Source: Unpublished tabulations of the October 1967, 1968, and 1969 Current Population Surveys of the Bureau of the Census, in which the occupations of younger persons, and the imputed earnings for the various occupations were related to levels of educational attainment. (Jaffe and Adams, 1972, p. 249)

Evidence on the economic returns of these vocational programs is, at best, indirect, and empirical studies on this topic would be extremely useful. Yet it is apparent that, in general, having two years of college is not half as good as having four years (Bowles, 1971b, Jaffe & Adams, 1972). Table 8, based on recent Census Bureau data, indicates that the recipient of five to seven terms of college is closer in income to a high school graduate than to a college graduate. Possibly, there is some sort of "sheepskin effect" associated with the attainment of a bachelor's degree. But whatever the reasons, having part of a college education seems to be of limited economic value. Whether this is also true for community college students in programs specially designed to prepare them for an occupation remains to be seen.(13)

THE SPONSORS OF THE VOCATIONAL MOVEMENT

Unlike the movement for open admissions to college, which received much of its impetus from mass pressure, there has been little popular clamor for community college vocational programs. Indeed, most junior college entrants see the two-year college as a way-station to a four-year college and shun occupational programs (see the next section). Despite this, there has been an enormous push to increase enrollment in community college occupational programs. This push from the top for more career education marks one of the major developments in the evolution of the community college movement.

The interest of the business community in encouraging occupational training at public expense is manifest. With a changing labor force which requires ever-increasing amounts of skill to perform its tasks and with manpower shortages in certain critical areas, private industry is anxious to use the community college as a training ground for its employees. An associate of the Space Division of the North American Rockwell Corporation makes the corporate viewpoint clear: "industry . . . must recognize that junior colleges are indispensible to the fulfillment of its needs for technical manpower" (Ryan, 1971:71). In the Los Angeles area, Space Division personnel and junior college faculty work together to set up curricular requirements, frame course content, determine student competence, and formulate "on-the-job performance objectives."

The influence of the business community on the junior college is exerted in part through membership of local industrial notables on community college boards of trustees. Hartnett (1969:28) reports that 33 percent of public junior college trustees are business executives and that over half of all community college trustees agree that "running a college is basically like running a business." Overt business interference in the affairs of the community college is, however, probably rare; the ideological influence of the business community, with its emphasis on pragmatism and economic efficiency, is so pervasive in the two-year college that conflicts between the industrial and educational communities would not normally arise. One imagines that Arthur M. Cohen (1971b:6), Director of the ERIC Clearinghouse for Junior Colleges, is hardly exaggerating when he says that when "corporate managers . . . announce a need for skilled workers . . . college administrators trip over each other in their haste to organize a new technical curriculum."

Foundations have also shown an intense interest in junior college vocational programs, an interest which is somewhat more difficult to explain than that of business and industry. The Kellogg Foundation, which over a period of years, has made grants to the community college movement totaling several million dollars (Gleazer, 1968:38), has a long-standing interest in career training. In 1959, the general director of the Kellogg Foundation noted approvingly that the "community college movement can do much to supply the sub-professionals, the technicians so necessary to the professions and industry in the years ahead" (Powell, 1965:17). Kellogg followed up on this interest in career education with grants to Chicago City Junior College in 1963 and 1964 for associate degree programs in nursing and business which came to $312,440 and $112,493 respecively (Sunko, 1965:42). In addition, in the late 1950's, Kellogg made a several hundred thousand dollar commitment to support the American Association of Junior Colleges, the national organization of the two-year college movement which has itself been a long-time advocate of vocational programs (Brick 1964).

The Carnegie Commission on Higher Education, financially sponsored by, but independent of, the Carnegie Corporation of New York, has also been active in sponsoring career education. In its widely read pamphlet, *The Open-Door Colleges*, the Carnegie Commission (1970), made explicit policy proposals for community colleges. Members of the Commission came out strongly for occupational programs, and stated that they "should be given the fullest support and status within community colleges" and should be "flexibly geared to the changing requirements of society" (1970:1). Later in the report (pp. 15-16) the Commission recommended that community colleges remain two-year institutions lest they "place less emphasis on occupational programs." Community colleges, the Commission said, "should follow an open-enrollment policy, whereas access to four-year institutions should generally be more selective." The net impact of these recommendations is to leave the tracking systems of higher education intact. Considering the class composition of the community college, to maintain the status quo in higher education tracking is, in essence, to perpetuate privilege (see Wolfe, 1971).

The influence of foundations in fostering vocational education in community colleges is difficult to measure precisely, but it is clear that they have been among its leading sponsors.(14) State master plans (see Hurlburt, 1969; Cross, 1970) have also done much to formalize the subordinate status of the community college within higher education and to encourage the growth of their vocational curricula. The federal government, too, has promoted vocational training in the two-year institutions. Federal involvement dates back at least to 1963. At that time, Congress authorized the spending of several hundred million dollars to encourage post-secondary technical education. More recently, the Higher Education Act of 1972 (pp. 77-78) authorized $850,000,000 over the next three years for post-secondary occupational education. In comparison, the entire sum authorized for the establishment of new community colleges and the expansion of old ones is less than one-third as much—$275,000,000.

The language of the Higher Education Act of 1972 makes clear just what is meant by vocational education:

> The term 'postsecondary occupational education' means education, training, or retraining ... conducted by an institution ... which is designed to prepare individuals for gainful employment as semi-skilled or skilled workers or technicians or sub-professionals in recognized occupations (including new and emerging occupations) ... but excluding any program to prepare individuals for employment in occupations ... to be generally considered professional or which require a baccalaureate or advanced degree. (p. 87)

The import of this definition of occupational education is to exclude four-year programs leading to a B.A. from funding. The intent of this legislation, which provides enormous sums of money for community college career education, is obvious: it is designed to fill current manpower shortage in the middle and lower-middle levels of the occupational structure.

The idea of career education which the U.S. Office of Education is "working to spread throughout elementary, secondary and at least community college circles" (Marland, 1972:217) is that the student, regardless of when he leaves the educational system, should have sufficient skills to enable him to be gainfully employed. The idea is a worthy one, but it implicitly accepts the existing system of social stratification. The philosophy of career education is that the proper function of the educational system is to respond to current manpower needs and to allocate people to positions characterized by large disparities in rewards. Commissioner of Education, Sidney Marland, observes that no more than 20 percent of all jobs in the 1970's will require a bachelor's degree; apparently, this is supposed to provide a rough index as to how many people should attend college for four years. Further, it is worth noting that career education does not seem to extend above the community college level. An idea whose "time has come," it somehow does not seem applicable to the sons and daughters of the middle and upper classes who attend four-year colleges and universities.

Federal sponsorship of vocational programs in the community college may have contributed to the development of a rigid track system (Cohen, 1971a:152). By prohibiting the allocation of funds to non-vocational programs, federal laws have deepened the division between transfer and occupational programs. This division fosters separate facilities, separate brochures, and separate administrations. The result is a magnification of the differences between transfer and vocational programs leading to a decline in the desirability of occupational training.

Also at the forefront of the movement to expand vocational programs in community colleges have been various national higher education organizations. The American Association of Junior Colleges (AAJC), almost since its founding in 1920, has exerted its influence to encourage the growth of vocational education. Faced with the initial problem of establishing an identity for two-year colleges, the AAJC set out to describe the unique functions of the junior college. Prominent among these was the provision of two-year occupational training at the post-secondary level. In 1940 and 1941 the AAJC sponsored a Commission on Junior College Terminal Education. According to Ralph Fields (1962), a long-time observer of the junior college, this commission was instrumental in lending legitimacy to vocational training in the community college.

In recent years, the AAJC has continued its active encouragement of occupational programs in the community college. Numerous pamphlets, training programs, and conferences on vocational training in the two-year college have been sponsored by AAJC. In that the AAJC, the leading national association of junior colleges, has probably done more than any other single organization to give definition to the community college movement, its enthusiasm for vocational training takes on particular importance.

The American Council on Education, the umbrella organization for the various associations of higher education, is considered by many to be the leading spokesman for American higher education. It, too, has given major support to post-secondary technical education. In 1963, the Council sponsored a study of the place of technical and vocational training in higher education. One of the conclusions of the report was that "two-year colleges, if they are to assume their proper and effective role in the educational system of the nation, should make vocational and technical education programs a major part of their mission and a fundamental institutional objective" (Venn, 1964:165). Edmund Gleazer, Jr. (1968:139), Executive Director of AAJC, points to this report as critical in gaining acceptance for vocational training within the higher education community.

Finally, many American universities have looked with favor on the development of the community college into a "comprehensive" institution with occupational programs in addition to its more traditional transfer programs. From the origins of the junior college in the late nineteenth and early twentieth centuries as an institution designed to extend secondary education for two years in order to keep the university pure, there has been a recognition among many university academics that it is in their interest to have a diversity of institutions in higher education (Thornton, 1960:46-50). A number of observers have noted that the community colleges serve as a safety valve, diverting students clamoring for access to college away from more selective institutions (Clark, 1960; Jencks and Riesman, 1968; Cohen, 1971b). Elite colleges neither want nor need these students; if separate institutions, or, for that matter, vocational programs within these institutions help keep the masses out of their colleges, then they are to be given full support.(15) Paradoxically, the elite sector of the academic community, much of it liberal to radical, finds itself in a peculiar alliance with industry, foundations, government, and established higher education associations to vocationalize the community college.(16)

THE RESPONSE TO VOCATIONAL EDUCATION

Despite the massive effort by leading national educational policy-makers to encourage the development of occupational education in the community college, student response to vocational programs has been limited. Estimates vary as to how many community college students are enrolled in career education programs, but the figures seem to range from 25 to 33 percent (Cross, 1970; Ogilvie, 1971; Medsker and Tillery, 1971). Over two-thirds of two-year college entrants aspire to a bachelor's degree, and a similar proportion enroll, at least initially, in college-parallel or transfer programs. Many of these students, of course, are subsequently cooled out, but few of them seem to prefer a vocational program to leaving the community college altogether.

Leaders of the occupational education movement have constantly bemoaned the lack of student enthusiasm for vocational education (Venn, 1964; Gleazer, 1968; Carnegie, 1970; Medsker and Tillery, 1971; Cross, 1971). The problem, they believe, is the low status of career training in a society that worships the bachelor's degree. Medsker and Tillery (p. 140), for example, argue that "negative attitudes toward vocational education ... are by-products of the academic syndrome in American higher education." Marland (1972:218) refers to the difficulty as "degree-fixation." The problem then, since it is one of an irrational preoccupation with obtaining a traditional four-year education, leads to an obvious solution: raising the status of vocational education. This proposed solution has been suggested by the Carnegie Commission on Higher Education, the Office of Education, the American Association of Junior Colleges, the American Council on Education, leaders of industry, and scholars in the field of community colleges.

Despite the apparent logic and simplicity of raising the status of vocational education, the task presents enormous difficulties. Minority students, though more likely to be enrolled in occupational programs than white students, seem especially sensitive to being channeled into vocational tracks. Overall, students are voting with their feet against community college vocational programs.

This is not an irrational obsession with four-year diplomas on the part of the students. It is not just snobbish prejudice; there are sound structural reasons for the low status of career education in the community college. At the base of an educational institution's prestige is its relationship to the occupational and class structure of the society in which it operates (Clark, 1962:80-83). The community college lies at the base of the stratification structure of higher education both in the class origins of its students and in their occupational destinations. Within the community college, the vocational curriculum is at the bottom of the prestige hierarchy—again, both in terms of social composition and likely adult status.

It is unrealistic, then, to expect that community college vocational programs, the bottom track of higher education's bottom track, will have much status. It is worth noting that the British, generally more hardheaded about matters of social class than Americans, faced the matter of educational status directly some years ago. In the 1950's in Great Britain, there was a great deal of talk about "parity of esteem" in English secondary education. The problem was to give equal status to grammar schools (college preparatory), technical schools (middle level managerial and technical), and secondary modern schools (terminal). After considerable debate, the British realized that "parity of esteem" was an impossible ideal given the encompassing class structure (Banks, 1955; Marshall, 1965).

The educational establishment's concern with the low status of occupational programs in the community colleges reveals much more about its own ideology than it does about the allegedly irrational behavior of students resistant to vocational education. A great deal of emphasis is placed on improving the public image of vocational education, but little attention is paid to the substantive matter of class differences in income, occupational prestige, power, and opportunities for autonomy and expression at the workplace. The Carnegie Commission, whose ideology is probably representative of the higher education establishment, blurs the distinction between *equality* and *equality of opportunity* (Karabel, 1972a:42). Discussing its vision of the day when minority persons will be proportionately represented in higher occupational levels, the Commission hails this as an "important signal that society was meeting its commitment to equality." The conception of equality conveyed in this passage is really one of equality of opportunity; the Commission seems less interested in reducing gross differences in rewards than in giving everyone a chance to get ahead of everyone else. The Carnegie Commission, reflecting the values not only of the national educational leadership but also of the wider society, shows concern about opportunities for mobility, but little concern about a reduction in inequality.

The submerged class conflict that exists between the sponsors of vocational education in the junior college, who represent the interests and outlook of the more privileged sectors of society, and community college students, many of them working class, occasionally becomes overt. At Seattle Community College in 1968-1969, the Black Student Union vigorously opposed a recommendation to concentrate trade and technical programs in the central (Black) campus while the "higher" semiprofessional programs were allocated to the northern and southern (white) campuses (Cohen, 1971a:142). Rutgers (Newark) was the scene in 1969 of extensive demonstrations to gain open admissions to a branch of the state university. The import of the case of Rutgers (Newark) was that the protests took place in a city where students already had access to an open-door community college (Essex) and a mildly selective state college (Newark State). What the students were resisting here was not being tracked within the community college, but rather being channeled into the community college itself.(17) The well-known struggle for open admissions at CUNY in the spring of 1969 was nor primarily for access per se, but for access to the more prestigious four-year institutions: City, Brooklyn, Queens, and Hunter.

The pattern in these isolated cases of manifest resistance to tracking within or between colleges is one of minority student leadership. In the United States, where race is a much more visible social cleavage than class, it is not surprising that Black students have shown the most sensitivity to tracking in higher education. Channeling of Black students to community colleges and to vocational programs within them is, after all, fairly visible; in contrast, the *class* character of the tracking system is much less perceptible. Were it not for the militancy of some minority students, it is likely that the conflict over vocational education would have long continued to manifest itself in enrollment patterns without becoming overt.

The class nature of the conflict over tracking has, however, not always been invisible. In Illinois in 1913, there was a battle over a bill in the state legislature to establish a separate system of vocational schools above the sixth grade. Business strongly backed the bill, sponsored by Chicago School Superintendent Edwin G. Cooley. The Chicago Federation of Labor, lobbying against the bill, expressed fear that it reflected

an effort on the part of large employers to turn the public schools into an agency for supplying them with an adequate supply of docile, well-trained,

> and capable workers (which) . . . aimed to bring Illinois a caste system of education which would shunt the children of the laboring classes at an early age first into vocational courses and then into the factories (Counts, 1928:167).

After a bitter fight, the bill was defeated in the legislature.

The tracking which takes place in the community college is, however, much more invisible than that proposed in the Cooley Bill. For one thing, the community college, by the very use of the word "college" in its title, locates itself squarely within the system of higher education and gives it at least the minimal status which comes from being a college rather than a technical school. For another, the apparent emphasis of the junior college on the transfer function leads to a perception of it as a way station on the road to a four-year college. This view of the community college as a place of transfer rather than a track is strengthened by the subtlety and smoothness of the cooling out process. The community college is a "comprehensive" institution; like the high school before it, it provides preparatory and terminal education in the same building and offers sufficient opportunities for movement between programs to obscure the larger pattern of tracking. Finally, the very age at which students enter the community college makes tracking a less serious issue; there *is* a difference between channeling an eleven-year-old child and channeling a young adult of eighteen.

Whatever the differences between high school and college tracking, there is a marked similarity in the rationales given in each case for curricular differentiation. The argument is that a common curriculum denies equality of opportunity by restricting educational achievement to a single mode which will inevitably lead to some form of hierarchy. In 1908, the Boston school superintendent argued:

> Until very recently (the schools) have offered equal opportunity to receive *one kind* of education, but what will make them democratic is to provide opportunity for all to receive such an education as will fit them *equally well* for their particular life work. (Cohen and Lazerson, 1972:69).

Similarly, K. Patricia Cross (1971:162), a leading researcher on the junior college, argues more than 60 years later:

> Surely quality education consists not in offering the same thing to all people in a token gesture toward equality but in maximizing the match between the talents of the individual and the teaching resources of the institution. Educational quality is not uni-dimensional. Colleges can be *different* and excellent too.

In principle, colleges can be different and excellent, too. But in a stratified society, what this diversity of educational experiences is likely to mean is that people will, at best, have an equal opportunity to obtain an education that will fit them into their appropriate position in the class structure. More often than not, those of lower class origins will, under the new definition of equality of educational opportunity, find themselves in schools or curricula which train them for positions roughly commensurate with their social origins.

The current movement to vocationalize the community college is a logical outgrowth of the dual historical patterns of class-based hierarchical differentiation in education and of educational inflation. The system of higher education, forced to respond to pressure for access arising from mobility aspirations endemic in an affluent society which stresses individual success and the democratic character of its opportunity structure, has let people in and has then proceeded to track them into community colleges and, more particularly, into occupational programs within these two-year colleges. This push toward vocational training in the community college has been sponsored by a national educational planning elite whose social composition, outlook, and policy proposals are reflective of the interests of the more privileged strata of our society. Notably absent among those pressuring for more occupational training in the junior college have been the students themselves.

THE DISTRIBUTIVE EFFECTS OF PUBLIC HIGHER EDUCATION

One of the benefits supposed to result from the democratization of access to higher education accompanying the growth of community colleges is a more just distribution of resources in the public sector of higher education. Before the advent of open door junior colleges, the argument goes, access to a college education was closely related to family income. However, now that everyone has a chance to go to college, class differences in attendance patterns should diminish, and we might expect differences in subsidies received from the public system of higher education to be minimized.

Hansen and Weisbrod (1969), in a study of the California system of public higher education, find that the three-track system of state university, state college, and community college results in poor people's paying for the education of the affluent. Position within the California tracking system is related to the amount of money spent on one's education; the cost of the first two years of education in the tripartite system is $2970, $2700, and $1440 at the university, state college, and community college levels respectively. Thus the higher ranking the institution, the more public money spent on the student.

Eligibility to attend the high-cost state university or the middle-cost state college system shows a generally linear relationship with family income. Table 9 shows that students from families with incomes of over $25,000 are about four times as likely to be eligible for the university and twice as likely to be eligible for the state colleges as are students from families with incomes under $4000. Further, the probability that a student will take advantage of his eligibility to enter the upper two tracks is also substantially related to his family income (Hansen & Weisbrod, 1969:74). Family income is thus related to which track a student attends and, indeed, to whether a student attends college at all. Among

California high school graduates, 41 percent of all high school graduates do not enter the system of public higher education.

Students in the higher tracks are more likely to persist in college and hence to get larger subsidies. Figures for the total higher education subsidy given to students in the three tracks are $4870, $3810, and $1050 from top to bottom. Since taxes in California are approximately proportional to income and since the probability of attending an expensive school is positively related to income, the net effect of the California system is to redistribute income from poor to rich.(18) Table 10 shows the net distributive effects of possibly the most celebrated state system of American public higher education. The real losers in this system are the families (average income $7900) without children in the Californian system of public higher education who receive a negative subsidy of $650. Junior college families, with average incomes of $8800 do slightly better than break even while families with children at the university, with incomes of $12,000 get an annual subsidy of $790.(19)

Again, the pattern revealed by examining the distributive effects of public higher education is part of a recurring historical process.(20) Katz (1968:53), analyzing the founding of the American high school in mid-nineteenth century Massachusetts, observes how the middle class was "spreading throughout the whole community the burden of educating a small minority of its children" The study by George S. Counts in the early twenties (1922:152) strikingly illustrates the historical parallel:

TABLE 9

Distribution of High School Graduates by Eligibility for Public Higher Education in California, by Type of Education and Family Income 1966

Family Income	Percentage Distribution of High School Graduates by Elibigility for	
	University of California	University of California and State Colleges
$ 0–3,999	10.7	28.0
4,000–5,999	11.5	26.3
6,000–7,999	11.9	30.5
8,000–9,999	16.2	33.2
10,000–12,499	19.4	37.1
12,500–14,999	22.5	39.8
15,000–17,499	27.9	45.4
17,500–19,999	29.5	45.1
20,000–24,999	33.3	46.1
25,000 and Over	40.1	54.3
Not Reported	13.3	28.0
All	19.6	36.3

Source: Hansen and Weisbrod (1969, p. 72)

TABLE 10

Average Family Incomes, Average Higher Education Subsidies Received, and Average State and Local Taxes Paid by Families, By Type of Institution Children Attend, California, 1964

	All Families	Families Without Children in California Public Higher Education	Families With Children in California Public Higher Education			
			Total	Junior College	State College	Univ. of California
1. Average Family Income	$8,000	$7,900	$9,560	$8,800	$10,000	$12,000
2. Average Higher Education Subsidy Per Year	–	0	880	720	1,400	1.700
3. Average Total State and Local Taxes Paid	620	650	740	680	770	910
4. Net Transfer (Line 2–Line 3)	–	-650	140	+40	+630	+790

Source: Hansen and Weisbrod (1969, p. 76)

> At the present time the public high school is attended quite largely by the children of the more well-to-do classes. This affords us the spectacle of a privilege being extended at public expense to those very classes that already occupy the privileged positions in modern society. The poor are contributing to provide secondary education for the children of the rich, but are either too poor or too ignorant to avail themselves of the opportunities which they help to provide.

Thus the stratified system of public higher education, like the class based system of secondary education before it, results in a redistribution of resources from poor to rich.

DISCUSSION

The recent Newman Report on Higher Education (1971:57) noted that "the public, and especially the four-year colleges and universities, are shifting more and more responsibility onto the community colleges for undertaking the toughest tasks of higher education." One of the most difficult of these tasks has been to educate hundreds of thousands of students, many of them of modest social origins, in whom more selective colleges and universities showed no interest. Community colleges have given these students access to higher education and have provided some of them a chance to advance their class position.

Despite the idealism and vigor of the community college movement, there has been a sharp contradiction between official rhetoric and social reality. Hailed as the "democratizers of higher education," community colleges are, in reality, a vital component of the class-based tracking system. The modal junior college student, though aspiring to a four-year diploma upon entrance, receives neither an associate nor a bachelor's degree. The likelihood of his persisting in higher education is *negatively* influenced by attending a community college. Since a disproportionate number of two-year college students are of working-class origins, low status students are most likely to attend those institutions which increase the likelihood that they will drop out of college. Having increased access to higher education, community colleges are notably unsuccessful in retaining their students and in reducing class differentials in educational opportunity.

If current trends continue, the tracking system of higher education may well become more rigid. The community college, as the bottom track, is likely to absorb the vast majority of students who are the first generation in their families to enter higher education. Since most of these students are from relatively low status backgrounds, an increase in the already significant correlation between social class and position in the tracking system of higher education is likely to occur. As more and more people enter postsecondary education, the community college will probably become more distinct from the rest of higher education both in class composition and in curriculum. With the push of the policy-planning elite for more career education, vocational training may well become more pervasive, and the community college will become even more a terminal rather than a transfer institution. These trends, often referred to as expressions of higher education's "diversity" and of the community college's "special and unique role" are the very processes which place the community college at the bottom of the class-based tracking system. The system of higher education's much-touted "diversity" is, for the most part, hierarchy rather than genuine variety (see Karabel, 1972a and 1972b), a form of hierarchy which has more to do with social class than educational philosophy.

The high rate of attrition at community colleges may well be functional for the existing social system. The cooling out function of the junior college, as Clark puts it, is what "such a college is about." Community colleges exist in part to reconcile students' culturally induced hopes for mobility with their eventual destinations, transforming structurally induced failure into individual failure. This serves to legitimize the myth of an equal opportunity structure; it shifts attention to questions of individual mobility rather than distributive justice. Cooling out, then, can be seen as conflict between working class students and standards that legitimize the position of the privileged—a veiled class conflict. Similarly, there is class conflict implicit in the differences over vocational education between the aspirations of students and the objectives of policy-makers. This has occasionally become overt, but the community colleges seem to serve their legitimizing function best when the conflict remains submerged.

Can the inability of the community college movement to modify the American class structure be overcome? An assessment of some specific reforms that have been proposed may yield some insight. One obvious reform would be to reverse the pattern that Hansen and Weisbrod (1969) document—simply to invest more money in the community colleges than in the four-year public institutions. The idea of this reform would be both to provide the highest quality education to those who have socioeconomic and cognitive disadvantages to overcome and to put an end to the pattern of poor people subsidizing relatively affluent people through public systems of higher education. This proposal, which may be justified on grounds of equity, is unlikely to make much difference either in terms of education or social class. A repeated finding in social science research, confirmed by both the Coleman Report (1966) and the recent Jencks (1972) study, is that educational expenditures seem to be virtually unrelated to cognitive development at the elementary and secondary levels, and there is no reason to believe that money is any more effective in colleges. However desirable a shift in resources from four-year colleges to community colleges might be on other grounds, it is unlikely to seriously affect the larger pattern of class-based tracking in higher education.

Another possibility would be to transform the community college into a four-year institution—the very proposal that the Carnegie Commission on Higher Education strongly opposes. The purpose of this reform would be to upgrade the status of the community college and to diminish the rigidity of the tracking system. Yet it is highly questionable whether making the junior college into a senior college would have any such effect; there are marked status distinctions among four-year colleges and, in all likelihood, the new four-year institutions would be at the bottom of the prestige hierarchy. Further, the creation of more four-year colleges would probably accelerate the process of educational inflation.

The proposal to vocationalize the community college exemplifies the dilemma faced by those who would reform the public two-year college. Noting that many community college students neither transfer nor get an associate degree, proponents of vocational education argue that the students should stop engaging in a uni-dimensional academic competition which they cannot win and should instead obtain a marketable skill before leaving the educational system. If one accepts the existing system of social stratification, there is an almost irresistible logic to the vocational training argument; there are, after all, manpower shortages to be filled and it *is* true that not everyone can be a member of the elite.

In a sense, the community colleges are "damned if they do and damned if they don't." The vocational educational reform provides a striking example of their dilemma, for the question of whether community colleges should become predominantly vocational institutions may well be the most critical policy issue facing the two-year institutions in the years ahead. If they move toward more career education, they will tend to accentuate class-based tracking. If they continue as "comprehensive institutions" they will continue to be plagued by the enormous attrition in their transfer curricula. Either way, the primary role of the colleges derives from their relation to the class structure and feasible reforms will, at best, result in minor changes in their channeling function.

That the community colleges cannot do what many of their proponents claim they are supposed to do does not mean that they can do nothing at all. They do make a difference for many students—providing them opportunities for better lives than their parents had. They are able to introduce some students, particularly those who are residential rather than commuter students, to ideas, influences, and ways of life that broaden their view of the world. And surely it is not beyond reason to think that better staff, counseling, and facilities could somewhat reduce the rate of attrition in the transfer curricula. It is not beyond hope to think that reform of the vocational tracks would encourage students not to fit like cogs into rigid occupational roles but to have some faith in themselves, their right to decent working conditions, and to some control over their own work so that they could shape the roles they are supposed to fit into. It may be that students and teachers intent on changing society could raise the consciousness of community college students about where they fit in the social system and why they fit where they do. All this is possible, important, and underway in many community colleges.

But as for educational reform making this a more egalitarian society, we cannot be sanguine. Jencks (1972) has shown that the effects of schooling on ultimate income and occupation are relatively small. Even if the community colleges were to undergo a major transformation, little change in the system of social stratification would be likely to take place. If we are genuinely concerned about creating a more egalitarian society, it will be necessary to change our economic institutions. The problems of inequality and inequality of opportunity are, in short, best dealt with not through educational reform but rather by the wider changes in economic and political life that would help build a socialist society.

Writing in favor of secondary education for everybody many years ago, R.H. Tawney, the British social historian, remarked that the "intrusion into educational organization of the vulgarities of the class system is an irrelevance as mischievous in effect as it is odious in conception." That matters of social class have intruded into the community college is beyond dispute; whether the influence of class can be diminished not only in the community college but also in the larger society remains to be seen.

NOTES

(1) Contrary to popular perceptions, American and European rates of social mobility, at least as measured by mobility from manual to non-manual occupations, are very similar. For data on this point see Lipset and Bendix (1959).

(2) See Ralph Turner's "Modes of Social Ascent through Education" (1966) for a discussion of how different norms in the United States and England lead to

patterns of "contest" and "sponsored" mobility.

(3) For an empirical study of hierarchical differentiation within higher education, see "Social Class, Academic Ability and College Quality" by Jerome Karabel and Alexander W. Astin (American Council on Education, Washington, D.C., forthcoming).

(4) The term "community college" is used in this study to refer to all *public two-year colleges*. Excluded from this definition are private two-year colleges and all four-year colleges and universities. In the text, the terms "junior college" and "two-year college" are used interchangeably with community college though they are not, strictly speaking, synonyms. The name community college has become the more frequently used because of the increasing emphasis of two-year public institutions on fulfilling local needs. Further, as the community college struggled to obtain a distinct identity and as greater stress was placed on two-year programs, the junior college label, which seemingly describes a lesser version of the four-year college geared almost exclusively to transfer, became increasingly inappropriate.

(5) Two of the most comprehensive recent studies of the influence of social class and ability on access to higher education are Sewell and Shah (1967) and Folger *et al.* (1970). George Counts (1922:149), in a classical empirical study of the American high school of a half century ago, concluded that "in very large measure participation in the privilege of a secondary education is contingent on social and economic status." Similarly, Michael Katz (1968), in a study of public education reform in nineteenth century Massachusetts, found that the early high school was overwhelmingly a middle class institution.

(6) We need to be cautious in interpreting this data; the aspirations of community college students may not be as deeply embedded as their counterparts at four-year colleges. There is a tendency in social research to reify data derived from questionnaires, even though the same response to an item may obscure differences in the intensity of the reply (e.g., two students may both check yes when asked if they aspire to a B.A., but one may merely like the idea while the other is committed to it). Further, there is a distinction between *aspirations*, which are frequently high, and *expectations*, which are often more realistic.

(7) Since these data include private two-year college students, they probably *underestimate* attrition at community colleges. Students at private junior colleges are somewhat higher than public two-year college students in both class background and academic ability (American Council on Education, 1971). A few of the studies reported in this paper aggregate public and private junior college data, but this poses little problem in that the inclusion of private institutions tends to provide a conservative estimate of differences between community colleges and four-year institutions. Further, since public colleges comprise well over 85 percent of total two-year college enrollment (HEW, 1970:33), it is highly unlikely that the inclusion of private junior colleges seriously affects the results of these studies.

(8) The fact that community colleges are almost all commuter rather than

residential institutions may contribute to their apparently negative impact on student persistence. Astin, in a personal communication, reports that much of the difference between two- and four-year colleges in attrition disappears when commuting is controlled. There may be a strain for the commuter student between the more academic world of college and the less intellectual world of family, neighborhood, and peers. One way ro resolve this conflict is to move into a residential setting, but a more common resolution of the problem seems to be to drop out of college altogether.

(9) In discussing the role of guidance in the junior college, it is interesting to observe the connection between the growth of the school counseling profession and education tracking. As long as the curriculum at a particular level of schooling remains unified, there is relatively little need for guidance. However, when a number of curricula leading to occupations of varying prestige come into being, counseling becomes a virtual necessity. It is worth noting in this connection the long-standing enthusiasm of the business community for guidance programs. George S. Counts, in a study entitled *School and Society in Chicago* (1928), noted the fervor with which the Chicago Association of Commerce, the city's dominant business association, supported the establishment of a program of vocational guidance in the public schools in the early twentieth century.

(10) When George L. Counts examined class differences in secondary schools in the early twenties, he wrote:

> These differences in the extent of educational opportunity are further accentuated through the choice of curricula. As a rule, those groups which are poorly represented in the high school patronize the more narrow and practical curricula, the curricula which stand as terminal points in the educational system and which prepare for wage-earning. And the poorer their representation in high school, the greater is the probability that they will enter these curricula. The one- and two-year vocational courses, wherever offered, draw their registration particularly, from the ranks of labor (Counts, 1922:143). See also Trow, 1966; Cohen and Lazerson, 1972; Greer, 1972.

(11) Minority students are also disproportionately enrolled in two of the lower rungs of the higher education tracking system—community colleges and unselective black colleges. Patterns of enrollment, of course, vary from region to region with community colleges dominant in the West and black institutions more prominent in the South. For data showing that the proportion of minority students decreases as one progresses up the three-track California system see Coordinating Council (1969:23) and Jaffe and Adams (1972:232).

(12) At the same time, however, it is easy to forget that *absolute* changes in occupation, income, and educational attainment can have important consequences in everyday life and may raise general levels of satisfaction. Having more people attend college, while not narrowing the educational gap in relative terms, may lead to a more enlightened populace. Keniston and Gerzon (1972)

attack the narrowly economic view of higher education and argue that important non-pecuniary benefits accrue from college attendance. Similarly, a change from a blue-collar to a white-collar economy may eliminate many menial tasks and hence lead to a greater job satisfaction. Finally, an absolute increase in the standard of living, while not necessarily abolishing poverty (which, as Jencks argues, is primarily a relative phenomenon), may result in a higher quality of life than was possible under conditions of greater scarcity.

(13) Grubb and Lazerson (1972) report that economic returns to vocational education are almost uniformly low, but their review does not include studies of programs at community colleges. Some skepticism as to the allegedly high incomes of graduates of occupational programs for blue-collar jobs may, however, be expressed. Contrary to popular mythology about the affluent worker, the proportion of male blue-collar workers earning more than $15,000 in 1970 was a miniscule 4 percent (Bureau of the Census, 1971:30). Only 3 out of 10 blue-collar workers earned more than $10,000 in 1970.

We do not know what economic rewards accrue to graduates of community college vocational programs, nor do we know much about the occupational and economic status of the community college drop-out. This is fertile ground for empirical inquiry. A longitudinal study of three groups of high school graduates—students who do not enter college, community college drop-outs, and community college entrants who obtain a degree (A.A. or B.A.)—matching students with similar personal characteristics, would do much to illuminate the effects of attending a community college.

(14) Karier (1972) has written a provocative essay on the role of foundations in sponsoring educational testing. The role of far-sighted foundations in fostering educational reform, possibly as a means of rationalizing the social order, is a topic worthy of careful investigation.

(15) Amitai Etzioni (1970), chairman of the Department of Sociology at Columbia University, expresses this point of view well: "If we can no longer keep the floodgates closed at the admissions office, it at least seems wise to channel the general flow away from four-year colleges and toward two-year extensions of high school in the junior and community colleges." Vice President Agnew (1970), in a speech attacking open admissions, approvingly cited this quotation.

(16) See Riessman's "The Vocationalization of Higher Education: Duping the Poor" for an analysis of the movement to turn the community college into a technical institution. For a brilliant article on the elitism of leftist academics toward working-class students see McDermott (1969).

(17) I am indebted to Russell Thackrey for pointing out the implications of the interesting case of Rutgers (Newark).

(18) A minor reversal of this pattern takes place in occupational programs within the community college. Morsch (1971:33) presents data showing that occupational programs in two-year colleges cost $756 annually compared with $557 for transfer programs. Since low status students are disproportionately enrolled in vocational programs, there may be some minor redistribution of

resources from rich to poor occurring.

(19) For a critique of Hansen and Weisbrod which used family income rather than college type as the independent variable see Pechman (1970). Using Hansen and Weisbrod's own figures, Pechman argues that the California system of public higher education does *not* result in a redistribution of resources from poor to rich. Windham (1970), however, applies Pechman's method of using family income rather than college type as the unit of analysis in a study of the Florida system and finds the state of Florida does indeed redistrubute resources in a regressive fashion. Whatever the net gains and losses by income class which occur when state tax systems are taken into account, it seems clear that the affluent *do* receive more benefits from state-supported systems of higher education than do the poor. Insofar as California and Florda have unusually large systems of free-access community colleges, the effects may be even more pronounced in states with more limited access to higher education.

(20) The case of public higher education, in which the middle class gains the greatest benefits, may be typical of the distributive effects of many social services in the modern Welfare State. See Titmuss (1964), Marshall (1965), and Blackburn (1969) for evidence showing that the prime beneficiaries of the British Welfare State are members of the middle class.

REFERENCES

Agnew, S. Toward a middle way in college admissions. Educational Record 51 (Spring, 1970), pp. 106-111.

American Council on Education, Office of Research. National norms for entering college freshmen—Fall 1966. ACE Research Reports, Vol. 2, No. 1. Washington, D.C.: 1966.

American Council on Education, Office of Research. The American freshman: National norms for Fall 1971. ACE Research Reports, Vol. 6, No. 6. Washington, D.C.: 1971.

Astin, A. W. Predicting academic performance in college. New York: Free Press, 1971.

Astin, A. W. College dropouts: A national profile. ACE Research Reports, Vol. 7, No. 1. Washington, D.C.: American Council on Education, 1972.

Astin, A. W. & Panos, R. J. The educational and vocational development of college students. Washington, D.C.: American Council on Education, 1969.

Banks, O. Parity and prestige in English secondary education. London: Routledge and Kegan Paul, Ltd., 1955.

Blackburn, R. The unequal society. In H. P. Dreitzel (Ed.), Recent sociology No. 1. London: Macmillan Company, 1969.

Blau, P. M. & Duncan, O. D. The American occupational structure. New York: Wiley, 1967.

Bowles, S. Contradictions in U.S. higher education. James Weaver (Ed.) Political economy: radical vs. orthodox approaches. Boston: Allyn & Bacon, 1972.

Bowles, S. Unequal education and the reporduction of the social division of labor. Review of radical political economics, 3 (Fall), 1971.

Brick, M. Forum and focus for the junior college movement. New York: Bureau of Publications, Teachers College, Columbia University, 1964.

Bureau of the Census. The American almanac. New York: Grosset & Dunlap, 1971a.

Bureau of the Census. Educational attainment: March 1971. Series P 20, No. 229. Washington, D.C.: U.S. Government Printing Office, 1971b.

Bureau of the Census. Undergraduate enrollment in two-year and four-year colleges: October 1971. Series P20, No. 236. Washington, D.C.: U.S. Government Printing Office. 1972.

Bushnell, D. S. & Zagaris, I. Report from Project FOCUS: Strategies for change. Washington, D.C.: American Association of Junior Colleges, 1972.

Carnegie Commission on Higher Education. The open-door colleges. New York: McGraw-Hill, 1970.

Clark, B.R. The open door college. New York: McGraw-Hill, 1960.

Clark, B.R. Educating the expert society. San Francisco: Chandler, 1962.

Cohen, A. M. et al. A constant variable. San Francisco: Jossey-Bass, 1971a.

Cohen, A. M. Stretching pre-college education. Social Policy (May/June, 1971b), pp. 5-9.

Cohen, D.K. & Lazerson, M. Education and the corporate order. Socialist Revolution, 2 (March/April, 1972). pp. 47-72.

Coleman, J.S., et al. Equality of educational opportunity. Washington, D.C.: U.S. Government Printing Office, 1966.

Collins, R. Functional and conflict theories of stratification. American Sociological Review 36 (December, 1971), pp. 1002-19.

Coordinating Council for Higher Education. The undergraduate student and his higher education: Policies of California colleges and universities in the next decade. Sacramento, Cal. 1969.

Counts, G.S. School and society in Chicago. New York: Harcourt, Brace, 1928.

Counts, G.S. The selective character of American secondary education. Chicago: University of Chicago Press, 1922.

Cross, K.P. The junior college student: A research description. Princeton, N.J.: Educational Testing Service, 1968.

Cross, K.P. The role of the junior college in providing postsecondary education for all. In Trends in postsecondary education. Washington, D.C.: U.S. Government Printing Office, 1970.

Cross, K.P. Beyond the open door. San Francisco: Jossey-Bass, 1971.

Department of Health, Education, and Welfare. Digest of educational statistics. Washington, D.C.: U.S. Government Printing Office, 1970.

Eckland, B.K. Social class and college graduation: Some misconceptions corrected. American Journal of Sociology, 70 (July, 1964), pp. 36-50.

Etzioni, A. The high schoolization of college. Wall Street Journal, March 17, 1970.

Fields, R.R. The community college movement. New York: McGraw-Hill, 1962.

Folger, J.K., Astin, H.S., & Bayer, A.E. Human resources and higher education. New York: Russell Sage, 1970.

Gleazer, E.J., Jr. This is the community college. Boston: Houghton Mifflin, 1968.

Greer, C. The great school legend. New York: Basic Books, 1972.

Grubb, W.N. & Lazerson, M. Educational and industrialism: Documents in vocational education. New York: Teachers College, Columbia University, in press.

Hansen, W.L. & Weisbrod, B.A. Benefits, costs, and finance of public higher education. Chicago: Markham, 1969.

Harris, N.C. The middle manpower job spectrum. In W.K. Ogilvie, and M.R. Raines (Eds.), Perspectives on the Community-Junior College. New York: Appleton-Century-Crofts, 1971.

Hartnett, R. T. College and University Trustees; Their Background, Roles, and Educational Attitudes. Princeton, N.J.: Educational Testing Services, 1969.

Havemann, E. & West, P. They went to college. New York: Harcourt, Brace, 1952.

Higher Education Act of 1972. Public Law 92-318. 92nd Congress, 659, June 23, 1972.

Hurlburt, A. L. State master plans for community colleges. Washington, D.C.: American Association of Junior Colleges, 1969.

Jaffe, A.J. & Adams, W. Two models of open enrollment. In L. Wilson and O. Mills (Eds.), Universal higher education. Washington: American Council on Education, 1972.

Jencks, C. & Riesman, D. The academic revolution. Garden City, N.Y.: Doubleday, 1968.

Jencks, C. *et al.* Inequality: a reassessment of the effect of family and schooling in America. New York: Basic Books, 1972.

Karabel, J. Perspectives on open admissions. Educational Record, 53 (Winter, 1972a), pp. 30-44.

Karabel, J. Open admissions: Toward meritocracy or equality? Change, 4 (May, 1972b), pp. 38-43.

Karabel, J. & Astin, A.W. Social class, academic ability, and college quality. Washington: American Council on Education, Office of Research, in press.

Karier, C.J. Testing for order and control in the corporate liberal state. Educational Theory, 22 (Spring, 1972), pp. 154-180.

Katz, M.B. The irony of early school reform. Boston: Beacon Press, 1968.

Keniston, K. & Gerzon, M. Human and social benefits. In L. Wilson and O. Mills, Universal Higher Education. Washington, D.C.: American Council on Education, 1972.

Knoell, D.M. & Medsker, L. L. Articulation between two-year and four-year colleges. Berkeley: Center for the Study of Higher Education, 1964.

Kolko, G. Wealth and power in America. New York: Praeger, 1962.

Lipset, S.M. & Bendix, R. Social mobility in industrial society. Berkeley: University of California Press, 1959.

Marland, S.P., Jr. A strengthening alliance. In L. Wilson and O. Mills (Eds.), Universal higher education. Washington, D.C.: American Council or Education, 1972.

Marshall, T.H. Class, citizenship, and social development. Garden City, N.Y.: Anchor, 1965.

McDermott, J. The laying on of culture. The Nation, March 10, 1969.

Medsker, L. L. & Trent, J.W. The influence of different types of public higher institutions on college attendance from varying socioeconomic and ability levels. Berkeley: Center for Research and Development in Higher Education, 1965.

Medsker, L. L. & Tillery, D. Breaking the access barriers. New York: McGraw-Hill, 1971.

Miller, H. Rich, man, poor man. New York: Thomas Y. Crowell, 1971.

Milner, M., Jr. The illusion of equality. San Francisco: Jossey-Bass, 1972.

Morsch, W.O. Costs analysis of occupational training programs in community colleges and vocational training centers. Washington, D.C.: Bureau of Social Science Research, 1971.

Newman, F., *et al.* Report on higher education. Reports to the U.S. Department of Health, Education, and Welfare. Washington, D.C.: U.S. Government Printing Office, 1971.

Ogilvie, W.K. Occupational education and the community college. In W.K. Ogilvie & M.R. Raines (Eds.), Perspectives on the Community-Junior College. New York: Appleton-Century-Crofts, 1971.

Pechman, J.A. The distributional effects of public higher education in California. Journal of Human Resources, 5 (Summer, 1970), pp. 361-37.

Pierson, G.W. The education of American leaders. New York: Praeger, 1969.

Powell, H.B. The foundation and the future of the junior college. In The foundations and the junior colleges. Washington, D.C.: American Association of Junior Colleges, 1965.

Reed, R. & Miller, H. Some determinants of the variation in earnings for college men. Journal of Human Resources, 5, Spring, 1970, pp. 177-190.

Riessman, F. The "vocationalization" of higher education: Duping the poor. Social Policy, 2, (May/June, 1971), pp. 3-4.

Rothbart, G.S. The legitimation of inequality: objective scholarship vs. black militance. Sociology of Education, 43 (Spring, 1970), pp. 159-174.

Ryan, P.B. Why industry needs the junior college. In W. K. Ogilvie & M.R. Raines (Eds), Perspectives on the Community-Junior College. New York: Appleton-Century-Crofts, 1971.

Schoenfeldt, L.F. Education after high school. Sociology of Education, 41 (Fall 1968), pp. 350-369.

Sewell, W.H. and Shah, V.P. Socioeconomic status, intelligence, and the attainment of higher education. Sociology of Education, 40 (Winter, 1967), pp. 1-23.

Sharp, L.M. Education and employment. Baltimore, Johns Hopkins, 1970.

Spaeth, J.L. The allocation of college graduates to graduate and professional schools. Sociology of Education, 41 (Fall, 1968), pp. 342-349.

Sunko, Theodore S. Making the case for junior college foundation support. In The Foundation and the junior college. Washington, D.C.: American Association of Junior Colleges, 1965.

Thornton, J.W., Jr. The community junior college. New York: John Wiley, 1960.

Titmuss, R.M. The limits of the welfare state. New Left Review, 23 (September/October, 1964), pp. 28-37.

Trent, J.W. & Medsker, L.L. Beyond high school. San Francisco: Jossey-Bass, 1968.

Trow, M. The second transformation of American secondary education. In R. Bendix and S. Lipset (Eds.), Class, status and power. New York: Free Press, 1966.

Turner, R. Modes of social ascent through education. In R. Bendix and S. Lipset (Eds.), Class, status and power. New York: Free Press, 1966.

Venn, G. Man, education and work. Washington, D.C.: American Council on Education, 1964.

Watson, N. Corporations and the community colleges: a growing liaison? Technical Education News, Vol. 29, No. 2 (April/May 1970), pp. 3-6.

Wegner, E.L. & Sewell, W.H. Selection and context as factors affecting the probability of graduation from college. American Journal of Sociology, 75 (January, 1970), pp. 665-679.

Willingham, W. Free-access higher education. New York: College Entrance Examination Board, 1970.

Windham, D.M. Education, equality and income redistribution. Lexington, Mass.: D.C. Heath, 1970.

Wolfe, A. Reform without reform: the Carnegie Commission on Higher Education. Social Policy, 2 (May/June, 1971), pp. 18-27.

Wolfe, D. The uses of talent. Princeton, N.J.: Princeton University Press, 1971.

THE DISTRIBUTION OF
EDUCATIONAL RESOURCES
IN LARGE AMERICAN CITIES

John D. Owen

A key determinant of success in achieving a balanced development of the nation's human resources is the extent to which poor people obtain, or fail to obtain, an equal share of educational services. It is well known that rich states provide more per pupil than do poor states, and that within states there is a positive relationship between educational expenditure per pupil and per capita income.(1) But variations in resources per pupil also take place within communities.(2) The evidence presented in this article suggests that, in large American cities, educational expenditures per child in public elementary school systems are somewhat larger in middle-class white neighborhoods than in those where most students are poor and nonwhite. Moreover, it is shown that this expenditure bias is not simply an artifact of price differentials between neighborhoods,(3) or of expenditure differentials which may reflect bureaucratic procedures but not educationally relevant differences in inputs. Rather, there is a significant tendency for higher quality educational resources to be assigned to middle-class white neighborhoods.

THE ANALYSIS

Abstract arguments could be put forth for expecting either an equal distribution of funds and resources in municipal educational systems (based on the character of elementary school education as a quasi-public good, which gives every citizen an interest in the educational attainment of the city's children) or a less than equal distribution (based on the character of education as a quasi-private good, which gives each parent a special interest in the education of his own child, as well as on a theory of city government which permits the city to put the private interest of some parents before that of others).(4) But when one turns from such abstract arguments about the underlying tendencies toward inequality or equality in municipal school systems to a more realistic description of the principles on which these systems allocate services and expenditures, it is rather obvious that equal treatment of all children is a most unlikely outcome.(5)

The major current expenditure of city school systems is on instruction, for the most part teachers' salaries.(6) In practice, the typical urban teacher assignment system concentrates the lowest-salaried teachers in the slums and ghettos.

The average American urban teacher's salary is determined almost entirely on the basis of his experience. There is a single city-wide salary scale, and ordinarily no financial incentives to accept inner-city assignments are offered, nor can a teacher's exceptional teaching ability substitute for experience in increasing his salary. In the absence of such rewards, most American cities permit their experienced teachers to request transfer to schools outside the ghetto, for most teachers prefer assignment to schools in white middle-class or upper working-class areas. This preference may reflect the teacher's racial or class attitudes; he may fear or dislike poverty-stricken ghetto neighborhoods; he may be aware that his training has been geared toward a well-equipped classroom of upper working-class and middle-class children and believe that he can perform with maximum effectiveness only in such a school; he may simply prefer a school near his home; or other factors may be operative. Add to these considerations the fact that requests for transfer are usually granted on the basis of seniority, and it can easily be seen that inexperienced teachers will be concentrated in poor non-white areas,(7) and that the average teacher's salary—and hence the average expenditure per pupil—will be lower in such districts.(8)

Differences among schools in the average level of experience of teachers or in their average salary levels (or, for that matter, in expenditure per pupil) measure only one aspect of differences in instructional quality. In his report, *Equality of Educational Opportunity*,(9) James Coleman found that a teacher's verbal ability was more important than experience in determining his effectiveness, and further that verbal ability of teachers had a rather low correlation with experience and salary. Thus it could be argued that an important aspect of discrimination is not included in this measure. But there are other features of the teacher assignment system which tend to concentrate the least able teachers in poor nonwhite areas. Apart from the general preference of many teachers for upper working-class and middle-class students, mentioned above, the more able teacher will frequently prefer to teach middle-class or white students because he feels that they are most highly motivated and challenging. If at the same time informal pressure is put upon the less able teachers to remain in slum or ghetto schools, the same result will follow.(10)

In this assignment process, the black teacher is a crucial factor. There is evidence that most black teachers do not share the white teachers' preference for white students.(11) Moreover, white parents generally have a stronger preference for white teachers than do black parents,(12) and white administrators frequently prefer to place black teachers in predominantly black schools (perhaps partially in response to the preferences of white parents). These attitudes become especially important when principals and others diverge from a straightforward seniority system of teacher assignments. There is some evidence that they do so and, at least in some cities, that when they do, black teachers are encouraged to remain in predominantly black schools.(13)

For these several reasons, one will expect to find black teachers teaching black students. When black teachers are equal or superior to white teachers in experience or verbal ability, this racial assignment pattern can constitute a major equalizing force in the city school system in the sense that black students are thus assured a supply of high quality teachers. When black teachers fall below whites in experience or verbal ability, however, their concentration in black schools does not fulfill this equalizing function.

Another dimension to the allocation of instructional resources is afforded by the teacher/student ratio: A persistent tendency for this ratio to be lowest in poor districts will also reduce the instructional expenditures per pupil. However, this ratio need not have a positive correlation with the neighborhood economic level. In Boston, for example, it was found that because of an open-enrollment policy which attracted pupils from all over the city to the better schools, the teacher/student ratio was higher in the slums than in less disadvantaged districts.(14)

Until recently, empirical data on the distribution of educational resources within cities have been difficult to obtain. However, several studies of individual cities have now been carried out.(15) Moreover, the Coleman Report has made available data on resource inputs in a large number of individual schools within a rather extensive sample of school systems.(16)

Data from the Report were drawn from elementary schools and their students in nine large cities;(17) they were supplemented with published data from the Bureau of the Census and other sources. Regression analysis was then used to measure the extent to which a school-expenditure variable and a number of school-quality variables were influenced by within-city variations in the economic and racial character of the families served by each school.

Average family income in the school attendance areas (Y_s) was used as a measure of neighborhood economic level.(18) Each regression was standardized for variations in city income. The percentage of white students (W_s) was used to measure the racial composition of the school. In a linear model, expenditure per student (or some other measure of input of educational resources) might then be estimated in a regression equation of the following type:

(1) $$I = a + bY_s + cW_s + u$$

where u stands for residual variation.

However, it has frequently been stated that the degree of discrimination

TABLE 1

	R^a	F

(1) Real expenditures per pupil on teacher salary (I)[b]

$I = -526.6 + .0173Y_s + 138.5W_s - 306.8W_sW_c$ .45 15.0

             (3.79)   (4.29)   (−5.19)

             [.43]   [.20]   [−.22]

(2) Real teacher salary (S)[b]

$S = -1932 + .227Y_s + 1124W_s - 1870W_sW_c$ .46 15.1

             (4.21)   (2.94)   (−2.67)

             [.20]   [.06]   [−.05]

(3) Teacher/student ratio (T)[b]

$T = .0288 + 144X10^{-5}Y_s + .00425W_s - .0169W_sW_c$ .25 4.5

             (2.67)   (1.11)   (−2.42)

             [.24]   [.04]   [−.05]

(4) Experience of teacher (E)

$E = 23.07 + .00123Y_s - .00273Y_c + 7.42W_s - 8.17W_sW_c$ .56 23.0

             (4.45)   (−2.39)   (3.34)   (−1.96)

             [.60]   [−1.64]   [.22]   [−.12]

(5) Verbal ability of teacher (V)

$V = -10.12 + .00044Y_s + .0038Y_c + 5.91W_s$

             (2.89)   (6.09)   (4.12)

             [.11]   [1.20]   [.10]

             $- 8.15W_sW_c + 4.86W_c$ .61 24.0

              (−2.79)   (4.12)

              [−.06]   [.10]

(6) Proportion of white teachers (W)

$W = -3.35 - .14X10^{-5}Y_s + .00047Y_c + .714W_s$

             (−.07)   (5.41)   (3.62)

             [−.01]   [5.24]   [.39]

             $- 1.21W_sW_c + 1.32W_c$ .62 25.1

             (−3.01)   (8.14)

             [−.32]   [.97]

Note: t ratios for the regression coefficients are given in parentheses. Elasticities calculated at the means are given in brackets.

[a] Correlation coefficients adjusted for degrees of freedom.

[b] Standardized for variations in city income level by the method of constrained regression.

against nonwhites rises as their proportion in the city population rises.(19) If the coefficient of racial discrimination can be approximated as a linear function of the percentage of white students in the city school system,

(2) $c=d+eW_c$

(where d might be expected to have a positive and e a negative value), then combining equations (1) and (2), educational input could usefully be estimated

(3) $I=a+bY_s+dW_s+eW_sW_c+u$

Table 1 gives some statistical results from this model. In the first equation, expenditures per pupil for salaries, standardized for variation in city income by the use of constrained regression,(20) are regressed against income in the school and the measure of racial composition. Elasticities calculated at the means of the variables are given, along with estimates of the regression coefficients.

Regression equation (1) suggests that there is significant discrimination against poor and nonwhite students in the allocation of instructional expenditures; in fact, the school income elasticity of salary expenditures (holding city income constant) of 0.43 is about half of some estimates of intercity elasticities of educational expenditures.(21)

The text table below gives an example of the effect of neighborhood income on salary expenditure per pupil in a typical city in this sample: An increase of $1,000 in income per family is accompanied here by an increase in salary expenditure per child of about $18.

Average Family Income in School Area	Expenditure per Pupil on Teacher Salary
$4,000	$158
6,000	193
7,500	219

The distribution of expenditures per pupil is of interest in itself as a measure of the extent to which financial resources are allocated unequally. But the distribution also reflects differences in educational quality, since per pupil salary costs rise both with the teacher/student ratio and with the average experience level of the faculty.

Turning to the racial composition variables, the elasticity of expenditures with respect to the proportion of white students in the school has a maximum value of about one-fifth. However, this comparison may tend to underestimate the relative importance of race, since the racial composition variable has a coefficient of variation that is more than five times that of neighborhood income. When the regression coefficients are standardized for this difference in relative variance, the influence of racial composition of the school appears to be somewhat greater than that of neighborhood income.

Since there is usually a negative correlation between income and non-white population in city neighborhoods, these results suggest that the gap between the poorer neighborhoods (defined as the average of low-income white and of black districts) and more prosperous neighborhoods (defined as the average of upper working-class and middle-class districts) is greater than that suggested by the income elasticity in equation (1), which was obtained by holding racial composition constant.

The measure of variation in salary expenditure per student was next broken down into its two components—teacher salary and teacher/student ratio—and estimated separately in regression equations (2) and (3). As expected, economic and social factors are more important determinants of salary than of teacher/student ratio. Salary has a school neighborhood elasticity of about one-fifth and a maximum elasticity with respect to the percentage of whites in the school of about one-sixteenth.

Equation (4) traces the variation in instructional expenditures a step farther by examining experience as a function of racial and economic factors. Since city-wide data on experience of teachers were not usually available, an attempt was made to standardize for variations in city income here (and in the following regressions) by introducing average family income in the city, Y_c, as an independent variable.(22)

Teacher experience has a neighborhood income elasticity of three-fifths. These results imply that a school serving an affluent neighborhood in which average family income is, say, 50 percent greater than in a poorer area will have a faculty whose average experience is about 30 percent higher.

Teacher experience has a closer relationship to the economic and racial character of school neighborhoods than does salary [see equation (4)], perhaps because above a certain level of experience most salary scales provide a somewhat less than proportionate increase in pay. Thus we find a teacher assignment pattern in which a large proportion of the teachers who have the most experience and who are earning the maximum salary are found in more affluent and white schools.

Thus the results presented in equations (1) to (4) are consistent with the hypothesis that neighborhood economic and racial characteristics are a significant factor in determining instructional expenditures per student. Experience of teachers is higher in the middle-class or white neighborhoods, and hence salary of teachers and instructional costs per pupil are also higher.

Some evidence of the influence of racial and economic factors on the distribution of teacher verbal ability among schools is offered in equation (5), where the dependent variable is the average score in a verbal ability examination given to teachers by the Coleman research team.(23) A fairly strong relationship between verbal ability and the racial and economic factors in the city and in a given school neighborhood is observed. There was an intercity income elasticity of 1.20. The income elasticity of the school area was much smaller, about one-tenth, but was still almost three times the estimate of its standard error.(24)

The racial composition of a given school is a significant factor in the assignment of verbally able teachers, and it becomes more important as the proportion of nonwhites in the city grows. The overall racial composition of a given school system is also a significant determinant of verbal ability [see regression equation (5)]. This result suggests that a 10 percent increase in the proportion of white students in city schools, holding other factors constant, will be associated with a 1 percent increase in the average verbal ability of city teachers.

The hypothesis that white teachers are more likely to select or to be assigned to schools in white, upper working-class neighborhoods is examined empirically in equation (6), which regresses percentage of white teachers in a school against the school and city income and race variables. As might be expected, the proportion of white teachers rises with the percentage of white students not only in the city but also in a given school; an increase in the proportion of white students in a school of 5 percent is associated with an increase in the proportion of white teachers of up to 2 percent.

One might ask to what extend the tendency for municipal education systems to segregate black teachers and students affects the distribution of teachers high in verbal ability, experience, and salary. In each city studied, average verbal ability, experience, and salary levels of white and nonwhite teachers were compared. If nonwhite teachers were rated lower on the average, and if they tended to be assigned to nonwhite students, then the lower experience, salary, and verbal ability averages in nonwhite schools are partially explained. As a second measure of the importance of teacher segregation, the independent variables in equations (2), (4), and (5) were used to explain the experience, salary, and verbal ability of black and of white teachers in separate regressions.

In the first comparison, the average black teacher was found to have about 8 percent less experience than the average white teacher and to be paid somewhat less as a result. Moreover, his score on the verbal ability test was considerably lower; the average differential was 3.60 points (this is greater than one standard deviation in the combined sample).(25) The results of the second comparison were equally striking. Whether verbal ability, experience, or salary of white teachers and of nonwhite teachers were used as dependent variables [equations (2), (4), and (5) were run with racially separated teacher data], no statistically significant relationship to the school-based independent variables (racial composition of students and average income in the school attendance area) was seen.(26) Taken together, these results indicate that in the large cities studied, a crucial factor in the lower verbal ability, experience, and salary of the average teacher in nonwhite areas is the high proportion of nonwhites teaching there.

This relationship could also help to explain the tendency, observed in Table 1, for the apparent difference in the level of resources allocated to nonwhite and white pupils to rise with the proportion of nonwhites in the city—at least if the assignment of black students to black teachers increases with the proportion of black students in the system. There is some empirical evidence that, in American cities, black teachers are in fact typically assigned to black students and, moreover, that as the proportion of black students in the school system increases, there is a more than proportionate increase in the hiring of black teachers, so that the ratio of black teachers to black students rises.(27) Taken together, the effect of these practices is that the proportion of black students with black teachers increases with the percentage of black students in the system. As a result, when black teachers average below white teachers in experience (or some other quality measure), there will be a larger gap in, say, the average experience level of teachers assigned to white and black students in those cities where the proportion of black students is high.

The most significant variables in any analysis of educational inequality are those associated with teacher quality, both because of their importance in the educational process and because of the weight of teachers' salaries in the educational budget. However, it is also useful to see to what extent, if any, the distribution of physical facilities either parallels the distribution of teaching resources or, alternatively, tends to offset the latter's inegalitarian tendencies. When data from the nine-city Coleman sample on three measures of physical quality—age of the plant, amount of school ground per student, and special facilities available in the school(28)—were each regressed against economic and racial variables,(29) a significant positive association was found between physical quality and income in the school neighborhood, although no relationship with the racial composition of the school or city was observed. On balance, these results suggest that the distribution of physical resources complements rather than compensates for the unequal distribution of teaching resources among schools.

CONCLUSION

The empirical evidence presented here is consistent with the hypothesis that instructional expenditures are distributed unequally and that school systems spend less on nonwhite and poor children than on other children in large American cities. The teachers with the most experience and the highest verbal ability scores are generally to be found in schools attended by the less-poor white children. An analysis of school plants indicates that the allocation of physical resources as well may be influenced by the economic characteristics of the school neighborhood.

The immediate cause of the economic and racial biases in the allocation of teaching resources appears to lie in the teacher assignment system: the single city-wide salary schedule, the allocation of attractive teaching posts to the most experienced teachers, and, in some cities, the informal pressures that are exerted to keep black teachers in black schools.

NOTES

(1) A number of cross-sectional studies of community demand for education have been carried out. See Werner Z. Hirsch, "Income Elasticity of Public Education," *International Economic Review* 2 (September 1961), pp. 230-39; Jerry Miner, *Social and Economic Factors in Spending for Public Education* (Syracuse, N.Y.: Syracuse University Press, 1963); and Thomas H. James et al., *Determinants of Educational Expenditures in Large Cities of the United States* (Stanford, Calif.: Technical Report to the U.S. Office of Education, Cooperative

Research Project No. 2389, 1965).

(2) In the literature on state and local finance it is frequently assumed that municipal expenditures for public services, including education, are equally distributed among the recipients. This assumption is sometimes then combined with data on taxes paid to different groups so as to show that the fiscal system of taxes and expenditure is, as a whole, less regressive than one would otherwise believe. See, for example, the analysis of educational expenditures in W. Irwin Gillespie, "Effect of Public Expenditures on The Distribution of Income," in Essays in Federalism, ed. Richard A. Musgrave (Washington: Brookings, 1965:122-86); and in Dick Netzer, Economics of the Property Tax (Washington: Brookings, 1966:256-57). See also the use of the Gillespie data in Paul A. Samuelson, Economics (New York: McGraw-Hill, 1967:167). However, this equal expenditure assumption is made without empirical justification. The distribution of educational resources described here and in the work cited in fn. 15 would tend to contradict it.

(3) Prices of educational resources would actually be likely to be higher in slum and ghetto areas. Land values are generally higher in the inner than in the outer city. More important, the teacher preferences described below suggest that if the price mechanism were used to assign teachers (rather than the bureaucratic procedure presently employed), higher salaries would be required, ceteris paribus, to assure equal teacher quality in the poorer neighborhoods.

(4) Some useful discussions of these problems are found in Milton Friedman, "The Role of Government in Education," in Capitalism and Freedom, ed. Milton Friedman (Chicago: 1962:85-107); W.C. Stubblebine, "Institutional Elements in the Financing of Education," Southern Economic Journal 32 (July 1965:15-35); B.A. Weisbrod, External Benefits of Public Education, Princeton University Research Report Series 105, Industrial Relations Section (Princeton, N.J.: Princeton University Press, 1964); M.V. Pauly, "Mixed Public and Private Financing of Education," American Economic Review 57 (March 1967:120-30); Walter Hettich, "Mixed Public and Private Financing of Education: Comment," and Pauly's "Reply," American Economic Review 59 (March 1969:210-13).

(5) Cf. the very useful discussion of these problems in Henry M. Levin, "Decentralization and the Finance of Inner-City Schools," Research and Development Memorandum No. 50, Stanford Center for Research and Development in Teaching.

(6) In the 91 largest school systems reporting for 1958-59, teachers' salaries accounted for over four-fifths of the expenditures for instruction. Average instructional expenditures accounted for three-quarters of average total current expenditures (see Gerald Kahn, "Current Expenditures Per Pupil in Public School Systems, Urban School Systems 1958-59," U.S. Department of Health, Education, and Welfare Circular No. 645 [Washington: 1961], Tables 2 and 3, pp. 15, 36).

(7) This career pattern is described in Howard S. Becker, "The Career of the Chicago Public School Teacher," American Journal of Sociology 57 (March 1952:471-72). See also Albert P. Blaustein, "Philadelphia," in U.S. Commission on Civil Rights, Civil Rights U.S.A./Public Schools North and West, 1962

(Washington: U.S. Government Printing Office, 1962); and Kenneth B. Clark, Dark Ghetto (New York: Harper & Row, 1965:134).

(8) In theory, the assignment of teachers can be controlled by administrators, including school principals. However, there is little evidence that the net effect of administrative influence is to encourage experienced teachers to seek transfers into slum schools or to discourage transfers from then.

(9) See James S. Coleman et al., Equality of Educational Opportunity (Washington: U.S. Government Printing Office, 1966).

(10) See Becker, "The Career . . . ," for an analysis of the reasons why the more able teachers leave and the less able teachers remain in slum schools.

(11) See, for example, Coleman et al., Equality of Educational Opportunity. Henry M. Levin, Recruiting Teachers for Large City Schools (Washington: Brookings, 1968), presents further evidence of the difference between the racial preferences of black and white teachers in ghetto schools. David Gottlieb, "Teaching and Students: The Views of Negro and White Teachers," Sociology of Education 37 (Summer 1964:345-53), found that while white teachers regarded their black pupils as "talkative, lazy, high strung, and rebellious," black teachers found them to be "happy, cooperative, energetic, and ambitious" (pp. 352-53).

(12) See A. Harry Passow, Toward Creating a Model Urban School System: A Study of the Washington, D.C., Public Schools (New York: Teachers College, Columbia University, 1968:64); Supplemental Studies for the National Advisory Commission on Civil Disorders (Washington: U.S. Government Printing Office, 1968:16, 36); and Richard E. Day, Civil Rights U.S.A./Public Schools Southern States, 1963/North Carolina, U.S. Commission on Civil Rights (Washington: U.S. Government Printing Office, 1964:33, 53-59).

(13) See Blaustein, "Philadelphia," pp. 154-70, "Discrimination Against Teachers." See also Becker, "The Career . . . " The informal pressures on black teachers are varied. However, both Becker and Blaustein agree that an important factor is the black teacher's fear that if he does succeed in transferring to a white school against the advice of its principal, the latter will interfere with his career by giving him low ratings, difficult classes, or the like.

(14) See Martin Theodore Katzman, "Distribution and Production in a Big City Elementary School System" (Ph.D. diss., Yale University, 1967).

(15) See Patricia Cayo Smith, Education and Income (New York: Viking, 1961); Jesse Burkhead, Thomas G. Fox, and John W. Holland, Input and Output in Large-City High Schools (Syracuse, N.Y.: Syracuse University Press, 1967); and Katzman, "Distribution and Production . . . "

(16) Coleman et al., Equality of Educational Opportunity.

(17) The quality of the data themselves has also been criticized: see Samuel S. Bowles and Henry M. Levin, "The Determinants of Scholastic Achievement—An Appraisal of Some Recent Evidence," Journal of Human Resources 3 (Winter 1968:3-24); and Bowles and Levin, "Equality of Educational Opportunity—More on Multicollinearity and the Effectiveness of Schools," Journal of Human Resources 3 (Summer 1968:393-400). See also James S. Coleman, "Equality of Educational Opportunity: Reply to Bowles and Levin,"

Journal of Human Resources 3 (Spring, 1968:237-46). In order to use these data for the present study, a number of corrections were made on the data tapes. These corrected data are described in a forthcoming report from the Johns Hopkins University Center for the Study of Social Organization of Schools. Within the Coleman sample, all elementary schools in the chosen cities were studied. Center cities were defined by their political boundaries.

(18) Estimated from Census tract data by using transparent overlays. Since neighborhood income levels were changing in the period from 1959, the Census year, to 1964, when the Equality of Educational Opportunity study was made, the estimates of family income based upon the Coleman Report questions on consumer durables in respondents' homes were used to correct the Census data for recent changes in income level.

(19) Cf. the discussion in G.S. Becker, The Economics of Discrimination (Chicago: University of Chicago Press, 1957). Becker found that this hypothesis was not supported in his study of earnings data.

(20) City-wide values for the dependent variables in regression equations (1) to (3) were first regressed against average family income in the city. The regression coefficients thus obtained were used to obtain values of the dependent variables net of the influence of city income. These values were then used as dependent variables in regressions (1) to (3). This method permitted the use of city-wide rather than sample values for the dependent variable in estimating the city income relationship, hence obtaining a more reliable result. It also served its conventional function of coping with any multicollinearity between city income and either neighborhood income or the racial composition variables.

(21) See the references in fn. 1. It has been suggested that the smaller size of the within-city elasticity affords a rough measure of the extent to which centralized administration of large-city educational systems has reduced inequality based on income differences.

(22) Both the school income and the city income variables were deflated by the U.S. Bureau of Labor Statistics city cost-of-living index. The deflated income data afford a more accurate measure of intercity variations in real income.

(23) This test was designed especially for the Coleman survey by the Educational Testing Service of Princeton, N.J. The purpose of this written examination was to measure the verbal facility of teachers.

(24) The smaller size of this income elasticity is not surprising, since the intracity variation is associated with a single labor market. Interregional variations in the supply of able teachers (which may be positively associated with income levels) do not contribute to the interschool variation.

(25) An adequate explanation of these racial differentials is, of course, beyond the scope of this study. The lower average experience level of black teachers is probably due to a more rapid increase in the hiring of black than of white teachers. It has been suggested that the lower verbal ability scores are accounted for by the recruitment of many black teachers who have been trained in segregated schools and colleges. Further explanations might be sought in a

possible cultural bias built into the test of verbal ability.

(26) A partial exception was found in the case of experience level of white teachers, where a relationship with income of the school neighborhood was found which was significant at the 5 percent level.

(27) The table below was based on data provided by the U.S. Civil Rights Commission for the public elementary schools of 69 cities. These data show that, as the proportion of black students in non-southern school systems increases, the ratio of black teachers to black students also incrreases. These teachers tended to be assigned to black students, so that the probability of a black child having a black teacher rose with the proportion of black students in the system.

Racial Segregation in the Assignment of Public Elementary
School Teachers in American Cities

% Black Students in Non-southern City Schools	% Black Teachers/% Black Students
1-10	.331
11-30	.497
31-50	.501
51-70	.863

Source: John D. Owen, Racial Patterns in the Assignment of Teachers in 69 American Cities (Baltimore: Johns Hopkins University Center for the Study of Social Organization of Schools, 1969).

(28) A weighted average of auditorium, cafeteria, and athletic facilities.

(29) The independent variables were those used in equations (4) to (6) of Table 1.

THE SCHOOLS AND
EQUAL OPPORTUNITY

Mary Jo Bane

Christopher Jencks

Americans have a recurrent fantasy that schools can solve their problems. Thus it was perhaps inevitable that, after we rediscovered poverty and inequality in the early 1960s, we turned to the schools for solutions. Yet the schools did not provide solutions, the high hopes of the early-and-middle 1960s faded, and the war on poverty ended in ignominious surrender to the *status quo*. In part, of course, this was because the war in Southeast Asia turned out to be incompatible with the war on poverty. In part, however, it was because we all had rather muddleheaded ideas about the various causes and cures of poverty and inequality.

Today there are signs that some people are beginning to look for new solutions to these perennial problems. There is a vast amount of sociological and economic data that can, we think, help in this effort, both by explaining the failures of the 1960s and by suggesting more realistic alternatives. For the past four years we have been working with this data. Our research has led us to three general conclusions.

First, poverty is a condition of relative rather than absolute deprivation. People feel poor and are poor if they have a lot less money than their neighbors. This is true regardless of their absolute income. It follows that we cannot eliminate poverty unless we prevent people from falling too far below the national average. The problem is economic inequality rather than low incomes.

Second, the reforms of the 1960s were misdirected because they focused only on equalizing opportunity to "succeed" (or "fail") rather than on reducing the economic and social distance between those who succeeded and those who failed. The evidence we have reviewed suggests that equalizing opportunity will not do very much to equalize results, and hence that it will not do much to reduce poverty.

Third, even if we are interested solely in equalizing opportunities for economic success, making schools more equal will not help very much. Differences between schools have very little effect on what happens to students after they graduate.

The main policy implication of these findings is that although school reform is important for improving the lives of children, schools cannot contribute significantly to adult equality. If we want economic equality in our society, we will have to get it by changing our economic institutions, not by changing the schools.

POVERTY AND INEQUALITY

The rhetoric of the war on poverty described the persistence of poverty in the midst of affluence as a "paradox," largely attributable to "neglect." Official publications all assumed that poverty was an absolute rather than a relative condition. Having assumed this, they all showed progress toward the elimination of poverty, since fewer and fewer people had incomes below the official "poverty line."

Yet, despite all the official announcements of progress, many Americans still seemed poor, by both their own standards and their neighbors'. The reason was that most Americans define poverty in relative rather than absolute terms. Public-opinion surveys show, for example, that when people are asked how much money an American family needs to "get by," they typically name a figure about half what the average American family actually receives. This has been true for the last three decades, despite the fact that real incomes (incomes adjusted for inflation) have doubled in the interval.

During the Depression the average American family was living on about $30 a week. A third of all families were living on less than half this amount, which made it natural for Franklin Roosevelt to speak of "one-third of a nation" as ill-housed, ill-clothed, and ill-fed. By 1964 mean family income was about $160 a week, and the Gallup poll found that the average American thought a family of four needed at least $80 a week to "get by." Even allowing for inflation this was twice what people had thought necessary during the Depression. Playing it safe, the Johnson administration defined the poverty line at $60 a week for a family of four, but most people felt this was inadequate. By 1970 inflation had raised mean family income to about $200 a week, and the National Welfare Rights Organization was trying to rally liberal support for a guaranteed income of $100 a week.

These changes in the definition of poverty were not just a matter of "rising expectations" or of people's needing to "keep up with the Joneses." The goods and services that made it possible to live on $15 a week during the Depression were no longer available to a family with the same real income ($40 a week) in

1964. Eating habits had changed, and many cheap foods had disappeared from the stores. Housing arrangements had changed, too. During the Depression many people could not afford indoor plumbing and "got by" with a privy. By the 1960s privies were illegal in most places. Those who still could not afford an indoor toilet ended up in buildings that had broken toilets. For these they paid more than their parents had paid for privies.

Examples of this kind suggest that the "cost of living" is not the cost of buying some fixed set of goods and services. It is the cost of participating in a social system. It therefore depends in large part on how much other people habitually spend to participate in the system. Those who fall far below the norm, whatever it may be, are excluded. Accordingly, raising the incomes of the poor will not eliminate poverty if the cost of participating in "mainstream" American life rises even faster. People with incomes less than half the national average will not be able to afford what "everyone" regards as "necessities." The only way to eliminate poverty is, therefore, to make sure everyone has an income at least half the average.

Arguments of this kind suggest not only that it makes more sense to think of "poverty" as a relative rather than an absolute condition but that eliminating poverty, at least as it is usually defined in America, depends on eliminating, or at least greatly reducing, inequality.

SCHOOLING AND OPPORTUNITY

Almost none of the reform legislation of the 1960s involved direct efforts to equalize adult status, power, or income. Most Americans accepted the idea that these rewards should go to those who were most competent and diligent. Their objection to America's traditional economic system was not that it produced inequality but that the rules determining who succeeded and who failed were often unfair. The reformers wanted to create a world in which success would no longer be associated with skin color, economic background, or other "irrelevant" factors, but only with actual merit. What they wanted, in short, was what they called "equal opportunity."

Their strategy for achieving equal opportunity placed great emphasis on education. Many people imagined that if schools could equalize people's cognitive skills this would equalize their bargaining power as adults. Presumably, if everyone had equal bargaining power, few people would end up very poor.

This strategy for reducing poverty rested on a series of assumptions that went roughly as follows:

    1. Eliminating poverty is largely a matter of helping children born into poverty to rise out of it. Once families escape from poverty, they do not fall back into it. Middle-class children rarely end up poor.

    2. The primary reason poor children cannot escape from poverty is that they do not acquire basic cognitive skills. They cannot read, write, calculate, or articulate. Lacking these skills, they cannot get or keep a well-paid job.

3. The best mechanism for breaking this "vicious circle" is educational reform. Since children born into poor homes do not acquire the skills they need from their parents, they must be taught these skills in school. This can be done by making sure that they attend the same schools as middle-class children, by giving them extra compensatory programs in school, by giving their parents a voice in running their schools, or by some combination of all three approaches.

Our research over the last four years suggests that each of these assumptions is erroneous:

1. Poverty is not primarily hereditary. While children born into poverty have a higher than average chance of ending up poor, there is still an enormous amount of economic mobility from one generation to the next. A father whose occupational status is high passes on less than half his advantage to his sons, and a father whose status is low passes along less than half his disadvantage. A family whose income is above the norm has an even harder time passing along its privileges; its sons are typically only about a third as advantaged as the parents. Conversely, a family whose income is below average will typically have sons about a third as disadvantaged as the parents. The effects of parents' status on their daughters' economic positions appear to be even weaker. This means that many "advantaged" parents have some "disadvantaged" children and vice versa.

2. The primary reason some people end up richer than others is not that they have more adequate cognitive skills. While children who read well, get the right answers to arithmetic problems, and articulate their thoughts clearly are somewhat more likely than others to get ahead, there are many other equally important factors involved. The effects of I.Q. on economic success are about the same as the effects of family background. This means, for example, that if two men's I.Q. scores differ by 17 points—the typical difference between I.Q. scores of individuals chosen at random—their incomes will typically differ by less than $2,000. That amount is not completely trivial, of course. But the income difference between random individuals is three times as large and the difference between the best-paid fifth and the worst-paid fifth of all male workers averages $14,000. There is almost as much economic inequality among those who score high on standardized tests as in the general population.

3. There is no evidence that school reform can substantially reduce the extent of cognitive inequality, as measured by tests of verbal fluency, reading comprehension, or mathematical skill. Eliminating qualitative differences between elementary schools would reduce the range of scores on standardized tests in sixth grade by less than 3 percent. Eliminating qualitative differences between high schools would hardly reduce the range of twelfth-grade scores at all and would reduce by only 1 percent the disparities in the amount of education people eventually get.

Our best guess, after reviewing all the evidence we could find, is that racial desegregation raises black elementary school students' test scores by a couple of points. But most of the test-score gap between blacks and whites persists, even when they are in the same schools. So also: Tracking has very little effect on test scores. And neither the overall level of resources available to a school nor any specific, easily identifiable school policy has a significant effect on students' cognitive skills or educational attainments. Thus, even if we went beyond "equal opportunity" and allocated resources disproportionately to schools whose students now do worst on tests and are least likely to acquire credentials, this would not improve these students' prospects very much.

The evidence does not tell us why school quality has so little effect on test scores. Three possible explanations come to mind. First, children seem to be more influenced by what happens at home than by what happens in school. They may also be more influenced by what happens on the streets and by what they see on television. Second, administrators have very little control over those aspects of school life that do affect children. Reallocating resources, reassigning pupils, and rewriting the curriculum seldom change the way teachers and students actually treat each other minute by minute. Third, even when the schools exert an unusual influence on children, the resulting changes are not likely to persist into adulthood. It takes a huge change in elementary school test scores, for example, to alter adult income by a significant amount.

EQUAL OPPORTUNITY AND UNEQUAL RESULTS

The evidence we have reviewed, taken all together, suggests that equalizing opportunity cannot take us very far toward eliminating inequality. The simplest way of demonstrating this is to compare the economic prospects of brothers raised in the same home. Even the most egalitarian society could not hope to make opportunities for all children appreciably more equal than the opportunities now available to brothers from the same family. Looking at society at large, if we compare random pairs of individuals, the difference between their occupational statuses averages about 28 points on the Duncan "status scale" (the scale runs from 0 to 96 points). The difference between brothers' occupational statuses averages fully 23 points on this same scale. If we compare men's incomes, the difference between random pairs averaged about $6,200 in 1968. The difference between brothers' incomes, according to our best estimate, probably averaged about $5,700. These estimates mean that people who start off equal end up almost as unequal as everyone else. Inequality is not mostly inherited: It is re-created anew in each generation.

We can take this line of argument a step further by comparing people who not only start off in similar families but who also have the same I.Q. scores and get the same amount of schooling. Such people's occupational statuses differ by an average of 21 points, compared to 28 points for random individuals. If we compare their incomes, making the additional assumption that the men have the same occupational status, we find that they differ by an average of about $5,300, compared to $6,200 for men chosen at random.

These comparisons suggest that adult success must depend on a lot of things besides family background, schooling, and the cognitive skills measured by standardized tests. We have no idea what these factors are. To some extent, no doubt, specialized varieties of competence, such as the ability to hit a ball thrown at high speed or the ability to persuade a customer that he wants a larger car than he thought he wanted, play a major role. Income also depends on luck: the range of jobs available when you are job hunting, the amount of overtime work in your plant, good or bad weather for your strawberry crop, and a hundred other unpredictable accidents.

Equalizing opportunity will not, then, do much to reduce economic inequality in America. If poverty is relative rather than absolute, equalizing opportunity will not do much to reduce poverty, either.

IMPLICATIONS FOR EDUCATIONAL POLICY

These findings imply that school reform is never likely to have any significant effect on the degree of inequality among adults. This suggests that the prevalent "factory" model, in which schools are seen as places that "produce" alumni, probably ought to be abandoned. It is true that schools have "inputs" and "outputs," and that one of their nominal purposes is to take human "raw material" (*i.e.*, children) and convert it into something more "useful" (*i.e.*, employable adults). Our research suggests, however, that the character of a school's output depends largely on a single input, the characteristics of the entering children. Everything else—the school budget, its policies, the characteristics of the teachers—is either secondary or completely irrelevant, at least so long as the range of variation among schools is as narrow as it seems to be in America.

These findings have convinced us that the long-term effects of schooling are relatively uniform. The day-to-day internal life of the schools, in contrast, is highly variable. It follows that *the primary basis for evaluating a school should be whether the students and teachers find it a satisfying place to be.* This does not mean we think schools should be like mediocre summer camps, in which children are kept out of trouble but not taught anything. We doubt that a school can be enjoyable for either adults or children unless the children keep learning new things. We value ideas and the life of the mind, and we think that a school that does not value these things is a poor place for children. But a school that values ideas because they enrich the lives of children is quite different from a school that values high reading scores because reading scores are important for adult success.

Our concern with making schools satisfying places for teachers and children has led us to a concern for diversity and choice. People have widely different notions of what a "satisfying" place is, and we believe they ought to be able to put these values into practice. As we have noted, our research suggests that none of the programs or structural arrangements in common use today has consistently different long-term effects from any other. Since the character of a child's schooling has few long-term effects, and since these effects are quite unpredictable, society has little reason to constrain the choices available to parents and children. If a "good school" is one the students and staff find satisfying, no one school will be best for everyone. Since there is no evidence that professional educators know appreciably more than parents about what is good for children, it seems reasonable to let parents decide what kind of education their children should have while they are young and to let the children decide as they get older.

Short-term considerations also seem decisive in determining whether to spend more money on schooling or to spend it on busing children to schools outside their neighborhoods. If extra resources make school life pleasanter and more interesting, they are worthwhile. But we should not try to justify school expenditures on the grounds that they boost adult earnings. Likewise, busing ought to be justified in political and moral terms rather than in terms of presumed long-term effects on the children who are bused. If we want an integrated society, we ought to have integrated schools, which make people feel they have a stake in the well-being of other races. If we want a society in which people are free to segregate themselves, then we should apply that principle to our schools. There is, however, no compelling reason to treat schools differently from other social arrangements, including neighborhoods. Personally, we believe in both open housing and open schools. If parents or students want to take buses to schools in other neighborhoods, school boards ought to provide the buses, expand the relevant schools, and insure that the students are welcome in the schools they want to attend. This is the least we can do to offset the effects of residential segregation. But we do not believe that forced busing can be justified on the grounds of its long-term benefits for students.

This leads to our last conclusion about educational reform. Reformers are always getting trapped into claiming too much for what they propose. They may want a particular reform—like open classrooms, or desegregation, or vouchers—because they think these reforms will make schools more satisfying places to work. Yet they feel obliged to claim that these reforms will also reduce the number of nonreaders, increase racial understanding, or strengthen family life. A wise reformer ought to be more modest, claiming only that a particular reform will not harm adult society and that it will make life pleasanter for parents, teachers, and students in the short run.

This plea for modesty in school reform will, we fear, fall on deaf ears. Ivan Illich is right in seeing schools as secular churches, through which we seek to improve not ourselves but our descendants. That this process should be disagreeable seems inevitable; a religion that promises anything less than salvation wins few converts. In school, as in church, we present the world as we wish it were. We try to inspire children with the ideals we ourselves have failed to live up to. We assume, for example, that we cannot make adults live in desegregated neighborhoods, so we devise schemes for busing children from one neighborhood to another in order to desegregate the schools. We all prefer conducting our moral experiments on other people. Nonetheless, so long as we confine our experiments to children, we will not have much effect on adult life.

IMPLICATIONS FOR SOCIAL REFORM

Then how *are* we to affect adult life? Our findings tell us that different kinds of inequality are only loosely related to one another. This can be either encouraging or discouraging, depending on how you look at it. On the discouraging side, it means that eliminating inequality in one area will not eliminate it in other areas. On the encouraging side, it means that inequality in one area does not dictate inequality in other areas.

To begin with, genetic inequality is not a major obstacle to economic equality. It is true that genetic diversity almost inevitably means considerable variation in people's scores on standardized tests. But this kind of cognitive inequality need not imply anything like the present degree of economic inequality. We estimate, for example, that if the only sources of income inequality in America were differences in people's genes, the top fifth of the population would earn only about 1.4 times as much as the bottom fifth. In actuality, the top fifth earns seven times as much as the bottom fifth.

Second, our findings suggest that psychological and cultural differences between families are not an irrevocable barrier to adult equality. Family background has more influence than genes on an individual's educational attainment, occupational status, and income. Nonetheless, if family background were the only source of economic inequality in America, the top fifth would earn only about twice as much as the bottom fifth.

Our findings show, then, that inequality is not determined at birth. But they also suggest that economic equality cannot be achieved by indirect efforts to manipulate the environments in which people grow up. We have already discussed the minuscule effects of equalizing school quality. Equalizing the amount of schooling people get would not work much better. Income inequality among men with similar amounts of schooling is only 5-10 percent less than among men in general. The effect is even less if we include women.

If we want to eliminate economic inequality, we must make this an explicit objective of public policy rather than deluding ourselves into thinking that we can do it by giving everyone equal opportunity to succeed or fail. If we want an occupational structure which is less hierarchical and in which the social distance between the top and the bottom is reduced, we will have to make deliberate efforts to reorganize work and redistribute power within organizations. We will probably also have to rotate jobs, so that no individual held power very long.

If we want an income distribution that is more equal, we can constrain employers, either by tax incentives or direct legislation, to reduce wage disparities between their best- and worst-paid workers. We can make taxes more progressive, and we can provide income supplements to those who do not make an adequate living from wages alone. We can also provide free public services for those who cannot afford to buy adequate services in the private sector. Pursued with vigor, such a strategy can make "poverty" (*i.e.*, having a living standard less than half the national average) virtually impossible. Such a strategy would also make economic "success," in the sense of having, say, a living standard more than twice the national average, far less common than it now is. The net effect would be to make those with the most competence and luck subsidize those with the least competence and luck to a far greater extent than they do today. Unless we are prepared to do this, poverty and inequality will remain with us indefinitely.

This strategy was rejected during the 1960s for the simple reason that it commanded relatively little popular support. The required legislation could not have passed Congress, nor could it pass today. That does not mean that it is the wrong strategy. It simply means that, until we change the political and moral premises on which most Americans now operate, poverty and inequality will persist at pretty much their present level. Intervention in market processes, for example, means restricting the "right" of individuals to use their natural advantages for private gain. Economic equality requires social and legal sanctions—analogous to those that now exist against capricious firing of employees—against inequality within work settings. It also requires that wage rates, which Americans have traditionally viewed as a "private" question to be adjudicated by negotiation between (unequal) individuals or groups, must become a "public" question subject to political control and solution.

In America, as elsewhere, the long-term drift over the past 200 years has been toward equality. In America, however, the contribution of public policy to this drift has been slight. As long as egalitarians assume that public policy cannot contribute to equality directly but must proceed by ingenious manipulations of marginal institutions like the schools, this pattern will continue. If we want to move beyond this tradition, we must establish political control over the economic institutions that shape our society. What we will need, in short, is what other countries call socialism. Anything less will end in the same disappointment as the reforms of the 1960s.

DESCHOOLING AND
THE DISADVANTAGED:
THE IMPLICATIONS
OF THE ILLICH PROPOSALS

Gertrude S. Goldberg

Ivan Illich has framed a declaration of educational independence: a guarantee of the "inalienable right" to learn what one chooses.(1) Illich maintains that in order to liberate the learner from the unnatural control of prescriptive and compulsory schooling, we must disestablish the public schools. Such a proposal departs radically from reforms like free schooling and even from the voucher system, which would break up school monopolies and replace them with competing educational structures.(2) The voucher system, according to Illich, "condemns itself by proposing tuition grants which would have to be spent on schooling."(3) Anything short of disestablishment and deschooling is insufficient because schools, no matter how free they claim to be, are always directed.(4)

Reforms like free schooling and the voucher system are designed to prepare workers and citizens more effectively for the same society, whereas deschooling is an attempt to effect major changes in political, economic, and cultural structures. Since Illich considers the school responsible for teaching men and women how to be modern producers and consumers, he views it as the major institutional bulwark of our false economy. The abolition of school, he holds, is an essential component of radical social change. Indeed, he insists that revolution in education can and must precede political change.

Were Illich's work an isolated plea for disestablishment or in itself less widely read, we might perhaps take his proposals less seriously and certainly less literally. A program so utopian, one that in the final analysis seems antithetical to the concept of society, is perhaps best regarded as a stirring manifesto, a means of mobilizing discontent with the present system and of channeling criticism in the direction of freer education. Yet, Illich devotes much space to describing the new relational structures that would replace school and would facilitate education that is free of social control. And he considers any program that does not include deschooling "demagoguery calling for more of the same."(5) In any case, many individuals are taking his proposals seriously, and other prominent critics are urging deschooling or educational change close to it.(6) Perhaps some of these individuals fail to distinguish between free schooling and education free of social control. Possibly they are unaware of the social and political implications of leaving direction with the learner. Or, some of them may not recognize that educational liberty would fail to benefit the disadvantaged, for it implies the differential ability to utilize freedom that we associate with inequality. Still others, perhaps willing to risk anarchy in order to free society of the undesirable controls that are now imposed by schools, may fail to scrutinize the assumption that radical change in education can precede political revolution. They seem to fall into the familiar trap of believing that schooling—or deschooling—can change society. By evaluating the salient attributes and implications of deschooling, we hope to raise the level of debate on these issues from that of eloquent declaration to rational dialogue.

EDUCATION AND SOCIAL CONTROL

Social control is intrinsic not only to schooling but to any system of education that is formally established by the community. As Anthony F.C. Wallace concludes, "there is . . . no human society on the face of the earth which concedes to *any* individual the right to learn anything he chooses."(7) Indeed, the definition of education often implies direction by others rather than control by the learner. For example, Durkheim defined education as "the influence exercised by adult generations on those that are not ready yet for social life."(8) The function of education he observed, is "to adapt the child to the social milieu in which he is destined to live . . . "(9)

Unless proponents of deschooling are merely urging freedom at all costs—because it is an "inalienable right"—they must also consider it adequate preparation for social life. Yet, Illich rejects both moral and technical education, the two types of direction which are traditionally associated with such preparation. What kind of social milieu, we ask, is implied by an education which does not concern itself with job training and with the values and norms of future citizens?

DE-MORALIZING SOCIETY

Moral education, when provided by the community, is an attempt to convey a set of socially-approved standards to all children in a society. Societal cohesion depends upon shared ideas and sentiments, on rules of conduct and goals of action which most people in a society can agree about. If the community ceases to provide moral education through its schools, it runs the risk not only of value conflict and societal fragmentation, but, depending upon the extent to which other institutions stress this form of socialization, of insufficient character training as well. Children in different social milieu may fail to learn the common values of a society, and ultimately, there may cease to be such a core of ideas and sentiments. Or the socialization of all or some groups may simply be deficient in moral influences. The implications of omitting morality from the educational system are different, depending upon whether one considers the teaching of group and community loyalties or the training of more general values and rules of conduct.

While proponents of deschooling find it officious for education to teach what is right and wrong in and out of school,(10) other critics of American socialization feel that children do not get enough of this kind of training anywhere. Urie Bronfenbrenner, for example, maintains that both school and family, the two potential agents for conveying socially-approved values, are not sufficiently potent influences.(11) Schools tend to restrict their role to subject matter in order to avoid the risk of religious persuasion, and families spend increasingly less time with their children. Instead, TV and peer group are more constant companions and more powerful influences. Thus the values of school and family are undermined by the often conflicting and usually more compelling message of media and youth culture. The implications of Bronfenbrenner's position is that a formal educational system without moral influence exacerbates the trend toward an upbringing which is already deficient in it. It leaves this function with a family system which wants to delegate more and more of its responsibilities to outside socializing agents, which are not only unwilling but probably incapable of doing the job. Indeed, Paul Goodman acknowledges that as bad as schools are, many homes are worse.(12)

There is little doubt that we risk increased societal fragmentation if we free education of moral control without assigning it to another community-wide institution. Durkheim, for example, argued that a society was impossible unless education provided this type of moral direction:

> If one attaches some value to the existence of society . . . education must assure, among the citizenry, a sufficient community of ideas and of sentiments, without which any society is impossible; and in order that it may be able to produce this result, it is also necessary that education not be completely abandoned to the arbitrariness of private individuals.(13)

It could perhaps be argued that we have available in our day, unlike that of Durkheim or Jefferson, media other than the school which can convey common ideas and sentiments to all. When Jefferson designed his three-year public-school system, it was necessary to create a new institution to weld a new democratic morality because there was no other single agency that would reach all young persons in the society. However, if we were to depend upon the media to teach common values and norms, we would first have to assure that it represents public rather than private interest, a goal that is very difficult to accomplish short of public ownership—which would be resisted even more than strict public regulation. In any case, the teaching of morality is probably best done by a live group media which affords interaction between an adult leader and a group of young people, as well as among the latter. Thus a school class or a youth group established in a community center is preferable to TV for teaching morality, despite the ubiquity of the media.

The ideas and sentiments to which Durkheim referred were respect for reason, for science, and for democratic principles. If these were the values that were conveyed by adult institutions, perhaps advocates of deschooling would be less eager to weaken the moral education that children get. Instead, school, parents, and TV often emphasize undesirable values: consumership, credentialism, and wasteful production, rather than values conducive to human development.(14) Instead of democratic principles our children learn a paternalistic patriotism, "how to feel like children of the same state."(15) They have been urged to achieve, not for their own development or for community welfare, but for national defense—in order to outpace our adversaries in space.

The crass and corrupt values that our children learn are, we feel, more alarming than either value conflict or weak exposure to such moral influences. It is not that school, family, and media disagree but that each fail to demonstrate the primacy of life over property, knowledge over credentialism, social worth over financial success, and truth over public relations. Were it not for the mild dissonance that some of our young people experience, they would be far more accepting than they are of adult ideas and sentiments that are the very antithesis of constructive human values. The question, then, is whether it is necessary to create anarchy in order to rid ourselves of anti-social moral education.

Different positions concerning the relationship between moral socialization and formal educational structures are associated with divergent attitudes toward the role of the peer group. Illich views school as the source, or at least the continuing stimulus, to age grouping and to separate childhood, which is really a modern phenomenon. "If there were no age-specific and obligatory learning institution, 'childhood' would go out of production."(16) The peer group that Illich would create by his new educational structures is composed of "partners in inquiry." It would take people out of neighborhoods and age-graded groupings and match them according to interest. Deschooling would break up the so-called "natural" peer group which is, to some extent, a product of school or of the mentality that regards friends as those who are born during the same school year or who attend the same class.

Bronfenbrenner, on the other hand, is concerned about the negative moral influences of the unsupervised peer group and would increase its exposure to adult influences. The Russian peer group, he reports, is graded and age-segregated, but it is supervised by adults and thus reflects rather than rejects societal values. One may consider Russian youth too conforming and docile, the products of a totalitarian society in which the State controls all institutions—family, media, school, peer group. Yet, one may nevertheless be worried about the impetus that deschooling would offer in this country, if not elsewhere, to an anti-social peer group.

There is reason to fear that many youngsters would not take up the option to learn what they wish or to join a group of partners in inquiry. Adolescent peer groups may resist corrupt adult values and may help us recognize the gap between creed and deed. But they can also become anti-social gangs which reflect adult corruption or their own brand of inverted values. Slum adolescents have long exhibited a tendency to become a separate society, alienated from parents and community institutions. The slum peer group is often a delinquent subculture, a gang committing anti-social acts akin to those that are increasingly engaged in by more affluent teen-agers.

It may, perhaps, be argued that disadvantaged groups, whose youth have traditionally been more oriented to the peer society than higher-status youngsters, would be affected more severely by the absence of moral education. It is true that lower-income parents, for understandable reasons, have less energy and time then middle-class parents to take on some of the moral functions the school now assumes. The responsibility for moral education may be a bigger burden for the lower-class family than for more advantaged groups, but it is doubtful that the school, though now assigned this function, succeeds in influencing the character training of disadvantaged youth. The values of the school are often out of context with the family and community interests of minority-group children; hence the proffered influence is usually rejected. Indeed, one goal of minority group parents who have attempted to achieve community control of local schools has been to increase continuity between home and school values.

If deschooling has only slightly different implications for the character training of higher and lower status groups, education that omits allegiance to the state does affect the disadvantaged differently. Our schools were established to teach men and women "those facts which history exhibiteth" in order that they might be able to discern tyranny and find the fervor to defend liberty.(17) Jefferson's educational system attempted to develop loyalty for what was, in retrospect, "a new nation conceived in liberty . . . " It was a democratic status quo that one should be proud to defend. Schools were established to teach principles akin to what Durkheim means by "ideas and sentiments which are at the base of democratic morality."(18)

The democratic morality that children learn, however, is particularly dissonant to disadvantaged groups. It is a distortion of democratic principles, the inculcation of respect for an established order that supports privilege in the name of "liberty and justice for all." It is the imposition of majority interest—or minority, depending on what groups are thought to benefit sufficiently—in the name of majority values. There is, of course, reason to question whether the new nation was responsive to all groups, particularly those without property. In any case, the teaching of patriotism to disadvantaged groups today, particularly to a racial caste, is an attempt to bind them to a status quo that does not meet their needs. Community control, which teaches blacks to be proud of their group and to consider themselves worthy of equal treatment, has made them aware of their disadvantages, of how democratic principles do not extend to them. It is not anti-democratic but anti-status quo.

Of particular importance to community control of education is what Anthony Wallace considers the supreme value in moral education: the stress on behavior that enhances the welfare of the group, or does not retard it.(19) Black-power strategists, who have influenced community control experiments, maintain that because black people have suffered as a group, their liberation lies in group action.(20) Integration, they claim, advances the individual, often a middle-class black, but leaves the great mass where they were and without potential leaders, who move up and out of the ghetto. In their view, such individual advancement robs the ghetto of those potential leaders who have been successful enough to move up and out.

It is possible that deschooled education would enable a significant minority to develop intellectual competence, which, in turn, might become an important group asset. The development of ideologies, the framing of strategies, and the documentation of disadvantage are all intellectual tasks which are vital to groups that are mobilizing themselves to overcome disadvantage. Yet, there is no reason to anticipate that egotistical, self-directed education would provide leaders for minority groups. For such an education fails to stress a commitment to one's group, a conviction that individual advancement must not be at the expense of group progress.

While moral education may be conducive to group loyalty, it often appears to handicap minorities by placing insufficient stress on intellectual or technical competence. Preference for one or the other type of learning emphasis for minority-group students depends upon how one conceives of individual and group advancement in a post-industrial society.

It is clear that certain educational decisions in areas where blacks have gained influence over local schools, as in Newark, stress different or additional learning matter from majority schools. The black-dominated Newark Board of Education voted to permit the Black Liberation flag to be flown in classrooms in which fifty percent or more students were black. The comment of Mayor Kenneth Gibson, also black—" . . . the flag remains as only a symbol that cannot teach children to read"(21)—suggests the conflict between moral and technical education for minority-groups in a society where majority emphasis is on training people to do jobs. It can be argued, on the one hand, that until the disadvantaged catch up in labor-market skills they remain behind. On the other hand, group power, made possible by solidarity, can get them the jobs without the credentials, particularly if skills are relatively unimportant. In the absence of clout, some will be discriminated against, even with the credentials.(22) Indeed, labor-market statistics have shown for some time that a high school diploma for a black is no particular advantage. A midway position on this issue is that enhanced group pride will contribute to group solidarity as well as to the ability to learn academic skills.

Programs that have succeeded in improving academic achievement of blacks have stressed the standard curriculum, and those which have enhanced self-image through emphasizing group culture and racial and ethnic pride have not necessarily remedied defects in formal education.(23) Yet, we have not measured which type of success, moral, technical, or intellectual, is more likely to lead to group or individual mobility, since we have tended to evaluate programs on the basis of academic rather than subsequent occupational or economic advancement. However, one program that has been viewed enthusiastically by many observers combines a highly disciplined standard curriculum with what is clearly the value emphasis of moral education. At Harlem Prep School for black teen-agers, educational achievement is not seen as a means of escaping from the community but of rendering it service.(24) For a disadvantaged group within a society that stresses job training for the majority (even though this may often consist of mere credentialing) it would seem a good strategy for schooling to combine both types of education.

As our discussion has shown, deschooling would have different implications for minority and majority groups. The more privileged groups do not need the public school to bind the loyalties of their children to existing societal arrangements. Indeed, their youth have often been educated privately. The public schools serve their interests by attempting to gain the allegiance of less privileged youth who, in the absence of such indoctrination, may be less accepting of their lot. Deschooling would thus free the poor of an education that teaches majority control. On the other hand, if disadvantaged groups were able to gain control of schools in their communities, they would have at their disposal an important resource for developing their own minority morality and, in turn, the group solidarity upon which advancement depends. Community control would gain them a positive resource rather than merely free them of a negative one. It is not that the poor need to be free of moral education but of majority control that is exerted through the educational system. They need minority rather than majority moral education.

Inasmuch as community control is very difficult to achieve and has been stricken down by State authorities where it was achieved on a local level, it seems unrealistic to base minority educational hopes on this option. However, a voucher system that would enable parents to establish such schools in their community, if they wish, would seem to offer the possibility of achieving some of the group goals that community control offers. The locus of choice would be the parent rather than society or local community, not the learner. However, without common morality and careful safeguards against racism, regular or reverse, the voucher system could be a new public license for discrimination and segregation.

It is also possible to argue that minority morality can be developed outside formal educational structures, through churches, social movements, youth serving agencies, etc. If intellectual competence were developed in school, perhaps these other institutions could encourage group solidarity and particularly influence potential leaders to put their education at the service of the community. While these agencies would provide minority morality, they would not obviate the problem of societal fragmentation, the lack of community-wide agencies to teach common morality. Competing ideologies are necessary and desirable in a society, but not in the absence of basic principles which all accept, no matter how much they disagree about subsidiary issues. Once again, though, it may be preferable to increase anarchy in order to flush out the corrupt value system.

If minority morality is strong enough, there may, as we have indicated, be less need to stress technical learning for the disadvantaged. Much depends upon whether one considers schooling necessary training for skills or required ritual for jobs. In the latter case, political power may gain what school credentials often fail to achieve, particularly for blacks. Deschooling proponents maintain that school is not needed to prepare workers for most jobs and that education for *all* groups can therefore be freed of unnecessary subservience to the labor market. In the following section, we shall discuss the implications of an education that is not geared to manpower development.

EDUCATION AND THE LABOR MARKET

The position that education need not be controlled for purposes of the labor market is based on two major assumptions. One, which we have already noted, is that people do not need a decade of schooling to prepare them for most jobs. What needs to be mastered could be learned on the job or in a far less protracted course of study than is now required, indeed compulsory. However, Illich bases his position on a more basic critique of the economic system. He argues that we do not need many of the present goods and services, that these products merely expand GNP and keep men employed. We are influenced, largely in school, to want these goods and services, but, according to Illich, we can do without many of the products and hence many of the jobs.

Illich is arguing that educational freedom is possible because modern technology enables man to relinquish the productive role. Producing the necessities of life has ceased to take up his time. The available hours can either be filled, as they are now, by stimulating a demand for and providing inessential services and wasteful goods. Or it can be used to make a limited range of more durable goods and to provide access to institutions which can increase the potential for human action. There will be much time for joyous leisure: not ennui, but intensive work and play. Such action is best promoted by learning which is an end in itself and which needs no external reinforcement. The learner is under no other control or curriculum than that which the subject of his choice dictates. In a society where men are to a great extent free of labor-market control, education which stresses intellectual and cultural development is functional. And schooling which does not prepare people to handle leisure is dysfunctional; it leads to wide-spread boredom and depression.

A choice that was unthinkable for man in earlier ages, that between unemployment and joyful, active leisure is "inevitable" for post-industrial man.(25) The choice of freedom is thus a necessity dictated by a particular state of industrial development and not a matter of a timeless value, an inalienable right. The question then is not whether we are for or against freedom but whether free education is a historical imperative.

WEALTH AND WELFARE IN A POST-INDUSTRIAL SOCIETY

This view of the post-industrial economy is quite similar to that of Robert Theobald and of the Triple Revolution group, although it is primarily concerned with education rather than with guaranteed income. Theobald and his colleagues have urged that we prepare for "freedom from work" by guaranteeing an income to everyone, in or out of the labor force.(26) Illich, though proposing the education for this post-industrial economy, never specifies how men are to support themselves if they are not among the few who produce durable goods and work in active institutions.

The failure to deal with the problem of income seems a major omission in view of the fact that we are not dealing with a "leisure class" but with a large sector of society that may be without jobs. Not only the poor, who are always fired first, but many others would find themselves without work. There is, of course, the possibility that what people learn out of choice, interest, or aptitutde will come to be valued by others and convertible into jobs and income—writing, sports, art collection, etc. Knowledge and competence would be the key to wealth rather than schooling and credentials. While choice might be influenced some by what would sell, labor market stimuli play a weaker role in the motivation for such vocations than in most other work. Many of these jobs could be learned through free education, and training for other work—the production of durable goods and of beneficial services—could be delayed or on-the-job; thus it would not contaminate or constrict the educational process. But, in the absence of any income guarantee—and even with a minimal one—the struggle for jobs would be fiercely competitive, and we might be forced to devise even more protacted rituals than schooling in order to select the "fittest."

NEED OR DEPENDENCY

Critics of the Triple-Revolution position have tended to consider it premature in view of the quantity of unmet needs in our society and all others. This debate hinges on the definition of need. Some years ago, Galbraith observed that advertising and salesmanship actively stimulate wants, that "production only fills a void that it has itself created."(27) Illich concurs, but he also considers many services unnecessary. He maintains that we are taught, primarily in school, to want and to depend upon institutional treatment. We learn that we must rely on experts rather than teaching ourselves, or ministering to others.

Although Illich does not deal with the problem of inequality, one may infer that if we were no longer taught to need such an excessive amount of goods, the poor would feel less deprived and the rich would be less greedy. Yet, the one group in our society that has shown the greatest indifference to post-industrial products (in addition to a few intellectuals) are contemporary, upper-status youth. Interestingly, their education has come closer to the one Illich proposes than that of the less-privileged classes, but they are also affluent enough to have been sated with goods. It is not clear whether freer education or increased distribution of wealth is more likely to make us less needy. There is little doubt that a system of education more geared to the development of inner resources would decrease the desire for superficial goods and increase resistance to advertised need. Yet, it is important to remember that for a great many people, especially the poor and near poor, needs remain unmet and uninflated.

The trend among social policy experts to redefine social need may seem to be symptomatic of a mentality that has become schooled to institutional treatment. Alfred Kahn, for example, argues that "social change creates new prerequisites for adequate social life in industrial communities."(28) He conceives of many social services as "social utilities" in order to emphasize that we should not consider ourselves any more inadequate or dependent because we need these services than those who need public utilities like roads, water supply, electricity, mail delivery. Martin Rein and S.M. Miller use the term "amenities" to emphasize that services enhance the quality of life rather than meet a narrowly conceived need.(29) A wealthy society, these social planners would argue, can do better than to define need in terms of scarcity; it can afford to provide modest services to all. Indeed, proponents of greater equality and of the welfare expansion they feel would accomplish this, find it strange to be put in the same camp with those who stimulate demand for commercial products—particularly since the inflation of such needs often keeps us from investing our surplus in welfare or from redistributing existing resources.

Whatever redefinition of social need has occurred, it would be incorrect to view school as the source of this expansion of increased dependency. It is also an illusion to think that deschooling would increase independence—or is it rugged individualism?

In our country, the school is the one service that is so completely a social utility—universal, provided without stigma of dependency, vitally needed by all—that it is no longer regarded as welfare.(30) Those who would move welfare in the direction of the utilities model would hope to emulate the schools in these respects, but they have not found that universal schooling teaches us to want very much welfare. We are still a "social-security state" in which the better and less coercive services go to those who establish their rights through attachment to the work force rather than through such universalistic criteria as citizenship, age, or need. If we made a few halting steps toward recognition of social insecurity, it was under the insurmountable pressure of a major depression and not as a result of manipulative schooling. Despite our commitment to universal schooling we are far less a welfare state than other societies that spend less on schooling and have provided compulsory education less long. It is, in fact, a major limitation of Illich's work that it fails to recognize significant differences in societies and differing educational needs depending upon the stage of industrial development and prevailing value orientations. The approach is sweeping in scope, but perhaps it is too global.

Although we do not share the view that the need for welfare services is inflated, we do consider the appetite for goods excessive and wasteful of natural resources. Indeed, HEW pollution is a misleading metaphor; some services may be destructive of people, but service industries do not deplete the environment. Furthermore, there is, as we shall describe later, a trend toward more *active welfare*, a concept which implies more service and more independence.

Although deschooling would not and should not decrease the need for social utilities, there are important reasons why education should give more freedom to the learner. Illich and others are correct in stressing that many jobs do not require schooling.(31) Indeed, an education that stressed morality or community service would probably do more to improve the job functioning of many workers than increased emphasis on skills training.(32) Freed from unnecessary labor-market constraints, education would enrich life, especially leisure, if it allowed the learner more latitude. For some, freedom would perhaps encourage intellectual development, which would be a desirable foundation for academic and professional work—one that may also increase sensitivity to the social consequences of such occupations. The cultivation of intellect is also likely to increase the ability to reject what is artificial, ugly, and false. And finally, as we have tried to indicate, potential leaders of disadvantaged groups need intellectual as well as moral education. Yet it is not clear whether deschooling would accomplish these desirable educational results. In the section that follows, we shall try to anticipate the educational effects of deschooling, particularly for those groups most handicapped by present schooling and other institutional arrangements.

THE EDUCATIONAL EFFECTS OF DESCHOOLING

Deschooled education is designed for a "well-motivated student who does not labor under a specific handicap" and who therefore "often needs no further human assistance than can be provided by someone who can demonstrate on demand what the learner wants to do."(33) Unlike present teachers, who are moralists, custodians, and therapists, deschooled educators would keep out of people's way, merely facilitating access to educational resources. The assumption is that without compulsory schooling, which distorts the natural impulse to learn, individuals will be motivated to seek partners in inquiry and teachers of skills. Illich observes that the ability to inspire others to learn is rarely combined with the capacity to impart a skill. But, since motivation is a given, it is the skills teacher who is the keystone of deschooled education.

SELF-MOTIVATION

We simply do not have enough experience with self-motivated learning to base an educational system on it. In all likelihood, some children need no more than the opportunity to pursue their learning interests by being helped to find skills teachers and partners in inquiry. Illich assumes that most are so motivated and that the rest are handicapped. Yet, for many children, perhaps the majority, mild direction may optimally serve what is probably moderate motivation. And still others, not necessarily handicapped, may require more forceful schooling.

Illich prefers delayed learning to external motivation or manipulation for those not eager to learn when they are young. He proposes an edu-credit card so that they can accumulate educational entitlements to be used later in life. Yet, the problems of motivation may be compounded if we desist from directed learning for the young who do not direct themselves. Jerome Bruner has observed that if certain basic skills are not mastered first, later more elaborate ones become increasingly out of reach.(34) Some late learners will go through all of the necessary steps, but the learning of such simple skills as number concepts and phonics is likely to be of inherent interest to the young, even if they do not ask to learn to read. The more mature learner must be sufficiently motivated to put up with the discomfort of learning simple skills when he is no longer a child.

THE MEANING OF MOTIVATION

A central issue in this discussion is what we mean by motivation. Is it the desire to learn the history of one's people, to play the piano, to speak a foreign language, to design a building? Or is it the interest in the skills which must be mastered in order to achieve these goals? Is motivation to play the piano enough to sustain the course of study that is dictated, not by arbitrary ritual or curriculum, but by the subject matter itself? Perhaps only the very avid and diligent can endure the endless practicing, not of music, but of isolated passages, scales, and arpeggios, without the encouragement, intervention, even prodding, of their teachers. We need to be far clearer about the meaning of motivation and its relationship to educational outcomes before we can blanketly urge self-directed learning for all.

DESCHOOLING AND THE DISADVANTAGED

We do not know how many children in any social class fit the model of the well-motivated learner, but Illich seems to think the poor are less likely than the affluent to take advantage of educational opportunities early in life. He observes that they "lack most of the educational opportunities which are casually available to the middle-class child"—conversation and books in the home, vacation travel, and a different sense of oneself.(35) In fact, he proposes the edu-credit card in order to "favor the poor." Evidently the impulse to learn is a natural one that can be easily distorted not only by an education which is probably more prescriptive in the case of the disadvantaged but by an environment that does not stimulate it. Or perhaps motivation depends upon such stimulation and cultivation.

Whether less able to be employed or to enjoy life, people will be handicapped so long as they delay their education. Furthermore, given the boundaries of the lives of the adult poor, one is not at all sanguine that their later experiences will provide them with the "casual advantages" they missed when they were young. If the environment is deficient in stimulation, why delay compensatory opportunities? Perhaps if they were followed by freer schooling or by direction that is motivated by educational rather than disciplinary goals, headstarts would be less likely to peter out.

The main beneficiaries of deschooled education will be those groups in which self-motivated learning has higher incidence. Indeed, many middle- and upper-class parents would welcome such education for their children, if not for the restive and roving poor. Deschooling would offer the better-motivated a tutorial system for which their parents would otherwise pay heavily. Free education may thus be like other publicly-provided equal opportunities—museums, libraries, cultural centers—that are unequally used. It will resemble these resources in that it will primarily benefit and subsidize the affluent who have developed the capacity to use them.

Although Illich maintains that deschooling is an essential component of any radical program in the seventies, those concerned with inequality in our society would want to rate any proposal on the basis of how it benefits the disadvantaged, whether or not this criterion is a mark of radicalism. Ironically, the trend toward more radical social criticism, of which Illich's work is a prominent example, has not necessarily signaled a shift toward greater concern for the poor. In the early sixties, emphasis was upon social reform, upon lessening disadvantage, which was defined largely in terms of quantitative deficit in income and education. As we have become concerned about the quality of our advantages, however, we have tended to become less aware of the quantity of others' disadvantages. Even though intended to favor the poor, deschooling would primarily improve the quality of upper-class education and might actually diminish the educational levels of the disadvantaged.

EDUCATIONAL AND SOCIAL CHANGE

The tendency to rely on cultural revolution is characteristic of some radical strategists who have perhaps become discouraged by the current decline of liberal and radical political activity. The "greening of America" is a revolution in attitudes or "consciousness" that may include political revolution in its final act, if at all.(36) Illich clearly wants to change the economic system and feels we can do so by deschooling, by ceasing to teach people to want meaningless goods and services. Until we learn this, he maintains, political change will only result in more of the same.

We have already indicated that deschooling would not necessarily break the consumer spiral and would not necessarily encourage equal educational or social outcomes. Yet, it seems important to show that radical changes in education, deschooling as well as any other, must be preceded by major political changes. The education which leads to the organization of disadvantaged constituencies must take place out of school and without deschooling.

POLITICAL RESISTANCE TO EDUCATIONAL CHANGE

Illich's belief that we can begin with educational change is partly dictated by expedience. He stresses that the school is under attack from many quarters and is thus a vulnerable institution. "The risks of revolt against school are unforseeable, but they are not as horrible as those of a revolution starting in any other major institution."(37) "School," he also writes, "is not yet organized for self-protection as effectively as a nation-state, or even a large corporation."(38)

Such a position overlooks the fact that a serious attack on any major institution would evoke political and corporate defenses. If, as Illich recognizes, the state has established the school in all societies, what reason is there to believe that its disestablishment would not be resisted by government?

While relatively vulnerable schoolmen may have control over educational decisions at the level of local government, the patterns of influence is very different at the State level, which has the say regarding important school policy. The State is not only the chief source of public school revenues but the seat of Constitutional authority to establish schools. Although States have delegated much authority to local school districts, the actual and potential control of education by State governments is vast. It includes not merely the power of the purse but influence over important areas like curriculum, certification, and consolidation of districts.(39) In this respect, it is important to point out that despite the successful mobilization of neighborhood groups in New York City, the State legislature flatly turned down community control proposals in the Spring of 1969.

There is little doubt that a basic decision such as one to abolish the public schools would arouse many potentially powerful actors at the State level. Many individuals do not exercise their influence over small educational issues because they are not dissatisfied with basic policies. In the case of disestablishment or any other major change, however, it seems unlikely that the economically powerful would be so unaware of the important social functions that school plays that they would merely welcome the opportunity to reduce their taxes. If they do not recognize how crucial a role school plays in shaping consumers and increasing GNP—they and the writer would probably accord more persuasiveness to commercial advertising—they are undoubtedly conscious of their dependence on it for purposes of social control. If schools fall short of inculcating patriotism and respect for the social order, the privileged would urge not disestablishment, but greater emphasis on moral education. The economically powerful also depend upon schools to teach prospective workers how to behave on the job, to screen employees through the credentialing system, and to teach skills which they may regard as basic education for the labor market. There is also the enormous constiuency of parents in all social classes who are certain to recognize that disestablishment of the school robs them of a daily babysitter for twelve years. In fact, there is reason to expect that if the State did not compel children to attend school, their parents would.(40)

THE SEQUENCE OF CHANGE

If we cannot and probably should not disestablish the schools, we do need to learn different values. Recent trends among consumers of goods and services suggest that people are becoming educated to new conceptions of their needs outside of school and that this new consciousness will lead to political mobilization. As a result of educational and organizational efforts by Ralph Nader and his associates, we are beginning to define our consumer needs differently and to free ourselves from persuasive advertising. In the area of welfare, minority leaders and "teachers of the poor" like George Wiley, Richard Cloward, and Frances Piven have helped public assistance clients to know their needs and rights, to demand cash benefits and to resist coercive case services.

We are learning that we are all disadvantaged as consumers of goods, that we have been under a mistaken illusion that if we organized ourselves as wage earners we would earn more money and hence more buying power and freedom. However, we will also stress consumer unions, when we recognize, as conservationists and consumer leaders are trying to teach us, that we do not have genuine choices of goods and services but merely the option of purchasing one of several identical goods that have been differentiated by what their advertisers choose to stress.

In the case of services we are not even under the illusion that present institutions offer us choices, but we are coming to recognize that there are alternatives to "take it or leave it" in welfare. The welfare rights groups have begun to demonstrate and to teach others that they are citizens and that there are political means, admittedly less direct than those of the market, of making institutions respond to their needs. They are also demonstrating that action, assertion, and independence are not inimical to institutionalized welfare. Our definition of self-help, unlike that of Illich, assumes institutional welfare—services and cash benefits—but associates it with these active efforts to make institutions responsive to individual and community needs. We need not risk *laissez-faire* or a fatuous regression to self-help and charitable private initiative in order to mitigate institutional control and over-dependency.(41) *Active welfare* is a humane alternative to coercive treatment and to societal neglect.

CONCLUSION

Illich will not succeed in disestablishing the school, but he is teaching us to deschool our values. With great force, he has shown us how schooled our minds and lives have become—how we substitute lessons for making music and instruction for playing the game. We are unable to recognize our worth unless we can judge it by the standards of the school. To a certain extent, we all resemble the young woman who felt lost because she could not rate herself as wife and mother—unlike school "where at least you got a grade." We have trouble teaching ourselves or learning informally with others. Assignments rather than the desire to learn or know are the only educational stimuli to which many are able to respond. Small wonder that some of us, schooled to an advanced age, find ourselves newly degraded each time we return to school. In order to justify their service, teachers must make students feel uneducated, no matter what their prior knowledge or experience is. Illich has helped us to recognize why we long to grow up, to obtain the last credential—the right never to regress to school again.

Deschooling proponents are not only offering a brilliant critique of contemporary schooling but are stimulating us to make education freer. Without basic political change, we can not disestablish the school; nor do we think it desirable to do so. In the meantime, we should attempt to find out what some of the educational effects of partial deschooling would be. We can develop experimental programs to test the results of freer education on selected groups of people, disadvantaged and privileged, educationally stimulated and apparently unmotivated. We can examine the effects of deschooling on the secondary level; less ambitiously, we can reduce the amount of required subjects, or offer some courses in the community rather than in the school. If the voucher system is tried experimentally, we can evaluate the effects of changing the locus of educational control from school and state to family and informal community. A voucher system would afford parents the right to choose among various alternatives for schooling their children: minority moral education, integration, technical education, apprenticeship, self-motivated learning, etc. It will, however, need to demonstrate its ability to encourage democratic pluralism rather than to license discriminatory division. With these experiments and others that freer learners, parents, and educators will be stimulated to devise, we can cease to justify educational freedom solely by declaring it an "inalienable right."

NOTES:

(1) Illich's proposals are set forth in Deschooling Society, New York: Harper and Row, 1970. Further and more recent elaboration of his ideas are found in "After Deschooling, What?" Social Policy, vol II, September/October, 1971, pp. 5-13.

(2) The Office of Economic Opportunity has given consideration to an experiment in which public education monies would be given directly to parents in the form of vouchers, or certificates, which the parents then could take to the school of their choice, public or private, as payment for their children's education, See, U.S. Department of Health, Education, and Welfare, Office of Economic Opportunity, A Proposed Experiment in Education Vouchers, OEO Pamphlet 3400-1, January 1971.

(3) Deschooling Society, p. 16.

(4) Illich is probably right in asserting the inevitability of directed schooling. In a study of free vs. directed schools, Nicolaus Mills concludes that freedom in

nondirected schools was "covert" rather than "overt." Freedom "was not leeway for the students to do as they pleased. Rather it was freedom to choose from a number of options: to discover what courses interested them, to learn at an individual rather than at a group pace." "Free Versus Directed Schools: Benefits to the Disadvantaged," IRCD Bulletin, September 1971, vol VII, No. 4, p. 9.

Paul Goodman holds the view that free schools, in the best cases, are "administrative gimmicks to get around compulsory education laws." ("What Rights Should Children Have?" The New York Review of Books, September 23, 1971, vol XVI, p. 21).

(5) Deschooling Society, p 75.

(6) Paul Goodman writes that the conclusions in Leila Berg's essay, "Moving Towards Self-Government," (Children's Rights: toward the Liberation of the Child, New York, Praeger, 1971, pp. 9-50) "argree with those of Holt, Dennison, Huberman, and myself. All of us have come to hanker after deschooling society altogether, except perhaps for socially deprived or psychologically disturbed children." (op. cit., p. 21).

As early as 1962, Goodman wrote: "Very many of the youth, both poor and middle class, might be better off if the system simply did not exist at all." (Compulsory Mis-Education and the Community of Scholars, New York: Vintage Books, 1962, p. 31.)

(7) Anthony F.D. Wallace, "Schools in Revolutionary and Conservative Societies," Social and Cultural Foundations of Guidance, edited by Esther M. Lloyd-Jones and Norah Rosenau, New York: Holt, Rinehart, and Winston, 1968, p. 197.

(8) Emile Durkheim, "Education: Its Nature and Role," Education and Society, translated and with an introduction by Sherwood D. Fox, Clencoe, Illinois: Free Press, 1956, p. 71.

(9) Ibid., p. 79.

(10) See Deschooling Society, p. 31.

(11) Urie Bronfenbrenner, Two Worlds of Childhood: U.S. and U.S.S.R., New York: Russell Sage Foundation, 1970, p. 100.

(12) Compulsory Mis-Education, p. 31.

(13) Durkheim, op. cit., pp. 79-80.

(14) A number of observors have pointed out that it is not so much that we fail to intone humanitarian ideals but that such teachings are hypocritical because our actions bely these stated values. Kenneth Kenniston, for example, has referred to the gap between social creeds and deeds. (Young Radicals: Notes on Committed Youth, New York: Harcourt, Brace & World, Harvest Book, 1968.)

(15) Deschooling Society, p. 31.

(16) Ibid., p. 28.

(17) Thomas Jefferson, "A Bill for the More General Diffusion of Knowledge," The Complete Jefferson, Containing His Major Writings, Published and Unpublished, except for His Letters, assembled and arranged by Saul K.

Padover, New York: Duell, Sloan & Pearce, 1943, p. 1048.

(18) Durkheim, op. cit., p. 81.

(19) Wallace, op. cit., p. 195.

(20) See, for example, Stokeley Carmichael and Charles V. Hamilton, Black Power: The Politics of Liberation in America, New York: Vintage Books, 1967, p. 54.

(21) "Black Symbol," New York Times, December 5, 1971, Section 4, p. 3.

(22) Using partial regression techniques to control for social origin and formal educational qualifications, Beverly Duncan and Otis Dudley Duncan found that Negroes fall significantly behind all other minorities and the majority (white native sons of native fathers) in occupational achievement or socio-economic status. The authors conclude: "The evidence of discrimination against the American Negro in the competition for jobs is diffucult to discount." ("Minorities and Process of Stratification," American Sociological Review, June 1968, vol 33, pp. 356-64.

(23) Nicolaus Mills, op. cit.

(24) Ibid., p. 7.

(25) Deschooling Society, p. 63.

(26) See, for example, Robert Theobald, editor, The Guaranteed Income: Next Step in Economic Evolution? New York: Doubleday, 1966.

(27) John Kenneth Galbraith, The Affluent Society, Boston: Houghton Mifflin, 1958, esp. "The Dependence Effect," pp. 152-60.

(28) Alfred J. Kahn, "Investments in People: A Social Work Persepctive," Urban Studies Center, Rutgers University, 1963, p. 6. See also, Theory and Practice of Social Planning, New York: Russell Sage Foundation, 1969, esp., pp. 178ff.

(29) Martin Rein and S.M. Miller, "Poverty, Policy, and Purpose: The Dilemmas of Choice," Social Policy: Issues of Choice and Change (essays by Martin Rein), New York: Random House, 1970, p. 225.

(30) Yet, education conforms to Eveline M. Burns' widely accepted definition of social welfare: ". . . any income, benefit, or service to individuals or families which is provided by the organized institutional methods in response to stimuli other than those operating in the economic market or arising out of the mutual obligations of the family or the relationships of individuals to individuals." "The Financing of Social Welfare," New Directions in Social Work, Cora Kasius, editor, New York: Harper, 1954, p. 132.

(31) See for example, Ivar Berg, Education and Jobs: The Great Training Robbery, New York: Praeger, 1970.

(32) However, no amount of moral persuasion will inculcate a commitment to community service when workers, especially if they are poor and black, are, in fact, excluded from full community membership.

(33) Deschooling Society, p. 68.

(34) Jerome Bruner, "Education as Knowledge Transmission," Social Foundations of Education: A Book of Readings, Cole Brembeck and Marvin Grandstaff, editors, New York: John Wiley, 1969, p. 16.

(35) Deschooling Society, p. 6.

(36) Charles Reich maintains that a revolution is taking place in people's "consciousness" or values. "It [the revolution] will originate with the individual and with culture and it will change the political structure as its final act." The Greening of America, New York: Random House, 1970, p. 4, and passim.

(37) Deschooling Society, p. 49.

(38) Ibid.

(39) Michael W. Kirst, "Introduction to Part II: Politics of Education at the State Level," The Politics of Education: at the Local, State, and Federal Levels, Kirst, editor, Berkeley, Cal.: McCutcheon, 1970, p. 215.

(40) Discussing the political and legislative prospects for deschooling may seem to lose sight of the rhetorical framework of deschooling proposals, particularly those of Illich. For the emphasis on rights connotes constitutional strategies and court action. Illich considers schooling ultimately the illegal right of one person to oblige another to attend a meeting. (Deschooling Society, p. 94). It may be that deschooling proponents can look to the courts to rule compulsory schooling illegal, just as integrationists found the Federal judiciary more responsive than the legislatures on any governmental level. However, deschooling, and certainly deschooled education may require positive legislation in addition to court rulings. Furthermore, even if the legislatures could be bypassed, implementation of any court decision depends upon politics—values, beliefs, and interests of the communities affected. (For a discussion of deschooling strategies, see Everett Reimer, School Is Dead: Alternatives in Education, Garden City, N.Y.: Doubleday, 1971, esp. "Stragegy for a Peaceful Revolution," pp. 173-84.)

(41) William Irwin Thompson observes that as minotiries of the right and left and dissident intellectuals attempt to escape state socialism they may be attracted to "Dr. Illich's anarchistic capitalism." "We Become What We Hate," New York Times, July 25, 1971, Section 4 p. 11.

II.
DEVELOPMENTAL
STATUS
AND
ABILITY

MALNUTRITION, LEARNING AND INTELLIGENCE

Herbert G. Birch

Research on the relation of nutritional factors to intelligence and learning has burgeoned over the past decade. Its resurgence after a period of nearly thirty years of quiescence which followed Patterson's (1930) review of studies conducted in the first three decades of the century reflects a number of social and historical currents. Newly emerging nations as well as aspiring underprivileged segments of the population in more developed parts of the world have increasingly come to be concerned by the association of social, cultural and economic disadvantage with depressed levels of intellect and elevated rates of school failure. Attention has variously been directed at different components of the combined syndromes of disadvantage and poverty in an effort to define the causes for such an association. Sociologists, psychologists and educators have advanced reasons for intellectual backwardness and school failure relevent to their particular concerns. They have pointed to particular patterns of child care, cultural atmosphere, styles of play, depressed motivation, particular value systems, and deficient educational settings and instruction as factors which contribute to lowered intellectual level and poor academic performance in disadvantaged children. The importance of such variables cannot be disputed and studies and findings relevant to them expand our understanding of some of the ways in which poor achievement levels are induced. However, it would be most unfortunate if by recognizing the importance of these situational, psychological and experimental components of the syndrome of disadvantage we were to conclude that they represented the whole of the picture or even its most decisive components. Any analysis of the content of poverty and disadvantage rapidly brings to our notice the fact that these negative features of the behavioral and educational environment take place within the pervasive context of low income, poor housing, poor health and, in general, defective circumstances for the development of the individual as a biologic organism who interacts with the social, cultural and educational circumstances.

Such considerations inevitably cause us to expand the range of our concern to include a fuller range of factors contributing to lowered intellect and school failure. In this larger perspective the health of the child and, in particular, his nutritional opportunities must assume a position of importance. It has long been recognized that the nutrition of the individual is perhaps the most ubiquitous factor affecting growth, health and development. Inadequate nutrition results in stunting, reduced resistance to infectious disease, apathy and general behavioral unresponsiveness. In a fundamental sense it occupies a central position in the multitude of factors affecting the child's development and functional capacity. It is therefore entirely understandable that in a period dedicated to the improvement of man and his capacities that renewed attention has come to be directed to the relation of nutrition to intelligence and learning ability.

As is almost always the case in new areas of inquiry, clarity of thought and concept has not kept pace with zeal. Confusion has resulted from extravagant claims as to the unique contribution of malnutrition to brain impairment and intellectual deficit. Further confusion has been contributed by those who have with equal zeal sought to minimize the importance of nutritional factors and to argue for the primacy of social, genetic, cultural, or familial variables in the production of deficit. Little that is useful emerges from such sterile controversy. It is a truism that malnutrition occurs most frequently in those segments of the population who are economically, socially and culturally disadvantaged. When lowered intellect is demonstrated in malnourished children coming from such groups, it is not difficult to ignore a consideration of the possible contribution of nutritional and health factors by pointing to the possibility that the children affected are dull because they are the offspring of dull parents; or that the general impoverishment of their environments has resulted in experiential deprivations sufficient to account for reduced intellectual function. Such an argument implies that the children are malnourished because their parents are dull and that their functional backwardness stems from the same cause as their malnutrition. On logical grounds one could of course argue the very opposite from the same bodies of data. However, to do so would not be to consider the issue seriously, but to engage in a debater's trick. The serious task is to disentangle, from the complex mesh of negative influences which characterize the world of disadvantaged children, the particular and interactive contributions which different factors make to the development of depressed functional outcomes. A responsible analysis of the problem, therefore, seeks to define the particular role which may be played by nutritional factors in the development of malfunction, and the interaction of this influence with other circumstances affecting the child.

Before considering the ways in which available research permit us to achieve this objective, it is of importance to clarify the term malnutrition. Characteristically, we in the United States tend to react to the word in terms of a crisis model. When we think of malnutrition our imaginations conjure up images of the Apocalypse. We have visions of famines in India, of victims of typhoons, and of young Biafrans starved by war. These images reflect only a highly visible tip of an iceberg. Intermittent and marginal incomes as well as a technology which is inadequate to support a population result less often in the symptoms characteristic of starvation than in subclinical malnutrition or what Brock (1961) has called "dietary subnutrition . . . defined as any impairment of functional efficiency of body systems which can be corrected by better feeding." Such subnutrition when present in populations is reflected in stunting, disproportions in growth, and a variety of anatomic, physiologic and behavioral abnormalities (Birch and Gussow, 1970). Our principal concern in this country is with these chronic or intermittent aspects of nutritional inadequacy.

In less highly developed regions of the world, and indeed in the United States as well, chronic subnutrition is not infrequently accompanied by dramatic manifestations of acute, severe, and if untreated, lethal malnutrition particularly in infants and young children. These illnesses variously reflected in the syndromes of marasmus, kwashiorkor, and marasmic-kwashiorkor are conditions deriving from acute exacerbations of chronic subnutrition which in different degrees reflect caloric deficiency, inadequacy of protein in the diet, or a combination of both states of affairs. Studies of children who recover from such disorders provide significant information on the effects of profound nutritional inadequacy on behavioral development.

In addition to the already mentioned conditions, malnutrition has classically been manifested as a consequence of the inadequate ingestion of certain essential food substances. The diseases of vitamin lack, such as scurvy, rickets, pellagra, and beri-beri, as well as the iron deficiency anemias are representative of this class of disorders.

None of the foregoing should be confused with the term hunger, which has often indiscriminately been used as a synonym for malnutrition. Hunger is a subjective state and should not be used as the equivalent of malnutrition, which is an objective condition of physical and physiologic suboptimum. Clearly, malnourished children may be hungry, but equally, hungry children may be well-nourished.

With these introductory considerations in mind we can now approach a series of questions. We shall be concerned with two issues: First, what is the state of sound knowledge of the relation of malnutrition in its various forms to intellect and learning and what is the significance of the evidence for psychology and education. And second, what are the implications of the evidence for improved functioning.

THE EVIDENCE

A number of model systems have been used to explore the relationship of malnutrition to behavior. At the human level these have consisted of a) comparative studies of well- and poorly-grown segments of children. In populations at risk of malnutrition in infancy; b) of retrospective follow-up studies of the antecedent nutritional experiences of well-functioning and poorly-functioning children in such populations; c) of intervention studies in which children in the poor risk populaton were selectively supplemented or unsupplemented during infancy and a comparative evaluation made of functioning in the supplemented and unsupplemented groups; d) follow-up studies of clinical cases hospitalized for severe malnutrition in early childhood; and e) intergenerational studies seeking to relate the degree to which conditions for risk of malnutrition in the present generation of children derived from the malnutrition or subnutrition experienced by their mothers when these latter were themselves children. Studies of human populations have been supplemented by a variety of animal models. These animal studies have been a) direct comparative follow-up investigations of the effects of nutritional difficulties in early life on subsequent behavioral competence and b) the study of the cumulative effects of malnutrition when successive generations of animals have been exposed to conditions of nutritional stress. The available evidence will be considered in relation to these investigative models.

In two of our reports (Cravioto, DeLicardie and Birch, 1966; Birch, 1970) we have reviewed many of the earlier studies which have sought to explore the association between malnutrition and the development of intellect and learning. Perhaps the most complete study of the relation of growth achievement to neurointegrative competence in children living in environments in which severe malnutrition and chronic subnutrition are endemic is our study of Guatemalan rural Indian children. The children lived in a village having a significant prevalence level of both severe acute malnutrition and prolonged subnutrition during infancy and the preschool years. At school age, relatively well-nourished children were identified as the better grown, and children with the highest antecedent risk of exposure to malnutrition identified as those with the lowest growth achievements for age. On the basis of this reasoning, two groups of children were selected from all village children in the age range 6 to 11 years. These groups encompassed the tallest and shortest quartiles of height distributions at each age for the total population of the village children. In order to avoid problems associated with the use of intelligence tests as measures of functioning in pre-industrial communities, levels of development in the tall and short groups were compared by means of evaluating intersensory integrative competence by a method developed by Birch and Lefford (1963). In this method of evaluation children are required to judge whether geometric forms presented in different sensory modalities are the same or different. Competence in making such judgments follows a clearly defined developmental course in normal children in the age range studied.

At all ages taller children exhibited higher levels of neurointegrative competence than did the shorter group. Overall, the shorter children lagged by two years behind their taller agemates in the competence which they exhibited in processing information across sensory systems.

In order to control for the possibility that height differences were reflecting differences in antecedent nutritional status rather than familial differences in stature, the child's height was correlated with that of the parents. The resulting correlation was extremely low and insignificant. This stands in marked contrast to the finding in the same ethnic group living in more adequate nutritional circumstances. Under these latter conditions the height of children correlates significantly with that of their parents.

Secondly, it was possible that the shorter children were, in the community at risk as well as in communities not at risk of malnutrition, merely exhibiting generalized developmental lag both for stature and for neurointegrative maturation. However, no differences in neurointegrative competence attached to differences in stature in the children not exposed to endemic malnutrition.

And finally, it was possible that the shorter children came from home environments significantly lower in socioeconomic status, housing and parental education, and that both the malnutrition and the reduced neurointegrative competence stemmed independently from these environmental deficits. When differences in these factors were controlled they did not erase the differences in intersensory integrative competence between children of different growth achievements for age in the community at nutritional risk.

Over the past several years replications of this study have been conducted in Mexico by Cravioto and DeLicardie (1968), and in India by Champakam et al. (1968). In addition, Cravioto, Espinoza and Birch (1967) have examined another aspect of neurointegrative competence and auditory-visual integration, in Mexican children of school age. Once again in children in communities at risk of malnutrition differences in growth achievement at shcool age were reflected in differences in auditory-visual integration favoring the taller children. These latter findings are of particular importance because of the demonstrated association between such competence and the ability to acquire primary reading skill (Birch and Belmont, 1964, 1965; Kahn and Birch, 1968).

A major consideration in interpreting the findings of all these studies is the fact that antecedent malnutrition is being inferred from differences in height rather than by direct observation of dietary intakes during the growing years. However, a multitude of data from earlier studies beginning with those of Boas (1910) on growth differences in successive generations of children of Jewish immigrants, of Greulich (1958) on the height of Japanese immigrants, of Boyd-Orr (1936) on secular trends in the height of British children, of Mitchell (1962, 1964) on the relation of nutrition to stature, of Boutourline-Young (1962) on Italian children, as well as the recent study of heights of 12-year-old Puerto Rican boys in New York City by Abramowicz (1969) all support the validity of such an inference.

It should be noted too that findings similar to those obtained in the Guatemalan and Mexican studies have been reported by Pek Hien Liang et al. (1967) from Indonesia, and Stoch and Smythe (1963, 1968) from South Africa. In the Indonesian study 107 children between 5 and 12 years of age all deriving from lower socioeconomic groups were studied. Forty-six of these children had been classified as malnourished during a previous investigation into nutritional status in the area carried out some years earlier. All children were tested on the WISC and Goodenough tests with scores showing a clear advantage for the better-grown and currently better-nourished children. Moreover, the data indicated that the shortest children were markedly overrepresented in the group that had been found to be malnourished in the earlier survey, with the largest deficits in IQ found to be associated with the poorest prior nutritional status.

Stoch and Smythe have carried out a semi-longitudinal study of two groups of South African Negro children, one judged in early childhood to be grossly underweight due to malnutrition, and the other considered adequately nourished. At school age, the malnourished children as a group had a mean IQ which was 22.6 points lower than that of the comparison group. Moreover, these relative differences were sustained through adolescence. Unfortunately, the interpretation of the findings in this study is made difficult because the better-nourished children came from better families and had a variety of nursery and school experiences unshared by the poorly grown children.

Comparative studies of differential cognitive achievement in better and less well-nourished groups in communities at high levels of subnutrition have been supplemented by a relatively large number of follow-up evaluations of children who had been hospitalized for serious nutritional illness (marasmus or kwashiorkor) in infancy. As will be recalled from our earlier remarks, marasmus is a disorder produced by an insufficient intake of proteins and calories and tends to be most common in the first year of life. Kwashiorkor—a syndrome produced by inadequate protein intake accompanied by a relatively adequate caloric level, or in its marasmic form associated with reduced calories as well, is more common in the post-weanling between 9 months and 2 years of age.

As early as 1960 Waterlow, Cravioto and Stephen (1960) reported that children who suffered from such severe nutritional illnesses exhibited delays in language acquisition. In Yugoslavia, Cabak and Najdanvic (1965) compared the IQ levels of children hospitalized for malnutrition at less than 12 months of age with that of healthy children of the same social stratum and reported a reduced IQ in the previously hospitalized group. Of perhaps greater interest was their report of a significant correlation between the severity of the child's illness on admission as estimated in his deficit of expected weight for age with depression of IQ in the school years. Indian workers (Champakam, et al. (1968) studied many variables in a group of 19 children who between 18 and 36 months of age had been hospitalized and treated for kwashiorkor. When compared at school age with a well-matched control group significantly depressed IQ was found in the children previously severely malnourished.

In order to control more fully for differences in the child's genetic antecedents microenvironment, which may still exist even when more general controls for social, class and general circumstances are used in the selection of a comparison group, we in two studies (Birch, Cravioto et al. in press, 1971) and Hertzig, Birch, Tizard and Richardson, in preparation, 1971) have compared children previosuly malnourished in infancy with their siblings as well as with children of similar social background. In the first of these studies intelligence at school age was compared in 37 previously malnourished Mexican children and their siblings. The malnourished children had all been hospitalized for kwashiorkor between the ages of 6 and 30 months. The siblings had never experienced a bout of severe malnutrition requiring hospitalization. Sibling controls were all within 3 years of age of the index cases. Full scale WISC IQ of the index cases was 13 points lower than that of the sibling controls. Verbal and Performance differences were of similar magnitude and in the same direction. All differences were significant at less than the 0.01 percent level of confidence. These findings are in agreement with those of the Yugoslav and Indian workers and the use of sibling controls removes a potential contaminant for interpretation.

In the second study, Hertzig, et al. (in preparation, 1971) a large sample of 74 Jamaican children, all males, who had been hospitalized for severe malnutrition before they were two years of age were compared with their brothers nearest in age, and with their classmates whose birthdate was closest to their own. All children were between 6 and 11 years of age at follow-up. On examination, neurologic status, intersensory competence, intellectual level, and a variety of language and perceptual and motor abilities were evaluated. Intellectual level was significantly lower in the index cases than in either the siblings or the classmate comparison groups. As was to be expected, the order of competence placed the classmate comparison group at the highest level, the index cases at the lowest, and the sibs at an intermediate level. The depressed level of the siblings in relation to classmates suggests one disadvantage in sibling studies. Clearly, the presence of a child hospitalized for severe malnutrition identifies a family in which all children are at a high level of risk for significant undernutrition on a chronic basis, the index child merely representing an instance of acute exacerbation of this chronic marginal state. Therefore, the index cases and sibs are similar in that they share a common chronic exposure to subnutrition and differ only in that the index cases have experienced a superimposed episode of acute nutritional illness as well. Thus, the use of sibling controls, in fact, does not compare malnourished with non-malnourished children. Rather, it determines whether siblings who differ in their degree of exposure to nutritional risk differ in intellectual outcomes and supports the view that graded degrees of malnutrition result in graded levels of intellectual sequelae.

Other follow-up studies of acutely malnourished children such as those of Cravioto and Robles (1965) in Mexico, Pollitt and Granoff (1967) in Peru, Botha-Antoun, Babayan and Harfouche (1968) in Lebanon, and Chase and Martin (1970) in Denver, have all been shorter-term follow-ups of younger children. Cravioto and Robles (1965) studied the developmental course of returning competence in children hospitalized for malnutrition during the period of their treatment and recovery while in hospital. Their findings indicated that behavioral recovery was less complete in the youngest children (hospitalized before 6 months of age) than in older children. They posed the possibility that this earliest period of infancy was the one most critical for insult to developing brain and thus to eventual intellectual outcome. However, the study of Jamaican children (in preparation—1971) does not have findings which supported this possibility. In that study approximately equal numbers of children having experienced an acute episode of malnutrition in each of the four semesters of the first two years of life were examined. Equivalent depression of IQ was found to characterize each of the groups when these were separated by age at hospitalization.

In the Lebanese (1968), Peruvian (1967) and Venezuelan (1963) short-term follow-up studies depression in intellectual level tended to be found in the index cases. In the American study (1970) and in a Chilean study (Monckeberg, 1968) the findings have shown depression in intellectual function in the preschool years in children hospitalized for malnutrition during the first year of life. The American investigators working in Colorado found that 20 children who had been hospitalized for malnutrition before the age of one year had a mean development quotient on the Yale Revised Developmental Examination which was 17 points lower than that achieved by a matched control group of children who had not been malnourished. All of these studies suggest strongly that malnutrition of severe degree in early life tends to depress the intellectual functioning at later ages.

In summary, the follow-up studies of children who have been exposed to hospitalization for a bout of severe acute malnutrition in infancy indicate an association of significant degree between such exposure and reduced intellectual level at school age. The studies, involving careful social class controls and sibship comparisons, suggest that it is not general environmental deprivation but rather factors which are uniquely related to the occurrence of severe malnutrition that are contributing to a depression in intellectual outcome. However, there is some indication that different degrees of recovery may be associated with different post-illness conditions. Thus, urban and rural differences in intellectual outcomes are reported in the sibship comparison studies of Jamaican children earlier referred to (in preparation, 1971).

The fact of such an association provides strongly suggestive but by no means definitive evidence that malnutrition directly affects intellectual competence. As Cravioto, DeLicardie and Birch (1966) have pointed out, at least three possibilities must be considered in the effort to define a causal linkage. The simplest hypothesis would be that malnutrition directly affects intellect by producing central nervous system damage. However, it may also contribute to intellectual inadequacies as a consequence of the child's loss in learning time when ill, of the influences of hospitalization, and of prolonged reduced responsiveness after recovery. Moreover, it is possible that particular exposures to malnutrition at particular ages may in fact interfere with development at critical points in the child's growth course and so provide either abnormalities in the sequential emergence of competence or a redirection of developmental course in undesired directions. Although certain of these possibilities (such as hospitalization and post-illness opportunities for recovery) can be explored in children, others for moral and ethical reasons cannot. Thus, it is impermissible to establish appropriate experimental models either for interfering with development at critical periods, or for inducing brain damage. The approach to these problems requires either detailed analyses of naturally occurring clinical models or the development of appropriate animal investigations.

Animal models of the effects of malnutrition on brain and behavior have been used to study the issue with a degree of control that is quite impossible in human investigation. In a series of pioneering investigations (Widdowson, 1966, Dobbing, 1964, Davison and Dobbing, 1966) have demonstrated that both severe and modest degrees of nutritional deprivation experienced by the animal at a time when its nervous system was developing most rapidly results in reduced brain size and in deficient myelination. These deficits are not made up in later life even when the animal has been placed on an excellent diet subsequent to the period of nutritional deprivation.

More recent studies (Zamenhof, 1968) as well as by Winick (1968) have demonstrated that the deprivation is also accompanied by a reduction in brain cell number. This latter effect has been demonstrated too in human brain in infants who have died of severe early malnutrition (Winick and Rosso, 1969).

Enzymatic maturation and development in brain is also affected, and Chase et al., (1967, 1970) have demonstrated defective enzyme organization in the brains of malnourished organisms.

In all of these studies the evidence indicates that the effects of malnutrition vary in accordance with the time in the organism's life at which it is experienced. In some organisms the effects are most severe if the nutritional insult occurs in the prenatal period, in others during early postnatal life.

Some confusion in the interpretation of evidence has occurred because of the use of different species, since in different organisms the so-called critical periods occur at different points in the developmental course. Thus, in pigs' brain, growth and differentiation is occurring most rapidly in the period prior to birth, whereas in the rat the most rapid growth occurs when the animal is a nursling. In human beings the period for rapid growth is relatively extended and extends from mid-gestation through the first six through nine months of postnatal life. In man, the brain is adding weight at the rate of one to two mg/minute at birth and goes from 25 percent of its adult weight at birth to 70 percent of its adult weight at one year of age. After this age, growth continues more slowly until final size is achieved. Differentiation as well as growth occurs rapidly during the critical periods, with myelination and cellular differentiation tending to parallel changes in size.

Since brain growth in different species is occurring at different points in the life course it is apparent that deprivations that are experienced at the same chronologic ages and life stages will have different effects in different species. Thus deprivation during early postnatal life will have little or no effect upon brain size and structure in an organism whose brain growth has largely been completed during gestation. Conversely, intrauterine malnutrition is likely to have only trivial effects on the growth of the brain in species in which the most rapid period for brain development has occurred postnatally. When these factors are taken into account, the data leave no doubt that the coincidence of malnutrition with rapid brain growth results in decreased brain size and in altered brain composition.

It would be unfortunate if brain growth in terms of cell number were to be viewed as the only definers of rapid change and thus of critical periodicity. In the human infant, neuronal cell number is most probably fully defined before the end of intrauterine life. Thereafter, through the first 9 months of postnatal life, cell replication is that of glial cells, a process which terminates by the end of the first year. However, myelination continues for many years thereafter as does the proliferation of dendrite branchings and other features of brain organization. It is most probable, therefore, that in man the period of vulnerability extends well beyond the first year of life and into the preschool period. Such a position is supported by the findings of Champakam et al. (1968). These workers, it will be recalled, found significant effects on intellect in their group of malnourished children who had experienced severe malnutrition when they were between 18 and 36 months of age.

Other workers who have used animal models have sought to study the effects of malnutrition on behavioral outcomes, rather than on brain structure and biochemical organization. The typical design of these studies are investigations in which animals have been raised upon diets which were inadequate with respect to certain food substances, or, in which general caloric intake has been reduced without an alteration in the quality of the nutriments. Such animals have then been compared with normally nourished members of the species with respect to maze learning, avoidance conditioning, and open field behavior. Unfortunately, most of the investigations have suffered from one or another defects in design which make it difficult to interpret the findings. Though in general the nutritionally deprived organisms have tended to be disadvantaged as learners, it is not at all clear whether this is the result of their food lacks at critical points in development or whether the differences observed stem from the different handling, caging, and litter experiences to which the well and poorly-nourished animals were exposed. Moreover, in a considerable number of studies food or avoidance motivation have been used as the reinforcers of learning. There is abundant evidence (Mandler, 1958; Elliott and King, 1960; Barnes, et al. 1968; Levitsky and Barnes, 1969) that nutritional deficiency in early life affects later feeding behavior. Consequently, it is difficult to know whether the early deprivation has affected food motivation or whether it has affected learning capacity. The use of learning situations which do not involve food, but are based upon aversive reinforcement, do not remove difficulties for interpretation, since early malnutrition modifies sensitivity to such negative stimuli (Levitsky and Barnes, 1970).

One must therefore recognize that at present, although the animal evidence suggests that early malnutrition may influence later learning and behavior, it is by no means conclusive. Moreover, when learning has been deleteriously affected the mechanisms through which this effect has been mediated is by no means clear. What is required is a systematic series of experiments in which behavioral effects are more clearly defined, and in which the use of proper experimental designs accompanied by appropriate controls permits the nature of the mechanisms affected to be better delineated.

Thus far both in our consideration of the human and animal evidence we have been considering the direct effects of nutritional deprivation on the developing organism. Clearly, this is too limited a consideration of the problem. It has long been known (Boyd-Orr, 1936) that nutritional influences may be intergenerational and that the growth and functional capacity of an individual may be affected by the growth experiences and nutrition of his mother. In particular the nutritional history of the mother and its effect upon her growth may significantly affect her competence as a reproducer. In its turn, this reproductive inadequacy may affect the intrauterine and birth experiences of the offspring.

Bernard (1952) working in Scotland has clearly demonstrated the association between a woman's nutritional history and her pelvic type. He compared one group of stunted women in Aberdeen with well-grown women and found that 34 percent of the shorter women had abnormal pelvic shapes conducive to disordered pregnancy and delivery as compared with 7 percent of the well-grown women with whom they were compared. Greulich, Thoms and Twaddle (1939) still earlier had reported that the rounded or long oval pelvis which appears to be functionally superior for childbearing was made more common in well-off, well-grown women than in economically less-privileged clinic patients. They further noted, as had Bernard, that these pelvic abnormalities were strongly associated with shortness.

Sir Dugald Baird and his colleagues in the City of Aberdeen, Scotland, have from 1947 onward conducted a continuing series of studies on the total population of births in this city of 200,000 in an effort to define the patterns of biologic and social interactions which contribute to a woman's growth attainments and to her functional competence in childbearing. More than 20 years ago Baird (1947) noted that short stature, which was five times as common among lower-class women than in upper-class women, was associated with reproductive complications. He pointed out (1949), on the basis of analyzing the reproductive performances of more than 13,000 first deliveries that fetal mortality rates were more than twice as high in women who were under five feet one inch in height than in women whose height was five feet four inches or more. Baird and Illsley (1953) demonstrated that premature births were almost twice as common in the shorter than in the taller group. Thomson (1959a) extended these observations by analyzing the relation between maternal physique and reproductive complications for the more than 26,000 births which had occurred in Aberdeen over a 10-year-period and found that short stature in the mother was strongly associated with high rates of prematurity, delivery complications and perinatal deaths at each parity and age level. He concluded that "it is evident that whatever the nature of the delivery the fetus of the short woman has less vitality and is less likely to be well-grown and to survive than that of a tall woman."

It was of course possible that these findings simply reflected differences in social class composition of short and tall women and were based upon differences in "genetic pool" rather than in stunting as such. To test this hypothesis the Aberdeen workers (Baird, 1964) re-examined their data for perinatal mortality and prematurity rates by height within each of the social classes for all Aberdeen births occurring in the 10-year-period from 1948 to 1957. They found that shortness in every social class was associated with an elevated rate of both prematurity and perinatal deaths. Concerned that the findings in Aberdeen might not be representative they also analyzed the data from the all-Britain perinatal mortality survey of 1958 and confirmed their findings. Moreover, Thomson and Billewicz (1963) in Hong Kong and Baird (1964) have substantiated the Aberdeen findings for Chinese and West African women respectively. Other findings on a similar vein from this series have been summarized by Illsley (1967).

The available data therefore suggest that women who are not well-grown have characteristics which negatively affect them as childbearers. In particular, short stature is associated with pregnancy and delivery complications and with prematurity. Since growth achievement within ethnic groups is a function of health history and in particular nutrition, it is clear that the mother's antecedent nutritional history when she herself was a child can and does significantly influence the intrauterine growth, development and vitality of her child. Moreover, an inadequate nutritional background in the mother places this child at elevated risk for damage at delivery.

It is instructive to consider the consequences for mental development and learning failure that attach to the most frequently occurring consequence of poor maternal growth—prematurity. Concern with the consequences of this condition is hardly new, with Shakespeare indicting it as one element in the peculiarities of Richard III, and Little (1862) linking it with the disorder we now call cerebral palsy. Benton (1940) reviewed the literature up to that time and found that though most students of the problem maintained that prematurity was a risk to later mental development, others could find no negative consequence attaching to it. At that time no resolution of disagreement could be made because most of the early studies had been carried out with serious deficiencies in design and in techniques of behavioral evaluation. Groups who were of low birth weights or early in gestational age were often compared with full-term infants who differed from them in social circumstances as well as in perinatal status. Estimates of intellectual level were made with poor instruments and often dependent on "clinical impression" or testimony from parents or teachers.

Serious and detailed consideration of the consequences of low birth for later behavioral consequences can properly be said to have been begun by Pasamanick, Knobloch, and their colleagues shortly after World War II. These workers were guided by a concept which they referred to as a "continuum of reproductive casualty." They argued that there was a set of pregnancy and delivery complications which resulted in death by damaging the brain and hypothesized that in infants who survived exposure to these risks "there must remain a fraction so injured who do not die, but depending on the degree and location of trauma, go on to develop a series of disorders extending from cerebral palsy, epilepsy and mental deficiency, through all types of behavioral and learning disabilities, resulting from lesser degrees of damage sufficient to disorganize behavioral development and lower thresholds to stress" (Pasamanick and Knobloch, 1960). In a series of retrospective studies prematurity and low birth weight were identified by them as being among the conditions most frequently associated with defective behavioral outcomes. They therefore, in association with Rider and Harper (1956) undertook a prospective study of a balanced sample of 500 premature infants born in Baltimore in 1952 and compared them with full-term control infants born in the same hospitals who were matched with the prematures for race, maternal age, parity, season of birth and socioeconomic status. Four hundred pairs of cases and controls were still available for years of age, and examinations of the sample indicated that at this age the prematures and full-term children continued to be matched for maternal and social attributes (Wiener, et al. 1965). Findings at various ages persistently showed the prematures to be less intellectually competent than the controls. At ages three to five the prematures were relatively retarded intellectually and physically and had a higher frequency of definable neurologic abnormalities (Knobloch, et al. 1959; Harper, et al. 1959). At ages six through seven, IQ scores to the Stanford-Binet test were obtained and at ages eight to nine, WISC IQs are available. At both age levels, lower birth weights were associated with lower IQs (Wiener, et al. 1965, 1968).

Although certain British studies such as that of McDonald (1964) and of Douglas (1956, 1960) appear to be somewhat discrepant with these findings reanalysis of their findings (Birch and Gussow, 1970) indicates a similar trend. More dramatic differences between prematures and full-term infants have been reported by Drillien (1964, 1965) but interpretation of her data is made difficult by complexities in the selection of the sample studied.

A number of analyses suggest that the effects of prematurity are not the same in different social classes, with children from the lowest social classes appearing to have subsequent IQ and school performances more significantly depressed by low birth weight than is the case for infants in superior social circumstances. This has been reported for Aberdeen births (Illsley, 1966; Richardson, 1968), and for Hawaiian children in the Kauai pregnancy study of Werner (1967). There appears to be an interaction between birthweight and family social condition in affecting intellectual outcome, but the precise mechanisms involved in this interaction are as yet unclear.

If the risk of deficient intellectual outcome in prematurity is greatest for those children who are otherwise socially disadvantaged as well, our concern in the United States with the phenomenon of prematurity must be increased. In 1962 more than 19 percent of non-white babies born in New York City had a gestational age of less than 36 weeks as compared with 9.5 percent of white babies, and in Baltimore this comparison was 25.3 percent in non-white infants as compared with 10.3 percent in whites (National Center for Health Statistics,

1964). In 1967 (National Center for Health Statistics, 1967) nationally, 13.6 percent of non-white infants weighed less than 2,500 grams as compared with 7.1 percent of white infants. Other relevant and more detailed analyses of the social distribution of low birth weight and gestational age on both national and regional bases, together with an analysis of their secular trends provides additional support for these relationships (Birch and Gussow, 1970). Thus, prematurity is most frequent in the very groups in which its depressing effects on intelligence are greatest.

On the basis of the evidence so far set forth it may be argued with considerable justification that one can reasonably construct a chain of consequences starting from the malnutrition of the mother when she was a child, to her stunting, to her reduced efficiency as a reproducer, to interuterine and perinatal risk to the child, and to his subsequent reduction in functional adaptive capacity. Animal models have been constructed to test the hypotheses implied in this chain of associations, most particularly by Chow and his colleagues (1968; Hsueh, 1967), as well as by (Cowley and Griesel, 1963, 1966). The findings from these studies indicate that second and later generation animals who derive from mothers who were nutritionally disadvantaged when young, are themselves less well-grown and behaviorally less competent than animals of the same strain deriving from normal mothers. Moreover, the condition of the offspring is worsened if nutritional insult in its own life is superimposed on early maternal malnutrition.

A variety of factors would lead us to focus upon the last month of intrauterine life as one of the "critical" periods for the growth and development of the central nervous system. Both brain and body growth together with differentiation are occuring at a particular rapid rate at this time. It has been argued, therefore, that whereas marginal maternal nutritional resources may be sufficient, adequately to sustain life and growth, during the earlier periods of pregnancy the needs of the rapidly growing infant in the last trimester of intrauterine existence may outstrip maternal supplies. The work of Gruenwald at al. (1963) among others, would suggest that maternal conditions during this period of the infant's development are probably the ones which contribute most influentially to low birth weight and prematurity. Such concerns have led to inquiries into the relation of the mother's nutritional status in pregnancy to the growth and development of her child. In considering this question it is well to recognize that as yet we have no definitive answer to the question of the degree to which maternal nutrition during pregnancy contributes to pregnancy outcome. Clearly, whether or not nutritional lacks experienced by the mother during pregnancy will affect fetal growth is dependent upon the size and physical resources of the mother herself. Well-grown women are most likely to have tissue reserves which can be diverted to meet the nutritional needs of the fetus even when pregnancy is accompanied by significant degrees of contemporary undernutrition. Conversely, poorly grown women with minimal tissue reserves could not under the same set of circumstances be expected to be able to provide adequately for the growing infant.

Children coming from familes in which the risks for exposure to malnutrition are high are unlikely to experience nutritional inadequacies only in early life. It is far more likely that earlier nutritional inadequacies are projected into the preschool and school years. Such a view receives support from numerous surveys as well as from recent testimony presented before the Senate Committee on Nutrition and Human Needs (1968-1970). Our knowledge of the degree to which children and families at risk continue to be exposed to nutritional inadequacies derive from a series of indirect and direct methods of inquiry. At an indirect level it can be argued that family diet in the main is very much dependent upon family income level. The report *Dietary Levels of Household in the United States* (1968) published by the United States Department of Agriculture underscores this proposition. According to a household survey conducted in the spring of 1965, only 9 percent of families with incomes of $10,000 and over a year were judged as having "poor diets." However, the proportion of poor diets increased regularly with each reduction in income level, with 18 percent of the families earning under $3,000 a year reporting poor diets, that is, diets containing less than two-thirds of the recommended allowance of one or more essential nutrients. Conversely, the proportion of "good" diets went from 63 percent in the $10,000 and over category down to 37 percent in the under $3,000 group. Of course, income alone is not an adequate indicator of socioeconomic status since in families with equal incomes more education appears to produce a better diet (Jeans, Smith & Stearns, 1952; Murphy & Wertz, 1954; Hendel, Burke & Lund, 1965). But, at the least such figures suggest that we must be seriously concerned with just how badly nourished are our poor in what we often claim is the "best-fed nation in the world."

Reports of the survey type may be supplemented by inquiries in which mothers are asked what they feed their families and how much of what kinds of food they purchase. Similarly actual food intakes may be estimated by requests for the retrospective recall of all foods eaten over the last 24 hours. Owen and Dram (1969) studying nutritional status in Mississippi preschool children found not only that the poorer children were on the average smaller than more affluent children but that their diets were significantly low in calories, vitamin C, calcium and riboflavin. Dibble, et al. (1965) in Onodaga County, New York found that among students drawn from a junior high school which was 94 percent Negro and predominantly laboring class, 41 percent had come to school without breakfast; but in two "overwhelmingly white" junior high schools, only 7 percent in one school and 4 percent in the other had skipped breakfast. In recent studies among teenagers in Berkeley, California, Hampton et al. (1967) and Huenemann et al. (1968) have found intakes of all nutrients declining with socioeconomic status, with Negro girls and boys having worse intakes than those in other ethnic groups. Huenemann also found that among junior and senior high school students studied over a two-year period 90 percent of the Negro teenagers had irregular eating habits and many appeared to be "fending for themselves."

Christakis et al. (1968) who carried out the first dietary study of New York school children in 20 years found that in an economically depressed district that the diets of 71 percent of children examined were poor and that less than 7 percent had excellent diets. Moreover, his data demonstrated that if the child's family were on welfare the likelihood of his having a poor diet was much increased.

The situation is not markedly different in the Roxbury district of Boston. In this area Meyers et al. (1968) studied the diets and nutritional status of 4th, 5th and 6th graders, about two-thirds of whom were black. Meals were ranked as "satisfactory" or "unsatisfactory." Four satisfactory ratings for a given meal over the 4-day period produced a "satisfactory" rating for the meal. Fifty-five percent of the children failed to get such a satisfactory rating for breakfast, 60 percent of them did not have satisfactory lunches, and 42 percent had less than four satisfactory evening meals in 4 days. "Satisfactory" scores declined with age for all meals, and Negroes generally had more unsatisfactory ratings than Caucasians. The schools had no school-lunch programs, and lunches were the poorest meals, with 33 percent of the children having two or more unsatisfactory lunch ratings in 4 days. During the 4-day period 64 percent of the children had less than two glasses of milk a day, 132 children had no citrus fruit and only 1 child had a green or yellow vegetable; 37 percent of the Negro and 46 percent of the Caucasian children had "unsatisfactory" intakes of the protein foods in the meat, fish, poultry, eggs, and legume group. "It is evident," the authors concluded, "that many of these children were eating poultry."

These data are illustrative and not atypical of the national picture. The preliminary reports deriving from the National Nutrition Survey serve to confirm these findings on a national scale. The evidence though scattered and of uneven quality indicates strongly that economically and ethnically disadvantaged children eat poorly in both the preschool and school age periods.

Direct clinical studies occurring largely within the Head Start Program serve to support the impression produced by the data of nutritional surveys. One way of examining possible sub-nutrition on an economical clinical basis is to define the prevalence of iron deficiency anemia. Hutcheson, (1968), reporting on a very large sample of poor white and Negro children in rural Tennessee, found the highest level of anemia among children around 1 year old. Of the whole group of 15,681 children up to 6 years of age, 20.9 percent had hematocrits of 31 percent, indicating a marginal status. Among the year-old children, however, the incidence of low hematocrits was even higher; 27.4 percent of the whites and 40 percent of the nonwhites had hematocrits of 31 percent or less, and 10 percent of the whites and one-quarter of the nonwhites had hematocrits of 30 percent or under, indicating a more serious degree of anemia. Low hemoglobin level was also most common among the younger children in a group whom Gutelius (1969) examined at a child health center in Washington, D.C. Iron-deficiency anemia, determined by hemoglobin level and corroborative red cell pathology, was found among 28.9 percent of the whole group of 460 Negro preschoolers, but children in the age group 12-17 months had a rate of anemia of 65 percent. Gutelius points out, moreover, that these were probably not the highest-risk children, since the poorest and most disorganized families did not come from well-baby care at all, and of those who did attend, the test group included only children who had not previously had a hemoglobin determination—that is, they were children judged to be "normal" by the clinic staff. Thus "many of the highest risk children had already been tested and were not included in this series."

Even in the summer 1966 Head Start Program, in which the incidence of other disorders was surprisingly low, (North, 1967) studies indicated that 20-40 percent of the children were suffering from anemia, a proportion consistent with the findings of various studies summarized by Filer (1969) as well as with the level of anemia found in a random sample of predominantly lower-class children coming into the pediatric emergency room on the Los Angeles County Hospital (Wingert, 1968). Anemia rates as high as 80 percent among preschool children have been reported from Alabama (Mermann, 1966) and Mississippi (Child Development Group of Mississippi, 1967).

It is clear from such evidence that some degree of malnutrition is relatively widespread among poor children; but we have already seen that the effects of inadequate nutrition on growth and mental development depend to a very large extent on the severity, the timing, and the duration of the nutritional deprivation. Inadequate as are our data on the true prevalence of malnutrition among children in this country, we are even less informed about its onset or about its severity and quality. The absence of such knowledge must not be taken to reflect the absence of the problem but rather the lack of attention which has been devoted to it.

IMPLICATIONS, PROGRAMS AND PROBLEMS

The evidence we have surveyed indicates strongly that nutritional factors at a number of different levels contribute significantly to depressed intellectual level and learning failure. These effects may be produced directly as the consequences of irreparable alterations of the nervous system or indirectly as a result of ways in which the learning experiences of the developing organism may be significantly interfered with at critical points in the developmental course.

If one were to argue that a primary requirement for normal intellectual development and for formal learning is the ability to process sensory information and to integrate such information across sense systems the evidence indicates that both severe acute malnutrition in infancy as well as chronic sub-nutrition from birth into the school years results in defective information processing. Thus, by inhibiting the development of a primary process essential for certain aspects of cognitive growth malnutrition may interfere with the orderly development of experience and contribute to a suboptimal level of intellectual functioning.

Moreover, an adequate state of nutrition is essential for good attention and for appropriate and sensitive responsiveness to the environment. One of the most obvious clinical manifestations of serious malnutrition in infancy is a dramatic combination of apathy and irritability. The infant is grossly unresponsive to his surroundings and obviously unable to profit from the objective opportunities for experience present in his surroundings. This unresponsiveness characterizes his relation to people, as well as to objects. Behavioral regression is profound; and the organization of his functions are markedly infantalized. As Dean (1960) has put it one of the first signs of recovery from the illness is an improvement in mood and in responsiveness to people—"the child who smiles is on the road to recovery."

In children who are subnourished one also notes a reduction in responsiveness and attentiveness. In addition the subnourished child is easily fatigued and unable to sustain either prolonged physical or mental effort. Improvement in nutritional status is accompanied by improvements in these behaviors as well as in physical state.

It should not be forgotten that nutritional inadequacy may influence the child's learning opportunities by yet another route, namely, illness. As we have demonstrated elsewhere (Birch & Cravioto, 1968; Birch & Gussow, 1970) nutritional inadequacy increases the risk of infection, interferes with immune mechanisms, and results in illness which is both more generalized and more severe. The combination of sub-nutrition and illness reduces time available for instruction and so by interfering with the opportunities for gaining experience disrupts the orderly acquisition of knowledge and the course of intellectual growth.

We have also pointed to intergenerational effects of nutrition upon mental development. The association between the mother's growth achievements and the risk to her infant is very strong. Poor nutrition and poor health in the mother when she was a girl result in a woman at maturity who has a significantly elevated level of reproductive risk. Her pregnancy is more frequently disturbed and her child more often of low birth weight. Such a child is at increased risk of neurointegrative abnormaility and of deficient IQ and school achievement.

Despite the strength of the argument that we have developed, it would be tragic if one were now to seek to replace all the other variables—social, cultural, educational, and psychological—which exert an influence on intellectual growth with nutrition. Malnutrition never occurs alone, it occurs in conjunction with low income, poor housing, familial disorganization, a climate of apathy, ignorance and despair. The simple act of improving the nutritional status of children and their families will not and cannot of itself fully solve the problem of intellectual deficit and school failure. No single improvement in conditions will have this result. What must be recognized rather is that within our overall effort to improve the condition of disadvantaged children, nutritional considerations must occupy a prominent place, and together with improvements in all other facets of life including relevant and directed education, contribute to the improved intellectual growth and school achievement of disadvantaged children.

REFERENCES:

Abramowicz, M. Heights of 12-year-old Puerto Rican boys in New York City: Origins of differences. Pediatrics, 43, 3:427-429, 1969.

Baird, D. Social class and foetal mortality. Lancet, 253:531-535, 1947.

Baird, D. Social factors in obstetrics. Lancet, 1:1079-1083, 1949.

Baird, D., and Illsley, R. Environment and childbearing, Proc. Roy. Soc. Med., 46:53-59, 1953.

Baird, D. The epidemiology of prematurity. J. Pediat., 65:909-924, 1964.

Barnes, R.H.; Neely, C.S.; Kwong, E.; Iabadan, B.A.; and Frankova, S. Postnatal nutritional deprivations as determinants of adult behavior toward food, its consumption and utilization. J. Nutr., 96:467-476, 1968.

Barrera-Moncada, G. Estudios sobre alteraciones del crecimiento y del desarrollo psicologico del sindrome pluricarencial (kwashiorkor). Caracas, Editora Grafos, 1963.

Benton, A.L. Mental development of prematurely born children: A critical review of the literature. Amer. J. Orthopsychiat., 10:719-746, 1940.

Bernard, R.M. The shape and size of the female pelvis. Transactions of the Edinburgh Obstetrical Soc. Edin. Med. J., 59,2:1-16, 1952 (Transactions bound at end).

Bevan, W. and Freeman, O. I. some effects of an amino acid deficiency upon the performance of albino rats in a simple maze. J. Genet. Psychol., 80:75-82, 1952.

Birch, H. G. and Lefford, A. Intersensory Development in Children. Monographs. The Society for Research in Child Development, 28:1-48, 1963.

Birch, H.G. and Belmont, L. Auditory-visual integration in normal and retarded readers. Amer. J. Orthopsychiatry, 44, 5:852-861, 1964.

Birch, H.G. and Belmont, L. Auditory-visual integration, intelligence and reading ability in school children. Percept. Mot. Skills, 20:295-305, 1965.

Birch, H.G. and Cravioto, J. Infection, nutrition and environment in mental development. In H.F. Eichenwald (Ed.) The Prevention of Mental Retardation Through the Control of Infectious Disease. Public Health Service Publication 1962. Washington, D.C.: U.S. Gov. Ptg. Office, 1968.

Birch, H.G. and Gussow, J.D. Disadvantaged Children: Health, Nutrition and School Failure. New York: Harcourt Brace and World, and Grune and Stratton, Inc., 1970, pp. 322.

Birch, H.G. Malnutrition and Early Development. In: Day Care: Resources for Decisions. Ed. Grotberg, E., Office of Economic Opportunity: Office of Planning, Research and Evaluation: Experimental Research Division, 340-372, 1971.

Birch, H.G.; Pineiro, C.; Alcalde, E.; Toca, T.; and Cravioto, J. Kwashiorkor in early childhood and intelligence at school age. Pediat. Res., 5:579-585, 1971.

Boas, F. Changes in the Bodily Form of Descendants of Immigrants.

Immigration Commission Document No. 208 Washington, D.C., U.S. Gov. Ptg. Office, 1910.

Botha-Antoun, E.; Babayan, S.; and Harfouche, J.K. Intellectual development relating to nutritional status. J. Trop. Pediat., 14:112-115, 1968.

Boutourline-Young, H. Epidemiology of dental caries: Results from a cross-cultural study in adolescents of Italian descent. New Eng. J. Med., 267:843-849, 1962.

Brock, J. Recent Advances in Human Nutrition. London: J. & A. Churchill, 1961.

Cabak, V. and Najdanvic, R. Effect of undernutrition in early life on physical and mental development. Arch. Dis. Child., 40:532-534, 1965.

Champakam, S.; Srikantia, S.G.; and Gopalan, C. Kwashiorkor and mental development. Amer. J. Clin. Nutr., 21:844-852, 1968.

Chase, H.P.; Dorsey, J.; and McKhann, G.M. The effect of malnutrition on the synthesis of a myelin lipid. Pediatrics, 40:551-559, 1967.

Chase, H.P. and Martin, H.P. Undernutrition and child development. New Eng. J. Med., 282:933-976, 1970.

Child Development Group of Mississippi: Surveys of Family Meal Patterns. Nutrition Services Division. May 17, 1967, and July 11, 1967, Cited in Hunger, USA.

Chow, B.F.; Blackwell, B,; Hou, T.Y.; Anilane, J.K.; Sherwin, R.W.; and Chir, B. Maternal nutrition and metabolism of the offspring: Sutides in rats and man. A.J.P.H. 58:668-677, 1968.

Christakis, G.; Miridjanian, A.; Nath, L.; Khurana, H.S.; Cowell, C.; Archer, M.; Frank, O.; Ziffer, H.; Baker, H.; and James, C. A nutritional epidemiologic investigation of 642 New York City children. Amer. J. Clin. Nutr., 21:107-126, 1968.

Cowley, J.J. and Griesel, R.D. The development of second generation low protein rats. J. Genet. Psychol., 103:233-242, 1963.

Cowley, J.J. and Griesel, R.D. The effect on growth and behavior of rehabilitating first and second generation low protein rats. Anim. Behav., 14:506-517, 1966.

Cravioto, J. and Robles, B. Evolution of adaptive and motor behavior during rehabilitation from kwashiorkor. Amer. J. Orthpsychiat., 35:449-464, 1965.

Cravioto, J.; DeLicardie, E.R.; and Birch, H.G. Nutrition, growth and neurointegrative development and experimental and ecologic study. Pediatrics, 38:2, Part II, Suppl. 319-372, 1966.

Cravioto, J.; Espinoza, C.G.; and Birch, H.G. Early malnutrition and auditory-visual integration in school age children. J. Spec. Ed., 2:75-82, 1967.

Cravioto, J. and DeLicardie, E.R. Intersensory Development in school age children. In N.S. Scrimshaw and J.E. Gordon (Eds.) Malnutrition, Learning, and Behavior. Massachusetts: MIT Press, 1968, pp. 252-269.

Davison, A.N. and Dobbing, J. Myelination as a vulnerable period in brain development. Brit. Med. Bull., 22, 1:40-44, 1966.

Dean, R.F.A. The effects of malnutrition on the growth of young children. Mod. Probl. Pediat., 5:111-122, 1960.

Dibble, M.; Brin, M.; McMullen, E.; Peel, A.; and Chen, N. Some preliminary biochemical findings in junior high school children in Syracuse and Onondaga County. New York: Amer. J. Clin. Nutr., 17:218-239, 1965.

Dobbing, J. The influence of early nutrition on the development and myelination of the brain. Proc. Roy. Soc., 159:503-509, 1964.

Douglas, J.W.B. Mental ability and school achievement of premature children at 8 years of age. Brit. Med. J., 1:1210-1214, 1956.

Douglas, J.W.B. "Premature" children at primary schools. Brit. Med. J., 1,2:1008-1013, 1960.

Drillien, C.M. The growth and development of the prematurely born infant. Baltimore: Williams & Wilkins, 1964, p. 376.

Drillien, C.M. Prematures in school. Pediatrics Digest, September, 1965, pp. 75-77.

Elliott, O. and King, J.A. Effect of early food deprivation upon later consummatory behavior in puppies. Psychol. Rep., 6:391-400, 1960.

Filer, L.J., Jr. The United States today: Is it free of public health nutrition problems? — anemia. A.J.P.H. 59:327-338, 1969.

Greulich, W.W.; Thoms, H.; and Twaddle, R.C. A study of pelvis type and its relationship to body build in white women. J.A.M.A. 112:485-492, 1939.

Greulich, W.W. Growth of children of the same race under different environmental conditions. Science, 127:515-516, 1958.

Gruenwald, P.; Dawkins, M.; and Hepner, R. Chronic deprivation of the fetus. Sinai Hosp. J., 11:51-80, 1963.

Gutelius, M.F. The problem of iron-deficiency anemia in preschool Negro children. A.J.P.H. 59:290-295, 1969.

Hampton, M.C.; Huenemann, R.L.; Shapiro, L.R.; and Mitchell, B.W. Caloric and nutrient intakes of teenagers, J. Amer. Diet. Ass., 50:385-396, 1967.

Harper, P.A.; Fischer, L.K.; and Rider, R.V. Neurological and intellectual status of prematures at three to five years of age. J. Pediat., 55:679-690, 1959.

Hendel, G.M.; Burke, M.C.; and Lund, L.A. Socio-economic factors influence children's diets. J. Home Econ., 57:205-208, 1965.

Hertzig, M.E.; Birch, H.G.; Tizard, J.; and Richardson, S.A. Growth sequelae of severe infantile malnutrition. 1971 (in preparation).

Hertzig, M.E.; Tizard, J.; Birch, H.G.; and Richardson, S.A. Mental sequelae of severe infantile malnutrition. 1971 (in preparation).

Hsueh, A.M.; Agustin, C.E.; and Chow, B.F. Growth of young rats after differential manipulation of maternal diet. J. Nutr., 91:195-200, 1967.

Huenemann, R.L.; Shapiro, L.R.; Hampton, M.C.; and Mitchell, B.W. Food and eating practices of teenagers. J. Amer. Diet. Ass., 53:17-24, 1968.

Hutcheson, H.A. and Wright, N.H. Georgia's family planning program. Amer. J. Nurs., 68:332-335, 1968.

Illsley, R. Early prediction of perinatal risk. Proc. Roy. Soc. Med., 59:181-184,

1966.

Illsley, R. The sociological study of reproduction and its outcome. In S.A. Richardson and A.F. Guttmacher (Eds.) Childbearing: Its Social and Psychological Aspects. Baltimore: Williams & Wilkins, 1967, pp. 75-135.

Jeans, P.C.; Smith, M.B.; and Stearns, G. Dietary habits of pregnant women of low income in a rural state. J. Amer. Diet. Ass., 28:27-34, 1952.

Kahn, D. and Birch, H.G. Development of auditory-visual integration and reading achievement. Percept. Motor Skills, 27:459-468, 1968.

Knobloch, H.; Rider, R.; Harper, P.; and Pasamanick, B. Neuropsychiatric sequelae of prematurity: a longitudinal study, J.A.M.A. 161:581-585. 1956.

Knobloch, J.; Pasamanick, B.; Harper, P.A.; and Rider, R. The effect of prematurity on health and growth. A.J.P.H. 49:1164-1173. 1959.

Levitsky, D.A. and Barnes, R.H. Effects of early protein calorie malnutrition on animal behavior. Paper read at meeting of American Association for Advancement of Science, Dec. 1969.

Levitsky, D.A. and Barnes, R.H. Effect of early malnutrition on reaction of adult rats to aversive stimuli. Nature, 225:468-469, 1970.

Liang, P.H.; Hie, T.T.; Jan, O.H.; and Giok, L.T. Evaluation of mental development in relation to early malnutrition. Amer. J. Clin. Nutr., 20:1290-1294, 1967.

Little, W.J. On the influence of abnormal parturition, difficult labour, premature birth, and asphyxia neonatorum on the mental and physical conditions of the child, especially in relation to deformities. Trans. Obstet. Soc. London, 3:293-344, 1862.

Mandler, J.M. Effects of early food deprivation on adult behavior in the rat. J. Comp. Physiol. Psychol., 51:513-517, 1958.

McDonald, A.D. Intelligence in children of very low birth weight. Brit. J. Prev. Soc. Med., 18:59-74, 1964.

Mermann, A.C. Lowndes County, Alabama, TICEP Health Survey, Summer 1966; and Statement Prepared for the U.S. Senate Sub-Committee on Employment. Manpower and Poverty. Washington, D.C.

Mitchell, H.S. Nutrition in relation to stature. J. Amer. Diet. Ass., 40:521-524, 1962.

Mitchell, H.S. Stature changes in Japanese youth and nutritional implications. Fed. Proc., 28:877, No. 27, 1964.

Monckeberg, F. Effect of early marasmic malnutrition on subsequent physical and psychological development. Chap. In Scrimshaw, N.S., Gordon, J.E. (Eds.) Malnutrition, Learning and Behavior. Cambridge: MIT Press, 1968, pp. 269-277.

Murphy, G.H. and Wertz, A.W. Diets of pregnant women: influence of socioeconomic factors. J. Amer. Diet. Ass., 30:34-48, 1954.

Myers, M.L.; O'Brien, S.C.; Mabel, J.A.; and Stare, F.J. A nutrition study of school children in a depressed urban district. 1. Dietary findings. J. Amer. Diet. Ass., 53:226-233, 1968.

National Center for Health Statistics. Vital Statistics of the United States, 1965. Washington, D.C., U.S. Gov. Ptg. Office, 1967.

National Center for Health Statistics: Natality Statistics Analysis, United States, 1962. Vital and Health Statistics, PHS Pub. No. 1000, Series 21, No. 1. Public Health Service. Washington, D.C.; U.S. Gov. Ptg. Office, 1964.

North, A.F. Project Head Start and the pediatrician. Clin. Pediat., 6:191-194, 1967.

Orr, J.B. Food, Health and Income. London: Macmillan, 1936.

Owen, G.M. and Kram, K.M. Nutritional status of preschool children in Mississippi: food sources of nutrients in the diets. J. Amer. Diet. Ass., 54:490-494, 1969.

Pasamanick, B. and Knobloch, H. Brain damage and reproductive casualty. Amer. J. Orthopsychiat., 30:298-305, 1960.

Patterson, D.G. Physique and Intellect. New York: Appleton-Century-Crofts, 1930.

Richardson, S.A. The influence of social environmental and nutritional factors on mental ability. In N.S. Scrimshaw and J.E. Gordon (Eds.) Malnutrition, Learning and Behavior. Cambridge: MIT Press, 346-360, 1968.

Pollitt, E. and Granoff, D. Mental and motor development of Peruvian children treated for severe malnutrition. Revista Interamericana de Psicologia, 1:(2), 93-102, 1967.

Senate Committee on Nutrition and Human Needs. cf. parts 1 et seq. 1968-70.

Stoch, M.B. and Smythe, P.M. Does undernutrition during infancy inhibit brain growth and subsequent intellectual development? Arch. Dis. Child., 38:546-552, 1963.

Stoch, M.B. and Smythe, P.M. Undernutrition during infancy, and subsequent brain growth and intellectual development. In N.S. Scrimshaw and J.E. Gordon (Eds.) Malnutrition. Cambridge: MIT Press, 1968, pp. 278-289.

Thomson, A.M. Diet in pregnancy. III. Diet in relation to the course and outcome of pregnancy. Brit. J. Nutr., 13:4:509-525, 1959a.

Thomson, A.M. and Billewicz, W.Z. Nutritional status, physique and reproductive efficiency. Proc. Nutr. Soc., 22:55-60, 1963.

Waterlow, J.C.; Cravioto, J.; and Stephen, J.K.L. Protein malnutrition in man. Advances in protein chemistry. New York: Academic Press, Inc. 15:131-238, 1960.

Werner, E. Cumulative effect of perinatal complications and deprived environment on physical, intellectual and social development of preschool children. Pediatrics, 39:490-505, 1967.

Widdowson, E.M. Nutritional deprivation in psychobiological development: Studies in animals. In: Deprivation in Psychobiological Development. Pan American Health Organization Scientific Pub. No. 134. Washington, D.C., WHO, 1966, pp. 27-38.

Wiener, G.; Rider, R.V.; Oppel, W.C.; Fischer, L.K.; and Harper, P.A. Correlates of low birth weight: Psychological status at 6-7 years of age. Pediatrics, 35:434-444, 1965.

Wiener, G.; Rider, R.V.; Oppel, W.C.; and Harper, P.A. Correlates of low birth weight: Psychological status at eight to ten years of age. Pediat. Res.,

2:110-118, 1968.

Wingert, W.A. The demographical and ecological characteristics of a large urban pediatric outpatient population and implications for improving community pediatric care. A.J.P.H. 58:859-876, 1968.

Winick, M. Nutrition and cell growth. Nutr. Rev., 26:195-197, 1968.

Winick, M. and Rosso, P. The effect of severe early malnutrition in cellular growth of human brain. Pediat. Res., 3:181-184, 1969.

Zamenhof, S.; Van Marthens, E.; and Margolis, F.L. DNA (cell number) and protein in neonatal brain: Alteration by maternal dietary protein restriction. Science, 160:322-323, 1968.

LONGITUDINAL DEVELOPMENT
OF VERY YOUNG CHILDREN
IN A COMPREHENSIVE DAY CARE PROGRAM:
THE FIRST TWO YEARS

Albert B. Robinson

Nancy M. Robinson

In September 1966 the Frank Porter Graham Child Development Center of the University of North Carolina at Chapel Hill opened a day care center offering comprehensive services to a small number of infants and very young children. This center was established as a pilot facility for a much larger multidisciplinary research project. The latter was to be devoted in part to a longitudinal intervention study of a sizable cohort of children ranging in age from birth to 13 years given education and comprehensive day care under conditions as optimal as could reasonably be devised (Robinson 1969). This study presents the assessment of the development of the 11 children admitted in 1966 and the 20 enrolled in 1967 and 1968. The data reflect the results of a complex experimental plan which combined several rather unusual characteristics:

1. Almost all Ss admitted as infants were selected before their birth, with the conditions only that the sample be roughly balanced for sex and race and that no gross anomalies be detected during the neonatal period. They entered day care when the mother returned to work, which ranged from 4 weeks to 6 months after the birth of the child.

2. The sample was broadly representative of the community's socioeconomic spectrum of Caucasian and Negro children of working mothers.

3. Comprehensive daytime care was given, including complete health care; children attended the center whether sick or well.

4. A carefully structured educational program, beginning in early infancy, constituted a strong focus of the center. Pilot curricula were developed in language, sensorimotor skills, perception and reading, scientific and numerical

concepts, music, art, and French.

5. The basic organizational pattern consisted of two cottages of up to 16 children of all ages represented in the center for basic activities such as eating, sleeping, and free play. All center children in the same family were housed together. Grouping by developmental level for instruction and play occurred for approximately 3 hours each day, children ages 2½-4½ going from their cottage to an educational unit.

6. Child-focused work with parents occurred through daily conversations with staff, frequent contacts with the pediatrician, and home visits by the public health nurse. There were also occasional newsletters, parent meetings, and parties.

SAMPLE SUBJECTS OF THE CENTER

During this pilot phase of the study, infants and 2-year-olds were admitted in order to provide for some heterogeneity. Most infants were selected through routine interviewing of all employed women receiving prenatal care in the university hospital, the only hospital in Chapel Hill. A few infants, and all older children, were admitted after applications by families not initially contacted prior to the birth of the child. Four infant siblings born to families already having a child in the center were automatically admitted. Efforts were made to keep each of the three annual waves (1966, 1967, 1968) as varied and balanced as possible in race, sex, and socioeconomic status.

During the fall of 1966 four children were admitted between the ages of 2.0 months and 5.5 months (mean age, 3.8 months) and seven others between 26 and 36 months (mean age, 28.7 months). In the fall of 1967, seven infants between 1.5 and 5.5 months old were admitted (mean age, 2.7 months), and five children who were 23-28 months of age (mean age, 25.6 months). In 1968, all eight new Ss were infants, 1.1—4.0 months (mean age, 2.1 months). Of the 31 children, 12 (7 Caucasian and 5 Negro) were admitted at age 2; 19 (8 Caucasian and 11 Negro) were admitted as young infants. One additional child, however, was a congenital athyreotic admitted before his condition was diagnosed at age 3 months. Borderline retarded, he is omitted from this report. One boy admitted at age 2 was withdrawn when his family moved 18 months later. He is included in the comparison with community controls, but not in the longitudinal analysis. By the end of the 2½-year period covered by this report, the 31 Ss ranged in age from a few weeks to 4½ years.

Twenty-four families were represented. Total incomes of the 12 Caucasian families (i.e., all adults with legal responsibility for child) ranged from $4,500 to above $40,000, the median family income for the 15 children being $10,976. Incomes of the 12 Negro families ranged from zero (unmarried student mothers) to $10,000, the median for the 16 children being $3,519. Median education for the Caucasian mothers was 14.5 years and for the Caucasian fathers, 16.5 years. Median education of the Negro mothers was 12.0 years, and of the Negro fathers, 11.0 years. One Caucasian child and four Negro children had no father in the home.

The dramatic differences between the Caucasian and Negro families in the sample are, in large part, a reflection of the disparities in this community. Its Caucasian wage earners are largely university staff and merchants, while its Negro population has traditionally performed supportive services. Community acceptance was also an issue, however. The early appeal of the center was to the poorer Negro parents, attracted by the low cost, and to the more affluent Caucasian parents, attracted by the potential benefits for their children. Eventually, however, the center's reputation began to attract blue-collar Caucasian parents and middle-class Negro parents. Included in the 1968 sample are, for example, the infant sons of a white policeman and of a Negro social worker.

CONTROL GROUPS

Two separate control groups were studied. One was followed from early infancy onward and is compared with center infants; the other was tested only once and was compared with center children who were at that time 2½-4½ years old.

From 1967, when pediatric services became available as part of the center's program, control groups of infants were selected by the same perinatal interviewing methods as center infants, an attempt being made to equate the annual waves as closely as possible on sex, race, number of siblings, education and occupation of parents, and number of rooms in the house. These groups were evaluated medically and psychologically on the same schedule as the center population, and additional health records were kept in conjunction with medical studies being carried out in the center. Complete medical supervision was given to the control children, in part to enlist the families' cooperation, but more important, to attempt to equalize medical care, the better to evaluate the effects of the enriched daily experience of the center children. Eleven control group infants were followed during the period of this report.

By 1968, the 16 oldest center Ss were 2½-4½. Four of these children had entered in 1966 as infants; 12 had entered in 1966 or 1967 at age 2. None had attended less than 1 year. As a rough comparison, a completely different group of noncenter children was matched with them individually on the basis of race, sex, parents' education and occupation, and the age at which the center child had last been given the Stanford-Binet and PPVT (see below). The controls were chosen from applicants to the center for whom there had not been space ($N = 5$), from friends of the family of the child for whom matching was sought ($N = 9$), and from another local day care center ($N = 2$). Mean CA of each group was 41 months, the mean within-pair age difference being 1.8 months. Exceedingly close matching on occupation and education of both parents was achieved, except that six control mothers were not currently employed.

The data reported here represent only the results of standardized testing over the period being considered. Tests were scheduled every 3 months to age 18 months, the Bayley mental scale, the Bayley motor scale, and the Bayley behavior profile (Bayley 1961) being completed on each occasion. Table 2 lists most of the subsequent tests administered to age 4½. In addition, several language-assessment measures were administered in June 1968 to the 14 oldest children (ages 2-7 to 4-3) and three additional tests (WPSSI, Frostig, Caldwell preschool inventory) were given at age 4.

Testing through age 18 months was conducted by the staff of the University of North Carolina Laboratory of Infant Behavior to which the infants were transported by a caretaker from the center or by the mothers of the control infants. Testing of center children 2 and over was conducted at the center by a member of its staff. The control children for the special one-time comparison with the older Ss were seen in their own homes or regular day care settings by the same examiner who tested the older center children. The Stanford-Binet and Peabody Picture Vocabulary Test (PPVT) were administered. Effort was made to establish rapport through an initial period of play and the presence, when apparently desirable, of a trusted adult. For almost all of the Negro children, whose homes had no telephones, the testing visit constituted the second to the fourth contact with the examiner, who had played with the child during each previous visit. Nevertheless, these comparison data suffer the obvious drawbacks of the greater familiarity of the examiner with the center Ss and the unknown practice effects of their previous testing.

TEST RESULTS

Test results for all children admitted as infants are shown in table 1, together with those for the control infants. A 2 X 5 analysis of variance (Dixon 1965) nested on treatments (center-control) with repeated measures on comparisons over time and using a general linear hypothesis to handle missing data values was applied to the infant test scores. Analysis of the Bayley mental scale scores yielded a between-groups F ratio of 7.99 (df 1/116, p = .01) for the treatments, an F ratio of 2.72 (df 4/116, p = .05) for the comparisons over time, and a nonsignificant interaction (F = 1.45, df 4/116). For the Bayley motor scale, the only significant F ratio (4.75, df 1/109, p = .05) occurred in the comparison of center and control groups. A t test of the mental scale scores at 18 months was significant at the .01 level, but a t test of motor scale scores at that age failed to reach significance at the .05 level. A t test of the small samples tested on the Stanford-Binet at 24 months also failed to reach significance.

In other words, scores for center and control Ss were significantly different on both tests, but a significant trend over time was found only on the mental scale, consisting of an initial rise for both groups, and a drop for the control group at the 18-month level. The suddenness of that drop probably accounts for the lack of significance in the interaction. The scores on the Bayley motor scale favored the center group but were less consistently different over time.

The test results for children admitted to the center at age 2 are described in table 2. Additional tests administered to the 1966 group at age 4-0 yielded the

TABLE 1

Test Results for Ss Admitted as Infants and Controls

Group	Bayley Mental Scale					Bayley Motor Scale					Stanford-Binet	
	6 Mo	9 Mo	12 Mo	15 Mo	18 Mo	6 Mo	9 Mo	12 Mo	15 Mo	18 Mo	24 Mo	30 Mo
Center:												
N	17	18	19	10	11	17	18	18	8	7	4	4
$\overline{X}$	108.00	115.94	112.16	116.60	115.18	110.94	109.22	99.61	107.62	107.29	116.25	117.25
SD	8.95	14.71	9.91	9.19	8.95	14.06	11.90	14.45	9.29	16.71	8.67	4.76
Control:												
N	11	11	11	10	8	11	11	11	10	8	4	...
$\overline{X}$	105.9	113.27	110.91	110.70	99.75	103.82	105.00	101.09	103.60	94.00	99.75	...
SD	10.15	12.23	9.97	8.79	11.61	13.11	11.45	14.96	10.95	7.17	11.23	...

TABLE 2

TEST SCORES OF CHILDREN ADMITTED AT AGE 2

TEST	ADMITTED 1966 (N = 6)					ADMITTED 1967 (N = 5)	
	2-6	3-0	3-6	4-0	4-6	2-6	3-0
Stanford-Binet							
$\overline{X}$	112.3	124.5	132.7	...	127.2	118.4	123.8
SD	23.5	20.2	17.5	...	13.4	23.1	13.9
PPVT							
$\overline{X}$	93.8	100.8	114.0	111.5	108.5	111.4	107.2
SD	15.5	19.7	7.2	6.9	6.9	17.9	10.8
ITPA							
$\overline{X}$	104.3	124.5	122.2	...	...	...	115.0
SD	14.0	17.0	12.8	...	...	...	15.0
Leiter							
$\overline{X}$	...	128.0	128.3	...	126.8	106.6	130.0
SD	...	19.6	16.4	...	8.7	26.1	14.9
Draw-a-Man							
$\overline{X}$	...	...	96.8	...	98.5	...	...
SD	...	...	15.3	...	9.9	...	...

following mean scores and standard deviations: Wechsler Primary and Preschool Inventory full scale IQ 124.6 (SD 12.4), verbal IQ 126.0 (8.8), performance IQ 117.7 (14.5); Frostig test of visual perception IQ 100.0 (20.9) and Caldwell preschool inventory, median percentile 90 (middle-class norms).

Scores on most primarily verbal measures were high, as shown by the Stanford-Binet (Terman & Merrill 1960), the verbal scale of the WPPSI (Wechsler 1967), the Caldwell preschool inventory (Caldwell 1967), and, as an exception, the nonverbal Arthur Adaptation of the Leiter scale (Arthur 1952). Peabody Picture Vocabulary Test (Dunn 1959) scores were consistently lower than the other measures.

On the nonverbal measures, most of the children's scores fell below their verbal scores. On the Frostig test of visual perception (Frostig, Lefever, & Whittlesey 1964), the draw-a-man test (Harris 1963), and portions of the Illinois Test of Psycholinguistic Abilities (McCarthy & Kirk 1961), this lower performance was evident. Sensorimotor items (Motor encoding, visual-motor sequential) were consistently the lowest of the mean ITPA scores, with the exception of the visual-motor association test, which is "motor" only to the extent that a pointing response is required. Similarly, on the WPPSI, the mean subscale scores for the seven children tested at age 4 ranged from a high of 16.43 on arithmetic to a low of 12.29 on geometric designs, the single exception being a mean score of 9.71 on the highly motoric mazes. The WPPSI performance IQ was approximately ½ SD below the mean verbal IQ.

The language assessment in June 1968 likewise revealed advanced verbal behavior. Of the 12 children given the Templin-Darley scale (Templin & Darley 1960), the score of each S was at or above CA level, the mean speech age exceeding the mean CA (42 months) by approximately 22 months. On the action-agent test (Gesell 1940), 10 of the 12 scored at age level or better, three Ss exceeding the CA by at least 6 months. On the Michigan Picture Language Inventory (Lerea 1958; Walski 1962) given to the seven oldest children, mean standard score of expression was +.96, while the mean comprehension standard score was +.65.

Test results for the 16 older center children and 16 matched controls are shown in figures 1 and 2. The most striking findings on both tests are the differences, on the order of two standard deviations, between the center Negro children and their controls. Mean Stanford-Binet IQs were 119.7 for these seven center children and 86.1 for their controls; both groups showed a marked clustering of scores (SDs 8.46 and 6.59, respectively). On the PPVT, center Negro children attained a mean IQ of 107.4 (SD 10.03) while that of the control Negro children was only 77.6 (SD 13.75). There was no overlap of scores

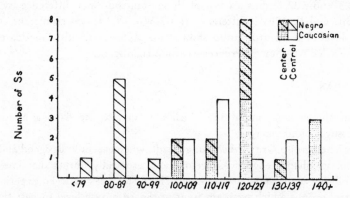

Fig. 1.—Stanford-Binet IQs of center and control children ages 2½–4½

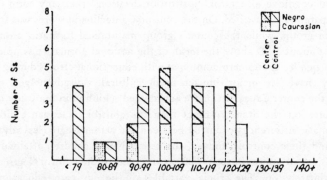

Fig. 2.—PPVT IQs of center and control children ages 2½–4½

between these groups on either test.

Differences between the nine Caucasian center children and their controls appeared on the Stanford-Binet but not on the PPVT. Mean IQs on the Stanford-Binet were 129.7 (SD 17.00) and 116.9 (SD 11.71), respectively. On the PPVT, mean IQ of the center Caucasian group was actually lower (108.1, SD 12.42) than that of the controls (110.2, SD 12.81).

According to an analysis of variance (Dixon 1965) of Stanford-Binet scores, F ratios were highly significant for their comparisons of racial groups ($F = 22.27$, df 1/28, $p <.001$) and center control groups ($F = 28.89$, df 1/28, $p <.001$), the significant interaction ($F = 5.81$, df 1/28, $p = .05$) highlighting the much greater magnitude of the difference between the Negro groups. In the analysis of scores on the PPVT, there were also significant effects of race ($F = 14.29$, df 1/28, $p = .001$) and of the center/control variable ($F = 9.90$, df 1/28, $p = .01$). The interaction term ($F = 13.14$, df 1/28, $p <.01$) demonstrated that the significant differences were limited to the Negro groups. Center Ss who were 3-6 and older attained somewhat higher scores on both tests than did center Ss 3-10 and younger (mean Stanford-Binet IQs 129.1 and 121.5, respectively; mean PPVT IQs 113.5 and 102.1), but a t test of these Stanford-Binet differences was not significant, and the PPVT difference ($t = 2.346$, df 14) was significant at only the .05 level. The control group showed no such age trends. Practice effects cannot be ruled out. Sex differences were not significant.

DISCUSSION

Within the serious limitations which characterize the data, a number of tentative suggestions emerge:

1. Enriched group care of the young infant, when carefully designed and fully staffed, may enhance cognitive development, especially during the time when verbal abilities are beginning to emerge. The differences between experimental and control groups which were apparent at the 18-month level suggest that the period before this may be a crucial one. Earlier concern about the possibility of detrimental cognitive effects of "institutionalization" (i.e., any form of group care) is apparently unjustified. On the contrary, a decline in scores was found for the control group, while the center's group maintained its status on cognitive measures at about 1 SD above the mean of the national normative sample.

2. High quality group care combined with educational efforts during ages 2-4 years may have its major impact upon culturally disadvantaged children. Although the center Caucasian (more advantaged) children in the study obtained higher scores on the Stanford-Binet than the control Caucasian children, the really dramatic differences occurred between the center Negro (less advantaged) children and their controls. Indeed, the center Negro children attained a mean Stanford-Binet of approximately 120, as opposed to the control Negro mean IQ of approximately 86. The crucial variables of the day care, educational, and health programs cannot be identified in this pilot study, but that the "package" made a difference in the lives of the children is unmistakable.

3. The major impact of the program was in verbal rather than motoric areas. The nonverbal scores of the center children were "normal" but not particularly advanced.

The lack of well-standardized instruments to assess social-emotional functioning of young children is a major handicap to a study of this nature. A series of attempts to devise a problem-behavior checklist or interview with the mothers was unsuccessful because of the inability of some poorly educated mothers, even with considerable prompting, to think in differentiated terms about their children's behavior. Overall evaluation by a team of psychoanalytically-oriented clinicians yielded interesting individual assessments which were based on limited observations of center children and did not yield useful research data. Similarly, detailed behavioral ratings by the staff, useful in many ways for longitudinal research, are not reported here because they yielded only within-group comparisons. There was unanimous agreement among all the staff, who were of diverse cultural and educational backgrounds, that as a group the children were extremely amicable, stable, and outgoing, and that none exhibited behavior deviant from the normal range of childhood behavior patterns.

A study such as the present one raises many more questions than it can answer. What are the long-range residuals of a program such as that provided by the center? In the long run, will the development of children who enter as infants differ significantly from that of children admitted at age 2, later, or not at all? What elements within the program are most effective? Can these elements be packaged and delivered more economically than through comprehensive full-day programs? What positive impact may the availability of reliable day care have on the stability of families, and on the mother's employment and personal adjustment? What are the immediate and delayed effects on the children's relationships with their parents? Major longitudinal research efforts will be required to anwer these compelling questions.

REFERENCES

Arthur, G.A. The Arthur adaptation of the Leiter international performance scale. Washington, D.C.: Psychological Service Center Press, 1952.

Bayley, N. Manual of directions for infant scales of development (temporary standardization). (Mimeographed.) Bethesda, Md.: National Institute of Neurological Diseases and Blindness, Collaborative Research Project, 1961.

Caldwell, B.M. The preschool inventory. Princeton, N.J.: Educational Testing Service, 1967.

Dixon, W.J. (Ed.) General linear hypothesis (BMDO5V). Biomedical Computer Program. Los Angeles, UCLA Health Sciences Computing Facility, 1965.

Dunn, L.M. Peabody Picture Vocabulary Test manual. Minneapolis: American Guidance Service, 1959.

Frostig, M.; Lefever, D.W.; & Whittlesey, J.R.B. A developmental test of visual perception for evaluating normal and neurologically handicapped children.

Perceptual and Motor Skills, 1964, 12, 383-394.

Gesell, A. The first five years of life. New York: Harper & Row, 1940.

Harris, D.B. Measuring the psychological maturity of children: a revision and extension of the Goodenough draw-a-man test. New York: Harcourt Brace & World, 1963.

Lerea, L. Assessing language development. Journal of Speech and Hearing Research, 1958, 1, 75-85.

McCarthy, J.J., & Kirk, S.A. Illinois test of psycholinguistic abilities. (Exp. ed.) Urbana: University of Illinois, Institute of Research on Exceptional Children, 1961.

Robinson, H.B. From infancy through school. Children, 1969, 16, 61-62.

Templin, M.C., & Darley, F.L. The Templin-Darley tests of articulation. Iowa City: University of Iowa Bureau of Education Research and Service, 1960.

Terman, L.M., & Merrill, M.A. Stanford-Binet intelligence scale. Boston: Houghton Mifflin, 1960.

Walski, W. Language development of normal children, four, five, and six years of age as measured by the Michigan Picture Language Inventory. Unpublished doctoral dissertation, University of Michigan, 1962.

Wechsler, D. A manual for the Wechsler preschool and primary scale of intelligence. New York: Psychological Corp., 1967.

CHILDREN'S SOCIOLINGUISTIC COMPETENCE AND DIALECT DIVERSITY

Susan M. Ervin-Tripp

Comparisons of social groups in the development of language and of cognitive functions mediated by or tested through language are common. These studies, to the extent that they focus on comparisons of underlying abilities, are only possible if the investigator has enough sociolinguistic knowledge to construct data-collecting situations which are comparable in a deep rather than superficial sense. These studies of children of varying social backgrounds can be contrasted with studies of sociolinguistic competence in pure form.(1) These need not be comparative at all. Their focus is the systematic relation of features of the children's language and the social milieu of speech, hearing, and talk about speech. Some of the major assumptions of this field have been developed in the works of Hymes [27, 28] and of Gumperz [20, 21], defining a field of ethnography of communication. In this chapter we shall focus on both comparative studies and developmental sociolinguistics and suggest some research problems which still face us, with particular attention to social dialects.

PROBLEMS OF BIAS

Linguistic bias. The first category of work, comparative studies, has attracted attention because American schools so often test and compare children's performances. But there has been great difficulty in finding ways of testing children's knowlege of language without using biased approaches. Most tests use communicative settings which are middle class, middle-class interviewers, middle-class kinds of tasks, middle-class language, and middle-class scoring criteria. It is very easy to find bleak examples of ignorance of work on social dialects and on social variation in the use of language, but hard to find alternative approaches for those who think they have to test.

One approach to the linguistic issue is to test development of features common to different languages. Let us suppose, for example, that we are concerned with the concept of location or of possession. Both of these structures, and at least eight others, can be identified in grammatical contrasts or classes in the earliest sentences of children in a variety of languages ranging from Samoan [31] to Luo in Kenya [5]. But if we are interested in the possessive, what approaches can we take?

1. The concept of possession is probably present well within the first eighteen months, but testing would require some nonverbal methods appropriate to the social group.

2. We might like to know how early children signal possession verbally by some distinct feature, any feature. Thus we might ask how early possession is a linguistically distinct feature.

3. We might ask how early a child comprehends specific linguistic contrasts as signaling possessive. The Torrey study [52] cited below asks this question but in a noncomparative framework.

4. We might ask how early the child signals possessive with the adult linguistic contrast of his home milieu. If his parents and siblings speak a nonstandard dialect of English, this might mean using order alone, or order and prosodic features, but not a suffix.

5. We might ask how early a child can systematically signal possession with a linguistic feature of some dialect or language not used regularly in his home but sometimes heard. For English speakers in a bilingual community it might be the Spanish possessive. For lower-class East Coast blacks it might be a possessive suffix. For Standard English speakers it might be the nonstandard variants.

An appropriate example is the work of Osser, Wang, and Zaid [43]. This was a study of rates of development in core grammatical transformations common to all dialects of English, such as relativization and passivization. The study compared middle-class white and lower-class black five-year-olds.

Many workers in child language question the likelihood of large differences in the average age of achievement of fundamental milestones (e.g., understanding verb-object, understanding relative clauses) or in ranges of variation in different social groups. There are two reasons for their doubt. One is the evidence of a considerable biological substrate for the maturation of language-learning abilities universal in humans [38], and the other is the evidence that the amount of direct reinforcement of language training seems to have little bearing, at least on grammatical development [7, 8]. Short of biological abnormalities(2) or deviant social conditions in a particular family that are pathological in the society, this theory would lead one to suspect underlying similarity of competence. Thus, those claiming differences must be particularly careful to use tests appropriate to the groups tested. There are many questions of interest in comparative studies outside of the hypothesis of difference, of course, such as universals of order and contingency for different features.

Osser, Wang, and Zaid developed some excellent methods for testing grammatical imitative skill and comprehension, aimed at specific grammatical features. But they made one serious mistake. The input was Standard English, so they used a type 4 test (like a parent's speech) for the middle-class children and a type 5 test (like the speech of the contact community) for the lower-class children and assumed they could make them comparable by some scoring rules. Differences in familiarity with the testing dialect must have thoroughly confounded developmental results.

One solution to this problem has been proposed by Joan Baratz (1). She constructed a set of idealized sentences "translated" into uneducated variants (wherever possible, in East Coast black speakers' phonology and grammar) and recorded by a middle-class white using a speech guise. Nobody speaks 100 percent nonstandard forms, so the input language was very artificial, but most of the children believed the speaker was black. The results show that whatever the unnaturalness of these materials, they were easier for black urban children in the third and fifth grades and harder for white suburban children in relatively segregated areas to imitate than was Standard English. Her study was not at all aimed at studying development of specific grammatical features, but at a gross test of grammatical competence and showing that the surface structure of the test is highly relevant if one wants to make such comparisons. She is clearly right.

The Baratz test included an extremely stereotyped approximation of home dialect and outside dialect materials for both groups, and she showed that for both it was easier to imitate pseudohome dialect materials. One could argue that until one is able to construct materials with which the minority group does better (like the nonstandard section of the Baratz test), one does not understand the unique features of the skills children acquire in those communities. Of course it is also the case that no sharply circumscribed "Standard English" is in use either by children or their parents and that both regional and class variation in "standard" exists. For example, we have found that preschoolers in working-class samples routinely change *which* to *that*, and we have noticed then that *which* is a relatively formal style not used much if at all with children. Out of an appropriate balance of items *known to be equally familiar* to component groups one might construct a more language-fair test for underlying structures than we now have.

Sociolinguistic bias. Sociolinguistic work has posed a much more difficult challenge to those who wish to make comparisons—one more difficult than equating familiarity with dialect features. Each community, even subgroups within communities like teenage gangs, may develop its own pattern of language use, its own set of speech events, its own valuing of skill. To take a simple example, suppose one wants to compare fluency or active vocabulary size in two groups. Presumably one can only assess fluency by discovering the social situation in which the person talks the most. Labov [33] has given a vivid example of a black child who was laconic with an older black from the same community and only became talkative when arguing with a friend. Assessment of vocabulary size in a small sample of speech would require finding the speech events within the culture of the children which maximally demand vocabulary diversity. An alternative might be to train the child to a new task which interested him and in effect ',resocialize" him, but then there would have to be some independent way of assessing success in this task. Jensen's comment [29] that the IQ of a lower-class black child might be raised ten points by spending many hours with him suggests that socialization to the task may be involved in a variety of ways which could be investigated.

An example of such an approach occurred to me while reading Labov's engrossing account of the rule structure for an insult game, "the dozens," involving Harlem males in the teenage street culture [37]. Playing the dozens requires sensitivity to syntactic patterns since success in the role of second party requires syntactic expansion, and in the role of third party some elements may remain constant but a semantic shift such as tense change or an anomalous but relevant lexical change can produce a successful effect. There is constant group evaluation and a high sense of skill.

Playing the dozens is not unique. "Rifting," "toasting," "rapping" are all speech events developed and labeled in black culture, all involving verbal creativity [32, 37]. Kochman [32] says that "rapping is distinctively a fluent and lively way of talking, always characterized by a high degree of personal style. To one's own group, rapping may be descriptive of an interesting narration, a colorful rundown of some past event." One can only guess that the features of successful rapping are both modeled and rewarded in lower-class black children's experience. The autobiographies of such diverse figures as Rap Brown and Dick Gregory attest the importance of such early training.

If verbal skills are transferable, tests should tap these fundamental skills. They could be validated against the group's ranking of the person on the relevant speech events. An example of such an extension appears in the recent research of Susan Houston using story-retelling methods [26]. She found that lower-class black children excelled white children in not just repeating the story elements but in enriching them to make a more vivid narrative. While she did not use the group validation method, she did look for a performance which is a plausible derivative of values in the community.

The argument here is that the route out of our linguistic and social myopia in constructing measures of language competence may be to draw on the speech events and linguistic structures of minority speakers. One problem of course is that the very fact that minority-group members themselves may regard their informal style (that heard by their children) as inappropriate to formal settings and tasks makes it harder to elicit "translations" or information about speech skills, except by ethnographic work. In such cases it would be much easier to go the other way, to first get materials, such as narratives, jokes, and picture descriptions in the most informal milieu. To take a simple case—Osser, Zaid, and Wang could get picture titles from speakers of black nonstandard dialects asked to talk to their own children. One cannot expect someone to sit in an office and be able to translate the formal sentences of the test into colloquial style since the natural vernacular style is usually not given to deliberate formal production. In test construction, the appropriate direction would be to start by searching for speech events, testing situations, and linguistic patterns familiar to the children to be tested. Full development and *independent validation* of the testing materials should take place within the reference population. It would be far easier to translate materials into middle-class and Standard English than to go the other direction.

In a recent comparision of standardized tests, Elsa Roberts [46] pointed out that in four commonly used ability tests for children, from 20 to 38 percent of the vocabulary items could be considered potentially subculture-specific, and in the ITPA (*Illinois Test of Psycholinguistic Abilities*) grammatical closure test, twenty-four out of thirty-three items may have forms with dialectal variants. The WPPSI (*Wechsler Preschool and Primary Scale of Intellegence*) sentence imitation test is also subject to dialect-based errors.

Our current language competence tests are second dialect tests for lower-class and especially for black children.(3) The accusations of bias that are being made are in many cases well-founded. Whenever a test is supposed to access fundamental linguistic and intellectual competence, it must be oriented directly to the speech community to be tested. Unless the speech skills and social performances required by the test are equally familiar to all tested children, the test is a biased estimate of underlying competencé.

DEVELOPMENTAL STUDIES

The development of tests for comparative work seems to be an example of applied developmental sociolinguistics. We have seen that adequate tests would have to draw on ethnographic developmental work. In basic research in developmental sociolinguistics, the principal assumption is that how people talk reflects directly both the regular patterns of their social networks and the immediate circumstances of speech. The first part is obvious; a child's interaction network is bound to influence his values about language and the repertoire he commands. The more we study speech in natural settings, the more we find systematic variation within every speaker, reflecting who he is addressing, where he is, what the social event may be, the topic of discussion, and the social relations he communicates by speaking.(4) The regularities in these features of speech make them as amenable to analysis as the abstracted rules called grammar. Competence in speaking includes the ability to use appropriate speech for the circumstance and when deviating from what is normal to convey what is intended. It would be an incompetent speaker who used baby talk to everyone or randomly interspersed sentences in baby talk or in a second language regardless of circumstance. It would be equally incompetent to use formal style in all situations and to all addresses in a society allowing for a broader range of variation.

With respect specifically to social dialects, we assume that all varieties of English are alike in many underlying features. The child in a community with social dialects of English is in a very different situation from an immigrant. Even though he may not understand all details of Standard English, those he fails to understand or use may be relatively superficial from a linguistic if not a social standpoint. In casual discourse, intelligibility of Standard English to a nonstandard features may often understand more of the surface features of speaker of another language. Since gross unintelligibility is not present, motives for learning may be different.

As a result of mass media and education, as well as pressures towards "proper" speech in many homes, we assume that children who use many nonstandard features may often understnad more of the surface features of Standard English than they reveal in their speech. In this sense a kind of bilingualism may exist at the comprehension level, as it does with those Spanish or Navaho speakers who can understand more than they produce.

Finally, we assume that social groups vary in the uses to which they most often put speech and in the value they attach to different uses, so that the range of uses of speech by a child is to be ascertained. On the other hand, certain values can be found universally in every social group. We ought to discover which speech events, for example, are evaluated aesthetically. We assume that aesthetic values are present in every society; whether they are focused on speech and, of so, on which kinds of speech, is to be learned.

PREVIOUS RESEARCH

Systematic correlates of variations in dialect features. In speakers with a wide repertoire of language or dialect variation, the internal linguistic structure of that variation and its co-occurrence with semantic and social features can be examined. Sam Henrie [24] found that deletion of verb affixes by five-year-old black children was related to semantic features of the utterance and was not a random feature. It has been known for some time [59] that the form *be* as in "He be outa school" is semantically contrasted with *is* and carries meaning that Standard English cannot easily translate. Henrie found that, by the age of five, children selected *be* most often for habitual actions ("they be sleeping") or distributed nontemporal states ("they be blue"), least often for momentary acts.

We have learned that the frequency of standard features may increase when (a) the child is role-playing doctor or teacher [30], (b) the child is in the schoolroom or being interviewed by an authority figure [25]. (c) the child is interviewed alone rather than in a group [37], (d) the interviewer uses only Standard English rather than variable speech [58]. Labov noted, for example, that in formal style black teenagers used the plural suffix more, though the redundant third-person verb marker remained infrequent. Since none of these studies except Labov's has focused on fine detail, we might be willing to pool them all as indicating a kind of formal-informal dimension. Fischer [14], for example, noted that New England three- to ten-year-old children increased their use of "-in" suffixes (fishin) over "-ing" suffixes (fishing) in the course of an interview, presumably relaxing into more casual style. Fischer noted, as others have, that girls in his group used the formal variant more often; Kernan's examples of formal features in role-playing usually involved girls.

This kind of variation corresponds to what Blom and Gumperz call situational switching and Houston [25] calls "register," where the primary determinants appear to be setting, situation, addressee, and topic. Overlaid on these features, which in bilinguals often generate sharp switching of languages, are variations in linguistic features like "-in" and "-ing" which may or may not form coherent styles. Gumperz calls these "metaphorical switching." These may be viewed as reflections of changes of function or intent within the particular interaction, that is, the variations between dialect features can be considered linguistic devices for realizing intent or social meaning. In a given conversation, different speech acts or structural units within the conversation and different foci or speech episodes often may be demarcated by changes in the frequency of socially significant speech variables. Blom and Gumperz [4] describe these phenomena with respect to dialect variation between a village dialect in Norway and Standard Norwegian. The phenomena are analogous to American dialect feature variation.(5)

An example of a simple analysis of classroom interaction (under John Gumperz's guidance) with these concepts may illustrate what I have in mind. Mary Rainey [45] studied a teacher in a black Head Start class. She selected the alternation between "-ing" and "-in" suffixes for observation, since they are related both to formality [14, 34] and to dialect. The teacher regularly used "-ing" in formal teaching and story reading, but in these situations she used "-in" when she was trying to get attention or closeness. Rainey calls "-ing" the *unmarked* or usual form for formal teaching. On the other hand, the unmarked form for informal or casual interaction was "-in" and in these situations "-ing" was used for marked emphasis. ("Where are *you* going, Ezekiel Cato Jones?") A contrast in *register* is the comparison of casual interaction with formal teaching; *marking* is the change in meaning indicated by a shift from the normal features of that register.

The notion that formality lies on a simple dimension seems well-founded empirically in Labov's studies. With addressee and setting constant, he was able to accomplish style changes in "-ing" and in phonological alternatives by topical changes (e.g., to a more emotional topic) or by task changes (to reciting a childhood rhyme, to reading) which affected the consciousness or "monitoring" of speech. Labov found in his Lower East Side New York study [34] that a full range of style variation in interviews was not adult-like until around fourteen or fifteen, but there is other evidence certainly that some variation exists before that time. Typically, children use the more informal forms more often than adults [35, 48, 59], as one would expect from their exposure to informal home situations.

In contrast to Labov's unidimensional view of monitoring, Claudia Kernan [30] has used this term in speaking of "monitoring black" and "monitoring white." These terms refer to speech which veers away from the normal expected, or unmarked vernacular. This monitoring is analogous to Blom and Gumperz's metaphorical switching. What are the social factors that go along with monitoring black? Some examples were parodying the speech of quoted persons to indicate their social characteristics.(6) On other occasions, speakers might be alluding to shared ethnic identiy.

Many black public figures like Dick Gregory and Bobby Seale are skilled at these allusions to ethnic identity through "monitoring black."(7) On the other hand, such allusions are common in every-day discourse, according to Kernan [30], and Gumperz has located instances in recordings made by a black community worker of interaction between his wife and teenage boys, for instance:

> You can tell me how your mother worked twenty hours a day and I can sit here and cry. I mean I can cry and I can feel for you. But as long as I don't get up and make certain that I and my children don't go through the same, *I ain't did nothin' for you*, brother. That's what I'm talking about.[19]

In speakers of Hawaiian pidgin, systematic register variation occurs between features of pidgin phonology, syntax, lexicon, and intonation and those features of Standard English known to the speaker, with social inputs such as age of addressee, relative status, familiarity, sex, and whether the addressee is an islander or mainlander. But within this registral variation, reference to shared, personal island experience even in a formal mainland setting can bring about style shift towards pidgin [42].

In a tape of Chicano bilingual interaction analyzed by Gumperz and Hernandez [19], loan words, exclamations, and sentence connectors were used as allusions to ethnic identity. These superficial items might even appear in relatively monitored speeches, such as political interaction. But in informal interaction where the speakers have no values deriding language switching, the bulk of the switching consists of changes in whole sentences or clauses underlying them. These code shifts have a social meaning similar to marking or style shifting in dialect variation. They can, for example, allude to ethnic identity and, depending on context, carry special meanings of confidentiality or personal involvement. In these cases the switching is often quite unconscious and affects a deeper level in the sentence production process. In dialect style shifting, the parallel between these superficial and deep shifts would be the contrast between the isolated use of single features like *be* or exclamations and lexical items compared to more pervasive changes in paralinguistic and phonological features affecting longer units of discourse.

Labov has commented that if a speaker masters a fully consistent standard register, he may be unable to switch to the vernacular except through the use of markers whose frequency is not like that in an unmarked vernacular. He loses his fine sense of context-defined inherent variation. In some of the black monitoring observed by Kernan, forms were used that were caricatures and which do not occur in any vernacular style.

The notion of marking or foregrounding information has been formally developed by Geoghegan [15]. He has found, in working on alternations in address forms, that one can identify a regular, expected, reportable, unmarked form which is predictable from social features such as setting, age, rank, sex, and so on. This would correspond to register or situational or unmarked style as used above. Register does not carry meaning because it is predictable from known social features. Deviations from the unmarked alternatives carry social information such as positive and negative affect, deference, and anger. Thus, "marking" is the same as Gumperz's metaphorical switches [4]. Kernan's "monitoring" carries information to the listener because it deviates from the speaker's usual style in that situation. In her examples, the information concerned attitudes toward addresses or persons referred to or quoted. Since these changes in speech are often unconscious, they can only be studied from taped natural conversations, not from informant reports.

Sociolonguistic development. I hope it is clear from this discussion of registers, styles, marking, and monitoring that these concepts are still being developed and changed and that attention to them will be fundamental in any research on children's understanding of the social aspects of language. Since work has beeen largely on adults, we do not know at how young an age and under what social conditions it is possible for speakers to show register or style variability in their speech.

My guess is that the first social features that will appear are major setting and addressee contrasts, since we find very early that bilingual children change language according to locations and persons. Martin Edelman, for example, examined the relation between reports of the expected language for given settings and language dominance as judged by fluency in emitting isolated words in a particular language associated with a given setting. The children were Puerto Rican bilinguals in New York, six to twelve. The pattern did not change with age, merely the amount of English dominance. Children knew significantly more English words for education and religion, but not for family and home.(8) Church, school, and home are unambiguous settings for which dominant language was reportable by the children.

In addition, when nursery school children role-play they often adopt consistent speech patterns in accordance with the social categories involved—mothers and babies, doctors, cowboys, teachers, puppets. These situational patterns are relatively stereotyped but do reveal quite early use of language with consistent feature changes. What we do not know is what features change and what social cues can be generalized beyond particular persons.

The instnaces we have observed of speech variation for intent may not be socially conventionalized in young children. One can only surmise how the metaphor they seem to express has been learned. For example, children will use infantilized style as a marker for dependency needs, but it is not clear whether this style is in fact drawn from the child's own earlier repertoire or is some stereotype of infant's speech. I have heard children of four years use telegraphic sentences to a foreigner just learning English and thought it an imitation, but Eurwen Price reports that four-year-old English monolinguals in a Welsh nursery school who assumed the Welsh teachers knew no English spontaneously spoke telegraphically, e.g., "Me cars now" [44:34], yet they clearly had not heard such speech from the fully bilingual teachers. The most striking feature of these style shifts is that they are transitory and that within a given conversation they may merely mark the onset of reversion to unmarked style.

We know that consistent code changes in second languages can be learned early very rapidly. Edward Hernandez, in Berkeley, has been studying a Chicano monolingual of three who became relatively bilingual within six months from nursery school exposure, though his English at that time was considerably simpler than his Spanish. We do not know how early or under what social conditions completely consistent control over the situational selection of two social dialects can be mastered. Part of the problem is that we know relatively little about the linguistic features of such competence. Greenlee, who observed bilingual five-year-olds, commented that they already had learned not to speak Spanish before outsiders, but that in her small sample of their own interaction there were code shifts for marking emphasis, indicating addressee, and quoting [16].

Stylistic consistency. In the more formal types of situations, bilinguals can learn relatively separated codes. Even metaphorical switching tends to be at fairly high syntactic nodes if both lexical alternatives are available to the speaker (i.e., he doesn't have to use vocabulary from one variety since he lacks words). Some bilinguals even have a range of formal to informal styles in both codes [18].

One of the major differences between the variation found in most bilinguals and in speakers with forms from various social dialects has been argued by Kernan [30]. She points out that there is a lack of co-occurrence restrictions, or stylistic consistency, in the samples of black speech. One changes register, or monitors, by increasing or decreasing the frequency of certain variables, sometimes categorically. But if one examines the variables which show stylistic variation, one finds the variants side by side. For example, "She has a morning class and a afternoon class, and she have their name taped down on a piece of cardboard" [30:52]. She found the same variation in preschoolers: "They seen the bird, saw the ducks." For these reasons, she does not think that standard variants are dialect borrowings, but rather that they are integral to the "be" dialect.

Labov, who has examined both individual and group styles in teenage and adult Harlem speakers, has been impressed by the inconsistency of their formal style features, especially in the formal test situations typical of schools. "Whenever a subordinate dialect is in contact with a superordinate dialect, answers given in any formal test situation will shift from the subordinate towards the superordinate in an irregular and unsystematic manner" [37].

Claudia Kernan also found, in classroom correction tests, that students had no stable notions of what the standard alternative was among the alternatives in their repertoire. Labov, McKay, Henrie, Kernan, and indeed everyone who has collected considerable samples of speech of dialect speakers have found that the full range of most standard forms will appear *some time* in their speech. That is, the problem of standard speech is in most cases not that the form is outside the repertoire but that the speaker *cannot maintain a consistent choice* of standard alternatives and not make slips. There is inadequate co-occurrence restriction between the standard forms whether they are dialect borrowings or not [59].

This is what we would expect if in fact the features that standard speakers use to identify standard and nonstandard speech are often used for metaphorical signaling by nonstandard speakers. They may hear a higher density of standard features as carrying a particular connotation in a given situation. But some features are *not* varied for this kind of meaning, and since various combinations of features co-occur there is no strong sense that any consistent style is required. In addition, there is considerable "inherent variation" according to Labov's work, which may not carry any connotations at all. In Standard English this inherent variation is not heard as marking the speaker as incompetent in Standard English, but since in any nonstandard English the variation includes features which are criterial to listeners' judgments of standardness, it appears to be socially inconsistent to outsiders.

In advising parents who rear bilingual children it is usual to point out that they should maintain consistency of speaker, occasion, and setting so that the child can be aided in predicting which form to use. But in the case of any nonstandard English the great bulk of the informal styles heard in the community by children contain a high degree of variability between standard and nonstandard features, since the variability is inherent in the dialect. A child who is to maintain a consistent choice of the standard alternative must mark it categorically in his storage, or at least have some linkages between forms which will make sequential occurrence of standard forms seem normal for him. If the child heard pure standard or nonstandard forms, this learning would not be a problem. He would learn the standard style as a second language with as brief and trivial interference as we normally find in immigrant children.(9) But this is not what he hears. He hears highly variable speech lacking in co-occurrence restrictions or predictability from segment to segment, at least at the grammatical level. Small wonder that many speakers are very uncertain as to which is standard and cannot do classroom correction tests comfortably.(10)

This line of thinking leads me to an outlandish proposal. If the problem is to identify "pure styles" and to store them with sufficient separateness to permit stylistic consistency, might it not be appropriate to help identify them by using "monitoring styles" of a sort, by having children role-play, parody, or use narrative styles in which a relatively extreme nonstandard without inherent variation on key features might seem appropriate and the other children could call them on failures? The converse would of course be role-playing a journalist, doctor, legislator, and so on, in Standard English grammar. The social appropriateness of such a move in a school might very well be questioned by parents who believe the school is the place for Standard English, but such games might enhance maximum adeptness in style switching. There is of course some precedent for permitting and encouraging a range of styles in dramatic play, even in school. In addition, there may be community tradition for such uses, as in the black speech act called "marking" [30] which parodies speech.

In courses helping adolescents to master register changes, Waterhouse [55] has found that even students who did not speak Standard English consistently were as a group critical of press releases in a role-played press conference if they contained nonstandard features like copula deletion. The group itself, without pressure from the teacher, exerted constraints on role-players to keep a consistent register. The method saves the actor from being teased about speaking Standard English and potentially may be transferred to situations where the teacher is not present.

The practice of giving students drills in Standard English, which has developed in some schools, is based on the assumption that the variants do not exist in their repertoire. It also assumes that there may be massive problems of failure of communication. But studies of social dilaects in fact show the frequency of nonstandard forms to be small but socially important because of prejudice against nonstandard speakers. Where the standard variants exist in the child's repertoire already, and where some already have markers of social meaning, the teacher has a special objective quite different from that of basic second-language learning. The teacher needs to find the most effective way to give a child training in situational switching which will allow him to use the forms consistently in writing and in speech situations where he may be affected by fatigue, fear, and by concentration on the content of what he is saying. That seems to be what parents want to happen.

If a child is forced to speak only Standard English, he is robbed of an essential rhetorical tool. An example from Gumperz and Hernandez [19] illustrates deliberate use of style shifting:

> Student (reading from an autobiographical essay): This lady didn't have no sense.
> Teacher: What would be another way of saying that sentence?
> Student: She didn't have any sense. But not this lady; she *didn't have no sense.*

The child who is bilingual or speaks a nonstandard variant has style variation available which signals social meaning which may be unexpressible in Standard English. Where these meanings have analogues in style shifts within Standard English the teacher who is able to understand the child's intent can view it as part of his task to enlarge his own and the child's repertoire to include several ways of signaling these meanings, depending on the audience.

Comprehension of features: Interpretation of studies of the possibilities of variation in produced speech requires better evidence on what features children can hear. Because of the evidence that many variants occur freely if unpredictably in children's output, it is sometimes assumed that all children understand all features of Standard English. Jane Torrey's work [52] using comprehension tests such as choice of pictures is a model for studying these problems. She found that sibilant suffixes had markedly different probabilities of being understood or produced, depending on their grammatical functions. Almost all the black children in her Harlem sample understood a plural suffix and produced it regularly, almost none understood or produced a verb suffix marking number, as in "the cat scratches," vs. "the cats scratch," and about half understood and produced the copula, the possessive, and the verb suffix denoting tense, as in "the boy shut the door" vs. "the boy shuts the door." Torrey has not reported the performances of children who usually hear Standard English to see if some developmental factors are present. This study, of course, isolates the features from contextual redundancy by selecting sentences in which only the suffix must be the cue, as one must to discover whether a particular linguistic cue can be interpreted alone.

The kind of evidence that Labov, Kernan, Baratz, and others have obtained, showing that in imitation tasks children *translate* into their own dialect, may be insufficient indication of comprehension of particualr features, since the sentences contain redundancy. For example, Baratz [1] found that white children translated "It's some toys out there" into "There are some toys out there," and black children often did the reverse. But this does not indicate that either group "understood" the first words, rather that the rest of the utterance made obligatory this form in their output. Error analysis of imitation materials with less redundancy would discover what syntactic and morphological features are employed. Torrey's findings are not inconsistent with the important fact that in everyday situations most Standard English may be intelligible grammatically to all black lower-class children, since in many situations language is redundant.(11)

A recent study by Weener [58] attempted to separate phonology from whatever semantic and syntactic sequential probabilities are tested by memory for "orders of approximimation" to English by six- and seven-year-olds. From the standpoint of syntactic differences, this method gives rather gross results and is unlikely to be sensitive to whatever syntactic differences occur in the formal output of lower-class black and middle-class white informants. The interesting finding in this study was that when asked to remember these strings of words, the lower-class black children and middle-class whites did equally well with the materials read by a middle-class white speaker, but the whites had trouble remembering the same materials read by a black speaker. That is, just as we might expect on social grounds, black children have more exposure to middle-class white phonology and could interpret it more easily than the suburban Detroit white children could interpret southern black speech.(12)

The Weener results remind us that the critical factors in adjusting to phonological differences, as in adjusting to "foreign accents," are likely to be experience and attitude toward the speaker. Studies of the mutual intelligibility of speakers in varieties of social settings allowing for both differences in contacts and in types of speech exposure and for differences in social attitudes towards the other group would inform us about factors causing changes in intelligibility in our pluralistic society. These studies need to focus on comprehension as such, not on output measures like the cloze procedure; and it would be helpful if they would distinguish finegrained feature interpretation (as of the plural marker in Torrey's work) from grosser referential intelligibility and the understanding of allusion and metaphor.

One of the most significant findings in Kernan's work and in recent studies by John Gumperz is that there is considerable informational or connotative content in choice among referential equivalents in the speaker's repertoire. A full competence in comprehending the speech of others includes these social interpretations. So far, most research on information-transmission has been focused on shapes, colors, and locations rather than on the equally systematic communication of hostility, affection, and deference. It is possible that the latter matters are of greater practical significance—for example, in the classroom where teacher and pupil need to communicate respect for each other. If teachers cannot understand when a pupil makes a conciliatory move, for instance, disaster could follow.

Subjective reaction tests. Along with studies of comprehension, we need more information about children's attitudes towards speech varieties and their sense of norms of register and style. There have been numerous studies in which people rate voices out of context (except of the topic) by Labov [34, 37], Tucker and Lambert [54], and Williams [57], for example. Such ratings necessarily tend to be of people or categories of people, since this is all the information the listeners can discover. It turns out to be the case, when specific features used in ratings are examined, that listeners tend to give "categorical" judgments, as Labov first pointed out. They will judge intelligence, ambition, and honesty just from "accent." They do not react to frequencies reliably but, as June McKay [40] has suggested, tend to pick out the "lowest" ranked social feature, even if it is rare, as an indicator of the speaker's social ranking—provided, of course, it is not contextually accounted for as "marking," such as parody, irony, humor. Williams has found that teachers tend to judge race from a few features. The work of Triandis, Loh, and Levin [53] and Lambert [39] implies that teachers will then treat the children by their group stereotype. From a practical standpoint, knowing which features are perceptually critical might help those who aim at giving the children the option of choosing when to be ethnically identifiable from phonology.

One of the fundamental ideas in sociolinguistics, as emphasized earlier, is that speech in fact and in its norms is context sensitive. We accept baby talk to infants but not to adolscents, As a measure of children's development of style norms, judgments of the sort just discussed need to be made where the social context is made clear in some way. It remains to be seen how children react to anomalies—by laughter, criticism, imitation perhaps. Children as young as five will criticize others who are role-playing for using the wrong terminology for the role, e.g., "You can't say 'honey'; you're the baby." Such studies are the judgmental analogue of the role-playing method of studying actually produced style and register changes, and the two kinds of studies should be paired to permit study of the extent to which judgments are finer than ability to produce the forms critical to the judgments. Labov [35] has found that by mid-teens speakers who did not themselves produce the most formal alternatives in New York phonology shared the opinion of the rest of the population on what variants were socially higher.

Claudia Kernan has commented that certain genres of folk literature, such as songs, poetry, and narratives would be ludicrous in Standard English, and Labov [34] found that childhood rhymes often forced use of the most casual vernacular. It would be of great value to know how sensitive are children to these social co-occurrence constraints, especially on genres brought into use from outside the school to enlarge the children's fluency in the classroom. If they react to some kinds of performances as sounding wrong in Standard English or vice versa—if some require Standard English—then efforts by the teacher to mismatch these types of discourse with the wrong style may make the children uncomfortable and silent. For these reasons studies of judgments may help guide teachers toward culturally appropriate varieties of language.

Functions of language. One of the major issues that has come to the fore in sociolinguistics and in applied work in education has been the question of varieties of language function. Bernstein [3] has pointed out that in England middle-class parents train children in a considerable amount of explicitness about referents, as though they were talking to a stranger or blind person and no shared assumptions obtained. The result of this training (possibly through the use of known-answer question drills) is that children perform verbal tasks very well in test situations with minimal verbal stimulation. The difference in stress on overelaboration of detail vs. terseness of description, based on shared assumptions, shows up in a variety of studies. Hawkins [22] found that lower-class English children described pictures with many "exophoric" pronouns, which required that the listener see the picture, as indeed he did. Middle-class pupils elaborated nouns and adjectives which specified information the examiner must already have known from seeing the picture. Williams and Naremore [58] found that when children were asked to be specific, class differences disappeared. But when terse questions were asked, the middle-class children assumed they should give complicated elaborate answers and the lower class, that only minimal necessary responses were needed. Labov has cited examples illustrating the bewilderment of a child taken into a room by a tester and told to "say what is in front of you" when both the tester and the child could see quite well what it was. The implication of course, is that children may have learned that the function of such communication is to convey information. If they have not been brought up on "known-answer" questions and taught to display their vocabulary and to disregard whether the hearer knows the information, they may not understand the intent of such questions.

Claudia Kernan described such an incident during her study of the speech of

Oakland black youngsters. She asked one child, "Where do you live?" and got a vague answer, "Over there," with a vaguely waved thumb. Shortly after, her husband asked the same question. The answer he got was, "You go down the stairs, turn left, walk three blocks . . . " What was the difference? Her husband had never been to the child's house—but she had picked the child up there.

Social-class differences in transmission of referential information may be a function of "set." If so, they can be easily changed by instruction or brief training. Studies by Cowan [10], Coulthard and Robinson [9], and Robinson [47] suggest that they are to some degree the effects of socially different ways of viewing the function of the act asked of them, or the "rules of the game." It is possible too, of course, that skill in the particular domain of vocabulary or previous experience with materials might aid in such performances.

Of considerable value to sociolinguistic work are studies of skills in language developed by children. For example, children often spontaneously play with sounds in the preschool years and invent games transforming songs by simplified transformations like pig Latin. Where these skills become socially organized, they may develop into identifiable speech categories: nursery rhymes, songs, sounding, toasting, rifting, or rapping. These in some cases include oral traditions, knowledge of which is part of the developing competence of children. These may include not only general stylistic features but sequential rules. Children's skills are repeatedly evaluated by peers and highly appreciated. Houston [25] has even argued that in the rural poor that she studied, lack of toys resulted in more storytelling, language games, and placing more value on linguistic creativity, spontaneous narrative, and improvisation. She has shown that black lower-class children excel in story enrichment during retelling [26]. Having recently seen a group of forty highly educated adults and their children around a campfire without even one person being skilled enough to carry on storytelling, I can believe education can produce cultural impoverishment!

Analysis of the structure of communication within communities could make us better able to draw events from children's repertoire into the schools, better able to use them in testing competence to identify biologically based retardation, and better able to understand how children interpret tasks they are given to do. Within these speech categories, stylistic variations involving the standard-nonstandard dimensions are important carriers of emotional significance. The ability to convey meaning depends on this range of variation. We can expect that as children have contact with members of varied social groups they will learn skill in a wider range of speech categories, learn each other's oral traditions, and learn devices for conveying information about social intent from each other's dialects. We are already seeing these changes in Berkeley children in integrated schools. Labov has pointed out that the black children he studied valued language highly for cleverness in besting others; this attitude, if fully understood by teachers, could, he proposed, be a basis for enlarging language competence.

Testing milestones. Tests were developed to predict success in schools as they were constituted and to assess achievements of the school. The need to compare the achievements of school entities and to pass the blame for failures onto the child probably will unfortunately guarantee that tests will continue to be used even when they are not needed for fundamental diagnosis. Diagnosis of biologically based retardation, assuming we have means of pedagogically treating such retardation, is an important function of tests. If this is to be done well, there need to be tests of basic milestones in competence which contain materials equated in dialect and social biases for the populations to be tested.

In contrast to previous attempts at culture-free testing, sociolinguistic research gives hope of finding how to create communicative settings, tasks, language, and scoring criteria that are fully compatible with the experience of the tested children and are validated *within* their own social group in cases of fairly clear group differences. Of course, ethnic and class categories do not bound homogeneous groups, so it is not clear in a diverse classroom which one it is appropriate to choose from a package of tests labeled lower-class black, middle-class black, Chicano, and so on. But at least such a pluralistic set might take us beyond the current middle-class white package!

As an example of the improvements of testing and teaching materials which might be gained from a realistic orientation to children's language use, we might cite the weaknesses of reading workbooks and tests. Items which rest on "comparing initial sound" or "rhyming words" depend on the probabilities that children will produce a very specific item of vocabulary for a given picture. They don't work as teaching materials or as valid tests unless the children do in fact "mediate" with these vocabulary items. Sensitive teachers have noticed repeatedly that a large proportion of these items do *not* elicit the expected names. The differences may be even larger where environmental and social differences exist. Such items are useless for teaching or testing without specific individual tutoring. Another example is the section in reading-recognition tests of word lists which are to be matched to pictures. Even if the words are read aloud, the items in some cases cannot be matched. But in this situation children rely on a single mediated name of the picture more than adults do. Probably such tests are often *not* tests of reading. In paragraph comprehension items, the syntax and content is often such that even if it were read aloud the child could not understand it. Such a test is not a pure test of reading skill. The evidence that children speaking social dialects cannot read may be largely based on invalid measures of reading ability. Of course, the effects of this evidence may be self-fulfilling if teachers believe dialect speakers have trouble learning to read.

Speech variation. We need much more work on the social conditions which alter the frequency of social variants in speech. We need work with children to see what are the social factors which increase and decrease ethnic identity markers in their speech at different ages.(13) It is not clear whether the monitoring of ethnic solidarity which Kernan describes has parallels in social categories like "working class" where there are no sharp socially defined boundaries. But there probably are parallels in all groups to the increase in vernacular usage under excitement that Labov has found.

Wider target populations. We need to extend sociolinguistic work to a wider variety of regions and groups. The problems of urban schools have for practical reasons led to lower-class black, Puerto Rican, and Chicano groups being at the focus of recent work. However, developmental sociolinguistics is appropriate to any child; upper-class children, both black and white, have stylistic variation in their speech, too, and they can be studied to gain basic information about age changes in the structure and function of speech variation. Any groups speaking nonstandard English are equally appropriate for the study of the relations between standard and nonstandard; areas of regional migration allow for group identity-marking through speech variables (e.g., migrants from Appalachia in Detroit). Since the social and the linguistic factors are slightly different in each of these groups, better generalizations about basic processes would be available if the range of groups studied was extended. There is a practical factor; such work is always contingent on collaboration or principal direction by ingroup members.

Code-switching training. We need to explore teaching methods for increasing competence in code switching and to find out the ages at which different methods are suitable for teaching. At present, unfortunately, most research on second-language learning has been so atheoretical and ad hoc that we know very little of basic relevance to questions of how different features of language can be learned. Role-playing and developing of tasks with appropriate registers that the children themselves recognize and reinforce (e.g., Waterhouse) are examples of possible methods to use. It is not clear when formal instruction, drills, individual tutoring, peer group learning, and teaching by older children from the same social group might be most effective. How does one learn appropriate frequencies where there is inherent variation?

One of the problems in suggesting changes in educational methods is the lack of close study of actual classroom interaction. Teachers are not conscious of the methods they use. Tapes and videotapes can provide a way to locate the effective features of current methods, methods chosen post hoc as most effective, or methods used in experimental studies. Since communication is not merely verbal, videotapes may considerably enrich our ability to interpret what happens in the classroom.

Comprehension. We need far more studies like Torrey's, exploring fully the range of comprehension of specific features of various types of English for various types of listeners. It would be of value to know whether teachers understand their pupils, for example, in terms of specific grammatical features.

Ethnography of literacy. We need to explore the place of reading and writing in the linguistic life of the child. Labov found Harlem teen-agers who did not know if their close friends were literate. Literacy was not necessary for the activities of the boys. Exploration of children's values about language might lead to ways of devising uses of language and, specifically, types of reading for beginners that are relevant to interests they already have; later one hopes that new interests arising from what they read will carry them further.

It is not clear how important *type* of language is in reading; adults frequently have strong attitudes that only Standard English is appropriate for reading. Navahos were for many years not especially receptive to efforts to make a written language of Navaho; English is for writing. Schools, of course, are not immune from adult community pressures; if it could be shown that literacy in the vernacular clearly aids literacy in Standard English, then the adults might be persuadable. Indeed, in community-controlled Navaho schools vernacular education and vernacular literacy have spurted recently.

Learning to read. We need to explore in detail the structural relations between the child's oral comprehension skills, his speech, and reading and writing. I know of no evidence that learning to *understand* written language (as contrasted with reading aloud) is generally affected by the child's dialect of English. In a recent study of third-graders, Melmed [41] asked them to read sentences containing key items and then to choose the appropriate picture. For example, a sentence might be, "I have six cats" or "He fell and tore his pants," and the picture items contrasted *six-sick* and *tore-toe*. Although in reading aloud they used black English phonology in 28 percent of the pairs, they chose the wrong picture in only 5.4 percent of cases for the same pairs. Thus their comprehension was not affected by the homonyms. Although black and white pupils differed significantly in both phonetic output and phonological discrimination in listening, they did not differ in oral and silent reading comprehension tests built around the hypothesis of homonym confusion.

We might expect there would be problems in spelling to the extent that spelling relies on phonological rather than visual memory. Phonological features like *l*-lessness and consonant cluster simplification affected auditory discrimination in Melmed's subjects and could affect the information they had stored about their aurally learned vocabulary. These items will have to be acquired by rote, visual, whole-word learning rather than completely rule-governed production, like *knife* and *would*.

Labov has pointed out that the underlying form is in many cases the same for standard and nonstandard words and only deletion rules apply. All children need to learn the relation between deletion and the spelled form; all English speakers learn there is no one-to-one relation between spelling and sound, and to depend to some extent on some sight vocabulary or contextual guessing. In other parts of the world where children speak a highly valued local dialect, learning to read a standard is no problem.

Two directions of research need exploration. One might be to explore the relation between common features in varieties of Standard English and the child's comprehension and production. We could test the child's specific feature knowledge as Torrey and Melmed have done and build materials related in systematic ways to this knowledge. I am not persuaded that social or regional dialects are related to having difficulties decoding inflectional suffixes in listening or reading. Labov has evidence that white boys as well as blacks do not readily interpret the -*ed* suffix in reading as a past tense indicator, especially in early adolescence and preadolescence. In cases where such grammatical features are not readily understood, they may not normally interfere with comprehension, given the redundancy of most texts, but they clearly are important in marginal cases and in writing. Specific instructional materials could focus on these issues.

A second possibility would be better investigation of the issues of teaching comprehension apart from reading aloud (which has to be unlearned later anyway). If part of the problem is the social one of punishment by teachers who do not recognize when speech is the child's equivalent of what is written, the teacher's judgment either must be changed or bypassed. In effect one would teach children to decode written symbols to their meanings via the path of *hearing* spoken words with what they read at first. Children would of course engage in sotto voce articulation while reading but they would not be directly punished or rewarded by the teacher for this vocal behavior.

Joan Baratz and William Stewart have proposed that children will learn to read faster if the grammatical structures used in primers are derived from their own output [2] or are structurally similar. Such materials could of course be prepared by teachers from stories told by the children with lexical normalization of spelling but not of syntax. We need detailed research with appropriate controls. With content and vocabulary controlled, does a child learn faster if the grammatical structures used come from his own output? What if they are like his most standard forms? His most nonstandard forms (as in the Baratz materials)? Variable, as verbatim materials would be? It is clear that different content,(14) different grammar but conventionalized orthography, different vocabulary and concept familiarity might all be at issue and should be studied separately. In these studies there needs to be knowledge of the spontaneous story-producing style of pupils, since a number of studies have shown relatively low frequencies of nonstandard variants and considerable variation between pupils.

Case histories of learning to read with details of teacher-child interaction might help us locate points of difficulty, identify over-generalization stages, and develop better theories of the reading process and, more important, better teacher training methods. It is to be hoped that detailed recordings will be available of children's performance as they learn to read the Baratz-Stewart materials.

It is quite possible that the structural features of the materials in terms of dialect are not important in themselves, given that children understand most Standard English structures and that many differences are superficial. Teachers and supervisors who have worked in many schools with minority pupils complain that the fundamental problem is that many middle-class teachers do not believe that poor children, especially nonstandard speakers, can easily learn to read. I could list a variety of types of observed behavior toward lower-class children that could be the kinds of discouraging cues that children emotionally understand or that more directly reduce the opportunity of the child to learn [19]. There are dramatic examples of teachers who have brought below-average IQ slum children to the third-grade level in reading while in first grade. We need to identify and videotape the teaching methods of such teachers and locate by experiment what are the key features of their methods and then teach with these videotapes.

If the Baratz-Stewart materials do result in faster learning, one reason might be their effects on teacher attitudes. If teachers believe the child has a language and a culture of his own that they themselves do not fully understand, they are less likely to treat him as "deficient." This may be a key difference in attitudes toward immigrant children and native ethnic minorities. One cannot teach this lesson by exhortation; teachers who begin to realize that the children know something they don't know may respect the children more. Therefore, research on the effects of teaching materials should include work on some sensitive indices (perhaps of the Lamber speech-guise type) of changes in social attitudes towards dialect speakers on the part of teachers and administrators.

Judgments. We need more research on the development of children's subjective reactions to language. How early and by what features do they identify categories of speakers? Are there sex differences, as so many studies have suggested, in the direction of greater preference for and use of formal variants by girls? How early can children, depending on their social experience, differentiate the Standard English of various ethnic groups? How do they evaluate it?

Speech norms. How do norms of appropriateness of speech variables to situation and meaning develop? While we know that children produce "baby-talk intonation" to babies when they are no more than twenty months old, we do not know how soon they react to misplaced baby talk as anomalous, or judge meanings on the basis of speech variables.

Teacher training. We need to explore for practical as well as theoretical reasons ways of training teachers to understand non-standard speech. Gumperz has made two proposals along these lines. One is that systematic nonstandard dialects be taught as second languages to teachers. The purpose would not be that the teachers produce these forms in the classroom, but that by learning them as "second languages" teachers would be brought to recognize their systematic character and their variability and to understand how they convey meaning. I believe also, from work on second-language teaching, that there might be a very strong attitudinal impact on the teachers. Learning a second language through methods of close imitation of native speakers is a dramatic personal experience. Success in imitation (within the range of adult articulatory rigidity) might be a sensitive measure of intergroup attitudes.

The second method proposed by Gumperz would be similar to some "sensitivity training" methods. Taped interaction between two groups of pupils or of teachers and pupils would be selected to show misunderstanding of the meaning of linguistic features and/or stylistic variation. For instance, suppose an excited child used more dialect features and the teacher heard these as hostile. Two groups of listeners could separately be asked to make judgments about the social meaning of each utterance. The differences in these judgments would bring to light systems of meaning that are not the same in the two groups and allow some learning about humor, irony, and insult. The significance of pitch changes, of marking of allusions, could begin to be apparent to trainees.

Teacher vernacular. We need to know more about the impact on children's attitudes of the teacher's use of the vernacular in the classroom. Some programs are already systematically teaching, for instance, "Pocho" to teachers.(15) In the case of nonstandard black features, Kernan's work suggests that nonstandard features out of context may have implications of ridicule, as for example if nonstandard grammar is used without associated phonological and paralinguistic features. Yet Baratz's method of teaching reading implies that the teacher knows how to speak nonstandard English appropriately.

Style consistency. We need to know how stylistic consistency can be learned, since children hear speech which is variable at home and among their friends. A good deal needs to be known about whether role-playing can increase consistency and whether a bipolar contrast between two relatively consistent "codes" is required or optimal for developing separately stored features, lexically, phonologically, and syntactically. The practical implications of more work on the learning of style rules are considerable.

Linguistic vs. social emphasis. Teacher training materials emphasizing formal categorial linguistic differences could have some negative effects on attitudes and educational practices. The formal differences between regional and social dialects are trivial and superficial in terms of the basic goals of the schools. The real educational problems may lie in the structure of the school and the operating classroom, in failures of social communication in the classroom, in strong beliefs about the knowledge, abilities, and attributes of speakers judged by their regional or social dialect [53]. If teachers mistakenly conclude that dialects are related to thought processes, that nonstandard speakers are like new immigrants and lack Standard English in their repertoire, or that all members of a given ethnic group are alike and have the same range of linguistic skills, then linguistically oriented materials will have reinforced social stereotypes and diverted attention from the real failures of the schools. For these reasons a high priority research area should be ethnography of classroom communication, and training about social dialects should include a sociolinguistic rather than formal perspective.

NOTES

(1) For theoretical discussions of communicative competence see Hymes [28]. For some research suggestions regarding developmental sociolinguistics see Slobin [40]. The term *sociolinguistic* rather than *communicative* is used here to exclude the many forms of skill in *non*linguistic communication which also undergo development and show up at an earlier age than conventional linguistic communication.

(2) With biological abnormalities we include birth damage, damage arising from malnutrition in gestation or infancy, damage from malnutrition of the maternal grandmother during pregnancy, damage from chronic illnesses, as well as genetically based brain deficiencies. From a social engineering standpoint it is important of course to differentiate these sources since something can be done about the systematic violence to the poor which results in malnutrition, illness, and the higher incidence of birth damage.

(3) Stewart [51] in particular has argued strongly that the number and importance of grammatical differences between nonstandard black English and any form of Standard English is greater, for historical reasons, than other social dialect differences.

(4) For further discussion of these points see Hymes [27] and Ervin-Tripp [12]. The furthese development of the importance of repertoire in social meaning has been in the work of John Gumperz [4, 17, 18].

(5) A striking finding of this study was that speakers valued the local vernacular highly and *could not believe* that they employed Standard Norwegian words and features for certain kinds of speech. The relation between the vernacular and a standard has been an educational issue in many parts of the world; studies in other places might often be relevant to developmental issues in the United States.

(6) A vivid example of completely unconscious marking which was not a direct imitation appeared in Labov's study of Lower East Side New York speech [35:97]. A Negro without ethnically distinctive speech told a story about a dangerous experience. In the dialogue he included he represented his own speech in his typical unmarked casual style, but he also represented his own speech of the person he feared, since that person was supposed to have threatened someone with a gun. This voice was rasping and rapid, with "country" southern Negro features. He later reported that the other person was—a Hungarian!

(7) An example from Bobby Seale, an expert at such monitoring, in a speech at a "Free Huey" rally: "If the United States government and the courts . . . did this they would have to choose black people from the black community to sit on their juries. They would have to choose some of them mothers who been working twenty years in Miss Ann's kitchen scrubbing floors like my mother done. They have to choose some of the hard-working fathers. They have to choose some of them brothers standing on the block out there wondering where they gonna git a gig!" In the discussion of press reports of the Black Panther Party, he says "the paper's going to call us thugs and hoodlums . . . but the brothers on the block . . . gonna say, them some out-of-sight thugs and hoodlums up there, and the brother on the block is going to say, who is these thugs and hoodlums. In fact, them dudes look just like me. In fact, I know John, George, Paul. In fact, I know Bobby Hutton. Hey, man, I know that dude, over there. Hey man, what you cats doin with them rods?" Voice quality and intonation change demarcates the quotation as well as the style shift apparent in a transcript [6]. This monitoring style was found in a rally with a largely black audience but not in a radio interview on the same subject matter.

(8) The discrepancy between the children's report about neighborhood language, which they rated as predominantly Spanish, and their word-fluency scores, which were significantly higher in English for the task of naming objects in the neighborhood, illustrates the problems of using tests rather than recordings of natural conversation. It is possible that most "doorstep conversations" common in the Puerto Rican neighborhoods were in Spanish but that vocabulary for nameable shops and objects was primarily English, and

likewise that considerable English was in fact used in conversations which speakers believed was Spanish. John Gumperz [18] has particularly emphasized the difference between questionnaire answers and actual behavior.

(9) Here we distinguish immigrant children from children in those bilingual communities where the same conditions of admixture of English and other forms may obtain in some cases. Many instances have been observed in which bilinguals cannot identify the language of the provenance of a form because it is used in both their codes.

(10) Kernan developed a method for identifying when speakers knew the "proper" standard form. She asked teen-agers to correct nonstandard sentences. She found that such forms as deleted copula, negative inversion (can't nobody jump), "ain't," and "done" plus participle, and hypercorrect verb suffix (they runs) were consistently identified, but the students were uncertain about many other forms. Labov [37] has had the same results, showing that some forms are stigmatized and are identified as nonstandard, but others are not.

Six-year old: She done ate up all of my potato chips.

Mother: Done ate! She has . . . have ate up all my potato chips. [30]

(11) This statement may sound overoptimistic. There are many registers outside of the everyday experience of most people. In the more open enrollment in universities, there may be many students encountering for the first time, with discouraging results, not only new vocabulary and subject matter, but also lecturers who use complex nominalizations and unusual types of sentence embeddings. The assumption that syntactic learning ends in childhood is not socially realistic, but there has been little systematic study of complex registers.

(12) In studies which disconnect syntax from phonology, there is a serious confounding because of the likelihood of some co-occurrence rules or rules-of-style consistency between the two levels. Nonstandard syntax with "standard" or media-announcer phonology is bizarre and quite different in meaning from nonstandard syntax and congruent phonology. In the same way, the standard syntax and stereotyped stage nonstandard phonology employed by Stern and Keislar [50] was so bizarre a combination that black children could not understand it very well. In the Weener study the syntax had no clear identity and the black speaker's phonology was a natural formal reading style.

(13) In some features there is a slight increase during adolescence [37] and greater register effect. We can expect that the peer culture will alter norms and that the progress from childhood to adult status will be affected not only by increasing knowledge (in relation to which children become more like adults with respect to formal style), but also by strongly age-graded attitudes about ingroup communication and by generational changes in norms that remain with the teen-agers when they are adults.

(14) Some primers have simply painted the faces of children for minority readers. A deeper change might entail using names and nicknames actually in use, culture content of interest to the children, but, most important, thematic cores that engage them. Teaching of minority folklore could have both properties of interest to ethnic identity and thematic relevance; on the other

hand, folklore whose themes arise from social conditions which are critically different can be as irrelevant as Dick and Jane and become a historical study but not personally engaging.

At the Social Dialect Conference, it was pointed out that black children like the *Five Chinese Brothers* because they were rewarded for cleverness, which is highly valued in black culture. It was mentioned that *Ping*, about a duck lost from his flock on a Chinese junk, appealed to Navahos. Possibly the metaphor of the duck parallels the flock in Navaho reservation experience. At least, one should not assume that such superficial features as geographical location or skin color in pictures determine the power of materials to engage a child's interest. Verbal games and folklore known to the parents and community resource people who can help develop school materials are not only a direct source of educational content, they can be a springboard to creative parallels to draw on for themes, formal structure, or interactive motives.

(15) A current program for Chicano teachers at Sacramento State College.

GLOSSARY

Categorial shifting. Definition of a register, code, or style contrast in terms of presence or absence rather than relative frequency of speech features.

Co-occurence constraints. Rules governing the predictability of linguistic features of one part of an utterance from another part to produce consistency of style or code.

Copula deletion. Absence of *is* or *are* in speech in some contexts in black English in environments where contraction is possible, according to specific conditioning factors in the linguistic and semantic context.

Exophoric pronouns. Pronouns with an extralinguistic "antecedent."

Inherent variation. Variable frequency of certain speech features like contraction, consonant deletions, syllable deletions contingent on linguistic and social determinants.

Lexical alternatives. Different vocabulary identical in reference but varying with code or register, e.g., bathroom vs. head.

Metaphorical switching. Style changes which have social meanings derived from the similar register or situational variation, e.g., baby talk has a metaphorical meaning that the addressee is loved like a baby or that the speaker is a baby.

Monitoring. Labov: Self-consciousness about speaking, which alters the relative frequencies of socially stigmatized or valued features. Kernan: Speech styles with ethnic identity allusions.

Paralinguistic. Concerning features outside of the conventional linguistic channel, e.g., pitch, rate, loudness, nonspeech vocalizations like laughter and coughs.

Phonology. The sound system of a language or dialect.

Register. (See Unmarked register.)

Relativization. Creation of a relative clause out of two independent predications.

Speech acts. Cultural units in interaction, such as greetings, jokes, requests, demands, praise.

Speech episode. Unit in ongoing interaction demarcated by change in participants, locus, activity, topic, or focus of attention.

Speech event. Cultural unit involving patterned sequences of speech acts, such as a church service, a class, a telephone conversation, a bridge game, storytelling.

Surface structure. The word or sound sequence of a sentence as uttered in contrast to the underlying meaning or to the semantic and grammatical relations the surface represents.

Syntactic nodes. In phrase-structure parsing of a sentence into constituents, nodes are superordinate units which are realized by units closer to the surface. A predicate or verb phrase is a higher node than a preposition or noun.

Unmarked register. The normal, usual speech pattern for a given constellation of setting, participants, and topic.

BIBLIOGRAPHY

[1] Baratz, Joan C. "A Bidialectal Task for Determining Language Proficiency in Economically Disadvantaged Negro Children." *Child Development* 40 (1969): 889-902.

[2] Baratz, Joan C., and Shuy, Roger W., eds. *Teaching Black Children to Read*. Washington: Center for Applied Linguistics 1969.

[3] Bernstein, Basil. "A Socio-linguistic Approach to Socialization: With Some References to Educability." In *Language and Poverty: Perspectives on a Theme*, edited by Frederick Williams, pp. 25-61. Chicago: Markham Publishing Co., 1970.

[4] Blom, J.P., and Gumperz, J.J. "Some Social Determinants of Verbal Behavior." *Directions in Sociolinguistics*, edited by J.J. Gumperz and D. Hymes, New York: Holt, Rinehart & Winston, in press.

[5] Blount, B.G. "Acquisition of Language by Luo Children." Language-Behavior Laboratory Working Paper No. 19. Berkeley: University of California, 1969.

[6] Brooks, Sammie. "A Study of the Rhetorical Styles of Bobby Seale, Chairman of the Black Panther Party for Self-Defense." Term paper, Rhetoric 152, University of California, Berkeley. 1971.

[7] Brown, R.; Cazden, C.B.; and Bellugi, U. "The Child's Grammar from I to III." In *Minnesota Symposia for Child Psychology*, vol. II, edited by J.P. Hill, pp. 28-73. Minneapolis: University of Minnesota Press, 1969.

[8] Cazden, Courtney. "The Neglected Situation in Child Language Research and Education." In *Language and Poverty: Perspectives on a Theme*, edited by Frederick Williams, pp. 81-101. Chicago: Markham Publishing Co., 1970.

[9] Coulthard, R.M., and Robinson, W.P. "The Structure of the Nominal

Group and the Elaboratedness of Code." *Language and Speech* II (1968): 234-50.

[10] Cowan, P. "The Link between Cognitive Structure and Social Structure in Two-Child Verbal Interaction." Symposium presented at the Society for Research on Child Development meeting, 1967.

[11] Edelman, M. "The Contextualization of Schoolchildren's Bilingualism." *Bilingualism in the Barrio*, edited by Joshua Fishman, Robert L. Cooper, Roxana Ma, et al., pp. 525-37. Final Report, Yeshiva University, Contract OEC-17-062817-0297, U.S. Department of Health, Education, and Welfare, 1968.

[12] Ervin-Tripp, Susan M. "An Analysis of the Interaction of Language, Topic, and Listener." In "The Ethnography of Communication," edited by J.J. Gumperz and D. Hymes. *American Anthropologist* 66 (1964): 86-102. (Pt. 2, No. 6.)

[13] ——————————. "Sociolinguistics." In *Advances in Experimental Social Psychology*, vol. 4, edited by Leonard Berkowitz, pp. 91-165. New York: Academic Press, 1968.

[14] Fischer, J.L. "Social Influences in the Choice of a Linguistic Variant." *Word* 14 (1958): 47-56.

[15] Geoghegan, W. "The Use of Marking Rules in Semantic Systems." Language-Behavior Laboratory Working Paper No. 26. Berkeley: University of California, 1969.

[16] Greenlee, Mel. "Rules for Code-Switching: A Pilot Study of Natural Conversation in Bilingual Children." Term paper, Rhetoric 260, University of California, Berkeley, 1971.

[17] Gumperz, J.J. "Linguistic and Social Interaction in Two Communities." In "The Ethnography of Communication," edited by J.J. Gumperz and D. Hymes. *American Anthropologist* 66 (1964): 137-53. (Pt. 2, No. 6).

[18] ——————————. "On the Linguistic Markers of Bilingual Communication." In *Problems of Bilingualism*, edited by J. Macnamara, pp. 48-57. Journal of Social Issues 23 (1967): pt. 2, pp. 48-57.

[19] Gumperz, J.J., and Hernandez, Edward. "Bilingualism, Bidialectalism, and Classroom Interaction." In *Language in the Classroom*, edited by C. Cazden. New York: Teacher's Press, in press.

[20] Gumperz, J.J., and Hymes, D. "The Ethnography of Communication." *American Anthropoligist* 66 (1964): pt. 2, no. 6.

[21] ——————————. *Directions in Sociolinguistics*. New York: Holt, Rinehart & Winston, in press.

[22] Hawkins, P.R. "Social Class, the Nominal Group and Reference." *Language and Speech* 12 (1969): 125-35.

[23] Heider, E. "Style and Effectiveness of Children's Verbal Communications within and between Social Classes." Ph.D. dissertation, Harvard University, 1969.

[24] Henrie, S.N. "A Study of Verb Phrases Used by Five Year Old Nonstandard Negro English Speaking Children." Ph.D. dissertation, University of

California, Berkeley, 1969.)

[25] Houston, Susan. "A Sociolinguistic Consideration of the Black English of Children in Northern Florida." *Language* 45 (1969): 599-607.

[26] ――――――――――. "Syntactic Complexity and Information Transmission in First Graders." *Child Development*, in press.

[27] Hymes, D. "Toward Ethnographies of Communication." In "The Ethnography of Communication," edited by J.J. Gumperz and D. Hymes. *American Anthropoligist* 66 (1964): 1-34. (Pt. 2, No. 6.)

[28] ――――――――――. *On Communicative Competence.* Conduct and Communication, No. 4. Philadelphia: University of Pennsylvania Press, in press.

[29] Jensen, A.R. "How Much Can We Boost IQ and Scholastic Achievement?" *Harvard Educational Review* 39 (1969): 1-124.

[30] Kernan, Claudia M. "Language Behavior in a Black Urban Community." Monographs of the Language-Behavior Laboratory, No. 2. Berkeley: University of California, 1969.

[31] Kernan, Keith. "The Acquisition of Language by Samoan Children." Language-Behavior Laboratory Working Paper No. 21. Berkeley: University of California, 1969.

[32] Kochman, Thomas. " 'Rapping' in the Black Ghetto." *Transactions* (February 1969): 26-34.

[33] Labov, W. "The Logic of Nonstandard English." In *Language and Poverty: Perspectives on a Theme*, edited by Frederick Williams, pp. 153-87. Chicago: Markham Publishing Co., 1970.

[34] ――――――――――. *The Social Stratification of English in New York City.* Washington: Center for Applied Linguistics, 1966.

[35] ――――――――――. "Stages in the Acquisition of Standard English." In *Social Dialects. and Language Learning*, edited by Roger Shuy, pp. 77-103. Champaign, Ill.: National Council of Teachers of English, 1965.

[36] ――――――――――. "The Study of Language in Its Social Context." *Studium Generale*, in press.

[37] Labov, W.; Cohen, P.; Robins, C.; and Lewis, J. *A Study of the Non-Standard English of Negro and Puerto Rican Speakers in New York City.* Final Report, OE-6-10-059. Columbia University, New York City, 1968.

[38] Lenneberg, E. *Biological Foundations of Language.* New York: John Wiley & Sons, 1967.

[39] Lambert, W. "A Social Psychology of Bilingualism." In *Problems of Bilingualism*, edited by J. Macnamara. *Journal of Social Issues* 23 (1967): pt. 2, pp. 91-109.

[40] McKay, June Rumery. "A Partial Analysis of a Variety of Non-standard Negro English." Ph.D. dissertation, University of California, Berkeley, 1969.

[41] Melmed, Paul. "Black English Phonology: The Question of Reading Interference." Ph.D. dissertation, University of California, Berkeley, 1970.

[42] Oishi, Jaynie, and Dorothy Kakimoto. "Pidgin and Pidgin Speakers." Term paper, Speech 164, University of California, Berkeley, 1967.

[43] Osser, H.; Wang, M.; and Zaid, F. "The Young Child's Ability to Imitate and Comprehend Speech: A Comparison of Two Subcultural Groups." *Child Development* 40 (1969): 1063-75.

[44] Price, Eurwen. "Early Bilingualism." In *Towards Bilingualism*, edited by C.J. Dodson, et al., p. 34. Welsh Studies in Education, Vol. 1, edited by Jack L. Williams. Cardiff: University of Wales Press, 1968.

[45] Rainey, Mary. "Style-switching in a Headstart Class." Language-Behavior Laboratory Working Paper No. 16. Berkeley: University of California, 1969.

[46] Roberts, Elsa. "An Evaluation of Standardized Tests as Tools for the Measurement of Language Development." Unpublished paper, Cambridge, Mass.: Language Research Foundation, 1971.

[47] Robinson, W.P. "Social Factors and Language Development in Primary School Children." In *Mechanisms in Child Language Development*, edited by Renira Huxley and Elizabeth Ingram. London: Academic Press, in press.

[48] Shuy, R.; Wolfram, W.; and Riley, W.K. *Linguistic Correlates of Social Stratification in Detroit Speech*. Final Report, OE-6-1347, 1967.

[49] Slobin, D.I., ed. *A Field Manual for Cross-Cultural Study of the Acquisition of Communicative Competence*. University of California, Berkeley, Associated Students' Bookstore, 1967.

[50] Stern, Carolyn, and Keislar, E. *An Experimental Investigation of the Use of Dialect vs. Standard English as a Language of Instruction*. OEO Project IED 66-1-12, 1968.

[51] Stewart, W. "Toward a History of American Negro Dialect." In *Language and Poverty*, edited by F. Williams, pp. 351-79. Chicago: Markham Publishing Co., 1970.

[52] Torrey, Jane. "Teaching Standard English to Speakers of Other Dialects." Second International Congress of Applied Linguistics, Cambridge, England, 1969.

[53] Triandis, H.D.; Loh, W.D.; and Levin, Leslie. "Race, Status, Quality of Spoken English, and Opinions about Civil Rights as Determinants of Interpersonal Attitudes." *Journal of Personality and Social Psychology* 3 (1966): 468-72.

[54] Tucker, R., and Lambert, W. "White and Negro Listeners' Reactions to Various American-English Dialects." *Social Forces* 47 (1969): 463-68.

[55] Waterhouse, J. "Report on a Neighborhood Youth Corps Summer Language Program, July 1-August 2, 1968." University of California, Berkeley. Mimeographed.

[56] Weener, P.D. "Social Dialect Differences and the Recall of Verbal Messages." *Journal of Educational Psychology* 60 (1969): 194-99.

[57] Williams, F. "Psychological Correlates of Speech Characteristics: On Sounding Disadvantaged." *Journal of Speech and Hearing Research*, in press.

[58] Williams, F., and Naremore, Rita C. "On the Functional Analysis of Social Class Differences in Modes of Speech." *Speech Monographs* 36 (1969): 77-101.

[59] Wolfram, W. *Detroit Negro Speech*. Washington: Center for Applied Linguistics, 1969.

CULTURAL DIFFERENCES AND INFERENCES ABOUT PSYCHOLOGICAL PROCESSES

Michael Cole

Jerome S. Bruner

Perhaps the most prevalent view of the source of ethnic and social class differences in intellectual performance is what might be summed up under the label "the deficit hypothesis." It can be stated briefly, without risk of gross exaggeration. It rests on the assumption that a community under conditions of poverty (for it is the poor who are the focus of attention, and a disproportionate number of the poor are members of minority ethnic groups) is a disorganized community, and this disorganization expresses itself in various forms of deficit. One widely agreed-upon source of deficit is mothering; the child of poverty is assumed to lack adequate parental attention. Given the illegitimacy rate in the urban ghetto, the most conspicuous "deficit" is a missing father and, consequently, a missing father model. The mother is away at work or, in any case, less involved with raising her children than she should be by white middle-class standards. There is said to be less regularity, less mutuality in interaction with her. There are said to be specialized deficits in interaction as well—less guidance in goal seeking from the parents (Schoggen, 1969), less emphasis upon means and ends in maternal instruction (Hess & Shipman, 1965), or less positive and more negative reinforcement (Bee, Van Egeren, Streissguth, Nyman & Leckie, 1969; Smilansky, 1968).

More particularly, the deficit hypothesis has been applied to the symbolic and linguistic environment of the growing child. His linguistic community as portrayed in the early work of Basil Bernstein (1961), for example, is characterized by a restricted code, dealing more in the stereotype of interaction than in language that explains and elaborates upon social and material events.

The games that are played by poor children and to which they are exposed are less strategy bound than those of more advantaged children (Eifermann, 1968); their homes are said to have a more confused noise background, permitting less opportunity for figure-ground formation (Klaus & Gray, 1968); and the certainty of the environment is sufficiently reduced so that children have difficulty in delaying reinforcement (Mischel, 1966) or in accepting verbal reinforcement instead of the real article (Zigler & Butterfield, 1968).

The theory of intervention that grew from this view was the idea of "early stimulation," modeled on a conception of supplying nutriment for those with a protein deficiency or avitaminosis. The nature of the needed early stimulation was never explained systematically, save in rare cases (Smilansky, 1968), but it variously took the form of practice in using abstractions (Blank & Solomon, 1969), in having dialogue where the referent objects were not present, as through the use of telephones (Deutsch, 1967; John & Goldstein, 1964), or in providing secure mothering by substitution (Caldwell et al., 1970; Klaus & Gray, 1968).

A primary result of these various deficits was believed to express itself in the lowered test scores and academic performance among children from poverty backgrounds. The issue was most often left moot as to whether or not this lowered test performance was easily reversible, but the standard reference was to a monograph by Bloom (1964) indicating that cognitive performance on a battery of tests, given to poor and middle-class children, yielded the result that nearly 80% of the variance in intellectual performance was accounted for by age 3.

DIFFERENCE INTERPRETATION

Such data seem to compel the conclusion that as a consequence of various factors arising from minority group status (factors affecting motivation, linguistic ability, goal orientation, hereditary proclivities to learn in certain ways—the particular mix of factors depends on the writer), minority group children suffer intellectual deficits when compared with their "more advantaged" peers.

In this section, we review a body of data and theory that controverts this contention, casts doubt on the conclusion that a deficit exists in minority group children, and even raises doubts as to whether any nonsuperficial differences exist among different cultural groups.

There are two long-standing precedents for the view that different groups (defined in terms of cultural, linguistic, and ethnic criteria) do not differ intellectually from each other in any important way. (It is assumed here that it is permissible to speak of minority group or poverty group "culture" using as our criterion Lévi-Strauss' (1963) definition: "What is called 'culture' is a fragment of humanity which, from the point of view of the research at hand . . . presents significant discontinuities in relation to the rest of humanity [p. 295]." We do not intend to enter into arguments over the existence or nature of a "culture of poverty," although such an idea seems implicit in the view of most deficit theorists.) First, there is the anthropological "doctrine of psychic unity" (Kroeber, 1948) which, on the basis of the "run of total experience," is said to warrant the assumption of intellectual equality as a sufficient approximation to the truth. This view is compatible with current linguistic anthropological theorizing, which concentrates on describing the way in which different cultural/linguistic groups categorize familiar areas of experience (Tyler, 1970). By this view, different conclusions about the world are the result of arbitrary and different, but equally logical, ways of cutting up the world of experience. From this perspective, descriptions of the "disorganization" of minorities would be highly suspect, this suspicion arising in connection with questions like, Disorganized from whose point of view?

Anthropological critiques of psychological experimentation have never carried much weight with psychologists, nor have anthropologists been very impressed with conclusions from psychological tests. We have hypothesized elsewhere (Cole, Gay, Glick, & Sharp, 1971) that their mutual indifference stems in part from a difference in opinion about the inferences that are warranted from testing and experimentation, and in part because the anthropologist relies mainly on data that the psychologist completely fails to consider: the mundane social life of the people he studies. As we shall see, these issues carry over into our criticism of the "deficit" theory of cultural deprivation.

A second tradition that calls into question culturally determined group difference in intelligence is the linguist's assertion that languages do not differ in their degree of development (Greenberg, 1963), buttressed by the transformationalist's caution that one cannot attribute to people a cognitive capacity that is less than is required to produce the complex rule-governed activity called language (Chomsky, 1966).

Although Chomskian linguistics has had a profound effect on psychological theories of language and cognitive development in recent years, psychological views of language still are considered hopelessly inadequate by working linguists. This criticism applies not only to psycholinguistic theory but to the actual description of linguistic performance on which theory is based. Needless to say, the accusation of misunderstanding at the descriptive level leads to accusations of absurdity at the theoretical level.

A third tradition that leads to rejection of the deficit theory has many sources in recent social sciences. This view holds that even when attempts have been made to provide reasonable anthropological and linguistic foundations, the conclusions about cognitive capacity from psychological experiments are unfounded because the performance produced represents a complex interaction of the formal characteristics of the experiment and the social/environmental context that determines the subject's interpretation of the situation in which it occurs. The need for "situation-bound" interpretations of experiments is emphasized in such diverse sources as sociology (Goffman, 1964) psychology (Brunswik, 1958), and psycholinguistics (Cazden, 1970). This is an important issue, which we will return to once illustrations of the "antideficit" view have been explored.

Perhaps the most coherent denial of the deficit position, coupled with compelling illustrations of the resourcefulness of the supposedly deprived and incompetent person, is contained in Labov's attack on the concept of "linguistic deprivation" and its accompanying assumption of cognitive incapacity (Labov, 1970).

It is not possible here to review all of Labov's evidence. Rather, we have abstracted what we take to be the major points in his attack.

1. *An assertion of the functional equality of all languages.* This assertion is applied specifically to his analysis of nonstandard Negro English, which has been the object of his study for several years. Labov provided a series of examples where young blacks who would be assessed as linguistically retarded and academically hopeless by standard test procedures enter conversations in a way that leaves little doubt that they can speak perfectly adequately and produce very clever arguments in the process.

2. *An assertion of the psychologist's ignorance of language in general and nonstandard dilects in particular.* Labov's particular target is Carl Bereiter (Bereiter & Englemann, 1966) whose remedial teaching technique is partly rationalized in terms of the inability of young black children to use language either as an effective tool of communication or thinking. Part of Labov's attack is aimed at misinterpretations of such phrases as "They mine," which Labov analyzed in terms of rules of contraction, but which Bereiter made the mistake of referring to as a "series of badly connected words [Labov, 1970, p. 171]." This "psychologist's deficit" has a clear remedy. It is roughly equivalent to the anthropological caveat that the psychologist has to know more about the people he studies.

3. *The inadequacy of present experimentation.* More serious criticism of the psychologist's interpretation of "language deprivation" and, by extension, his whole concept of "cultural deprivation" is contained in the following, rather extensive quote:

> this and the preceeding section are designed to convince the reader that the controlled experiments that have been offered in evidence [of Negro lack of competence] are misleading. The only thing that is controlled is the superficial form of the stimulus. All children are asked, "What do you think of capital punishment?" or "Tell me everything you can about this." But the speaker's interpretation of these requests, and the action he believes is appropriate in response is completely uncontrolled. One can view these test stimuli as requests for information, commands for action, or meaningless sequences of words. . . . With human subjects it is absurd to believe that identical stimuli are obtained by asking everyone the same question. Since the crucial intervening variables of interpretation and motivation are uncontrolled, most of the literature on verbal deprivation tells us nothing of the capacities of children [Labov, 1970, p. 171].

Here Labov is attacking the experimental method as usually applied to the problem of subcultural differences in cognitive capacity. We can abstract several assertions from this key passage: (a) Formal experimental equivalence of operations does not insure de facto equivalence of experimental treatments; (b) different subcultural groups are predisposed to interpret the experimental stimuli (situations) differently; (c) different subcultural groups are motivated by different concerns relevant to the experimental task; (d) in view of the inadequacies of experimentation, inferences about lack of competence among black children are unwarranted.

These criticisms, when combined with linguistic misinterpretation, constitute Labov's attack on the deficit theory of cultural deprivation and represent the rationale underlying his demonstrations of competence where its lack had previously been inferred.

One example of Labov's approach is to conduct a rather standard interview of the type often used for assessment of language competence. The situation is designed to be minimally threatening; the interviewer is a neighborhood figure, and black. Yet, the black 8-year-old interviewee's behavior is monosyllabic. He is a candidate for the diagnosis of linguistically and culturally deprived.

But this diagnosis is very much situation dependent. For at a later time, this same interviewer goes to the boy's apartment, brings one of the boy's friends with him, lies down on the floor, and produces some potato chips. He then begins talking about clearly taboo subjects in dialect. Under these circumstances, the mute interviewee becomes an excited participant in the general conversation.

In similar examples, Labov demonstrated powerful reasoning and debating skills in a school dropout and nonlogical verbosity in an acceptable, "normal" black who has mastered the forms of standard English. Labov's conclusion is that the usual assessment situations, including IQ and reading tests, elicit deliberate, defensive behavior on the part of the child who has realistic expectations that to talk openly is to expose oneself to insult and harm. As a consequence, such situations cannot measure the child's competence. Labov went even further to assert that far from being verbally deprived, the typical ghetto child is

> bathed in verbal stimulation from morning to night. We see many speech events which depend upon the competitive exhibition of verbal skills—sounding, singing, toasts, rifting, louding—a whole range of activities in which the individual gains status through the use of language. . . . We see no connection between the verbal skill in the speech events characteristic of the street culture and success in the school room [Labov, 1970, p. 163].

Labov is not the only linguist to offer such a critique of current theories of cultural deprivation (see, e.g., Stewart, 1970). However, Labov's criticism raises larger issues concerning the logic of comparative research designs of which the work in cultural/linguistic deprivation is only a part. It is to this general question that we now turn.

The major thrusts of Labov's argument, that situational factors are important components of psychological experiments and that it is difficult if not impossible to infer competence directly from performance, are not new ideas to psychologists. Indeed, a concern with the relation between *psychological processes* on the one hand and *situational factors* on the other has long been a kind of shadow issue in psychology, surfacing most often in the context of comparative research.

It is this question that underlies the oft-berated question, What do IQ tests measure? and has been prominent in attacks on Jensen's (1969) argument that group differences in IQ test performance are reflective of innate differences in capacity.

Kagan (1969), for example, pointed to the work of Palmer, who regularly delays testing until the child is relaxed and has established rapport with the tester. Jensen (1969, p. 100) himself reported that significant differences in test performance can be caused by differential adaptation to the test situation.

Hertzig, Birch, Thomas, and Mendez (1968) made a direct study of social class/ethnic differences in response to the test situation and demonstrated stable differences in situational resposnes that were correlated with test performance and were present even when measured IQ was equivalent for subgroups chosen from the major comparison groups.

Concern with the particular *content* of tests and experiments as they relate to inferences about cognitive capacity occurs within the same context. The search for a "culture-free" IQ test has emphasized the use of universally familiar material, and various investigators have found that significant differences in performance can be related to the content of the experimental materials. Price-Williams (1961), for example, demonstrated earlier acquisition of conservation concepts in Nigerian children using traditional instead of imported stimulus materials, and Gay and Cole (1967) made a similar point with respect to Liberian classification behavior and learning.

Contemporary psychology's awareness of the task and situation-specific determinants of performance is reflected in a recent article by Kagan and Kogan (1970). In a section of their paper titled "The Significance of Public Performance," they are concerned with the fact that "differences in quality of style of public performance, although striking, may be misleading indices of competence [p. 1322]."

Although such misgivings abound, they have not yet crystallized into a coherent program of research and theory nor have the implications of accepting the need to incorporate an analysis of situations in addition to traditional experimental manipulations been fully appreciated.

EXTENDED IDEA OF COMPETENCE

Labov and others have argued forcefully that we cannot distinguish on the basis of traditional experimental approaches between the underlying competence of those who have had a poor opportunity to participate in a particular culture and those who have had a good opportunity, between those who have not had their share of wealth and respect and those who have. The crux of the argument, when applied to the problem of "cultural deprivation," is that those groups ordinarily diagnosed as culturally deprived have the same underlying competence as those in the mainstream of the dominant culture, *the differences in performance being accounted for by the situations and contexts in which the competence is expressed.* To put the matter most rigorously, one can find a corresponding situation in which the member of the "out culture," the victim of poverty, can perform on the basis of a given competence in a fashion equal to or superior to the standard achieved by a member of the dominant culture.

A prosaic example taken from the work of Gay and Cole (1967) concerns the ability to make estimates of volume. The case in question is to estimate the number of cups of rice in each of several bowls. Comparisons of "rice-estimation accuracy" were made among several groups of subjects, including nonliterate Kpelle rice farmers from North Central Liberia and Yale sophomores. The rice farmers manifested significantly greater accuracy than the Yale students, the difference increasing with the amount of rice presented for estimation. In many other situations, measurement skills are found to be superior among educated subjects in the Gay and Cole study. Just as Kpelle superiority at making rice estimates is clearly not a universal manifestation of their superior underlying competence, the superiority of Yale students in, for example, distance judgments is no basis for inferring that their competence is superior.

We think the existence of demonstrations such as those presented by Labov has been salutary in forcing closer examination of testing situations used for comparing the children of poverty with their more advantaged peers. And, as the illustration from Gay and Cole suggests, the argument may have quite general implications. Obviously, it is not sufficient to use a simple equivalence-of-test procedure to make inferences about the competence of the two groups being compared. In fact, a "two-groups" design is almost useless for making any important inferences in cross-cultural research, as Campbell (1961) has suggested. From a logical view, however, the conclusion of equal cognitive competence in those who are not members of the prestige culture and those who are its beneficiaries is often equally unwarranted. While it is very proper to criticize the logic of assuming that poor performance implies lack of competence, the contention that poor performance is of *no* relevance to a theory of cognitive development and to a theory of cultural differences in cognitive development also seems an oversimplification.

Assuming that we can find test situations in which comparably good performance can be elicited from the groups being contrasted, there is plainly an issue having to do with the range and nature of the situations in which performance for any two groups can be found to be equal.

We have noted Labov's conclusion that the usual assessment of linguistic competence in the black child elicits deliberate defensive behavior and that he can respond effectively in familiar nonthreatening surroundings. It may be, however (this possibility is discussed in Bruner, 1970), that he is unable to

utilize language of a decentered type, taken out of the context of social
interaction, used in an abstract way to deal with hypothetical possibilities and to
spell out hypothetical plans (see also Gladwin, 1970). If such were the case, we
could not dismiss the question of different kinds of language usage by saying
simply that decontextualized talk is not part of the natural milieu of the black
child in the urban ghetto. If it should turn out to be the case that mastery of the
culture depends on one's capacity to perform well on the basis of competence
one has stored up, and to perform well in particular settings and in particular
ways, then plainly the question of differences in the way language enters the
problem-solving process cannot be dismissed. It has been argued, for example, by
Bernstein (1970) that it is in the nature of the very social life of the urban
ghetto that there develops a kind of particularism in which communication
usually takes place only along concrete personal lines. The ghetto child, who by
training is likely to use an idiosyncratic mode of communication, may become
locked into the life of his own cultural group, and his migration into other
groups consequently becomes the more difficult. Bernstein made clear in his
most recent work that this is not a question of capacity but, rather, a matter of
what he calls "orientation." Nevertheless, it may very well be that a ghetto
dweller's language training unfits him for taking jobs in the power- and
prestige-endowing pursuits of middle-class culture. If such is the case, then the
issue of representativeness of the situations to which he can apply his
competence becomes something more than a matter of test procedure.

A major difficulty with this line of speculation is that at present we have
almost no knowledge of the day-to-day representativeness of different situations
and the behaviors that are seen as appropriate to them by different cultural
groups. For example, the idea that language use must be considered outside of
social interactions in order to qualify as abstract, as involving "cognition," is
almost certainly a psychologist's fiction. The work of contemporary sociologists
and ethnolinguists (Garfinkle, 1967; Hymes, 1966; Schegloff, 1968) seems
conclusively to demonstrate the presence of complex contingent thinking in
situations that are all too often characterized by psychologists as consisting of
syncretic, affective interactions. Until we have better knowledge of the cognitive
components that are part of social interactions (the same applies to many
spheres of activity), speculations about the role of language in cognition will
have to remain speculations.

In fact, it is extraordinarily difficult to know, save in a most superficial way,
on the basis of our present knowledge of society, what is the nature of situations
that permit control and utilization of the resources of a culture by one of its
members and what the cognitive skills are that are demanded of one who would
use these resources. It may very well be that the very definition of a subculture
could be put into the spirit of Lévi-Strauss' (1963) definition of a culture:

> What is called a subculture is a fragment of a culture which from the point
> of view of the research at hand presents significant discontinuities in
> relation to the rest of that culture with respect to access to its major
> amplifying tools.

By an amplifying tool is meant a technological feature, be it soft or hard, that permits control by the individual of resources, prestige, and deference within the culture. An example of a middle-class cultural amplifier that operates to increase the thought processes of those who employ it is the discipline loosely referred to as "mathematics." To employ mathematical techniques requires the cultivation of certain skills of reasoning, even certain styles of deploying one's thought processes. If one were able to cultivate the strategies and styles relevant to the employment of mathematics, then that range of technology is open to one's use. If one does not cultivate mathematical skills, the result is "functional incompetence," an inability to use this kind of technology. Whether or not compensatory techniques can then correct "functional incompetence" is an important, but unexplored, question.

Any particular aspect of the technology requires certain skills for its successful use. These skills, as we have already noted, must also be deployable in the range of situations where they are useful. Even if a child could carry out the planning necessary for the most technically demanding kind of activity, he must not do so if he has been trained with the expectancy that the exercise of such a skill will be punished or will, in any event, lead to some unforeseen difficulty. Consequently, the chances that the individual will work up his capacities for performance in the given domain are diminished. As a result, although the individual can be shown to have competence in some sphere involving the utilization of the skill, he will not be able to express that competence in the relevant kind of context. In an absolute sense, he is any man's equal, but in everyday encounters, he is not up to the task.

The principle cuts both ways with respect to cultural differences. Verbal skills are important cultural "amplifiers" among Labov's subejcts; as many middle-class school administrators have discovered, the ghetto resident skilled in verbal exchanges is a more than formidable opponent in the battle for control of school curriculum and resources. In like manner, the Harlem youth on the street who cannot cope with the verbal battles described by Labov is failing to express competence in a context relevant to the ghetto.

These considerations impress us with the need to clarify our notion of what the competencies are that underlie effective performance. There has been an implicit, but very general, tendency in psychology to speak as if the organism is an information-processing machine with a fixed set of routines. The number and organization of these routines might differ as a function of age, genetic makeup, or environmental factors, but for any given machine, the input to the machine is processed uniformly by the routines (structures, skills) of the organism.

Quite recently, psychologists have started to face up to the difficulties of assuming "all things are equal" for different groups of people (concern has focused on difference in age, but the same logic applies to any group comparisons). The study of situational effects on performance has forced a re-evaluation of traditional theoretical inferences about competence. This new concern with the interpretation of psychological experiments is quite apparent in recent attempts to cope with data inconsistent with Piaget's theory of cognitive development. For example, Flavell and Wohlwill (1969) sought to distinguish between two kinds of competence: First, there are "the rules, structures, or 'mental operations' embodied in the task and . . . [second, there are] the actual mechanisms required for processing the input and output [p. 98]." The second factor is assumed to be task specific and is the presumed explanation for such facts as the "horizontal decalages" in which the same principle appears for different materials at different ages. The *performance* progression through various stages is presumably a reflection of increases in both kinds of competence, since both are assumed to increase with age.

The same general concern is voiced by Mehler and Bever (1968). They ask,

> How can we decide if a developmental change or behavioral difference among adults is really due to a difference in a structural rule, to a difference in the form of the expressive processes or a difference in their quantitative capacity [p. 278] ?

Their own work traces the expression of particular rules in behavior and the way the effect of knowing a rule ("having a competence") interacts with dependence on different aspects of the input to produce "nonlinear trends" in the development of conservation-like performance.

Broadening psychological theory to include rules for applying cognitive skills, as well as statements about the skills themselves, seems absolutely necessary.

However, the extensions contemplated may well not be sufficient to meet all of Labov's objections to inferences about "linguistic deprivation." In both the position expressed by Flavell and Wohlwill and by Mehler and Bever, "competence" is seen as dependent on situational factors and seems to be a slowly changing process that might well be governed by the same factors that lead to increases in the power of the structural rules or competence, in the older sense of the word. Yet in Labov's example, the problem is considerably more ephemeral; Labov gives the impression that the subjects were engaged in rational problem solving and that they had complete control over their behavior. He is claiming, in effect, that they are successfully coping with *their* problem; it simply is not the problem the experimenter had in mind, so the experimenter claims lack of competence as a result of his own ignorance.

Acceptance of Labov's criticisms, and we think they should be accepted, requires not only a broadening of our idea of competence, but a vast enrichment of our approach to experimentation.

NECESSITY OF A COMPARATIVE PSYCHOLOGY OF COGNITION

If we accept the idea that situational factors are often important determinants of psychological performance, and if we also accept the idea that different cultural groups are likely to respond differently to any given situation, there seems to be no reasonable alternative to psychological experimentation that bases its inferences on data from comparisons of both experimental and situational variations.

In short, we are contending that Brunswik's (1958) call for "representative design" and an analysis of the "ecological significance" of stimulation is a prerequisite to research on ethnic and social class differences in particular, and to any research where the groups to be compared are thought to differ with respect to the process under investigation prior to application of the experimental treatments.

Exhortations to the effect that college sophomores with nonsense syllables and white rats in boxes are not sufficient objects for the development of a general psychological theory have produced, thus far, only minor changes in the behavior of psychologists. The present situations seem to *require* a change.

An illustration from some recent cross-cultural research serves as an illustration of one approach that goes beyond the usual two-group design to explore the situational nature of psychological performance.

Cole et al. (1971, p. 4) used the free-recall technique to study cultural differences in memory. The initial studies presented subjects with a list of 20 words divided into four familiar, easily distinguishable categories. Subjects were read the list of words and asked to recall them. The procedure was repeated five times for each subject. A wide variety of subject populations was studied in this way; Liberian rice farmers and school children were the focus of concern, but comparison with groups in the United States was also made.

Three factors of the Kpelle rice farmers' performance were remarkable in these first studies: (*a*) The number recalled was relatively small (9-11 items per list); (*b*) there was no evidence of semantic or other organization of the material; (*c*) there was little or no increase in the number recalled with successive trials.

Better recall, great improvement with trials, and significant organization are all characteristic of performance of the American groups above the fifth grade.

A series of standard experimental manipulations (offering incentives, using lists based on functional rather than semantic classes, showing the objects to be remembered, extending the number of trials) all failed to make much difference in Kpelle performance.

However, when these same to-be-recalled items were incorporated into folk stories, when explicit grouping procedures were introduced, or when seemingly bizarre cuing procedures were used, Kpelle performance manifested organization, showed vast improvements in terms of amount recalled, and gave a very different picture of underlying capacity. Cole et al. (1971) concluded that a set of rather specific skills associated with remembering disconnected material out of context underlies the differences observed in the standard versions of the free-recall experiment with which they began. Moreover, they were able to begin the job of pinpointing these skills, their relevance to traditional activities, and the teaching techniques that could be expected to bring existing memory skills to bear in the "alien" tasks of the school.

CONCLUSION

The arguments set forth in this study can now be brought together and generalized in terms of their bearing on psychological research that is "comparative" in nature—comparing ages, cultures, subcultures, species, or even groups receiving different experimental treatments.

The central thesis derives from a reexamination of the distintion between competence and performance. As a rule, one looks for performance at its best and infers the degree of underlying competence from the observed performance. With respect to linguistic competence, for example, a single given instance of a particular grammatical form could suffice for inferring that the speaker had the competence to generate such instances as needed. By the use of such a methodology, Labov demonstrated that culturally deprived black children, *tested appropriately* for optimum performance, have the same grammatical competence as middle-class whites, though it may be expressed in different settings. Note that negative evidence is mute with respect to the status of underlying capacity—it may require a different situation for its manifestation.

The psychological status of the concept of competence (or capacity) is brought deeply into question when one examines conclusions based on standard experiments. Competence so defined is both situation blind and culture blind. If performance is treated (as it often is by linguists) only as a shallow expression of deeper competence, then one inevitably loses sight of the ecological problem of performance. For one of the most important things about any "underlying competence" is the nature of the situations in which it expresses itself. Herein lies the crux of the problem. One must inquire, first, whether a competence is expressed in a particular situation and, second, what the significance of that situation is for the person's ability to cope with life in his own milieu. As we have had occasion to comment elsewhere, when we systematically study the situational determinants of performance, we are led to conclude that cultural differences reside more in differences in the situations to which different cultural groups apply their skills than to differences in the skills possessed by the groups in question (Cole et al., 1971, Ch. 7).

The problem is to identify the range of capacities readily manifested in different groups and then to inquire whether the range is adequate to the individual's needs in various cultural settings. From this point of view, cultural *deprivation* represents a special case of cultural *difference* that arises when an individual is faced with demands to perform in a manner inconsistent with his past (cultural) experience. In the present social context of the United States, the great power of the middle class has rendered differences into deficits because middle-class behavior is the yardstick of success.

Our analysis holds at least two clear implications of relevance to the classroom teacher charged with the task of educating children from "disadvantaged" subcultural groups.

First, recognition of the educational difficulties in terms of a *difference* rather than a special kind of intellectual disease should change the students' status in the eyes of the teacher. If Pygmalion really can work in the classroom (Rosenthal & Jacobson, 1968), the effect of this change in attitude may of itself produce changes in performance. Such difference in teacher attitude seems to be one prime candidate for an explanation of the fine performance obtained by

Kohl (1967) and others with usually recalcitrant students.

Second, the teacher should stop laboring under the impression that he must create new intellectual structures and start concentrating on how to get the child to *transfer* skills he already possesses to the task at hand. It is in this context that "relevant" should mean something more than a way to motivate students. Rather, relevant materials are those to which the child already applies skills the teacher seeks to have applied to his own content. It requires more than a casual acquaintance with one's students to know what those materials are.

The Soviet psychologist, Lev Vygotskii (1962), took as the motto of his well-known monograph on language and thought an epigraph from Francis Bacon: Neither hand nor mind alone, left to themselves, amounts to much; instruments and aids are the means to perfection (*Nec manus nisi intellectus sibi permissus multam valent; instrumentibus et auxilibus res perficitur*). Psychologists concerned with comparative research, and comparisons of social and ethnic group differences in particular, must take seriously the study of the way different groups organize the relation between their hands and minds; without assuming the superiority of one system over another, they must take seriously the dictum that man is a cultural animal. When cultures are in competition for resources, as they are today, the psychologist's task is to analyze the source of cultural difference so that those of the minority, the less powerful group, may quickly acquire the intellectual instruments necessary for success of the dominant culture, should they so choose.

REFERENCES

Bee, H.L., Van Egeren, L.F., Streissguth, A.P., Nyman, B.A., & Leckie, M.S. Social class differences in maternal teaching strategies and speech patterns. Developmental Psychology, 1969, 1, 726-734.

Bereiter, C., & Englemann, S. Teaching disadvantaged children in the preschool. Englewood Cliffs, N.J.: Prentice-Hall, 1966.

Bernstein, B. Social class and linguistic development: A theory of social learning. In A.H. Halsey, J. Floyd, & C.A. Anderson (Eds.), Education, economy and society. Glencoe, Ill.: Free Press, 1961.

Bernstein, B. A sociolinguistic approach to socialization: With some references to educability. In F. Williams (Ed.), Language and poverty. Chicago: Markham, 1970.

Blank, M., & Solomon, F. A tutorial language program to develop abstract thinking in socially disadvantaged preschool children. Child Development, 1969, 40, 47-61.

Bloom, B.S. Stability and change in human characteristics. New York: Wiley, 1964.

Bruner, J.S. Poverty and childhood. Merrill-Palmer Institute Monographs, 1970.

Brunswik, E. Representative design in the planning of psychological research. Berkeley: University of California Press, 1958.

Caldwell, B.M., et al. Infant day care and attachment. American Journal of Orthopsychiatry, 1970, 40, 397-412.

Campbell, D. The mutual methodological relevance of anthropology and psychology. In F.L.K. Hsu (Ed.), Psychological anthropology. Homewood, Ill.: Dorsey Press, 1961.

Cazden, C. The neglected situation. In F. Williams (Ed.), Language and poverty. Chicago: Markham Press, 1970.

Chomsky, N. Cartesian linguistics. New York: Harper & Row, 1966.

Cole, M., Gay, J., Glick, J., & Sharp, D.W. The cultural context of learning and thinking. New York: Basic Books, 1971.

Deutsch, M. The disadvantaged child. New York: Basic Books, 1967.

Eifermann, R. School children's games. Washington, D.C.: Department of Health, Education, and Welfare, 1968.

Flavell, J.H., & Wohlwill, J.F. Formal and functional aspects of cognitive development. In D. Elkind & J.H. Flavell (Eds.), Studies in cognitive development. New York: Oxford University Press, 1969.

Garfinkle, H. Studies in ethnomethodology. Englewood Cliffs, N.J.: Prentice-Hall, 1967.

Gay, J., & Cole, M. The new mathematics and an old culture. New York: Holt, Rinehart & Winston, 1967.

Gladwin, T. East is a big bird. Cambridge: Belnap Press, 1970.

Goffman, E. The neglected situation. In J. Gumperz & D. Hymes (Eds.), The ethnology of communication. American Anthropologist, 1964, 66 (6, Pt. 2), 133.

Greenberg, J. Universals of language. Cambridge: M.I.T. Press, 1963.

Hertzig, M.E., Birch, H.G., Thomas, A., & Mendez, O.A. Class and ethnic differences in the responsiveness of preschool children to cognitive demands. Monographs of the Society for Research in Child Development, 1968, 33(1, Serial No. 117).

Hess, R.D., & Shipman, V. Early experience and socialization of cognitive modes in children. Child Development, 1965, 36, 869-886.

Hymes, D. On communicative competence. (Report of a Conference on Research Planning on Language Development among Disadvantaged Children) New York: Yeshiva University Press, 1966.

Jensen, A. How much can we boost IQ and scholastic achievement? Harvard Educational Review, 1969, 39, 1-123.

John, V.P., & Goldstein, L.S. The social context of language acquisition. Merrill-Palmer Quarterly, 1964, 10, 265-275.

Kagan, J. Inadequate evidence and illogical conclusions. Harvard Educational Review, 1969, 39, 274-277.

Kagan, J., & Kogan, N. Individuality and cognitive performance. In P. Mussen (Ed.), Manual of child psychology. New York: Wiley, 1970.

Klaus, R., & Gray, S. The early training project for disadvantaged children: A report after five years. Monographs of the Society for Research in Child Development, 1968, 33(4).

Kohl, H. 36 children. New York: New American Library, 1967.

Kroeber, A.L. Anthropology. New York: Harcourt, Brace, 1948.

Labov, W. The logical non-standard English. In F. Williams (Ed.), Language and poverty. Chicago: Markham Press, 1970.

Levi-Strauss, C. Structural anthropology. New York: Basic Books, 1963.

Mehler, J., & Bever, T. The study of competence in cognitive psychology. International Journal of Psychology, 1968, 3, 273-280.

Mischel, W. Theory and research on the antecedents of self-imposed delay of reward. In Progress in experimental personality research. Vol. 3. New York: Academic Press, 1966.

Price-Williams, D.R.A. A study concerning concepts of conservation of quantities among primitive children. Acta Psychologia, 1961, 18, 297-305.

Rosenthal, R., & Jacobson, L. Pygmalion in the classroom. New York: Holt, Rinehart & Winston, 1968.

Schegloff, E.A. Sequencing in conversational openings. American Anthropologist, 1968, 70, 1075-1095.

Schoggen, M. An ecological study of three-year-olds at home. Nashville, Tenn.: George Peabody College for Teachers, November 7, 1969.

Smilansky, S. The effect of certain learning conditions on the progress of disadvantaged children of kindergarten age. Journal of School Psychology, 1968, 4(3), 68-81.

Stewart, W.A. Toward a history of American Negro dialect. In F. Williams (Ed.), Language and poverty. Chicago: Markham Press, 1970.

Tyler, S. Cognitive anthropology. New York: Holt, Rinehart & Winston, 1970.

Vygotskii, L.S. Thought and speech. Cambridge: M.I.T. Press, 1962.

Zigler, E., & Butterfield, E. Motivational aspects of changes in IQ test performance of culturally deprived nursery school children. Child Development, 1968, 39, 1-14.

PATTERNS OF MENTAL ABILITIES:
ETHNIC, SOCIOECONOMIC, AND
SEX DIFFERENCES

Margaret E. Backman

Past research has shown that males and females exhibit characteristic patterns of mental abilities; however, comparatively few studies have considered the patterns of mental abilities that distinguish different ethnic and socioeconomic groups (Anastasi, 1958).

One such study, conducted by Lesser, Fifer, and Clark (1965) found characteristic patterns of mental abilities for first grade children from different ethnic backgrounds (Chinese, Jewish, Negro, and Puerto Rican). The ethnic patterns differed in shape and average level. Socioeconomic status (SES) was not related to the shape of the patterns, but those of higher SES tended to have higher mean scores on the mental ability tests. A replication study (Stodolsky and Lesser, 1967) confirmed these results on a sample of Negro and Chinese first graders; however, no common ethnic pattern emerged for samples of lower- and middle-class Irish-Catholics.

It was felt that examining the patterns of mental abilities of students beyond the first grade would contribute to the understanding of the development of mental abilities. Thus, the present study was designed to investigate the relationships of ethnicity, SES, and sex to patterns of mental abilities of adolescents.

SUBJECTS

The subjects were 2,925 twelfth grade students from among those who had participated in Project TALENT, a study of 4.5% of the U.S. students in grades

9 through 12 in the spring of 1960 (Schoenfeldt, 1968). Approximately 100,000 students in each grade had been given a two-day battery of tests and inventories gathering information on their abilities, interest, and backgrounds.

The present sample was restricted to those who had responded to a follow-up survey five years after graduation, as information on ethnic background was not collected until that time. The sample was composed of 1,236 Jewish-whites, 1,051 non-Jewish-whites, 488 Negroes, and 150 Orientals.

SES was defined by the Project TALENT Socioeconomic Environment Index (Flanagan, Cooley, Lohnes, Schoenfeldt, Holdeman, Combs and Becker, 1966; Shaycoft, 1967). The Index has a mean of 100 and a standard deviation of 10 for twelfth graders, and reflects father's education and occupation, mother's education, family income, value of the home, and number of specific facilities and economic goods in the home, such as a television set, radio, and typewriter.

Data had originally been obtained from Project TALENT for a sample of 3,086 respondents: This included only those for whom information on all essential variables was available; since a large majority of the students were non-Jewish-white, data were obtained for only a 5% sample of that group. As there were only a small number of students at the extreme ends of the SES scale, it was not considered feasible to make comparisons of extreme SES groups. Also, although the SES distributions of the ethnic groups overlapped, the Jewish whites tended to be displaced toward the upper end of the SES scale and the Negroes toward the lower end. To control for differences in SES the analysis was restricted to those in the middle range of the SES scale. The resulting sample of 2,925 students was divided into two groups: upper-middle SES and lower-middle SES, which covered 80-99 and 100-119 respectively on the SES scale.

PATTERNS OF MENTAL ABILITIES

Factor analysis of 60 information, achievement, and aptitude tests administered to the students in Project TALENT had yielded 11 orthogonal ability factors (Lohnes, 1966). Factor scores are reported on a scale with a mean of 50 and standard deviation of 10 for high school students, grades 9-12 combined.

Six of the factors were examined for the presence of patterns in specific ethnic, SES, and sex groups. The other five factors not included in the present study were primarily measures of information in areas considered relatively unimportant as dimensions of mental ability: Hunting-Fishing, Color-Foods, Etiquette, Games, and a factor called Screening which had its highest loading on a test designed to identify illiterates and uncooperative subjects.

The six mental ability factors examined were: Verbal Knowledges (VKN)–a general factor, but primarily a measure of general information; English Language (ENG)–a measure of grammar and language useage; Mathematics (MAT)–a measure of high school mathematics with a minimum of computation; Visual Reasoning (VIS)–a measure of reasoning with spatial forms; Perceptual Speed and Accuracy (PSA)–a measure of visual-motor coordination under speeded conditions; and Memory (MEM)—a measure of short-term recall of verbal symbols.

STATISTICAL PROCEDURES

The statistical model was a 4 x 2 x 2 x 6 fixed effects analysis of variance in which ethnicity, SES, and sex were treated as between-subjects variables and the mental ability factors were treated as a within-subjects variable (Block, Levine and McNemar, 1951; Myers, 1966, Ch. 8). Differences in the shapes of the patterns of mental abilities were reflected by the interactions of ethnicity, SES, and sex with the mental ability factors. Differences in the levels of the patterns of mental abilities were reflected by the main effects of ethnicity, SES, and sex, and their interactions.

Estimates of ω^2, the proportion of the total variance accounted for by the variables and their interactions, were also obtained (Hays, 1965, pp. 406-407; Schutz, 1966).

Hays (1963, p. 408) recommends having equal numbers of observations per cell in an analysis of variance; equal cell frequencies are considered advantageous in that the resulting experimental design is orthogonal and the assumption of homogeneity of variances can be violated without serious risk. The present sample was composed of 16 subgroups when stratified according to ethnicity (four levels), SES (two levels), and sex (two levels). As there was a great disparity in the numbers of subjects in the different subgroups, the procedure called replicated sampling was used to obtain equal cell frequencies (Cochran, 1963, pp. 383-385, Kish, 1965, pp. 127-132). According to this procedure, the subjects within each of the 16 subgroups were randomly divided into 4 subsamples or replicated samples. Each replicated sample was "regarded as a single complex unit, the sample [subgroup] being in effect a simple random sample of those complex units, with uncorrelated errors of measurement between different complex units" (Cochran, 1963, p. 385).

Since all the 2,925 subjects were used, the group means, computed by summing over replicated samples, were very reliable. The standard deviations reported in Table 1 were based on deviations of the means of the four replicated samples from their own mean. These deviations squared were considered estimates of the error variance, as they did not include systematic variance related to the effects of ethnicity, SES, and sex. Although the standard deviations were based on an equal number of replicated samples, they did differ considerably for ethnic groups because of the wide variation in the number of subjects in each group. The standard errors of the mean in Table 2 and the confidence intervals in Figures 1 and 2 were obtained by squaring and pooling the standard deviations in Table 1 (Hays, 1963, pp. 209-210).

RESULTS AND CONCLUSIONS

Ninety percent of the total variance was accounted for by the main effects and interactions of the variables (Table 3). Sex accounted for a much larger

TABLE 1

Patterns of Mental Abilities by Ethnicity, SES, and Sex

Ethnic group	N^a	VKN		ENG		MAT		VIS		PSA		MEM	
		$\bar{X}$	SD^b	$\bar{X}$	SD^b	$\bar{X}$	SD^b	$\bar{X}$	SD^b	$\bar{X}$	SD^b	$\bar{X}$	SD^b
Males, Upper-middle SES													
Jewish-white	542	61.7	0.5	41.5	0.5	73.0	0.8	53.5	1.2	50.7	1.7	41.0	0.8
Non-Jewish-white	280	56.2	0.9	40.7	0.9	65.0	2.0	58.0	0.8	48.0	2.5	45.0	1.1
Negro	43	53.0	4.5	36.5	4.4	55.0	3.4	53.2	2.0	49.5	5.5	44.0	2.9
Oriental	31	53.2	2.5	44.5	2.0	72.5	4.3	55.7	2.2	50.5	2.6	45.5	5.8
Males, Lower-middle SES													
Jewish-white	116	59.0	2.1	40.7	0.5	67.0	3.1	51.0	1.4	48.7	0.5	41.2	0.9
Non-Jewish-white	227	51.7	2.0	41.7	1.2	61.5	0.5	58.5	1.2	48.0	0.8	45.2	1.2
Negro	130	44.7	2.2	41.0	1.4	54.5	2.3	51.0	0.8	50.0	1.8	46.5	1.0
Oriental	37	50.2	1.5	40.7	2.8	62.7	6.6	55.0	2.5	48.0	2.1	46.2	2.6
Females, Upper-middle SES													
Jewish-white	491	55.2	0.9	60.7	0.9	48.7	1.2	40.5	0.5	52.7	0.5	54.7	0.9
Non-Jewish-white	282	52.2	0.5	61.0	0.0	42.5	0.5	46.0	0.8	51.2	0.5	56.2	1.7
Negro	73	45.5	1.7	57.5	1.2	40.5	2.3	40.0	2.1	51.7	2.0	55.2	1.7
Oriental	30	47.2	3.2	62.5	3.1	52.2	4.9	44.5	4.9	50.2	2.9	58.5	5.0
Females, Lower-middle SES													
Jewish-white	87	52.7	0.5	60.2	1.5	46.0	4.0	39.0	2.9	52.0	3.7	54.2	0.9
Non-Jewish-white	262	47.5	1.0	61.0	0.8	39.2	1.7	45.0	0.8	50.7	0.9	57.2	0.9
Negro	242	40.7	0.5	55.2	1.2	39.2	0.5	36.2	0.5	52.5	2.3	56.0	2.7
Oriental	52	45.5	1.0	62.2	2.5	49.0	1.4	42.5	4.2	52.7	3.3	56.2	3.0

[a] Number of subjects; data based on 4 replicated samples per subgroup
[b] Based on deviations of the means of the 4 replicated samples in each subgroup

TABLE 2

Patterns of Mental Abilities of Ethnic, SES, and Sex Groups

Group	VKN		ENG		MAT		VIS		PSA		MEM	
	$\bar{X}$	$SE_{\bar{X}}^c$	$\bar{X}$	$SE_{\bar{X}}^c$	$\bar{X}$	$SE_{\bar{X}}^c$	$\bar{X}$	$SE_{\bar{X}}^c$	$\bar{X}$	$SE_{\bar{X}}^c$	$\bar{X}$	$SE_{\bar{X}}^c$
Ethnic group[a]												
Jewish-white	57.1	0.3	50.8	0.2	58.6	0.7	46.0	0.4	51.0	0.5	47.8	0.2
Non-Jewish-white	51.9	0.3	51.1	0.2	52.1	0.3	51.8	0.2	49.5	0.4	50.9	0.3
Negro	46.0	0.7	47.5	0.6	47.3	0.6	45.1	0.4	50.9	0.8	50.4	0.6
Oriental	49.0	0.6	52.5	0.7	59.1	1.2	49.4	0.9	50.3	0.7	51.6	1.1
SES[b]												
Upper-middle	53.0	0.4	50.6	0.4	56.2	0.5	48.9	0.4	50.5	0.5	50.0	0.5
Lower-middle	49.0	0.3	50.3	0.3	52.4	0.6	47.2	0.4	50.3	0.4	50.3	0.3
Sex[b]												
Male	53.7	0.4	40.9	0.4	63.9	0.6	54.5	0.3	49.1	0.5	44.3	0.5
Female	48.3	0.3	60.0	0.3	44.6	0.5	41.7	0.5	51.7	0.4	56.0	0.4

a Data based on 16 replicated samples per ethnic group

b Data based on 32 replicated samples per SES and sex group

c Based on pooled estimates of the error variance computed from Table 1 for the subgroups that constitute the larger groups reported in this table

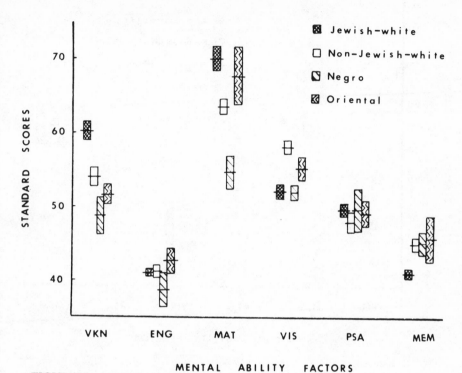

FIGURE 1.
Patterns of mental abilities of twelfth grade students by ethnic group: males.
Vertical bar represents 95 percent confidence interval; horizontal line in center
of bar represents group mean.

proportion of the total variance than did either ethnicity or SES. Sex was
significantly (p<.001) related to both the shape and the level of the patterns.
The relationship of sex to the shape of the patterns accounted for 69% of the
total variance. Females received higher mean scores on ENG, PSA, and MEM,
and males received higher mean scores on VKN, MAT, and VIS (Table 2). The
relationship of sex to the level of the patterns was considered to be unimportant
as it accounted for .00 of the total variance when rounded to two significant
figures.

Ethnicity, the only other variable showing a substantial effect on the
patterns, accounted for 13% of the total variance: 9% associated with shape and
4% associated with level. The pattern of mental abilities of the Jewish-whites was
characterized by high mean scores on VKN and MAT and low mean scores on
VIS and MEM (Table 2). The pattern of mental abilities of the Orientals was
characterized by a high mean score on MAT; little difference was noted among
their mean scores on the other mental ability factors. Negroes received higher
mean scores on PSA and MEM than on the other factors; their mean scores on

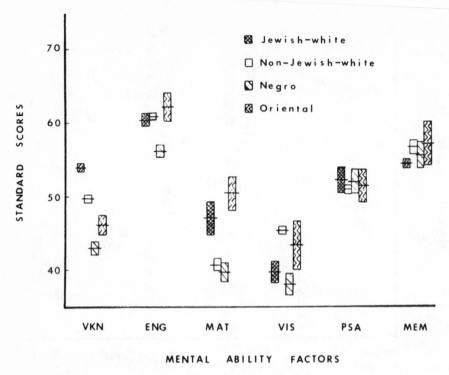

FIGURE 2.
Patterns of mental abilities of twelfth grade students by ethnic group: females.
Vertical bar represents 95 percent confidence interval; horizontal line in center
of bar represents group mean.

the other factors did not differ from each other to any great extent. There was
little variation among the mean scores on the six mental ability factors for the
non-Jewish-whites; this was expected as the factor scores had been standardized
on a sample that was predominantly non-Jewish-white.

A Scheffé test revealed that the average level of the pattern of mental abilities
of the Negroes (47.9) was significantly lower (p<.01) than the average level of
the patterns of mental abilities of the other ethnic groups (Jewish-whites—51.9;
non-Jewish-whites—51.2; and Orientals—52.0).

The combined effects of ethnicity and sex are illustrated in Figures 1 and 2.
Differences between the means were considered to be due to chance if the
confidence intervals overlapped. It should be pointed out that the interaction of
ethnicity and sex accounted for only 1% of the total variance and was
considered unimportant.

Although the patterns of mental abilities of the SES groups differed
significantly in both shape and level (p<.001), these differences accounted for

TABLE 3

Analysis of Variance and Estimated Proportion of Total Variance
Accounted for by the Variables

Source of variation	df	Mean square	F	Est. ω^2
Ethnicity (A)	3	364.95	56.32***	.04
SES (B)	1	250.26	38.62***	.01
Sex (C)	1	44.01	6.79*	.00
A × B	3	5.45	.84	.00
A × C	3	3.64	.56	.00
B × C	1	3.01	.46	.00
A × B × C	3	11.42	1.76	.00
Between-replicated samples error	48	6.48		
Mental ability factors (D)	5	259.85	45.75***	.05
A × D	15	157.40	27.71***	.09
B × D	5	58.79	10.35***	.01
C × D	5	3,428.05	603.52***	.69
A × B × D	15	10.17	1.79*	.00
A × C × D	15	15.30	2.69**	.01
B × C × D	5	9.54	1.68	.00
A × B × C × D	15	5.93	1.04	.00
Within-replicated samples error	240	5.68		

*p<.05   **p<.01   ***p<.001

only 2% of the total variance and were judged to be too small to be important.
The interaction of ethnicity and SES also did not account for a sufficient
proportion of the total variance to be considered meaningful (ω^2 = .00). The
remaining 5% of explained variance was related to the variation among mean
scores for the total sample: VKN–51.0; ENG–50.5; MAT–54.3; VIS–48.1;
PSA–50.4; and MEM–50.1

DISCUSSION

The results of the present study revealed that for a given ethnic group males
and females tended to exhibit patterns of mental abilities characteristic of their
sex; these patterns were only slightly modified by ethnic background. The
relationship of SES to the patterns of mental abilities—although statistically
significant—was considered too weak to be important. Had a wider range of SES
been studied, a stronger relationship between SES and the patterns of mental
abilities might have been found.

In contrast, Lesser et al. (1965) reported that "no marked pattern differences
emerged when [first grade] boys and girls were compared" (p. 65). First grade

children from different ethnic groups did, however, exhibit characteristic patterns of mental abilities; SES was related to the level but not the shape of the patterns.

Thus, differences between the sexes apparently become more marked with age. In addition, it appears that sex may play a greater role in the development of patterns of mental abilities than either ethnicity or SES. Although previous research had reported characteristic patterns of mental abilities for adolescent males and females, it was unexpected that sex would account for such a large proportion of the total variance (69%), as compared to ethnicity (13%) and SES (2%). An examination of tests with loadings on the specific factors may shed some light on this question.

For example, the higher mean score of the males on VKN probably reflects the large percentage of tests with loadings on the factor that would be expected to favor males, e.g., tests of information about the military (.59), aeronautics and space (.50), outdoor activities (.50), sports (.48), and electricity and electronics (.36). The tests with high loadings on ENG and MAT measure to a large extent school related experiences, and different curricula followed by males and females. For example, the sex differences on MAT may reflect the common situation in which fewer females than males study mathematics beyond the usually required ninth grade algebra (National Center for Educational Statistics, 1968); by twelfth grade, in addition to not knowing the advanced mathematics required for a high score on MAT, the females may have forgotten much of the algebra studied several years earlier.

When interpreting the results of this study, one should keep in mind that the sample was rather select. Using a sample of students who were in the twelfth grade and who were also respondents to a follow-up survey would be expected to bias the results toward higher SES and higher mental ability factor scores (Flanagan *et al.*, 1967, Appendix C). Bias related to SES was reduced by restricting the sample to the middle range on the SES scale. When the respondent sample was compared to a sample of twelfth graders representative of the total twelfth grade population, the level of the pattern of mental abilities of the respondent sample was only about one-tenth of a standard deviation higher than that of the other sample (Lohnes, 1966, Ch. 7). The respondents, as expected, also had higher mean scores when compared to a sample of nonrespondents subsequently interviewed by Project TALENT field representatives. The shapes of the patterns, however, were similar for respondents and nonrespondents from specific ethnic and sex groups (Backman, 1970). Thus, it does not appear that using a respondent sample seriously biased the results of this study.

It is also important to point out that the present study was not designed to answer questions regarding heredity and environment; ethnic groups were defined sociologically and not biologically, and there was no way to determine the contributions of heredity and environment to the variation among ethnic groups on the mental ability factors. Although the groups were approximately matched on score on an index of SES, differences could still be due to SES factors not measured by the index. Also, groups that can be identified according to physical characteristics—such as males and females—are differentially reinforced by society; the social implications of the physical differences can play an important role in the development of characteristic abilities.

REFERENCES

Anastasi, A. Differential psychology: Individual and group differences in behavior. (3rd ed.) New York: Macmillan, 1958.

Backman, Margaret E. Relationships of ethnicity, socioeconomic status, and sex to patterns of mental abilities. Unpublished doctoral dissertation, Teachers College, Columbia University, 1970.

Block, J., Levine, L., & McNemar, Q. Testing for the significance of psychometric patterns. Journal of Abnormal and Social Psychology, 1951, 46, 356-359.

Cochran, W.G. Sampling techniques. (2nd ed.) New York: Wiley, 1963.

Flanagan, J.C., Cooley, W.W., Lohnes, P.R., Schoenfeldt, L.F., Holdeman, R.W., Combs, J., & Becker, S.J. Project TALENT one-year follow-up studies. (Final report to the U.S. Office of Education, Cooperative Research Project No. 2333.) Pittsburgh: Project TALENT Office, University of Pittsburgh, 1966.

Hays, W.L. Statistics for psychologists. New York: Holt, Rinehart, & Winston, 1963.

Kish, L. Survey sampling. New York: Wiley, 1965.

Lesser, G.S., Fifer, G., & Clark, D.H. Mental abilities of children from different social-class and cultural groups. Monographs for the Society for Research in Child Development, 1965, 30(4).

Lohnes, P.R. Measuring adolescent personality. (Interim report 1 to the U.S. Office of Education: Cooperative Research Project No. 3051.) Pittsburgh: Project TALENT Office, University of Pittsburgh, 1966.

Myers, J.L. Fundamentals of experimental design. Boston: Allyn & Bacon, 1966. National Center for Educational Statistics, Digest of educational statistics. Washington, D.C.: United States Government Printing Office, 1968, No. FS 5.210: 10024-68. P. 34.

Schoenfeldt, L.F. A national data resource for behavioral, social, and educational research. Palo Alto: American Institutes for Research, 1968.

Schutz, R.E. The control of "error" in educational experimentation, School Review, 1966, 74, 150-158.

Shaycoft, M.F. The high school years: Growth in cognitive skills. Pittsburgh: American Institutes for Research and University of Pittsburgh, Project TALENT Office, 1967.

Stodolsky, S.J., & Lesser, G. Learning patterns in the disadvantaged. Harvard Educational Review, 1967, 37, 546-593.

RACE, SOCIAL CLASS, AND I.Q.

Sandra Scarr-Salapatek

The heritability of intelligence in white, middle-class populations of school-aged children and adults has been repeatedly estimated to account for 60 to 80 percent of the total variance in general intelligence scores, however measured (1-4). Yet Jensen (3, pp. 64-65) has noted many limitations to the available data on heritability.

> It is sometimes forgotten that such [heritability] estimates actually represent *average* values in a population that has been sampled and that they do not necessarily apply either to differences *within* various subpopulations or to differences *between* subpopulations. ... All the major heritability studies have been based on samples of white European and North American populations, and our knowledge of intelligence in different racial and cultural groups within these populations is nil. For example, no adequate heritability studies have been based on samples of the Negro population of the United States [italics added].

After carefully examining the intelligence data on the black and white populations, Jensen (3, 4) hypothesized that the average genetic potential of the black population may not be equal to that of the white population. Others (5, 6) have interpreted the same racial differences in mean IQ (Intelligence quotient) within an environmental framework, often naively and without good evidence for their competing hypotheses. Dislike of a genetic hypothesis to account for racial differences in mean IQ scores does not equal disproof of that hypothesis. Evidence for genetic or environmental hypotheses must come from a critical examination of both explanations, with data that support one.

As every behavioral geneticist knows, the heritability of a behavioral characteristic is a function of the population in which it is measured (7, 8). There is no reason to assume that behaviors measured in one population will show the same proportion of genetic and environmental variances when measured in a second population whose distributions of genetic or environmental characteristics, or both, differ in any way from those of the first population. Racial and social class groups are, for many purposes, sufficiently different populations to make a generalization from one to another highly questionable (9-11).

The sociological literature on social class and racial differences in style of life, nutrition, child-rearing practices, and the like describes *population* differences in distributions of environments. These population differences must affect the development of phenotypic (observed) IQ (12) and the relative proportions of genetic and environmental variances in IQ scores.

Distributions of genotypes for the development of behavioral characteristics may also vary from one population to another. Except for single-gene characteristics such as Huntington's chorea, microcephaly, and the like, we know very little about genotypic variability among populations for behavioral development. Because identified single-gene characteristics are known to occur with varying frequencies among populations, it is assumed that genes for polygenic characteristics may also be distributed somewhat differently among groups.

The sources of within-group and between-group variation can be assessed, although they are seldom effectively studied. Thoday (13, pp. 4-5) reviewed the problems of cross-population studies and concluded:

> While discontinuous variables such as blood groups present us with little difficulty [in studying differences between populations], continuous variables such as IQ are a different matter, for it is not possible with these to identify specific genotypes and it is therefore not possible to determine gene frequencies. Furthermore, there are always environmental as well as genetic causes of variation. We may measure the relative importance of environmental as well as genetic causes of variation or heritability within a population, and if the heritabilities are very high, that is, variation is almost entirely a consequence of genetic variety, we may know more than if they are low. But even if they are high, as with fingerprint ridge counts, we are already in difficulties with population comparisons, for there is no warrant for equating within-group heritabilities and between-group heritabilities.

In this article, I outline important concepts and methods in the study of individual and group variation and describe a new study of genetic and environmental variances in aptitude scores in black and white, and advantaged and disadvantaged populations.

TWO MODELS OF IQ, SOCIAL CLASS, AND RACE

There are two major, competing hypotheses for predicting the relation among social class, race, and IQ—the environmental disadvantage hypothesis and the genotype distribution hypothesis. Both hypotheses make differential predictions about the proportions of genetic and environmental variance in IQ within lower and higher social class groups.

The term "environmental disadvantage" refers to the largely unspecified

Model 1: Environmental advantage as the determinant of group differences in IQ.

Assumptions:

    1. Genotypic distribution by social class for phenotypic IQ of children (no differences).

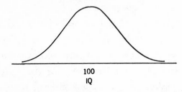

    2. Environmental effects on the development of IQ by SES (large effect).

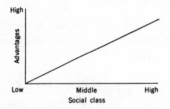

Prediction: Lower h^2 in disadvantaged groups.

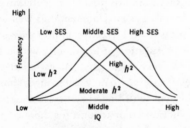

Fig. 1. Environmental disadvantage, model 1 (h^2 is heritability for twins; SES is socioeconomic status).

Model 2: Genetic differences as the primary determinant of group differences in IQ.

Assumptions:

    1. Genotypic distribution by social class for phenotypic IQ of children (differences).

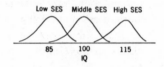

    2. Environmental effects on the development of IQ by SES (small effect).

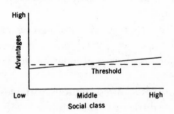

Prediction: Equal h^2 in all groups.

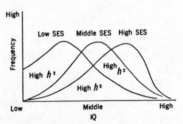

Fig. 2. Genetic differences, model 2 (h^2 is heritability for twins; SES is socioeconomic status).

complex of environmental factors associated with poverty that prevents an organism from achieving its optimum development. The biological environmental disadvantages have been reviewed by Birch and Gussow (14), and references to social environmental disadvantages have been reviewed by Deutsch, Katz, and Jensen (15).

Race and social class are terms that refer to socially defined subgroups of the human population. Reproduction is more likely to occur between people in the same subgroup than between people in different subgroups. There is no question that races are partially-closed breeding groups with a great deal more endogamy than exogamy (10). It is also true that social class groups (groups whose members have attained a certain educational and occupational status) within races practice more endogamy than exogamy (11). Social mobility from generation to generation does not upset the notion of social classes as somewhat different breeding groups, in terms of IQ levels, because the distribution of IQ's within each occupational level is reestablished in each generation of adults (16). Brighter children in families at all but the top social levels tend to be upwardly mobile, whereas duller siblings at all but the bottom class level tend to be downwardly mobile (17). Social class groups may be thought of as endogamous primarily for IQ (as expressed in occupational and educational achievements).

Social class groups may represent both different distributions of parental genotypes for IQ and different rearing environments for children. Although fathers' average IQ scores may vary by 50 points or more from top professional groups to unskilled laborers, their children's average IQ's differ by 25 points or less (16, 17).

The mean differences in children's IQ's by social class reflect differences in both parental genotypes and rearing environments, which covary to a large extent in the development of IQ. Crucial evidence on the genetic and environmental components from adopted children is very limited, but Skodak and Skeels (18) revealed a 20 point rise in the IQ of adopted children over that of their biological mothers. The distribution of adopted children's IQ's was also shifted beyond the values expected by regression to a mean above the average of the population, presumably by their better social environments.

Social class groups, then, are subdivisions of races and represent different distributions of parental genotypes, as well as different rearing environments. There is no comparable statement that can be made about racial groups: whereas races represent different rearing environments, no statements can be made concerning different distributions of parental genotypes for IQ. Since there is no direct test possible for distributions of genotypic IQ (13), it is impossible to assert that such distributions for the two races are "equal" or "different." Races do constitute different rearing environments in two respects. First, proportionately more blacks than whites are socially disadvantaged, thus more black children are reared under lower-class conditions; second, being black in the United States may carry with it a special burden not inflicted on any white.

The environmental disadvantage hypothesis assumes that lower-class whites and most blacks live under suppressive (19, 20) conditions for the development of IQ. In brief, the disadvantage hypothesis states: (i) unspecified environmental factors affect the development of IQ, thereby causing the observed differences in mean IQ levels among children of different social classes and races; (ii) blacks are more often biologically and socially disadvantaged than whites; and (iii) if disadvantage were equally distributed across social class and racial groups, the social class and racial correlations with IQ would disappear. The environmental disadvantage hypothesis predicts that IQ scores within advantaged groups will show larger proportions of genetic variance and smaller proportions of environmental variance than IQ scores for disadvantaged groups. Environmental disadvantage is predicated to reduce the genotype-phenotype correlation (21) in lower-class groups and in the black group as a whole.

The genetic differences hypothesis, as it applies to social class groups within races, centers on the issues of assortative mating by IQ and selective migration, based on intelligence, within the social structure. Social class differences in mean IQ are assumed to be principally genetic in origin and to result from the high heritability of IQ throughout the population, assortative mating for IQ, and a small covariance term that includes those educational advantages that brighter parents may provide for their brighter children (3, 10). Social class differences in phenotypic IQ are assumed to reflect primarily the mean differences in genotype distribution by social class; environmental differences between social class groups (and races) are seen as insignificant in determining total phenotypic variance in IQ. Therefore, the proportion of genetic variance in IQ scores is predicted to be equally high for all social class groups (and for both races). Figures 1 and 2 present models 1 and 2, respectively, as they apply to social class.

In model 1, there are assumed to be equal distributions of genotypes across social classes. In model 2, there are assumed to be unequal distributions of genotypes for IQ, the lower class having proportionally more genotypes for low IQ and the upper social groups having proportionally more genotypes for high IQ. Environmental effects of social class are posited to be strong in model 1 and very weak in model 2.

COMPETING PREDICTIONS

Both models account for the observed social class data on IQ, but they make competing predictions about the proportion of genetic variance. In model 1, environmental factors are predicted to reduce the mean and the heritability of IQ in the lower social class groups and raise both in the higher social groups. Model 2 predicts equally high heritabilities for all groups, regardless of rearing environments and regardless of mean scores. Estimated heritabilities by social class and race provide a new way of evaluating the adequacy with which the two hypotheses account for observed differences in mean IQ by social class. Racial differences may also be examined if the following rationale is always considered.

To the extent that the *same* environmental factors are assumed to affect the development of IQ in the same way in both black and white populations, predictions can be made about the sources of racial differences in mean IQ scores. If certain biological deprivations (such as low weight at birth, poor nutrition) are known to be more prevalent in lower class groups of both populations and more prevalent among blacks than whites, then the two models can make differential predictions about the effects of these sources of environmental variance on the proportion of genetic variance in each population. Given a larger proportion of disadvantaged children within the black group, the environmental disadvantage hypothesis must predict smaller proportions of genetic variance to account for differences in phenotypic IQ among blacks than among whites, as whole populations. Since the genotype distribution hypothesis predicts no differences in the proportion of genetic variance for social class groups within the races, it should predict the same proportions of genetic variance in the two races.

To the extent that *different* environmental factors are assumed to affect the development of IQ in black and white populations, or the same environmental factors are assumed not to affect the development of IQ in the same way, or both, no differential predictions about the origin of racial differences can be made by the two models. If all black children are disadvantaged to an unknown degree by being reared as blacks in a white-dominated society, and no white children are so disadvantaged, it is impossible to estimate genetic and environmental variances between the races. Only if black children could be reared as though they were white, and vice versa, could the effects of different rearing environments on the genotype distribution of the two races be estimated.

Some combinations of models 1 and 2 may be found to account best for phenotypic variability within and between groups. The clear opposition of models 1 and 2 as explanations for the same IQ, racial, and social class data was presented to demonstrate the differential predictions that can be generated about proportions of genetic variance in different populations.

TWIN SAMPLE

An alphabetic roster of all students enrolled in the Philadelphia public schools in April 1968 was examined for children with the same last name, the same birth dates, and the same home address. Children who met the three criteria were identified as twins.

Of the 250,258 children in kindergarten through grade 12, 3042 were identified as twins, including 493 opposite-sex pairs and 1028 same-sex pairs.

The racial distribution of these twins was 36 percent white and 64 percent black. The corresponding figures for the entire public school population were 41 percent white and 59 percent black. The twins' racial distribution was discrepant from the total population by 5 percent, which can be accounted for by the substantially higher rate of fraternal twinning among blacks (22).

In a large sample of twins it is tactically difficult to differentiate the monozygotic and dizygotic groups directly. Direct approaches to zygocity could be discarded in favor of the indirect, statistical approach, which is advocated by

Burt (2), Vandenberg (23), Sandon (24), and Husen (25). The reasoning is as follows: the percentage of opposite-sex pairs is known in any complete population survey. By applying the Weinberg formula, the proportion of monozygotic twins can be easily obtained (21). There will always be approximately the same proportion of same-sex pairs as opposite-sex pairs because of the distribution of sexes. It is then a simple matter to estimate the percentage of monozygotic pairs as follows: 100 − 2 (percent of opposite-sex pairs) = percent of monozygotic pairs. Percentage estimates for monozygotic and dizygotic groups were done separately for each racial group.

Once the proportion of monozygotic and dizygotic twins is known, the correlations for same-sex and opposite-sex groups can be used to estimate the correlation coefficients for monozygotic and dizygotic twins within the same-sex sample. By converting correlation coefficients to z scores, the same-sex intraclass coefficient can be approportioned according to the percentages of monozygotic pairs in the same-sex group, so that:

$$r_{izs} = \frac{\% \, SS_{dz}(r_{ioz}) + \% \, SS_{mz}(X)}{\% \, SS_{mz+dz}}$$

On the basis of seven independent studies including more than 1000 pairs of same-sex and 100 pairs of opposite-sex twins, Burt (2) found the average correlations for intelligence to be .76 and .57 respectively. From these coefficients, he was able to estimate the correlation for monozygotic and dizygotic groups as .89 and .56 respectively. These estimates match very closely the correlations found for intelligence in samples of monozygotic and dizygotic twins whose zygosity had been determined by blood-grouping procedures.

In the Philadelphia sample, 30 percent of the white pairs and 34 percent of the black pairs were found to be of opposite sexes. Therefore, by the Weinberg formula, 40 percent of the whites and 32 percent of the blacks were estimated to be monozygotic pairs. The higher proportion of monozygotic twins in the white population matched the figures reported (24) for a complete age-group of British children taking the 11+ examinations.

The final samples were considerably smaller than the original 1521 pairs found, for several reasons. First, since standardized tests were not administered to the kindergarten or first-grade groups, 282 pairs were lost. Second, one or

Table 1. Final sample pairs by race and test scores.

Test scores	Black	White
Aptitude only	315	194
Achievement only	129	75
Aptitude and achievement	191	88
Total pairs	635	357

Table 2. Means and standard deviations (σ) of national scores for individuals by race.

Aptitude test	Black ($N = 1006$)		White ($N = 560$)	
	Mean	σ	Mean	σ
Verbal	30.3	18.2	45.9	21.2
Nonverbal	32.7	19.1	47.9	21.8
Total	28.9	18.5	46.1	20.8

both members of 124 pairs were found to be enrolled in special classes, to whom the tests used in this study were not given (26). Third, the absence of one or both twins on the days that tests were administered eliminated an additional 123 pairs. Combined losses of 529 pairs reduced the final sample to 992 pairs with aptitude or achievement scores, or both, for each twin, as shown in Table 1.

SOCIAL CLASS MEASURES

Within both the black and white groups, social class variables were used to assign pairs to relatively advantaged and disadvantaged groups. The public school data on parental occupation, income, and education were incomplete and too unreliable for these purposes. Instead, census tract information from the 1960 U.S. Census was used.

Table 3. Mean and standard deviations (σ) of national scores on combined aptitude tests for individuals by race and social class (Q indicates quartile).

Statistics	Black			White		
	Below (*N* = 634)	Middle (*N* = 236)	Above (*N* = 134)	Below (*N* = 114)	Middle (*N* = 106)	Above (*N* = 340)
			Verbal			
Mean	29.0	30.9	35.3	36.4	43.9	49.8
σ	(17.7)	(17.2)	(20.8)	(18.6)	(22.6)	(20.4)
Q	15-28-39	19-31-43	23-32-46	22-38-50	28-42-56	38-41-63
			Nonverbal			
Mean	32.0	32.7	35.9	38.3	44.5	52.2
σ	(19.2)	(18.7)	(19.3)	(18.0)	(22.5)	(21.5)
Q	17-32-44	20-32-46	20-34-50	25-39-50	29-43-59	36-51-68
			Total			
Mean	27.7	29.7	33.0	34.8	43.4	50.9
σ	(18.1)	(18.1)	(20.3)	(16.9)	(21.4)	(20.2)
Q	15-26-39	15-30-41	19-29-47	23-37-47	29-42-56	38-52-65

Every pair had a census tract designation for which median income and educational data were available. Although census tracts in an urban area are designed to provide maximum homogeneity within tracts, they are still imperfect measures of individual SES (socioeconomic status) characteristics. Relatively advantaged and disadvantaged groups could be designated by neighborhood SES, however, since peer assocations and school characteristics would be reflected in the census tract data. To the extent that the social disadvantage hypothesis pertains to the life-style, in addition to within-family environment, the census tract data were appropriate.

Social-class assignment was made by establishing a median level of income and educational characteristics for the total number of census tracts from which the twin sample was drawn, regardless of race. Cross-tabulations of above- and below-median levels of income and education provided three groups: one below the census tract medians for both income and education; one above the medians of both; and a third above in one and below in the other. On this basis, the three groups were designated as below median, above median, and middle status.

APTITUDE AND ACHIEVEMENT TESTS

Results from several tests were available in the 1968-69 school year for children in the Philadelphia school district from second through twelfth grade (27). All children in grades three through eight who were in regular academic classrooms were given the Iowa Tests of Basic Skills, which test long-term development of intellectual skills (28). These are highly reliable group tests (29) that are used to measure scholastic achievement in many school districts across the nation. The vocabulary, reading, language total, arithmetic total, and composite scores were obtained. A total of 319 black and 163 white pairs had scores on all subtests for each twin.

Since a different aptitude test was given in every second school grade, it was impossible to obtain a sufficiently large number of pairs for reliable test-by-test results. It was decided, therefore, to combine aptitude test results across tests and age ranges, and to treat them as age-appropriate, equivalent forms of the same test. This radical decision was based primarily on the roughly equivalent structure of the aptitude tests. All have at least two principal subtests, a verbal and a non-verbal (or numerical), as well as a total score. Some tests, such as the Differential Abilities Test, have additional subtests to measure spatial, mechanical, and other abilities not included in more scholastically-oriented tests, such as the School and College Ability Tests. Thus, the total scores based on all subtests are not strictly equivalent; nor are the nonverbal tests, which may be based primarily on arithmetic reasoning or may include abstract reasoning as well. The verbal scores are the most nearly equivalent from test to test, and thus are the most reliable for comparisons across grades.

No a priori assumptions were made about the appropriateness of standardized aptitude tests for different social-class and racial groups. Although there exists a popular notion that standardized tests are less predictive of scholastic achievement in disadvantaged groups, this has generally been unsupported by research (30). This hypothesis was tested, however, by examining the correlations between aptitude and achievement scores for each racial and social-class group.

Since the generalizations were never intended to exceed the limits of aptitude test and IQ scores, no extensive discussion of the epistemological issue, "What do IQ tests measure?" will be attempted here. Suffice it to say that variance in IQ and aptitude test scores have been shown to have strong genetic components in other studies of white populations, and that the appropriateness of these measures for other racial and social-class samples will be considered in the results section.

Statistics in studies of twins are based on the variances in scores among individuals of different genetic and environmental relatedness. The total phenotypic variance in the populations studied can be apportioned into between-family and within-family variances for both same- and opposite-sex twins. The comparison of between- and within-family mean squares is usually expressed as an F ratio

$$r_1 = \frac{\sigma_b^2 - \sigma_w^2}{\sigma_b^2 + \sigma_b^2} = \frac{F-1}{F+1}$$

The intraclass correlation expresses the proportion of variance arising from family influences, both genetic and environmental. It compares the between-family variances minus the within-family variances to the total phenotypic variance in the population from which the related persons are drawn.

$$r_1 = \frac{\sigma_b^2 - \sigma_w^2}{\sigma_b^2 + \sigma_w^2} = \frac{F-1}{F+1}$$

where σ_b^2 is the mean squares between pairs, and σ_w^2 is the mean squares within pairs.

The comparison of intraclass correlation coefficients and variance ratios for two or more related sets of individuals leads to the calculation of heritability estimates. The heritability of a trait is an expression of the ratio of total genetic variance to total phenotypic variance.

In the simplest form for studies of twins, the restricted model for broad heritability (h_r^2) was defined by

$$h_r^2 = \frac{2(r_{imz} - r_{idz})}{1 - \sigma_E^2}$$

where r_{imz} is the intraclass correlation for monozygotic pairs, r_{idz} is the intraclass correlation for dizygotic pairs, and σ_E^2 is the percentage of variance due to errors in measurement. In this study, σ_E^2 was estimated to be .073, or the minimum unreliability for group aptitude tests.

Another version of the h^2 statistic for broad heritability using twins was offered by Jensen (31) to include the available data on assortative mating for IQ in the white population. The assortative-mating model for data on twins takes into account the positive correlation between IQ scores of parents, which are generally found to be around .40. Nonrandom mating patterns produce a genetic correlation between siblings that is somewhat higher than the .50 expected under mating patterns that are random with respect to IQ. The formula for computing the heritability coefficient with assortative mating (h_a^2) is

$$h_a^2 = \frac{c(r_{imz} - r_{idz})}{1 - \sigma_E^2}$$

Table 4. Intercorrelations of test scores by race and social class [nonverbal (NV), total (T), vocabulary (Vo), reading (R), language (L), arithmetic (A), composite (C)].

Black

Test	Aptitude			Achievement			
	Verbal	Non-verbal	Total	Vocabulary	Reading	Language	Arithmetic
Below-median group (N = 351)							
NV	.57						
T	.84	.87					
Vo	.56	.44	.54				
R	.56	.47	.59	.64			
L	.59	.54	.64	.67	.67		
A	.53	.58	.62	.57	.66	.67	
C	.64	.57	.67	.82	.84	.86	.83
Middle group (N = 125)							
NV	.71						
T	.90	.89					
Vo	.54	.47	.56				
R	.64	.56	.66	.66			
L	.67	.54	.65	.66	.75		
A	.60	.53	.60	.64	.72	.73	
C	.70	.59	.70	.83	.89	.90	.85
Above-median group (N = 51)							
NV	.53						
T	.82	.86					
Vo	.60	.35	.53				
R	.62	.56	.68	.71			
L	.68	.55	.71	.74	.87		
A	.55	.65	.68	.61	.81	.77	
C	.67	.57	.71	.83	.94	.93	.87

White

Test	Aptitude			Achievement			
	Verbal	Non-verbal	Total	Vocabulary	Read-[*]ing	Language	Arithmetic
Below-median group (N = 60)							
NV	.44						
T	.81	.83					
Vo	.53	−.04	.31				
R	.62	.30	.51	.61			
L	.76	.28	.61	.69	.79		
A	.67	.37	.59	.58	.77	.79	
C	.75	.26	.58	.81	.87	.92	.89
Middle group (N = 43)							
NV	.57						
T	.88	.85					
Vo	.81	.49	.71				
R	.84	.59	.79	.88			
L	.71	.51	.69	.75	.85		
A	.60	.52	.63	.64	.71	.77	
C	.78	.61	.77	.86	.93	.94	.85
Above-median group (N = 147)							
NV	.66						
T	.81	.88					
Vo	.71	.49	.59				
R	.68	.53	.60	.78			
L	.69	.61	.66	.73	.74		
A	.70	.70	.74	.66	.71	.78	
C	.77	.64	.72	.87	.90	.88	.87

Table 5. Analysis of variance of aptitude scores of twin pairs by race.

Mean squares	Black		White	
	Same sex	Opposite sex	Same sex	Opposite sex
		Verbal		
	($N = 333$)	($N = 169$)	($N = 192$)	($N = 82$)
σ_b^2	129.1	113.7	149.4	133.2
σ_w^2	38.2	44.8	29.6	33.9
F	3.38	2.54	5.05	3.93
r_i	0.543	0.435	0.669	0.594
r_{ims}		0.653		0.719
		Nonverbal		
	($N = 332$)	($N = 169$)	($N = 192$)	($N = 82$)
σ_b^2	130.5	115.2	149.7	131.7
σ_w^2	39.6	39.4	33.8	26.8
F	3.30	2.92	4.42	4.92
r_i	0.535	0.490	0.631	0.662
r_{ims}		0.594		0.601
		Total		
	($N = 334$)	($N = 169$)	($N = 193$)	($N = 82$)
σ_b^2	127.4	119.2	168.0	156.9
σ_w^2	35.1	31.2	23.7	28.4
F	3.62	3.82	7.10	5.53
r_i	0.567	0.585	0.753	0.694
r_{ims}		0.544		0.791

where $c = 1/1 - p$, or 2.222, when $p = .55$; and σ_E^2 is the percentage of variance due to errors in measurement.

If the heritability of a trait is known, the total variance can be apportioned into four major components: within-family genetic variance (σ_{wg}^2), within-family environmental variance (σ_{we}^2), between-family genetic variance (σ_{bg}^2), and between-family environmental variance (σ_{be}^2). Regardless of the absolute size of the total variance, the proportions of variance can be estimated (32).

DISTRIBUTIONS OF SCORES

An initial look at the distribution of scores within the samples of twins from Philadelphia indicated that the scores were far from normal. The low mean value, especially in the black population, and the skew of the distributions required careful normalization of the scores before any heritability analyses could be attempted. Thus, the results are reported in three sections: first, the distributions of scores and their transformations; second, the analyses of data on twins; and third, the heritability and estimated proportions of variance in the scores by race and social class.

The distributions of aptitude scores, based on national norms were divided first by race and then by race and social class. The means and standard deviations of the scores were markedly different by race; the mean aptitude scores of whites were slightly below the national mean of 50, while the mean aptitude scores of blacks were one standard deviation $(\sigma = 19)$ below the national mean. There was almost one standard deviation between the means of the two races. The standard deviations of the whites were slightly higher than those of the blacks, as Jensen (3, 4) and others have noted; but the ratios of standard deviations to the means (proportional variance) were higher in the black than in the white groups (see Table 2).

On measures of aptitude, the racial groups had surprisingly large differences, once social class was considered (Table 3). The mean of the below-median (in income and education) white group equalled or surpassed the mean of the above-median black children on verbal, nonverbal, and total aptitude scores. The quartile (q) boundaries showed the distributions of below-median whites and above-median blacks to have similar properties, except that the total variance among advantaged black children was somewhat higher than that among disadvantaged whites.

The social-class divisions among whites separated the aptitude means of the subpopulations by approximately four-fifths of a standard deviation. The comparable divisions among blacks produced a difference of one-quarter of a standard deviation between children below and above the medians for the 280 census tracts in which the twins lived. Social-class groups of children were far more differentiated among whites than among blacks, despite the same criteria for assignment.

Comparisons across racial groups showed that disadvantaged white children scored in a pattern similar to that of black children, while the middle and above-median white groups had much higher means. Variances were not reliably different across races.

Compared to the national distribution, the twins in Philadelphia scored poorly. Instead of mean scores of 50, all black groups and white groups of below-median and middle status had mean performance scores in the 20 to 40 range. Only the above-median whites had mean scores close to the national average. A comparison of the means and variances of the twins' scores with those of all Philadelphia children showed that the twins were indeed representative of their respective racial and social-class groups, and were only slightly handicapped by their twinship.

Since the scores based on national norms were skewed within the Philadelphia samples, the scores for each test were normalized, separately by racial groups, to a mean of 50 and a standard deviation of 10, in order to develop comparable data for blacks and whites. Since the means and variances of the two racial groups were arbitrarily set as equal, there was no longer any differences based on race in the distributions of scores. In every test, there were significant social-class differences and significant class-by-race interaction terms, which reflected the fact that social-class differences in mean scores were much greater among whites than blacks.

Correlational analyses of all test scores by race and social class were done to examine the equivalence of measurement among groups. As Table 4 shows, the patterns of correlation among aptitude and achievement scores were quite

Table 6. Analysis of variance of verbal aptitude scores of twin pairs by race and social class.

Mean squares	Black		White	
	Same sex	Opposite sex	Same sex	Opposite sex
		Below-median group		
	($N = 211$)	($N = 107$)	($N = 41$)	($N = 16$)
σ_b^2	120.7	102.9	81.8	105.8
σ_w^2	41.7	42.1	28.7	31.0
F	2.89	2.44	2.85	3.41
r_1	0.486	0.419	0.481	0.546
r_{1mz}		0.558		0.430
		Middle and above-median group		
	($N = 123$)	($N = 62$)	($N = 153$)	($N = 70$)
σ_b^2	136.0	134.0	154.1	119.9
σ_w^2	32.2	49.4	29.8	34.5
F	4.23	2.71	5.17	3.47
r_1	0.618	0.460	0.676	0.553
r_{1mz}		0.753		0.749

Table 7. Analysis of variance of nonverbal aptitude scores of twin pairs by race and social class.

Mean squares	Black		White	
	Same sex	Opposite sex	Same sex	Opposite sex
		Below-median group		
	($N = 211$)	($N = 107$)	($N = 41$)	($N = 16$)
σ_b^2	128.9	120.3	111.1	87.8
σ_w^2	41.4	37.8	34.8	20.7
F	3.11	3.19	3.20	4.25
r_1	0.513	0.523	0.524	0.619
r_{1mz}		0.508		0.445
		Middle and above-median group		
	($N = 123$)	($N = 62$)	($N = 152$)	($N = 68$)
σ_b^2	132.5	107.8	149.9	122.3
σ_w^2	36.3	42.2	33.6	28.1
F	3.65	2.55	4.46	4.34
r_1	0.570	0.437	0.634	0.625
r_{1mz}		0.698		0.642

Table 8. Analysis of variance of total aptitude scores of twin pairs by race and social class.

Mean squares	Black		White	
	Same sex	Opposite sex	Same sex	Opposite sex
		Below-median group		
	($N = 212$)	($N = 107$)	($N = 41$)	($N = 16$)
σ_b^2	122.7	109.7	83.1	109.1
σ_w^2	38.1	27.5	20.5	24.7
F	3.22	3.99	4.05	4.42
r_1	0.526	0.599	0.604	0.631
r_{1mz}		0.434		0.585
		Middle and above-median group		
	($N = 123$)	($N = 62$)	($N = 155$)	($N = 70$)
σ_b^2	130.6	137.4	174.7	139.1
σ_w^2	30.1	37.5	24.5	29.2
F	4.34	3.66	7.13	4.76
r_1	0.625	0.571	0.754	0.653
r_{1mz}		0.680		0.813

similar in all groups, regardless of race or social class. It is difficult to argue that the dimensions of performance measured in the different racial and social-class groups were not comparable. The most parsimonious explanation of similar patterns of correlations is that there are similar underlying dimensions. It is impossible to argue that "nothing" is being measured by these tests in disadvantaged groups, because the prediction from aptitude to achievement scores is approximately as good in the below-median as in the middle black groups, and is certainly as good in the black groups as it is in the white groups.

ANALYSES OF TWINS BY RACE

The four major groups of same-sex and opposite-sex, black and white twins were treated separately for the first set of analyses. Analyses of variance comparing within-pair and between-pair variances were applied to each test score in the four groups. Table 5 gives the twins' results by race for the three aptitude scores. Intraclass correlations for the monozygotic group are estimated by the method described earlier.

Same-sex twins were, in general, more similar than were opposite-sex pairs. In both the black and white groups, the presence of monozygotic pairs in the same-sex group increased their correlation above that of the opposite-sex dizygotic pairs, so that the estimated monozygotic correlation was higher than the dizygotic correlation for four of the six comparisons. The two exceptions are total aptitude score for the blacks and nonverbal aptitude for the whites. Correlations between the two children in each same-sex and opposite-sex black pair were consistently lower than for their white counterparts. Black twins were not found to be as similar to each other as white twins, when compared to randomly paired members of the same groups.

ANALYSES OF TWINS BY RACE AND SOCIAL CLASS

It was hypothesized in model 1 that social-class conditions of life would affect twin similarities and resulting estimates of genetic variances. The potentially restricting effects of lower-class life on the development of genetically based individual differences could tend to reduce within-pair correlation coefficients in the lower-class groups, whereas better environmental opportunities could allow a greater range of phenotypic individual differences in the middle-class groups. Model 2 predicted that similar proportions of genetic variance would be found across social-class groups because mean differences in scores were assumed to arise from differences in genotype distributions.

Within-pair similarities were analyzed for those pairs below the median and then for those of middle and above status combined—the small number of black pairs above the median made it advantageous to combine the latter two groups. Tables 6, 7, and 8 give the analysis of variance results of the aptitude tests for the below-median and the combined middle and above-median groups for both races.

Table 9. Estimated heritability ratios by race and social class for aptitude scores.

Aptitude test scores	Black					White				
	r_{ios}	r_{iss}	r_{ims}	h_r^2	h_a^2	r_{ios}	r_{iss}	r_{ims}	h_r^2	h_a^2
				Below-median group						
Verbal	0.419	0.486	0.558	0.309	0.343	0.546	0.481	*	*	*
Nonverbal	0.523	0.513	*	*	*	0.619	0.524	*	*	*
Total	0.599	0.526	*	*	*	0.631	0.604	*	*	*
			Middle and above-median group							
Verbal	0.460	0.618	0.753	0.651	0.723	0.553	0.676	0.749	0.436	0.484
Nonverbal	0.437	0.570	0.698	0.580	0.644	0.625	0.634	0.642	0.038	0.042
Total	0.571	0.625	0.680	0.242	0.269	0.653	0.754	0.813	0.356	0.395
				All						
Verbal	0.435	0.543	0.653	0.470	0.522	0.594	0.669	0.719	0.270	0.299
Nonverbal	0.490	0.535	0.594	0.224	0.249	0.662	0.631	*	*	*
Total	0.585	0.567	*	*	*	0.694	0.753	0.791	0.209	0.232

* Cannot be estimated.

Table 10. Percentage of variance in verbal aptitude scores for opposite-sex twins by race and social class.

Source	Disadvantaged			Advantaged		
	Between family	Within family	Total	Between family	Within family	Total
			Black			
Genetic	18.8	15.5	34.3	39.7	32.6	72.3
Environmental	23.1	42.6	65.7	6.3	21.4	27.7
Total	41.9	58.1	100.0	46.0	54.0	100.0
			White			
Genetic	*	*	*	24.0	19.6	43.6
Environmental	54.6	45.4	*	31.3	25.1	56.4
Total	54.6	45.4	*	55.3	44.7	100.0

* Cannot be estimated.

In the below-median SES groups of both races, the same-sex correlation exceeded the opposite-sex coefficient only once (black verbal aptitude). The failure of opposite-sex correlations to exceed same-sex coefficients left the estimated monozygotic correlations and heritability statistics indeterminant. It is unlikely that the correlations for monozygotic twins were lower than those for the same-sex dizygotic twins, but it is senseless to assign a value when 4_{ios} is greater than r_{iss}. The most likely interpretation of this result is that the greater genetic correlation between monozygotic twins was not sufficient to increase the same-sex correlations above the values obtained for opposite-sex twins. Thus, genetic factors cannot be seen as strong determinants of aptitude scores in the disadvantaged groups of either race.

In the middle- to above-median SES groups, the same-sex correlations exceeded the opposite-sex correlations for all three aptitude scores in both races. The most likely inference from these data is that both genetic and environmental components of variance contributed to the similarity of within-pair scores in the advantaged group. For the disadvantaged group, the failure of same-sex correlations to exceed opposite-sex coefficients makes it doubtful that the proportion of genetic variance in the lower-class group equals that of the advantaged group.

Total variance was generally larger in the advantaged than in the disadvantaged groups of both races. For whites, total variance was larger in all six comparisons of advantaged and disadvantaged groups. For blacks, total variance was larger in four of six comparisons. This finding reflects the greater phenotypic variability of advantaged children, as predicted in model 1. The intraclass correlations were found to be comparable for blacks and whites within classes (see Table 9).

Assuming that the comparison of estimated monozygotic correlations and opposite-sex dizygotic correlations can be used to estimate heritability ratios, the proportion of genetic to total variance was calculated by the restricted and assortative mating formulas. Table 10 gives the intraclass correlations and estimated heritabilities for aptitude scores by race and social class.

As noted earlier, the proportion of genetic variance in disadvantaged groups was low, but indeterminant—except for verbal aptitude among blacks. Aptitude scores in advantaged groups all showed heritability estimates of greater than zero, except in the non-verbal scores of whites. Verbal aptitude scores had the highest heritability for both blacks and whites.

Based on the estimated heritability ratios, genetic and environmental variances can be apportioned. The apportionment between and within families is based on the ratio of between-family to total variance, expressed in the intraclass correlation. Only opposite-sex pairs were used, because their correlations were known to be based on a common inheritance of about 55 percent.

From Tables 11, 12, and 13, one can see that the percentage of total variance attributable to genetic sources was always higher in the advantaged groups of both races. In most cases, genetic variance could not be estimated for the aptitude scores of lower-class children. For both advantaged and disadvantaged children, however, there were approximately equal variances between and within families, the between-family variance being somewhat larger more often. Thus, the major finding of the analysis of variance is that advantaged and disadvantaged children differ primarily in what proportion of variance in aptitude scores can be attributed to environmental sources.

To check on the validity of the findings, the aptitude data were analyzed separately for male-male and female-female pairs who were found to have correlations of similar magnitude. The overall results of the study were not due to the greater similarity of male or female pairs, as seen in Table 14.

GENOTYPE-ENVIRONMENT INTERACTION

While neither model 1 nor model 2 predicted statistical interaction, a combination of the two models could predict an interaction between genotypes

Table 11. Percentages of variance in nonverbal aptitude scores for opposite-sex twins by race and social class.

Source	Disadvantaged			Advantaged		
	Between family	Within family	Total	Between family	Within family	Total
			Black			
Genetic	*	*	*	35.4	29.0	64.4
Environmental	52.3	47.7	*	8.3	27.3	35.6
Total	52.3	47.7	*	43.7	56.3	100.0
			White			
Genetic	*	*	*	2.3	1.9	4.2
Environmental	61.9	38.1	*	60.2	35.6	95.8
Total	61.9	38.1	*	62.5	37.5	100.0

* Cannot be estimated.

Table 12. Percentages of variance in total aptitude for opposite-sex twins by race and social class.

Source	Disadvantaged			Advantaged		
	Between family	Within family	Total	Between family	Within family	Total
			Black			
Genetic	*	*	*	14.3	11.7	26.0
Environmental	59.9	40.1	*	42.7	31.3	74.0
Total	59.9	40.1	*	57.0	43.0	100.0
			White			
Genetic	*	*	*	21.5	17.5	39.0
Environmental	63.1	36.9	*	43.5	17.5	61.0
Total	63.1	36.9	*	65.0	35.0	100.0

* Cannot be estimated.

Table 13. Analysis of variance of aptitude scores for same-sex pairs by race.

Mean squares	Black		White	
	Male ($N = 139$)	Female ($N = 194$)	Male ($N = 96$)	Female ($N = 96$)
		Verbal		
σ_b^2	144.3	119.0	162.5	134.8
σ_w^2	43.1	34.7	34.7	24.4
F	3.35	3.43	4.68	5.52
r_1	0.540	0.549	0.648	0.693
		Nonverbal		
σ_b^2	131.6	129.1	156.3	144.6
σ_w^2	47.6	33.7	28.7	39.0
F	2.76	3.83	5.45	3.71
r_1	0.468	0.586	0.690	0.575
		Total		
σ_b^2	127.6	127.3	202.0	135.0
σ_w^2	43.0	29.5	26.1	21.2
F	2.97	4.31	7.75	6.36
r_1	0.496	0.623	0.771	0.728

and environments in producing phenotypic ability. Wiseman (33) has suggested that children with lower IQ's are less affected by environmental deprivations than are children with higher IQ's. If lower IQ children are less affected by differential family environments, then the between-family variance and the correlations between siblings with lower IQ's will be smaller than among siblings with higher IQ's, on whom family environment presumably has a greater effect. Burt (34) reported a correlation of .61 between siblings both of whose IQ's were above 100, and a correlation of .43 between siblings with IQ's below 100.

The possible explanations for these findings include (i) restriction of total variance in the group with lower IQ's because of a "floor effect" in the tests used; (ii) larger within-pair variances for children with lower IQ's as a function of a poor family environment; and (iii) smaller between-pair variances for children with lower IQ's as a function of less responsiveness to different family environments.

A test for restriction in total variance was made by dividing all opposite-sex pairs into those with both twins above the mean of 50 and those with both twins below. Mixed cases were eliminated from the samples. Neither black nor white twins with aptitude scores below the mean had lower total variances than the above-mean groups. Since total variances were equal in the two groups, a test of the interaction hypothesis could be made.

To test for the effects of lower IQ alone on patterns of sibling correlation in the white group, only those children with social class ratings at the median and above were included. Intraclass correlations for the 22 white, advantaged, opposite-sex pairs with aptitude scores below 50, and the 31 above 50 were found to be consistently different. As Table 14 shows, siblings below the aptitude mean had consistently lower correlations between their scores than siblings above the mean. The lower correlations between siblings with lower IQ's were not a function of social class, but of smaller between-pair variances, primarily. This suggests that white children with lower IQ's are less susceptible to environmental differences between families than are children with higher IQ's, even in an advantaged population. There was no evidence of interaction between IQ and environment in the black population.

MEAN SCORES AND GENETIC VARIANCE

The lower mean scores of disadvantaged children of both races can be explained in large part by the lower genetic variance in their scores. A "deprived" or unfavorable environment for the development of phenotypic IQ unfavorably affects mean scores, phenotypic variability, genetic variance in phenotypes, and the expression of individual differences (21, pp. 64-65). No study of human family correlations to date has looked at all of these effects of suppressive environments. In a landmark study of mice, however, Henderson (8) has demonstrated that suppressive environments reduce the amount of genetic variance in performance, reduce phenotypic variability, and reduce mean performance scores. The percentage of genetic variance in the scores of standard-cage-reared animals was one-fourth that of animals with enriched environments (10 percent versus 40 percent). Not only did genetic variance account for a larger portion of the variance among animals with enriched environments, but their performance on the learning task was vastly superior to that of their relatively deprived littermates.

Although generalizations from genetic studies of the behavior of mice to genetic studies of the behavior of human beings are generally unwarranted (because mechanisms of development vary greatly among species), the role that a better rearing environment played in the development of genetic individual differences among Henderson's mice finds an obvious parallel with the effects of advantaged SES homes in this study.

From studies of middle-class white populations, investigators have reached the conclusion that genetic variability accounts for about 75 percent of the total variance in IQ scores of whites. A closer look at children reared under different conditions shows that the percentage of genetic variance and the mean scores are very much a function of the rearing conditions of the population. A first look at the black populations suggests that genetic variability is important in advantaged groups, but much less important in the disadvantaged. Since most blacks are socially disadvantaged, the proportion of genetic variance in the aptitude scores of black children is considerably less than that of the white children, as predicted by model 1.

"Disadvantage" has been used as a term throughout this paper to connote all of the biological and social deficits associated with poverty, regardless of race. As long as these environmental factors were considered to be the same, and to act in the same way on children of both races, then racial differences in scores could be discussed. Unquantified environmental differences between the races—either different factors or the same factors acting in different

Table 14. Analysis of variance of white, advantaged, opposite-sex twins, by aptitude level.

Mean squares	Both < 50 ($N = 22$)	Both $\geqq 50$ ($N = 31$)
	Verbal	
σ_b^2	54.8	65.7
σ_w^2	30.1	20.3
F	1.82	3.24
r_1	0.291	0.528
	Nonverbal	
σ_b^2	44.7	59.4
σ_w^2	18.7	20.9
F	2.39	2.84
r_1	0.41	0.479
	Total	
σ_b^2	34.6	57.5
σ_w^2	17.8	19.8
F	1.94	2.90
r_1	0.320	0.487

ways—preclude cross-racial comparisons. Informed speculation is not out of order at this point, however.

Those cultural differences between races that affect the *relevance* of home experience to scholastic aptitudes and achievement may be of primary importance in understanding the remaining racial differences in scores, once environmental deficits have been accounted for. In a series of studies of African children's scholastic performance, Irvine found that many sources of variation that are important for European and American scores are irrelevant for African children (35, p. 93).

> Of environmental variables studied in population samples, including socio-economic status, family size, family position, and school quality, only school quality showed significant and consistent relation to ability and attainment tests. Other sources of variation were irrelevant to the skills being learned.

For the black child in Philadelphia, the relevance of extrascholastic experience is surely greater than it is for the tribal African. But one may question the equivalence of black and white cultural environments in their support for the development of scholastic aptitudes. As many authors of an environmental persuasion have indicated (6, 36), the black child learns a different, not a deficient, set of language rules, and he may learn a different style of thought. The transfer of training from home to school performance is probably less direct for black children than for white children.

The hypothesis of cultural differences in no way detracts from the predictive validity of aptitude tests for the\scholastic achievement of black children. The correlations between aptitude and achievement are equally good in both racial groups. But the cultural differences hypothesis does speak to the issue of genetic and environmental components of variance. If most black children have limited experience with environmental features that contribute to the development of scholastic skills, then genetic variation will not be as prominent a source of individual phenotypic variation; nor will other between-family differences, such as SES level be as important as they are in a white population. School-related experiences will be proportionately more important for black children than for white children in the development of scholastic aptitudes. The Coleman report (37) suggested that scholastic environment does have more influence on the performance of black children than it does on the performance of white children. The generally lower scores of black children can be fit adequately to the model 1 hypothesis, with the additional interpretation of cultural differences to account for the lower scores of black children at each social-class level.

The differences in mean IQ between the races can be affected by giving young black children rearing environments that are more conducive to the development of scholastic aptitudes. Or the differences in performance can simply be accepted as differences, and not as deficits. If there are alternate ways of being successful within the society, then differences can be valued variations on the human theme (38), regardless of their environmental or genetic origins. Haldane (39) has suggested that, ideally, different human genotypes would be found to respond most favorably to different environmental conditions—that genotype-environment interactions would exist for many human characteristics. From a genetic point of view, varied adaptations are useful to the species and permit the greatest flowering of indivdual differences. Socially invidious comparisons, however, can destroy the usefulness of such differences.

Group differences in mean scores and phenotypic variability that exist because of environmental deprivation can and should be ameliorated. To the extent that children are not given supportive environments for the full development of their individual genetic differences, changes can be made in their prenatal and postnatal environments to improve both their overall performance and the genetic variance in their scores. If all children had optimal environments for development, then genetic differences would account for most of the variance in behavior. To the extent that better, more supportive environments can be provided for all children, genetic variance and mean scores will increase for all groups. Contrary to the views of many naive environmentalists, equality of opportunity leads to bigger and better genotype-phenotype correlations. It is toward this goal that socially concerned citizens should work.

REFERENCES AND NOTES

(1) L. Erlenmeyer-Kimling and L. F. Jarvik, Science 142, 1477 (1963); S. G. Vandenberg, in Genetics, D. Glass, Ed. (Rockefeller Univ. Press, New York, 1968), pp. 3-58; Acta Genet. Med. Gemellol. 19, 280 (1970).

(2) C. Burt, Brit. J. Psychol. 57, 137 (1966).

(3) A. R. Jensen, Harv. Educ. Rev. 39, 1 (1969a).

(4) A. R. Jensen, in Disadvantaged Child, J. Hellmuth, Ed. (Brunner-Mazel, New York, 1970), vol. 3, pp. 124-157.

(5) T. F. Pettigrew, A Profile of the Negro American (Van Nostrand, Princeton, N. J., 1964)

(6) S. Baratz and J. Baratz, Harv. Educ. Rev. 40, 29 (1970).

(7) M. Manosevitz, G. Lindzey, D. Thiessen, Behavioral Genetics; Method and Research (Appleton-Century-Crofts, New York, 1969).

(8) N. Henderson, J. Comp. Physiol. Psychol. 3, 505 (1970).

(9) I. Gottesman, in Handbook of Mental Deficiency: Psychological Theory and Research, N. Ellis, Ed. (McGraw-Hill, New York, 1963). pp. 253-295; F. Weizmann, Science 171, 589 (1971).

(10) I. Gottesman, in Social Class, Race, and Psychological Development, M. Deutsch, I. Katz, A. Jensen, Eds. (Holt, Rinehart & Winston, New York, 1968), pp. 11-51.

(11) C. V. Kiser, Eugen, Quart. 15, 98 (1968).

(12) A genotype is the genetic makeup of an individual. The term may refer to one, several, or all loci. Genetic variance refers to the differences among individuals that arise from differences in genotypes. A phenotype is the sum

total of all observable characteristics of an individual. Phenotypic variance refers to the observable differences among individuals.

(13) J. Thoday, J. Biosoc. Sci. 1 (Suppl.), 3 (1969).

(14) H. Birch and J. Gussow, Diasdvantaged Children: Health, Nutrition and School Failure (Harcourt, Brace & World, New York, 1970).

(15) M. Deutsch, I. Katz, A. Jensen, Eds., Social Class, Race and Psychological Development (Holt, Rinehart & Winston, New York, 1968).

(16) C. Burt, Brit. J. Statist. Psychol. 14, 3 (1961); R. Herrnstein Atl. Mon. 228, 43 (September 1971).

(17) J. Waller, thesis, University of Minnesota (1970).

(18) M. Skodak and H. Skeels, J. Genet. Psychol. 75, 85 (1949).

(19) Suppressive environments are those which do not permit or evoke the development of a genetic characteristic. "Suppose, for example, that early experience in the manipulation of objects is essential for inducing hoarding behavior. Genetic differences in this form of behavior will not be detected in animals reared without such experience" (21, p. 65).

(20) J. L. Fuller and W. R. Thompson, Behavior Genetics (Wiley, New York, 1960).

(21) The genotype-phenotype correlation is generally expressed as the square root of the heritability of a characteristic in a given population ($p_{ng} = \sqrt{h^2}$).

(22) H. Strandskov and E. Edelen, Genetics 31, 438 (1946).

(23) S. G. Vandenberg, quoted in C. Burt (2).

(24) F. Sandon, Brit. J. Statist. Psychol. 12, 133 (1959).

(25) T. Husen, Psychological Twin Research (Almquist and Wiksele, Stockholm, 1959).

(26) Of the 124 pairs in special classes, one or both members of 99 pairs were enrolled in "retarded educable" and "retarded trainable" classes. The racial distribution of the "retarded" twins was 80 percent black and 20 percent white, which represents a 15 percent discrepancy from the racial distribution of twins in the public schools. The exclusion of "retarded" twins attenuates the sample and restricts the conclusions of the study to children in normal classrooms.

(27) Aptitude tests used in this study are Primary Mental Abilities (2nd grade): *verbal meaning, perceptual speed, *number facility, spatial relations, and *total: Lorge-Thorndike Intelligence Tests (4th grade): *verbal, *non-verbal, and *total: Academic Promise Tests (6th grade): abstract reasoning, numerical, *nonverbal total, language usage, verbal, *verbal total, and *total; Differential Abilities Tests (8th grade); *verbal reasoning, *numerical ability, abstract reasoning, space relations, mechanical reasoning, clerical speed and accuracy, language usage, and *total (scholastic aptitude); School and College Ability Tests (10th grade): *verbal, *quantitative, and *total: Test of Academic Progress (12th grade): *verbal, *numberical, and *total. Achievement tests used are Iowa Tests of Basic Skills (3rd through 8th grades): *vocabulary, *reading comprehension, *language total, work-study skills, *arithmetic total, and *composite (average of five scores). Asterisks indicate scores reported.

(28) H. Stevenson, A. Friedrichs, W. Simpson, Child Develop. 41 625 (1970).

(29) O. Buros, Ed. The Sixth Mental Measurements Yearbook (Gryphon Press, Highland Park, N.J. 1965).

(30) J. Stanley, Science 171, 640 (1971).

(31) A Jensen, Proc. Nat. Acad. Sci. U.S. 58, 149 (1967).

(32) My gratitude for Prof. V. Elving Anderson and Dr. Paul Nichols for suggesting this analysis.

(33) S. Wiseman, in Genetic and Environmental Factors in Human Ability, J. Meade and A. Parkes, Eds. (Oliver and Boyd, London, 1966), pp. 64-80.

(34) C. Burt, Brit. J. Educ. Psychol. 13, 83 (1943).

(35) S. Irvine, J. Biosoc. Sci. 1 (Suppl), 91 (1969).

(36) S. Houston, Child Develop. 41, 947 (1970); F. Williams, Ed. (Markham, Chicago, 1970), pp. 1–10; C. Cazden, ibid., pp. 81-101.

(37) U.S. Commission on Civil Rights, Racial Isolation in the Public Schools (Government Printing Office, Washington, D.C., 1967).

(38) D. Freedman, in Progress in Human Behavior Genetics, S.G. Vandenburg, Ed. (Johns Hopkins Press, Baltimore, 1968), pp. 1–5.

(39) J.B.S. Haldane Ann. Eugen. 13, 197 (1946).

(40) My gratitude goes to Heidelise Rivinus and Marsha Friefelder, who collected much of the data; to William Barker and Melvin Kuhbander, who ran many of the analyses; to Professors I. I. Gottesman, Arthur R. Jensen, Harold W. Stevenson, Leonard Heston, V. Elving Anderson, Steven G. Vandenberg, and Lee Willerman, and to Dr. Paul Nichols, all of whom critically read an earlier draft of this article. The research was supported by a grant from the National Institute of Child Health and Human Development (HD-04751).

III.
TEACHERS
AND
SCHOOLS

NOTES TOWARD A PROCESS
OF AFRO-AMERICAN EDUCATION

Thomasyne Lightfoote Wilson

As with any attempt to jolt and reorient a people's thinking, this paper must take the risk of offending those, including brothers and sisters, who adhere to one or more of three sets of assumptions regarding education and social change. I refer to those who see education as training rather than as the evolution of a probing, analytic, reflective individual and collective consciousness; those who desire the destruction of people, property, and institutions in the name of revolution, without serious concern for individual and social reconstruction after the revolution; and those reactionaries who respond to the prospect of social change with "white lashes" rather than any willingness to examine and eradicate institutionalized practices that fail to serve the well-being of all citizens. These latter patriots believe it to be inherently wrong to critically unearth inequitable practices in the distribution of wealth, the provision of educational opportunity, and the administration of justice.

Perhaps it would be presumptuous to ask persons who operate within the staid mentalities above to consider a process of education that is uniquely Afro-American, but we do implore others to open their minds and hearts to thought processes that search for positive selfness, truth, and confident Being as foundations of education and community. Such processes oppose the notion of "proving" the total worth of one's Black selfness to other Blacks and to alien institutions within the American community.

This paper attempts to identify some of the historical and cultural elements that point toward an Afro-American process of developmental education. Our goal is to begin to specify and legitimize those educative tasks that help clarify an Afro-American communal framework which involves all the people in education. In this paper we are just beginning to delineate the underlying principles for an Afro-American educational process. We shall attempt to trace that process from a historio-cultural framework and contrast it to the current Anglo educational system, and finally we draw attention to the necessity of restructuring the community's values and attitudes toward both students and educational institutions. This approach draws from the roots of our Black existence.(1) It is this existence that we should reclaim in our homes, schools, and Afro-American communities. Throughout, we must remember that we are not proving anything to anyone but ourselves (although America might incidentally profit from this personal and Black institutional self-clarification).

Although some of us have conceived of education as a means for making a sovereign nation, and a few of us have dreamed of it as a means for achieving true freedom,(2) we have only begun to envision education as a process for establishing corporate communality, i.e. our institutional and socio-cultural identity. This position rejects the chauvinistic practices characteristic of nationalism. What we seek is a kind of sovereignty of Afro-American *being* within a social system that preserves the selfhood of all peoples.(3)

HISTORIO-CULTURAL BASES OF AFRO-AMERICAN EDUCATION

Let me caution against the belief that diverse cultural content as found in public schools today represents a viable base for creating Afro-American identity. At a time when Afro-Americanism is in vogue and all types of printed materials *about* Blacks are reaping commercial harvests for their authors, it might seem unduly radical for me to reject nearly all of these highly generalized and selective works. Yet many of these writings are no more than palliative white leaves, "white books with black covers." The truth is that widespread and accurate knowledge or acceptance of Afro-American culture as well as that of Indian-Americans, Mexican-Americans, Japanese-Americans, and other peoples of color has never been allowed to develop in American schools. The limited acceptance of Black works by Anglos is too often a form of "academic tokenism."(4) Certainly, the essence of Afro-Americanism as a cultural entity with its own educational process has not been acknowledged, much less accepted in the American social system. In fact, it has been necessary to "justify" even the admission of the already distorted versions of Afro-American content that are finally beginning to appear in elementary and secondary curricula. That is to say we still find that the American educational system requires justifications much like the following, given more than a century ago:

> He who writes the history of the world must not neglect to observe and
> describe this black stream of humanity which ... poured into America
> from the Sudan. It has fertilized half a continent with its labour, and set a
> world on fire ... it has influenced the progress of commerce, culture and
> morality in Europe and the United States and transformed a Federation into
> a Nationality.(5)

This need to justify Blacks implies fundamental social resistance to Afro-Americanism in American institutions. We need to clarify the valid historio-cultural bases upon which our Afro-American education rests, and these bases will have to be found outside of America's educational boundaries. Consequently, the major goal is not simply to identify culturally relevant content for Afro-American teachers and learners, but to help them use evolving thought processes to seek dynamic new values and appropriately evolving and meaningful life styles. The instruction provided by the total community should be directed toward this goal; it should allow each generation of learners to develop abilities to interpret phenomena in a self-clarified manner. The resulting confidence in self as a thinker and prime mover should enable the learner to deal with success and failure realistically; it should help the learner replace antagonistic and destructive behavior with his or her own constructive arts.

This task cannot be accomplished by attempting to clarify self through specific cultural artifacts alone, such as Afro hair styles, dashikis, lappas, bubbas, "black is beautiful" slogans, and soul food (okra, palm oil, black-eyed peas, etc.)(6) Enduring bases and values can only emerge from less tangible factors. They must emanate from the essence of the Black man's folkways, *ways* by which the Black man can be identified historically as one who: 1. believes man should relate to man—he subscribes to interdependent sharing and caring for one another in human organizations such as the extended family(7); 2. has behaved as a partner with nature(8)—his practices are more usufructuary than exploitative with land and property(9); 3. uses time and space for the enhancement of intra-group relations rather than being controlled by time and space(10); and 4. is conscious of unity among and between all things.

The first posited value, grounded in Afro-American folkways, aids in defining a basically Afro-American school, the school district as a community-family. This "community" is conceived of as that total group of persons, diverse in aspirations, motivations, and skills, who identify with and care for each other and who function as an extended-family in order to encourage the overall development of the community's children. Corporate communality is exemplified at the Nairobi Day School in East Palo Alto, for example,(11) by the morning assembly where parents come and sit with the children to chat and sing, to exchange commitments and to get a little happy feeling inside. This assembly is a kind of hallelujah session, a distinctive communality growing out of the Afro-American tradition. This group of persons, though unrelated by blood, constitutes an educational extended family which seeks to encourage the positive personal and socio-cultural development of all its members. This entails guiding educational experiences from conception through adulthood, and will eventually involve resocialization of adults through continuing parent-child education. It stresses the expansion of the emotional, physical, artistic, linguistic, computational, vocational, and other expressive abilities, skills, concepts, and values for all ages in the community-family.

Rather than foster exploitative tendencies among children and people, curricula based upon an Afro-American process in the Ravenswood city school district as well as in the Nairobi Day School emphasize man's partnership with nature. This second value means, for instance, teaching the young to optimally utilize and recycle goods and self, as the grandmothers and mothers of the Nairobi Day School do when they instruct boys and girls on how to make something from nothing—used clothing and junk items. More broadly, it means reordering the psycho-emotional relationships connected with daily interaction among teachers, students, parents, and the community agents. It is a means of guiding each complementary family member to realize that he or she must not use any other member of the community-family to satisfy his or her *ego-trip* needs.

The third value is the use of time and space for intra-group enhancement. Scheduling, per se, in the traditional Anglo education, fits a Western concept of time. However, in large areas of Africa, time is not so many marks on the clock; it is not the quantification of the period between sun up and sun down. Instead, it is what is done, the use to which that "time" is put. Time is a more functional concept there. Similarly in the Nairobi Day School you do not necessarily study reading on Monday morning at 9 o'clock. If it appears that teacher and students are "out of it," they decide together what to do. Perhaps they go out and see what is happening to a tree, how it has changed from Friday until today. Time is not a constraint; it is conceived in terms of its functionality for learning and sharing with the environment.

The fourth value posited in the Afro-American process of education stresses comprehensive unity among all elements (man, natural phenomena, time and space). This fourth value speaks against divisiveness and superiority-inferiority hierarchies among members of the community. Our process would not foster a kind of unity that would be defined in terms of total similarities of interest, skills, and personalities among Blacks. Instead, it would foster diversities, all of which would be supported by different educational approaches, personnel, and places to educate.

Using the implicit socialization approaches above as our point of departure we present a challenge to Western education: an educational process that presumes to provide specific Afro-American values and practices for Afro-Americans. Our basic premise is that Western education's values and instructional behaviors and content are antithetical to authentic Afro-American socialization, culture, and education.

Historically, Afro-American existence is rooted in an African context that constantly reflected the "cultural ways" to be learned. The transmission of these folkways was shared by mothers, fathers, uncles, aunts, grandparents, community artisans, diviners, neighbors, tribal chiefs in the village-community, as well as the teachers from the tribe in the initiation schools.(12) Decisions were shared not only about *what* was to be taught, but *how* and *why*. All facets of the culture pervaded the curricular content and process, and this "curriculum" was transmitted by a prismatic range of culture bearers; all of them possessed interdependent skills, attitudes, and values that encompassed the major aspects of the people's folkways.(13)

It is clear that the above values and practices do not fit into the American educational scheme.(14) They do not condone unequal access to education. They are incompatible with heretofore accepted criteria of humane and quality education. Until now, Anglo social and economic predominace in America has effectively obscured the need to put any but mainstream content in the curriculum. The resulting neglect, ignorance, and suppression of nondominant cultures have been psychologically and culturally devastating for Afro-Americans. For centuries we extracted our "identity" from the false images available to us,(15) and we knew next to nothing about the significance of Afro-American values in education. Our educational perspectives mirrored those of Anglos. We seemed satisfied to let the dominant society define *us*. It is time to remind ourselves that even when Anglos waxed philanthropic in the 1870's, they (and we) perceived Afro-American education as something for "special people," instituted to keep us in our places at the bottom of the social scale. Education for us involved little planning beyond the amount of hours to be spent on a limited range of subjects, usually agricultural or vocational.(16) At best, it was a tool to remake Afro-Americans in the images of Anglos. Some Afro-Americans saw education as the instrument for making persons of color super people—better than Euro-Americans. We thought this would be accomplished through teaching the classics.(17)

Some current idioms challenge and blur our selfness and educational goals even further. For instance, we now know that our process of education must be stripped of any kinship with Anglo education's theme of "do your own thing." Such an individualistic approach outside the corroboration and collaboration of the community-family unit whether at home or in the community, is antithetical to the Afro-American process. In the true Afro-American process of education there can be no selfish exploitation of others; nor can there be exploitation of an environment which is viewed as complementary to the unity of man.

Our process of education stresses the continuity of existence as persons relate to persons within groups; first at home, then with peers, and later with older adults of the community. Through identification and positive interaction with the home-community-school environments, the individual can begin to experience personal and *group integrity* (socio-cultural group identity). He can begin to recognize personal worth, and differentiate success and failure as he receives the support of community-family members. Hence, our Afro-American education is concerned with *how* personal achievement is experienced as well as with what is experienced. We are proposing that a familial setting of interdependent and collaborative points of identification, goals, and behaviors, must not only foster achievement, but should enrich human caring experiences as well.(18) This is not to say that our educational process would disregard personal initiative and invention, for its aim is to lead individuals towards self-direction, creativity, and individual responsibility. Nevertheless, such individualization, if it is to retain the "human touch," must be realized through caring-family interrelationships that build mutual trust, set a balance between group and individual goals, and retain collaborative behaviors that demonstrate community-family oriented feelings and concerns. In practice, Afro-American education will include the sharing of labor, laughter, and hope, the identification of a personal and group Afro-American selfness, and specification of self-initiated goals and frameworks for the realization of these goals. Individuals will have opportunites to be joyful together, to gain patience in disappointments, to make decisions, to recognize the consequences of appropriate and inappropriate decisions, and to learn to care about oneself and others.

PERSONNEL, STRUCTURE, AND SOCIALIZATION PHASES

Afro-American education must begin at infancy, as the child begins to enter into the enculturative social relationships in his immediate extended family and in the community. Personnel for the Afro-American process of education consists of successive community-family educators (see Diagram 1) who will serve from infancy through adulthood. As children grow, the focus of their education shifts. For children of normal school age, the school will focus on educational activity, observation, and sensing, but the successful socialization of the children (and the resocialization of adults in the community) depends upon community members maintaining the conception that they are *always* educators. The viable transmission of our norms to the young and to psychologically confused Afro-American adults depends at least upon two aspects of awareness on the part of educational personnel: first, that each "family member" perceive that he or she *is* is a family member, and second, that each member be willing to teach another Brother or Sister. Every participant in a social unit within the community must serve an educative function; as such each person is committed to teach what he or she knows to someone else in the community—in a home, park, library, public school, alternative school, or in some other community unit or agency.

It should be understood here that the term "family member" is not used in the "nuclear family" sense, for the latter is a Western-type enclosure of blood relations. In our Afro-American process of education, the term "family member" connotes caring-familial behaviors among all who identify with the community family. These identity points stretch from the home to the community on to the school units such as classrooms, multi-units within the school,(19) and the total school district. These levels of *educational family memberships* hint at a bridge between a few of the more innovative educational approaches and the quality education we seek.(20)

"Family membership" will assume structural dimensions according to what is appropriate for a particular school family or a school district family. However, planners should make certain that the functional educative definitions, duties, and discipline of "family members" (especially as they evolve into policies, procedures, and programs for a district) will conform to horizontal and complementary service relationships that lead to self-imposed goals and evaluation for group excellence. Planners should avoid bureaucratic and

DIAGRAM 1

Personnel for Afro-American Process of Education

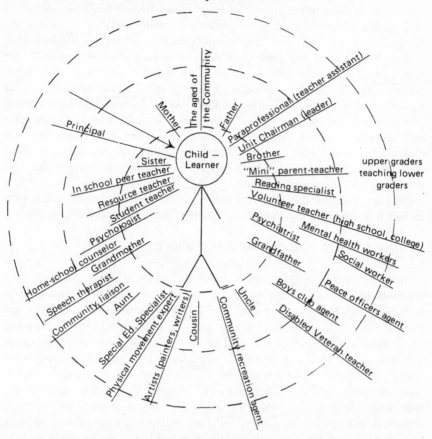

hierarchical models that inhibit the kinds of interactive feelings that would occur in supportive families. When hierarchical and discrete line-staff models are used, teachers, students, and principals begin to strive to please their superiors rather than to develop familial units for providing consistent intragroup improvement through developmental education.

There are four phases of socialization, all of which aim to increase prismatic flows of interaction, shared developmental planning, respect for all abilities, and awareness of one's duty to make a personal commitment to teach others. The first phase, for children from birth to age five, emphasizes assisting extended families in establishing a secure and stimulating environment for the infant. These goals entail guiding parents to learn about children's growth and developmental capabilities. The assumption here is that some degree of intervention in the family will be necessary.

Phases two through four, for five- to nine-year-olds, nine- to thirteen-year-olds, and thirteen- to twenty-year-olds, emphasize interdependent relations and responsibilities among all of the successive community family educators. In these phases, community educators strive to sensitize children to their responsibilities as constructive actors and contributors ("mini" parents and teachers), rather than passive recipients of favors from adults. For example, each community educator will participate in the education of others, especially the young. Each educator will be involved in three basic forms of activity: interrelating with peers in activities related to self-identification and in duties regarding social, cultural, linguistic, and recreational learning functions; working directly on educational committees with peers and adults in teaching functions; and coordinating his own objectives as to vocation, life-style, and philosophy—which will probably include continual education through community college programs. However, this community college education should not be perceived as the schooling that occurs in the usual Anglo community college today. Our community college is distinctly different. It rests on beliefs in self-cleansing, Black identification, and building the community.

THE SEARCH FOR TRUTH AND BLACK IDENTITY

If Afro- (and Anglo) Americans wish to become open to reasonable and equitable approaches to education and social change, it will be necessary to undergo *self-cleansing*, or re-focusing of perspectives. We need to redefine and reorient our wills, feelings, values, reactive inclinations, social concepts, preferences and prejudices, as well as our personal goals and aspirations. Self-cleansing involves a thorough self-examination and truthful reshaping of the "eyes" through which we perceive the self and the world, and the *ways* through which we shall establish a more communal existence. These perspectives initially deal with visual acuity—what we physically see, including, for instance, elemental forms, sizes, structures, and hues. After this stage, if we can bring ourselves to visualize our identities, folkways, and life-styles, we might begin to conceive their boundaries and the outlines of our broader value-systems.

Superficially, these initial visual aspects of one's world-view do not seem complicated. Certainly they are less mentally, morally, and socially taxing than the complex processes that seek soul perspectives. The latter question and move to counter the *causes* of the personal and institutional "conscience crisis" of our time. This crisis, as shown in various levels of distortion, is a general phenomenon in contemporary America; it is a condition of confused *soul vision*: the distortion of affective judgment, of selfness, and of interpretations of the world, and the twisting of one's perceptions and conceptualizations of truth. This soul vision, misshapen by intellectual distortions, diminishes the possibility of expanding one's own positive self-image, and it imprisons the will to allow the diversity of *other* human beings' cultures and *selves* to be free.

There are various levels of distortion (see Diagram 2). Misconceptions of family and kin values lead to beliefs in ascribed privileges for one family or group to the exclusion of another. In the socio-political sphere, perceptual distortions predispose us to acquiesce to limited civil rights and the exclusion of minority groups from decision-making. In religion our institutions parody the one-God, one-way, elect-versus-damned philosophy of mainstream society. More broadly, distorted social vision leads to beliefs about separateness and distinctions about reality. Then we reify the words that partially describe our experience and consequently limit the possibility of creative thinking to make cultural pluralism possible. We learn early to make the kinds of distinctions about speech, dress, manners, and other appearances and behaviors that mask the essential unity of all things—a unity which can be understood best through perceiving human differences through undistorted soul vision.

Those most anxious to "make it" socially are often the least capable of perceiving self and others clearly. They are especially likely to respect and praise socially-proclaimed "superior" intellects, families, social strata, and cultural ways—and especially fearful of maintaining a self different from that which the culturally-dominant group dictates.

DIAGRAM 2

Learning to Think Straight: Reorganising Levels of Distortions in Our Vision

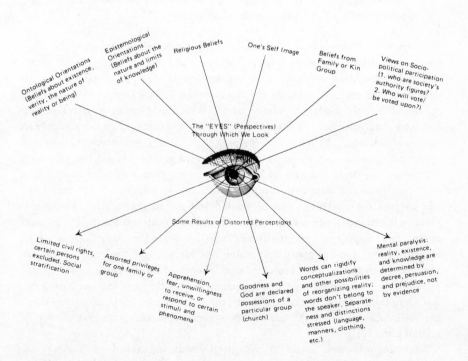

It is easy to see why personal cleansing is a first step. When an individual is distracted from truth by a commitment to distorted perceptions, he is victimized by this very commitment. Even an Afro-American capable of "getting along" emerges with an impaired ability to precisely and forcefully declare, without violence, the cultural components that express the essence of our Afro-American heritage.

Of course, to recommend that Afro-Americans get to know their levels of distortion is not to ignore the concomitant need to restructure the broader American social context—the socially devastating hierarchical stratification, institutional racism, etc.—in which Afro-American communities must exist. But at present, not only does it seem reactive to use most of our energy to assault Anglo values, it is short-sighted. When we reflect upon the distance that we (Afro-Americans) must go to clarify (to and for ourselves) our identity, and when we note that the gap between Haves and Have-Nots is widening, not narrowing, despite all the violence, we begin to realize how great our task of self-identification and implementation is. Our points of identity must still be clarified by us for our children. The education that will transmit these "points" must be engendered. If, for some, the identity question has gone underground, we must unearth it. As one African writer aptly put it:

> Before the African could come into his own, he had to break out of the shell in which others had sought to contain him; he had to destroy the stereotyped idea of himself as an inferior being.(21)

There is a difference between knowing one's Black self and "playing the role" of a revolutionary—one who expends time and energy in rhetoric about destroying Anglo institutions. This becomes most clear in actual practice in education and social change. At the Ravenswood School District, for example, we asked Nairobi College students to work alongside other teachers of the district to motivate unmotivated children to learn. This required the students to put their "assumed" belief about "helping the brothers and sisters to know and appreciate themselves and their community" into practice. It did not take long for these students to discover which persons among them possessed Black selves that were clear and committed enough to design educational experiences within and beyond the classroom that motivated and guided the children. Those few junior educational leaders with clear self and socio-cultural identities designed instructional approaches ranging from "cross age-grade" teaching (helping older students to set familial-group responsibilities for younger students) to regular afternoon school in the junior leaders' homes. During these home-school sessions, young students took turns teaching all that they had learned during the day from their friends, teachers, parents, the garbage man, birds, dogs, etc. Thus, the sessions emphasized the use of one's personal power to observe all that is around him.(22)

Cleansing of one's levels of distortion needs to extend to institutional cleansing and reorientation after criteria are established regarding equitable

GUIDELINES FOR NAIROBI COLLEGE JUNIOR EDUCATIONAL LEADERS IN THE RAVENSWOOD CITY SCHOOL DISTRICT

These are performance competencies and the scale by which Junior Educational Leaders can determine if they are doing adequate justice in serving our young Brothers and Sisters within the School District.

EACH JUNIOR EDUCATIONAL LEADER (LEARNER) WILL:

1. BE ON TIME* to meet students, teacher, or other educational leaders with whom he will work. He/she should work faithfully EVEN WHEN A SUBSTITUTE TEACHER SERVES AT THE ABSENCE OF THE MAIN TEACHER AND PARA-PROFESSIONALS.

2. KEEP HIS PROMISE AND COMMITMENT to the hours, persons, and programs of which he has become a part.

3. NOT REQUEST OR ACCEPT LUNCH PERMITS: these permits belong to the young Sisters and Brothers.

4. EAT WITH STUDENTS at Lunchtime and assist students on the playground.

5. SHARE HIS IDEAS AND EXPERIENCES in attempting to serve our children by producing quality education in a community-family or extended-family atmosphere.

6. Learn new ways of operating in his chosen SITUATION FOR EDUCATIONAL LEARNING (school or District office).

7. DISPLAY HONESTY, INTEGRITY, AND PROFESSIONALISM: he will not tattle, gossip, or carry information that is incorrect into the community and upset parents and others. All misunderstanding will be discussed openly with the persons concerned.

8. SHOW GOOD JUDGMENT, RELIABILITY, AND ENTHUSIASM in his school, classroom, or other task.

9. MOTIVATE OR ATTEMPT TO MOTIVATE OTHERS to better serve our children.

SCALE EXCEPTIONAL	Very good	Average	Low Motivation	POOR
5	4	3	2	1

*We are working toward getting personal commitments that are not bound by time alone.

behavior of institutional agents. The more honest and equitable their behavior, the better the chances of sustaining participation and commitment of the "clients." Social participation retains its dynamic character when parents, students, teachers and all community-family members set positive and satisfying goals, define specific educative tasks, foster maximum communication among members, and engender an atmosphere of just treatment for all. The "guidelines" for junior educational leaders (see p. 335) indicate what this may mean in a community college for Afro-Americans.

We are well aware of the need for individual and societal cleansing in every phase of the dominant culture in this nation, but I am appealing to us—Afro-Americans. Our traditional values and folkways offer us means to recapture ourselves; moreover, the creation of more humane, caring, constructive, and real educational experiences which the process of Afro-American education proposes would provide a model which America sorely needs. A truly Afro-American process of education will not come easily, particularly since so many Afro-Americans have become more American than African in their acquisitiveness. Nevertheless, we must pursue the goal of corporate communality, for this goal involves acceptance of and respect for diverse peoples, a willingness to teach and learn from others, and a commitment to share and communicate.

Euro-American education continues to preclude a pluralistic curricular approach. This has meant social devastation for minorities, and it is to this narrow humanism that the Afro-American "process" model offers an alternative. To the extent that we accept a "process" model of humaneness and communality we may rebuild the level of trust necessary for a pluralistic community. In any case, during this period of social examination Afro-Americans must loudly declare that *we* shall legitimize our existence, and others shall no longer determine for us the words we shall speak, the values we claim, and the beliefs we shall transmit to our children.

NOTES

(1) For convenience the terms "Afro-American" and "Black" are used interchangeably. However, this author prefers *Afro-American* as a more appropriate cultural and geographic designation for our people. At times, as in this paragraph, "Black Man" will refer to all persons of African descent.

(2) See W.E.B. DuBois, "Suppression of the African Slave Trade in America, 1838-1870." Unpublished dissertation, Harvard University, Cambridge, Mass., 1896. Also see DuBois's "Message" in which he dreams "of a world of infinite and invaluable variety." He writes, "But more especially far above and beyond this, in a realm of true freedom: in thought and dream, fantasy and imagination; in gift, aptitude, and genius—all possible manner of difference, topped with freedom of soul to do and be, and freedom of thought to give to a world and build into it, all wealth of inborn individuality . . . to stop this freedom of being is a blow at democracy . . . There can be no perfect democracy curtailed by

color, race, or poverty." In W.E.B. DuBois, The World and Africa: An Inquiry into the Part Which Africa Has Played in World History (New York: International Publishers, 1965), p. 261.

(3) For a discussion of how one might preserve the selfhood of all peoples within a nation-state, and how wealth, land, and political power might be equitably distributed, see J. Nyerere, Education for Self-Reliance (Dar es Salaam, Tanzania: Government Printer, 1967), and Reinhard Bendix, Nation-Building and Citizenship (New York: Anchor Books, 1969), pp. 175-356.

(4) It is not uncommon for Anglo-American curricular directors to include Ebony or perhaps Black World among the suggested reading materials for their school systems, but the writings of certain Blacks might be banned from their library shelves (e.g., E. Cleaver's Soul on Ice or H. Rap Brown's Die Nigger Die).

(5) W. Winwood Reade, The African Sketch-Book, Vol. 2 (London: Smith, Elder, 1873), p. 511.

(6) See George P. Murdock, Africa: Its Peoples and their Cultural History (New York: McGraw-Hill, 1959), pp. 23 ff.

(7) Extrafamilial kinship obligations are common in Africa. Cf. James Gibbs (ed.), Peoples of Africa (New York: Holt, Rinehart and Winston, 1965) and Paul Bohannan, Africa and Africans (New York: The Natural History Press, 1964), Chap. 10.

(8) See Basil Davidson, "The Balance with Nature," The African Genius (Boston: Atlantic Monthly Press, 1969), pp. 54-67.

(9) Cf. Gunter Wagner's discussion of collective ownership among the Bantu of Kavirondo (Kenya) in African Political Systems, Meyer Fortes and E.E. Evans-Pritchard, eds. (London: Oxford University Press, 1940). See R.F. Stevenson, Population and Political Systems in Tropical Africa (New York: Columbia University Press, 1968).

(10) See Daniel F. McCall, Africa in Time-Perspective: A Discussion of Historical Reconstruction from Unwritten Sources (New York: Oxford University Press, 1969), pp. 110-111. Cf. John Gay, "Classification and Thought" (of the Kpelle tribe) Liberian Studies 1 (December, 1967), 20-23. Also see John Gay and Michael Cole, The New Mathematics and an Old Culture: A Study of Learning among the Kpelle (New York: Holt, Rinehart & World, 1967).

(11) Nairobi Day School was initiated in East Palo Alto, California in 1965 under the leadership of Mrs. Gertrude Wilks and The Mothers for Equal Education. Much of Dr. Wilson's thinking is derived from her first-hand experience as consultant to the school.

(12) Augustus Caine, "A Study and Comparison of the West African 'Bush' School and the Southern Sotho Circumcision School." Unpublished Master's Thesis, Evanston, Illinois: Northwestern University, 1959. Cf. Mark Hanna Watkins, "The West African 'Bush' School," American Journal of Sociology, XLVIII (May, 1943), 1666-1675. Reprinted in George Spindler (ed.), Education and Culture (New York: Holt, Rinehart and Winston, 1964), pp. 426-443.

(13) We have noted that essential and valid historio-cultural bases for our

Afro-American process of education will not be found in Western education, or in the bulk of current writings on the Black man's experience. Instead, valid bases must be excavated and compiled from less contaminated sources. Truthful bases might be sought in a number of sources. In archaeology: L.S.B. Leakey, Adam's Ancestors (New York: Longmans, Green & Co., 1935); regarding the oral tradition: Jan Vasina, R. Mauny and L.V. Thomas eds.), The Historian in Tropical Africa (London: Oxford University Press, 1964); in glotto-chronology: Dell Hymes, "Lexicostatistics So Far," Current Anthropology, I (1960), pp. 3-44; in musicology: Ralph H. Metcalfe, "The West African Roots of Afro-American Music," The Black Scholar, I (June, 1970), pp. 16-25; in Black Theater, Floyd Gaffney, "Black Theatre: Commitment and Communication," The Black Scholar, I (June, 1970), pp. 10-15; Mercer and Stephen Henderson, The Militant Black Writer (Madison: The University of Wisconsin Press, 1969); in Afro-American anthropology: Norman E. Whitten and John F. Szwed (eds.), Afro-American Anthropology: Contemporary Perspectives (New York: The Free Press, 1970); in discussion of African land holding practices, myths, rituals and ideologies: L.V. Thomas, "De Quelques Attitudes Africaines En Matière D'Histoire Locale," in J. Masina, R. Mauny and L.V. Thomas (eds.) The Historian in Tropical Africa, 1964.

(14) For the values in American education, see Howard Becker, "Social Class Variations in the Teacher-Pupil Relationship," Journal of Educational Sociology, 25 (April, 1952), pp. 451-465. Also see Talcott Parsons, "The School Class as a Social System: Some of its Functions in American Society," Harvard Educational Review, 29 (Fall, 1959), pp. 297-318.

(15) See Melville J. Herskovits, The Myth of the Negro Past (Boston: Beacon Press, 1958).

(16) Randal's poem epitomizes what was thought to be Black education:

> "It seems to me," said Booker T.,
> "It shows a mighty lot of cheek
> To study chemistry and Greek
> When Mister Charlie needs a hand
> To hoe the cotton on his land,
> And when Miss Ann looks for a cook,
> Why stick your nose inside a book?"

Dudley Randal, "Booker T. and W.E.B." in Black Voices: An Anthology of Afro-American Literature, A. Chapman, ed., (New York: Mentor Books, 1968), p. 470 ff.

(17) In America, the "re-making of Blacks" began with non-legitimate indices for humane values—exploitation of people and things, emphasis on white skins and money as important acquisitions, and association with European objects and knowledge. Cf. "Group Identity in the United States," in Color and Race, John H. Franklin, ed. (Boston: Beacon Press, 1968), pp. 249-263. See Edward W. Blyden, Christianity, Islam and the Negro Race (London: W.B. Whittingham and Co., 1888).

(18) The term "family members will be discussed later with regard to

educational personnel. Cf. McClelland's "achievement motive" as a view toward *personal* achievement. David McClelland, The Achieving Society (Princeton, N.J.: Van Nostrand Publishers, 1961).

(19) See Herbert J. Klausmeier, Richard Morrow, and James E. Walter, "Individually Guided Education in the Multiunit Elementary School: Guidelines for Implementation" (Madison, Wis.: Wisconsin Department of Public Instruction, 1968).

(20) Some works that complement our efforts are: Klausmeier, Morrow, and Walter (*op. cit.*), J.C. Baratz, "Who Should Do What to Whom . . . and Why?" in A.C. Aarons, B. Gordon, and W. Stewart, eds., Linguistic-Cultural Differences and American Education, Special Anthology by the Florida FL Reporter, Spring/Summer, 1969. Also see The Continuous Progress Concept of Seattle's Middle Schools in David Fraser, *et. al.*, "Middle School Overview," Seattle Public Schools, 1969; J.S. Bruner, Toward a Theory of Instruction (New York: W.W. Norton, 1968); H. Taba *et al.*, Teaching Strategies and Cognitive Functioning in Elementary School Children, Coop. Research Project No. 2404 (Washington, D.C.: HEW Department, 1966).

(21) Ayo Ogunsheye: "The African Personality: Ideology and Utopia," Paper presented to International Symposium on African Culture, Ibadan, Nigeria, December 1960, p. 1, mimeographed. See R. Blauner, "Black Culture: Myth or Reality?": in N. Whitten and J.F. Szwed (eds.), Afro-American Anthropology (New York: Macmillan, 1969), and Lee Rainwater, ed., Soul (Chicago: Transaction Books, Aldine Press, 1970).

(22) See K. Yamamoto, ed., The Child and His Image: Self Concept in Early Years (Boston: Houghton Mifflin, 1972); G. Weinstein and M.D. Fantini, eds. Toward Humanistic Education (New York: Praeger, 1970), pp. 66-121. Also see William C. Kvaraceus, *et al.*, Negro Self-Concept: Implications for School and Citizenship (New York: McGraw-Hill Book Co., 1965).

CHILDREN IN HARLEM'S
COMMUNITY-CONTROLLED SCHOOLS

Marcia Guttentag

Views of the poor reflect two competing social ideologies—one elitist, the other egalitarian. Each has an implicit social and an implicit psychological theory. The elitist ideology assumes that people stand where they do in the social system because of biological or psychological determinism. Men on top have risen because of virtue, intelligence, or character. People at the bottom are there because they lack those qualities. Changes in the system would not enable people to change their positions. In contrast, the egalitarian view holds that social systems strongly shape behavior, particularly those systems which determine who has power. A redistribution of power would have many behavioral effects. For that reason, an adherent of the egalitarian view emphasizes participation in its effects, especially the participation of the powerless.

There currently are strong proponents of each point of view, sometimes called the Cambridge Circle vs. the New York radicals, though these differences go back to Hamilton and Jefferson. A quick test of whether someone belongs to one or the other school is to identify his evaluation of what happened during the late 1960s when poverty programs were in their heyday. Elitists view those years as a messy and disappointing failure. Egalitarians see the same events as having provided a necessary training ground for disenfranchised poor and minorities. Community Action Programs gave the poor an opportunity to learn political realities, provided them with money so they could organize, and introduced them to the experience of wresting power from public organizations. Today's militancy among these groups was nurtured by those programs.

The poor, more than any other segment of society, are bound to the functioning of public organizations. These government agencies—federal, state, and local—have the public as their consumers. The jobs of many of the poor are in or obtained through public organizations. Welfare, state employment agencies, public hospitals, and schools impinge on their lives daily.

The situation of the poor in cities used to be different. At one time, immigrant laborers could become established as small entrepreneurs. Local political parties offered jobs or services for the one thing the poor could give that did not require capital—their votes. Educational credentials were not the *sine qua non* for upward mobility.

Today there are few opportunities for the uneducated poor in cities. Business ventures require capital. Manufacturing has fled. Civil service has commandeered the jobs which once were at the fingertips of the politicans.

Since their fate is now tied to the public organizations, the poor try to gain some measure of control over them. The struggle involves such issues as: Who shall run them? To whom shall they be accountable? How shall decisions be made within them? Who hired to work in them? According to what criteria?

Egalitarians support the poor in this struggle, believing that particpatory democracy is the solution and that the poor themselves should have a large measure of power in these decisions. Elitists argue that the control of these organizations is best left in the hands of professionals. Underlying this issue is the larger problem of what the optimal size of the unit in urban organizations should be and how such organizations can become more responsive to the needs of their consumers.

At present, we have few data which can be used to support either the egalitarian or elitist position. Often in the battle over these issues, only the conflict is recorded in the consciousness of the public and social scientists. How then are the controversies over public organizations to be resolved?

One possibility is to see each change in a public agency as a potential social experiment and to use the data from it to create new organizational forms. Such experiments in social change are generated in two very different ways. One approach is to impose them from above, usually with official blessing and endorsement—government agencies approve, even if people outside the agency do not. These experiments may be of long duration and frequently are studied by social scientists. (Many studies of school integration are of this type.) But public organizations do not initiate experiments in which power is given to people outside the agency. These organizations have a natural intransigence toward participation; it is inefficient, untidy, and politically explosive.

Fortunately, there are other social changes, not officially sanctioned, which can also be seen as natural experiments. Like community control, they come into being because of pressure from non-establishment groups. They create real changes in the structure of a public organization—usually in who makes the decisions, who has the money, and who gets the jobs. They occur in schools, in welfare, and in community mental health and are accompanied by a shift in power and accountability. Their key theme is participation in decision-making by the people served. Not surprisingly, they are short-lived because public organizations have a way of subverting them. And also not surprisingly, these experiments in social change are little studied by social scientists.

Why? They don't last a comfortable length of time. Social scientists are inside some of the very organizations which are challenged. Multiple perspectives are required, because the point of view adopted affects the choice of variables and the methods used. Social scientists share the views of established institutions and are acquainted with the elites and the organizational professionals. The perspective of the outsider—the point of view of the powerless—is difficult to adopt. No organization gives up power willingly, so there is always an ugly struggle. Thus these unsanctioned social experiments are generally announced and later condemned in the newspapers. Without evidence, they are often discarded as noisy failures—as was community control of schools in Harlem.

Yet these unsanctioned experiments are likely to provide the most useful data of all on new forms for urban organizations. That is because they directly address the most critical problems of these organizations: consumer power to make decisions, size, responsiveness, and accountability.

To illustrate what such experiments can yield, the following summarizes a series of studies on community control done at the request of and in close collaboration with the community school board of the Intermediate School 201 (IS-201) district. Seven studies were conducted in which the IS-201 district was compared with a neighboring but centrally controlled school district, both in Harlem. We can then consider the effects of community control and its likely future, and return to the question of why it and other unsanctioned social experiments should contribute to decisions on the structure of public organizations in cities.

COMMUNITY CONTROL OF SCHOOLS IN NEW YORK CITY

Education is a route to social mobility. Parents in the inner city want their children to succeed in school. They distrust the central school administration, usually made up of people different from them in social class and ethnic background. They want a say in the schools. Yet, they are confronted by school professionals who make all the decisions. Community control of schools in New York City is an example of an experiment in which parents and local community people did, for a brief time, acquire power over the conduct of their public schools.

It was accompanied by conflict of many kinds, the most pronounced between the professional-educational bureaucracy and the community boards and parents of three poor areas in New York City. From the viewpoint of newspapers and public, community control was only a political struggle. Was there more to it than the disordered surface of events?

The IS-201 Board asked some basic questions about the effects of community control on schools and children. Were community controlled schools different from other schools? How were children affected by experiences in these schools? Did the schools create a sense of community, in contrast to the anomie of other

New York city schools?

Parents said the purpose of community control was to change the schools and, in doing so, to benefit the children. Their long-term aim was improvement of the quality of education.

Effects on children are of interest from several points of view. In New York City the size of minority populations is so great that integrated schools are unlikely under any plan. One must ask whether there are alternative forms of school organization which have beneficial effects on children. Is community control one of these?

One objective of the study was to understand how the schools functioned at several different levels. To do so required measurement of general school characteristics and specific features of subsystems, such as parent involvement, teacher-pupil interactions, and children's expectancies and achievements.

In the late 1960s, three groups of schools in New York City were designated "community controlled": Ocean Hill-Brownsville, Intermediate School 201, and Two Bridges. In contrast to the typical New York City school district with 30,000 children, each of these districts had between four and eight thousand children. Local elections for school board membership were held for the first time since 1900. Each district elected a local community school board. Throughout the country, demonstration school districts have community boards which are more representative of the ethnic populations in their schools than are typical urban school boards (see Table 1).

The IS-201 board was representative of the community. Its 21 elected members included parents, teachers, community representatives, and one school administrator. Membership on the board roughly reflected the educational and social class make-up of the community.

The elected local board gained some direct control over fiscal, personnel, and curricular matters. A grant from the Ford Foundation gave each district a small measure of independence from the New York City Board of Education. The IS-201 district additionally received funds from Rockefeller, Carnegie, New York, Field, and Episcopal foundations along with support from the Michael Schwerner Fund, Warner Fund, Columbia University Urban Center, U.S. Office of Education, and State and City educational authorities.

TABLE 1
Ethnic Composition of Schools and School Boards

Percentage Nonwhite	6 Urban School Districts	Demonstration Districts
Pupil Population	57	56
School Board Members	23	61

Note—Data for these comparisons are from Gittell et al. (1971).

TABLE 2
Ethnic Backgrounds of Lay Board Members, Pupils, and
Community in IS-201 District (Percentages)

Source	Black	Puerto Rican	Other
Pupils	83	16	1
Board Members	73	20	7
Community	92	7	1

In the IS-201 district in Harlem, community organizations and parent groups had become heatedly involved in the local schools when a new junior high school was built several years before. Over parental protests, the school was placed where it could not become an integrated school. After this occurred, community groups demanded autonomy for their schools, and the IS-201 schools became one of the three experimental community controlled districts.

Seven studies were conducted in these schools for the IS-201 governing board. Among the studies were: organizational climate in the schools; parent use of school buildings; administrator's use of time; health and other innovative programs in the schools; teacher-pupil interaction in classrooms, and pre-school and grammar school children's expectancies. A neighboring school district in Harlem with pupils of similar SES and ethnic background was used for comparison.

ORGANIZATIONAL CLIMATE IN THE SCHOOLS

The organizational climate study, conducted by C. Steinhoff and M. Roberts, used Stern's (1963) Organizational Climate Index, a measure of the environmental press as experienced by individuals in an organization. Stern's (1963) Activities Index, an individual self-descriptive measure, also was used. The two instruments share a common taxonomy and supplement one another as reciprocal measures of the individual's characteritstics and his perception of his environment. Only three of the five elementary schools in IS-201 yielded enough returns to be represented.

Compared with a sample of New York City elementary schools for which normative data were available, two of the IS-201 schools in the district provided a significantly stronger expressive climate and one which was stronger in development press. The third school was average compared with the reference population. Sub-scales showed IS-201 schools provided a climate characterized by intellectual activity, social action, individual responsibility, and open-mindedness. Faculty members in these schools described themselves as having personal needs of intellectual aspiration and competitiveness. They perceived the climate of the schools to be supportive of their personal needs.

The self descriptions of IS-201 teachers compared with other New York City teachers also are of interest. IS-201 teachers saw themselves as significantly higher in acceptance of criticism and in purposefulness. They believed they were

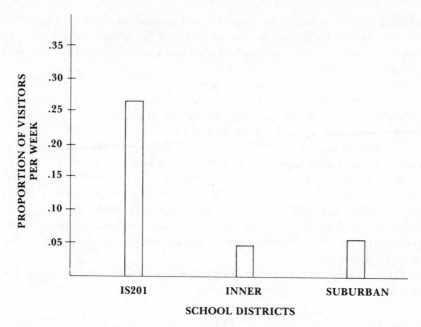

FIGURE 1.
School visitors per week relative to enrollment (based on Rothenberg's study).

more organized and self-reliant.

These findings are surprising because the comparison sample was biased in the direction of middle-class schools. Nevertheless, it was the IS-201 schools, with a lower-class population, which showed the stronger expressive climate and placed greater stress on intellectual matters, on achievement standards, and on personal dignity. In Stern's terms, the IS-201 schools had a press for achievement, change, tolerance, objectivity, and sensuality. This translates into a juicier, more vivid environment, one with more sights and sounds, one less repressively controlled.

PARENT INVOLVEMENT IN IS-201 SCHOOLS

In their fight to obtain community control, one of the strongest arguments marshalled by community groups was that inner-city schools tend to be closed to parents. Community groups wanted an open atmosphere where parents would be able to communicate directly with school staff through the district level. It was hoped that this would create greater involvement in school affairs on the part of parents. It would also permit community residents to rely on their own observations about what happened in the schools. School board members then could be held directly accountable.

The parent involvement study, done by Marilyn Rothenberg, investigated the use of school buildings by visitors. Observations were made on randomly selected days in community controlled and comparison districts. The survey included the name of each person who entered the school, his purpose, the identity of persons seen, the length of stay, and whether the person had a child attending the school.

Observations also were made for after-school-hours use as well as in the evening, when types of activity and numbers of people involved were recorded. To supplement the survey data, the calendars of administrators were examined for the names of groups and individuals they had seen.

Two compariosn school districts were used: the neighboring school district in Harlem and a suburban school district with the same number of schools.

The number of visitors for randomly selected days was totalled and divided by school enrollemnt to make possible a comparison of proportions. In the IS-201 district there was one visitor for every four pupils; in the two comparison districts, one visitor for every 20 pupils. The relative number of visitors to the community controlled schools was overwhelmingly greater than either comparison district.

Table 3 shows the percentages of visitors classified by stated purpose. The first three categories are of greatest interest.

TABLE 3
Percentage of Visitors by Purpose and School Category

Purpose	School Category		
	IS-201	Urban Controls	Suburban Controls
Parent/Child	49	7	52
Parent/Re: Child	10	36	9
Organizational/Parent	10	7	20
Health	2	0	2
Professional	16	14	9
Other	13	36	8

Note—Data are from parent involvement study conducted by M. Rothenberg.

The category, *Parent/Child*, includes visits by parents primarily to deliver a child, to take a child from school, or to bring something to him. It provides an indication of the ease with which parents entered the schools in IS-201. About half of all visitors were parents who entered the building when walking their children to or from school. This contrasts with 7 percent for the urban control schools. This activity was encouraged at IS-201. Parents often brought their children to the classroom and remained for a while. At pickup time parents arrived early and spent time observing or helping. People in this category averaged a stay of more than ten minutes.

Parent/Re: Child includes only those parent visits to discuss a child, usually his misbehavior, with a teacher or principal. These were not casual visits; they were requested by school personnel. In IS—201, few parents came to discuss the behavior of their child.

Organizational/Parent includes parents' visits for group activities, such as observing a class unit, PTA meeting, or parent education. Some visitors in this category said they were there to help in the reading course, or with multi-media. Still others said they were there "to look in on the children" or "to visit a class."

In the (urban) comparison schools, the most frequent category was that of parents entering the school to discuss a child's misbehavior. In the suburban school district the breakdown of visitors by purpose was not unlike that of IS-201.

Were parents who came to the IS–201 schools representative of the low SES families in the neighborhood or were they just the better educated ones? Parents were asked to write a brief phrase about why they had come to the school. Linguistic analysis of these showed that they were representative.

School administrators in IS-201 and the comparison district had diverse attitudes toward this study. In IS-201, they were concerned only that the study might hinder parents' access to the buildings or deflect them even briefly from their purpose in coming to the schools. In contrast, an administrator of the comparison schools agreed to the survey with the comment that she didn't know how profitable the study would be because when parents come to the school "they are liable to be too angry" to sign the survey—implying that they came only when summoned.

COMMUNITY USE OF SCHOOLS

All schools in the IS-201 complex had active afternoon, evening, and weekend centers open to the community, all with a large range of activities. Activities were diverse and encouraged participation by people of all ages and interests. The school buildings were vital community centers. The study of administrator's calendars showed a great many community organizational contacts and much time spent with parents and students.

In contrast to the comparison district, school staff devoted a considerable time to telling the community what was going on in the schools. Flyers were sent to homes on a variety of topics. Adults in the community felt free to enter the schools and took advantage of this opportunity. Many assumed responsibility for part of an educational program. The amount of face-to-face contact between parents and staff was much greater than in the comparison schools. Parents and teachers worked together with fewer status differences.

One can infer that parents perceived the schools to be less anonymous and alienating than schools in the comparison district. Parents of low SES, with limited education, usually are hesitant to enter the schools and rarely participate in school activities. IS-201 differed sharply from this pattern.

Big city school systems suffer from a lack of flexibility and a limited number of innovative programs, though cities are most in need of them. Proponents of community control believed that it would permit innovative educational programs which would be related to local needs. In the absence of a centralized bureaucracy, many more such programs were expected.

This proved to be the case (see Gittell, 1971). We studied several in the IS-201 district. I will briefly mention two and discuss the health program more fully.

Programs initiated in each demonstration district ranged from brief to long-term. For example, IS-291 had a "teach-out," to demonstrate the school curriculum to the community. On a spring day, classes were held outside on the school mall and in the street. A great many people observed these lessons.

A variety of programs in reading and math were initiated in schools in the district. One school, which used the Gattegno reading method, showed a dramatic increase in reading achievement.

Of the number of these programs we assessed, the health program can serve an an illustration. This study was carried out by Liebman. In a suburban area where general health is good and children see private physicians frequently, a health program in the schools would arouse little comment. In Harlem, however, health services in the schools are inadequate or nonexistent. Despite unusually high rates of tuberculosis, sickle cell anemia, and vision and hearing problems, few children ever receive examinations. The IS—201 district initiated a system of diagnostic examinations and established relationships with nearby hospitals, medical schools, and colleges. For the present study, a one-fifth sample of the school population was selected. Of the children sampled, 87% had received visual screening tests and 97% auditory tests at the time of the study. Serious visual or hearing problems were found in 10%. Diagnostic examinations revealed that there were physical problems at a rate of 54 per 100 children. At the time of our study 41% of these problems had been treated. Most children had received immunizations for the first time. Free eyeglasses were provided.

Findings were similar on all the innovative programs studied. There were many more of them, and those we studied were highly effective.

TEACHER-PUPIL CLASSROOM INTERACTION

Were the classrooms of IS-201 different? Wiser and Fanin conducted a study of teacher-pupil interactions in the community controlled school and the comparison district. Interaction analysis, using the Flanders-Dunbar technique (Flanders, 1960), was the observation system used in the classrooms in each school. This technique codes both teacher and pupil talk and the contingency relationships between them. Black and white, male and female teachers were sampled.

In IS-201, student-initiated talk was more often directly followed either by teacher praise or teacher acceptance of the student's ideas, a highly significant finding. Furthermore, although teacher's race was significantly related to verbal behavior in the comparison schools, this was not true of the community controlled schools.

These findings suggest that a social climate had been created in the community controlled schools which was more powerful than the individual characteristics of teachers, for in the comparison district race predicted interaction patterns. Children in the community controlled classrooms were exposed to a distinctive academic and social experience, one which was more strongly positive than that in comparison schools.

Each of the previously mentioned studies of the IS-201 district schools indicated that these schools were markedly different from those of the neighboring district. Teachers and administrators perceived them to have a stronger, freer intellectual atmosphere and a more growth-inducing climate. Parents were actively involved in school programs and had free access to the schools. The schools themselves had more varied and successful innovative programs. Teacher's responses to pupils were more positive.

CLARK AND CLARK REPLICATION

Given the school characteristics reported above, what were the effects on children?

A flurry of studies in recent years have replicated the Clark and Clark doll preference and identification studies (1947). Nearly all have found that black preschool children, at least those who live in cities, now prefer black dolls and accurately identify them. In fact one recent study (Fox & Barnes, 1972) has shown that Chinese children are much more likely to choose white dolls and to make derogatory statements about same-race dolls than are black children.

Therefore it is not surprising that when we replicated the Clark and Clark study with preschool children, no differences in racial identification were found between the IS-201 preschool children and those in the comparison district. But on racial preference, the IS−201 preschool girls showed a stronger preference for their own race dolls than did the controls. The same was true for boys, though it was not as pronounced as it was for girls.

All children in Harlem are exposed to a strong emphasis on black pride; most have black dolls, One would not expect to find differences between preschool children in the IS-201 and comparison district. That such differences were found suggests that the special social climate of these schools had penetrated even to the preschool level, where girls, as usual, showed the greatest responsiveness to social inputs.

ACHIEVEMENT

We turn now to changes in the achievements and expectancies of older children in the grammar and junior high schools of IS-201. Achievement often is treated as the only important output of schools. Although higher achievement certainly was one of the aims of the community board, it was by no means the only one. As well as improved achievement, the board also wanted schools that were open to parents, and a change in classroom and school atmosphere.

Achievement results must be pieced together from two sources, neither of which provides adequate information. The first is the standard achievement testing given throughout New York City. It does not provide valid data. All the community controlled districts were hostile toward the standardized achievement tests sent from the City Bureau of Educational Research. Many teachers did not administer them. Others gave them carelessly or idiosyncratically.

A second source is a study of achievement in IS-201 conducted by the Psychological Corporation in the spring of 1971. In this study, teachers gave special achievement measures to preschool, kindergarten, and first grade children. New York City group tests were used for higher grades. To provide a comparison population, children who had been in the complex for three successive years were compared with those who had been in the complex for only two years. This analysis aimed to reveal the effect of different amounts of educational experience in the IS-201 schools.

Generally, the gap between national norms and the norms of New York City schools increases by grade. In 1968-69 one-fourth of all children in elementary schools were two or more years behind in reading, an increase from the previous year's figure of one-fifth of all children. In the IS-201 schools, however, first and second graders reached national norms in both reading and arithmetic. In one school of the complex, the mean in reading surpassed the national norm by two months. While New York City's achievement norms declined in 1968-69, reading achievement levels at IS-201 did not decline. Moreover, some individual schools in IS-201 showed considerable advances. A school which had a special reading program showed a rise in reading level for the entire school. Second and third grade children were reading at nearly a full year above the national norm. Between 1969 and 1971, the means for successive pupil groups at the same grade levels in the IS–201 district increased from second to sixth grade level.

To evaluate the effect of community control on achievement, the most useful information is the comparison of the achievement scores of children in the district for three years with those in the district for a shorter period. The three-year children had means significantly higher than the average child in their grade.

To summarize, despite the scattered and fragmented nature of the achievement data, achievement in the community controlled schools apparently improved over the three-year period of their existence. One school in the district was significantly above national norms for reading. Children who had been in the district for three years showed significantly higher reading and math scores than did other children. Moreover, IS-201 did not share in the general decline in New York City achievement scores. The picture was best for young children in kindergarten and first grade; for children from second to sixth grade it was somewhat better than the comparison schools. Seventh and eighth-grade children did not show similar gains.

"Expectancies" are what children think will happen to them—in school, with adults, in the political arena, and in the future. The cluster of expectancies called "locus of control" accounts for much of the variance in the academic achievement of poor and minority children. Locus of the control refers to the child's belief that chance, luck, and other external factors as opposed to his own actions, intentions, and other internal factors determine what happens to him.

The research literature indicates that changes in expectancies are associated with changes in academic achievement. The Coleman report (1966) suggested that expectancies are more internal for children who attend integrated schools. Other studies show that expectancies can become more internal after children experience control over what happens to them. Undoubtedly there are many situations which can affect expectancies.

Expectancies of poor and minority children are more complex and differentiated than those of middle-class children. They also are more responsive to environmental changes.

Do community controlled schools affect children's expectancies? Community control provided parents with greater power and particiaption in the schools. Children in the IS—201 schools had the opportunity to see their parents in autonomous roles. It seemed reasonable that children's own beliefs about their likelihood of success in the schools should be altered by these experiences. If this were so, then long term changes in academic achievement were possible even if no immediate effects were apparent.

When this study began, no expectancy questionnaires had been standardized on a large population of poor, urban and minority children. Therefore several instrumentation studies were done with large samples of such grade school, poor, urban,and minority children, in which all relevant children's expectancy scales were used. In each of these studies, it was found that expectancy scores made an appreciable contribution to achievement variance.

Children in the community controlled and comparison districts received expectancy questionnaires in 1970 and 1971. These questionnaires contained items distilled from previous studies and a number of others written together with the IS-201 board.

No differences were found between the districts for total expectancy scores, but there were many significant subscale and item differences. For example, on a subscale of expectancies of personal effectiveness, means for the IS-201 children were all signifcantly higher.

Were children more aware of the active and influential roles of parents and teachers? If they were, then IS-201 children should have made more external choices on items relating to school and parents and should not have differed from the controls on non-school-related questions. Table 4 shows some illustrative data on this question. Each tally for the two districts represents a significant Chi-square for treatment effects for a single item.

Every one of 13 significant Chi-squares for school-related items is in the external direction for IS-201 pupils and in the internal direction for controls. On non-school-related items, there is no systematic difference for internality—externality. Clearly, IS-201 pupils responded vigorously to the changed school environment, especially to the influence of parents and teachers on school performance.

One can get a better idea of the meaning of this finding from the content of some items. On one, IS-201 pupils attribute a child's learning something quickly in school to the teacher's clear explanation. On another, they attribute difficulty in working arithmetic problems to the teacher's having given problems that were too hard.

TABLE 4

Differences in Locus of Control Between IS-201
and Comparison Schools

	School-Related Items	
	External response	Internal response
IS-201	13	0
Comparison Schools	0	13
	Non-School-Related Items	
	External response	Internal response
IS-201	12	11
Schools	11	12

Note—Frequencies represent the number of items having significant Chi-Squares in the labeled direction.

There are some straightforward implications to be drawn from the expectancy findings and some questions left open by them. The clarity of results leaves no doubt that the changed school environment was directly perceived and responded to by children in IS-201 schools. School related items sharply differentiated IS-201 from comparison children. Whenever IS-201 children made causal attributions which required a choice between teachers or parents and themselves, they overwhelmingly placed the locus of cause in adults. Teachers and parents were a more salient feature of the school environment to these children.

In previous studies, children's external expectancies about success in school generally are associated with low achievement; internal expectancies are related to higher academic achievement, at least for middle-class children. If poor children's expectancies mirror reality, they must believe that external circumstances make a difference in whether they succeed in school. The data just reported show a new combination: a shift toward more external expectancies about who has power in the schools (parents and teachers) combined with higher academic achievement. In IS-201 schools, the children's perception of teachers' and parents' responsibility for the schools was correlated with higher academic achievement.

Externality of school expectancies for lower-class children has different meanings in different contexts. When the child believes the school is alien, that adults are remore or hostile, and that what he does will not influence what happens to him, his external expectancies are linked to lower academic achievement. When, however, he perceives the school to be accepting of him, and, his parents support the school and have some power in it, his realistic appreciation of this changed school environment is reflected in external expectancies and higher achievement.

IS-201 children thus attribute the success or failure of their school performance to parents, teachers, and the school rather than to their own characteristics. This is especially revealed in answers to expectancy questions on blame for failure. IS-201 children, much more often than controls, place blame for a specific failure on parents, teachers, or the school; the IS-201 children were not self-blaming. Similarly, they more often gave credit to teachers for their own good performance than did comparison children.

CONCLUSIONS

No one of the studies just reported can stand by itself. Taken together they show that a major social change with far-reaching effects had taken place in the community-controlled schools. This change created a radically different school structure. Despite many problems, the IS-201 schools were doing what the community school board wanted them to do. They were more innovative; the school climate was more intellectual and stimulating; teacher pupil interaction, more positive. Parents made their presence known in the schools; they were frequently in the schools for a variety of constructive purposes. Children showed somewhat higher academic achievement. The school children were acutely aware of the power and salience of parents and teachers in their schools. An outsider had the impression of one cohesive group from school board members to pupils, all committed to and enthusiastic about the IS–201 schools.

IS-201 no longer exists. It was swallowed up into a larger school district following a change in New York State law. This law created a weakened form of school decentralization throughout New York City. The law permitted elected boards, but these were stripped of the fiscal, personnel, and curricular power which the experimental community controlled districts had assumed. District size was considerably larger.

The state legislature passed the weak decentralization law as a way of ridding New York City of the troublesome experimental districts, and, at the same time, placating critics of centralization. In the process of incorporation into the larger district, all of IS-201's special programs were dismantled. Ironically, the district into which IS-201 was absorbed had served as the comparison school district in the studies just reported.

In New York City, as in other parts of the country, decisions about community control are settled solely in the political sphere. The decision to abolish the experimental districts was made in the absence of data on the effects of this experiment on schools and children. It was made in complete awareness of the intense conflict which had erupted between organizational professionals and inner-city residents. It was clear to the lawmakers that community control experiments attempted to shift the power of educational policy decisions to new groups.

The political future of community control is an uncertain one. There are at least two possible future outcomes, and undoubtedly more. One likely outcome is that within the next ten years teachers, school administrators, and central school board members will be much more representative of the population of children in the schools. This trend is accelerating in most urban centers. When ethnic minorities see board members, teachers, and administrators from their own groups, the demands for community control of schools in cities may decline. From this point of view, demands for community control represent a transitional phase in the ethnic make-up of public organizations in cities.

The second—and I think a more likely—outcome is that even when ethnic homogeneity exists, experiments in community control will continue. Pressure for community control today is found in ethnically homogeneous school systems. This continued pressure is to be expected, since differences in social class between the poor and professionals in charge of the schools are likely to remain. The problem of the gap between centralized decision-making and the attitudes and desires of the consumers of education will continue, as will the issue of the sheer size of educational and other public organizations in cities.

Therefore it is worth asking why the experiment in community control just reported was successful. There were, I think, two reasons. The first was the small size of the community controlled district. In Harlem most informal social organization is linked to the block in which a person lives. People do not drive, they walk or take the subway to their destinations. Thus in Harlem a small school district in which the schools are within walking distance maximizes the likelihood of face-to-face contact between parents and school personnel, as was apparent in IS-201.

Undoubtedly the optimal size of a public organization varies according to a number of technological, physical and social characteristics of the population it serves. The purpose of the agency, who it serves, where it is located, and the social organization of the community are a few of the many factors which should be balanced in the identification of optimal size. At present this is not done; most ecological considerations are ignored. Decisions about size are currently made on political and intra-organizational grounds, not on the basis of optimal psychological size. More data are needed on the critical variables and weights which should enter into size decisions; thus a variety of natural experiments must be studied.

The second reason for the success of IS-201 was the powerful and shared ideological commitment of people in the district. It originated with the history of the district when community organizations banded together to fight a common enemy—the central school board—in the dispute over the placement of the "integrated" school. The community's commitment was maximized during the life of the district by the successful policy of active parent participation and involvement in the schools. Such shared ideological commitments had pervasive effects throughout the school organization.

Yet one cannot discover such an ideology without looking for it. Let me illustrate. The ghost of reductionism lingers on in research with children. Research continues to be conducted as though children were isolated from the larger social system, as though they were immune to the ideology and rules which govern the whole social context. Generally only the immediate environment of the classroom is studied. Explanations of children's attitudes and behaviors extend only to the face-to-face level of interactions. Yet it is the social and ideological system within which these interactions are embedded which provides the truest and most general explanation for the observed interactions.

Ideology counts even with children. They do respond to a major change in the distribution of power in a school district. If in the study of IS-201 only teacher-pupil interactions had been studied, or only achievement scores reported, little would be known about community control of schools in Harlem. Such single results ignore the "why" of it all.

Philosophers of human action, the symbolic interactionists, Goffman, Garfinkel, and many others, stress how important both the social context and the implicit rules which govern behavior are in understanding the meaning and thus the explanation of individual behavior. These ideas apply with equal force to the understanding of social systems of every size. The growth of a vigorous ideology in IS-201 was also undoubtedly helped by the small size of the district.

The study of just one natural experiment in community control has been reported. This experiment happened to have been successful. Undoubtedly, many unsanctioned social experiments are failures. Nevertheless, these fleeting, unsanctioned experiments in participation must be studied. They can provide some partial answers to the problems of urban organizations—size, complexity, centralization, and accountability. Decisions about organizational changes in the future should be made on the basis of more than elitist or egalitarian biases. In the absence of data, elitist views win.

REFERENCES:

Clark, K., & Clark, M.P. Racial identification and preference in Negro children. In T.M. Newcomb & E.L. Hartley (Eds.), Readings in social psychology. New York: Holt, 1947.

Coleman, J.S., et al. Equality of educational opportunity. Washington, D.C.: U.S. Government Printing Office, 1966.

Flanders, N.A. Teacher influence, pupil attitudes, and achievement. Minneapolis: University of Minnesota, 1960. (Mimeo)

Fox, D.J., & Barnes, V.B. Racial preference and identification of black, American Chinese, and white children. Unpublished manuscript, CUNY, 1972.

Gittell, M. et al. Demonstration for social change: An experiment in local control. New York: Institute for Community Studies, Queens College, CUNY, 1971.

Stern, G.G. Measuring noncognitive variables in research on teaching. In N.L. Gage (Ed.), Handbook of research on teaching. Chicago: Rand McNally, 1963.

SOCIAL DISTANCE AND
SOCIAL INEQUALITY IN A GHETTO
KINDERGARTEN CLASSROOM:
AN EXAMINATION
OF THE 'CULTURAL GAP' HYPOTHESIS

Ray C. Rist

A widely used approach in the analysis of the relationship between the ghetto school teacher and the pupils with whom she is in daily contact is that of the "cultural gap" hypothesis. This hypothesis, associated with such men as Davis (1952) and Riessman (1962), proposes that the ghetto school teachers are middle-class in their occupational status and cultural values, while their pupils are described as overwhelmingly from the lower class and, consequently, adhere to lower-class values and attitudes. Since, it is argued, the values of the middle class and those of the lower class are so widely divergent, there exists a cultural gap between teacher and pupils.

Becker (1952), Coleman et al., (1966), Hollingshead (1949), Leacock (1969), Rist (1970), Stein (1971), and Warner et al. (1944), among others, have all demonstrated that the social-class position of the student does in fact affect his role within the social system of the public school. These writers have documented, in both elementary and secondary schools, the critical importance of social-class position in relation to academic achievement, participation in school activities, formulation of peer cliques, and interactional patterns with teachers. In sum, the findings suggest that academic success in school is directly related to one's social-class position—the higher the class, the higher the probability of academic success. James Coleman (et al., 1966: 325) spoke to this point when he noted:

> One implication stands out above all: That schools bring little influence to bear on a child's achievement that is independent of his background and

general social context; and that this very lack of independent effect means that the inequalities imposed on children by their home, neighborhood, and peer environment are carried along to become the inequalities with which they confront adult life at the end of school. For equality of edcuational opportunity through the schools must imply a strong effect of schools that is independent of the child's immediate social environment, and that strong independent effect is not present in American schools.

It is the goal of the paper to demonstrate within one urban kindergarten classroom the manner in which those "inequalities imposed on children" were not overcome but, in fact, reinforced. The cultural and status distance between teacher and pupils generated a learning milieu where "some could do it and some could not," depending upon the degree of differentness one possessed from the teacher.

To date, the empirical verification of the cultural gap hypothesis has been tenuous at best. *A serious shortcoming in substantiating the position results from those researchers who have advocated the presence of such a gap failing to demonstrate explicitly how the "gap" is manifested within the classroom setting.* That is, any number of studies are cited which demonstrate that there are significant differences in the socioeconomic status rankings of the teacher and the vast majority of her pupils. Note is also made of the exceedingly high dropout rate of these low-income youth from school, with the implication being that the teacher and the students were not able to communicate effectively; the students became frustrated and dropped (or were pushed) out. But the *process* by which such teacher-pupil interactional dynamics occur over time is yet to be sufficiently documented. With the lack of verification from direct classroom observations, the theoretical formulation essentially rests on the secondary data analysis and thus remains open to vigorous dispute. It is the purpose of this paper to move beyond the discussion of the cultural gap hypothesis based on secondary data analysis and subject it to a scrutiny based on direct observation of classroom interaction within an urban black school. By such direct observation, it is hoped that a significant methodological shortcoming can be at least partially overcome.

Della-Dora (1966: 270), Jackson (1968: 28), and Riessman (1962: 82-84) have all noted that one manifestation of status and cultural differences between the teacher and her pupils is the presence of "social distance." If such a contention is correct, and it is assumed within this paper that it is, then frequent and overt manifestations of social distance would suggest the presence of a cultural gap, while the infrequent presence of such distance would negate this assumption. (It is assumed that there would inevitably occur some degree of social distance between the teacher and pupils due to a number of differentials such as age, role, authority, and the option for legitimized use of physical force.) The validity of the hypothesis would not appear to rest upon the substantiation of the presence of distance, but evaluating the degree of its frequency and intensity (compare Banton, 1967: 315-333).

Parenthetically, Mannheim (1957: 47) notes that social distance may take one of two primary forms—an external or spatial distance on the one hand, and an internal or mental distance on the other. The whole variety and diversity of social and cultural life as it pertains to such phenomena as social differentiation and social status would be inexplicable without the construct of social distance. Lacking such a conceptualization, one could speak of a variety of objects and persons, but not their interrelationships within a social world. As Mannheim (1957: 52) notes, the enforced distancing of persons from one another is a pattern of organization essential to the existence and continuity of a highly stratified social structure.

Data for this study were collected over the length of one academic year by means of twice-weekly visits of one and one-half hours to the kindergarten classroom of a group of black children. During the visits to the classroom, a continuous handwritten account was taken of interaction and activity as they occurred. Smith and Geoffrey (1968) have termed this method of classroom observation "microethnography." Additionally, interviews were conducted with both the kindergarten teacher and the principal at the school. No mechanical devices were utilized to record classroom activities or interviews.

I believe that it is methodologically necessary, at this point, to clarify what benefits can be derived from nonparticipant observation of a single group of children. An apparent weakness of the vast majority of studies of urban education is that they lack any longitudinal perspective. The complexities of the teacher-pupil interactional process which evolves over time within a classroom cannot be discerned with a single two- or three-hour observational period. Also, education is a social process that cannot be reduced merely to variations in IQ scores over a period of time. At best, IQ scores can give indication of potential, not of process. I also would contend that the particular school and classroom described in this study are not atypical from others in urban black neighborhoods. They bear strong resemblance to those described in the academic literature on urban schools (compare Eddy, 1967; Fuchs, 1969; Leacock, 1969; Levy, 1970; Moore, 1967), as well as that of the popular literature (compare Haskins, 1969; Kohl, 1967, Kozol, 1967).

The district superintendent of the city public schools selected the school in which this study occurred along with four others as available to the research team. All five of the selected schools were visited during the study, and intensive observations were conducted in four of them. The principal of the school reported upon in this study commented that he believed I was quite fortunate to have the opportunity to observe in his school since, he noted, his staff "was equal to any in the city." He made special reference to the kindergarten teacher as "one of the best." Finally, as an additional benefit of detailed longitudinal study, there was the enhanced possibility of gaining further insights into the various adaptive mechanisms employed by black children to an institution oriented toward white, middle-class values.

The school which the kindergarten children attend is located in a predominantly low-income area of the city that has a 98% black population within its census district. The enrollment in the school, which was built in the early part of the 1960s, fluctuates near 900. There are 26 teaching staff in addition to a librarian, 2 physical education instructors, the principal, and an assistant principal. A speech therapist, a social worker, a nurse, and a doctor are all at the school on a part-time basis and are employed by the city Board of Education. All administrators, teachers, staff and pupils are black (the author is Caucasian). Of the nearly 900 pupils, just under 500 (55%) come from families which receive funds from Aid to Dependent Children, a form of public welfare.

SOCIAL DISTANCE: CLASSROOM MANIFESTATIONS

The spatial arrangement of the classroom gave clear expression to a number of social distinctions between the teacher and pupils. The pupils sat at long tables (composed of individual desks pushed together) facing the blackboard at the front of the room. The teacher's desk was at the rear of the room behind the children. When at her desk, she was in a position to have the children under observation. However, the children were unable to observe her activities with the same ease. Windows were confined to the rear wall of the room. Wall space to the right and left of the children contained storage areas as well as bulletin boards.

The kindergarten child's space of free movement was generally restricted simply to his seat at a table. The child was assigned to a particular location, which he occupied throughout the class session. He kept his school paraphernalia in a drawer under the table, but since it was unlocked and open to inspection, it by no means provided the child with a personal and private storage place (for documentation of similar circumstances, compare Eddy, 1967: 72-74). Additionally, several children during the school year exchanged seats because the teacher told them to do so.

The teacher's area or region of movement within the classroom was not restricted. She spent much time in the front of the room by the blackboard. In this area, she not only assigned work to the children, but also occasionally had the children present their work for her correction in front of their peers. The spatial arrangement reflected the role of the teacher as one who was distinct from the children and had areas of movement apart from those allowed for the children. The teacher in this class was in a position to move without restraint into the restricted area of the children either to reward, criticize, or supervise. The pupils, on the other hand, were not supposed to leave their seats without first gaining permission from the teacher.

The permanent seating of the children in the classroom on the eighth day of school took on additional significance when it is noted that they appear to have been seated based on a number of social-class criteria independent of any measurement of cognitive capacity and ability to perform academic tasks. These criteria are codified in Table 1.

It is evident from these data that there were a number of children within the class who came from homes where both parents were present, income levels were

TABLE 1
DISTRIBUTION OF SOCIAL CLASS VARIABLES
BY SEATING ARRANGEMENT

Factors	Seating Arrangement [a]		
	Table 1	*Table 2*	*Table 3*
Income			
(1) Families on welfare	1	2	4
(2) Families with father employed	6	3	2
(3) Total family income below			
$3,000 per year[b]	0	4	7
(4) Total family income above			
$12,000 per year[b]	4	0	0
Family Size			
(1) Both parents present	6	3	2
(2) Average number of siblings in family	3-4	5-6	6-7
(3) Families with one child	3	1	0
Education			
(1) Father ever high school	5	2	1
(2) Father ever college	1	0	0
(3) Mother ever high school	7	6	5
(4) Mother ever college	4	0	0

a. There are nine children at table 1, eleven at table 2, and ten at table 3.
b. Estimated from stated occupation.

in the middle class, and the parents had at least high school education or beyond. These children the teacher placed at the first table (table 1) and referred to them as her "fast learners." Her resultant preferential treatment of this group (e.g., recieving approximately two-thirds of all classroom teaching time, receiving less than a third the number of rebukes given to those at the other tables, and touching them more frequently), appeared to be derived from her assumption that certain social and cultural factors were highly significant in determining learning ability within the school. There also appears to be the basis to claim that such differential treatment may ensure a self-fulfilling prophecy within the class whereby those expected to do well did so. It is perhaps not unimportant to reiterate that the seating assignments for the academic year were made on the eighth day of school. At the end of the school year, the teacher noted:

> I guess the best way to say it is that very few children in my class are exceptional. I guess you could notice this just from the way the children were seated this year. Those at table 1 gave consistently the most responses throughout the year and seemed most interested and aware of what was going on in the classroom.

Those children who were placed at tables 2 and 3 were progressively dissimilar in social-class characteristics from those at table 1. At table 2, and even more so at table 3, were children from broken homes, families supported by Aid to Dependent Children funds, low levels of education, and families with large numbers of siblings. The teacher appeared to believe that these characteristics were not conducive to academic performance and thus placed them at the two tables she indicated were served for "slow learners." The teacher also commented on the children at these two tables and noted:

> It seems to me that some of the children at table 2 and most of the children at table 3 at times seem to have no idea of what is going on in the classroom and are off in another world all by themselves. It just appears that some can do it and some cannot. I don't think that it is the teaching that affects those that cannot do it, but some are just basically low achievers.

Though the blackboard stretched along one side of the room in front of all three tables, the assignments and drawings done by the teacher were consistently on the board space in front of those children at table 1. Thus those at table 2 and even more so at table 3 had difficulty in observing the teacher's blackboard activities. As an example of the way in which this situation also contributed to ensuring that the labels given by the teacher to the various groups of children remained intact (though I do not wish to impute that it was done deliberately), the seating location of Lilly may demonstrate the penalty those at the last table in particular had to pay (the names of all teachers and students are pseudonyms. Names are provided to indicate that the discussion relates to the experiences of living persons, and not to fictitious characters developed by the author).

> Lilly stands up out of her seat. Mrs. Caplow asks Lilly what she wants. Lilly makes no verbal response to the question. Mrs. Caplow then says rather firmly to Lilly, "Sit down." Lilly does. However, Lilly sits sideways in the chair (so she is still facing the teacher). Mrs. Caplow instructs Lilly to put her feet under the table. This Lilly does. Now she is facing directly away from the teacher and the blackboard where the teacher is demonstrating to the students how to print the letter "O."

The teacher appeared to decide very early in the school year which children in her class were going to be "successful" students and which were going to be "failures." The criteria which led to her decisions seemingly included her intuitive evaluation of the child's intellectual potential as only one of a number of factors. The social contingencies physical hygiene, darkness of skin, social status of parents, the frequency and intensity of interaction with both the teacher and other students, and the ability of the child to utilize standard American English as opposed to reliance on Black American English were of equal, if not greater, importance in evaluating the child's potential educatability. Those children who possessed any of the traits of poor physical hygiene, dark skin, low family status, low social interactional patterns, or infrequent use of standard American English were all evaluated by the teacher as being "slow learners."

One example of the way in which social contingencies influenced the child's chances for educational achievement concerned whether the child came from a family which subsisted on public welfare. A roster of all welfare-supported children tentatively registered for the kindergarten class was supplied to the teacher before school began. Both the teacher and the school administration were then involved periodically in filing reports with the city welfare department as to the child's attendance, physical appearance, and apparent nutritional level. Also, on the official school transcript of the child, there was clearly marked in red pencil, if a child came from a home which received welfare funds, the letters "A.D.C."

In the classroom at the beginning of the year, the teacher did not place a single child from a welfare home at the first table for "fast learners." Rather, two were placed at table 2 and four were placed at table 3. I believe that the teacher's stereotyped impressions of how a child from a welfare home could learn was a critical variable in her relegating that child to a table for "slow learners." At no time during the remainder of the school year did the teacher ever "advance" any welfare child to a higher table. In a very real sense, the child had been "stigmatized" as a low achiever by the teacher before school ever began, again aiding in the emergence of a self-fulfilling prophecy. The social handicap which the welfare child brought with him into the classroom resulted in relegation to a table for those "low achievers" who had "no idea of what is going on."

LINGUISTIC RESTRICTIONS

Within the kindergarten classroom, the teacher explicitly indicated that she wished the children to converse only in standard American English (S.A.E.). That is, she did not want the children in conversation either among themselves or with her to use Black American English (B.A.E.). One group of children, those at table 1, appeared to meet her requirement in that they, within the classroom, spoke in the manner she desired. Several of the children at table 2 and all of those at table 3, however, were not able to converse in S.A.E. It appeared that they spoke only in B.A.E. It should be noted that the students at table 1 appeared to be bilingual in that they spoke S.A.E. when in the presence of the teacher, but "code-switched" into B.A.E. when with the other students. (The teacher also appeared to be bilingual but switched into B.A.E. only on those occasions when she wished to discipline the class or individual students within it.)

With the restrictions the teacher placed upon the children as to their mode of speech, there was often a disruption of communication between her and the students at tables 2 and 3. She frequently insisted that a child remain silent unless he would give his answer in S.A.E. It is obvious that these linguistic restrictions have certain educational aims in mind, but they also appear to have resulted in the creation of barriers of communication between teacher and pupils (compare Rist, 1972; Kobrick, 1972). The teacher's occasional deprecation and suppression of the child's language may have created a situation where the child either remained silent or else regressed to a less verbal stage to avoid humiliation in front of peers. The data suggest that, as the social barriers between teacher and pupils intensified, the amount of communication significantly decreased. For example, in one observational period of an hour in May, not a single act of communication was initiated by the teacher toward those children at either table 2 or 3 save twice commanding "sit down." The intensity of distance between the teacher and those children at the last two tables may well have hindered the development of language skills by the children. This is no mean situation for, as Berger and Luckman (1967:36) note, "Language . . . is the most important sign system of human society."

PEER RELATIONSHIPS

By the end of the school year a number of the children who sat at table 1 were beginning in an almost imperceptible manner to fashion their own relationships with the children at tables 2 an 3 after that of the teacher. That is, though they themselves were at a distance from the teacher, they were closer to her than were those at tables 2 and 3. Several of the children at the first table also appeared to realize that there was not a "spontaneous" seating arrangement of the children by the teacher, but, rather, that the children were grouped according to some criteria. The following examples are of the children from table 1 who belittled or degraded those children from tables 2 and 3 in some fashion. I did not observe any incident of a child from either table 2 or 3 ever directing a derogatory remark toward a child at the first table.

> Mrs. Caplow says, "Raise your hand if you want me to call on you. I won't call on anyone who calls out." She then says, "All right, now who knows that numeral? What is it, Tony?" Tony makes no verbal response but rather walks to the front of the classroom and stands by Mrs. Caplow. Gregory calls out, "He don't know. He scared." Then Ann calls out. "It sixteen, stupid." (Tony sits at table 3; Gregory and Ann sit at table 1.)

> Jim starts to say out loud that he is smarter than Tom. He repeats it over and over again. "I smarter than you. I smarter than you." (Jim sits at table 1; Tom sits at table 3.)

> Milt came over to me and told me to look at Lilly's shoes. I asked Milt why I should and he replied, "Because they so ragged and dirty." (Milt is at table 1; Lilly at table 3.)

> When I asked Lilly what it was that she was drawing, she replied, "A parachute." Gregory interrupted and said, "She can't drawn nothin'."

The problems of those children in the class who had been labeled low achievers by the teacher were confounded by the fact that a number of their peers also turned against them. If this is the situation for children who are five years old, labeled by the teacher and ridiculed by their classmates, the implications for the labeled child's reaction toward school and education are clear. The advent of anticipated failure has begun.

SOCIAL-PSYCHOLOGICAL CONSIDERATIONS

Extrapolating a typology proposed by Lewin (1936:44), one may view the teacher and children as both having had distinct areas of regions that were either accessible or nonaccessible to one another. The peripheral layers of the individual's personality and life events which were available for communication (and examination) were greater for the child than for the teacher. The children had more peripheral regions with permeable boundaries, and they had fewer private regions secure from scrutiny. On the other hand, the status and role of the teacher reduced her accessibility to the children. This resulted in proportionately fewer regions open to communication. Her degree of insulation from the child's communications was both stronger and more defined than vice versa. The teacher was much more able to remove herself from the children than they were from her. Only the peripheral surface regions (as opposed to the private regions) of the teacher were accessible to the children. Thus the concept of social distance can be extended to help delineate private from public sectors of life. If this extension is accepted, one can say that, within the classroom, the private life of the child was greatly reduced, while that of the teacher was not.

> Mrs. Caplow says, "Now aren't mothers nice?" James says, "Mine not. She mean." Mrs. Caplow then says, "Oh, children, wait a minute. James is going to tell us why his mother is mean." She then says, "James, tell us why your mother is mean to you."

With the central and peripheral regions corresponding respectively with the private and public spheres of life, the lack of sufficient similarity of accessible regions for the teacher and pupils led on occasion to a breakdown of understanding and communication. With the regions of accessibility clearly differentiated between teacher and child, it appeared that experiences and events occurred almost exclusively in one region or the other, but not simultaneously. Thus, in the classroom, the daily perfunctories could be conducted between the teacher and a number of the children without establishing a personal relationship. As a consequence, the teacher was in a position which facilitated impersonal manipulation and control of the children. Mrs. Caplow had on occasion displayed little respect for the private lives of the children. Yet she defensively guarded her own private life.

Fred says to Mrs. Caplow, "Mrs. Caplow, you have any children?" Mrs.

Caplow says, "No, I don't Fred," and Fred says, "Why not?" Mrs. Caplow says, "I just don't."

The desire on the part of the pupils for closeness with the teacher was occasionally thwarted by her maintenance of distance.

The child who is involved in putting pegs in the peg board shows her work to the teacher. She [the teacher] does not respond but walks to the desk.

Gregory again calls out, "I saw an elephant at Sherman's farm. Also I was on a horsey." The teacher disregards him.

It appeared that for the majority of the children, the classroom was a place of uncertainty and fear due to the lack of personal relationships and maintenance of social distance between themselves and the teacher. As Levi-Strauss (1964:79) wrote:

When social distance is maintained, even if it is not accompanied by manifestation of disdain, insolence or aggression, it is in itself a cause of suffering; for such social distance is [at] variance with the fact that all social contact carries with it an appeal and that this appeal is at the same time a hope for a response.

Underlying the social interaction between the teacher and the child, there appeared to be what Goffman (1959: 240) called a "fundamental dialectic." That is, when one person enters into interaction with another, the person will want to discover and learn the facts of the situation within which he finds himself. If this information is known, the person will make allowances for, and accommodate himself in, the interests of his own self-presentation during the period of interaction. Yet the children in the classroom (especially those at tables 2 and 3) were kept at such distances from the teacher that they were unsure of her expectations of them as students. Thus, they were unable to gain the cues, hints, and expressive gestures from the teacher as necessary predictive devices to guide them in meeting her expectations. Not being able to participate in the dialectic, the children were increasingly ignored by the teacher, which resulted in the children having even fewer opportunities to learn the necessary expectations. The cyclical nature of the decreasing interaction continued.

Those children at tables 2 and 3 who became increasingly withdrawn from classroom activities were ignored by the teacher and allowed to drift under the guise that "they do not have the experiences and ability to talk, and they are not prepared to act out in a group." On the other hand, the teacher focused attention on the several children who came from middle-class homes to a greater extent than on those of the lower classes. Essentially, the teacher believed that "to those who have, there shall be given." A middle-class child was occasionally singled out as an example that the rest of the class should attempt to emulate.

(It is Fire Prevention Week and the teacher is trying to have the children say so. The children make a number of incorrect responses, a few of which follow): Jim, who had raised his hand in answer to the question "Do you know what week it is?" says, "October." The teacher says, "No, that's the name of the month. Jane, do you know what special week this is?" and Jane responds, "It cold outside." Teacher says, "No, that is not it either. I guess I will have to call on Pamela. Pamela, come here and stand by me and tell the rest of the boys and girls what special week this is." Pamela leaves her chair, comes and stands by the teacher, turns, and faces the rest of the class. The teacher puts her arm around Pamela, and Pamela says, "It's fire week." The teacher responds, "Well, Pamela, that is close. Actually, it is Fire Prevention Week."

The child's main symbol of power and authority within the school was the teacher. Since the teacher and many of the children did not have much sense of a relationship, the use of commands and directions often remained somewhat impersonal.

As I arrived in the classroom at 8:30, the first thing that I heard Mrs. Caplow say was, in a rather firm voice, "Boy, bring that coat here."
Then she says, "Okay, now let's sing it through the regular way again." So this time as she begins to sing, she gets up from her bench and begins to walk around through the group, turning heads, pinching ears, and almost shouting into the child's face so he will sing back to her. She hangs right over the children when she says, "Okay, I want to see them right here."

Likewise, the response of the teacher to children, who attempt to escape physically or withdraw psychologically from the classroom and its activities suggested a lack of empathy on her part.

Betty, a very poorly dressed child, has gone outside and hidden behind the door. Mrs. Caplow sees Betty leave and goes outside to bring her back. She says, in an authoritative and irritated voice, "Betty, come right here now." When the child returns, Mrs. Caplow seizes her by the right arm, brings her over to the group, and pushes her down to the floor. Betty begins to cry.... The teacher now shows the group a large poster board with a picture of a white child going to school.

Because of the social role and status of the children within the class, they were in no position to question the actions of the teacher. They had no recourse to change what they found undesirable. Consequently, the alternatives open were, as mentioned, either escape or withdrawal.

The children are supposed to make United Nations flags. They have been told that they do not have to make exact replicas of the teacher's flag.

They have before them the materials to make the flags. Lilly and James are the only children who have not yet started to work on their flags. Presently, James has his head under his desk and Lilly simply sits and watches the other children. Now they are both staring into space . . . Five minutes later, Lilly and James have not yet started, while several children have already finished. . . . A minute later, with the teacher telling the children to begin to clean up their scraps, Lilly is still staring into space.

CONCLUSIONS

The data presented in this paper appear to warrant two major conclusions, with the second proceeding from the first. The first is that the "cultural gap" hypothesis appears to have merit and can be substantiated, in part, by the analysis of observations conducted within this particular kindergarten classroom. The reservation that the hypothesis can be substantiated "in part" results from a constraint of the analysis being based on the observations within only one classroom. A second constraint appears to be derived from the operationalization of the theoretical concept of a cultural gap by means of examining manifestations of social distance. Though I believe that social distance is a significant index of cultural variation between the middle-class teacher and the lower-class student, it is not the sole manifestation. Additional study will have to examine patterns of discipline, modes of reward and punishment, satisfaction of the child's dependency needs, teacher's self-image, and the reinforcement of stereotypes as to what kinds of children the teacher perceives are able to learn. These, I believe, will provide further insights into the degree of intensity of cultural differences between the teacher and children. A third constraint on categorically accepting the cultural gap hypothesis is that there was not observed a single level of social distance between the teacher and students within the kindergarten classroom. This constraint influences the second major conclusion of the study.

Social-class differences play an important role in the school experience of the child, and such differences may significantly affect the child's opportunity for success (or failure) within the classroom milieu. There appeared to be clear differences between the level of intensity of distance maintained by the teacher between herself and those children at table 1 as opposed to the enforced distance between herself and those children at tables 2 and 3. Those children from dissimilar social-class backgrounds appeared to experience the classroom situation in quite different ways. It may be suggested that the pattern of social organization present within the kindergarten classroom in fact sustained the class differences of the large society with a definite gap, not only between the teacher and those children at tables 2 and 3, but also between the children at table 1 and those at the remaining two tables. Thus one finds, from the very beginning of the school experience of this particular group of low-income children, the school perpetuating what it is theoretically committed to dissolve—class barriers which reinforce inequality.

REFERENCES

Banton, M. (1967) Race Relations. New York: Basic Books.

Becker, H.S. (1952) "Social class variations in teacher-pupil relationship." J. of Educational Sociology 25: 451-465.

Berger, P. and T. Luckman (1967) The Social Construction of Reality. Garden City, N.Y.: Doubleday Anchor.

Coleman, J.S. et al. (1966) Equality of Educational Opportunity. Washington, D.C.: Government Printing Office.

Davis, A. (1952) Social Class Influences Upon Learning. Cambridge, Mass.: Harvard Univ. Press.

Della-Dora, D. (1966) "The culturally disadvantaged: educational implications of certain social-cultural phenomena," in S. Webster (ed.) The Disadvantaged Learner. San Francisco: Chandler.

Eddy, E. (1967) Walk the White Line. Garden City, N.Y.: Doubleday Anchor.

Fuchs, E. (1969) Teachers Talk. Garden City, N.Y. Doubleday Anchor.

Goffman, E. (1959) The Presentation of Self in Everyday Life, Garden City, N.Y.: Doubleday Anchor.

Haskins, J. (1969) Diary of a Harlem Schoolteacher. New York: Grove.

Hollingshead, A. (1949) Elmtown's Youth. New York: John Wiley.

Jackson, P. (1968) Life in Classrooms. New York: Holt, Rinehart & Winston.

Kobrick, J. (1972) "The compelling case for bilingual education." Saturday Rev. (April 29): 54-58.

Kohl, H. (1967) 36 Children. New York: New American Library.

Kozol, J. (1967) Death at an Early Age. Boston: Houghton Mifflin.

Leacock, E. (1969) Teacher and Learning in City Schools. New York: Basic Books.

Levy, G. (1970) Ghetto School. New York: Pegasus.

Levi-Strauss, C. (1964) "Les structures elementaires de la parente Paris: presses universitaries de France" in L. Coser and B. Rosenberg, Sociological Theory (L. Coser and G. Frazer, translators) New York: Macmillan.

Lewin, K. (1936) Principles of Topological Psychology. New York: Harper.

Mannheim, K. (1957) Systematic Sociology, New York: Grove.

Moore, A. (1967) Realities of the Urban Classroom. Garden City, N.Y.: Doubleday Anchor.

Riessman, F. (1962) The Culturally Deprived Child. New York: Harper & Row.

Rist, R.C. (1972) "Black English for black schools: a call for educational congruity," in R.C. Rist (ed.) Restructuring American Education. New Brunswick, N.J.: Trans-Action Books.

Rist, R.C. (1970) "Student social class and teacher expectations: the self-fulfilling prophecy in ghetto education." Harvard Educational Rev. 40, 3:411-451.

Smith, L. and W. Geoffrey (1968) The Complexities of an Urban Classroom. New York: Holt, Rinehart & Winston.

Stein, A. (1971) "Strategies of failure." Harvard Educational Rev. 41, 2:158-204.

Warner, W.L., R. Havighurst and M. Loeb (1944) Who Shall be Educated? New York: Harper & Row.

SCHOLASTIC AND PSYCHOLOGICAL EFFECTS OF A COMPENSATORY EDUCATION PROGRAM FOR DISADVANTAGED HIGH SCHOOL STUDENTS: PROJECT ABC

Alden E. Wessman

While compensatory education programs for disadvantaged students have developed rapidly in a variety of school and college settings, relatively little evaluative research has appeared that provides adequate knowledge about their specific character and results. This paper will report the main findings from a four-year study of one such program: Project ABC.

"Project ABC: A Better Chance" was established in 1963 by 21 independent secondary schools and Dartmouth College, with the support of the Rockefeller Foundation. During its initial five years, 1964-68, Project ABC enrolled 1218 students, and expanded to include 5 colleges offering a summer transitional program, and 106 private and 8 public secondary schools which the students subsequently entered. Like other such programs, it experienced rapid expansion and cutbacks of federal funds; but it has continued through private support, though on a diminished scale. The program is unusual in certain respects. It seeks to recruit students who, though they may be handicapped by poor schooling and limited opportunity, have shown scholastic potential and motivation. Also, it differs from other summer programs for compensatory education in that it does not return the students to their local high schools in the fall, but rather provides all who do sufficiently well with scholarships to secondary schools.

When the present study was begun little evidence was available concerning the consequences of such compensatory programs. Therefore the major research aims for the evaluation of Project ABC were to assess realistically its operation and results including: the nature of the program; selection and characteristics of the students; characteristics associated with success and failure; and the scholastic and psychological consequences. The detailed account, including considerable representative interview material, is in the final project report (Wessman, 1969). The major findings and conclusions will be presented here.

The research was carried out on an entire group of 82 boys who began the summer transitional program at Dartmouth College in 1965 and entered 39 preparatory schools that fall. Detailed information was obtained from tests and interviews on the entering students and by means of a systematic two-year follow-up. The design included comparable psychological testing of a smaller matched control group who remained at their local high schools.

"SUBJECTS": CHARACTERISTICS OF ABC STUDENTS

The 82 ABC students were disadvantaged boys: 70% Negro, 10% White, 10% American Indian, 9% Puerto Rican, and 2% Oriental; ages 12 to 16 at entrance. Home communities were predominantly urban ghettos or rural areas throughout the country that were economically impoverished with inadequate local schools and limited opportunities. Median reported family income was $4,320, with about one-third on welfare or reporting incomes below $3,000. Median parental education level was eleventh grade, and 38% of the boys came from broken homes. Father's occupations were mainly unskilled manual labor or low status white collar jobs. Mothers were predominantly housewives; with most working mothers in unskilled labor, largely as domestics, or in low level white collar jobs.

Though coming from impoverished backgrounds and substandard schools, the ABC boys were regarded as having shown ability or "promise" and the desire to advance educationally. Their initial Otis "I.Q." scores averaged 115, with a range from 92 to 132. Cooperative English Achievement Test percentiles averaged in the 70's on appropriate national high school norms, and in the 40's on preparatory school norms on the same tests.

In analysis of standardized test data from the follow-up, it was possible to match 23 control subjects with a sub-sample of 23 ABC students. Because there had been considerable difficulties in relocating and retesting the control pool, it was decided to match *only students continuing in secondary school* (with ABC students in the private schools and controls in their local schools). The 23 pairs were matched on initial *I.Q.* scores (within 5 points), on *age* (within 5 months), and on *race* (with 19 Negro pairs, 3 Puerto Rican pairs, and 1 American Indian pair). There were no significant differences on the initial measures between the two matched groups.

Random assignment to control or "experimental" groups was not attained. Though both groups came from the common pool of program applicants, the ABC students were selected for admission by the independent schools which wished to maintain their autonomy rather than being assigned students. So it was decided to do the best possible job of matching ABC boys with available controls, after the data were completely gathered, but before any follow-up data were scored or analyzed. The test findings summarized later are based on analysis of three sets of change scores: 1) scores for the *entire ABC group* successfully retested (77 of the original 82 boys, including 65 of the 66 continuing in the program and 12 of the 16 dropouts); 2) scores of the 23 boys in the *ABC sub-group;* and 3) scores of the 23 boys in the *matched control group.*

NATURE OF THE ABC SUMMER PROGRAM

The eight-week summer program at Dartmouth College was designed to prepare students for the transition to boarding school life. It concentrated on strengthening abilities in English, reading, and mathematics. The program was rigorous and demanding, but with small classes and an unusual degree of individual help. The staff was racially mixed, with all teachers experienced at the secondary school level. Black and white Dartmouth undergraduates were resident tutors in the dormitories and organized recreational activities. Dormitory life and daily schedules were designed to familiarize the boys with the characteristics of boarding schools.

The 39 independent schools the ABC boys entered that fall included most of the best known and outstanding private schools in the United States. They are mainly in the Northeast and have a predominantly upper-middle and upper class clientele. The schools feature intensive classroom work in small groups, close faculty-student relationships, considerable athletic emphasis, fairly closely regulated living conditions, and tightly organized study and recreational schedules. Though the boys' academic programs were typical of other students at the schools with no special remedial programs, those who might need extra help and attention received it and placements were made in accord with their level of preparation.

INTERVIEWS WITH ABC STUDENTS AND SCHOOL STAFF

Of the 82 entering boys, all 80 who completed the first summer were interviewed at its end. And in the subsequent two-year follow-up, 79 were reinterviewed.

In both interviews a standard schedule was followed with set opening questions on the various topics, but with considerable freedom in the follow-up questions. The first interview covered: family and home community, prior schooling, recruitment and experience in the summer program, and future plans and anticipations. The follow-up interview at the private schools covered the initial transition, subsequent scholastic work, extracurricular activities and sports, social adjustment, feelings about home and family, personal changes, and future plans and expectations. The follow-up interviews with boys who had dropped out included additional questions regarding reasons they had left, and experiences and feelings since returning home. All interviews were conducted by the writer, a white psychologist in his mid-thirties, who had become familiar to all the boys as an interested and sympathetic observer. The boys were assured of the confidential nature of information volunteered and were encouraged to be frank.

In the two-year follow-up, the writer conducted standardized interviews with administrative and teaching staff at the private schools who knew each boy well. There was access to the student's records. Topics included scholastic work, extra-curricular activities and sports, dormitory and social life, general adjustment and problems, and personal changes observed. Special emphasis was placed on consideration of difficulties and problems.

From these interview data, criterion ratings and classification groups were developed. The first was an *overall academic performance rating* made at the time of the faculty interviews, with particular attention to the full transcript of the student's grades and with the consensus and agreement of the school staff members. A 7-point rating from "1," Failing or Academic drop-out, to "7," Outstanding, excellent, "A," was used.

A second classification was concerned with changes in scholastic performance. This *classification of academic trends* into five groups was developed during the coding as typical patterns emerged from the set of interviews; however it was made before there was any analysis of objective test data.

The third classification was a *social adjustment rating* based both on the faculty reports and the students' own testimony. Usually these were in good agreement; but when there were discrepancies, most weight was given to the more unfavorable account. This 7-point rating scale ran from "1," Dropout because of serious social adjustment problems, to "7," Outstanding, unusually fine social adjustment.

A battery of standardized educational and psychological tests was administered on two occasions: 1. during the spring before the initial summer program and 2. again two years later. The test-retest data were obtained for 77 of the original 82 ABC boys, plus the 23 matched Controls.

The scholastic tests included the Otis *Self-Administering Test of Mental Ability, Higher Examination* (1928), and the Educational Testing Service *1960 Cooperative English Test.* Alternate forms were used for retesting. The psychological inventories used were the Cattell and Belloff *High School Personality Questionnaire* (HSPQ) (1962) and the Gough *California Psychological Inventory* (CPI) (1957). Only the ABC students took the CIP. Other tests were administered in the battery, but as their results are of less interest, they will not be reported here.

RESULTS

Attrition during the first two years was 20%. By the beginning of the fourth year 26% had dropped out of the program, 41% were continuing in independent schools, and 33% were attending college.

The main data come from the two-year follow-up at which time the break-down of the boys' status in the program showed: 2% left during the initial summer program, 6% were not recommended to go on to independent school at end of summer program, 1% were recommended to attend independent school but chose not to attend, 10% attended independent school but dropped out (or about to be dropped), 79% continued in independent school, and 1% graduated from independent school and attending college.

SCHOLASTIC PERFORMANCE IN PRIVATE SCHOOL

The boys' scholastic record during the first two years was mixed, ranging from failure to outstanding success according to the faculty reports. On the *overall academic performance rating*, the distribution of the 82 boys was:

%	N	Rating
12	10	Outstanding, excellent, A
7	6	Very good, B or B+
18	15	Fairly good, above average, C+ or B−
16	13	Average, fair, C
20	16	Below average, D+ or C−
7	6	Near failing, barely pass, D or D−
20	16	Failing or Academic drop-out, E
100	82	

The direction of the scholastic changes was a matter of greater interest. The inductive *classification of academic trends* over the two years showed the following distribution for the 82 boys:

%	N	Group
26	21	"POOR," consistent low level academic performance
11	9	"DECLINE," definite fall in academic performance
9	7	"SO-SO" or "Mediocre," no great changes in low average academic performance
30	25	"GAINS," definite improvement in academic performance
24	20	"GOOD," consistent high level academic performance
100	82	

The reports indicated a moderate level of overall success regarding scholastic change, but they cannot support uncritical claims of uniform gains. There were definite failures, with about a quarter of the students consistently poor and showing little improvement. And small groups showed continuing mediocre performance or a definite fall in their work. About a quarter were good students to begin with and remained good, improving at their already high levels. Only about 30% were reported as showing distinct gains and fit the program's "ideal model" of a disadvantaged boy who would succeed in overcoming the obstacles of previous poor schooling. As these reports indicated, 54% of the boys were making consistently good academic progress or distinct gains.

In the interviews with the ABC boys, 80% reported the work harder than at their previous schools but they reported smaller classes, more individual help, and better teaching than formerly. Most (88%) felt they were treated the same as the other students at their school, 8% felt they received some special attention or extra help, and only 4% felt they received unusual attention or were judged by lower standards. About one third were pleased with their records, but the other two-thirds had varying degrees of mixed feelings or dissatisfaction. Most students reported no great scholastic problems; but those who did report some problems (36%) cited lack of academic motivation and poor study habits as the main difficulties. A small number (8%) felt the work was beyond their abilities, and 6% reported that adjustment problems hindered their academic progress. Roughly 70% felt they had remained poor or become distinctly worse.

INTELLIGENCE AND ACHIEVEMENT TEST CHANGES

Test-retest data over the two-year period showed no significant change in mean Otis IQ score for the ABC students (112.7 to 112.3); but the Control group showed a slight, but statistically significant, drop of three points (111.9 to 108.6, $p < .01$). Similarly the various Cooperative English achievement test percentile scores showed only minor changes for ABC students and Controls. Thus these standardized educational tests of scholastic ability showed no appreciable relative gains for the ABC students after two years in the program.

SOCIAL ADJUSTMENT TO PRIVATE SCHOOL

Based on the staff and student interviews, the *social adjustment rating* showed the following distribution:

%	N	Rating
15	12	Outstanding, unusually fine social adjustment
15	12	Very good, no problems evident, doing very well
18	15	Quite good, no serious problems evident, doing quite well
21	17	Mixed, minor problems, generally "O.K."
15	12	Difficult, definite major problems
5	4	Very difficult, serious and continuing problems
12	10	Drop-out because of serious social adjustment problems
100	82	

Thus according to these combined reports: roughly 30% had major social adjustment difficulties, 40% had transient minor adjustment problems, and 30% had apparently experienced little difficulty and made an easy adjustment.

Faculty members were somewhat more sanguine about the boys' adjustment than were the boys themselves, but generally were aware of the more serious problems. The majority of the boys said that the summer program had been good preparation for boarding school life. Regarding their new schools: 60% said they felt they really belonged, 30% felt somewhat apart, and 10% felt very much apart and alone. About a quarter reported various unpleasant experiences with other students at the school, primarily hazing and excessive teasing. About 40% reported encountering major incidents of prejudice and racial discrimination by other students, but 35% said they had enountered none.

PERSONAL AND SOCIAL CHANGE

Faculty reports on observed changes in ABC boys were predominantly positive in roughly 75% of the cases, mixed in 15%, and predominantly negative in 10%. The main positive changes cited were: more at ease and confident; academic improvement; more experienced and broader; more aware and perceptive; and more articulate and better able to express self. In the 25% where negative changes were reported, they were mainly; more tense and anxious; discouraged and defeated; more alienated and cynical; and more complacent and snobbish.

In 75% of the cases the ABC boys themselves reported the experience as beneficial, in 17% mixed, and in 6% as definitely harmful. Many were enthusiastic and appreciative, stating it had been a major transition point in their lives. About half said they had changed a great deal. They gave predominantly positive reports of change, including in order of frequency: increased academic competence; greater social awareness; more direction and higher goals in life; wider cultural background; greater social ease; more self-awareness; more political awareness; increased tolerance; and increased articulateness. However, 26% reported greater tension and anxiety; 15% discouragement with their limitations; and 10% less drive and dedication. Smaller numbers reported disillusionment and alienation, smugness and complacency, or social withdrawal. A few students were clearly in great conflict and deeply troubled. The increased anxiety and tension reported by a quarter was generally attributed to increased academic pressure and competition, uncertainty regarding future chances, and the strain of adjusting to the uncertainties of a different social and racial environment.

About 40% of the boys reported feeling more critical of their former communities. But only 20% said they felt more distant from their families, and most felt the same or even closer and more appreciative. About half said they experienced difficulties in the transitions between school and home. About 60% maintained contact with friends at home, who generally tended to be similar college-oriented boys. Compared with their responses from two years previously, more students were undecided about future vocational plans. There were decided shifts away from science and technology, toward managerial and business careers. Generally they had become more optimistic about their chances, though most were worried about future success.

The personality inventory scores showed many striking and statistically significant changes for the ABC boys that were not found for the Controls. On the Cattell HSPQ, all the Anxiety-related measures were increased, with significant changes on the factor scales indicating: emotionality (C), reactivity to threat (H), apprehensiveness and worry (O), tension and drive (Q4); with a particularly striking change on the combined second-order factor "Anxiety" scale. But paradoxically there was also a significant increase on casualness (Q3).

In addition, on the Gough CPI (with no comparable Control group data), there were significant increases on: capacity for status; social presence; self-acceptance; tolerance; achievement via independence; and flexibility. There were significant decreases on socialization, self-control; and achievement via conformance.

The pattern of these many significant changes on the personality inventories may be interpreted as indicating that the ABC boys became more tense and driven, yet paradoxically more self-assured and independent. They appear to reflect both the personal stress and benefits of having encountered and coped with new and highly demanding situations.

SUBSEQUENT COLLEGE ADMISSIONS

The original research design had planned to follow the ABC students into college. Unfortunatley, cutbacks in research funds made this impossible. However it can be reported that all of the 27 boys (33% of the total group) who had graduated from private schools by the end of the third year were attending college the next fall. All were receiving scholarship aid. College placement of a few boys with poor records was difficult, but the majority were attending high quality institutions throughout the country.

As already noted, program attrition was 20% in the first two years, and 26% by the beginning of the fourth year. Of these drop-outs approximately 60% left because of scholastic difficulties predominantly, and 40% because of social adjustment problems.

Scholastic difficulties in some cases were due to low ability, but most often to poor motivation and lack of self-discipline. In all but one case, the dropouts resumed high school at home and were expected to graduate with generally undistinguished records.

The adjustment problems of the drop-outs varied, but were predominantly homesickness and dislike of boarding school atmosphere and restrictions. Racial tensions appeared of significance in only a few instances. There were a few cases of marked emotional conflict where the social adjustment strains may have been a contributing factor; and one case of excessive disruptive influences on other students that led to expulsion from the initial summer program. Interviews revealed that some dropouts, particularly among the American Indian boys, initially had little desire to leave home and the relevance of the program to their lives and personal desires was questionable.

Boys who had dropped out did not appear to be suffering obvious bad effects. Most reported occasional mild regrets, but had returned to the community and resumed their former lives without much difficulty. A few were clearly relieved to be home again. Though most dropouts expressed predominantly positive attitudes toward the program, it appeared to have had minimal effects, positive or negative, on their lives.

DISCUSSION

The findings have made it clear that educational miracles did not occur. According to the two-year reports only about 30% of the boys actually fit the program's ideal of motivated "academic risks" who would improve their scholastic performance through better teaching and their own hard work. Another 24% were consistently good students from the beginning and continued to do well. Both groups, of course, merit scholarship support and would appear in certain respects to justify the program. The remaining 46% had done mediocre or poor work, and in some cases had even declined scholastically. For them the program appeared to have minimal or negative effects on scholastic performance. The intelligence and English achievement test data showed no substantial relative gains for the group as a whole, only the usual expected improvement reflected in the test norms. Thus it appears, all things considered, that the program cannot be credited with producing marked scholastic gains.

The unimpressive scholastic results confirm the need for realistic appraisal of the contributions and limitations of such endeavors, and for recognition of their often complex and varied consequences (Katz, 1968). Despite the great expansion of compensatory education programs occurring in the 1960's (Gordon, 1968; Rees, 1968), relatively few programs have reported the findings of careful evaluative research. The findings that have appeared (Wrightstone, et. al., 1964; Gordon, 1968, pp. 393-397; Hunt & Hardt, 1969; White, 1970) are also quite sobering.

Beyond the matter of just the scholastic results is the more important question of the effects of such programs on the lives and personalities of the student involved. Here the research literature is even more sparse. And our conclusions from the present study must be tentative. A two-year span is only a short time in which to judge consequences that may be extremely varied, subtle, and only manifested over a period of years. Certainly the immediate life situation of the ABC students was dramatically altered. Most managed to adjust reasonably well, with less than a third having serious problems and only a few obviously in deep conflict. Undoubtedly a large measure of this success was attributable both to careful initial screening and to the supportive treatment they received. In three-quarters of the cases, both faculty and students were convinced of the beneficial effects of the transition.

The positive changes reported included increased self-confidence and social ease, greater awareness, more direction and higher goals, increased tolerance and flexibility. However, a quarter of the boys reported feeling more tense, anxious, and driven; and the personality inventory data for the group also showed significant changes indicative of greater anxiety and tension. The findings make it clear that boys had indeed made significant personal gains, but often at a price in terms of effort and strain. They were already exceptional boys in their former surroundings; their experience in their new environments made them even more unusual. Such social marginality with contrasting experiences in vastly different worlds can create problems and conflicts, but it can also produce increased social awareness and resiliency. The writer was often impressed by the growth in perceptiveness and articulateness in many of these young men after two years. It is perhaps in these human terms that such endeavors must ultimately be judged.

REFERENCES

Cattell, R.B. & Belloff, H. High school personality questionnaire ("HSPQ"). (2nd ed.) Champaign, Ill.: Institute for Personality and Abilities Testing, 1962 (Forms A and B).

Educational Testing Service, Cooperative Test Division, Cooperative English tests, (1960 ed.) Princeton, N.J.: Educational Testing Service, 1960. (Forms 2A and 2B for grades 9-12, Reading Comprehension and English Expression in single combined booklet).

Gordon, E.W. Programs of compensatory education. In M. Deutsch, I. Katz & A.R. Jensen (Eds.) Social class, race, and psychological development. New York: Holt, Rinehart & Winston, 1968.

Gough, H.G. California psychological inventory ("CPI"). Palo Alto, Calif.: Consulting Psychologists Press, 1957.

Hunt, D.E. & Hardt, R.H. The effect of Upward Bound programs on the attitudes, motivation, and academic achievement of Negro students. Journal of Social Issues, 1969, 25 (3).

Katz, I. Factors affecting Negro performance in the desegregated school. In M. Deutsch, I. Katz & A.R. Jensen (Eds.) Social class, race, and psychological development. New York: Holt, Rinehart, & Winston, 1968.

Otis, A.S. Otis self-administering test of mental ability, New York: Harcourt, Brace, & World, 1928. (Higher Examination for high school students and college freshmen, forms A and B.)

Rees, H.E. Deprivation and compensatory education: A consideration. Boston: Houghton and Mifflin, 1968.

Wessman, A.E. Evaluation of Project ABC (A Better Chance): An evaluation of Dartmouth College-Independent Schools scholarship program for disadvantaged high school students. Office of Education, Bureau of Research, U.S. Department of Health, Education and Welfare, Project 5-0594, final report, April 1969. (Available through ERIC Document Reproduction Service, 4936 Fairmont Ave., Bethesda, Maryland 20014, as document ED-031-549).

White, S.H. The national impact study of Head Start: In J. Hellmuth (Ed.) Disadvantaged child, vol. 3: Compensatory Education: a national debate. New York: Brunner-Mazel., 1970.

Wrightstone, J.W., et. al. Evaluation of the Higher Horizons program for underprivileged children. New York Board of Education, Bureau of Educational Research, 1964. (Cooperative Research Project No. 1124).

FREE VERSUS DIRECTED SCHOOLS:
BENEFITS FOR THE DISADVANTAGED?

Nicolaus Mills

Between 1965 and 1968 over three billion dollars were spent in U.S. schools to offset the disadvantages of about six million children. . . . It is the most expensive compensatory program ever attempted anywhere in education, yet no significant improvement can be detected in the learning of these "disadvantaged" children.(1)

There is, to be sure, a certain faddishness in the fact that the question of free versus directed schools should now have the importance it does. As Joseph Featherstone recently observed, "The responses [to this controversy] tend to fall into the stereotyped categories of a cultural cold war. . . . Hip people like the idea of open classrooms, because they seem to give children freedom; straight people fear the supposed absence of order, discipline, and adult authority."(2) The question of free versus directed schools is not a faddish one as far as the educational needs of disadvantaged children go, however. For it arises at a time when the failures of massive governmental efforts to solve the current school crisis are more apparent than ever, and there is a need, both political and psychological, to develop on a controlled scale school programs that can show positive results.(3)

What follows in this paper is an attempt to analyze twelve such programs, all of which in varying degrees have proved successful. The middle and largest section of this paper is concerned with what generalizations can be made about such programs: Do free schools provide a better emotional environment for disadvantaged children and directed schools offer more help in developing cognitive skills? Is one school generally superior to the other in educating disadvantaged children, or is some combination of the two most desirable? Are free schools as free and directed schools as directed as they claim to be, or are both usually hybrids?

> The informal English schools demonstrate in practice what Dewey argued in theroy: that a deep and genuine concern for individual growth and fulfillment not only is compatible with but indeed demands an equally genuine concern for cognitive growth and intellectual discipline, for transmitting the cultural heritage of the society.(4)

> Unfortunately, the history of education is paved with good intentions that have led to failure. Those who know the limitations of people as well as of educational methods are well aware that no miracle can assure easy success.(5)

The twelve schools surveyed in this section have been chosen because they provide an indication of the broad range of free and directed school programs now being developed for disadvantaged children of all ages. The schools are analyzed in terms of a scale that starts with the most directed classroom situation and moves toward the freest. The scale is approximate rather than absolute, however, the differences between schools at both ends being obvious, the differences between schools in the middle often being debatable. Whenever possible test scores are used to measure the academic successes the schools have had, but this hard data has not been relied on to the exclusion of more intangible factors—such as what students themselves think about a school. Indeed, the most suspect experimental programs are those which produce an immediate rise in test scores but no changes in the disadvantaged student's feelings about himself or his relationship to society.

THE AMIDON ELEMENTARY SCHOOL

The Amidon Program, developed by Dr. Carl F. Hansen during the time he was Superintendent of Schools for the District of Columbia, represents an effort to return to what Hansen calls the "sanity of order and logic in curriculum organization and to the wisdom of teaching subject matter to children in direct and effective manner."(6) The program is characterized by an approach to education that is not only highly disciplined but highly traditional.

The Amidon School began as part of a redevelopment program in Southwest Washington, but when the school was finished before the housing around it, a decision was made to let Amidon serve the city at large and be a model in elementary school education. Thus, when Amidon opened in the fall of 1960, its 469 pupils came from 110 different schools. Seventy percent of them were nonwhite, and of these, all but a few were black. The only truly distinguishing feature of the Amidon school was that most of the students came to it because their parents had applied for them to do so. Otherwise, the Amidon students were representative of those who attend the Washington public schools.(7)

The curriculum of the Amidon School was developed to center on basic subjects with "life adjustment" as a secondary concern. As Superintendent Hansen noted:

> The Amidon concept is definiteness in curriculum, so that what is to be learned is, at least in a basic way, spelled out for the pupil. No fuzzy and unrestricted roaming for undefined facts and elusive ideas is to be found when the Amidon system is fully developed . . . the student knows what is expected of him, and that he is to be taught with a direction and certainty which will help him to be successful in doing what is expected of him.(8)

The preciseness of the stated Amidon curriculum was, moreover, matched by an equal preciseness in the running of the school. The two subjects most emphasized at Amidon were "language and numbers"; music and art were treated as secondary concerns. Students were groups by ability, and then placed in classes in which the primary emphasis was on teaching the whole class at once. Even recess was run in such a way that unsupervised play was replaced by "directed instruction in physical education."(9)

Individual instruction at Amidon was thus minimized. Each subject was given a predetermined time allotment, and teachers were expected to stick to their lesson plans. The "basic cycle" at Amidon was one in which, "The teacher is to teach what is to be learned. The pupil is to study, practice, and know what is to be learned. The pupil is to be tested on what he has learned. The teacher is to reteach as needed." Added to this regime were textbooks designed to further relieve the teacher from "the unsuitable responsibility of judging for herself what should or should not be taught."(10)

The strictness of the Amidon program did not, however, generally seem repressive to students, parents, or teachers. While teachers felt that reading books within a class should be done at a variety of levels, on no other basic matter did they dispute the conditions under which they worked. From both students and parents there were some objections to the discipline at Amidon, but mostly there was overwhelming approval of the order it created and a willingness to take related matters, such as homework, very seriously. The results of achievement tests given the Amidon students substantiate the progress they did make. In a school system in which students are usually well below national norms, 82 percent of the Amidon scores equalled or excelled national scores, and in the verbal areas Amidon emphasized, reading, spelling, word discrimination, the results were best of all. Equally revealing is the fact that, based on intelligence scores (I.Q. at Amidon ranged from 44 to 132), 74 percent of the Amidon students tested exceeded expectancy levels and 6 percent equalled them, making a total of 80 percent at or above predictable levels.(11)

Recently Carl Bereiter has gone on record in favor of "maintaining schools for skill-learning purposes, at greatly reduced levels of support, and putting the money saved into other kinds of free cultural resources, with children set free most of the day to take advantage of them"(12) The Bereiter-Engelmann Academically-Oriented Preschool studied here reflects, however, only a very directed approach to the problem of educating disadvantaged children.

The school is based on the belief that disadvantaged children "must progress at a faster than normal rate if they are to catch up" with other children. What this means in practice for Bereiter and Engelmann is:

> If disadvantaged children are to learn at faster than normal rate, they are going to have to learn from experiences of some other kind than those which have been responsible for the learning of more privileged children—experiences that are more potent generators of significant learning, experiences that can be compressed into a small period of time without losing their effectiveness.(13)

The kinds of experiences Bereiter and Engelmann have in mind are those which focus upon certain formal academic objectives and relegate all nonacademic matters to a secondary position. They are very candid in admitting that this step means abandoning the traditional preschool concern with the whole child.

The Bereiter-Engelmann School, begun in 1965 in Urbana, Illinois, reflects a working out of this philosophy. Fifteen children were chosen to be taught according to the Bereiter-Engelmann method. They were selected from a predominantly black school district in which income was generally low. The fifteen children (average age four years, six months) came from families in which older brothers and sisters were having school problems and home was considered "unfavorable educationally."(14) From the beginning the children were given an intensive, highly directed program of instruction in basic language skills, reading, and arithmetic. Each of these subjects was taught as a separate class with its own teacher. The classes were 15 minutes in length, later expanding to 20 minutes as the children became adjusted to the routine. Singing was the only other major activity (with specially written songs to give additional practice in skills being taught in the classes). The total time spent in school was two hours, five days a week.(15)

Although there were only five students in each class, grouping was still done by ability. Children were able to get individual attention, but the class was teacher-oriented and run at a pace set by the teacher. The classrooms were arranged so as not to be distracting, and there were a limited number of toys available. As Bereiter and Engelmann note:

> Classes were generally run in a business-like, task-oriented manner. Each period the childrn shifted to a different teacher for a different subject. The school thus resembled more nearly a high school than an elementary school, and was certainly in striking contrast to the "mother and her brood" atmosphere of many nursery schools.(16)

In addition, all other phases of the school—from snack time to toilet periods—were run to reinforce the academic programs. Discipline was strict, and there was a system of rewards for good behavior in the classroom.

The performance of the children on a number of tests indicates the academic progress they made. On the Illinois Test of Psycholinguistic Abilities they began more than a year and a half behind their age group, and at the end of seven months of schooling, they were approximately normal on the verbal subtests of ITPA and six months above average on Vocal Encoding. At the end of nine months the children were given the Wide Range Achievement Test. In reading 11 of the children scored at or above the beginning second grade level. On I.Q. tests the children went from an average score of 93 before the program began to an average score of slightly over 100 by the end of the program. In short, there was no academic area in which clear and important gains were not made. As for social development, while it was not a prime concern of the school, the children, nonetheless, showed striking gains in their ability to get along with each other at play and at work.(17)

THE INSTITUTE FOR DEVELOPMENTAL STUDIES

Under the direction of Martin Deutsch, New York University's School of Education has run a teaching program for children (K-3) since 1962-63. The program is based on the belief that the "lower-class child does not have the same coping mechanisms [as the middle-class child] for internalizing success or psychologically surviving failure in the formal learning setting. . . . Further, because of the differences in preparation, he is more likely to experience failure.(18)

To correct what Deutsch calls the "stimulus deprivation" and "environmental disadvantage" of the lower-class child, the Institute has put into practice a program of "intervention." The program rejects as appropriate to the disadvantaged child a school environment in which warmth and affection are the primary ingredients and development is thought of as an "unfolding process." Instead, the program concentrates on stimulating cognitive processes that have not been developed by the earlier experiences of the disadvantaged child.(19) The developmental model that underlies most of the Institute's procedures and materials is a Piaget-based three-step learning sequence that consists of a sensorimotor stage in which perceptual discrimination through the use of concrete materials is stressed, a perceptual stage, which focuses on finer discriminations through contrasting stimuli of colors, shapes, and sounds, an ideational-representation stage, where the child learns to relate things on a verbal and conceptual level with a minimum of concrete aid.(20)

In practice the Institute's program is very specific and touches on all phases of the school day—from room arrangements to reading material. As Fred Powledge has noted, "Everything that occurs in an intervention classroom, ideally, is intellectual fodder, an ingredient in the antidote of stimulus deprivation."(21) From the use of pictures and mirrors (to give the child a sense of himself) to the manner in which, according to one instructor, the children "cognitively eat," the Institute emphasizes what will stimulate the language growth, concept formation, and perceptual discrimination it ultimately wants to develop.

The manner in which this intervention is carried on is not, however, intended to alienate the disadvantaged child from his home or neighborhood. To the contrary, there is a deliberate attempt at the Institute to draw parents and community people into the school programs, to have them as teachers or teachers' aides, and to make sure that educational materials, such as story books, do not have the usual white, middle-class bias.(22) The results of this carefully worked out program, as reflected in a variety of tests, show very positive gains made at the Institute, particularly during the first year of school. On the Illinois Test of Psycholinguistic Abilities, for example, virtually all of the children who undergo intervention do markedly better than a control group getting regular schooling. The test scores of the Institute's pupils are not, however, all the Institute could wish for. At certain later stages in their development, some of the advantages the Institute children have over the control group are due less to gains they have made than losses in progress on the part of the control group.(23)

THE PERRY PRESCHOOL PROJECT

The Perry Preschool Project in Ypsilanti, Michigan, was an experimental program designed to compensate for functional retardation in children from disadvantaged families. It began in 1962 and was terminated in 1967. During the five years of the project, 123 children were studied. Fifty-eight of these children were in the experimental program (which for each of them lasted two years), and 65 were in the control group. The children selected were black and from families (for the most part very poor) which had low scores on a Cultural Deprivation Scale. The mean Stanford-Binet I.Q. score for the children was 79.(24)

The preschool curriculum was derived mainly from Piagetian theory and focused on cognitive objectives. Emphasis was placed on the teacher gearing classroom activity to the individual child, but this effort was not allowed to subvert the program's concern with verbal stimulation rather than social behavior. Indeed, one of the strongest characteristics of the project was that teachers maintained a constant verbal communication pattern with each child, even when he did not respond. In addition to the regular morning of school, there was also a 90-minute home session that the project's teachers had with the children and their parents each week. These sessions were designed both to give teachers a better understanding of a particular child's educational needs and to involve parents in the program.(25)

While there were some differences in the teaching techniques used, these differences were minor rather than major. Teachers were required to prepare a lesson plan based on the Piagetian curriculum at least a week in advance, and the

Perry School staff constantly met as a group. Team teaching was the rule, and teachers taught the entire time they were in the classroom, avoiding serial teaching. In addition team teaching was supervised by an older teacher as well as a member of the Perry School research staff.(26) Cognitive skills served to divide the children, with the more advanced group taking units for language use, auditory discrimination, and complex dramatic play and the less advanced group spending time in basic skill training and simple pre-math concepts. There was also a period in the day in which children were free to select from one of four activity centers: the house-keeping area, the clock area, the art area, and the pre-academic (quiet) area.(27)

Children who participated in the program experienced immediate and significant improvement in cognitive functioning as measured on the following tests: Stanford Binet, Leiter International Performance Scale, Peabody Picture Vocabulary Test, Illinois Test of Psycholinguistic Abilities. This improvement in functioning continued through the first three years of regular schooling, but after that point, the control group did just as well. Children in the preschool experimental group also performed significantly better on the California Achievement Test than children in the control group during the first three years of schooling, but here too it is important to make a qualification. This gain was derived primarily from the performance of the experimental girls. Children who went through the experimental program also seemed to adjust to school more easily than the control group. This gain appears, however, to be directly related to their academic performance, which makes school less of a trial for them than the control group.(28)

THE AFRICAN FREE SCHOOL PROGRAM

The African Free School program, conducted in classrooms at the Robert Treat School in Newark, consists of an African Free School experimental class and a control group established for the purposes of comparative evaluation. The program began in 1970 and is now being refunded.

The students in the program at the time of its first evaluation were 56 in number and all of African-American racial origin. At the start of the program the achievement levels of the students were from two to four years behind national norms. The children in the program averaged 12.5 years in age, and the program included students from the fifth to eighth grades. Most of the AFS experimental group was born in Newark, and the control group was evenly divided between those born in Newark and those born elsewhere.(29)

The staffing of the program was geared to provide an equal number of personnel for the AFS experimental program and the control group. Each class was assigned a certified teacher and four teacher's aides. In the control group the teacher-aides assisted the teacher in carrying on regular classroom activities, while in the AFS class the teacher-aides took a more active part in the instruction by assuming responsibility for various phases of the curriculum. Both groups were ungraded. The control group was taught in accord with the regular

Newark curriculum, the AFS class in accord with a curriculum designed to satisfy the standard curriculum and to allow for the introduction of Afro-American instruction.(30)

The AFS experimental program was based on a total learning environment in which a close relationship between teachers, students, and parents was emphasized. The teacher-aides allowed for individual attention to be given whenever special problems arose. In the AFS class students were required to respond to questions with a prescribed ritual that stressed group responses and repetitive answers. The specific curriculum of the AFS program consisted of the following courses and activities: "Swahili, History (with emphasis on African and African-American), Literature (emphasis on African and Africa-American and Asian), customs and concepts (which teaches unity, self-determination, collective work and responsibility, cooperative economics . . . travelogue (going by film and book to places all over the world with an emphasis on places where black people are), Simba Wachanga (boys: drill, physical training and health studies; girls: African-American and African dance troupe, health studies and hygiene), Seventh wonder (guest speakers who come from all walks of life) . . . remedial programs in mathematics, arts, and crafts."(31)

In terms of the AFS goals of teaching "racial dignity and pride without teaching racism" and of "improving emotional achievement of students," the experimental program has been a marked success. The AFS class shows a much higher level of self-confidence and self-image than the control group, and has been well motivated to keep up with the program (they have a low absence rate). On the other hand, the academic achievement of the AFS experimental class has not been equal to that of the control group. In word skills the AFS group lost ground when measured in terms of the Metropolitan Achievement Test, and in problem solving their gains were significantly less than those of the control group. In reading and computational skills, they were also behind the control group, but not in a serious way. What these results indicate is that so far the learning gains of the AFS experimental group do not seem likely to remedy defects in their formal education.(32)

THE MONTESSORI PROGRAM FOR THE DISADVANTAGED

The Montessori programs that have been instituted in disadvantaged areas are not directed in the traditional sense of being teacher-oriented or outwardly restrictive of children's freedom. Yet, they follow a very thoroughly planned format, and the result is a subtle but continuous direction of all classroom activity. George Stevens has described this arrangement in an essay on the "Implications of Montessori for the War on Poverty":

> The Montessori educational format, then, preserves the freedom of the individual child while introducing him into a highly structured learning environment. The children can choose to work alone or together or not at all. However, by virtue of the structured learning apparatus, the freedom is

only relative. Everything in the prepared environment is designed to interest the child in learning; therefore, he is in fact being channeled into certain lines of intellectual and personal development. The child's freedom is really a matter of choosing which aspect of his culture he wishes to master first and in what manner he wishes to master it.(33)

What this Montessori direction, with its emphasis on sensorial development and autoinstructional materials, means in practice has been spelled out by Lena Gitter in her pamphlet, "A Strategy for Fighting the War on Poverty." The program that Gitter describes is one that has its basis in a "prepared environment" in which everything from furniture to educational materials has been designed to suit the child. At the heart of the program lies what the Montessori Schools call Sensorial Exercises and Practical Life Exercises. The first of these exercises stresses the fact that until a child actually experiences an object, there is no point in having him give it a name. He must first have a correct sensory understanding of an object and then be able to label it with the correct word. In the prepared Montessori environment equipment is available for the child to isolate and use specific senses, and later on, when the child is able to do more advanced work, there are such things as sandpaper letters for his use.

The Practical Life Exercises involve a variety of day-to-day skills (washing, shoe polishing, setting the table) which are designed not only to make the child feel more comfortable in his environment but to build up his confidence about himself. Their relationship to the Montessori program is vital, for they reinforce the patterns of learning and order established in the other exercises and stress the fact that in the Montessori program there is no division between the mastery of cognitive skills and the development of sensorial awareness.(34)

The degree to which a Montessori program can help disadvantaged children learn has been documented by Dr. Henry S. Johnson in his study, "The Effects of Montessori Techniques on Culturally Disadvantaged Children." Dr. Johnson's report is on the Clovis Montessori School in Fullerton, California. The program itself was six weeks in duration, and 80 percent of the children in it were of Mexican-American heritage. At the conclusion of the program the children showed I.Q. gains of 7 to 19 points and gains in perceptual-motor skills of six months. Indeed, they made progress in virtually every area tested (a more modest success was a three-month gain on a Wide Range Arithmetic Test).(35)

THE W. J. MAXEY BOYS TRAINING SCHOOL

This program at the W.J. Maxey School at Whitemore Lake, Michigan, is another case of a situation in which students are given great leeway and also are subjected to a format that is highly directed. The program is based on the assumption that teaching disadvantaged students to read and write English through formal instruction in a class that meets once a day and relies on "classical" texts is bound to fail.

The English in Every Classroom Program alters this procedure. To begin with, it uses newspapers and periodicals as its basic reading material. While traditional texts are not excluded, the program assumes that its primary goal is to encourage reading in any form and that this effort means dealing with the magazines and newspapers that are most widely available. Writing follows along similarly untraditional lines. Papers are required every other day in all subjects other than English. Some of these papers are passed on to be read by the student's English instructor, who corrects for grammar and rhetoric, other papers are read for content by non-English teachers, and still others are filed away unread. (This latter practice is done to emphasize doing writing as valuable in itself.) Students also keep a journal in which they are required to write at least two pages each week. These journals may be read by the English teacher, but only if the student wishes. The result is a program in which "diffusion" and "saturation" are the two working principles. The diffusion refers to the variety of the reading matter. The saturation refers to the fact that the reading and writing of English pervade all activities at the Maxey school.(36)

That such an approach to English is social rather than literary in its emphasis is freely admitted by Dan Fader, the creator of the English in Every Classroom Program. But the program as put into practice has not been undisciplined or unsystematic in its aims. The list of books at Maxey (2,200 titles and 7,500 volumes for 280 boys) has been carefully chosen and modified, and the responsibilities of the teaching staff for developing a basic literacy among the students (ages 12 to 18 with an average reading level at fourth grade prior to the program) are more rather than less than in a traditional public school.(37)

The results of tests given both a control group and selected students from the Maxey School show the benefits of the English in Every Classroom Program. The boys from the Maxey School show not only a much stronger sense of self-image but a greater improvement in learning skills. On a Verbal Proficiency Test the scores of the Maxey boys go up 20 percent, while those of the control group go down. On the Stanford Achievement Test both groups improve over the course of the year, but the boys at Maxey make more than twice the progress of the control group.(38)

THE FREE SCHOOLS OF PRINCE EDWARD COUNTY

The Free Schools of Prince Edward County (Virginia) went into operation in 1963, four years after the county made a decision to close its public schools rather than integrate them. The schools were opened as a result of pressure from blacks in Prince Edward County and from the Kennedy administration. At a news conference in 1963 the President noted, "There are only four places in the world where children are denied the right to attend school: North Vietnam, Cambodia, North Korea, and Prince Edward County."(39) William vanden Heuvel, then an assistant to the Attorney General, was instrumental in arranging backing for the project, and Neil Sullivan was persuaded to accept the position of Superintendent of the Free Schools. The staff of the Free Schools reflected a similarly broad background. Half were from Virginia and half were from out of state, recruited from public school systems as well as organizations like the Peace Corps.

The aim of the Free Schools was not only to give black children in Prince Edward County an education but, as much as possible, to make up for what they had missed over the previous four years. While the organization of the school did not involve radical innovation, it did involve a format free from the usual conventions and a learning environment in which discipline problems were virtually nonexistent. A nongraded program was initiated to provide continuous learning for students and to allow flexibility in advancement. Students were grouped according to ability and stage of academic advancement rather than by age, and they were allowed to move on to new levels as soon as they had mastered the content skills of the preceding one. At the same time, team teaching was instituted, thus making it possible to vary the size of classes and to allow teachers to work individually with students. The subject of greatest concern in the Free Schools was language arts work, and a major portion of the day was allotted to this area. Math, social studies, science, and fine arts were the other basic academic areas. In these areas a special emphasis was put on acquiring the concepts of the course rather than on developing particular skills.(40)

Of the 1,578 students in the Free Schools all but a few were black. Many had never been to school at all, and most had not received instruction during the four years the Prince Edward County schools were closed. The average income for a black family in Prince Edward County in 1963 was $1,800, and during the summer before the Free Schools opened I.Q. tests administered to 800 of the county's black children showed the mean I.Q. to be 69—"borderline defective."(41) The teaching program at the Free School provided excellent results, however. In ten months time, students advanced on an average of two years scholastically (in terms of their test scores), and in a number of cases progress was three and four years. Moreover, the greatest strides were made in the last rather than the first five months of school, an indication that had the school been able to continue longer, results might even have been better. Of the graduating class of twenty-three twelve had plans to continue their education, and for them there was an abundance of scholarship help.(42)

HARLEM PREP

Founded in 1967 through the sponsorhip of the New York Urban League, Harlem Prep was created to provide an alternative education for Harlem youths who had rejected traditional school programs. The provisional charter which the New York State Department of Education granted Harlem Prep describes its purposes in the following terms:

> To establish, conduct, operate, and maintain a non-sectarian, private college preparatory school for boys and girls between the ages of 16 and 21 who have dropped out of school and who, in the opinion of the

administration of the school, can be motivated to complete secondary education, to provide such education for such boys and girls, and to develop liaison with a number of colleges eager and willing to accept such graduates.(43)

From its original enrollment of 49 students, Harlem Prep has grown to an enrollment of 400 students, ranging from 17 to 40 years of age. Money is still a problem for the school which is housed in a former supermarket on Eight Avenue in Central Harlem, but as a result of grants from Standard Oil of New Jersey, the Ford Foundation, the Chase Manhattan Foundation, and other sources, Harlem Prep is now on a sounder basis than at any time in its history.(44)

The students at Harlem Prep are given both a great deal of freedom and responsibility and at the same time are subjected to a highly disciplined curriculum. Along with teachers, students plan and evaluate material to be studied in class. They organize and elect their own student council and write their constitution. They also have real economic and political power outside the classroom. They elect a representative to the Board of Trustees, raise funds for meeting the school's budget, administer money in the student welfare account, and are represented at faculty conferences. The classes at Harlem Prep are conducted in an open area, without walls or partitions. Students are free to visit classes other than their own, and if they wish, to take part in them. The curriculum at Harlem Prep involves the usual number of basic subjects (English, Math, Science), but it also reflects the special interests of its students through courses in Black Theatre, Swahili, and African Studies.(45)

The freedom and responsibility which the students at Harlem Prep exercise reflects, however, their closeness with one another and the faculty. As one student noted, "Harlem Prep really is a family—and not one just in name."(46) The emblem of the school, MOJA, LOGO, Unity, Brotherhood, is indicative of the atmosphere within it. Indeed, Harlem Prep emphasizes the fact that the education it provides is not intended as a means of escaping the community but a means of allowing students to develop so they may return to the community and render it service.

Thus, while students have a great deal of leeway and real power, graduation is contingent upon their demonstrating the capacity for doing college work and establishing a record "for consistent attendance and punctuality" in school. A student is expected to make up material in any class he misses, and there is no way around the material Harlem Prep feels is basic for a college education. The results speak for themselves. All of Harlem Prep's graduates go on to college, and to date very few of them have dropped out. This record is far and away the most impressive and practical indication by an alternative school for disadvantaged students of its capacity for developing a program that provides a high level of education. That three years after its founding, a graduating class of 116 Harlem Prep students should be accepted with scholarships to 139 different schools (in many cases more than one college was interested) is proof that colleges, too, find

Harlem Prep an extraordinary place.(47)

THE CAM ACADEMY

The CAM (Christian Action Ministry) Academy in Chicago was founded in 1967 to teach students who dropped out or were pushed out of the public school system. It is located in a building in the area of Chicago which was burned during the riots that followed the shooting of Martin Luther King. The school's flyer bills it as a "second-chance, nongraded highschool with qualified teachers" and an "Afro-American emphasis."(48) The Academy is particularly interested in those who wish to continue their education after they have left it.

CAM's courses are divided into three levels, and students are placed according to results on the California Test Bureau's Test of Adult Basic Education. At level one Basic Math, English I, II or Reading, a Writing Workshop, and Observation and Inquiry must be completed. At level two a student must take introduction to Science, Introduction to Culture, Humanities, Art, Advanced Writing, Drama, and Current Events. Level three consists of indivdual research projects in Advanced Science, Humanities, and Culture, which are done under a teacher's supervision. Prior to level three students, however, also receive close personal attention and move at their own pace. Attendance is voluntary, and the classes are informal in nature.(49)

The teaching at CAM is in addition highly innovative in a number of areas. The Writing Workshop, for example, avoids the traditional grammar and punctuation emphasis of such classes and concentrates on "image making" and speed writing. A course in Educational Psychology, open to all students who have taken one other course at CAM is designed to get students involved in curriculum research and development. The course focuses on the psychology of learning and classroom techniques, and the students involved in it spend one period a day teaching their own classes or working as research assistants.(50)

CAM's enrollment, 72 in its first year, 170 in its second, is modest by standard high school proportions, but its relative smallness is the key to its success. The special attention CAM gives to its students enables it to have excellent results. In its first year, for example, CAM graduated 35 students with its own certificate (which guarantees a tenth-grade reading level) and 22 of these students then went on to college. CAM's graduates have a higher reading average than the graduates of Chicago's public schools, and in addition to going on to college, most of them take and pass the Chicago public school examination, which is offered as the equivalence of a high school diploma. What makes these figures particularly noteworthy is that, although the men entering CAM average 10.2 years in the Chicago public schools and the women 8.8 years, their scores place them at the seventh grade level in reading, math, and language.(51)

The Pennsylvania Advancement School takes in students from the fifth to eighth grades who have been performing below capacity in their regular schools. Most of the pupils in it are black and from low-income families. It originally began in Winston-Salem, North Carolina with a $500,000 grant from the

Carnegie Corporation, but interference from the North Carolina Board of Education (The Advancement School was the first integrated boarding school in the South) caused it to move to Philadelphia. It is now run as a nonprofit corporation with a board of directors and is under a contract with the School District of Philadelphia. It has 43 staff members, and serves from 150 to 220 students. Except for becoming a day school rather than a residential school, the Advancement School has generally followed its original format. The school is located on the third and fourth floors of what was once a factory.(52)

The Advancement School concentrates on the emotional growth of its students and makes extensive use of group therapy, role playing and psychodrama. Subjects are treated as a "process" rather than a narrow body of learning. There is an emphasis on making a student's own experiences and interests part of the course. Thus, history and geography at the Advancement School have centered on Philadelphia itself and included such subjects as the rise of street gangs in the city. There has also been a reading-boxing course in which the students themselves boxed, went to boxing matches, and then read books on boxing.(53)

What all of this means in practice is that in the five or six courses students take per 14 week term they learn mainly through action. The courses involve a variety of experiences in which students must either interact with each other (as in improvisational drama) or else practice what they are learning: write plays and not just read them, make cameras and develop photos, conduct science experiments. The "planned environment" that the student initially encounters in the advancement school is one that has been set up to stimulate him, but it is in turn an environment which he is free to change and respond to in individual ways. In no course at the Advancement School is the content organized into a set sequence at the beginning of a term, and students are continually encouraged to develop a curriculum that interests them. Indeed, students of the Advancement School are often used as teachers in it and at nearby elementary schools.(54)

The academic results of the Pennsylvania Advancement School are generally modest. The most extensive report to date is a follow-up study of 175 boys who spent a 14-week term at the school. When they returned to their original schools, 96 pupils or 55 percent of the group improved, 15 pupils showed no change, and 64 pupils went downhill. The Advancement School contends that these results show that nearly two-thirds of the time it was able to stop a downward academic spiral. On the other hand, what these figures mean in fact is an average gain of 1/5 a grade point for students (functioning below par when they entered the Advancement School.(55) Reading tests administered to another group of boys from the Advancement School show similar results. In general the improvement in reading scores was modest and did no more than keep pace with what the boys were doing prior to the Advancement School. The one notable exception in this case was the reading-boxing class in which the boys showed an 8/10 of a year reading improvement on the Durrell-Sullivan Reading Test after three months work.(56)

The First Street School in New York reflects the most intensive commitment by any school in this study toward granting its students real freedom. In the words of First Street's Director, George Dennison:

> Perhaps the single most important thing we offered the children at First Street was hours and hours of unsupervised play. By unsupervised I mean that we teachers took no part at all, but stood to one side and held sweaters. We were not referees, or courts of last resort.(57)

In practice the First Street School abandoned virtually all the structure of a traditional school:

> We abolished tests and grades and Lesson Plans. We abolished Superiors too—all that petty and disgusting order of the school bureaucracy. . . . We abolished homework (unless asked for); we abolished the category of truant.(58)

The abandonment of such a structure by the First Street School was, however, positive in nature and based on the belief that "in doing this, we laid bare the deeper motivations and powers which contribute to what might be called 'internal order,' i.e., a structuing of activities based upon the child's innate desire to learn."(59)

The First Street School Faculty conceived of the school as a total environment for growth:

> where the public school conceives of itself merely as a place of instruction, and puts severe restraints on the relationships between persons, we conceived of ourselves as an environment for growth, and accepted the relationships between the children and ourselves as being the very heart of the school.(60)

The size of the school made it possible for faculty to find the time to be close to students. First Street began with nine students and ended up with 23. It had three full and one part-time teacher, and others who came in to assist for classes in singing, dancing, and music. The classes were according to age: 5 to 8, 8 to 10, 10 to 13, with students free to go to different classes if they felt like it. The school was located on the Lower East Side, and both faculty and the children lived nearby. The majority of the students were nonwhite and poor, and all had had problems in the public schools. The parents of the First Street School were not initially committed to the school's libertarian approach, but as the year went on and the students began liking school, the parents' feelings changed, and there arose a closeness between them and the First Street teachers.(61)

The results of the First Street School are difficult to assess in the absence of any hard test data from the school, but they were clearly positive in nature. The emotional problems of most of the children in the school diminished considerably, and progress in turn was made in a variety of formal skills, particularly reading. On the other hand, as George Dennison has acknowledged, "We can boast of very little in the way of long-range effects." The First Street School lasted only two years, and so came to provide very little continuity in the lives of the children it helped. While some of them managed to keep the gains they made, others slipped back to where they had been before the school started.(62)

> It may well be that certain levels of literacy and ability in arithmetic constitute "fundamentals" for survival in America. . . . But it does not follow that learning these things can be achieved by a single set of techniques. . . . More defensible is the assumption that, while drill, order, and tight discipline may be suitable for some students and teachers, they may be destructive for others; that "permissive" classes or Deweyan practice may work well with certain personalities but not with everyone.(63)

> A final word on the faddishness of our educational concerns. The appearance of new ideas, such as the clamor for oepn, informal schools, does not cancel out old ideas. "Open education" will be a sham unless those supporting it address themselves to recurring, fundamental problems, such as the basic inequality and racism of our society.(64)

It would be very reassuring if this study of free and directed schools could conclude with a definitive statement on which type of school is better suited for disadvantaged children. But clearly there is, as yet, no evidence for a generalization of this sort. One has directed schools like the Bereiter-Engelmann Preschool with outstanding academic success and directed schools like the Newark African Free School, where formal gains are extremely limited despite striking changes in student morale. The same variety of results is true for the free schools. Some, like the Pennsylvania Advancement School, barely make academic inroads. Others, like Harlem Prep, leave little to be desired in all phases of education. The only conclusion supported by this survey is one that reinforces previous evidence on the question of free versus directed schools: in terms of conventional tests and cognitive skills, students educated in directed schools tend to do slightly better than those educated in free schools, but the difference is slight and in no way supports a claim for the overall superiority of one or the other kind of school.(65)

What can be usefully said about free and directed schools and the needs of the disadvantaged is then not so much a matter of comparing systems of education but of pointing out what freedom and directedness mean in successful educational practice. In this regard it is fair to say that directedness has shown itself to be a vital element in the teaching of cognitive skills to disadvantaged children. This is true not only of the programs which are unequivocal about the nature of their directedness, but also of the programs which stress freedom. Indeed, it was difficult to find a successful program in which directedness was not part of the teaching process. Even at a libertarian school like First Street, the director had no qualms about asserting "adult" direction when he thought it was required and telling one of his students it was time to begin reading lessons. The most significant distinction in this area was not between directedness and nondirectedness but between overt direction, like that at the Amidon Elementary School, and covert direction, like that in the Montessori Head Start programs. Similar observations may be made with regard to the question of freedom. Very clearly in a number of schools the freedom students were given was responsible for changes in their motivation and self-esteem. But freedom in these cases was not leeway for the students to do as they pleased. Rather it was freedom to choose from a number of options: to discover what courses interested them, to learn at an individual rather than at a group pace. It was not unusual for students in a free school to end up doing many of the same things they would have in a directed school.

In practical terms what these observations suggest, however, is not simply that in the great majority of cases the free versus directed school controversy involves hubrid rather than "purist" forms of education. They also suggest that, if disadvantaged children (or for that matter, middle-class children) are to profit from the programs going on in free and directed schools, it will be necessary for individual public school systems to adopt a flexible attitude toward such programs: to use them only as they serve particular needs and not be swayed by pedagogical fashion.

NOTES:

(1) Ivan Illich, Deschooling Society (New York, 1971), pp. 4-5.

(2) Joseph Featherstone, "Open Schools—II: Tempering a Fad," The New Republic, 165 (September 25, 1971), p. 19.

(3) In a sample of 1,000 compensatory programs tested for the period 1963 to 1968, only 21 were found to meet a criterion of improved intellectual or academic functioning. See David P. Weikart, "Comparative Study of Three Preschool Curricula," Paper delivered at the biennial meeting of the Society for Research Development, Santa Monica California, March, 1969, p. 1.

(4) Charles E. Silberman, Crisis in the Classroom (New York, 1970), p. 220.

(5) Quoted in Fred Powledge, To Change a Child (Chicago, 1967), p. 22.

(6) Carl F. Hansen, The Amidon Elementary School (Englewood Cliffs, 1962), p. 66.

(7) Ibid., pp. 68-73.

(8) Ibid., pp. 91-92.

(9) Ibid., pp. 15-21

(10) Ibid., pp. 59-159.

(11) Ibid., pp. 201-234.

(12) Carl Bereiter, "Education and the Pursuit of Reality," Interchange, 2 (1971), p. 44.

(13) Carl Bereiter and Siegfried Engelmann, Teaching Disadvantaged Children

in the Preschool (Englewood Cliffs, 1966), pp. 9-10.

(14) Ibid., p. 52.

(15) Ibid., pp. 52-53

(16) Ibid., p. 59.

(17) Ibid., pp. 52-54.

(18) Fred Powledge, To Change a Child, p. 15.

(19) Ibid., p. 31.

(20) A Harry Passow, "Early Childhood and Compensatory Education," Reaching the Disadvantaged Learner, ed. A Harry Passow (New York, 1970), p. 42.

(21) Fred Powledge, To Change a Child, p. 78.

(22) Ibid., pp. 72-75.

(23) Ibid., pp. 96-110.

(24) David P. Weikart, Dennis J. Deloria, Sarah A. Lawser, and Ronald Wiegerink, Longitudinal Results of the Ypsilanti Perry Preschool Project (Ypsilanti, Michigan), pp. 14-16.

(25) Ibid., pp. 140-141.

(26) Ibid., pp. 137-140.

(27) A Harry Passow, "Early Childhood and Compensatory Education," p. 45.

(28) David P. Weikart and others, Longitudinal Results, pp. 130-131.

(29) Communications Technology Corporation, African Free School Evalution Regular Year (July 1971), pp. 2-9.

(30) Ibid., p. 2.

(31) Ibid., p. 6.

(32) Ibid., pp. 14-19.

(33) George L. Stevens, "Implications of Montessori for the War on Poverty," Montessori for the Disadvantaged, ed. R.C. Orem (New York, 1968), p. 42.

(34) Lena Gitter, A Strategy for Fighting the War on Poverty (Washington, D.C., 1968), pp. 19-20.

(35) Henry S. Johnson, "The Effects of Montessori Techniques on Culturally Disadvantaged Head Start Children," OEO Report (Washington, 1965), pp. 59-61.

(36) Dan Fader and Elton McNeil, Hooked on Books: Program and Proof (New York, 1968), pp. 5-26.

(37) Ibid., pp. 53-55.

(38) Ibid., pp. 212-213.

(39) Neil V. Sullivan, Bound for Freedom (Boston, 1965), p. 65.

(40) Edmund Gordon, Report on the Free Schools of Prince Edward County (mimeograph on file at Teachers College, Columbia), pp. 24-26.

(41) Neil Sullivan, Bound for Freedom, pp. 85-106.

(42) Ibid., p. 211.

(43) Ann M. Carpenter and James Rogers, "Harlem Prep: An Alternative System," High School, ed. Ronald Gross and Paul Osterman (New York, 1971), p. 274.

(44) The New York Times (June 10, 1971), p. 45.

(45) Ann Carpenter and James Rogers, "Harlem Prep," p. 277.

(46) Ibid., p. 280.

(47) The New York Times (June 10, 1971), p. 45.

(48) Jon Wagner, "The CAM Academy," Radical School Reform, ed. Ronald and Beatrice Gross (New York, 1971), p. 323.

(49) Ibid., pp. 324-325.

(50) Ibid., pp. 326-330.

(51) Ibid., p. 324.

(52) Farnum Gray, "The Pennsylvania Advancement School," Radical School Reform, ed. Ronald and Beatrice Gross (New York, 1971), pp. 307-310.

(53) Wanda Gray, P.A.S. Laboratory School, 1967-70 (Philadelphia, 1970), pp. 19-20.

(54) Ibid., pp. 20-31.

(55) An Interim Follow-Up Study of Recent Graduates from the Pennsylvania Advancement School by Research Department Pennsylvania Advancement School (Philadelphia, 1970), pp. 1-11.

(56) A Study of Pennsylvania Advancement School Reading Programs by Research Department Pennsylvania Advancement School (Philadelphia, 1970), pp. 1-16.

(57) George Dennison, The Lives of Children (New York, 1969), p. 83.

(58) Ibid., p. 98.

(59) Ibid., pp. 97-98.

(60) Ibid., p. 4.

(61) Ibid., pp. 9-12.

(62) Ibid., pp. 274-275.

(63) Peter Schrag, "End of the Impossible Dream," Saturday Review, LIII (Sept. 19, 1970), p. 94.

(64) Joseph Featherstone, "Open Schools—II: Tempering A Fad," p. 21.

(65) Joseph Featherstone, "Open Schools—I: The British and Us," The New Republic, 165 (September 11, 1971), p. 23.

PARENTS AS EDUCATORS: EVIDENCE FROM CROSS-SECTIONAL, LONGITUDINAL AND INTERVENTION RESEARCH

Earl S. Schaefer

An awareness of the major role of the parent as educator is emerging from child development research. Research findings now suggest the need to return to a traditional comprehensive definition of education as opposed to a restricted, professional and institutional one. Definitions of education such as "the act or process of rearing or bringing up . . . " and "the process of providing with knowledge, skill, competence or usually desirable qualities of behavior and character . . . " (Webster's Third New International Dictionary of the English Language, Unabridged. Springfield, Mass.: G. & C. Merriam Co., 1965) apply to the activities of parents as well as professional teachers. However, the classroom model of education has focused on the school-age child in the classroom, in company with a professional educator, learning academic subjects through formal instruction in order to earn academic credentials. Webster's definitions of educator, "one skilled in teaching" and "a student of the theory and practice of teaching" are currently applied primarily, if not exclusively, to the professional educator. Accumulating research on parent behavior and child development now suggests the need to develop a life time and life space perspective on education which recognizes the major educational role of parents.

A review of recent trends in early childhood and early education research may explain the increasing interest in the educational role of parents. From research findings, a rationale for early education can be developed emphasizing provision of experience that contributes to intellectual development. One response, from a classroom perspective, is to speed the development of preschool education. Other responses are to develop enriched day care programs and child-centered home tutoring programs. Although these programs have led to immediate gains in mental test scores, evaluations after termination of the intensive child-centered enrichment show significant declines in IQ. Such findings have led to recognition of the need for continued education in order to foster continued development (Klaus & Gray, 1968; Schaefer, 1970).

The development of programs to train parents to foster the intellectual development of their children has been yet another major response to the need for early and continuing education of the child. Whether brief parent training programs will be sufficient to have long-term effects upon parents' education of their children is as yet undetermined. Perhaps a comprehensive system of education that integrates the collaborative efforts of the family, the community, the mass media, and the schools must be developed to provide a continuing educational impact upon the child.

The history of education also suggests a need to develop a comprehensive view that recognizes the role of parents in the educational process. The initial *thesis* of education through life experience in the family and community was followed by the *antithesis* of academic education in the schools. As a result, the educational professions and institutions often assume a restricted classroom perspective rather than the more comprehensive life time and life space perspective on education. Child development research now suggests that academic education in the schools will not solve the problems of low academic achievement of disadvantaged groups, again suggesting the need to support the child's education in the family and community. Increasing recognition of the impact of the mass media, particularly television, and of their potential effectiveness in education, also suggests the need for the development of a *synthesis* that will strengthen and integrate the educational contributions of various social units.

Increasing awareness of the role of the parent in the child's education is shown by an analysis of parental involvement in early education (Hess et al., 1970). Parental roles in the classroom education of children—parents as supporters, service givers, and facilitators; parents as teacher aides and volunteers in the classroom: and parents as policy makers and partners in the operation of the school—were differentiated from more independent roles of parents as learners and parents as teachers of their own children. The research reviewed here strongly supports the need to view parents as students of educational methods and as teachers in their own right. An analysis of major characteristics of children's interaction with parents also supports the view that parents are teachers and increases the credibility of findings concerning parental influences on child development. The combination of these different characteristics of parent-child interaction suggests that their cumulative impact upon the child's development would be substantial. Contrasting these characteristics of parent-child interaction with characteristics of children's interaction with the child care and education professions and institutions suggests that strengthening and supporting family care and education of the child should be a major focus in child development programs.

Reviews of the extensive literature on maternal deprivation by Bowlby (1951), Yarrow (1961), and Ainsworth (1962) have contributed substantially to understanding deprivation and its effects. Ainsworth's review suggests distinction of: "(a) insufficiency of interaction implicit in deprivation; (b) distortion of the character of the interaction, without respect to its quantity; and (c) the discontinuity of relations brought about through separation." Ainsworth recognized that various combinations of these types of deprivation occur. Converging conceptual models for parent behavior derived from ratings support Ainsworth's categories for they clearly distinguish hostile detachment (including neglect and ignoring) from hostile involvement (including nagging and irritability) (Schaefer, 1971). Recent studies suggest a further distinction between the amount of emotional support and the amount of educational stimulation provided by parents. Lack of educational stimulation seems to be related to school achievement problems while lack of emotional support is more closely related to emotional problems (Werner, Bierman & French, 1971).

Table I

Major Characteristics of the Parent's Interaction with the Child

Priority	Parents influence the early development of relationships, language, interests, task-oriented behaviors, etc.
Duration	The parent's interactions with the child usually extend from birth to maturity.
Continuity	The parent-child interaction is usually not interrupted, particularly in early childhood, apart from brief separations. Concern about such interruptions has led to research on maternal separation and deprivation.
Amount	The total amount of time spent in parent-child interaction, particularly one-to-one interaction, is usually greater than with other adults.
Extensity	The parent shares more different situations and experiences with the child than do other adults.
Intensity	The degree of involvement between parent and child, whether that involvement is hostile or loving, is usually greater than between the child and other adults.
Pervasiveness	Parents potentially influence the child's use of the mass media, his social relationships, his exposure to social institutions and professions, and much of the child's total experience, both inside and outside the home.
Consistency	Parents develop consistent patterns of behavior with their children.
Responsibility	Both society and parents recognize the parent's primary responsibility for the child.
Variability	Great variability exists in parental care of children, varying from extremes of parental neglect and abuse to extremes of parental acceptance, involvement, and stimulation.

Hess (1969), based on an extensive review, has developed a list of parent behaviors that have been found to be related to intellectual development and academic achievement. Similar lists of parental variables can be found in studies by Rupp (1969) and Wolf (1964) and in others summarized elsewhere in this review. The Hess list is as follows:

A. *Intellectual Relationship*
 1. Demand for high achievement
 2. Maximization of verbal interaction
 3. Engagement with and attentiveness to the child
 4. Maternal teaching behavior
 5. Diffuse intellectual stimulation
B. *Affective Relationship*
 1. Warm affective relationship with child
 2. Feelings of high regard for child and self
C. *Interaction Patterns*
 1. Pressure for independence and self-reliance
 2. Clarity and severity of disciplinary rules. (The literature that was interpreted as "clarity and severity of disciplinary rules" could be interpreted instead as setting of high standards and enforcement of rules, rather than severity, which may imply hostility or rejection.)
 3. Use of conceptual rather than arbitrary regulatory strategies

INTRA-FAMILY RESEMBLANCE

Roff's (1950) review of intra-family resemblances in personality characteristics has provided a great deal of evidence that parents influence the development of attitudes, opinions, and interests in their children. Hartshorne et al. (1930) found relatively high correlations between parents and children in a test of moral knowledge and opinion and Newcomb and Svehla (1937) found substantial correlations between parents and children in attitudes toward the church, war, and communism. Somewhat lower correlations have been found between fathers and sons in vocational interests and even lower, but usually positive correlations, in personality inventory scores. Reports by high school children about their own use and their parent's use of psychoactive drugs suggest that patterns of heavy drug use are heavily influenced by parental example (Smart & Fejer, 1970). Children who reported that their mothers used tranquilizers nearly every day were eight times as likely to report their own use of tranquilizers as were children who reported that their mothers never used tranquilizers. Use of one psychoactive drug by parents, both mothers and fathers, was found to influence use of many other psychoactive drugs by their children. Thus, Smart and Fejer (1970) suggested that "A likely hypothesis is that students are modeling their drug use after parents' use. . . . "

In the area of intellectual and language development, relatively stable differences in mean mental test scores between socioeconomic groups emerge in the second and third year of life (Terman & Merrill, 1937; Hindley, 1965). This may be interpreted as evidence of the early and continuing influence of parental stimulation. Studies show that the mean IQs of different groups tend to remain stable during the school years (Terman & Merrill, 1937; Kennedy, 1969), or the mean IQs of disadvantaged groups may even decline in regions of relative deprivation (Coleman, 1966). Apparently, the typical school does not improve the level of intellectual functioning that is established and maintained by the family and community under these circumstances. Schaefer (1970), from a summary of findings on early language development and intellectual development concluded, "The evidence of the coincidence of the emergence of early language skills with the emergence of mental test differences between social groups, of the relationship of verbal skills with socioeconomic status, ethnic groups, IQ scores, reading achievement and academic and occupational success, supports a conclusion that the education of the child should begin prior to or at the beginning of early language development." Relations between maternal behavior and child language behavior at five months (Rubenstein, 1967) and 10 months of age (Tulkin, 1971) can be interpreted as evidence of influence of parent behavior upon early language development and, perhaps, later cognitive development.

CHILDREN IN INSTITUTIONS AND ADOPTIVE HOMES

Another source of evidence showing the educational influence of parents is the study of language development of children reared in institutions (Skeels et al. 1938; Pringle & Bossio, 1958). Skeels et al. reported: "At most ages the orphanage children had a vocabulary only one-fourth to one-half that of Iowa City children of average intelligence and the same age. Explanations of this extreme retardation were advanced; namely, that the orphanage situation was characteristically deficient in the factors known to be associated with good language development—such factors as adult-child ratio, parent goals for child achievement, standard of acceptability of verbal expression, number of hours being read to and being told stories, breadth of experiences, and extensions of environment." Skeels et al. pointed out that study of the orphanage group "demonstrates to some extent what average homes operating in an average social milieu accomplish in the way of mental stimulation, by showing what may happen when children are bereft of such influences."

Other studies by Skeels (1940) and his coworkers at the University of Iowa provided additional data on the role of the environment in intellectual development. A study of infants in an institution for higher level retarded girls (Skeels & Dye, 1939) who received a relatively high stimulation from patients and staff, as contrasted to infants who received relatively little stimulation in an orphanage, showed substantial IQ increases in the stimulated group and substantial decreases in the unstimulated group. Subsequently, most of the stimulated group were adopted while the unstimulated group remained in the orphanage. A follow-up showed very large differences in the social competence of the two groups at maturity (Skeels, 1966). Not only the early stimulation in the institution, but also the continued stimulation in the adoptive homes, contributed to the intellectual functioning and social competence of the experimental group.

A study by Skeels and Harms (1948) of children in good adoptive homes whose natural parents were either mentally retarded or of very low socio-economic status yielded surprising results. The adopted children of mentally retarded natural mothers achieved a mean IQ of 105.5, children whose natural fathers were laborers had a mean IQ of 110.3, and children with both laborer fathers and mentally retarded mothers had a mean IQ of 104.1. Mental retardation in the children "with known inferior histories" who were placed in adoptive homes in infancy was no greater than that of a random sample of the population and the frequency of superior intelligence was somewhat greater than would be expected. Skodak and Skeels (1949) also reported a 20-point IQ difference between adopted children and their natural mothers, with a maternal mean of 86 and a child mean of 106. These data suggest that a radical change in environment can produce a major change in intellectual functioning between generations.

Despite the substantial differences between mean IQs of the adopted children and their natural mothers, Skodak and Skeels reported higher correlations between the IQs of the adopted children and those of their natural mothers than with characteristics of the adoptive parents. Thus, the data indicate that genetics may determine the potential for intellectual developments but the quality of the environment may determine the level of intellectual functioning that is achieved.

CROSS-SECTIONAL STUDIES

A number of cross-sectional studies have provided detailed analysis of parent variables that are related to children's mental test scores. Milner (1951) interviewed both mothers and children to determine family variables that were related to high and low language scores on the *California Test of Mental Maturity*. High scoring children had more books, were read to more often, had more meal time conversation with parents, and received less harsh physical punishment. Interpretation of the findings is obscured by the great differences in socioeconomic status between low and high scoring groups. Milner recognized the problem in her statement, "The findings listed above may be restated, substituting for the words *mothers of low scorers and high scorers*, the words *lower-class mothers and middle-class mothers* respectively." Milner's study suggests that different socio-economic groups have different patterns of parent behavior that are partially determined by their adaptation to their life situation but also are related to their children's intellectual development.

Kent and Davis (1957) interviewed parents of samples of school children, juvenile offenders, and psychiatric outpatient clinic referrals and classified the type of discipline used as normal, demanding, over-anxious, and unconcerned. The parents of the school children showed the highest percentage of normal discipline, the parents of the juvenile offenders showed the highest percentage of unconcerned discipline, and the parents of the psychiatric outpatient clinic referrals showed the highest percentages of demanding and over-anxious discipline. Among the school sample, children of demanding parents had the highest IQ scores and had higher verbal than performance scores; children of unconcerned parents had the lowest IQ scores and reading scores. This study suggests that insufficiency of emotional support and intellectual stimulation results in lower intelligence and academic achievement than moderate degrees of distortion—demanding and overanxious discipline—but both insufficiency and distortion may be related to different types of maladjustment.

Interviews and mailed questionnaires focusing upon parental rejection and punitiveness have been correlated with *California Test of Mental Maturity* scores (Hurley, 1965;1967). An association between parent rejection and low mental test scores was found for different measures and for different samples, with higher correlations between the mother's education and the daughter's IQ and low correlations for the higher educational groups of parents. Although a number of studies support the conclusion that rejection tends to be negatively related to intellectual development (Baldwin, Kalhorn & Breese, 1945; Bayley & Schaefer, 1964; Kagan & Freeman, 1963; Kagan, 1964; Honzig, 1967), different findings for different socioeconomic groups and for boys and girls in different studies suggest a possible interaction between socioeconomic group, sex of child, and parent behavior as these influence the intellectual development and academic achievement of children. Perhaps different socioeconomic groups have different expectations for boys and girls that are related to parent behavior and child development.

Interviews with parents of fifth grade children about family educational processes (Dave, 1963; Wolf, 1964) have isolated a number of parental variables that are related to academic achievement and intellectual development. Family process was found to be more highly related to intelligence and achievement than was socioeconomic status. Rupp (1969) tested hypotheses about the relation of parent practices to reading success through a questionnaire study of a range of socioeconomic groups. Cultural-pedagogical patterns of child rearing were related to socioeconomic status within the lower socioeconomic groups, but not within the higher socioeconomic groups in which the fathers had at least high school educations. A second study of children from very low socioeconomic groups from the first grade of the primary school also showed significant relations between parent behavior and attitudes and the children's reading achievement.

Although the cross-sectional studies of parent behavior and child development yield consistent findings, their interpretation is unclear. The results may reflect the parent's response to the child's behavior rather than parental influence upon the child's development. Further, methods that have been used in these studies—interviews, questionnaires, and inventories—may not yield valid information on the parents' behavior. The longitudinal studies that have used repeated observations of a parent's actual behavior as observed in familiar situations, provide more valid data upon which to interpret parent influences on child development.

LONGITUDINAL STUDIES

Analysis of data collected in several early longitudinal studies show significant correlations between observations of maternal behavior in early childhood and the child's subsequent mental test scores (Baldwin, Kalhorn & Breese, 1945; Bayley & Schaefer, 1964; Honzig, 1967; Kagan & Freeman, 1963; Kagan, 1964). Since the maternal behavior was often observed prior to the appearance of the correlations with the children's intelligence, it is less likely that the parent behavior is a response to the child's intelligence. Small sample sizes, inconsistent results for boys and girls, difficulties in controlling for social class in these small samples, and the utilization of the data for purposes not foreseen at the time they were collected, have limited the usefulness of these early studies. However, the major trends in the significant relations found between parent behavior and the child's intellectual growth have been replicated in several major studies.

A longitudinal study of ability and educational attainment of approximately 5,000 children born in 1946 in England, Scotland, and Wales documents the influence of the home and of the school (Douglas, 1964). Significant differences between social classes were found in standards of infant care and management, use of medical services, interest in the child's school progress, age at which the parents wished the child to leave school, and the desire for the child to enter grammar school—higher standard, academic education. Children of manual working-class parents showed a relative decline in tests of mental ability and school achievement between eight and 11 years of age. They also had a lower chance of going to grammar school even when measured ability was controlled. The parents' interest in their children's school progress was measured by frequency of mothers' visits to the school, requests to speak to the principal as well as the teacher, and by fathers' visits. These showed striking differences between social classes. The author concluded that "The influence of level of parents' interest on test performance is greater than that of any of the three other factors—size of family, standard of home (housing), and academic record of the school—which are included in this analysis, and it becomes increasingly important as the children grow older." After controlling for socioeconomic level of the family, variations in the children's test scores were much more related to variations in degree of parent interest than to variations in the quality of the schools.

Another English longitudinal study, reported by Moore (1968), concerned material gathered from home visits. Toys, books, and experiences available to the child were rated, as were example and encouragement in the home for the development of language, emotional atmosphere of the home, and general adjustment of the child at two and a half years of age. Although these qualities of home influences were only slightly related to the child's early intelligence test scores, the relations with reading quotient at seven years and IQ at eight years were substantial. The family variables gave better predictions of IQ and reading, even after controlling for social class, than did maternal vocabulary or education. The control for social class and the early data on family variables increase the credibility of the interpretation that parent practices influence the child's development.

Werner, Bierman and French (1971) presented a longitudinal study of the effects of perinatal complications and of socioeconomic status, educational stimulation, and emotional support upon achievement problems, learning problems, and emotional difficulties of children. Socioeconomic status, educational stimulation, and emotional support showed moderate inter-correlations ranging from .37 to .57. These were all significantly related to school achievement and learning problems (IQ, perceptual, and language problems) at 10 years of age with the highest relations for educational stimulation. Emotional problems were most highly related to lack of emotional support. The findings that the child's learning, achievement, and emotional problems were more related to indices of family environment than with socioeconomic status is similar to Douglas' (1964) and Moore's (1968) findings. The authors also concluded that "Ten times more children had problems attributed to the effects of a poor environment than to the effects of serious perinatal stress." Relations between perinatal stress and the child's competence decreased with age but relations of environmental factors and competence increased with age. At 20 months of age only a four-point difference in IQ was found between children from the least and most favored environments but at 10 years of age a 20-point difference was found between children who received the least and most educational stimulation in the home.

Hess (1969) has summarized some of the significant findings from a short-term longitudinal study that correlated measures on 160 middle-class and lower-class mothers collected at the child's age of four years with the child's school performance two to four years later. Among the variables that were related significantly to reading readiness, reading achievement and grades given by teachers were availability and use of home educational resources, the mother's personal optimism and number of out-of-home activities. Maternal behaviors in teaching the child use of an *Etch-A-Sketch* that were related to later achievement included number of models shown the child, number of specific turning directions, orientation to the task, praise and encouragement, and specificity of maternal feedback. Maternal language scores and indices of affection—support toward the child, warmth in block-sorting task, and affectionateness in teaching tasks—also predicted later school achievement. Apparently the mother's teaching behavior, the experiences she provides, and the model she sets for the child are important influences.

Evidence that low intelligence test scores are not only developed but maintained by adverse environments of neglect and cruelty has been reported by Clarke and Clarke (1959). Their studies of mentally retarded adolescents and young adults show an average IQ increase of 16 points during the six-year period after they left their adverse home environments with 33 percent showing IQ increments of 20 points or more. The Clarkes interpret their results as showing recovery from deprivation and state that "the amount of measured recovery can be taken as a minimal estimate of original damage" with the probability that the data are an underestimate of damage. The Clarkes' data are valuable not only for showing the extent to which adverse environments can influence intellectual development but also for showing the possibility of at least partial recovery, even in early maturity.

INTERVENTION RESEARCH

An increasing number of researchers are turning from descriptive and correlational studies of parent behavior and child development to research on programs that, through varied methods, teach parents methods for fostering the intellectual development and academic achievement of their children. Klaus and Gray (1968) utilized visitors actively to engage parents in the education of their own children as a supplement for a preschool program. Significant differences were found in mental test scores between the control children and those who had been involved in both the preschool and home visitor programs. Although the amount of difference between experimental and control groups decreased after termination of the special program, differences between groups persisted during the first years of elementary education. Evidence of vertical diffusion, i.e., that the younger children in the experimental group families also showed more rapid development, was found. The authors expressed guarded optimism about the long-range effects of two or three years work with the mothers, stating that the disadvantaged mother may be unable to provide a home situation that would maintain the development of the child and that the schools are, in general, unable to provide alone for the education of the child. Their concluding statement is an excellent summary of the evidence from intervention research,

> ... the evidence is overwhelming in indicating that ... performance results from the continual interaction of the organism with its environment. Intervention programs, well conceived and executed, may be expected to make some relatively lasting changes. Such programs, however, cannot be expected to carry the whole burden of providing adequate schooling for children from deprived circumstances; they can provide only a basis for future progress in schools and homes that can build upon that early intervention.

More recently, Gray (1970) has contrasted a preschool program with a program that taught mothers to foster the development of their children. The home program showed equal effectiveness at far lower cost as well as allowing vertical diffusion to younger children in the family and horizontal diffusion through the neighborhood. Gray's results suggest that a home program that teaches a mother to teach her child might either be an alternative or a supplement for a preschool program.

Weikart and Lambie (1969) have utilized trained educators to teach parents how to support their child's education in conjunction with half-day preschool programs. The combined programs, after successive refinement over a period of years, have resulted in mean IQ gains of up to 30 points in low IQ disadvantaged children. Weikart and his colleagues are currently working with parents of infants in the first year of life to determine the effectiveness of very early parent-centered intervention but have not yet reported the results.

Gordon (1968) has used paraprofessional parent educators to teach parents specific infant education exercises during the first year of life. The *Griffith Mental Development Scales* at 12 months of age showed significant differences between the experimental group and a control group, with significant differences in eye-hand, personal-social, and hearing-speech skills and little difference in locomotor and performance skills. The design of this project will evaluate the effects of intervention during the first, second, and third years of life and will evaluate the effects of brief early intervention as contrasted to continued intervention.

Levenstein (1970) conceptualized books and toys as "Verbal Interaction Stimulus Materials," had toy demonstrators use the carefully selected materials in home visits with mothers, had mothers use them under the supervision of the demonstrator, and encouraged mothers to use the materials that were left in the home. With approximately 32 visits over a seven-month period her two- and three-year-old subjects showed a mean IQ gain of approximately 17 points—from an IQ of 85 to 102. Levenstein also found that the child's IQ level can be maintained or increased by a reduced number of visits the following year. In Levenstein's initial studies, professional social workers were used as toy demonstrators but in more recent studies paraprofessionals have been trained for that role. Karnes, Teska, Hodgins and Badger (1970) worked with small groups of mothers of infants in the first and second year of life on child-centered educational activities and materials. Cooperation and attendance was lower for working mothers and only 15 of the initial group of 20 mothers completed the second year of the program. Highly significant differences in IQ were found between the experimental group of children and matched controls and the experimental group and their sibling controls. The authors expressed caution about long-term effects as contrasted to the long-term effects of the preschool programs at later ages but concluded " . . . the results of the study suggest that a program of mother training can do much to prevent the inadequate cognitive and linguistic development characteristic of the disadvantaged child."

The promising results of these parent-centered intervention programs show that working with mothers is an effective method for producing gains in intellectual functioning. Parent-centered, as contrasted to child-centered, early intervention programs have equal immediate effectiveness, greater long-term effectiveness, are less expensive, and produce vertical and horizontal diffusion through the family and community. However, the longer the time interval between the intervention and the evaluation, the less significant the effects of the program. These results suggest not only the need for early and continuing education of the child but also early and continuing support for parents in their roles as educators of their own children and as students of the theory and practice of education in the home.

A major question about the future of intervention programs designed to increase parental effectiveness in the education of their children is whether these programs would have significant effects in upper socioeconomic groups as well as in disadvantaged groups and whether intensive parental stimulation contributes substantially to superior levels of functioning as well as fostering average levels of functioning. Evidence by Moore (1968) that early parent behaviors are related to intelligence and reading achievement even after controlling for socioeconomic status and by Douglas (1964) that degree of parental involvement in the child's education is related to mental test scores at 10 years in all socioeconomic groups suggests that intervention to improve parent education would have significant effects in all socioeconomic groups. Fowler (1962) reviewed records of "25 superior IQ children, all of whom learned to read by the age of three. . . . Of these, 72 percent had definitely enjoyed a great deal of unusually early and intensive cognitive stimulation. For the other 28 percent evidence regarding the quality and quantity of stimulation was lacking in the records." Current intervention research on disadvantaged groups should be extended to other socioeconomic groups to obtain evidence of the degree to which intellectual functioning can be changed in more varied populations. The result of that study would suggest whether programs to improve parental education should be offered to all or only to disadvantaged groups.

SUMMARY

The accumulating evidence suggests that parents have great influence upon the behavior of their children, particularly their intellectual and academic achievement, and that programs which teach parents skills in educating their children are effective supplements or alternatives for preschool education. These data should influence future education policies and programs. A critical decision will be whether to devote manpower and money to child-centered extensions of academic education or to develop a comprehensive system of education that strengthens and supports parental education in the home, effective use of the mass media, and collaboration between the school, the home, and the mass media. This review suggests that an exclusive focus upon academic education will not solve the major educational problems. A major task for our child care and educational institutions and professions will be the development of a support system for family care and education. Major changes in professional roles and responsibilities, in training, and in educational policies and programs will be required to achieve a goal of equal education in the home as well as in the school.

REFERENCES

Ainsworth, M.D. The effects of maternal deprivation: A review of findings and controversy in the context of research strategy. In Deprivation of Maternal Care: A Reassessment of its Effects. Public Health Papers, 14, Geneva: World Health Organization, 1962.

Baldwin, A.L., Kalhorn, J. & Breese, F.H. Patterns of parent behavior. Psychol. Monogr., 1945, 58, 3.

Bayley, N. & Schaefer, E.S. Correlations of maternal and child behaviors with the development of mental abilities: Data from the Berkeley Growth Study. Monogr. Soc. Res. Child Develpm., 1964, 29, 6.

Bowlby, J. Maternal care and mental health. 2nd ed. Geneva: World Health Organization: Monograph Series, No. 2, 1951.

Clarke, A.D.B. & Clarke, A.M. Recovery from the effects of deprivation. Acta Psychologica, 1959, 16, 137-144.

Coleman, J.S. Equality of Educational Opportunity. Washington: U.S. Government Printing Office, 1966.

Dave, R.T. The identification and measurement of environmental process variables that are related to educational achievement. Unpubl. doctoral dissertation, Univ. of Chicago, 1963.

Douglas, J.W. The Home and the School: A Study of Ability and Attainment in the Primary School. London: MacGibbon & Kee, 1964.

Fowler, W. Cognitive learning in infancy and early childhood. Psychol. Bull., 1962, 59, 116-152.

Gordon, I.J. Early child stimulation through parent educators. A progress report to the Children's Bureau. U.S. Dept. of H.E.W., Gainesville, Fla. 1968,

Gray, S. Home visiting programs for parents of young children. Paper presented at the meeting of the National Association for the Education of Young Children. Boston, 1970.

Gray, S.W. & Klaus, R. The early training project: A seventh year report. John F. Kennedy Center for Research on Education and Human Development, George Peabody College, 1969.

Hartshorne, H., May, M. & Shuttleworth, F.K. Studies in the Organization of Character. New York: MacMillan, 1930.

Hess, R.D. Parental behavior and children's school achievement; implications for Head Start. In E. Grothberg (Ed.), Critical Issues in Research Related to Disadvantaged Children. Princeton: Educational Testing Service, 1969.

Hess, R.D., Block, M., Costello, D., Knowles, R.T. & Largan, D. Parent involvement in early education. In Edith H. Grothberg (Ed.) Day Care: Resource for Decisions. Washington: Office of Economic Opportunity, 1971.

Hess, R.D., Shipman, V.C., Brophy, J. & Bear, R.B. (In collaboration with A. Adelberger). The cognitive environment of urban pre-school children: follow-up phase. Report to Children's Bureau. Social Security Administration, U.S. Dept. of H.E.W., 1969.

Hindley, C.B. Stability and change in abilities up to five years: Group trends. J. Child Psychol. Psychiat., 1965, 6, 85-99.

Honzig, M.P. Environmental correlates of mental growth: Prediction from the family setting at 21 months. Child Develpm., 1967. 38, 337-364, 1967.

Hurley, J.R. Parental acceptance-rejection and children's intelligence. Merrill-Palmer Qtrly., 1965, 11, 19-31.

Hurley, J.R. Parental malevolence and children's intelligence. J. Consult. Psychol., 1967, 31, 199-204.

Irwin, O. Infant speech: Effect of systematic reading of stories, J. Speech Hearing Res., 1960, 3, 187-190.

Kagan, J. Erratum. Child Develpm., 1964, 35, 1397.

Kagan, J. & Freeman, M. Relation of childhood intelligence and social class to behavior during adolescence. Child Develpm., 1963, 34, 899-901.

Karnes, M.B. & Badger, E. Training mothers to instruct their infants at home. In M.B. Karnes (ed.), Research and Development Program on Preschool Disadvantaged Children. Project Report to the U.S. Dept. of H.E.W., 1969.

Karnes, M.B., Teska, I.A., Hodgins, A.S. & Badger, E.D. Educational intervention at home by mothers of disadvantaged infants. Child Develpm., 1970, 41, 925-935.

Kennedy, W.A. A follow-up normative study of Negro intelligence and achievement. Monogr. Soc. Res. Child Develpm., 1969, 34, 2.

Kent, N. & Davis, D.R. Discipline in the home and intellectual development. Brit. J. Med. Psychol., 1957, 30, 27-34.

Klaus, R.A. & Gray, S.W. The educational training program for disadvantaged children: A report after five years. Monogr. Soc. Res. Child Developm., 1968. 33, 4.

Levenstein, P. Cognitive growth in preschoolers through verbal interaction with mothers. Am. J. Orthopsychiat., 1970, 40, 426-32.

Milner, E.A. A study of the relationship between reading readiness in grade one school children and patterns of parent-child interaction. Child Develpm., 1951, 22, 95-112.

Moore, T. Language and intelligence: A longitudinal study of the first eight years. Part II: Environmental correlates of mental growth. Human Develpm., 1968, 11, 1-24.

Newcomb, T. & Svehla, G. Intra-family relationships in attitude. Sociometry, 1937, 1, 271-283.

Pringle, M.L. & Bossio, V. A study of deprived children. Vita Humana, 1958, 1, 65-92.

Roff, M. Intra-family resemblance in personality characteristics. J. Psychol. 1950, 30, 199-227.

Rubenstein, J. Maternal attentiveness and subsequent exploratory behavior of the infant. Child Develpm., 1967, 38, 1089-1100.

Rupp, J.C.C. Helping the Child to Cope with the School: A Study of the Importance of Parent-Child Relationships with Regard to Elementary School Success. Croningen: Walters-Noordhoff, 1969.

Schaefer, E.S. Need for early and continuing education. In V.M. Denenberg, (Ed.), Education of the Infant and Young Child. New York: Academic Press, 1970.

Schaefer, E.S. Development of hierarchial configurational models for parent behavior and child behavior. In J.P. Hill (Ed.), Minnesota Symposia on Child Psychology, Vol. V., Minneapolis: Univ. of Minnesota Press, 1971.

Shramm, W., Lyle, J. & Parker, E.W. Television in the Lives of Our Children. Stanford: Stanford Univ. Press, 1961.

Skeels, H.M. Some Iowa studies of the mental growth of children in relation to differentials of the environment: A summary. In G.M. Whipple (Ed.), Intelligence: Its Nature and Nuture. 39th Yearbook, Part II, National Society for the Study of Education. 1940. 281-308.

Skeels, H.M. Adult status of children with contrasting early life experiences. Monogr. Soc. Res. Child Development. 1966, 31, 3.

Skeels, H.M. & Dye, H.B. A study of the effects of differential stimulation on mentally retarded children. Proceedings of the American Association on Mental Deficiency. 1939, 44, 114-136.

Skeels, H.M. & Harms, I. Children with inferior social histories; their mental development in adoptive homes. J. Genetic Psychol., 1948, 72, 283-294.

Skeels, H.M., Updegraff, R., Wellman, B.L. & Williams, H.M. A study of environmental stimulation: An orphanage preschool project. Univ. of Iowa Studies in Child Welfare. 1938, 15, No. 4.

Skodak, M. & Skeels, H.M. A final follow-up of one hundred adopted children. J. Genetic Psychol., 1949, 75, 85-125.

Smart, R.G. & Fejer, D., Drug use among adolescents and their parents: Closing the generation gap in mood modification. Paper presented at the meeting of the Eastern Psychiatric Research Association, Nov., 1970.

Terman, L.M. & Merrill, M.A. Measuring Intelligence: A Guide to the Administration of the New Revised Stanford-Binet Tests of Intelligence. New York: Houghton Mifflin, 1937.

Tulkin, S.R. Infant's reaction to mother's voice and stranger's voice. Social class differences in the first year of life. Paper presented at the meeting of the Society for Research in Child Development. Minneapolis, April 1971.

Weikart, D.P. & Lambie, D.Z. Ypsilanti-Carnegie Infant Education Project Progress Report. Dept. of Research & Development. Ypsilanti Public Schools, Ypsilanti, Mich., 1969.

Werner, E.E., Bierman, J.M. & French, F.E. The Children of Kauai. A Longitudinal Study from the Prenatal Period to Age Ten. Honolulu: Univ. of Hawaii Press. 1971.

Wolf, R.M. The identification and measurement of environmental process variables related to intelligence. Unpubl. doctoral dissertation, Univ. of Chicago, 1964.

Yarrow, L.I. Maternal deprivation: Toward an empirical and conceptual reevaluation. Psych. Bull., 1961, 58, 459.

TEACHER TRAINING DESIGNS
FOR IMPROVING INSTRUCTION
IN INTERRACIAL CLASSROOMS

Mark A. Chesler

Perhaps the most important instructional issue in racially desegregated schools is how best to improve students' academic learning and social relations within this particular context. It is a task which requires continuing confrontation and change toward the elimination of personal and institutional racism in schools, as well as new instructional styles and content that serve better the hopes for a pluralistic society. If desegregation is a viable alternative to low-quality segregated education, it must be made to work and work well for all students. If we cannot make it work, it is an unfeasible priority that should give way to other designs.

Some recent studies (Hansen, 1960; Stallings, 1959; U.S. Commission on Civil Rights, 1967) suggest that black students' achievement scores rise in newly desegregated situations. However, it is also clear that many special barriers to academic growth are present in these changing classrooms (I. Katz, 1964; Katzenmeyer, 1963). A newly desegregated school thrusts black, brown, and white youngsters alike into those "threatening" environs which their peers and parents (even the media) have warned them about. The range of potentially threatening phenomena present may include: pressures attendant on students leaving one educational environment and moving into another, and the need to adjust to new travel routes, buildings, and peers; pressures generated by white, black, and brown students' feelings of anxiety about being with persons of another race, and the need to deal with a reality from which they have been sheltered by geography, economy, and mythology; pressures on white students and teachers to see blacks and browns as less competent and able in academic spheres; and antidesegregation pressures created by increasing white emigration from urban areas, and movements for ethnic pride and control in the black or brown community. These issues are present in interracial classrooms in cities of different sizes and in schools of urban and suburban character.

The phenomena above not only illustrate problems; they also suggest areas of challenge and potential growth in an interracial classroom. The possibility exists that through guided classroom interaction students' interracial attitudes may become more positive and accepting. We speak of guided interaction because it is clear that one cannot depend on "natural" contact and relations to improve school racial patterns—certainly not immediately.(1) Most of what is natural in American race relations is distrustful, oppressive, and separatist; desegregation itself is a departure from our natural social patterns, and other breaks with tradition are vital.

Recent reports of newly desegregated classrooms verify some of the negative views (or changes in views) of race relations that may accompany interracial experiences. The sudden entrance of black students has caused some white students to be unfriendly and hostile to persons they perceived to be interlopers or sources of threat. This may have been especially true among white students who are themselves socially or academically insecure. Some black students have come away from desegregated experiences with more pessimistic and/or negatively realistic views of the potential for racial harmony.(2) Surely there are instances of positive change as well, but to accomplish it requires great skill, energy, and patience on the part of all members of the school or classroom social system.

Teachers' responsibilities for guiding and promoting positive learnings in an interracial situation are very clear. In a number of ways, teaching in the interracial classroom is like teaching in any other classroom; similar problems of instructional competence, diagnostic knowledge of one's students, relations with students, management of peer relations, and effective evaluation arise.(3) A teacher who is a skilled and fully competent professional has a good start on being successful in an interracial situation. But the interracial classroom is different from other more homogeneous situations. Although there is insufficient research to state them boldly and to rank these differences in importance, the following list seems reasonable:

1. Since the cultural heritage and reality of mutual ignorance and distance—if not antagonism and fear—between the races probably are present in the minds and views of all Americans, the teacher must wrestle with his or her own preconceived views of people of another race.(4)

2. In a similar fashion, student peer relations are likely to be constrained and affected by the same set of racist attitudes and behaviors.

3. Since few schools of education offer courses focusing on racial aspects of education, most teachers are not prepared by their preservice experiences or training for this instructional challenge.

4. There may be few professional peers who have had experience in teaching an interracial class, and thus few colleagues with whom to share fears, hopes,

tactics, successes, and failures.(5)

5. There may be few available sources of special expertise relevant to the particular problems faced by teachers of interracial classrooms. Most schools that have and will have desegregated facilities find themselves experiencing new "pains," without a body of tradition and experience to call upon to help handle problems.

6. The structure and content of American education presents a white-dominated institution whose racism surrounds and constrains all antiracist acts individual teachers may try to invent.(6)

7. Militant advocates of racially distinctive and/or separate education continually raise doubts, for students and educators, about the viability and stability of desegregated classes and curricula. White teachers especially may have to cope with the local community's desire to replace them; black and brown teachers may face demands to be loyal to new definitions of ethnic pride.(7)

Clearly, teachers are in a position to affect, positively or negatively, the results obtained from working on these special problems. But because of their training, experience, and perhaps inclination, they will not be able to contribute to positive outcomes without some special instruction. In these circumstances, it seems most appropriate to consider ways of helping teachers change their behavior and teach more successfully in interracial classroom situations. In the remainder of this paper, we examine retraining programs that may provide such help and we try to suggest the particular advantages and drawbacks of each program or method. We do not focus on the content of "how to teach," but on "how to prepare or train teachers for teaching."(8) Moreover, our concern is with designs that could be used in most school systems as they are currently organized. We do not discuss here more radical and embracing proposals for structural reform in schools, such as revision of certification standards to permit the utilization of paraprofessionals or nonprofessionals, suburban-urban amalgamation, decentralization of urban school systems and transfer of decisions directly to the community, power confrontations with the educational establishment, involvement of students in making major school decisions, curriculum restructuring, or time sharing with free or freedom schools.

In this discussion of teacher retraining, we delineate change targets and describe training methods or strateties. *Targets* are persons or relations representing the foci of teacher change efforts; they include forces which, when altered, could permit or induce teacher change about racial matters in the classroom. *Strategies* represent ways of proceeding to encourage, permit, or create teacher change. The chart in Figure 1 presents a matrix composed of a number of potential targets and strategies, and the delineation of these constitutes the discussion in this paper.

Each of the aspects of persons or relationships on the horizontal axis in Figure 1 can be the target of efforts to change teachers. Some focus on teachers very directly; others focus on the professional and organizational environment within which teachers function. None of these targets is mutually exclusive, and

FIG. 1.   *Targets and Strategies for Teacher Change in Interracial Situations*

STRATEGIES   **TARGETS**

	Knowledge of Students	Teachers' Own Feelings	Teaching Practices	Peer Relations	Relations with Administration	Community Relations
Books						
Other Materials						
Laboratory Training Groups						
Survey Feedback						
Peer-Sharing Sessions						
Team Formation						
Confrontation–Search						
Problem-Solving Exercises						
Derivations from Behavioral Science Research						
External Consultants						

any program should conceivably include several at once.

KNOWLEDGE OF STUDENTS

One of the necessary foci of a teacher training program is a clarification and explanation of the characteristic attitudes and behaviors of youngsters in the classroom. Haubrich (1963, pp. 246-247), for instance, probably understates the problem as he points out that "there seem to be gaps in the orientation and preparation of teachers for urban schools which leave the new teacher 'at sea' with respect to methods, curricula, and approaches to the 'discipline' problem." One aspect of knowledge to close these gaps could be a review of the different cultural styles in the youngsters' (or group of youngsters') families or backgrounds. The attempt to provide general information must avoid the traps of vagueness and stereotyping, a difficulty magnified by scientists' typical concern for making generalizable statements. Another form of knowledge is data regarding the current attitudes and values of youngsters in class, including assessments of attitudes toward self and school, toward classmates and teacher, and toward specific racial issues in school or community.(9)

Schmuck (1968) in particular stresses the importance of student peer relations, or classroom group processes, as a crucial target of teacher retraining efforts. Detailed and specific reports or locally collected data on how white and black classmates, or future classmates, view the prospects or realities of an interracial classroom are very relevant here. Teachers working in predominantly black or brown schools will need to be especially cognizant of community pressures and movements which affect students' views of the school and racial relations. Teachers who understand different racial groups' expectations and discrepancies in perceptions of each other and the school can develop a better sense of how they themselves affect such groups, and therefore, have a sounder base for classroom planning. In some cases, knowledge of students may also help teachers plan their careers and roles. Whites must reconsider their utility in all or mostly black and brown schools, and those without special skills and roles may need to transfer.

TEACHERS' OWN FEELINGS

Another necessary target of plans for teacher change is a self-examination of each individual's personal feelings and values about racially potent matters. Persons—white, black, or brown—who teach in public or private school classrooms are all part of American society; this society has been built and is maintained upon racially separate living, working, and schooling patterns. The racist views and behaviors of white Americans have been analyzed in several recent books (Knowles & Prewitt, 1969; Terry, 1970). Teachers can be expected to have the same racist feelings as do most white Americans; a few articulate white teachers have carefully documented their own and colleagues' confusion and fear in largely black classes and schools (Kaufman, 1964; Kendall, 1964; Rubinstein, 1969). Certainly, we can expect that these views affect the kinds of alternatives that these teachers are able to invent or modify for use in the classroom. The common expectation that open confrontation of racial feelings is a Pandora's box of destruction and chaos, for instance, inhibits many teachers from dealing with students' real feelings in class.

Haubrich (1963) notes prospective teachers' desires to be located in a good school, where students are like themselves, and Becker (1952) describes this concern as the basis for many teachers' career mobility patterns. In addition, Foley (1965) discusses the negative expectations many teachers hold of disadvantaged or minority group youngsters and speculates upon the development of a self-fulfilling prophecy.(10) The teacher who expects poor student performance often may create it by his or her own fear or lack of enthusiasm. The student senses this judgment and is not motivated to exceed or exert himself—thus confirming the teacher's worst expectations. White teachers often hold low expectations for their black charges, but this is by no means merely a racial phenomenon. Black or brown teachers who are in stable professional roles also often underestimate the ability of lower-class students. The stereotyping of black, brown, and white and rich and poor youngsters happens across the board and in a vicious circle.

For some teachers, these views are held consciously and are close to the surface; for others, they are submerged deeply and seldom recognized. Serious examination may not lead always to changed views, but it may help teachers to understand the potential effects of their views in the classroom and to control their expression of them.(11)

Many educators and designers of educational change efforts take it for granted that more adequate knowledge of oneself, one's role, and one's youngsters will lead directly to improved classroom practive. But there are many teachers who fail to bridge the gap between increased knowledge or new intentions and new behavior. For them, the gap may be caused by lack of motivation, lack of skill, or other barriers present in the school system. Among the most important of these is the professionals' elitist assumption of unilateral control of students and of the processes of instruction. Students and parents have many new ideas for schools, and their inclusion in the educational process can create and encourage a wider repertoire of more effective practices and resources.

We do not wish to suggest that teachers need a detailed cookbook for classroom use, but some specific focus upon the development of teaching procedures and concrete and feasible suggestions is needed in any training program. Translating theoretical propositions, research findings, or new insights about oneself into behavioral implications relevant for the classroom is a highly developed skill, and most teachers do not have it.(12) Moreover, changes in teaching are not merely mechanical adjustments. They typically require change in complex behavioral patterns and the examination and alteration of values as well. The difficulties involved in deciding to teach differently—and actually teaching in new ways—are by no means simple to overcome.

PEER RELATIONS

Another crucial change target is relationships with professional peers. Many teachers who generate exciting ideas for use in their own classrooms never have the opportunity to share these ideas with their colleagues. Without this opportunity for sharing, and without the possibility of giving or receiving feedback, the potential resources and assistance of peers may be lost. In fact, as Chesler and Fox (1967) point out:

> Peers and friends help in many ways to define the situation for the individual. They define possible and permissible personal and organizational behavior and provide social rewards and punishments. In addition, colleagues' positive reactions help the individual to perceive himself as a respected and valued professional ... such a setup fosters a continuing cycle of change and support, invention and sharing of ideas (p. 26).

Collaborative work on school committees and associations and more informal networks of social and travel arrangements appear to be related positively to a willingness to be public about new classroom ideas. These issues may be especially poignant on an interracial staff. A segregated staff or an interracial staff fearful and unwilling to confront and counter its racism establishes a negative model of race relations for students. Efforts of teachers to be helpful in the advancement of one another's professional competence may require new structures and styles of organizational management. We may need to move away from schools as they are now structured, with an educational leader (principal) who manages a staff of teacher-workers; we need to explore instead more decentralized and plural forms of peer initiative and responsibility. Several other perspectives on the need for organizational changes to support individual retraining efforts are described in Buchanan (1967) and Schmuck (1968).

RELATIONS WITH THE ADMINISTRATION

The character of the school administration is clearly another potential change target in efforts to improve classroom racial relations. Principals and superintendents of schools can obviously play key roles in facilitating and supporting teacher change. Administrators can help by providing extra resources to relieve teachers from some daily routines and funds and positive support for training programs. Moreover, they can help set a systemic atmosphere that encourages extra training and generates institutional support for later efforts to try out new things with youngsters and with peers. It is clearly not enough for principals to "feel" a certain way about these matters; teachers are constantly attuned to the nuances of administrator reward or punishment, and supervivisors must publicly and obviously demonstrate their concern (Chesler, Schmuck, & Lippitt, 1963).

The tone set by administrators influences not only teachers but students. For instance, consider these black youngsters' reports from newly desegregated schools in the Deep South:

> The principal never brought up the question of integration; if he did, he tried to hide it. So the kids kind of rejected us. I didn't have any friends; maybe this was because of the principal also.
>
> The atmosphere this year is very different from last year, I guess, because of the change in principals. . . . I guess the new principal doesn't try to hide the situation that is involved, like the old one. You who came in this year are fortunate because he will talk to you about anything you want. He is trying to get the two races to come together. I think that may be what changed the atmosphere. When you hide things it makes people go around not saying things to each other. Now everybody can talk to one another (Chesler, 1967, pp. 6-7).

Sometimes the principal acts as a model for teachers and students to follow in their efforts to decide how to behave in new and threatening circumstances. The creation and maintenance of an effective desegregated teaching and service staff is obviously an important step in this regard.

The white principal in a largely black community faces special problems, just as do white teachers. Community pressure for black professional leadership is natural in such circumstances, and educators unprepared for impersonal attacks on this basis will be unable to exert any effective leadership in school affairs.

Some white principals can and do work well in largely black communities, and some cannot. One's self-regard, anticipation of staff, student, and community reactions—and skill in responding to them—are relevant training foci. Black principals leading interracial staffs in largely white neighborhoods may have similar needs and corresponding approaches.

COMMUNITY RELATIONS

A final focus for change efforts is the community within which the particular school or school system operates. Perhaps a more delimited aspect of this topic, one that is more manageable within the context of this report, is school-community relations. In understanding and modifying youngsters' classroom behavior, teachers need to consider how youngsters can change apart from related change in their social surroundings: if new peer relations are explored and created in class but not realized in extra-classroom situations, the resultant discrepancy may be painful for everyone involved. Some students will not be able to experiment with new classroom behaviors because of restraints, inhibitions, or admonitions by parents and neighborhood leaders. Moreover, teachers who attempt classroom changes may have to deal with resistance and opposition from their own families and social community. Several creative teachers and administrators have reported experiences of community vilification as a result of their efforts to better intergroup relations in and out of class. White, black, or brown pressures for separatism, whether couched in rationales of fear and defense of standards, or of ethnic pride and protection, will undoubtedly adversely affect the classroom situation. Although these forces are different in suburban, barrio, and ghetto environs, they similarly strengthen student distance, weaken teacher resolve, and threaten massive school disruption.

Many educators try to preserve their own autonomy by keeping the community ignorant about what they are doing in the schools. One result of this posture is that both community and school system are systematically deprived of mutual resources and potential help. Parent-teacher organizations represent one easily accessible institution that might constitute a forum to discuss issues relevant to school change and to build support for new ideas and programs. Other community organizations and leaders can facilitate the success of change programs. Reciprocally, the school can enter into community affairs by championing positions on economic and legislative matters that support a quality desegregation effort. The major problem seems to be one of enabling teachers and the school system to see and use the community's members and agents as collaborators and potential helpers, instead of as perennial enemies.

The mere existence of a white-staffed school in a largely black neighborhood is evidence of institutional racism. Whether this can be overcome by different staffing patterns or by active community connections is unclear. At the very least, the staff should solicit the desires and goals of the community and involve parents in the design and conduct of in-service programs.(13)

Fig. 2. Teacher-reported Barriers to Effective Sharing of Desegregation Plans[a]

Within Oneself

—————— I lack conviction about the need or value of desegregation.

—————— I lack knowledge or background about Negroes, the community, or the decision to transfer students.

—————— I have high and/or inflexible standards for classroom performance and expect that Negroes won't meet these.

—————— I am a young teacher and therefore am reluctant to tell older teachers what to do; or as an older teacher I feel that young teachers hesitate to suggest their plans to me.

—————— I lack confidence about what I am doing in class and fear incompetence in knowing answers.

—————— I resent the extra energy required to go to planning meetings, to share with colleagues, and the like.

Within Others

—————— Some of my colleagues will criticize my leadership.

—————— Some of my colleagues don't recognize the problems.

—————— Some of my colleagues want to be left alone; they feel the proper role of a professionally trained teacher is one of self-sufficiency.

—————— Some of my colleagues are prejudiced.

—————— Some of my colleagues resent extra time required for meetings or to share with colleagues.

—————— Some of my colleagues express resistance in ways I do not know how to handle.

Within the Administration

—————— The policy about school desegregation isn't clear.

—————— Policy about my role as influencer of staff leaders isn't clear.

—————— There is a lack of strong support for a staff-sharing program.

—————— There is a lack of direction for change efforts; someone should tell us what to do and how to do it.

—————— There is a lack of support for teacher initiative in the classroom or to share with colleagues.

—————— There is a lack of money for extra time, school meetings, and so on.

Within the Community

—————— There is a great gap between the school and most of the community with regard to standards for education, values about desegregation, and the like.

—————— White parents resist desegregation.

—————— Negro parents resist desegregation.

—————— The resistance of parents to busing needs to be met and faced by the administration's justification and legitimation of what we are doing as a school and as teachers.

—————— Social class differences introduce misunderstandings and more barriers.

—————— There is much prejudice in the community.

[a] This list was originally created and reported in Chesler and Wissman (1967).

Many of the targets outlined in Figure 1 have been reported by teachers as constituting barriers to their own personal and professional invention and growth efforts. The horizontal axis of that figure can be illustrated in greater detail by the forces experienced and reported by several groups of teachers in Figure 2.

The distinction between barriers internal to the person and those located in the social and organizational environment is an important guide for change efforts. Teachers' specification of such barriers lends added complexity to the columns of Figure 1; data on these barriers can help designers of change efforts focus on real and delineated targets. Clearly these barriers must be reduced and/or converted into facilitative forces to produce professional growth and change that will extend from the classroom through the school. How to accomplish this is the concern of the next section of this paper, a review of strategies for teacher retraining.

STRATEGIES

The list of strategies on the vertical axis of Figure 1 does not exhaust either the actual or potential range of current retraining methods. Moreover, as noted with regard to the targets above, several varied strategies can and should be combined or used sequentially in a particular change program.

BOOKS

The traditional strategy most frequently relied upon for increasing educators' skills involves new written materials. Every year staffs are virtually inundated with books expounding every conceivable type of message. To date, there have been few that have focused explicitly on interracial relations in the classroom. The most useful works are probably the pioneering volume by Giles (1959) and the more recent effort by Noar (1966). Among the tremendous variety of recent books on disadvantaged or deprived youngsters, those by Beck and Saxe (1965) and Kontos and Murpjy (1967) seem to be particularly useful to teachers. These works give attention to theoretical issues and include a selection of fairly pragmatic and concrete articles. Noar's work deals with many classroom problems realistically but fails to provide any conceptual or operative scheme that would enable the teacher to go beyond these examples to future efforts on his own. Since racism continues to be a fundamental dynamic of our society, materials exploring race relations should be useful for anyone seeking change in self or school.

But almost all books are just that—books. They are verbal distillations and abstractions of experience that are rarely provocative, and not necessarily generative of change efforts. There is no clear evidence that such stimuli can, in any serious way, help create instructional change. The best we can hope for is to use such material as reference guides in a more provocative program or as jumping-off points for other strategies.

Films, photographs, and recordings represent another variant in the general category of material resources for retraining teachers. One of the greatest dangers in utilizing such materials is the temptation to let them speak for themselves. Material resources do not and cannot stand alone; they should be accompanied by some kind of discussion or practice. Such resources must be seen and used as tools by teachers and discussion leaders; they should become part of a comprehensive training program and not simply used as additive material or separate experiences. Used in these ways, audiovisual materials can communicate findings or phenomena more directly than can books and other resources.

An interesting series of mixed-media packages is currently being prepared and published by Addison-Wesley Publishing Company.(14) This entire cluster of units containing recorded and printed materials on the problems of youth is designed to stimulate discussion around critical questions, to disseminate innovative practitioner efforts, and to present research findings and theory. The units also provide skill training exercises, to enable teachers and discussion leaders who are listening and watching to adapt the materials to their particular situations and concerns. These materials do not focus explicitly upon interracial interaction but would engender a more sophisticated understanding of youth in general. Several provocative new films and programs on race relations and education may also have value for retraining programs.(15)

LABORATORY TRAINING

A third strategy for teacher change is the use of laboratory training methods, particularly sensitivity training groups. T Groups come in all shapes and forms, with a variety of foci, ranging from concentration on intrapersonal or interpersonal dynamics through concern with task- or skill-centered learning and organizational development. What seems common to all such groups is the members' attempts to give and receive feedback with peers and to consider making changes in their own interpersonal styles through an analysis of what they feel and see occurring in their small groups.(16) Advocates of this technique hope that sufficient interpersonal trust can be developed for persons to be honest and open about their racial views. Such openness is probably a precondition for testing one's views with others, for getting feedback and clarification, and for trying out new behavior. Since one of the key issues in most change programs is the confrontation and exploration of whites' views of racism, antiracist training has become a part of some recent laboratory training programs.(17)

Most reports of the design and use of such methods in the retraining of school teachers and administrators are documentary commentaries, but they are rich in illustrative detail.(18) The general lack of well-designed research, however, especially when coupled with the zeal and fervor sometimes articulated by laboratory participants, has led some observers to doubt the method's utility for change in personal prejudices about race. But research is being developed; Rubin

(1967) reports once instance of the use of T Groups to increase racial insight and reduce prejudice among adults.(19)

Most adherents of laboratory training now go well beyond the use of T Groups as the sole device in a reeducation program. Role playing and skill practice exercises are among those techniques also used in more comprehensive efforts to help people achieve change. Under the protection of playing out an "artificial" drama, players can take risks in experimenting with new behaviors that ordinarily might be threatening. Skill practice exercises also utilize a deliberately structured situation and a norm of experimentation to support learning and trying out new behavior. Ellis and Burke (1967) and Heller (1971) report their success in programs involving such techniques to help prepare teachers for interracial schools.

SURVEY FEEDBACK

Another strategy that has been used successfully in a variety of change programs is the feedback of survey results. Essentially this strategy involves collecting data about the performance or processes of a client system, and then feeding back those data, with interpretations, into the client system. The assumption is that under appropriate conditions persons who can now see their own performance data may be able to make changes in a direction more fulfilling and satisfying for them. This method most often has taken the form of social scientists' collecting data and sharing findings with practitioners. Survey feedback techniques have been utilized extensively with industrial and educational organizations (see especially Mann, 1962; Miles, Calder, Hornstein, Callahan, & Schiavo, 1966; and Neff, 1965), and there are also several reports of its utility in retraining classroom teachers (Flanders, 1965; Gage, Runkel, & Chatterjee, 1963). The teachers' personal views and behavior in regard to racial matters in school may be assessed and shared via a series of tests or checklists recently developed for educators' use (Winecoff & Kelly, 1969). As with some of the other change strategies examined here, there are several reports of programs using feedback techniques but relatively few well-designed research studies showing whether change has occurred, or just how these programs may have contributed to that change.

PEER SHARING

The establishment of opportunities for productive sharing of views and practices may also encourage teacher change. By sharing we mean more than mere information exchange; although teachers often talk together they seldom make use of those conversations to focus on the development of professional skill and experitse.(20) Especially with regard to racial matters, it will be necessary to develop a climate supportive of meaningful personal exploration and the establishment of new staff norms.

The traditional notion that a teacher is (and should be) a fully autonomous professional increases the personal risk involved in asking a peer or supervisor for help. Moreover, this conception of the teacher's role also operates to inhibit some teachers from sharing their ideas with others, lest they appear arrogant and omniscient rather than helpful or curious. These barriers to sharing, and those already presented in Figure 2, may be reduced by creating both conditions of high priority for professional growth and high trust in colleagues. These conditions are most likely to be generated when school administrators themselves place a high priority on professional growth and can communicate a respect for peer resources and expertise. A program to encourage sharing among teachers probably can best be built upon (a) the articulation and recognition by peers and authorities of a superordinate "need to know" what others are doing—a need to fill the gaps in common ignorance; (b) the creation of a climate of interpersonal intimacy and trust among colleagues, where difficulties can be admitted and resources shared without competition and judgment; (c) the reorientation of professional role relations to include the view that teachers are learners and that colleagues are partners in a learning process; and (d) extra payment or other rewards for teachers committed to and engaged in the leadership of such activities.

The greatest amount of teacher innovation and adoption seems to occur in schools that deliberately provide opportunities for peer professional exchange, enhancement of feelings of involvement and influence in school policy making, and support from teachers' peer groups and principals. These support systems greatly facilitate the sharing of ideas with colleagues, and teachers who learn about new practices under these conditions are more likely to adapt or to adopt them for use in their own classrooms (Chesler & Barakat, 1967). Failure to organize, publicize, and use teachers' own expertise constitutes a waste of key educational resources, as well as a further diminution of teachers' perceived competence and esteem.

TEAM FORMATION

A corollary to the encouragement of peer-sharing processes is the formation of small groups or teams that have some formal professional responsibility. Research from a number of industrial and governmental settings stresses the relevance of such groupings for feelings of social cohesiveness, for a sense of adequacy of performance, and for satisfaction with one's work.(21)

In educational systems these teams can work together to deal with important school organizational, as well as instructional, issues. For instance, teams of teachers can plan parent-school meetings, can represent a staff to the superintendent's office, can make decisions about school racial policy, and can advocate a meaningful professionalism that encourages expertise without control; they can also plan and support the kinds of peer-sharing sessions discussed above. Nonteacher team members, such as students and community members, can add relevant perspectives that go beyond the biases of professional educators. Some of the most relevant skills that could facilitate teacher planning in this regard include: (a) helping a peer identify classroom racism, (b) diagnosing organizational problems, and (c) establishing colleague and community support for change. Clearly these skills can be taught; with such expertise at hand, school administrators may be influenced to provide the opportunity for their practice in new forms of school organization.

CONFRONTATION AND SEARCH

Some organizational change experts suggest starting a renewal or change process with a "confrontation-search" design. Essentially, this involves a real, engaging presentation of a dilemma or serious problem. In this context, many recent teacher training designs include the presence of black and white youngsters as experts or co-trainees. Relevant materials might also include tape recordings and reports of comments made by black and white students describing their feelings about teachers, race relations, or life in a newly desegregated classroom.(22) Then participants are provided with a range of resource materials potentially applicable to an elaboration, investigation, and/or resolution of the confrontation. The individual or collective search through such materials reflects and defines the direction of members' major interests. Search or resource materials for teachers might include colleagues who have had such experiences; a compendium of potentially useful classroom practices; social science reports; and parents, community leaders, and youngsters themselves.

Another approach to confrontation strategies in training situations has utilized the phenomena of race pride, fear, and separatism as positive learning devices. Within a training design, time may be set aside for meetings of racial caucuses. These caucuses often occur spontaneously in interracial settings, but they can be preplanned as well. Caucuses of all black, all brown, or all white teachers, students, or parents may define their collective interests, perceptions, or grievances and then present them to other caucuses. Such a strategy reduces the tendency to see racial or status differences as personal idiosyncrasies, and it stresses collective differences. Moreover, when whites are forced to work in caucuses with whites they are more likely to deal with themselves, and less likely to fantasize about or project onto blacks and browns. These designs also duplicate some of the highly confronting events that now occur in schools.

PROBLEM-SOLVING EXCERCISES

One particularly useful strategy for retraining classroom teachers which may grow out of such a search focuses on the use of personal or organizational systems of problem solving. Schmuck, Chesler, and Lippitt (1966) list a five-phase problem-solving process: 1. identifying classroom problems, 2. diagnosing classroom problems, 3. developing a plan, 4. taking action, and 5. feedback and evaluation. This empirical-rational approach places a premium upon step-by-step analysis of contemporary states of affairs preliminary to action-taking. For teachers who often operate on purely intuitive or traditionally authoritative grounds, there is every possibility that classroom teaching can be dramatically improved through the learning of this self-training methodology. A similar model for use with members of an entire school system has been suggested by Jung, Fox, and Lippitt (1967); *see also* Shaevitz (1967) and Watson (1967). The major hope of most problem-solving strategies is that once skills of this sort have been taught, teachers or administrators can continue to apply them to new situations. Continued systematic practices or ongoing retraining events are probably needed.

DERIVATIONS FROM BEHAVIORAL SCIENCE

A variant of the problem-solving process has recently been proposed by scientists concerned with ways in which behavioral science knowledge and methods can be utilized to improve social practice. A focus on the process by which practical suggestions can be derived from research findings has been suggested by Jung and Lippitt (1966, pp. 25-29). These authors stress the fact that "research findings seldom provide direct answers about what the educator should do in dealing with a problem." Teachers have to go beyond the data or empirical generalizations to derive implications relevant to their own classrooms.

An example of a useful research finding might be: persons from divergent ethnic or task groupings may be able to collaborate if a situation encourages them to commit themselves to superordinate goals that are of a higher priority than personal goals or fears.(23) The problems of deriving classroom practices from this finding include specifying what such terms mean for the classroom and then devising instructional problems that operationalize such terms. For instance, what are some naturally diverse goals or group formations in the classrooms? What could be a superordinate goal? A class that decides to take communal responsibility for raising funds for a war orphan or for poor people might so commit every person to this work that other problems in social interaction could become secondary. Boys and girls, rival club members, blacks and whites, students and teachers, may all be able to foreswear intergroup bickering and distance in their attempt to attain this embracing goal. In the process of this work they may also discover the possibility of collaboration that might affect other elements of classroom life.

Undoubtedly it would be useful if scientists were able to present a list of educational and social scientific findings considered relevant for the interracial classroom.(24) But even if this were done, it would only be the first step in the derivation process. School people would then need to specify and program these findings to create classroom strategies. Most appropriately, these alternative strategies should be clarified again with the scientist, in order to check the accuracy of their derivation from the original findings or conceptual model.

It is possible to begin this derivation process from the practioner's point of view as well. In this variant a teacher may identify a problem and articulate some needs for knowledge relevant to it. When the scientist brings his expertise to bear on these inquiry areas, the derivation of action alternatives can begin again. In either case, this strategy of educational change requires the development of a new collaborative form—a new marriage between scientists and practitioners.

EXTERNAL CONSULTANT

In any of these strategies, it is possible to employ an external consultant to help deal with the problems attendant upon racial change in the schools. Unfortunately, many educational leaders request such temporary and external agents, hoping these persons will *solve* their problems for them. Most of the time this is an impossible task—a judgment in which even the most casual observer would concur. But the need to be helped may be so great as to overcome rational considerations.

Consultants commited to a person's or a system's continuing ability to grow and develop must teach clients ways of *solving their own* problems.(25) This clearly cannot be accomplished by a quick meal of all the "right" answers, even if such a menu were available. Perhaps a helpful activity in this regard might involve a short course for educational practitioners on "how to use a consultant." Such an experience might assist school systems to build key external resources into their ongoing educational change strategies in more meaningful ways. Consultant expertise might well focus on the more refined or precise design of teacher programs, such as those discussed here. If a panel of consultants from various institutions or disciplines were collected, they would bring a rich and varied set of resources to bear on the critical problems of designing teacher learning and relearning experiences.

SOME CONCLUDING DESIGN PROBLEMS AND RECOMMENDATIONS

Many of the educational change strategies described in this paper have been tried and reported without benefit of clear research on their actual effects. Moreover, some of the particular combinations of possible targets and strategies may not even have been attempted. It is clear, however, that the problems of racial change and improved educational management cannot wait for long-range research and evaluation efforts. Educators must, on the basis of the best intelligence they can muster, make this leap to action, partly on the basis of rational speculation and partly on faith.

A number of the strategies discussed here have not been tried with specifically interracial populations or concerns. That they have not is testimony to the reluctance with which even forward-looking educators have heretofore dealt with matters of race relations in the schools. But those principles and strategies which have facilitated other forms of school and teacher change should be relevant to race relations problems as well. Although some problems take on a peculiar hue, and some new priorities and problems undoubtedly arise, the fact that teachers are dealing with interracial issues should not mitigate seriously the value of sound designs originally used for other purposes of educational change.

Neither list of targets or strategies is mutually exclusive; in fact, the most effective retraining designs may include multiple targets and strategies. The combination of several rows and columns in Figure 1 and the simultaneous use of several boxes is probably most effective. To take the first target as an example, a *teacher's knowledge about youngsters* may be improved by reading, by receiving survey data on his own class, by engaging in research retrieval activities, and/or by talking with other teachers working with similar students. Given teachers' probable resistance to publicly admitting their own views of racial matters, the second target—a *teacher's own values*—may be best dealt with through laboratory training, confrontation episodes, or survey feedback strategies; books, other teachers, and consultants may not be particularly helpful in this instance. Of course, any particular design utilized by a school system will need to be a unique blend of targets and strategies that best meet that system's special characteristics and goals. It might be well for any school system starting out in these directions to experiment with a variety of designs and a variety of ways of creating designs. The creation of a program is a task for which an external consultant's expertise may be especially important and useful.

Another important feature of the designs and strategies discussed here is their implicit reliance upon long-term involvement. Some of these designs have been tried in one-day, two-day, one-week, or one-month programs. Longer programs permit more extended inquiry and practice, but they are not always feasible within the normal operating and financial conditions that predominate in schools. Regardless of the specific strategy, one-shot efforts and isolated training institutes have very little chance of enabling changed attitudes and roles or the best of new intentions and desires to be translated into new classroom behaviors or new organizational forms. Teachers attempting to change need the continuing support that can be provided by a series of meetings and a total system commitment to change efforts. In this sense, the improvement of teaching is only one component in a system's effort to be more responsive to the demands of a racially heterogeneous society. To focus overmuch on teachers may detract attention from other change targets in a school system.

Finally, all of the designs outlined here can be implemented within the context of the contemporary educational establishment. There is every reason to believe that community members and educators of various persuasions can collaborate somewhere within this context. Attempts to alter educational roles and structures through desegregation, decentralization, or other means will succeed only if we can train and retrain more sympathetic, skillful, and effective teachers. However, there is no reason to assume that all the initiative and planning for such change can and will come from school administrators and faculties. Educational change often does not occur until collaboration is induced by community- and student-generated confrontations and power politics. Teacher training programs built on that base may take different forms but be implemented more quickly and with a greater sense of commitment. Until school systems successfully plan, refine, and utilize designs for teacher retraining, student and community protests will continue to press coercive and justified demands for dramatic change in the teaching profession.

NOTES

(1) Some of the early research in housing and summer camp situations which supports this proposition is summarized in Selltiz and Cook (1963).

(2) Some of these students' changes in Northern and Southern situations are reported in Chesler and Segal (1967); Lombardi (1963); and Webster (1961).

(3) A more detailed discussion of some of these issues appears in Schmuck, Chesler, and Lippitt (1966).

(4) The proposition that teachers often hold low estimates of minority youngsters' abilities and communicate them to these students is presented in Bloom, Davis, and Hess (1965); HARYOU (1964); and Niemeyer (1962).

(5) "Sharing" as used here refers to more than information exchange; it also implies the establishment of a professionally helpful and reciprocal interpersonal relationship. The positions that many problems and fears are not shared, that teachers often do not exchange and critique colleagues' styles and techniques, and the importance of such sharing for professional growth and competence are discussed by Chesler and Barakat (1967) and by Fox and Lippitt (1967).

(6) The structure of institutional racism in schools is largely overlooked in educational literature. It is addressed in Citron (1969); Ortego (1971); Rossi, Berk, Boesel, Eidson, and Groves (1968); and Wilcox (1967).

(7) *See* the positions outlined in Pettigrew (1969). Linkage to issues of local community control is provided by Wilcox (1969).

(8) There is little research and few efforts at the derivation or retrieval of instructional practices directly relevant to the particular problems of the interracial classroom. Several useful books that have begun these tasks include Beck and Saxe (1965), Giles (1959), and Noar (1966).

(9) For a broad range of examples of variables and instruments classroom teachers may find useful in this regard, *see* Fox, Luszki, and Schmuck (1966).

(10) *See also* Rosenthal and Jacobson (1968) and U.S. Commission on Civil Rights (1967).

(11) Coles (1963) reports ways in which Southern white teachers wrestled with the control of their antidesegregation views in order to fulfill their professional commitments to equal educational treatment.

(12) This position is amplified and remedial suggestions are offered in Jung and Lippitt (1966).

(13) This need is articulated, although with no practical suggestions for satisfying it, in Haubrich (1969) and Hogan (1969).

(14) The World of Troubled Youth, Reading, Mass.: Addison-Wesley. Units in this series include The Vicious Cycle, 1966; The In-Betweeners, 1967.

(15) For example, the films High School by F. Wiseman (Cambridge, Mass.: OSTI Films) and The Way It Is (New York: National Educational Television Corporation). *See also* Venditti's (1970) simulation game on multi-ethnic problems.

(16) More elaborate discussions of the theory and practice of laboratory learning methods and sensitivity training groups can be found in Bradford, Gibb,

and Benne (1964) and in Schein and Bennis (1965).

(17) Among the organizations providing such training are the NTL Institute for Applied Behavioral Science ("Program for the Reduction of Individual and Organizational Racism") and New Detroit, Inc., with Detroit Industrial Mission ("Conference on New White Consciousness").

(18) An especially interesting and sensitive report is by Keen and Wagner (1968). TV documentaries of training group processes have been prepared under the direction of Knowles, M. T Group 15 (Boston: WBZ [Group W] Radio, 1969); and Birnbaum, M. Where Is Prejudice? (New York: National Educational Television Corporation).

(19) For excellent reports discussing and annotating research in the general area of human relations training *see* Harrison (1971), and Durham, Gibb, and Knowles (1967).

(20) Fox and Lippitt (1967) do, however, provide several examples of sharing (see especially Chapter 7). Another example of sharing between schools or school systems is reported by Shepard and Hunnicut (1966).

(21) This literature is reviewed and conceptualized quite clearly by Katz and Kahn (1966) and by Likert (1961).

(22) *See* examples of such materials in Chesler (1967) and Fuchs (1966). A similar resource used in college classes involved a series of brief essays written by white and Negro collegians about their feelings toward people of another race (Chesler, 1966).

(23) Just such a finding results from several experiments with adolescent social organizations, reported in Sherif (1966) and Sherif, Harvey, White, Hood, and Sherif (1961).

(24) A good start on a list dealing with classrooms in general has been prepared by Schmuck (1966). The fact that most educational researchers are white may help to explain the gaps and biases in available literature.

(25) Reports relevant to problems incurred in such efforts include those by Chesler (1970), Gouldner (1961) G. Lippitt (1959), and R. Lippitt (1959).

REFERENCES

Beck, J., & Saxe, R. (Eds.) Teaching the culturally deprived pupil. Springfield, Ill.: Charles C. Thomas, 1965.

Becker, H. The career of the Chicago public school teacher. Amer. J. Sociol., 1952, 57, 470-477.

Bloom, B., Davis, A., & Hess, R. Compensatory education for cultural deprivation. New York: Holt, Rinehart & Winston, 1965.

Bradford, L., Gibb, J., & Benne, K. (Eds.) T-group theory and laboratory method: Innovation in re-education. New York: Wiley, 1964.

Buchanan, P. The concept of organizational development or self-renewal as a form of planned change. In G. Watson (Ed.), Concept for social change. Washington, D.C.: National Training Laboratories, 1967.

Chesler, M. (Ed.) How do you Negroes feel about whites, and how do you whites feel about Negroes? Ann Arbor: Institute for Social Research, The Univer. of Michigan, 1966.

Chesler, M. In their own words. Atlanta, Ga.: Southern Regional Council, 1967.

Chesler, M. The school consultant: Change agent or defender of the status quo? Integrated Educ., July-August 1970, 8, 19-25.

Chesler, M., & Barakat, H. The innovation and sharing of teaching practices, I: A study of professional roles and social structures in schools. Ann Arbor: Institute for Social Research, The Univer. of Michigan, 1967.

Chesler, M., & Fox, R. Teacher peer relations and educational change. Nat. Educ. Assoc. J., 1967, 56, 25-26.

Chesler, M., & Segal, P. Characteristics of Negro students attending previously all-white public schools in the deep South. Ann Arbor: Institute for Social Research, The Univer. of Michigan, 1967.

Chesler, M., & Wissman, M. Teacher reactions to school desegregation preparations and processes: A case study. Ann Arbor: Institute for Social Research, The Univer. of Michigan, 1967. Mimeo.

Chesler, M., Schmuck, R., & Lippitt, R. The principal's role in facilitating innovation. Theory into Practice, 1963, 2, 269-276.

Citron, A. The rightness of whiteness. Detroit, Mich.: Michigan-Ohio Regional Educational Laboratory, 1969.

Coles, R. The desegregation of Southern schools. Atlanta, Ga.: Southern Regional Council and Anti-Defamation League of B'nai B'rith, 1963.

Durham, L., Gibb, J., & Knowles, E. (Eds.) A bibliography of research on human relations training, 1947-1967. In Explorations in human relations training and research, No. 1. Washington, D.C.: National Training Laboratories, 1967.

Ellis, B., & Burke, W. A. A design for training discussion leaders. NTL Training News and Notes, 1967, 11, 1-3.

Flanders, N. Helping teachers change their behavior. Ann Arbor: School of Education, The Univer. of Michigan, 1965.

Foley, W. Teaching disadvantaged pupils. In J. Beck and R. Saxe (Eds.), Teaching the culturally deprived pupil. Springfield, Ill.: Charles C. Thomas, 1965. Pp. 89-108.

Fox, R., & Lippitt, R. The innovation and sharing of teaching practices, II: Stimulating adoption and adaptation of selected teaching practices. Ann Arbor: Institute for Social Research, The Univer. of Michigan, 1967.

Fox, R., Luszki, Margaret B., & Schmuck, R. Diagnosing classroom learning environments. Chicago: Science Research Associates, 1966.

Fuchs, E. Pickets at the gate. New York: Free Press, 1966.

Gage, N.L., Runkel, P., & Chatterjee, B. Changing teacher behavior through feedback from pupils: An application of equilibrium theory. In W.W. Charters and N.L. Gage (Eds.), Readings in the social psychology of education. Boston: Allyn and Bacon, 1963. Pp. 173-181.

Giles, H. The integrated classroom. New York: Basic Books, 1959.

Gouldner, A. Engineering and clinical approaches to consulting. In W. Bennis, K.

Benne, and R. Chin. The planning of change. New York: Holt, Rinehart & Winston, 1961.

Hansen, C. The scholastic performance of Negro and white pupils in the integrated public schools of the District of Columbia. Harvard Educ. Rev., 1960, 30, 216-236.

Harrison, R. Research on human relations training: Design and interpretation. J. appl. Behav. Sci., 1971, 7 (1), 71-85.

HARYOU (Harlem Youth Opportunities Unlimited, Inc.). Youth in the ghetto. New York: HARYOU, 1964.

Haubrich, V. Teachers for big city schools. In A.H. Passow (Ed.), Education in depressed areas. New York: Teachers College Press, 1963. Pp. 246-247.

Haubrich, V. Preparing teachers for disadvantaged youth. In R. Green (Ed.), Racial crisis in American education. Chicago: Follett Educational Corp., 1969. Pp. 126-146.

Heller, S. The effects of a five-day institute on the attitudes of black and white public school participants. Knoxville, Tenn.: Equal Opportunities Planning Center, 1971.

Hogan, E. Racism in educators: A barrier to quality education. In R. Green (Ed.), Racial crisis in American education. Chicago: Follett Educational Corp., 1969. Pp. 147-166.

Jung, C., & Lippitt, R. The study of change as a concept in research utilization. Theory into Practice, 1966, 5, 25-29.

Jung, C., Fox, R., & Lippitt, R. An orientation and strategy for working on problems of change in school systems. In G. Watson (Ed.), Change in school systems. Washington, D.C.: National Training Laboratories, 1967. Pp. 89-106.

Katz, D., & Kahn, R. The social psychology of organizations. New York: Wiley, 1966.

Katz, I. Review of evidence relating to effects of desegregation on the intellectual performance of Negroes. Amer. Psychologist, 1964, 19, 381-399.

Katzenmeyer, W. Social interaction and differences in intelligence test performance of Negro and white elementary school pupils. Dissertation Abstracts, 1963, 24, 1905.

Kaufman, B. Up the down staircase. Englewood Cliffs, N.J.: Prentice-Hall, 1964.

Keen, E., & Wagner, R. Sensitivity training in a seminar with black and white students. Bucknell Univer., 1968. Mimeo.

Kendall, R. White teacher in a black school. Chicago: Henry Regnery Co., 1964.

Knowles, L., & Prewitt, K. Institutional racism in America. Englewood Cliffs, N.J.: Prentice-Hall, 1969.

Kontos, P., & Murphy, J. (Eds.) Teaching urban youth. New York: Wiley, 1967.

Likert, R. New patterns of management. New York: McGraw-Hill, 1961.

Lippitt, G. A study of the consultation process. J. Social Issues, 1959, 10, 43-50.

Lippitt, R. Dimensions of the consultant's job. J. Social Issues, 1959, 10, 5-12.

Lombardi, D. Factors affecting change in attitude towards Negroes among high school students. J. Negro Educ., 1963, 32, 127-136.

Mann, F. Studying and creating change. In W. Bennis, K. Benne, and R. Chin, The planning of change. New York: Holt, Rinehart & Winston, 1961. Pp. 605-615.

Miles, M., Calder, P., Hornstein, H., Callahan, D., & Schiavo, S. Data feedback and organizational change in a school system. Paper read at American Sociological Association meeting, Miami, Florida, August 1966.

Neff, F. Survey research: A tool for problem diagnosis and improvement in organizations. In A. Gouldner and S. Miller (Eds.), Applied sociology: Opportunities and problems. New York: Free Press, 1965. Pp. 23-38.

Niemeyer, J. Some guidelines to desirable elementary school reorganization. In Programs for the educationally disadvantaged. Washington, D.C.: U.S. Government Printing Office, 1962.

Noar, G. The teacher and integration. Washington, D.C.: National Education Association, 1966.

Ortego, P. Schools for Mexican-Americans: Between two cultures. Saturday Rev., April 17, 1971, pp. 62-64; 80-81.

Pettigrew, T. Racially separate or together? Integrated Educ., 1969, 7, 36-56.

Rosenthal, R., & Jacobson, L. Pygmalion in the classroom. New York: Holt, Rinehart & Winston, 1968.

Rossi, P., Berk, D., Boesel, D., Eidson, B., & Groves, W. Between black and white: The faces of American institutions in the ghetto. In Supplemental Studies for the National Advisory Commission on Civil Disorders. Washington, D.C.: U.S. Government Printing Office, 1968.

Rubin, I. The reduction of prejudice through laboratory training. J. appl. Behav. Sci., 1967, 3 (1), 29-50.

Rubinstein, B. Coming of age in blackness. Integrated Educ., 1969, 7, 58-69.

Schein, E., & Bennis, W. Personal and organizational change through group methods: The laboratory approach. New York: Wiley, 1965.

Schmuck, R. Some generalizations from research on the socialization of youth. Philadelphia: Temple Univer., 1966.

Schmuck, R. Helping teachers improve classroom group processes. J. appl. Behav. Sci., 1968, 4 (4), 401-435.

Schmuck, R., Chesler, M., & Lippitt, R. Problem-solving in the classroom. Chicago, Ill.: Science Research Associates, 1966.

Selltiz, C., & Cook, S. The effects of personal contact on intergroup relations. Theory into Practice, 1963, 2, 158-166.

Shaevitz, M. School system personnel as scientific inquirers. Ann Arbor: Institute for Social Research, The Univer. of Michigan, 1967. Mimeo.

Shepard, S., & Hunnicut, G. Institute on Urban Elementary School Desegregation (Summary Report). Syracuse, N.Y.: Syracuse Univer., 1966.

Sherif, M. In common predicament. Boston: Houghton Mifflin, 1966.

Sherif, M., Harvey, O.J., White, B., Hood, W., & Sherif, Carolyn. Intergroup conflict and cooperation: The Robbers' Cave experiment. Norman: Univer. of Oklahoma Press, 1961.

Stallings, F. A study of the immediate effects of integration on scholastic achievement in the Louisville public schools. J. Negro Educ., 1959, 28, 439-444.

Terry, R. For whites only. Grand Rapids, Mich.: Eerdmans Publishing Co., 1970.

U.S. Commission on Civil Rights. Racial isolation in the public schools, Vol. I. Washington, D.C.: U.S. Government Printing Office, 1967.

Venditti, F. Solving multi-ethnic problems: A simulation game for elementary and high school teachers. New York: Anti-Defamation League of B'nai B'rith and Friendly House Publishers, 1970.

Watson, G. Toward a conceptual architecture of a self-renewing school system. In G. Watson (Ed.), Change in school systems. Washington, D.C.: National Training Laboratories, 1967.

Webster, S. The influence of interracial contact on social acceptance in a newly integrated school. J. educ. Psychol., 1961, 52, 292-296.

Wilcox, P. Teacher attitudes and student achievement. Teachers College Record, 1966-1967, 68, 371-379.

Wilcox, P. The thrust toward community control of the schools in black communities. In R. Green (Ed.), Racial crisis in American education. Chicago: Follett Educational Corp., 1969. Pp. 299-318.

Winecoff, H., & Kelly, E. Teachers, free of prejudice? Take this test and see. Integrated Educ., 1969, 7, 30-36.

RELATIONS
BETWEEN LANGUAGE ATTITUDES
AND TEACHER EXPECTANCY

Frederick Williams
Jack L. Whitehead
Leslie Miller

Considerable research evidence has accululated in recent years which provides information on the relationships between language or dialect features and persons' attitudes toward, and expectations of, speakers of a particular language or dialect. In one well-known study (Lambert, Hodgson, Gardner, and Fillenbaum, 1960) listeners evaluated the speech of French and English speakers on such traits as good looks, intelligence, dependability, and self-confidence, unaware that the speech samples were provided by perfectly coordinate bilingual speakers. It was found that English and French listeners evaluated the English samples more favorably than the French samples provided by the same speakers. Similar research has since been conducted on Jewish-accented English speech (Anisfeld, Bogo, and Lambert, 1962) and upon selected American dialects (Tucker and Lambert, 1969) in which it was found that the standard or unaccented speech samples were rated more favorably by all listener subgroups. More linguistically oriented research in this area has been conducted by Labov (1966) who selected five phonological variables which were known to be socially stratified in New York speech, and then presented samples of speech containing these variables to listeners who were asked to rate the speaker according to his probable occupation. Occupations ranged from "television personality" to "factory worker," which was presumably also a range from prestigious to nonprestigious forms of speech. As anticipated, the socially stratified phonological variables were excellent predictors of the prestige level of occupation assigned to the speaker.

Research of the foregoing type most relevant to the present investigation was conducted by Williams (1970) on teachers' attitudes toward children's dialect features. Scaling techniques for assessing teachers' attitudes were developed by presenting small groups of teachers with samples of continuous speech obtained from the audio tapes of a dialect research project (Shuy, Wolfram, and Riley, 1967), then having the teachers describe their general impressions of the children whom they heard. Adjectives drawn from the teachers' descriptions were subsequently used in the development of a set of semantic differential scales. An example of such a scale is as follows:

THE CHILD SEEMS: unsure___:___:___:___:___:___:___confident

A subsequent factor analytic assessment of teachers' uses of the scales in rating samples of children's speech revealed that although the teachers tended to discuss children's speech in terms of numerous referents and adjectives, their scaled ratings reflected only two relatively global evaluative dimensions: *confidence-eagerness* and *ethnicity-nonstandardness*. The validity of these two dimensions was substantiated to an interpretable degree by the fact that quantified characteristics of the speech samples could be used as reliable predictors of teachers' ratings. For example, the infrequency of hesitation phenomena was among the best predictors of ratings of confidence-eagerness, while selected phonological nonstandardizations (e.g., *d* for *th* sound substitutions) were the best predictors of ratings of ethnicity-nonstandardness.

The foregoing results led to a number of questions for further research, one of which was how teachers' attitudes toward different dialects might be related to expectancy of pupils' classroom performance. This question seemed particularly significant in view of the issues raised by Rosenthal and Jacobson(1) in *Pygmalion in the Classroom* (1968). Could dialect attitudes be associated with expectations of pupils' performance in particular subject matter areas? In designing research to answer this overall question, several other factors were considered. Among these was the methodological assumption that videotapes, as against audio tapes, would provide a closer approximation to the actual classroom stimulus situation for making generalizations about teachers' attitudinal behavior.(2) There was also the issue of whether the two-factor judgmental model of confidence-eagerness and ethnicity-nonstandardness would emerge with videotapes and with different populations of teachers and pupils. If the model were obtained, how would judgments vary as a function of teacher experience and ethnicity? A final question was the degree to which stereotyping could be said to play a role in teachers' evaluations of children's language. To what degree might a teacher simply report her attitudinal predispositions in evaluating a child from a particular ethnic group, rather than carefully evaluating the details of what is presented for assessment?

The present investigation was designed to answer the foregoing questions based upon data from a field study in which teachers from schools selected within Central Texas evaluated videotape speech samples of Black, Anglo, and Mexican-American children sampled from middle and low status homes.

Videotape samples. Mainly for purposes of comparability with the earlier studies (Williams, 1970), language samples were drawn from male fifth and sixth grade school children. These children were sampled from low and middle status families, representing Black, Mexican-American, and Anglo(3) ethnic groups. This representation was based upon known speech differences associated with income, status, and ethnic groups predominating in particular schools in Austin, Texas. Children were interviewed in a living room-like atmosphere in a research facility located on the University of Texas campus. The linguistic interview was conducted by an Anglo female in her mid-twenties who was identified to the children as a teacher. The sequence of the interview was designed to elicit continuous speech in a semi-formal speech style as described by Shuy, Wolfram, and Riley (1968, pp. 39-57). The children responded to two questions which have been used in previous dialect study: 1. "What kinds of games do you play?" 2. "What are some of your favorite T.V. programs?" Given responses to these opening questions, the child was encouraged to engage in conversation by open-ended questions (e.g., "How do you play baseball?" "What happened on Gunsmoke?"). All children were given a five to ten minute warmup prior to the introduction of the above questions. Videotaping was accomplished by a hidden camera (the children learned afterwards that they had been videotaped). From 41 videotaped interviews, 23 were selected as characteristic of the speech typically associated (by dialect criteria) with children from each of six groups, these representing children from middle and low status homes and the three ethnic groups. Within each of these six subgroups there were four children. Eventually four test sequences were prepared such that each tape contained a random sequence of six stimuli, including one child from each of the six subgroups. The average length of an individual child's language sample was two minutes.

Evaluation form. Similar to the scale development procedure described for the earlier study (Williams, 1970), small groups of teachers were presented with videotapes and were asked to comment freely on their impressions of the children. Adjectives from these comments were used in the development of a series of semantic differential scales, which in turn were used by teachers in a series of pilot studies (Williams, Whitehead, and Traupmann, 1971; Williams, Whitehead, and Miller, 1971a). Results of these pilot studies again indicated clusters of scales pertinent to the two-factor model of confidence-eagerness and ethnicity-nonstandardness. Ten scales, divided evenly between the two factors, were selected for use in the study. These were as follows.

(Confidence-Eagerness)
    THE CHILD SEEMS: unsure-confident
    THE CHILD IS: passive-active
    THE CHILD SEEMS: reticent-eager to speak
    THE CHILD SEEMS: hesitant-enthusiastic
    THE CHILD SEEMS TO: dislike-like talking

(Ethnicity-Nonstandardness)

   THE LANGUAGE OF THE CHILD'S HOME IS PROBABLY: marked ethnic-standard style

   THE CHILD SOUNDS: non-Anglo-like—Anglo-like

   THE CHILD'S HOME LIFE IS PROBABLY: unlike-like yours

   THE CHILD'S FAMILY IS PROBABLY: low-high social status

   THE CHILD SEEMS CULTURALLY: disadvantaged-advantaged

The above scales randomized with five additional filler scales constituted the first portion of the evaluation instrument.

   The second portion of the instrument requested that the teacher-evaluator assign the child to class levels in nine different subjects. For this purpose, the evaluator was given a one to five code defined as follows:

   1=remedial class
   2=below average class
   3=average class
   4=above average class
   5=far above average class

These class level assignments were made for each child in each of the nine subject matter areas—*art, grammar, physical education, social studies, mathematics, spelling, music, composition,* and *reading*.

   The evaluation scales and the class assignment appeared on a single evaluation sheet reproduced on a Digitex form to provide for automatic key punching. There was one evaluation form for each teacher's rating of a child's videotape or ethnic stereotype. Evaluation booklets contained a first page for demographic data; the second page explained the guise for the experiment, and the third page instructed Ss how to use the response scales. Following these instructional pages were three evaluation forms, each of which had a label of an ethnic group in the upper right hand corner (Mexican-American, Anglo, Black). It was assumed that a teacher's rating of the speech that she would anticipate from a child of a particular ethnic group or based upon experiences with children of a particular ethnicity would represent a suitable approximation of that teacher's stereotype. The remaining six pages were evaluation forms numbered one through six corresponding to the six videotapes that were to be presented to the teachers.

SUBJECTS

   The teachers were from fifteen elementary schools in the Central Texas area. A promise of anonymity prevents the identification of the individual schools, but some 60% of the teachers were from towns under 35,000 in population, while the remainder were from larger areas. A total of 175 teachers participated in the evaluations which were included in the present analyses.(4) A desire for teacher stratification by ethnicity and experience level led to the division of this total number of teachers into five experience groups (0-4 years, 5-9, 10-19,

20-29, over 30) with 25 Anglo teachers and 10 Black teachers within each.

PROCEDURES

Data gathering. Teachers' evaluations were provided within the context of an in-service training program on the topic of "language differences in children." Instructions and the videotape evaluations themselves comprised the first segment of this program. Testing was followed by the instructional materials for the in-service training, which drew in part from the videotapes which had been presented to the teachers. Evaluations were gathered in subgroups of teachers averaging approximately ten persons per session.

Data gathering took place in the schools, and most often in a space set aside in a library. Typically, two researchers conducted the evaluation session, having been introduced to the teachers as the staff for the in-service training session. The videotapes and the booklets were presented to the teachers as materials for the in-service training session along with the instruction which encouraged the teachers' frank opinions of these children in terms of the items on the evaluation sheet. Following instructions in the use of the evaluation form, teacher-evaluators were told to begin marking the first three sheets of the evaluation booklet, each of which contained a label representing children of a particular ethnic group. The teachers were asked to provide evaluations of their average or anticipated experiences with children in each of these groups. It should be noted that teachers had the option of marking the neutral point on any of the evaluation scales and a "no-decision" option on the placement in the various graded classes. Videotapes were played through an 11-inch monitor with sufficient time after each selection for evaluators to complete their response scales. Each teacher-evaluator responded to one of the four tape sequences which incorporated a child in each of the ethnic groups and each of the two status levels. The four stimulus tapes were systematically rotated such that each was used with equal frequency.

Response scoring. Teachers' reponses to semantic differential scales were scored by assigning a one through seven scale to the response entries where the one was arbitrarily associated with a cell adjacent to the less desirable adjective. (These adjectives appeared on the left side in the preceding list.) The numeric assignemts used by the teachers for the graded classes were used directly in the subsequent statistical analyses. Whenever teachers marked the "no decision" option, their scores were treated as missing data, which in subsequent statistical analyses involved the incorporation of the mean of the distribution of scores on that scale as the least biased score estimate.

IDENTIFICATION OF EVALUATIVE DIMENSIONS

The existence of the two-factor judgmental model was confirmed by a factor analysis of the intercorrelations among the semantic differential data. In this analysis, unities were placed in the diagonal of the correlation matrix, and factors with latent roots greater than one were rotated with Varimax criteria. The results of the analysis are presented in Table 1 in the form of a rotated matrix of the factor structure. As in the prior audio tape study (Williams, 1970) and in the videotape study leading to the development of the instrument (Williams, Whitehead, and Traupmann, 1971), the two-factor model had dimensions interpretable as *confidence-eagerness* and *ethnicity-non-standardness*. Given evidence of the judgmental model, the ten scale scores were reduced to two factor scores by summing over the five scales that had been identified with each of the two factors. Accordingly, factor scores for confidence-eagerness could range from 5 to 35, where the higher the score, the greater the rated confidence-eagerness of the child. Scores on ethnicity-nonstandardness represented the same range; however, a high score would represent a lesser amount of ethnicity-nonstandardness associated with the stimulus.

Table 1

Rotated Factor Matrix of Teacher Responses to 10
Semantic Differential Scales

| | Factors | |
Variables	I	II
1. unsure	.73	.27
2. marked ethnic style	.12	.83
3. non-Anglo-like	.12	.81
4. home life unlike yours	.24	.79
5. passive	.72	.16
6. reticent	.85	.18
7. low social status	.50	.63
8. hesitant	.81	.22
9. disadvantaged	.51	.63
10. dislike talking	.71	.14
Percentage of total variance	(35.3%)	(29.7%)

RATING DIFFERENCES

An assumption of the study was that children from low-status families would typically be rated as less confident and eager and more ethnic-nonstandard than children from middle-status families, and that Anglo children would be rated differently on these two variables as compared with children from the Black and Mexican-American speech communities. A test of this assumption as well as the research question of effects of teacher ethnicity and experience level was undertaken in the form of two identical four-way analyses of variance, one each for the confidence-eagerness and the ethnicity-nonstandardness factor scores, with teacher experience and teacher ethnicity as between subjects variables and child status and child ethnicity as within subjects variables. A summary table of

Table 2

Analyses of Variance of Confidence-Eagerness
and Ethnicity-Nonstandardness Ratings

		Confidence-Eagerness		Ethnicity-Nonstandardness	
Source	d.f.	MS	F	MS	F
Between-Ss					
A (experience)	4	57.0	1.1	57.9	1.1
B (teach. ethnicity)	1	141.1	2.6	322.1	6.4**
AB	4	48.5	.9	25.1	.5
error	165	54.2		50.6	
Within-Ss					
C (child status)	1	5751.3	83.5**	1745.4	35.6**
AC	4	161.0	2.3	63.1	1.3
BC	1	32.2	.5	2.7	.1
ABC	4	46.1	.7	139.4	2.8*
error	165	68.8		49.0	
D (child ethnicity)	2	554.7	11.1**	6571.8	86.2**
AD	8	41.4	.8	46.7	.6
BD	2	17.1	.3	422.1	5.5**
ABD	8	20.7	.4	37.4	.5
error	330	50.1		76.2	
CD	2	928.6	27.7**	186.7	7.3**
ACD	8	25.7	.8	15.9	.6
BCD	2	96.8	2.9	59.6	2.3
ABCD	8	32.9	1.0	27.3	1.1
error	330	33.6		25.7	

**p $<$.01
*p $<$.05

the two analyses is presented in Table 2.

Confidence-eagerness ratings. Analysis of confidence-eagerness ratings revealed that there were no significant differences among means due to teachers' level of experience (0-4 yrs. = 23.0; 5-9 = 23.3; 10-19 = 22.3; 20-29 = 22.8; $>$30 = 22.2), teacher ethnicity (Black = 23.0, Anglo = 22.5), nor any interactions between these variables. Neither did these variables interact with any of the child characteristics. In short, confidence-eagerness ratings appeared independent of the teacher characteristics included in this study.

As assumed earlier, there were differences in ratings according to child status and ethnicity. The interpretation of these was found within the significant interaction between these two variables, the means of which are compared in Table 3. Children from the low status groups were, on the average, rated lower in confidence-eagerness than children from the middle status families. In the low status groups, as expected, Anglo children were generally rated higher in confidence-eagerness than the children from the minority groups. However, this assumption was not sustained in the middle status groups. Here there was a reversal with the Black children rated as slightly more confident and eager than the Anglo children, but both were rated as significantly higher than Mexican-American children.

Table 3

Means of Confidence-Eagerness Ratings
in the Child Status by Ethnicity Interaction

Ethnicity:		Anglo	Black	Mexican-American
Status:	Low	23.0_c*	18.3_a	20.2_b
	Middle	26.1_d	27.6_e	23.3_c

* Means with common subscripts are not significantly ($p < .05$) different from one another (Duncan Multiple Range Test).

Ethnicity-nonstandardness ratings. There were no significant differences in ethnicity-nonstandardness ratings according to teacher experience (Table 2). There was a significant three-way interaction which involved the teacher ethnicity variable with the variables of teacher experience and child status. The examination of the pattern of the twenty means involved in this interaction revealed that low status children were generally rated as more ethnic and nonstandard than middle status ones. However, the magnitude of these differences varied in an uninterpretable pattern according to particular combinations of teacher experience and ethnicity.(5)

Additionally, there was a significant (Table 2) difference in ratings of ethnicity-nonstandardness according to the ethnicity of the teacher (Black = 20.1; Anglo = 18.6). Significant differences also were found in the interaction of teacher ethnicity and child ethnicity (Table 4). Here the general pattern was that although Black and Anglo teachers tended to rate Anglo children as less ethnic and nonstandard as compared to minority group children, Black teachers rated the minority group children as less ethnic and nonstandard as compared with the Anglo teachers' ratings. In short, either Anglo teachers perceived Black and Mexican-American children as more ethnic-nonstandard, or Black teachers perceived them as less so, or both.

As in the case of the confidence-eagerness ratings, the assumption of status differences among the children was confirmed. The means of a significant child status by ethnicity interaction are given in Table 5. Here it is shown that low status children were rated, on the average, as more ethnic-nonstandard than the children from middle status families. Anglo children were rated as less ethnic-nonstandard, as compared with the Black and Mexican-American children.

As described earlier, it was assumed that teachers' ratings of their average and expected experiences with children as labeled for the three ethnic

Table 4

Means of Ethnicity-Nonstandardness Ratings
in the Teacher Ethnicity by Child Ethnicity Interaction

Teacher Ethnicity:		Anglo	Black
Child Ethnicity:	Anglo	25.8_c*	24.5_c
	Black	14.2_a	17.7_b
	Mex.-Am.	17.5_b	19.0_b

* Means with common subscripts are not significantly ($p < .05$) different from one another (Duncan Multiple Range Test).

Table 5

Means of Ethnicity-Nonstandardness Ratings
in the Child Status by Ethnicity Interaction

Ethnicity:		Anglo	Black	Mexican-American
Income Level:	Low	23.7_d*	13.7_a	17.7_b
	Middle	26.6_e	18.2_{bc}	18.9_c

* Means with common subscripts are not significantly ($p < .05$) different from one another (Duncan Multiple Range Test).

groups would provide data approximating the stereotypes of these children in terms of the two-factor model. An assessment of the relation between these stereotyped ratings and the ratings of the videotaped presentations was undertaken by the calculation of a regression of the latter scores upon the former. Separate equations were calculated for the variables of confidence-eagerness and ethnicity-nonstandardness. Further, separate equations were calculated for both of these within the two child status groups.

Findings. Results of the regression equations (Table 6) were interpreted as follows: 1. A statistically significant but negligible magnitude of correlation was found between stereotyped ratings on confidence-eagerness and the ratings of videotapes of low status children. 2. No correlation on confidence-eagerness was observed between stereotypes and videotapes for the children from middle-income families. 3. By contrast, stereotyped ratings of ethnicity-nonstandardness showed moderate correlations with videotaped ratings for both low and middle status groups of children.

The general answer to questions of stereotyping was that there is a moderate degree of relation between stereotyped ratings of ethnicity-nonstandardness and videotaped ratings of the children.

Based upon intercorrelations among the class assignments to the

Table 6

Prediction of Videotape Ratings from Stereotype Ratings

	Coefficients			
Rating/Subgroup	a	b	R	R^2
Confidence-Eagerness				
(low status)	15.8	.200	.19**	.037
(middle status)	22.9	.042	.04	.002
Ethnicity-Nonstandardness				
(low status)	9.2	.500	.48**	.232
(middle status)	12.1	.389	.40**	.157

**$p < .01$ with d.f. = 503

Table 7

Predictions of Class Level Assignemts from
Confidence-Eagerness and Ethnicity-Nonstandardness Ratings

			Relative Contributions	
Stimulus Class	R	R^2	Confidence-Eagerness	Ethnicity-Nonstandardness
Videotapes				
Language Arts	.70**	.488	.17	.32
Math-Soc. St.	.61**	.377	.16	.21
Music-Art-P.E.	.36**	.129	.12	.01

**$p < .01$ for d.f. = 1156

subject matter areas, it was possible to reduce the nine subject variables to three. These were: *Language-arts* (average assignments in grammar, spelling, composition and reading); *Language-arts-related* (mathematics, social studies); and *Non-language arts* (music, arts, physical education). As implied by these labels, it was assumed that intercorrelations among the individual assignments were evidence of a general differentiation of subject matter according to the degree of involvement of language arts. These averaged scores were subsequently employed in three two-variable regression equations, each one corresponding to a regression of class-level assignments in a subject area upon the videotape ratings of confidence-eagerness and ethnicity-nonstandardness. Results (Table 7) of the three equations were interpreted in terms of multiple correlation coefficients, determination coefficients, and the relative proportions of variance predicted by confidence-eagerness and ethnicity-nonstandardness ratings.

Findings. Although graded class assignments in all three areas could be predicted upon the basis of the language evaluations, two patterns were evident in these results. One apparent generalization was that, as might be expected, the more the subject matter areas are directly related to language arts the better the evaluation of the child's language serves as a predictor of teacher expectancy. A second generalization was that the more a subject area involves language arts, the more ratings of ethnicity-nonstandardness rather than confidence-eagerness will serve as a dominant predictor of teacher expectancy.

DISCUSSION

In summary, generalizations of the results were as follows: 1. As found in past studies, teachers tended to give global evaluations of language samples along dimensions identified as confidence-eagerness and ethnicity-nonstandardness. 2. Teacher experience appears unrelated in any interpretable way to ratings of confidence-eagerness or ethnicity-nonstandardness. 3. Teacher ethnicity and child ethnicity interact in terms of minority group children being rated generally less ethnic-nonstandard by Black teachers than by Anglo teachers. 4. Only in evaluations of ethnicity-nonstandardness do teachers' stereotype ratings of children appear to be related to ratings of videotape language samples. 5. Teachers' expectations of children's performance in subject matters are partially predictable upon the basis of language attitudes; the degree of prediction increases when the subject matter area is directly within the language arts.

The close association between teachers' language attitudes and expectations in language arts subjects can be viewed within several of the issues which have emerged from contemporary urban language studies (Labov 1966; Shuy, et al. 1967). The main linguistic variable in these studies has been dialect, which is presumed to be a function of the grammatical system that a child is using. Another variable is fluency, which is performance variation related to the formality of the speech situation. It seems worth speculating that the two dimensions of evaluation found in the present and earlier studies are attitudinal correlates of two of the main variables found in urban lauguage studies. That is, ratings of confidence-eagerness seem to reflect perception of fluency in a situation. Ratings of ethnicity-nonstandardness may be a direct reflection of the grammatical characteristics exhibited in the child's language. This correspondence between language characteristics and language attitudes prompts considerations of a major problem discussed in many contemporary urban language studies. This is the tendency of teachers and educational researchers to confuse language differences with deficits. As argued by the urban language researchers, most minority group children are developing quite normal and adequate linguistic systems to meet the demands of their individual speech communities. Although it may be accurate for a teacher to evaluate a child's language as ethnic and nonstandard or reticent, it may be quite inaccurate to always expect this performance in all speech situations.

The moderate relation between stereotyped ratings of ethnicity-nonstandardness and ratings of the videotapes suggests that teachers to some degree may be fulfilling their own expectations even in the evaluations of children. This predisposition, too, requires further exploration. To what degree in evaluating the speech of the child do teachers differ in their capability of being sensitive to dialect variations relative to their stereotyped attitudes? Evidence in the present research shows a greater variability among Black teachers' ratings than among those of Anglo teachers. Perhaps this is a function of the Black teachers' more direct experience with both standard and Black dialects of English.

One of the most practical implications of this research is that given the relationship between language attitudes and teacher expectancy, there is a suggestion that the study of language variations in children, particularly minority group children, and attitudinal correlates be introduced into the curricula of teacher training. To prevent language attitudes from serving as false prophecies, or worse yet becoming themselves self-fulfilled prophecies, teachers should be trained to be sensitive to the variations in social dialects and the variations in performance. Language evaluation, which incorporates the attitudinal side of the social dialect coin, could be included as part of the teacher training process. The present project not only points to the need for such training but provides a number of ideas for implementation and evaluation of the results of the training.

NOTES

(1) The authors are well aware of the controversy surrounding this study; see, for example, Fleming and Anttonen (1971).

(2) This, of course, meant that teachers were no longer responding strictly to speech samples, but to dress, visual cues of ethnicity, and the like. The effects of the visual image are a topic of another report (Williams, Whitehead, and Miller, 1971b).

(3) These are common labels in Central Texas. The term "Anglo" as used here refers to Caucasian children.

(4) Eighteen Mexican-American teachers were also tested in the field work, however, this sample was too small for inclusion in the present analyses. Separate analyses are reported in Williams, Whitehead, and Miller (1971a).

(5) To save space these means are not reproduced here. They are reported in Williams, Whitehead, and Miller (1971a), p. 71.

REFERENCES

Anisfeld, M., Bogo, N., & Lambert, W.E. Evaluational reactions to accented English speech. Journal of Abnormal and Social Psychology, 1962, 65, 223-231.

Fleming, E.S., & Anttonen, R.G. Teacher expectancy or My Fair Lady. American Educational Research Journal, 1971, 8, 241-252.

Labov, W. The social stratification of English in New York City. Washington, D.C.: Center for Applied Linguistics, 1966.

Lambert, W.E., Anisfeld, M., & Yeni-Komshian, G. Evaluational reactions of

Jewish and Arab adolescents to dialect and language variations. Journal of Personality and Social Psychology, 1965, 2, 84-90.

Lambert, W.E., Hodgson, R.C., Gardner, R.C. & Fillembaum, S. Evaluational reactions to spoken languages. Journal of Abnormal and Social Psychology, 1960, 60, 44-51.

Rosenthal, R., & Jacobson, L. Pygmalion in the classroom. New York: Holt, Rinehart, and Winston, 1968.

Shuy, R.W., Wolfram, W.A., & Riley, W.K. Linguistic correlates of social stratification in Detroit speech. U.S. Office of Education Cooperative Research Project No. 6-1347, Michigan State University, 1967.

Shuy, R.W., Wolfram, W.A., & Riley, W.K. Field techniques in an urban language study. Washington, D.C.: Center for Applied Linguistics, 1968.

Tucker, G.R., & Lambert, W.E. White and Negro listeners' reactions to various American-English dialects. Social Forces, 1969, 47, 463-468.

Williams, F. Psychological correlates of speech characteristics: On sounding "disadvantaged." Journal of Speech and Hearing Research, 1970, 13, 472-488.

Williams, F., Whitehead, J.L., & Miller, L.M. Attitudinal correlates of children's speech characteristics. Final Report, U.S.O.E. Project OEG-0-70-2868 (508). Austin, Texas: University of Texas, Center for Communication Research, March 1971(a).

Williams, F., Whitehead, J.L., & Miller, L.M. Ethnic stereotyping and judgments of children's speech. Speech Monographs, 1971, 38, 166-170, (b).

Williams, F., Whitehead, J.L., & Traupmann, J. Teachers' evaluations of children's speech. Speech Teacher, 1971, 20, 247-254.

THIRTY-SIX TEACHERS:
THEIR CHARACTERISTICS, AND OUTCOMES
FOR BLACK AND WHITE PUPILS

Nancy St. John

One aspect of school desegregations that has been much neglected by researchers is the influence of teachers on the adjustment of children to interracial classrooms. Social scientists have long recognized the potentially important role of the leader in any desegregated situation (Allport, 1954; Dean and Rosen, 1955; Yarrow and Yarrow, 1958) and of the teacher in the desegregated classroom (Taba, 1955; Katz, 1957; Clark, 1965). That teachers can have a great influence on minority group children can also be inferred from such research evidence as Gottlieb's (1964) finding that white teachers perceived ghetto children more negatively than did black teachers, Amos' (1952) report that Negro pupils believed teachers to be more unfavorable to them than did white pupils or than their teachers themselves claimed to be, and the Davidson and Lang (1960) demonstration of a relation between children's perceptions of their teachers' feelings towards them and their actual achievement. Researchers also find that children perform better if their teachers expect them to do so (Rosenthal and Jacobson, 1968) or dispense praise and positive reinforcement (Clark and Walberg, 1966). Such studies suggest that in the desegregated classroom characteristics of the teacher will affect the achievement, self-concept and interracial behavior of both minority group and minority group pupils. But this prediction remains largely untested.

It is not only in regard to the adjustment to an integrated situation that the effect of a teacher on his pupils is insufficiently documented. There is also little evidence of teacher effectiveness in regard to any other kind of outcome. Sarane Boocock (1966) reviews 25 years of research only to conclude, "Very little seems to be known about the relationship between what teachers do in the classroom and the subsequent behavior of students" (p. 6). Other reviewers agree (Biddle, 1964; Wynne, 1969; Rosenshine and Furst, 1970). A major finding of the Coleman Report (1967) was that only a small part of the school-to-school variance in pupil achievement is attributable to school factors, although characteristics of teachers (especially their verbal ability) account for more variance than any other school factor and more for minority than for majority group pupils. Unfortunately, the EEOS data do not allow the matching of teachers with their own pupils. McPartland (1968) in his reanalysis of this data, achieved a degree of matching by grouping teachers in a school according to the racial proportion of the students they said they taught. He found no relation between the verbal competence of teachers and pupils when classroom racial and social class composition was held constant.

In short, though a relation between quality of teaching and quality of learning appears axiomatic, it has proven hard to demonstrate. It may be even harder to study the process in the desegregated classroom, where teaching and learning both have racial components. Nevertheless, this was the aim of this paper. Specifically, observers' ratings of 36 teachers of interracial sixth grade classrooms are related to their pupils' academic growth, self-concept and interracial friendship behavior.

PROCEDURES

The study was part of a larger investigation into the achievement and attitudes of children in interracial sixth grade classrooms in a large Northern city. Eighteen schools were randomly drawn from cells in a matrix representing the racial and social class distribution of those elementary schools in the city with five or more black sixth graders. Two classrooms were selected from each school (again randomly). The final sample included all 956 children in these 36 classrooms, of whom 497 were white, 411 Negro, and 48 of other ethnic backgrounds (Chinese, Puerto Rican, etc.). The classrooms varied from 7 to 100 in the percentage of black children enrolled and from lower to middle in mean socioeconomic status (SES). School racial mixture and SES were to a degree independent. Among the schools of lowest SES half were majority white, and among the schools with many middle class pupils one was all-black.

The 36 classes were observed each for a week by one of a staff of eight. For four days the staff member ("first observer") sat in a back-row desk, kept a running narrative of activities and behavior, scored teacher-pupil and pupil-pupil interaction, interviewed the teacher, and administered attitude and sociometric tests to pupils. On one day she exchanged classrooms with the staff member assigned to the other sixth grade room in the same school ("second observer"). At the end of the week both observers wrote summary comments on the teachers' academic policies and differential treatment of white and black pupils and scored them on a modified version of Ryans (1960) Characteristics of Teachers Scale. Neither observer had examined pupils' test scores and grades before rating the teacher; a third staff member copied these data from the school records.

TEACHER CHARACTERISTICS

The major independent variable of this analysis, teacher characteristics, are factor scores derived from the ratings the teachers received from "first" observers on the Ryans Scale. This is a semantic differential instrument on which teachers were rated 1 to 7 according to their position on 13 qualities. (See Table 1.) Observers were also asked to give each teacher an overall score. Overall and on the separate characteristics there is good range, but a tendency towards positive ratings. No one of the eight observers showed consistent bias toward the top or bottom of the scale, and the four observers who covered the most classrooms each used a range of 5 points in their overall ratings.

Table 1

Zero Order Correlation of Independent Evaluations of
Teachers (First and Second Observer, First Observer
and Mother), by Characteristics

	25 First and Second Observers		35 First Observers and Mothers
	N	r	r
Autocratic-Democratic	22	.22	.21
Aloof-Responsive	22	.49*	.34
Dull-Stimulating	25	.58*	.28
Partial-Fair, Generally	21	.36	.26
Partial-Fair, Racially	18	.47	.16
Unsympathetic-Understanding	20	.64**	.40*
Harsh-Kindly	25	.70**	.36*
Inarticulate-Fluent	25	.16	.15
Uncertain-Confident	25	.46*	.27
Disorganized-Systematic	22	.48*	.21
Inflexible-Adaptable	18	.57*	.22
Pessimistic-Optimistic	20	.74**	.34
Narrow-Broad	20	.64**	.11
Overall Score	25	.68**	35 .29

*Statistically significant at the .05 level.
**Statistically significant at the .01 level.

Three procedures were used to test the reliability and validity of ratings: 1. Narrative accounts of classroom interaction and interview replies of teachers were examined and found to corroborate the evaluations of the teachers. 2. The independent evaluations of first and second observers of the same classrooms were compared (see Table 1). Overall agreement was fairly high (r = .68) For six teachers the two evaluations are identical, and for fifteen others only off by one point. Together this is 84% of the overall ratings. Agreement is less high on the separate items than overall, but even here 67% of the ratings are the same or only off by one point.(1) There is greatest accord on Pessimistic-Optimistic and Harsh-Kindly. There is least accord on Articulate-Fluent, Autocratic-Democratic, and Partial-Fair (Generally). These aspects of teaching behavior are either hard to judge in a short span or capable of divergent interpretations. 3. A further test of the validity of the scores was afforded by interviews with a random sub-sample of 4 black and 4 white mothers for each classroom. Evaluations of their child's teacher by mothers were later coded according to the same overall scale as that used by classroom observers. In six classrooms the average mother's rating was the same as that of the main observer. The ratings were 1 off fifteen times, 2 off ten times and 3 off four times. Observers gave the teachers higher ratings than did mothers 28 times and lower ratings 11 times. The zero order correlation for the ratings of the mothers and observers is .29 overall (see Table 1). All in all, although it was not possible to establish beyond doubt the validity of the observers' ratings of teachers, there was some support for accepting them at face value.

TABLE 2

Orthogonally Rotated Factor Loadings on Teacher Characteristics.

	FACTOR	LOADINGS	
	1	2	3
	Child-	Task-	
Teacher Attributes	Oriented	Oriented	Fair
Autocratic - Democratic	.808	.193	.210
Aloof - Responsive	.912	.179	.181
Dull - Stimulating	.511	.739	.202
Partial - Fair, Generally	.600	.204	.603
Partial - Fair, Racially	.334	.176	.813
Unsympathetic - Understanding	.868	.195	.172
Harsh - Kindly	.923	.082	.152
Inarticulate - Fluent	.128	.901	.164
Uncertain - Confident	.011	.755	.415
Disorganized - Systematic	.139	.507	.679
Inflexible - Adaptable	.702	.431	.255
Pessimistic - Optimistic	.908	.170	.155
Narrow - Broad	.301	.813	.065
Overall	.700	.589	.256

A factor analysis(2) of the 13 ratings of teachers by observers revealed both strong intercorrelation among items and the presence of three distinct sub-scales, labeled Child-oriented, Task-oriented, and Fair. Table 2 shows the factor loadings. The Child-oriented teacher has high ratings on these dimensions:

democratic, responsive, understanding, kindly, adaptable, fair, and optimistic. The Task-oriented teacher was rated fluent, confident, broad and stimulating. The Fair teacher was rated systematic and fair, both generally and in regard to race. The factor scores are the units utilized in the subsequent analysis. The reader should bear in mind that the labels are shorthand for the factors and thus for observer ratings of teachers on a number of qualities found to vary together.

Background characteristics of the teachers showed considerable diversity except in regard to race. All were white, but only half were women. In age they ranged from mid-twenties to mid-sixties, in experience as a teacher from less than one year to over thirty years. Twenty held masters degrees; thirteen served as assistant principals as well as sixth grade teachers. Nineteen were of Irish origin; twenty-one had attended elementary school in this city (11 parochial and 10 public); and half were from white collar, half from blue collar, parental homes. In view of such diversity, an association between certain status characteristics and the ratings by observers seemed likely. In fact, no such relationship appeared. Although cross-tabulations indicated some association between background and ratings on some variables, there was also a range of teacher quality across all background characteristics. Moreover, no strong selective factor appears to have resulted in a clustering of the most highly rated teachers in middle class schools or (within schools) in classes for the academically able.(3)

PUPIL OUTCOMES

The dependend variables of the study are four measures of the academic growth of pupils and four measures of their attitudes. For each measure of academic performance there are two readings (Time 1 and Time 2). For the correlational analysis, growth is a Time 2 minus Time 1 score. For the regression analysis, the Time 2 score is the dependent variable and the Time 1 score was entered into the equations as one of the independent variables.

1. *Reading Achievement*—Grade-equivalent scores on Metropolitan Achievement Test, fall and spring, grade six (Paragraph and Word Meaning sub-tests averaged).

2. *GPA*—Average academic mark, grades 2-5 or 6.

3. *Conduct*—Average conduct mark, grades 2-5 or 6.

4. *Attendance*—Number of absences (reversed), grades 4-5 or 6.

5. *Academic Self-Concept*—Self-placement on 10-runged ladder representing "sixth graders in this school, the best students at the top (10) and the worst students at the bottom."

6. *"My teacher thinks I am"*—Pupil's mean estimate (1-5) of teacher's responses on 10-item semantic differential scale.(4)

7. *Fate Control*—Summary score on three true-false items adapted from Coleman, *et al.* (1966) to measure sense of environmental control.(5)

8. *Friendliness to Other Race*—Difference between mean friendship rating (1-5) given to classmates of own and other racial group.

The relation between characteristics of the 36 teachers and outcomes for their pupils was examined by means of zero order correlations, analysis of variance, and multiple regression analysis. Table 3 shows, for each race separately, the correlations between the three rotated factor scores for teacher ratings and measures of individual pupil growth and attitudes.

TABLE 3

Zero Order Correlations for Teacher Characteristics and Individual Pupil Achievement or Attitudes, by Race.

| | TEACHER CHARACTERISTICS (FACTOR SCORES) | | | | | |
| | WHITE PUPILS[a] | | | BLACK PUPILS[b] | | |
	Oriented Child-	Oriented Task-	Fair	Oriented Child-	Oriented Task-	Fair
Class % White	—.35**	—.21**	.10	—.22**	.15**	—.12*
Class SES	.01	—.10*	—.02	.17**	.05	—.07
Fall Reading Score	—.04	—.08	.11*	.09	.07	.03
Reading Growth	.01	—.02	.02	.25**	.05	—.05
Improved GPA	.06	—.01	.07	—.11	.10	.05
Improved Conduct	.15**	—.02	.06	.10	.05	.18**
Improved Attendance	.00	.00	—.14**	.11	—.06	—.03
Academic Self-Concept	—.05	—.01	.09	.08	—.05	—.04
"My Teacher Thinks I Am"	—.03	.08	.05	.12*	—.12*	.05
Fate Control	.00	—.03	—.03	.10	.03	.10
Friendliness to Other Race	—.03	—.05	.09	—.02	.03	.00

[a]N's vary between 373 and 497.
[b]N's vary between 304 and 412.

For white pupils only 2 of the 24 coefficients reached statistical significance, both at the .01 level: conduct improved under Child-oriented teachers and attendance deteriorated under Fair teachers. For blacks 4 of the 24 coefficients reached significance level, two of these at the .01 level: pupils felt that Child-oriented teachers thought well of them, but that Task-oriented teachers did not. Their conduct improved under Fair teachers. But the strongest relationship for black pupils was that between teacher orientation to the child and growth in reading.

Coleman (1966) found that, of all measures of teacher quality available in the EEOS data, verbal ability of teachers was most related to the verbal ability of pupils in the same school. But the present study which matches teachers and pupils by classroom and measures change over a six-month period, finds no zero order relation between teachers' ratings on fluency and pupils' gain in reading comprehension. Nor do we find that length of experience, another frequent measure of teaching quality, contributes to growth. Instead for blacks it is kindliness (r = .35), adaptability (r = .42) and optimism (r = .41) that are the significant factors. Another variable that is significantly related to their reading growth is the teacher's response to an interview item, "Are test scores a good indication of a pupil's ability?" Teachers who answer *No* have pupils with largest gains (r = .45).

Analysis of variance confirmed the possibility that pupil-oriented teaching contributed to black growth in reading. In the fall 17% of the variance in black reading scores was between classrooms; in the spring 28% was between classrooms. It is plausible to infer that the difference might be due at least in part to the influence of teachers. However, since class percent white is significantly related to ratings of teachers on all three dimensions (especially to scores on child-orientation) and since there is also some association between class SES or level of reading achievement and teacher ratings, the apparent relation between teacher and pupil characteristics may be spurious and the result of their joint association with these background characteristics.

A multiple regression analysis was then performed of mean classroom reading achievement on teacher characteristics, controlling on classroom percentage white and mean SES and mean IQ. Since the difference between two test scores is known to be unreliable, the dependent variable is not reading growth fall to spring. Instead spring reading is the dependent variable and fall reading is entered into the equations as an independent variable. The results shown in Table 4 indicate that controlling on other variables does not diminish the teacher-pupil relationship. Black pupils made significantly greater gains in reading under Child-oriented teachers, but white children apparently did best under teachers labeled Task-oriented.

Finally we ran individual level regression equations for the four measures of achievement and four measures of attitudes entering as independent variables sex, individual SES, classroom SES, classroom percentage white and relevant prior measures of achievement, as well as teacher factor scores. We recognize that analysis using individual scores rather than classroom means is in a sense inappropriate here, since teacher scores are the same for all pupils in class. But our focus in this research is the pupil, not the teacher, and analysis by classroom means ignores the separate effects on his achievement of individual and group background characteristics. In the interracial classroom the interplay of these variables may be crucial. Therefore, we show in Table 6 the contribution to a pupil's growth of 3 types of teaching with individual and group SES both controlled.(6)

For white pupils reading showed significant growth under Task-oriented and conduct under Child-oriented teachers. Under Fair teachers, academic self-concept and sense of control were low and friendliness to the other race high.

For whites the number of coefficients significant at the .05 and .01 levels could almost have occurred by chance. For blacks the fact that three coefficients

TABLE 4

Standardized Regression Coefficients for *Mean* Classroom Spring Reading Achievement Scores of Pupils on Characteristics of Their Teachers, by Race (Mean, SES, IQ, Fall Reading Scores and Class % White Entered in Equation).

The r's in Table 4 are zero-order. The effect of teachers on black reading gains becomes clearer when we examine the partial r's, as the independent variables are stepped into the equations. Table 5 shows that the point at which the child-oriented teacher makes a difference for blacks is after Fall reading scores are controlled. In other words, the relationship is not due to a selective factor which matches certain teachers with certain pupils. It is *gain* in reading, not level of reading achievement, that is related to type of teaching.

	WHITE PUPILS[a]			BLACK PUPILS[b]		
	r zero order	β	t-value	r zero order	β	t-value
Mean Fall Reading	(.89)	.44**	2.12	(.77)	.71**	5.13
Mean IQ	(.87)	.43**	2.55	(.63)	.21	1.44
Class % White	(.57)	.06	.60	(.17)	.03	.29
Mean SES	(.25)	.00	.01	(.31)	—.00	—.01
TEACHER DIMENSIONS						
Child-Oriented	(—.08)	—.02	—.30	(.14)	.25*	2.11
Task-Oriented	(.30)	.19*	2.53	(.18)	.03	.32
Fair	(.08)	.02	.32	(.02)	—.16	—1.55
		$R^2 = .865$			$R^2 = .719$	

[a] d.f = 26
[b] d.f = 28

TABLE 5

Zero Order and Partial r's for *Black* Spring Reading Scores and Seven Independent Variables as They Are Stepped into Equation.[a]

STEP	0	1	2	3	4	5-7
Entering Variable	Zero Order	SES	IQ	Fall Reading	Class % W	3 Teacher Character-istics
SES	.31	.31	.08	.06	.05	—.00
IQ	.63	.59	.60	.25	.25	.21
Fall Reading	.77	.75	.63	.61	.61	.71
Class % W	.17	.25	.13	—.03	—.02	.03
Child-Oriented Teacher	.14	.06	.02	.37	.38	.25
Task-Oriented Teacher	.18	.19	.12	.08	.08	.03
Fair Teacher	.02	—.01	—.24	—.29	—.29	—.16
R^2		.10	.41	.64	.64	.72

[a] Betas above line and Partial r's below line.

TABLE 6

Standardized Regression Coefficients for Individual Pupil Outcomes
on Teacher Characteristics, by Race (Sex, IQ, Family SES, Classroom
SES and % White Entered In all Equations, also Prior Achievement
Where Relevant).

| | TEACHER CHARACTERISTICS (FACTOR SCORES) | | | | | |
| | WHITE PUPILS | | | BLACK PUPILS | | |
	Child-Oriented	Task-Oriented	Fair	Child-Oriented	Task-Oriented	Fair
Reading Growth	—.02	.06*	—.00	.14**	.07*	—.03
Improved GPA	.05	.03	.02	—.09**	—.02	—.03
Improved Conduct	.12*	—.02	.02	.10*	—.08	.12**
Improved Attendance	.03	—.00	—.10	.09*	—.02	—.01
Academic Self-Concept	.00	.02	—.15**	—.09	.04	.01
"My Teacher Thinks I Am"	.02	—.09	.04	.14*	—.13*	.07
Fate Control	.02	.04	—.09*	.04	—.01	.10*
Friendliness to Other Race	.00	—.04	.09*	.01	—.03	—.01

*Significant at the .05 level.
**Significant at the .01 level.

reach the .01 level and five others the .05 level suggests that more than chance is
probably at work. Having a pupil-oriented teacher contributes significantly to
improved conduct and attendance, as well as to reading growth, and to belief in
teacher approval. Having a Task-oriented teacher contributes positively to
reading, but negatively to belief in teacher's approval. Having a Fair teacher
contributes to improved conduct and sense of environmental control.

CONCLUSION AND DISCUSSION

The evidence tends to support the proposition that teachers play an
important role in the interracial classroom and contribute more to the academic
growth of black than of white children. One important finding is the necessity of
distinguishing between various dimensions of teaching behavior. A factor
analysis of the ratings of teachers on a modified Ryans Scale by observers who
spend a week in each classroom produced three clear factors. The label
Child-oriented was assigned the factor with high weights on kindly, optimistic,
responsive, understanding, democratic and adaptable. Task-oriented is shorthand
for the factor with high loadings on fluent, broad, stimulating and confident.
"Fair" refers to the factor in which ratings on racially fair, generally fair, and
systematic were high. Both zero order correlation and multiple regression
analyses indicate that these factors correlate with pupil outcomes quite
differently for blacks and whites.

For blacks, child-orientation or interpersonal competence in teachers contributes significantly to reading growth and seems to lead to improved conduct and attendance and belief in teacher's approval. Fairness in teachers contributes to improved conduct and sense of environmental control, as well as to friendliness from white classmates. Task-orientation or subject competence contributes to black reading growth, but shows a low negative correlation with other variables. The fact that neither the verbal fluency of teachers (as rated by observers) nor the length of their experience is associated significantly with pupil outcomes, whereas subjective but independent ratings by observers are significantly related to outcomes, suggests that future studies of equality of educational opportunity should use the anthropologist's observational tools, rather than depend on more "objective" or quantifiable indices of teaching quality.

Since the sample of classrooms was small and many of the differences not statistically significant even in individual level analysis, there should be further tests of the effects of teaching style in the interracial classroom. In particular other partial relationships deserve close scrutiny, as there are many other qualities of schools, teachers and pupils than those which were here controlled which may explain or place a condition upon the relationship.

Of course, one obvious variable that should be explored is the race of the teacher. In this study not one teacher in 36 randomly selected classrooms was black. Such a built-in control was in one sense a methodological advantage, but at the same time severely limits the generalizability of the findings.

NOTES

(1) Fox (1966) reports the following agreement between independent observers using the Ryans check list in the New York Open Enrollment Study:

35.2% identical
41.2   "   within 1 point
23.6   "   "   2 points
5.3   "   "   3 points

(2) The original factor solution was principal components with one in the principal diagonal. The rotation was orthogonal varimax. Latent Root:

Factor 1 - 8.392
Factor 2 - 2.089
Factor 3 - 0.883

(3) Heterogeneous grouping is standard practice in the elementary classrooms of the city.

(4) Sad - Happy   Bad - Good
Lazy - Hard-working   Unsure - Sure
Mean - Kind   Unsuccessful - Successful
Proud - Not Proud   Not a Good Student - A Good Student
Stupid - Smart   Follower - Leader

(5) *True-False*:

Good luck is more important than hard work for success.

People like me don't have much of a chance to be successful in life.

When I make plans I am almost sure I can make them work.

(6) The analysis was also performed using classroom mean scores and showed very similar differences, but the only betas that reached the .05 level of significance with 33 degrees of freedom were those for reading growth.

REFERENCES

Allport, Gordon W. The nature of prejudice. Cambridge, Mass.: Addison-Wesley Publishing Co., 1954.

Amos, Robert T. The accuracy of Negro and white children's predictions of teachers' attitudes toward Negro students. Journal of Negro Education, 1952. 21, 125-135.

Biddle, Bruce J. The integration of teacher effectiveness research. In Biddle and Ellena (Eds.), Contemporary research on teacher effectiveness. Holt, Rinehart, and Winston, 1964.

Boocock, Sarane S. Toward a sociology of learning: A selective review of existing research. Sociology of Education, 1966, 39, 1-45.

Clark, Carl A., & Walberg, Herbert J. The effects of increased rewards on reading achievement and school attitudes of potential dropouts. Paper presented at American Psychological Association Convention, September 2, 1966.

Clark, Kenneth B. Dark ghetto: Dilemmas of social power. New York: Harper and Row, 1965.

Coleman, James S., et al. Equality of educational opportunity. Washington, D.C.: U.S. Department of Health, Education, and Welfare, 1966.

Davidson, Helen H., & Lang, Gerhard. Children's perceptions of their teacher's feelings toward them related to self-perception, school achievement and behavior. Journal of Experimental Education, 1960, 29, 107-118.

Dean, John P., & Rosen, Alex. A manual of intergroup relations. Chicago: University of Chicago Press, 1955.

Fox, David J. Free choice open enrollment elementary schools. Evaluation of New York City School District educational projects funded under Title I of the Elementary and Secondary Education Act of 1965, August 31, 1966 (mimeo).

Gottlieb, David. Teaching and students: The views of Negro and white teachers. Sociology of Education, 1964, 37, 345-353.

Katz, Irwin. The socialization of motivation in minority group children. Nebraska symposium on motivation. University of Nebraska, 1967.

McPartland, James. The segregated student in desegregated schools: Sources of influence on Negro secondary students. The Johns Hopkins University, 1968.

Rosenshine, Barak, & Furst, Norma. Current and future research on teacher performance criteria. In B.O. Smith (Ed.), Research on teacher education: A symposium. Englewood Cliffs, New Jersey: Prentice-Hall, in press.

Rosenthal, Robert, & Jacobson, Lenore. Pygmalion in the classroom. Holt,

Rinehart and Winston, 1968.

Ryans, D.G. Characteristics of teachers. Washington D.C.: American Council on Education, 1960.

Taba, Hilda. With perspective on human relations. American Council on Education, 1955.

Wynne, Edward. School output measures as tools for change. Education and Urban Society, 1969, 2, 3-21.

Yarrow, Leon J., & Yarrow, Marian Radke. Leadership and interpersonal change. The Journal of Social Issues, 1958, 14, 47-59.

EXAMINER EFFECT
IN I.Q. TESTING
OF PUERTO RICAN
WORKING-CLASS CHILDREN

Alexander Thomas
Margaret E. Hertzig
Irving Dryman
Paulina Fernandez

The use of a standardized instrument to determine the level of measured intelligence makes it possible to compare the performance of an individual child with that attained by the standardization population. Although the correctly prescribed use of standard test procedures reduces variability and insures some degree of comparability, a considerable body of evidence suggests that a child's performance level may be affected by a variety of factors operative within the testing situation *per se*. (9) Of particular interest in this connection is the nature of the examiner's contribution to the determination of outcome. Sex, (4) race, (7, 8) and experience have all been identified as relevant examiner variables. In addition, much information indicates that the behavior of the tester may have a facilitating or debilitating effect upon the performance of the testee. (11, 12, 13, 15) Thus it would appear that meaningful interpretation and application of an IQ score would depend not only upon knowledge of the score itself, but also upon some understanding of the circumstances in which it was obtained, as well as of the examiner who obtained it.

Knowledge of the examiner's role perhaps assumes particular importance in evaluating the intellectual test performance of disadvantaged children. Not only do children from lower socio-economic segments of society generally perform less well than middle-class children on standardized tests of intelligence, (1, 2, 10) but their very manner and style of coping with cognitive demands differs as well. (6) Such children may be particularly vulnerable to variations in examiner behavior. Our interest in the problem of examiner influences on the level of measured intelligence in disadvantaged children arose when, in the course of investigating aspects of cognitive functioning in Puerto Rican working-class children of school age, we observed what appeared to be a systematic difference in the IQ scores reported by two examiners. The present paper derives from the further exploration of this observation.

Specifically, we will: 1. compare the intelligence test performance of Puerto Rican working-class children when evaluated by two examiners; 2. study differences in the situations created by these examiners, and in the children's behavior in response to them, that might account for the observed differences in performance level; and 3. explore the relation between the performances obtained by the two examiners and the level of cognitive functioning attained on standardized tests of reading achievement administered in school.

SUBJECTS AND METHODS

The subjects were 116 school children (62 boys and 54 girls) from 72 families of Puerto Rican working-class origin residing in New York City. The children, who were between the ages of 6-0 and 15-11 years, consisted of all but two of the offspring of these families who were within this age range at the time of study. The families have participated in long-term studies of the behavioral and intellectual development of their children over the past ten years. The major characteristics of these families, reported in detail elsewhere, (6) will be briefly summarized here. Over 85% of the parents were born in Puerto Rico, and came to New York in their late teens. Currently, over 80% of the families live in low-income public housing projects. Less than 25% of the parents have completed high school. Over 95% of the fathers are employed, and of these almost two-thirds are unskilled workers. Less than 10% of the mothers work, either full or part-time. Thirteen of the families have been disrupted, twelve through separation or divorce, and one as the result of the death of the mother.

The data derive from several sources.

THE WECHSLER INTELLIGENCE SCALE FOR CHILDREN

The sample as a whole. The Wechsler Intelligence Scale for Children was administered to all of the children by one of two examiners. Examiner A tested 71 children (37 boys and 34 girls), while Examiner B evaluated 45 children (25 boys and 20 girls). The children tested by Examiners A and B did not differ significantly with respect to either age or sex.

Both examiners were female, of Puerto Rican origin, fluent in Spanish and English, and had comparable experience in administering and scoring the WISC. The children were tested in the examiners' homes, both located in upper middle-class high-rise apartment buildings adjacent to the lower Harlem area. However, while Examiner B had never met any of the children before testing them, Examiner A had known the children and their families for many years as a result of her participation in other phases of our ongoing longitudinal studies.

The retest sample. Nineteen children (8 boys and 11 girls) were selected for intensive study of the relation of examiner-child interactions to the level of measured intelligence. Of these, nine had originally been examined by A and ten by B. These children were selected from separate alphabetical lists of the children tested by each examiner in a manner that insured that the IQ and age distributions of the sub-samples were comparable to those of the groups as a whole. Each of these children was retested by the other examiner. The mean interval between original and retesting was 13.9 months. In no case was the interval less than six months. Each examiner was told that the reason for retesting was "a routine check" and no hint was given as to our interest in differences in examiner behavior and their possible relation to outcome.

Psychological reports. At the close of each testing session, including both the original examinations and the reevaluations, the examiners prepared a report that included a summary of the results of intellectual assessment as well as their impressions of the child's behavior during the testing session and their reactions to him.

Additional data on cognitive functioning of the total sample of 116 children were obtained through a search of the school records. In the course of this search all scores of standardized tests of reading achievement were recorded, together with the date of administration and the school grade of the child at the time of testing.

RESULTS

A comparison of the IQ scores attained by the 71 children originally tested by Examiner A and the 45 children contemporaneously evaluated by Examiner B revealed systematic differences. As Table 1 demonstrates, the mean full-scale, verbal and performance IQs reported by Examiner A are all at least ten points higher than those reported by B. These differences are in all cases significant at less than the .001 level of confidence.

Table 1

Mean WISC IQ's Obtained by Examiner A and Examiner B

WISC IQ	Tester A[a]	Tester B[b]	t	p
Full Scale	97.17 ± 11.10	80.47 ± 11.44	7.73	<.001
Verbal Scale	96.51 ± 12.56	79.09 ± 10.16	8.17	<.001
Performance Scale	98.61 ± 12.41	86.09 ± 13.76	4.95	<.001

[a]N=71, [b]N=45

As would be expected from these mean differences, the distributive characteristics of the scores reported by A and B are markedly different as well. Table 2 shows that 65% of the children tested by A achieved scores in the average range, while only 15% of the children tested by B did so. Moreover, only

5% of the children tested by A had scores that were borderline or defective, in contrast to 45% of the children examined by B.

Table 2

Proportion of Subjects at Different Full-Scale IQ Levels
Attained by Examiner A and Examiner B

Classification	A^a	B^b
Very Superior	0%	0%
Superior	1	0
Bright Normal	10	2
Average	65	15
Dull Normal	18	38
Borderline	4	27
Mental Defective	1	18

^{a}N=71, ^{b}N=45

The mean WISC subtest scores attained by the children examined by A and B are presented in Table 3, where it may be seen that the children tested by A achieved significantly higher scores on all ten subtests. The greatest absolute differences in mean scores were found on the vocabulary, comprehension, and similarities sub-tests. Moreover, when the mean subtest scores reported by each examiner were ranked from the lowest to the highest and the ranks compared, RHO was only 0.261. This low and insignificant rank order correlation suggests that in addition to differing clearly with respect to the magnitude of the scores obtained, the children tested by Examiners A and B also exhibited differences in the general patterning of relative strengths and weaknesses. Particularly striking in this connection is that although similarities and comprehension were the two subtests responded to best by the children tested by Examiner A, they received ranks of only five and two respectively when B was the examiner.

THE RETEST SAMPLE

The reliability of the above findings was assessed through a consideration of the performance of nineteen children who were tested by both Examiners A and B. In Table 4, the full-scale, verbal, and performance IQs, as well as the mean sub-test scores reported by each of the examiners of these nineteen children, are presented. As may be seen in the data of Table 4, in every instance the scores attained by the children when examined by A were higher than those attained when the same children were examined by B. However, because of the smaller number of children involved in the retest sample, only seven of the thirteen comparisons reached statistically significant levels of difference. Nevertheless, an examination of the individual paired records revealed that in every instance the scores obtained by A were higher than those obtained by B. The superiority of

Table 3

Mean WISC Sub-Test Scores

WISC Subtests	Tester A[a]	Tester B[b]	t	p
Information	7.77 ± 2.21	6.91 ± 2.25	2.00	<.05
Comprehension	10.81 ± 2.74	6.39 ± 1.98	9.95	<.001
Arithmetic	8.59 ± 2.55	7.36 ± 1.93	2.95	<.01
Similarities	11.42 ± 3.52	7.44 ± 2.86	6.62	<.001
Vocabulary	8.41 ± 2.55	3.31 ± 2.14	11.51	<.001
Picture Completion	9.29 ± 2.96	7.73 ± 2.65	2.93	<.01
Picture Arrangement	9.53 ± 2.67	8.40 ± 2.67	2.20	<.05
Block Design	9.71 ± 2.17	8.60 ± 2.80	2.26	<.05
Object Assembly	10.32 ± 2.92	7.98 ± 3.50	3.73	<.001
Coding	10.18 ± 2.85	7.56 ± 2.94	4.70	<.001

[a]N=71, [b]N=45

Table 4

Mean FS, V, P, and Sub-Test Scores of Children Tested by Both Examiners

	A[a]		B[a]			
	Mean	SD	Mean	SD	t	p
Full Scale (FS)	95.05	21.18	81.26	18.17	2.15	<05
Verbal (V)	92.68	21.29	78.06	14.13	2.47	<05
Performance (P)	97.89	19.79	87.79	20.57	1.54	NS
Information	7.84	3.57	6.53	2.69	1.33	NS
Comprehension	9.89	4.33	6.41	2.11	+3.15	<01
Arithmetic	8.61	3.22	6.94	1.96	+1.94	<10
Similarities	9.95	4.38	6.32	3.64	2.78	<01
Vocabulary	7.63	3.96	4.12	3.39	2.95	<01
Picture Comp.	9.21	2.76	8.21	4.42	0.84	NS
Picture Arrangement	9.00	3.33	7.96	2.96	1.29	NS
Block Design	10.21	3.52	9.32	4.11	0.72	NS
Object Assembly	10.05	4.35	7.11	3.57	2.28	<05
Coding	10.42	3.44	8.89	3.56	1.35	NS

[a]N=19

+ Because of a significant difference in the variances the Cochran correction of the "t" test was used.

the children's performance with A as the examiner was independent of the order of testing and occurred whether A had administered the original examination or the retest.

Thus, despite the fact that both examiners were equivalent with respect to sex, ethnicity, fluency in Spanish and English, and amount of clinical experience, Examiner A was consistently able to elicit a higher level of performance from the children than was Examiner B. In an effort to identify the possible sources of these differences, we investigated features of the testing situation created by the two examiners and the reactions of the children to them.

SOURCES OF DIFFERENCE

Examiners' description of the testing session in psychological reports. The psychological test reports prepared immediately after the testing sessions were analyzed with regard to the examiners' descriptions of the children's behavior. The reports of seventeen children tested by both examiners provided the basic data for this analysis. With respect to the quality of the examiner-child interaction, we devised an adjective checklist of positive and negative terms and phrases used by the examiners in preparing their reports. The positive terms included: *friendly, pleasant, warm, spontaneous, relaxed, relates well,* and *comfortable.* The negative terms included: *shy, hostile, rigid, aloof, stubborn, passive, reserved, quiet,* and *reticent.* In each report we determined the number of positive and negative descriptive statements about the child's relation to the examiner in the test situation. These data are summarized in Table 5, where it may be seen that the total number of statements made by the two examiners was very similar. However, over 57% of the statements made by Examiner A were positive, in contrast to 45% of those made by Examiner B, a difference significant at less than the 0.001 level of confidence, indicating that Examiner A was more likely to report having established a positive interactive relation with the child.

Table 5

Examiners' Descriptions of Behavior During Testing

A			B				
Positive Statements	Total Statements	Percent Positive	Positive Statements	Total Statements	Percent Positive	z	p
58	83	57.2	41	90	45.6	3.23	<001

In order to examine the differences in the ways in which the two examiners evaluated test performance and described the childrens' approach to test demands, another adjective checklist was prepared, again derived from the actual terms used by the examiners in their reports. The terms were again generally categorized as positive and negative. The positive expressions included: *involved in tasks, expressed interest, complied with demands, persisted with difficult tasks, maintained interest,* and *listened to instructions.* The negative descriptions included: *non-involved, uninterested, rejected demands, did not persist, gives up easily, disorganized,* and *easily distracted.* The number of positive and negative statements made by each examiner was determined. The relevant data are presented in Table 6, where it may be seen that of a total of 72 statements describing test performance by Examiner A, 97% were positive in character. In contrast, only 67% of the 62 relevant statements made by Examiner B could be so classified. This difference is significant at less than the 0.001 level of confidence and indicated that the reported behavior of the children with respect to the ways in which they approached the test demands was different with the two examiners.

Table 6

Examiners' Description of Test Performance

A			B				
Positive Statements	Total Statements	Percent Positive	Positive Statements	Total Statements	Percent Positive	z	p
70	72	97.2	42	62	67.7	4.59	$<.001$

Examiners' descriptions of the testing session through retrospective interview. The two examiners were interviewed in order to obtain a retrospective description of how each had conducted the testing session. Careful questioning revealed that, although both examiners had operated within the boundaries of the rules of standardized test procedure, they appeared to differ markedly with respect to the manner in which they made initial contact with the child and sustained his interest in the situation. Despite the fact that A already was acquainted with the children, she reported that she spent considerable time with each child before beginning formal testing. She greeted the child in a lively and friendly manner, engaging him in conversation at once. She encouraged the child to ask questions about herself, the apartment, and features of the test itself. If the child did not bring up any questions, A made sure to spend time showing him around the apartment and describing the contents. She tried to create the atmosphere of a game, and made every effort to draw the child into the test situation as a joint pleasant activity. In the course of the actual testing, Examiner A reported that she encouraged the child to try again if his initial response was an "I don't know." Moreover, she tried to be sensitive to the child's needs, and she organized breaks and rest periods if she felt the child was tired.

In contrast, Examiner B described herself as being reserved and quiet. She approached the children seriously. Although she emphasized that she replied willingly to spontaneous questions, she reported that she did so in an impersonal manner and did not pursue conversations unrelated to the formal testing session. She tended to follow a set routine that varied little from child to child. Examiner B reported that she tended to remain silent if the child hesitated or responded, "I don't know." She then went on to the next item without encouraging the child to try, stating that she felt that, "Encouragement at that time would not bring them closer to the answer. It would be almost an act of cruelty . . . to encourage would continue the child's embarrassment."

These descriptions by the two examiners of their methods of orientating the child to the testing situation and coping with his failures to respond to items indicate that the two differed considerably. Examiner A tried to establish a warm, friendly, and mutually cooperative relationship in which the child was encouraged to do well. Examiner B described herself as attempting to establish a friendly but impersonal situation in which formalized rules were followed quite rigidly and in which the child was protected from having to cope with his own inadequacies.

CHILDREN'S BEHAVIOR DURING TESTING

As indicated above, the analyses of the psychological reports prepared by Examiners A and B strongly suggest that the children did in fact behave differently in the different testing situations. However, as these analyses were based upon the examiner reports of the children's behavior, the question arises as to whether the children actually behaved in these different ways or whether the two examiners merely differ in their interpretation of similar types of behavior. We sought to resolve this question through an examination of the WISC protocols themselves. The data to be reported derive from the analysis of nineteen pairs of the response records of children tested by both examiners. Only the responses to the verbal sub-test items were considered.

Table 7

Length of Responses Made to Examiners A and B on Verbal Scale of the WISC

Subtest	A Longer	Equal	B Longer	Exp. Freq. In Each Cell (N=19)	x^2	p
Information	10	9	0	6.33	9.58	$<$001
Comprehension	14	5	0	6.33	15.90	$<$001
Similarities	16	2	1	6.33	22.22	$<$001
Vocabulary	14	5	0	6.33	15.90	$<$001
Total	54	21	1	25.33	56.56	.001

Length of response: The first analysis of the WISC protocols concerned the length of the responses made by the children to the verbal items of the WISC scale when presented by the different examiners. The average length of the responses made to each of the verbal subtests was determined, and the records were classified as to whether the responses were longer to Examiner A, longer to

Examiner B, or of equal length. Because of the number of items presented by the two examiners often differed, the computation of average length was made only for those items presented by both. The relevant data are presented in Table 7, where it may be seen that for each sub-test of the verbal scale, more children made longer responses when the items were presented by Examiner A. The actual frequencies obtained differ from chance expectancy at less than the 0.001 level of confidence.

Table 8

Proportion of Items on the WISC Verbal Scale Responded to By "I Don't Know" in Children Examined By A and B

Subtest	A			B				
	"IDK"	Total	%	"IDK"	Total	%	z	p
Information	39	322	12.1	55	291	18.9	2.23	<.05
Comprehension	8	227	3.5	7	140	5.0	0.69	NS
Arithmetic	6	206	2.9	15	186	8.0	2.26	<.05
Similarities	6	215	2.8	25	164	15.2	4.38	<.001
Vocabulary	96	422	22.7	76	327	23.2	0.16	NS
Total	155	1392	11.1	178	1108	16.1	3.62	<.001

"I don't know" responses. Table 8 presents data on the relative frequency with which "I don't know" responses were made to each of the examiners. The number of terminal "I don't know" responses made by the children in the different examining situations to each of the verbal sub-tests was determined. Responses of "I don't know" that were followed by an attempt at an answer were not counted. The total number of items presented for each situation was also determined. Table 8 indicates the proportion of this total that were "I don't know" for each examiner. As may be seen in Table 8, for the verbal scale as a whole the children made a greater proportion of "I don't know" responses to Examiner B than to Examiner A, a difference significant at less than the 0.001 level of confidence. This direction of difference was sustained for all of the verbal subtests and in three of the five comparisons was statistically significant as well.

RELATION OF IQ SCORES TO ACADEMIC ACHIEVEMENT

The subjects for the following analysis are 57 children whose IQs were determined by Examiner A, and 26 children tested by Examiner B. They represent that portion of the total sample who had received a standardized reading achievement test in school within two years of the date of IQ determination. In over three-quarters of the cases the standardized test was the Metropolitan Reading Achievement test. The school grades of the children at the

Table 9

School Grades at the Time of Achievement Testing

Grade	A			B		
	M	F	Total	M	F	Total
1	3	1	4	3	0	3
2	3	5	8	2	4	6
3	4	5	9	2	2	4
4	6	7	13	5	4	9
5	2	3	5	2	1	3
6	2	5	7	0	6	6
7	3	5	8	0	1	1
8	0	0	0	0	0	0
9	2	1	3	0	0	0
Total	25	32	57	14	18	32

time of achievement testing are presented in Table 9.

The number of males and females tested by the two examiners did not differ significantly. However, Examiner B had determined the IQs of fewer children in the older grades than did Examiner A.

For each child a difference score was computed between his reading achievement as measured by the standardized test and his actual school grade in terms of months and years. The range of difference scores was -3 years 9 months to $+3$ years 2 months for the children whose IQs were measured by Examiner A, and -3 years 0 months to $+0$ years 11 months for the children tested by Examiner B. The difference scores were ranked separately for the two groups of children, with the positive scores receiving lower ranks. Similarly the IQ scores were ranked for each examiner, also from the highest to the lowest. Rank order correlations between this measure of academic achievement and IQ were determined for each examiner and are presented in Table 10.

As the data in Table 10 indicate, the correlations for both examiners are positive and statistically significant. However, the RHO for the children tested by Examiner B is larger and accounts for 25% of the variance, as contrasted to only 9% of the variance accounted for by children tested by Examiner A.

The range of school grades of the children at the time of testing was very

Table 10

Rank Order Correlation Between IQ and Academic Achievement
In Children Tested By Examiners A and B

Examiner	N	df.	RHO	p
A	57	55	0.316	$< .02$
B	26	24	0.548	$< .01$

large and not comparable in the two groups. One factor influencing the degree of reading retardation is the number of years the child has been in school; therefore, a second analysis was done, limiting consideration to those children who were in the fourth and fifth grades at the time of achievement testing.

The results of this second analysis are presented in Table 11, where the differences previously described have become more sharply evident. For Examiner B, the correlation between IQ and academic achievement is significant at less than the 0.01 level of confidence and accounts for almost 50% of the variance. In contrast, for the children tested by Examiner A, the correlation between measured intelligence and academic achievement accounts for less than 20% of the variance and does not reach the 0.05 level of statistical significance. Thus the IQ scores obtained by Examiner B correlate with standardized measures of academic achievement better than do those of Examiner A.

DISCUSSION

The findings of the present study clearly indicate that different examiners can elicit significantly different levels of performance on standardized tests of intelligence in Puerto Rican working-class children. Despite the fact that both examiners were equivalent with respect to sex, ethnicity, fluency in Spanish and

Table 11

Rank Order Correlations Between IQ and Academic Achievement in Fourth and Fifth Grade Children Tested by Examiners A and B

Examiner	N	df.	RHO	p
A	18	16	0.453	<10
B	12	10	0.768	<01

English, and amount of clinical experience, the scores obtained by Examiner A were consistently higher than those obtained by Examiner B. The two examiners were found to have initiated and conducted the testing sessions in very different ways, although both operated within the boundaries of the rules of standardized test procedure. Examiner A spent considerably more time with the child before beginning formal testing than did Examiner B. While A tried to create the atmosphere of a game in which both she and the child participated, B was much more formal, insisting upon the child's participation in task-orientated activities directed by her. Furthermore, Examiner A actively encouraged the child to try when his first response was, "I don't know," while B tended to accept "I don't know" responses by proceeding to the next item.

The reports of the children's behavior during the testing period also differed markedly. Examiner A reported the children tested by her to be significantly more spontaneous, relaxed, and friendly during the testing session than they were when tested by Examiner B. In addition, when A conducted the examination the children were reported to be significantly more interested and persistent in the face of difficulty than when B was the examiner. Furthermore, when examined by A the children gave longer responses and made fewer "I don't know" statements to the items of the verbal sub-scales of the WISC than when tested by B.

These differences in the behavior of the children when tested by the different examiners would appear to be a direct consequence of the examiners' behavior during the sessions. The evidence indicated that Examiner A was warm, interested, friendly, and concerned in her behavior, and the children responded by similar expressions of interest and enjoyment. In response to encouragement they amplified and elaborated their verbalizations and sought to modify their "I don't know" answers.

Examiner B, on the other hand, established a neutral emotional relationship with the children and tried to limit her involvement with them to the test material proper. This may have not only inhibited spontaneous verbalizations, but also verbalization in response to cognitive demands. Furthermore, the reluctance of Examiner B to ask the child to try again after an "I don't know" response may have discouraged persistence in the face of difficulties.

These differences in examiner-child interaction appear to have contributed significantly to the differences in the level of measured intelligence obtained by the two examiners. Greater verbalization increases the opportunity of saying something right. Also, repeated effort after an initial expression of ignorance also increases the possibility of success. This tendency is most dramatically illustrated by the fact that the greatest differences in performance level of the children were on the comprehension and similarities sub-scales. Thus, the examiner's ability to initiate and sustain interest in the cognitive tasks, to encourage working in the face of initial refusal, and to stimulate verbalization would appear to maximize the level of cognitive performance.

Our findings are reminiscent of those reported by Zigler and Butterfield (17) in a study of changes in the Stanford-Binet test performance of culturally disadvantaged children of nursery school age. These workers contrasted the IQ scores obtained when "optimizing" rather than "standardized" testing procedures were employed. The "optimizing" procedure consisted in altering the order of items presented so as to insure some degree of initial success and to maximize the number of successes early in the testing procedure. Non-responsiveness was countered by gentle encouragement, which was continued until it was felt that maximal responsiveness had been obtained. In the "standardized" situation the examiner attempted to be neutral though friendly to the children. Encouragement was confined to those situations specifically indicated in the manual of instructions. The measures used by Zigler and Butterfield to facilitate performance appear to be very similar to those employed spontaneously by our Examiner A, while their "standardized" procedure closely approximated the behavior of Examiner B. In their study, as well as in our own, significantly higher levels of measured intelligence were obtained when "optimizing" procedures were employed. Thus the use of measures to facilitate the performance of disadvantaged children on standardized intelligence tests appears to be effective.

In both the Zigler and Butterfield study and in our own, examiner style was found to affect the intellectual test performance of disadvantaged children.

It cannot be assumed that this examiner effect on IQ test performance will be similar for all groups of children. In fact, in our studies of the cognitive behavior of middle-class children the mean IQ scores obtained by three different examiners in the testing of 116 children were identical, despite the fact that the examiners' testing styles and ways of making contact varied considerably. This finding is only suggestive, inasmuch as the retesting procedure used with the Puerto Rican children was not done.

An additional finding of the present study is that the IQ scores obtained by Examiner B correlate better with reading achievement as measured by standardized group tests administered in school, than do the IQs obtained by Examiner A. Little or no opportunity for maximizing performance is possible during the administration of such group tests of academic achievement. This could account in part for the fact that the children's performance on such tests was closer to the results obtained by examiner B than by Examiner A. In addition, it is also probable that the procedures used by most teachers in routine classroom instruction more closely resemble those of Examiner B, suggesting that her test scores may represent a more accurate reflection of what is actually learned under such instructional conditions.

It has become increasingly clear that mere exposure to opportunities and situations that have been successful in promoting school learning in middle-class children has not significantly raised the academic achievement level of disadvantaged children. (3, 5, 16) To deal with the problem of school failure in disadvantaged children requires more than an analysis of specific cognitive defects and the remediation of such defects. It is also necessary to take into account the learning characteristics of the children, including their particular manner of coping with demands for cognitive functioning. (6) Our study indicates that the performance level of disadvantaged children on standardized tests of intellectual functioning can be raised by employing examination procedures that are congruent with their spontaneous cognitive styles. This suggests that the academic achievement of such children may also be improved by the use of similar techniques of instruction in school. Our findings thus point to one possible direction of attack upon the enormous problem of school failure and underachievement in disadvantaged children.

REFERENCES

(1) Baughman, E. and Dahlstrom, W. 1968. Negro and White Children: A Psychological Study in the Rural South. Academic Press, New York.

(2) Birren, J. and Hess, R. 1968. Influences of biologic, and psychological, and social deprivation upon learning and performance. In Perspectives on Human

Deprivation: Biological, Psychological and Sociological. National Institute of Child and Human Development, National Institute of Health, Public Health Service, United States Department of Health, Education, and Welfare.

(3) Blank, M. and Salomon, F. 1968. A tutorial language program to develop abstract thinking in socially disadvantaged preschool children. Child Developm. 39: 379.

(4) Cieutat, V. and Flick, G. 1967. Examiner differences among Stanford-Binet items. Psychological Report 21:613-622.

(5) Hertzig, M. 1971. Aspects of cognition and cognitive style in young children of differing social and ethnic backgrounds. In Defects of Cognition, J. Hellmuth, ed. Brunner-Mazel, New York.

(6) Hertzig, M. et. al., 1968. Class and ethnic differences in the responsiveness of preschool children to cognitive demands. Monographs of the Society for Research in Child Development 33(1):Serial No. 117.

(7) Katz, I., Henchy, T. and Allen, H. 1968. Effects of race of tester, approval-disapproval, and need on Negro children's learning. J. Pers. Soc. Psychol. 8:38-42.

(8) Katz, I., Roberts, S. and Robinson, J. 1965. Effects of task difficulty, race of administrator and instructions on digit-symbol performance of Negroes. J. Pers. Soc. Psychol. 2:53-59.

(9) Lesser, G., Fifer, G. and Clark, D. 1965. Mental abilities of children from different social class and cultural groups. Monographs of the Society for Research in Child Development 30(4):Serial No. 102.

(10) Loevinger, J. 1940. Intelligence as related to socio-economic factors. In 39th Yearbook, National Society for the Study of Education, Part 1, pp. 159-210.

(11) Phares, J. and Rotter, J. 1956. The effect of the situation on psychological testing. J. Cons. Psychol. 20:291-293.

(12) Sarason, I. 1962. Individual differences, situational variables, and personality research. J. Abnorm. Soc. Psychol. 65:376-78.

(13) Sarason, I. and Nunard, J. 1963. Interrelationships among subject, experimenter, and situational variables. J. Abnorm. Soc. Psychol. 67:87-91.

(14) Smith, H., May, T. and Lebovitz, L. 1966. Testing experience and Stanford-Binet scores. J. Ed. Measurement 3:229-233.

(15) Smith, W. and Rockett, S. 1958. Test performance as a function of anxiety, instructor, and instruction. J. Ed. Res. 52: 138-141.

(16) Wilkerson, D. 1964. Prevailing and needed emphasis on research on the education of disadvantaged children and youth. J. Negro Ed. 33:346-357.

(17) Zigler, E. and Butterfield, E. 1968. Motivational aspects of changes in IQ test performance of culturally deprived nursery school children. Child Developm. 39:1-14.

IV.
SCHOOL DESEGREGATION,
ACADEMIC ACHIEVEMENT,
AND RACIAL ATTITUDES

THE EVIDENCE ON BUSING

David J. Armor

The legal basis of the national policy of integration—and of the school busing issue today—is the declaration of the Supreme Court in 1954 that

> to separate [black children] from others of similar age and qualifications solely because of their race generates a feeling of inferiority as to their status in the community that may affect their hearts and minds in a way unlikely ever to be undone.

Few decisions of the Court have provoked so much controversy for so long, or have had so much impact on the way of life of so many persons, as the case of *Brown v. the Board of Education of Topeka*, where this doctrine is stated. Policy makers have used it to restructure political, economic, and social institutions. Groups have rioted and states have divided over actions, direct and indirect, that have flowed from this ruling. And social scientists have proudly let it stand as a premier axiom of their field—one of the few examples of a social theory that found its way into formal law.

Few persons, perhaps, know of the role played by the social sciences in helping to sustain the forces behind desegregation. It would be an exaggeration to say they are responsible for the busing dilemmas facing so many communities today, yet without the legitimacy provided by the hundreds of sociological and pyschological studies it would be hard to imagine how the changes we are witnessing could have happened so quickly. At every step—from the 1954 Supreme Court ruling, to the Civil Rights Act of 1964, to the federal busing orders of 1970—social science research findings have been inextricably interwoven with policy decisions.

And yet, the relation between social science and public policy contains a paradox in that the conditions for adequate research are often *not* met until a policy is in effect, while the policy itself often cannot be justified until supported by the findings of science. In consequence, the desire of scientists to affect society and the desire of policy makers to be supported by science often lead to a relation between the two that may be more political than scientific. Further, this can mean that the later evaluation research of a social action program may undo the very premises on which the action is based—as is the case somewhat in the Coleman Report on the effect of schools on achievement. There are obvious dangers for both social science and public policy in this paradox. There is the danger that important and significant programs—which may be desirable on moral grounds—may be halted when scientific support is lacking or reveals unexpected consequences; conversely, there is the danger that important research may be stopped when the desired results are not forthcoming. The current controversy over the busing of schoolchildren to promote integration affords a prime example of this situation.

The policy model behind the Supreme Court's 1954 reasoning—and behind the beliefs of the liberal public today—was based in part on social science research. But that research did not derive from the conditions of induced racial integration as it is being carried out today. These earlier research designs were "ex post facto"—i.e., comparisons were made between persons already integrated and individuals in segregated environments. Since the integration experience occurred *before* the studies, any inferences about the effects of *induced* integration, based on such evidence, have been speculative at best. With the development of a variety of school integration programs across the country there arose the opportunity to conduct realistic tests of the integration policy model that did not suffer this limitation. While it may have other shortcomings, this research suffers neither the artificial constraints of the laboratory nor the causal ambiguity of the cross-sectional survey. The intent of this essay is to explore some of this new research and to interpret the findings. What we will do, first, is to sketch the evolution of the social science model which became the basis of public policy, and then review a number of tests of this model as revealed in recent social science studies of induced school integration and busing.

THE INTEGRATION OF POLICY MODEL: STAGE I

The integration model which is behind current public policy is rooted in social science results dating back to before World War II. The connections between segregation and inequality were portrayed by John Dollard (1937) and Gunnar Myrdal (1944) in the first prestigious social science studies to show how prejudice, discrimination, segregation, and inequality operated to keep the black man in a subordinate status. Myrdal summarized this process in his famous "vicious circle" postulate: White prejudice, in the form of beliefs about the inferior status of the black race, leads to discrimination and segregation in work, housing, and social relationships; discrimination reinforces social and economic inequality; the resulting inferiority circles back to solidify the white prejudice that started it all. The vicious circle theory was the integration policy model in embryonic form.

Along with these broad sociological studies there also appeared a number of psychological experiments which were to play a crucial role in the policy decisions. The most notable were the doll studies of Kenneth and Mamie Clark (1947). They found that preschool black children were much less likely than white children to prefer dolls of their own race. Though this tendency tapered off among older children, the Clarks concluded that racial awareness and identification occurred at an early age and that the doll choices suggested harmful and lasting effects on black self-esteem and performance. Other studies confirmed these early findings (Proshansky and Newton, 1968; Porter, 1971). These studies added a psychological dynamic to explain the operation of the vicious circle: Prejudice and segregation lead to feelings of inferiority and an inability to succeed among the blacks; these sustain inequality and further reinforce the initial white prejudice. In other words, segregation leads to serious psychological damage to the black child; that damage is sufficient to inhibit the kind of adult behavior which might enable the black man to break the circle.

How could the circle be broken? This question plagued a generation of social scientists in quest of a solution to America's race problems. Of a number of studies appearing after the war, two which focussed upon the effects of segregation and integration upon white racial attitudes had especial impact. The first was a section of Samuel Stouffer's massive research on the American soldier during World War II (1949). Stouffer found that white soldiers in combat companies with a black platoon were far more likely to accept the idea of fighting side by side with black soldiers than were white soldiers in non-integrated companies. The second was the study by Morton Deutsch and Mary Evans Collins (1951) of interracial housing. Comparing residents of similar backgrounds in segregated and integrated public housing projects, they found that whites in integrated housing were more likely to be friendly with blacks, to endorse interracial living, and to have positive attitudes towards blacks in general then were whites living in the segregated projects. Though neither of these studies could ascertain the beliefs of these individuals *prior* to integration, neither author had reason to believe that the integrated whites differed from the segregated whites before the former's experience with blacks. They concluded, therefore, that the positive results were due to the effect of interracial *contact* and not to prior positive belief.

The culmination of this research was Gordon Allport's influenctial work, *The Nature of Prejudice*, (1953). Using the work of Stouffer, Deutsch and Collins, and others, he formulated what has come to be known as the "contact theory":

> Contacts that bring knowledge and acquaintance are likely to engender sounder beliefs about minority groups. . . . Prejudice . . . may be reduced

by equal status contact between majority and minority groups in the pursuit of common goals. The effect is greatly enhanced if this contact is sanctioned by institutional supports (i.e., by law, custom, or local atmosphere), and if it is of a sort that leads to the perception of common interests and common humanity between members of the two groups.

The clear key to breaking the vicious circle, then, was contact. By establishing integrated environments for black and white, white prejudice would be reduced, discrimination would decline, and damaging effects upon the black child's feelings and behavior would be reduced.

While the Supreme Court based its 1954 decision upon the narrower relationship between legally sactioned segregation and psychological harm, it is clear that the *modus operandi* by which the damage would stop is implied by the contact theory. With the 1954 decision, then, contact theory became an officially sanctioned policy model, and the Southern public school systems became prime targets for its implementation.

THE INTEGRATION POLICY MODEL: STAGE II

In the eyes of the Northerner, segregation had always been a Southern problem. The Supreme Court's action at first reinforced this belief, since state-sanctioned school segregation was rare outside the South. But events in the 1960's changed this for good. While the modern civil rights movement began in the South, its zenith was reached in the March on Washington in the late summer of 1963. Organized to dramatize the failure of court action to end segregation in the South, the March brought together 250,000 persons in the most impressive organized protest meeting in the history of the United States, and showed President Kennedy and the Congress the deep and massive support for anti-discrimination legislation.

The Congress answered this appeal by passing the Civil Rights Act of 1964, the strongest such act since the Reconstruction period. The Act included strong sanctions against discrimination in education, employment, housing, and voting (the last supplemented by the Voting Rights Act of 1965), and while its thrust was still aimed at the South, it also set standards that could be used against de facto segregation in the North (for example, the Title VI provisions directed the withholding of federal funds from localities which intentionally maintain segregated schools—and this has recently been applied to the city of Boston). Equally important, it set in motion a social science study that was to have an immense impact upon public policy in the North as well as the South. As part of the Act, the Congress commissioned the United States Office of Education to conduct a survey "concerning the lack of equal educational opportunities for individuals by reason of race, color, religion, or national origin in public educational institutions at all levels in the United States. . . ." Sociologist James Coleman was selected to head a team to design and conduct the survey.

The Coleman Report (1966), as it has come to be known, contained striking evidence of the extent of school segregation not only in the South but in all parts of the country. While the South was more segregated than the North, fully 72 percent of black first graders in the urban North attended predominantly black schools. The report also confirmed one of the basic assumptions of the Stage I model: that black students performed poorly compared to white students. Using results from a variety of achievement tests, Coleman reported that throughout all regions and all grade levels, black students ranged from two to six years behind white students in reading, verbal, and mathematics performance. Equally, black students were shown to have lower aspirations, lower self-esteem about academic ability, and a more fatalistic attitude about their ability to change their situation.

The Coleman study, however, also reported some findings that surprisingly were not in accord with the early model. For one thing, black children were already nearly as far behind white children in academic performance in the *first* grade as they were in later grades. This raised some question about whether school policies alone could eliminate black/white inequalities. Adding to the significance of this finding were the facts that black and white schools could not be shown to differ markedly in facilities or services, and that whatever differences there were could not be used to explain the disparities in black and white student achievement. This led Coleman to conclude that

> schools bring little influence to bear on a child's achievement that is independent of his background and general social context; and this very lack of an independent effect means that the inequalities imposed on children by their home, neighborhood, and peer environment are carried along to become the inequalities [of their adult life].

While the findings about segregation and black/white differences have been widely publicized and largely accepted, this concluding aspect of Coleman's findings has been ignored by educational policy makers. Part of the reason may derive from the methodological controversies which surrounded these findings (e.g., Bowles and Levin, 1968), but the more likely and important reason is that the implications were devastating to the rationale of the educational establishment in its heavy investment in school rehabilitative programs for the culturally deprived; the connection between public policy and social science does have its limitations.

We must return to the policy makers one more time for an important input into the final policy model. In 1965, President Johnson requested the United States Commission on Civil Rights to conduct an investigation into the effects of de facto segregation in the nation and to make recommendations about how it might be remedied. He expressed hope that the findings "may provide a basis for action not only by the federal government but also by the states and local school boards which bear the direct responsibility for assuring quality education." The Commission recommendations, in its 1967 volume entitled *Racial Isolation in the Public Schools*, constitute the most comprehensive policy statement to date on the subject of school integration; it is the policy which is, indeed, being followed by many states and local school boards throughout the country.

Using data from the Coleman study and several other original studies prepared for the Commission, the report concluded that

> Negro children suffer serious harm when their education takes place in public schools which are racially segregated, whatever the source of such segregation may be. Negro children who attend predominantly Negro schools do not achieve as well as other children, Negro and white. Their aspirations are more restricted than those of other children and they do not have as much confidence that they can influence their own futures. When they become adults, they are less likely to participate in the mainstream of American society, and more likely to fear, dislike, and avoid white Americans. The conclusions drawn by the U.S. Supreme Court about the impact upon children of segregation compelled by law—that it "affects their hearts and minds in ways unlikely ever to be undone"—applies to segregation not compelled by law.

To remedy this situation, the Commission recommended that the federal government establish a uniform standard for racial balance and provide financial assistance to states that develop programs to meet the standard. The Commission did not recommend a precise standard, but it did suggest that the standard be no higher than 50 percent black in any single school. Likewise, the Commission did not specifically recommend that busing be the method whereby integration is accomplished. But the realities of residential segregation in many cities throughout the nation offered little alternative to the use of busing if these integration standards were to be attained.

This, then, became the basis for the integration policy model as applied to public schools. While the implementation of racial balance programs has differed from one locality to the next, the underlying rationale of all these programs is similar to that first formulated by the Supreme Court and extended by the Civil Rights Commission. The full policy model may be summarized as follows: The starting point is white prejudice consisting of stereotyped beliefs about black people. These beliefs lead to discriminatory behavior in employment, housing, schooling, and social relationships in general. Discrimination in turn leads to social and economic inequality on the one hand, and segregation on the other hand. Inequality and segregation are mutually reinforcing conditions, reflecting not only the judicial doctrine that separation is inherently unequal, but also the social reality that segregation of a deprived group can cut off channels and networks that might be used to gain equality. Segregation and inequality combine to cause psychological damage in children resulting in lower achievement, lower aspirations, and less self-esteem. As the child grows older, this damage leads, on the one hand, to further social and economic inequalities in the form of inadequate education and inferior jobs and, on the other hand, to black alienation, prejudice, and hostility towards whites. This in turn leads to increased white prejudice (the vicious circle) and a general polarization of race relations. Given these cause and effect relations, the elimination of segregation in schooling should act as a countervailing force for black students by increasing achievement, raising aspirations, enhancing self-esteem, reducing black/white prejudices and hostility, and enabling black students to find better educational and occupational opportunities. It then follows that social and economic inequalities would be lessened and the vicious circle would be bent if not broken.

It must be stressed that this model is construed from public policy. While many of the causal relationships assumed in the model are, indeed, based on many years of scientific research in psychology and sociology, it is doubtful that any two specialists in the field of race relations would agree on all of the components of the model. Be that as it may, it is more to the point to stress that we are not setting out to test the *full* model. *We are specifically interested in those aspects of the model that postulate positive effects of school integration for black students; namely, that school integration enhances black achievement, aspirations, self-esteem, race relations, and opportunities for higher education.* We do not have data on the effects of integration on adults, nor on the effects of other types of integration, such as neighborhood housing, employment, and other forms. More important, the school integration programs we review here have two important characteristics in common that may limit generalizability. First, they are examples of "induced" integration as opposed to "natural" integration. Induced integration is brought about by the decision of a state or local agency to initiate a school integration program (sometimes voluntary, sometimes mandatory), rather than by the "natural" process whereby a black family makes an individual decision to relocate in a predominantly white community. Second, all of these programs have had to use varying amounts of busing to accomplish integration. This makes it difficult to separate out the potential effects of busing, if any, from the integration experience *per se*. In other words, *we will be assessing the effects of induced school integration via busing*, and not necessarily the effects of integration brought about by the voluntary actions of individual families that move to integrated neighborhoods. This is a more limited focus, yet induced integration, usually necessitating some amount of busing, is precisely the policy model that has been followed (or is being considered) in many communities throughout the country.

THE DATA

Many of the cities which desegregated their schools to achieve a racial balance have conducted research programs to evaluate the outcomes of desegregation. It is from these studies that we can derive data to test the school and busing hypotheses stemming from the integration policy model. Since the evaluations were conducted independently, the variables studied and the research designs differ from one study to the next, and the quality of the research and the reports varies considerably. Accordingly, we have been selective in choosing studies to include in our analysis. Our choices have been guided by two considerations: 1. A study must employ a longitudinal time-span design, with the same tests administered at different times during the integration experience so that *actual* changes can be assessed; and 2. a study must have a control group for comparison with integrated black students. The ideal control group, of course, would consist of black students who are identical to the integrated students in every way except for the integration experience. Since such studies are rare, an "adequate" control group for our present purposes is either a group of non-bused black students who are reasonably comparable to the bused black students, or a group of white students in the same school as the bused black students. In the latter case, the effects of integration are revealed in the changes in the black/white differential for the measure in question.(1)

The data we will use can be classified into two parts. The first part consists of findings from a study of Boston's METCO program, for whose research design, execution, and analysis we are partly responsible (Walberg, 1969; Armor and Genova, 1970).(2) The data are more complete and offer a more thoroughgoing test of the policy model than many other studies we have seen. The METCO program buses black students of all age levels from Boston to predominantly white middle-class schools in the suburbs. Approximately 1500 black students and 28 suburban communities have participated since the program began in 1966; the study from which our data will be taken covers the period from October 1968 to May 1970. The study used a longitudinal design that called for achievement testing for all students and a questionnaire for the junior and senior high students in three waves: the first at the beginning of the school year in October 1968; a second in May 1969; and a third in May 1970. (For a variety of reasons, the achievement testing was not done for the third wave.) The questionnaire covered several areas, including academic performance, aspirations and self-concept, relations with and attitudes toward white students, and attitudes toward the program.

The METCO study also included a small control group consisting of siblings of the bused students matched by sex and grade level.(3) The fact that the siblings were from the same families as the bused students means that there is an automatic control for social class and other tangible and intangible family factors. Since the high application rate usually prevented the busing program from taking more than one applicant per family, we had reason to believe that the control students would not differ substantially from the bused students along the important dimensions of ability, aspirations, and so forth. This belief is confirmed by the findings presented in the next section.

In addition to the data for black students, there are also data from a single cross-sectional study done in the spring of 1969 to assess the impact of the program on white sophomores in eight of the suburban schools (Useem, 1971 and 1972). We will cite some of the findings from the Useem study whenever such comparisons seem relevant.

The second part of the data comes largely from reports on integration programs in four other Northern cities throughout the country.(4) In 1964,

White Plains, New York, closed down one racially imbalanced inner-city elementary school and began busing the children to predominantly white inner-city schools; the study we cite covers a two-year period from 1964 to 1966 (White Plains Public Schools, 1967). In Ann Arbor, Michigan, there was a similar pattern: A racially imbalanced elementary school was closed in 1965 and the students were bused to predominantly white schools; the study covers a one-year period with a three-year follow-up (Carrigan, 1969). A program in Riverside, California, followed a graduated program of closing its racially imbalanced elementary schools and integrating its predominantly white schools; the program began in 1965 and the study covers a five-year period (Purl and Dawson, 1970; Gerard and Miller, 1971). The fourth program, Project Concern, is similar to METCO. Elementary school children from two inner cities (Hartford and New Haven, Connecticut) are bused to suburban schools in surrounding towns; this program began in 1966—the studies selected cover two years for Hartford (Mahan, 1968) and one year for New Haven (Clinton, 1969). In addition to these five major studies, we will also refer at certain points to studies of other integration programs that seem relevant. One such study is an evaluation of A Better Chance (ABC), a program which places high-ability black students in white preparatory schools in the Northeast (Perry, 1972). This evaluation research used techniques and instruments similar to those used in the METCO study; therefore comparisons with ABC may be more valid than comparisons with some of the other studies.

To test the integration policy model we can group our findings under five major headings—the effects of busing and integration on: 1. academic achievement; 2. aspirations; 3. self-concept; 4. race relations; and 5. educational opportunities. In addition, we will examine a sixth area, program support. In each case, we shall compare bused students with the control groups to assess those changes that might be uniquely associated with the effects of induced integration.

THE FINDINGS: ACHIEVEMENT

None of the studies were able to demonstrate conclusively that integration has had an effect on academic achievement as measured by standardized tests. Given the results of the Coleman study and other evaluations of remedial programs (e.g., Head Start), many experts may not be surprised at this finding. To date there is no published report of *any* strictly educational reform which has been proven substantially to affect academic achievement; school integration programs are no exception.

The changes in reading achievement for elementary and secondary students in METCO program are shown in Figures 1 and 2.(5) For the elementary students, the grade-equivalent gains for bused third and fourth graders after one year are somewhat greater than those for the control group (.4 to .3), but this is not a statistically significant difference. For grades 5 and 6 the situation is reversed; the control group outgained the bused group (.7 and .5), but again the difference is not significant. We can see that the control group is somewhat higher initially for both grade levels, but this difference, too, is not significant.(6)

In the case of high school students, the bused group scores somewhat higher than the control groups initially (but not significantly so).(7) Nonetheless, the gain scores present no particular pattern. While the bused junior high students increased their grade-equivalent score from 7.5 to 7.7, the control group improved from 7.4 to 7.5; the bused gain is not significantly different from that for the control group. For senior high students the effect is reversed; the control students gain more than the bused students (9 percentile points compared to 4 points), but again the gains are not statistically significant for either group.

The results for reading achievement are substantially repeated in a test of arithmetic skills; the bused students showed no significant gains in arithmetic skills compared to the control group, and there were no particular patterns in evidence.

The White Plains, Ann Arbor, and Riverside studies also found no significant changes in achievement level for bused students in the elementary grades when comparisons were made with control groups. Although the White Plains report did show some achievement gains among the bused students, these were not significantly different, statistically, from gain scores of inner-city black students in 1960. Moreover, when comparisons were made with white students in the integrated schools, the black/white achievement gap did not diminish during the period of the study. The Ann Arbor study compared bused black student gains to white gains and to black student gains in a half-black school.(8) The bused students did not gain significantly more than the black control group, nor did their gains diminish the black/white gap in the integrated schools. On the contrary, a follow-up done three years later showed that the integrated black students were even further behind the white students than before the integration project began.(9) The Riverside study compared minority students (black and Mexican-American) who had been integrated for differing number of years with the city-wide mean (which consisted of about 85 percent white students). The minority/white gap had not diminished for fourth graders who had been integrated since kindergarten; the gap in 1970 was as great as it was in 1965 when the program began (Purl and Dawson, 1971). Similar results occurred for minority pupils at other grade levels with differing numbers of years in the integration program.

Studies in the fifth program, Project Concern, showed mixed results. A study of the Hartford students compared bused black students who received special supportive assistance with non-bused inner-city black students (Mahan, 1968). (Although two separate one-year periods were covered, problems with missing data allow valid comparisons for only one full academic year, fall 1967 to spring 1968). The bused students showed significant IQ gains only in grades two and three; the gains in kindergarten and grades one, four, and five were either insignificant or, in two cases, favored the control group. In a study of New Haven students, second and third grade students were randomly assigned to bused and non-bused conditions and were given reading, language, and arithmetic tests in October 1967 (when the busing began) and again in April 1968 (Clinton, 1969). Of the six comparisons possible (three tests and two grades), only two showed significant differences favoring the bused students.(10)

While none of these studies are flawless, their consistency is striking. Moreover, their results are not so different from the results of the massive cross-sectional studies. An extensive reanalysis of the Coleman data showed that even without controlling for social class factors, "naturally" integrated (i.e.. non-bused) black sixth-grade groups were still one and one-half standard deviations behind white groups in the same schools, compared to a national gap of two standard deviations (Armor, 1972). This means that, assuming the Coleman data to be correct, the *best* that integration could do would be to move the average black group from the 2nd percentile to the 7th percentile (on the *white* scale, where the average white group is at the 50th percentile). But the social class differences of integrated black students in the Coleman study could easily explain a good deal of even this small gain. Other investigators, after examining a number of studies, have come to similar conclusions (St. John, 1970).

While there are no important gains for the METCO group in standardized test scores, there were some important differences in school grades (See Fig. 3). Even though the bused secondary school students have somewhat higher test scores than the control group, the bused group was about half a grade-point *behind* the control group in 1969, and the bused students dropped even further behind by 1970.(11) The average control student is able to maintain a grade average at above a B— level in the central city, while the average bused student in the suburbs is just above a C average. Although it is not shown in the Figure, from the Useem study we can estimate the average white student *academic* grade average (i.e., excluding non-academic courses—an exclusion not made for the black students) at about 2.45, or between a B— and C+ average.

Again, if we take into account the Coleman findings, we should not be too surprised. Since black students of the same age are, on average, behind white students in all parts of the country with respect to academic achievement, we should expect their grades to fall when they are taken from the competition in an all-black school to the competition in a predominantly white school. In addition, the bused students may not be adequately prepared for this competition, at least in terms of the higher standards that may be applied in the suburban schools.

ASPIRATION AND SELF-CONCEPT

In the METCO study we found that there were no increases in educational or occupational aspiration levels for bused students (see Figs. 4 and 5); on the contrary, there was a significant decline for the bused students, from 74 percent wanting a college degree in 1968 to 60 percent by May 1970. The control panel actually increased its college aspirations over the same period, but this is probably not a meaningful finding. (The cross-sectional data show a slight decline for the control group in 1970; this cautions us about our interpretation).

At the very least, we can conclude that the bused students do not improve their aspirations for college. The same is true for occupational aspirations, and in this case both the bused students and the controls show a similar pattern. We should point out, however, that the initial aspiration levels are already very high; Coleman found that only 54 percent of white twelfth graders in the urban North aspired to college, and 53 percent expected a professional or technical occupation. Therefore, even the slight decline we have found still leaves the bused students with relatively high aspirations compared to a regional norm. Moreover, when achievement is taken into account, black students actually have higher aspirations than white students at similar levels of achievement (Armor, 1967; Wilson, 1967). In this respect, some educators have hypothesized that integration has a *positive* effect in lowering aspirations to more realistic levels; of course, others would argue that any lowering of aspirations is undesirable. However, we shall see in a later section that the METCO students were more likely to start college than the control group.

Since the other cities in our review included only elementary students, they do not provide data on regular educational or occupational aspirations.(12) But two of the studies did examine a concept closely related to aspirations—"motivation for achievement." The findings of the Ann Arbor and Riverside studies corroborate the pattern of high aspirations for black children in both the pre- and post-integration periods. In addition, the Ann Arbor researchers concluded that the overly high aspiration of black boys may have been lowered by the integration experience. The Riverside study, on the other hand, concluded that there were no significant changes in achievement motivation.

In the METCO study we also found some important differences with respect to academic self-concept (Fig. 6). The students were asked to rate how bright they were in comparison to their classmates. While there were some changes in both the bused and control groups, the important differences are the gaps between the bused students and controls at each time period. The smallest difference is 15 percentage points in 1970 (11 points for the full cross-section), with the control students having the higher academic self-concept. Again, this finding makes sense if we recall that the academic performance of the bused students falls considerably when they move from the black community to the white suburbs. In rating their intellectual ability, the bused students may simply be reflecting the harder competition in suburban schools.

Both the Ann Arbor and Riverside studies made much more extensive inquiry into the realm of self-esteem of black children, although there were no directly comparable data for our academic self-concept measure. The Riverside study did report that, in a special test, minority children (black and Mexican-American) tended to choose white students more often than black students as "the [ones] with good grades." While we will not go into detail on the many other measures used in these studies, we can summarize their findings briefly as follows: 1. Minority children do tend to have lower self-esteem before integration, particularly in the later elementary grades; and 2. integration does not seem to affect the self-esteem measures in any clearly consistent or significant way.

One of the central sociological hypotheses in the integration policy model is that integration should reduce racial stereotypes, increase tolerance, and generally improve race relations. Needless to say, we were quite surprised when our data failed to verify this axiom. Our surprise was increased substantially when we discovered that, in fact, the converse appears to be true. The data suggest that, under the circumstances obtaining in these studies, integration heightens racial identity and consciousness, enhances ideologies that promote racial segregation, and reduces opportunities for actual contact between the races.

There are several indicators from the METCO study that point to these conclusions. The question which speaks most directly to the 50 percent racial balance standard suggested by the Civil Rights Commission asked: "If you could be in any school you wanted, how many students would be white?" Figure 7 reports the percentage which responded in favor of 50 percent or fewer white students. While both the control and the bused students started out fairly close together in 1968 (47 percent and 51 percent, respectively), two school years later the bused students were 15 percentage points *more* in favor of attending *non-white* schools than the controls (81 percent compared to 66 percent), although the differential change is not statistically significant. The changes for the controls (both the panel and the full cross-sections) indicate that the black community as a whole may be changing its attitudes toward school integration, but the bused students appear to be changing at a more rapid rate. Ironically, just as white America has finally accepted the idea of school integration (Greeley and Sheatsley, 1971), blacks who begin experiencing it may want to reject it.

That these changes reflect ideological shifts is supported by Figures 8 and 9. The bused students are much more likely to support the idea of black power than the control students, going from a difference of 11 points in 1969 to 36 points in 1970. We were also able to construct a Separatist Ideology Index from responses to a series of statements about black/white relations (e.g., 1. "Most black people should live and work in black areas, and most whites should live and work in white areas." 2. "Black and white persons should not intermarry.") The scores range from 0 (anti-separatist) to 4 (pro-separatist). From 1968 to 1970 the control group barely changes, increasing from 1.4 to 1.5. The bused group, however, changed from 1.4 to 1.8—a statistically significant change of about one half a standard deviation. This is the clearest indication in our data that integration heightens black racial consciousness and solidarity.

The changes do not appear to be in ideology alone. From 1969 to 1970 the bused students reported less friendliness from whites, more free time spent with members of their own race, more incidents of prejudice, and less frequent dating with white students (Fig. 10). In other words, the longer the contact with whites, the fewer the kinds of interracial experiences that might lead to a general improvement in racial tolerance.

To what extent might these changes be a result of negative experinces with white students in the schools? We do not doubt that there has been considerable hostility shown by certain groups of white students. Nonetheless, although the evidence is not complete, what we have indicates that the white students themselves were negatively affected by the contact. Support for the busing program was generally high among white sophomores in the eight high schools studied, especially among middle-class students in the college preparatory tracks (Useem, 1972). For example, 46 percent of all students were "very favorable" to METCO (only 11 percent were "not favorable"); 73 percent felt METCO should be continued; and 52 percent agreed that there should be more METCO students (20 percent disagreed and 27 percent were not sure). But those students who had direct classroom contact with bused black students showed *less* support for the busing program than those without direct contact. In fact, the kind of students who were generally the most supportive—the middle-class, high-achieving students—showed the largest decline in support as a result of contact with bused black students. This finding is based on cross-sectional data and does not indicate a change over time, but it is suggestive of the possibility that a general polarization has occured for both racial groups.

The data from the Ann Arbor and Riverside studies give some support to these findings, although again there were no directly comparable measures. Moreover, it is unlikely that the concept of ideology is relevant to elementary students. The Ann Arbor study included a sociometric test, whereby children could indicate how much they liked each classmate. Black students at all grade levels suffered a loss of peer status when they switched from a segregated to an integrated school, although the results were statistically significant only for second and third grade girls and fourth and fifth grade boys. That is, these black children were liked less by their new white peers than by their previously all-black peers. Also, the level of acceptance was considerably lower for black students than for white students. On the other hand, the black students tended to be more positive about their white peers after integration, although the changes are not statistically significant.

The Riverside data more clearly support the conlcusion that integration heightens racial identity and solidarity. Data from a test in which children rate pictures of faces portraying various ethnic and racial groups showed that fewer cross-racial choices were made after integration than before integration. For example, one rating task required that the children choose the face that they would "most like for a friend." Both black and white children tended to choose their own race to a greater extent after one year of integration than before integration (Gerard and Miller, 1971). The Riverside study also concluded that these effects were stronger with increasing age; that is, the cross-racial choices declined more in the later grades than in the earlier grades.

To avoid any misinterpretation of these findings, we should caution that the measures discussed here do not necessarily indicate increased *overt* racial hostility or conflict. This may occur to some extent in many busing programs, but our impression based on the METCO program is that overt racial incidents initiated by black or white students are infrequent. The polarization that we are describing, and that our instruments assess, is characterized by ideological solidarity and behavioral withdrawal. Our inferences pertain to a lack of racial togetherness rather than to explicit racial confrontations or violence. While it is conceivable that a connection may exist between these ideological shifts and open racial conflicts, such a connection is not established by the studies reviewed.

There are two other qualifications we must place on the interpretation of these data. First, as of 1970 the *majority* of the bused METCO students still supported general integration ideology. Only 40 percent of the METCO students would ideally prefer schools with a majority of black students (compared to 28 percent of the controls); 60 percent of METCO students believe that "once you really get to know a white person, they can be as good a friend as anyone else" (compared to 78 percent of the controls); and 58 percent of METCO students do not agree that "most black people should live and work in black areas, and most white should live and work in white areas" (compared to 71 percent of the control students).

The main point we are making is that the integration policy model predicts that integration should cause these sentiments to *increase*, while the evidence shows they actually *decrease*, leaving the bused students *more opposed* to integration than the non-bused students. Only further research can determine whether this trend will continue until the majority of bused students shifts to a general anti-integration ideology.

Second, group averages tend to obscure important differences between individual students. While we do not deny the existence of racial tension and conflict for some students, other students and families (both black and white) have had very meaningful relationships with one another, relationships made possible only through the busing program. It is very difficult, indeed, to weigh objectively the balance of benefit and harm for the group as a whole. The main point to be made is that a change in a group average does not necessarily reflect a change in every individual group member.

LONG-TERM EDUCATIONAL EFFECTS

In view of the fact that most of the short-term measures do not conclusively demonstrate positive effects of busing in the area of achievement, aspirations, self-concept, and race relations, it becomes even more important to consider possible longer-term changes that may relate to eventual socio-economic parity between blacks and whites. Since no busing program has been in operation for more than seven years or so, this area, obviously, has not been studied extensively. There are, however, some preliminary findings on long-term educational effects. Specifically, two studies have investigated the effects of integration on college attendance and some tentative conclusions have emerged.

Seniors from the 1970 graduating class in the METCO program, as well as the seniors in the 1970 control group, formed samples for a follow-up telephone interview in the spring of 1972. Approximately two-thirds of both groups were contacted, resulting in college data for 32 bused students and 16 control group students. The results of the follow-up are striking and they are summarized in

Figure 11. The bused students were very much more likely to start college than the control group (84 percent compared to 56 percent), but by the end of the second year the bused students resembled the control group (59 percent compared to 56 percent). In other words, the METCO program seems to have had a dramatic effect upon the impetus for college, and many more of the bused students actually started some form of higher education. But the bused drop-out rate was also substantially higher, so that towards the end of the sophomore year the bused students were not much more likely to be enrolled full-time in college than the control group.

In spite of this higher drop-out rate, the bused students were still enrolled in what are generally considered higher-quality institutions. That is, 56 percent of the bused students were in regular four-year colleges, compared to 38 percent for the control group. An even greater difference was found for those enrolled in full universities (which include a graduate school). The figures are 47 percent and 12 percent for bused and control students, respectively.

Similar findings emerged from a special college follow-up study of the ABC program (Perry, 1972). A group of ABC students were matched with a control group of high-ability black students not in the ABC program. Since ABC is a highly selective program, the matching was carried out so that the ABC and control groups had very similar family backgrounds, socio-economic status, and achievement levels. Approximately 40 matched pairs were followed until their first year of college (academic year 1971-72). All of the ABC students entered college, whereas only half of the control group did so. While it is too early to assess differential drop-out rates, it is very clear from the data that even if half of the ABC students drop out of college, the quality of colleges attended by the ABC students is considerably higher than those attended by the control group. Of the matched pairs attending college, two-thirds of the ABC students attended higher-quality institutions.

Neither of these studies is large enough, of course, to draw any definite conclusions. But there does seem to be some strong evidence that middle-class suburban or prep schools have an important "channeling" effect not found in black schools. The effect is probably due to better counseling and better contacts with college recruiting officers. Whatever the reason, black students attending such schools may have doors opened for them that are closed to students attending predominantly black schools. Given the lack of positive effects in other areas, these findings may have great significance for future busing programs, and further research is urgently needed.

PROGRAM SUPPORT

Although it is not explicitly part of the integration policy model we are testing, it seems appropriate to consider the extent of the support for the busing program among the students and communities involved. As might be expected from the changes already described, there was a general decline in the enthusiasm for the METCO program over time, with the bused students showing greater changes than the controls: 80 percent of the bused group said they were "very favorable" to the program in 1968, compared to 50 percent by 1970. Yet we cannot infer from this alone that there is a decline in support for the program. The drop-out rate in the METCO program is almost non-existent in spite of some of the changes we have reported. The families involved in the program appear to feel that their children will get a better education in the suburbs in spite of the inconvenience and the problems. Our data indicated that the most important reason cited by the bused students for being in the busing program was to receive "a better education." Moreover, this did not change as much as many of our other indicators from 1969 to 1970; 88 percent said this was a "very important" reason in 1969, and 81 percent indicated the same in 1970. Very few reported that "getting out of the city" or "more contact with whites" were important reasons for being in the program.

In other words, the justification of the program in the black community has little to do with the contact-prejudice components of the policy model; instead, busing is seen in the context of enlarging educational opportunities for the black students.

We do not have much systematic data from the white receiving schools other than those cited earlier (i.e., a sample of white sophomore students was generally supportive of the program in 1969). It is our impression, however, that most of the 28 communities that receive METCO students are enthusiastic about the program, and only a few communities have turned down the opportunity to participate. The other programs reviewed receive moderate to strong support from the community and participants. In Project Concern the drop-out rate was only 10 percent, half of which was due to the program directors' initiative in withdrawing students. After two years of urban-to-suburban busing, nine additional suburban towns chose to participate and over 1,000 additional elementary school children were bused to suburban schools. In White Plains both black and white parents expressed more positive than negative attitudes about integration, although black parents were more favorable to the program than white parents after two years of desegregation. In Ann Arbor the black parents felt more positive toward the program after one year of desegregated schooling, but the children were slightly less positive than they were prior to the integration experience. In both groups, however, support was high; only 20 percent of each group expressed negative attitudes toward the program.

We must conclude that the busing programs we have reviewed seem to have considerable support from both the black and white communities. In most cases, black parents were highly supportive of the various busing programs. Like the students in our own study, black parents stressed quality education as the most important benefit of such programs, whereas white parents in receiving schools tended to stress the experience of coming into contact with other races. We must point out, however, that *none* of the programs reviewed involved *mandatory* busing of white students into black communities; cities facing this situation might present a very different picture of white support. Moreover, it is unlikely that many in the black community have seen the data on achievement reported here; much black support may be based upon premises regarding academic gain which our findings call into question. Whether or not black support will be affected by such findings remains to be seen.

SOCIAL CLASS AND OTHER BACKGROUND FACTORS

Most of the data we have presented so far summarize the effects of busing on all students considered as a single group. A question might be raised about whether these effects (or lack of same) are consistent for all students regardless of their background. In particular, it might be hypothesized that social class differences between black and white students can explain the changes (or lack of changes) we have reported. We shall briefly indicate the major trends for students of different social class and other characteristics, such as sex and age level.

It is difficult to separate race and social class, since black families as a group tend to be lower than white families on most socio-economic measures. To the extent that the distinction can be made, however, no uniquely social class factors have been reported that would contradict the findings presented so far. The Riverside study selected a group of white students whose social class scores were less than or equal to the minority students; achievement test scores of the black students were still significantly lower than the low-SES white students (although the original difference was diminished somewhat; Gerard and Miller, 1971). For the METCO data, special analyses were made of the race relations changes among bused students who were children of blue-collar as compared to white-collar workers; no significant differences emerged. What small changes there were usually revealed that the black students from white-collar families changed more (in a negative direction) than those from blue-collar families.

There is also the possibility that, contrary to the assumptions behind many school integration programs, some of the predominantly white schools to which black students are sent are in fact worse than the inner-city black schools. In the METCO study there were no data to examine this issue in detail, but it is our impression that perhaps only one ot two suburbs would approximate the inner-city socio-economic level. In any event, while there were some differences from one town to another in the absolute levels of the various measures, there were no important variations in the *changes* over time that appeared to be related to any socio-economic differences in the communities.

With the exception of achievement test scores, there was some sex and age differential on various measures both before and after integration; but there were no important differences in the relative *changes* in these groups due to integration. That is, in METCO we found that girls generally had a more difficult time adjusting to the program (reflected in lower program support, stronger separatist ideology, and less contact with white students). There seemed to be some important differences in cross-sex, cross-race relationships, which were better between black boys and white girls than between white boys and black girls. This situation seems to have left some black girls with resentful feelings over white girls "stealing their men." But the amount of interracial contact was small for both groups, and, more important, the *changes* in our race relations measures for bused students were about the same for both boys and girls. A similar finding emerged for age levels. Younger students were somewhat more supportive of the program and were more positive on the various race relations measures than older students, but the degree and direction of *change* were similar for all ages. This was true for the METCO secondary school data as well as the Riverside elementary school data.

In sum, while there were some over-all differences according to the sex and age levels of students in busing programs, the effects of busing on *changes* (if any) in achievement and attitudes tended to be uniform for all groups.

It seems clear from the studies of integration programs we have reviewed that four of the five major premises of the integration policy model are not supported by the data, at least over the one- to five-year periods covered by various reports. While this does not deny the possibility of longer-term effects or effects on student characteristics other than those measured, it does mean that the model is open to serious question.

The integration policy model predicted that achievement should improve as black students are moved from segregated schools to integrated schools. This prediction was based in part upon the classical works of Kenneth Clark and others which argue that, because of segregation, black students have lower regard for themselves. It was also based in part upon reanalyses of the Coleman data which showed that black students achieve less than white students, but that black students in integrated schools achieve more than black students in segregated schools. But four of the five studies were reviewed (as well as the Berkeley and Evanston data discussed in footnote 4) showed no significant gains in achievement scores; the other study had mixed results. Our own analyses of the Coleman data were consistent with these findings (see Armor, 1972).

Although there were no gains in general standardized achievement scores that we might attribute to integration, neither were there any losses for black or white students. Unfortunately, we cannot say the same about academic grades of black students. The grades of the METCO secondary students in suburban schools dropped considerably. We did not measure the bused students' grades before they entered the program, but the fact that their test scores are somewhat *higher* than the control group's offers substantial evidence that this difference does represent a change. Along with this change we observed a difference in academic self-concept that seems to indicate that the bused students are aware that they are experiencing more difficult competition in the suburbs. While we might expect this result if we believe the Coleman finding of black/white achievement differences, it does not mean there is no problem. It is possible that there are psychological consequences of this increased competition that may be harmful to black children. Being moved from an environment where they are above average to one in which they are average or below may be frustrating and discouraging. It might be one of the reasons why the bused black students have become less supportive of the program and more supportive of black separatism.

We tested this latter possibility by examining the relationship between support for the Black Panthers and academic grades in our 1970 sample from METCO (see Fig. 12). Consistent with our findings, the bused students are more favorable to the Panthers than the control group. But among the bused students we find that the METCO group which has college aspirations but which has a C average or below stands out clearly as more pro-Panther than the other groups. In other words, the increased militancy and anti-integration sentiments among the bused students may arise partly from the fact that their aspirations remain at a very high level even though their performance declines to the point where they may question their ability to compete with whites at the college level. The fact that this group is proportionally a large one (about 25 percent of the total bused group compared to 13 percent for the analogous control group) may be an indication of a potentially serious problem.

The integration policy model predicted that integration should raise black aspirations. Again, our studies reveal no evidence for such an effect. Unlike poor achievement, however, low aspirations do not appear to be much of a problem. The black students in our busing program seem to have aspirations as high as or higher than white students. If anything, given their academic records in high school, these aspirations may be unrealistic for some students. The emphasis on equality of educational opportunity may be pushing into college many black students whose interests and abilities do not warrant it. The fact that only half of the 1970 METCO seniors are still enrolled in four-year colleges (after over 80 percent had started) may attest to this possibility.

The integration policy model predicted that race relations should improve as the result of interracial contact provided by integration programs. In this regard the effect of integration programs seems the opposite of that predicted. It appears that integration increases racial identity and solidarity over the short run and, at least in the case of black students, leads to increasing desires for separatism. These effects are observed for a variety of indicators: attitudes about integration and black power; attitudes towards whites; and contact with whites. The trends are clearest for older students (particularly the METCO high school students), but similar indications are present in the elementary school studies as well. This pattern holds true for whites also, insofar as their support for the integration program decreases and their own race preferences increase as contact increases.

It is this set of findings that surprised us most. Although many recent studies have questioned the meaning of black/white differences in achievement and aspirations, to our knowledge there have been no research findings which challenged the contact theory. The idea that familiarity lessens contempt has been a major feature of liberal thought in the western world, and its applicability to racial prejudice has been supported for at least two decades of social science research. It may be true that, under certain conditions, greater contact will lead to a reduction of prejudicial feelings among racial or ethnic groups. But the induced integration of black and white students as it is being carried out in school today does not fulfill the conditions.

In all fairness to the Allport contact theory, it must be said that he placed many qualifications upon it. One major qualification was that the contact must be made under equal-status conditions. Many behavioral scientists might assume that an integration program presumes equality of status, at least in the formal sense that all races are treated equally and have equal access to educational resources. But there is another way to look at status. Integrating black and white students does very little, in the short term, to eliminate the *socio-economic* and *academic* status differentials between black and white students that exist before integration. Therefore, we have to question whether integration programs for black and white children fulfill the equal-status conditions as long as socio-economic and academic inequalities are not eliminated. Allport warned that contact under the wrong conditions can reinforce stereotyped beliefs rather than reduce them; this may be occurring in our current integration programs. In other words, the social class differences between blacks and whites—the differences that integration programs are supped to eliminate eventually—may heighten the sense of black identity and solidarity, leading to an increasing opposition to integration.

What Allport did not say, but what his emphasis on equal-status conditions may imply, is that contact between two groups with strong initial prejudices may increase prejudice to the extent that stereotypes are reflected by actual group differences. For black students, initial stereotypes about white students as snobbish, intellectual, and "straight" may be partially confirmed by actual experience; the same may be true for white stereotypes of black students as non-intellectual, hostile, and having different values. We might make the same observations about some of the other ethnic and religious conflicts we see in the world today, particularly the Protestant-Catholic conflict in Northern Ireland and the Israeli-Arab battles in the Middle East. It is certainly true in these cases that the amount of contact has not lessened the hostilities; it seems to have heightened them to dangerous levels in the first place.

Why has the integration policy model failed to be supported by the evidence on four out of five counts? How can a set of almost axiomatic relationships, supported by years of social science research, be so far off the mark? Part of the reason may be that the policy model has failed to take into account some of the conditions that must be placed upon contact theory; but we believe that there may be other reasons as well having to do with 1. inadequate research designs, 2. induced versus "natural" factors, and 3. changing conditions in the black cultural climate.

Most of the methodological procedures which have been used to develop various components of the integration policy model are not adequate. The single most important limitation is that they have been cross-sectional designs. That is, the studies have measured aspects of achievement or race relations at a single point in time, with causal inferences being drawn from comparisons of integrated groups with segregated groups. Such inferences are risky at best, since the cross-sectional design cannot control for self-selection factors. For example, the Coleman study showed that integrated black students had slightly higher achievement than segregated students, but it is more than likely that families of higher-achieving students move to integrated neighborhoods in the first place (for reasons of social class or other issues involving opportunity). Thus the cause-and-effect relationship may be the opposite to that suggested by the U.S. Civil Rights Commission report. In the Deutsch and Collins housing study, which found that integrated whites were more tolerant of blacks than segregated whites, it is possible that self-selection factors were operating which led the more tolerant white persons to choose the integrated housing project in the first place. It is fair to say that none of the studies before the ones we have reviewed had an opportunity to study the effects of large-scale induced integration over a reasonable period of time. Yet this is the only way the effects of integration can be sorted out from differences which may originally exist between any two groups of persons.

The second reason for our findings in the race relations realm may have to do with the relatively contrived nature of current school integration programs. In all of the programs reviewed, the integration has been induced by the actions of state or local agencies; it has not occurred in a more natural way through individual voluntary actions. The use of busing, the relatively instantaneous transition from an all-black to an all-white environment, the fact of being part of a readily identifiable group in a new and strange setting, may all combine to enhance racial solidarity and increase separatist tendencies for black students. (We might find a very different picture for black families that move into predominantly white neighborhoods and allow their children some time to adjust to the new environment.) On the other hand, this set of mechanisms would not explain why white student attitudes in the receiving schools also tended to become less favorable to black students, as shown in the Ann Arbor, Riverside, and METCO studies. Moreover, these mechanisms—if they are, in fact, operating—do not invalidate our evaluation of those current policies that focus precisely on induced school integration.

The final major reason why the integration policy model may fail is that the racial climate has changed drastically in the years since the Allport work and the Supreme Court decision. The most noteworthy change, of course, has been in the attitudes of black people. Although the majority of blacks may still endorse the concept of integration, many younger black leaders deemphasize integration as a major goal. Black identity, black control, and black equality are seen as the real issues, and integration is regarded as important only insofar as it advances these primary goals. Some black leaders, albeit the more militant ones, feel that integration might actually defeat attainment of these goals by dispersing the more talented blacks throughout the white community and thereby diluting their power potential. Integration is also seen as having white paternalistic overtones and as the means whereby the white man allays his guilty conscience while ignoring reform on the really important issues. Given these sentiments, school integration programs are seen by blacks not as a fulfillment of the goal of joining white society, but only as a means of obtaining better educational opportunities, which would ultimately lead to a more competitive position in the occupational and economic market.

Integrated schools *per se* are not the real issue; if schools in the black community provided education of the same quality as those in white communities, blacks would not be so interested in busing programs. In fact, when we asked students in the METCO program this question, almost 75 percent said they would prefer to attend their own community school if it were as good as the suburban schools. Of course, it is by no means clear that the suburban schools actually offer better education. Any improvement in facilities or teacher quality (the ultimate importance of which is called into question by the Coleman report) may be counteracted, as our data show, by stiffer competition and a more hostile and unfriendly student atmosphere. Black leaders who view school integration only as a means to better opportunity must take these other factors into account.

In the context of these new black attitudes, the Allport model may not be applicable, and contact with white students provided by induced school integration may enhance ideological tendencies towards separatism. The reality of contact seems to sensitize black students to the heightened racial identity and separatism that has been growing in the black community since the late 1960's. The explanation may be, in part, that the large socio-economic differences between black and white students are fully recognized only when contact enables them to witness these differences. The difficulty of bridging this gap, coupled with the knowledge that they are viewed by whites as having lower status, leads black students to reject white standards and relationships. They turn inward, as it were, stressing the uniqueness and value of their own race, shutting off contact with whites, and embracing a point of view which endorses separatism as a means toward preserving and elevating their own position. Those black students not in contact with whites may exhibit some of these tendencies due to the over-all contact with white society, but the lack of direct contact postpones the problem or avoids it altogether. This type of "contact-conflict" model may be used to explain the conflicts which occur between two different cultural groups which come into direct contact (e.g., Catholics and Protestants in Northern Ireland; Israelis and Arabs in the Middle East). Whether or not it is applicable on a larger scale, it would fit the data better and would provide a more realistic model for the school integration case.

It would be a mistake, of course, to view the increased racial solidarity of black students as a completely negative finding. The differences between black and white cultures make a certain amount of culture conflict inevitable and even necessary if an integrated society is to be realized. In fact, it would be reasonable not to expect conflict—which always accompanies the contact of two cultures—only if we did not believe that a distinct black culture exists in America. Although this belief was held at one time by a large number of social scientists, it is not so popular today. There is now growing recognition that a black culture does exist, at least in the eyes of many blacks, and that this culture stresses values, goals and behavioral patterns that differ considerably from those of the predominant white culture (Jones, 1972; Metzger, 1971).

Up to this point, we have said little about the one positive finding of our research, the "channeling" effect whereby black students who attend white middle-class schools tend to get into higher quality colleges (even though they may not finish college at a higher rate than segregated black students). This finding should be heartening to those who have believed that integration does provide educational opportunities not found in inner-city black schools, although the finding must be considered a tentative one since it has been shown in only two fairly small studies. Also, the positive effects are limited to the college-bound, so that there still may be a question about the benefits of integration for the non-college-bound black students. And it may be that the "channeling" effect works only when the number is relatively small. Nonetheless, this kind of longer-term effect—and perhaps others as yet undiscovered—may turn out to provide a basis for certain types of integration plans.

POLICY IMPLICATIONS

It is obvious that the findings of integration research programs have serious implications for policy. Given the momentum which has built up over the last few years for the school integration movement, however, it is likely that in some quarters the data we have presented will be attacked on moral or methodological grounds and then summarily ignored. In other quarters the data may be met with rejoicing over the discovery of a club which can be used to beat back the pro-integration forces. But we hope these extreme reactions will be avoided and that a more balanced interpretation of our findings will prevail.

The most serious question is raised for mandatory busing (or induced integration) programs. If the justification for mandatory busing is based upon an integration policy like the one we have tested here, then that justification has to be called into question. The data do not support the model on most counts. There may be justifications for school integration other than those in the integration policy model, but then the burden must fall upon those who support a given school integration program to demonstrate that it has the intended effects (with no unintended, negative side-effects). It also must be demonstrated that any such program is at least supported by the black community.

We want to stress this last point. Decisions must be based upon feelings of the black community as well as the white community. Many liberal educators have been so intent on selling integration to reluctant white communities that they risk the danger of ignoring the opinion of the black community. While many black leaders favor school integration, there are also many black persons who would much prefer an upgrading of schools in their own community. The recent (March 1972) Natinal Black Political Convention in Gary, Indiana, condemned mandatory busing and school integration, arguing that such plans are racist and preserve a black minority structure. These views may not represent the entire black community, but they are indicative of the complexity and heterogeneity of black political opinion.(13) Whether or not a white community wants integration (and there are obviously many that do not), we must take into account the feelings of the group on whose behalf integration is advocated.

Although the data may fail to support mandatory busing as it is currently justified, these findings should not be used to halt voluntary busing programs. For one thing, we have stressed that the studies of integration so far have been over fairly short periods (one to five years), and there are possibilities of longer-term effects which are not visible until adulthood (not to speak of effects on characteristics not measured by the present research). More important, however, we have tentatively demonstrated one very significant longer-term benefit of integration for college-bound blacks. The "channeling" effect, if substantiated by further research, could form a substantial basis for voluntary programs whose focus is upon the college-bound black student. Even for this subgroup, of course, we have documented the trend towards separatist ideology. But the gain in educational opportunity may well outweigh this consequence in the eyes of the black community, as indeed it does now for programs like METCO. In fact, some persons will view these ideological changes, as well as any conflict that may accompany them, as an inevitable consequence of contact between two different cultures. If blacks and whites are ever to live in an integrated culture, they must begin learning and accepting their differences; and this cannot happen without contact. If contact engenders a certain amount of racial friction, many persons will feel the gains from school integration—both long-term and symbolic—more than make up for it.

To these questions of the symbolic and long-run benefits of induced school integration, the existing studies provide no answer. What they do show is that, over the period of two or three years, busing does not lead to significant measurable gains in student achievement or interracial harmony (although it does lead to the channeling of black students to better colleges). The available evidence thus indicates that busing is not an effective policy instrument for raising the achievement of black students or for increasing interracial harmony. On the other hand, the existing studies do not rule out the possibility that in the longer run, or in other respects, busing may indeed prove to have substantial positive consequences.

The available evidence on busing, then, seems to lead to two clear policy conclusions. One is that massive mandatory busing for purposes of improving student achievement and interracial harmony is not effective and should not be adopted at this time. The other is that voluntary integration programs such as METCO, ABC, or Project Concern should be continued and positively encouraged by substantial federal and state grants. Such voluntary programs should be encouraged so that those parents and communities who believe in the symbolic and potential (but so far unconfirmed) longrun benefits of induced integration will have ample opportunity to send their children to integrated schools. Equally important, these voluntary programs will permit social scientists and others to improve and broaden our understanding of the longer-run and other consequences of induced school integration. With a more complete knowledge than we now possess of this complicated matter, we shall hopefully be in a better position to design effective public education policies that are known in advance to work to the benefit of all Americans, both black and white.

Even in voluntary school integration programs, however, our data indicate that certain steps should be taken which might help alleviate the problems of achievement and race relations. Wholesale integration without regard to achievement levels of white and black students can lead to potentially frustrating experiences. Some selectivity might be desirable so that both groups reflect a similar achievement capacity. Although a certain amount of racial problems may be inevitable, full education of both groups about the possibilities and causes of differences might ameliorate the kind of polarization that would endanger the program.

One must also consider the possibility that other types of integration programs may be more successful. We have said since the outset that our data do not necessarily apply to neighborhood integration brought about by the individual choice of black families. It is possible that such programs would be more successful over the long run, at least in terms of race relations. Being a member of the community might tend to ameliorate black feelings of separateness that are fostered in the relatively contrived busing situation. Whether or not this kind of program could also change standardized achievement levels remains to be seen. Since the differences between black and white achivement are so large and consistent across so many different settings and studies, we must entertain the possibility that no plan of school integration will lessen this gap. Research will have to be continued in this area before the full causal mechanisms are understood and a firm basis is established on which social action can accordingly be planned.

Although we have been critical of some aspects of the connection between social science and public policy in the integration movement, we do not want to imply that their connection should be lessened. On the contrary, the real goals of social science and public policy are not in opposition; the danger is rather that the connection may not be close enough to enable us to make sound decisions. Society can only benefit by those ties which combine the advantage of scientific knowledge with a clear awareness of its limitations.

NOTES

(1) In spite of these precautions, we must still warn that it is difficult to make comparisons and generalizations when data are derived from different studies. Also, all of the studies we review were done in Northern cities, so that our findings may not be generalizable to the South. Nonetheless, the studies do reveal sufficiently clear and consistent findings in certain areas to enable at least a preliminary assessment of the effects of induced integration in de facto segregated cities of the North.

(2) The data summarized in the reports cited were subjected to extensive reanalysis for the present study.

(3) The number of junior and senior high students participating in the METCO study are as follows: wave one, 357 bused (80 percent of the total population) and 112 controls (54 percent of the eligible population); wave two, 229 bused (51 percent) and 67 controls (32 percent); wave three, 492 bused (87 percent) and 232 controls (65 percent). Because of clerical errors in relating achievement tests to questionnaires, the questionnaire data for waves one and two are based on about 10 percent fewer respondents in each group. Given the low turnout rates for wave two and other factors (drop-outs, graduates, transfers from control to bused status), our panel of secondary school students with achievement data for both testing periods consists of 195 bused students and 41 control students; for the questionnaire data the panel consists of 135 bused students with data from all 3 waves and 36 control students with data from wave one and wave three. (Only 16 students in the control group had questionnaire data from all three waves. Of the initial sample of control students, over a third had either graduated or transferred into the busing program by the third wave.) In addition, achievement data for elementary grades is available for panels of 147 bused students (66 percent of the wave one sample) and 41 controls (44 percent). Given the relatively small proportion of both bused and control students in the panels, there is the chance that the panels are not representative of the full population of bused students and their matched siblings. In the comparisons we make in the next section, therefore, we shall also present data from the complete cross-sections for all waves. The bused panel does not differ significantly from the full cross-section of bused students, and the control panel differs in no way that would affect our main conclusions. In other words, the cross-sectional data can be used as a check on the panel data; the absence of any divergency between the two sets of findings indicates that the attrition of the panels does not invalidate the panel findings. (Analysis was carried out on the 240 bused students who were in both waves one and three, representing 74 percent of the wave one sample, and there were no important differences between these results and the results from the smaller three-wave panel.)

(4) Research reports for a number of widely-discussed busing programs were not included for various reasons. For example, the Berkeley, California, busing program has not been systematically studied; a report is available, however, which shows that black student achievement is as far behind (or *further* behind) white achievement after two years of integration as before integration (Dambacher, 1971). A study of the Rochester busing program also lacked a proper pre-test design (Rochester City School District, 1970). The study had pre-test and post-test achievement scores from *different tests*, and control groups with generally lower pre-test scores; and it used analysis of covariance to make adjustments for post-test scores. Such statistical adjustments do not necessarily eliminate initial differences between the bused and control groups. A third study—of the Evanston integration program—was received too late for inclusion (Hsia, 1971). This report did show, however, that after two to three years of integration, integrated black students were still as far—or farther—behind white students as before integration. This research also confirmed the reduction in

black academic self-concept after integration and the tendency for black student grades to decline. We know of no other studies of induced school integration in the North which have the research design necessary for establishing cause and effect relationship—to wit, a longitudinal design with a control group.

(5) About half of the elementary students and two thirds of the secondary students were new to the program in 1968. However, there were no differences in gain scores for the newly-bused compared to the previously-bused students.

(6) Initial differences between the newly-bused and the previously-bused revealed no particular pattern; for third and fourth graders the previously-bused were higher by .15 points, but for fifth and sixth graders the newly-bused were higher by .5 points; in any event there were no statistically significant differences in gain scores.

(7) The newly-bused students were somewhat higher than the previously-bused initially for both junior and senior high students (.3 and 2.5, respectively), but the differences were not significant.

(8) The control school was a "naturally" integrated school with an increasing proportion of black students; it was scheduled to be closed down the following year.

(9) The pattern of black achievement falling further behind white achievement at later grade levels has been extensively documented (Coleman, 1966; Rosenfeld and Hilton, 1971).

(10) Even these two significant results might not have occurred if the data had been analyzed differently. The author controlled for pre-busing scores using analysis of covariance rather than analyzing gain scores (see footnote 4). Since the author did not present pre-test means, we cannot know if the bused and control groups differed initially.

(11) The grade-point system used here has an A as 4 points, B as 3 points, and so on.

(12) The Ann Arbor study did include a measure of occupational aspiration, but the variation was so great (not to speak of the coding problems presented by such choices as "superman" and "fairy princess") that interpretation was difficult.

(13) A recent Gallup Poll reported that 46 percent of a national non-white sample are opposed to busing for racial balance; 43 percent were in favor, and 11 percent were undecided (August 1971).

REFERENCES

Allport, Gordon W., 1954. The Nature of Prejudice, Cambridge, Massachusetts, Addison-Wesley.

Armor, David J., 1967. "The Racial Composition of Schools and College Aspirations of Black Students," Appendix C2 of Racial Isolation in the Public Schools, Government Printing Office, U.S. Commission on Civil Rights, Washington, D.C.

Armor, David J., 1972. "School and Family Effects on Black and White

Achievement," in Frederic Mosteller and Daniel P. Moynihan, eds., On Equality of Educational Opportunity, New York, Random House.

Armor, David J. and William J. Genova, 1970. "METCO Student Attitudes and Aspirations: A Three-Year Evaluation," unpublished manuscript.

Bowles, Samuel and Henry Levin, 1968. "The Determination of Scholastic Achievement: An Appraisal of Some Recent Evidence," The Journal of Human Resources, Vol. III, No. 1.

Carrigan, Patricia M., 1969. "School Desegregation via Compulsory Pupil Transfer: Early Effects on Elementary School Children," Final Report for Project No. 6-1320, Contract No. OEC-3-6-061320-0659, U.S. Office of Education.

Clark, Kenneth B. and M.P. Clark, 1947. "Racial Identification and Preference in Negro Children," in T.M. Newcomb and E.L. Hartley (eds.), Readings in Social Psychology, New York, Holt, Rinehart, and Winston.

Clinton, Ronald R., 1969. "A Study of the Improvement in Achievement of Basic Skills of Children Bused from Urban to Suburban School Environments," unpublished Master's Thesis, Southern Connecticut State College.

Coleman, James, et al, 1966. Equality of Educational Opportunity, Washington, D.C., U.S. Government Printing Office.

Dambacher, Arthur D., 1971. "Comparison of Achievement Test Scores made by Berkeley Elementary Students, Pre and Post Integration," unpublished report, Berkeley Unified School District, Berkeley, California.

Deutsch, Morton and Mary Evans Collins, 1951. Interracial Housing: A Psychological Evaluation of a Social Experiment, University of Minnesota Press.

Dollard, John, 1937. Caste and Class in a Southern Town, New York, Doubleday.

Gerard, Harold and Norman Miller, 1971. "Factors Contributing to Adjustment and Achievement in Racially Desegregated Schools," unpublished manuscript, Department of Psychology, University of California at Los Angeles.

Greeley, Andrew M. and Paul B. Sheatsley, 1971. "Attitudes toward Racial Integration," Scientific American, Vol. 225, No. 6.

Hsia, Jayjia, 1971. "Integration in Evanston, 1967-71." Educational Testing Services, Evanston, Illinois.

Jones, James, 1972. Prejudice and Racism, Reading, Massachusetts, Addison-Wesley.

Mahan, Thomas W., 1968. Project Concern—1966-1968, Hartford Public Schools.

Metzger, L. Paul, 1971. "American Sociology and Black Assimilation: Conflicting Perspectives," American Sociological Review, LXXVI, 627-647.

Myrdal, Gunnar, 1944. An American Dilemma, New York, Harper and Bros.

Perry, George, 1972. "A Preliminary Evaluation of the Effects of ABC on

College Attendance," unpublished report. A Better Chance, Boston.

Porter, Judith, 1971. Black Child, White Child, Harvard University Press.

Proshansky, Harold and Peggy Newton, 1968. "The Nature and Meaning of Negro Self-Identity." in Deutsch, et al, eds., Social Class, Race and Psychological Measurement, New York, Holt, Rinehart, and Winston.

Purl, Mabel and Judith Dawson, 1971. "The Achievement of Pupils in Desegregated Schools," unpublished manuscript, Riverside Unified School District, California.

Rochester City School District, 1970. "Final Report: A Three-Year Longitudinal Study to Assess a Fifteen Point Plan to Reduce Racial Isolation," Rochester, New York.

Rosenfeld, Michael and Thomas L. Hilton, 1971. "Negro-White Differences in Adolescent Educational Growth," American Educational Research Journal, Vol. VIII.

St. John, Nancy, 1970. "Desegregation and Minority Group Performance," Review of Educational Research, Vol. 40, 111-134.

Stouffer, Samuel A., et al, 1949. The American Soldier, Princeton University Press, Vol. II.

U.S. Commission on Civil Rights, 1967. Racial Isolation in the Public Schools, Washington, D.C., Government Printing Office.

Useem, Betsy, 1971. "White Suburban Secondary Students in Schools with Token Desegregation," unpublished Ph.D. Thesis, Graduate School of Education, Harvard University.

Useem, Betsy, 1972. "Correlates of Racial Attitudes Among White High School Students," unpublished manuscript.

Walberg, Herbert J., 1969. "Student Achievement and Perception of Class Learning Environments," unpublished manuscript, METCO, Boston.

White Plains High Schools, 1967. "White Plains Racial Balance Plan Evaluation," White Plains, New York.

Wilson, Alan B., 1967. "Educational Consequences of Segregation in a California Community," Appendix C3 in Racial Isolation in the Public Schools, Government Printing Office, U.S. Commission on Civil Rights, Washington, D.C.

FIGURE 1. *Reading Achievement—Elementary.*[a]

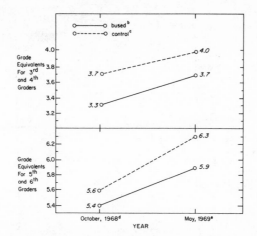

[a]Metropolitan Achievement Tests; no statistically significant gains when bused compared to controls for either age group.
[b]N=88 for Third-Fourth graders and 59 for Fifth-Sixth graders.
[c]N=14 for Third-Fourth graders and 27 for Fifth-Sixth graders.
[d]Full cross-sections for grades:
      3-4: bused 3.4 (N=131); control 3.7 (N=38)—not significant (sd= .96)
      5-6: bused 5.5 (N=90); control 5.4 (N=55)—not significant (sd=1.5).
[e]Full cross-sections for grades:
      3-4: bused 3.7 (N=111); control 3.8 (N=23)—not significant (sd=1.1)
      5-6: bused 6.0 (N=74); control 5.8 (N=52)—not significant (sd=1.7).

FIGURE 2. *Reading Achievement—Junior and Senior High.*

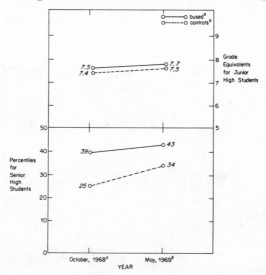

[a]N=123 for junior high and 72 for senior high (no statistically significant changes).
[b]N=27 for junior high and 14 for senior high (no statistically significant changes).
[c]Full cross-section for junior high: bused 7.5 (N=197); control 7.4 (N=74)—n. s. (sd=1.9)
  Full cross-section for senior high: bused 36 (N=160); control 28 (N=35)—n. s. (sd=24).
[d]Full cross-section for junior high: bused 7.7 (N=143); control 7.3 (N=47)—n. s. (sd=1.9)
  Full cross-section for senior high: bused 44 (N=86); control 34 (N=20)—n. s. (sd=25).

FIGURE 3. *Grade Point Average—Junior and Senior High.*

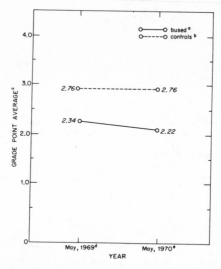

^aN=165; statistically significant change (.01 level).
^bN=23; no significant change.
^cSelf-reported; a grade of A is 4.0, B is 3.0, etc.
^dFull cross-section: bused 2.33 (N=210); control 2.73 (N=59)—significance at .001 level.
^eFull cross-section: bused 2.20 (N=467); control 2.59 (N=228)—significance at .001 level.

FIGURE 4. *Per Cent Wanting a Bachelor's Degree.*

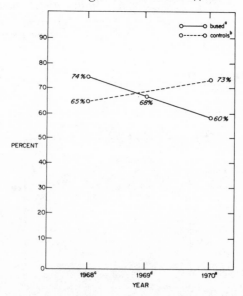

^aN=132; bused changes significantly different from control changes (.02 level).
^bN=34.
^cFull cross-section: bused 71% (N=323); controls 68% (N=87)—not significant.
^dFull cross-section: bused 69% (N=211); controls 68% (N=60)—not significant.
^eFull cross-section: bused 60% (N=486); controls 56% (N=228)—not significant.

FIGURE 5. *Per Cent Expecting a Professional or Technical Occupation.*

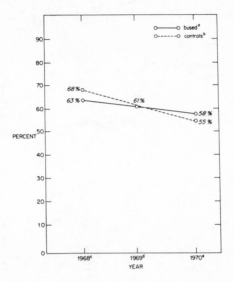

[a]N=130; bused changes not significantly different from control changes.
[b]N=31.
[c]Full cross-section: bused 63% (N=311); controls 55% (N=91)—not significant.
[d]Full cross-section: bused 62% (N=203); controls 52% (N=58)—not significant.
[e]Full cross-section: bused 66% (N=482); controls 66% (N=228)—not significant.

FIGURE 6. *Per Cent Feeling More Intelligent than Classmates.*

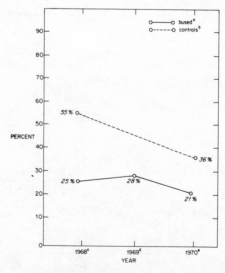

[a]N=130; bused changes not significantly different from control changes.
[b]N=33.
[c]Full cross-section: bused 25% (N=320); controls 47% (N=99)—significance under .01.
[d]Full cross-section: bused 31% (N=211); controls 42% (N=60)—not significant.
[e]Full cross-section: bused 23% (N=483); controls 34% (N=230)—significance under .01.

FIGURE 7. *Per Cent Wanting to be in a School with no More than 50 Per Cent White Students.*

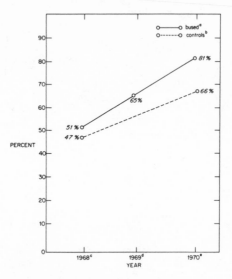

[a]N=133; bused change not significantly different from control change.
[b]N=36.
[c]Full cross-section: bused 56% (N=323); controls 56% (N=97).
[d]Full cross-section: bused 67% (N= 209); controls 59% (N=61)—not significant.
[e]Full cross-section: bused 71% (N=485); controls 62% (N=229)—significance under .001.

FIGURE 8. *Per Cent Favoring Black Power.*

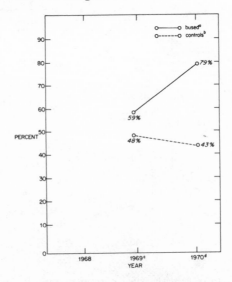

[a]N=167; bused change significantly different from control change (.05 level).
[b]N=21.
[c]Full cross-section: bused 59% (N=211); controls 52% (N=59)—not significant.
[d]Full cross-section: bused 76% (N=479); controls 55% (N=220)—significance under .001.

FIGURE 9. *Separatist Ideology Index.*

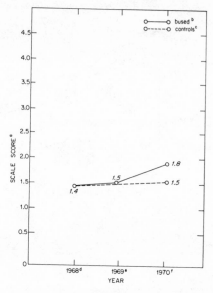

^aA score of 4 indicates strongest separatist feelings; reliability = .76; sd = .8.
^bN=135; bused change significantly greater than control change (under .01 level).
^cN=34.
^dFull cross-section: bused 1.4 (N=324); control 1.4 (N=97)—not significant.
^eFull cross-section: bused 1.6 (N=213); control 1.5 (N=60)—not significant.
^fFull cross-section: bused 1.8 (N=489); control 1.5 (N=230)—significance under .001.

FIGURE 10. *Bused Students Relations with White Students.*

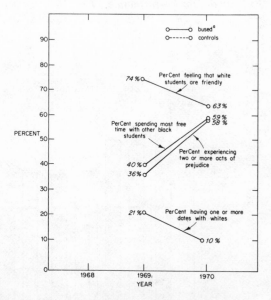

^aN's range from 146 to 159; all changes significant at or under .02 level.

FIGURE 11. *Per Cent Attending College Full-time.*

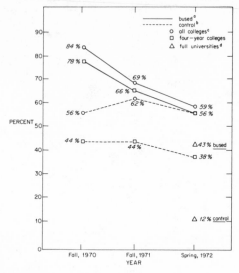

[a]N=32 for all time periods.
[b]N=16 for all time periods.
[c]Includes 2-year junior college; bused change significantly greater than control change (.05 level).
[d]Universities with a graduate program.

FIGURE 12. *Percentage of Bused and Control Students Who Sympathize with the Black Panthers, by College Plans and Academic Performance.*

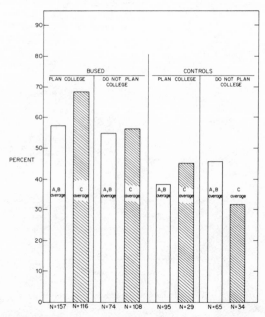

BUSING:
A REVIEW OF THE EVIDENCE

Thomas F. Pettigrew

Elizabeth L. Useem

Clarence Normand

Marshall S. Smith

David Armor's "The Evidence on Busing," (*The Public Interest*, No. 28, Summer 1972) presented a distorted and incomplete review of this politically charged topic. We respect Armor's right to publish his views against "mandatory busing." But we challenge his claim that these views are supported by scientific evidence. A full discussion of our reading of the relevant research would be too lengthy and technical for the non-specialist. We must limit ourselves here to outlining and discussing briefly our principal disagreements with Armor, which center on four major points.

First, his article begins by establishing unrealistically high standards by which to judge the success of school desegregation. "Busing," he claims, works only if it leads—in *one* school year—to increased achievement, aspirations, self-esteem, interracial tolerance, and life opportunities for black children. And "busing" must meet these standards in *all* types of interracial schools; no distinction is made between *merely desegregated* and *genuinely integrated* schools.

This "integration policy model," as it is labeled, is *not* what social scientists who specialize in race relations have been writing about over the past generation. Indeed, Armor's criteria must surely be among the most rigid ever employed for the evaluation of a change program in the history of public education in the United States.

Second, the article presents selected findings from selected studies as "*the* evidence on busing." The bias here is twofold. On the one hand, the few studies mentioned constitute an incomplete list and are selectively negative in results. Unmentioned are at least seven investigations—from busing programs throughout the nation—that meet the methodological criteria for inclusion and report *positive* achievement results for black students. These seven studies are widely known.

On the other hand, only cursory descriptions are provided of the few investigations that are reviewed. Mitigating circumstances surrounding black responses to desegregation are not discussed. For example, we are not told that educational services for the transported black pupils were actually *reduced* with the onset of desegregation in three of the cited cities. In addition, negative findings consistent with the paper's anti-busing thesis are emphasized, while positive findings from these same cities are either obscured or simply ignored. Newer studies from three of the cited cities showing more positive results are not discussed.

Positive findings are also obscured by the utilization of an unduly severe standard. The achievement gains of black students in desegregated schools are often compared with white gains, rather than with the achievement of black students in black schools. But such a standard ignores the possibility that *both* racial groups can make more meaningful educational advances in interracial schools. Indeed, this possibility actually occurs in three of the cities mentioned by Armor. Yet he does not inform us of this apparent dual success of desegregation; instead, "busing" is simply rated a failure because the black children did not far outgain the improving white children.

Third, the paper's anti-busing conclusions rest primarily on the findings from one short-term study conducted by Armor himself. This investigation focused on a voluntary busing program in metropolitan Boston called METCO. Yet this study is probably the weakest reported in the paper. Our reexamination of its data finds that it has extremely serious methodological problems.

Two major problems concern deficiencies of the control group. To test the effects of "busing" and school desegregation, a control group should obviously consist exclusively of children who neither are "bused" nor attend desegregated schools. But our check of this critical point reveals that this is not the case. Among the 82 control students used to test the achievement effects of METCO at all 10 grade levels, we obtained records on 55. Only 21 of these 55 actually attended segregated schools in the tested year of 1968-69. Many of the 34 (62 percent) desegregated children by necessity utilized buses and other forms of transportation to get to school.

Incredible as it sounds, then, Armor compared a group of children who were bused to desegregated schools with another group of children which included many who *also* were bused to desegregated schools. Not surprisingly, then, he found few differences between them. But this complete lack of adequate controls renders his METCO research of no scientific interest in the study of "busing" and school desegregation. Since this METCO investigation furnished the chief "evidence" against "busing," Armor's conclusions are severely challenged by this point alone.

Serious, too, is an enormous non-response rate in the second test administration, a problem alluded to by Armor only in a footnote. For the elementary students, only 51 percent of the eligible METCO students and 28 percent of the eligible "control" students took part in both of the achievement test sessions. The achievement results for junior and senior high students are also rendered virtually meaningless by the participation of only 44 percent of the eligible METCO students and 20 percent of the eligible "control" students. Compare these percentages to the survey standard of 70 to 80 percent, and one can appreicate the magnitude of the possible selection bias introduced into the METCO results by the widespread lack of student participation. Efforts to compensate for these high non-response rates through the use of cross-sectional samples that also suffer from extensive non-response are insufficient.

There are other problems in the METCO study. Some children were included who initially performed as well as the test scoring allowed and therefore could not possibly demonstrate "improvement"; in fact, these pupils comprise one sixth of all the junior high pupils tested for achievement gains in reading. Moreover, the conditions for the third administration of the attitude tests were different for the METCO students and the "controls": The former took the tests at school and the latter took them at home with their parents as proctors. Even apart from the severe control group problems, then, the faulty research design makes any conclusions about differences in racial attitudes between the two groups hazardous.

The inadequate discussion of the METCO study in Armor's article makes it virtually impossible for even the discerning reader to evaluate it properly. We uncovered its many errors only from unpublished earlier materials and from reanalyzing the data ourselves. The METCO discussion is inadequate in other ways. Differential statistical standards are employed, with less rigorous standards applied to findings congruent with the article's anti-busing thesis; attitude differences among METCO schools are not shown; and misleading claims of consistency with other research findings are made.

From this assortment of "evidence," Armor concludes authoritatively that "busing" fails on four out of five counts. It does not lead, he argues, to improved achievement, grades, aspirations, and racial attitudes for black children; yet, despite these failures, he admits that desegregated schools do seem somehow to lead more often to college enrollment for black students.

The picture is considerably more positive, as well as more complex, than Armor paints it. For example, when specified school conditions are attained, research has repeatedly indicated that desegregated schools improve the academic performance of black pupils. Other research has demonstrated that rigidly high and unrealistic aspirations actually deter learning; thus, a slight lowering of such aspirations by school desegregation can lead to better achievement and cannot be regarded as a failure of "busing." Moreover, "militancy" and "black consciousness and solidarity" are not negative characteristics, as Armor's article asserts, and their alleged development in desegregated schools could well be regarded as a further success, not a failure, of "busing." Finally, the evidence that desegregated education sharply expands the life opportunities of black children is more extensive than he has indicated.

Consequently, Armor's sweeping policy conclusion against "mandatory busing" is neither substantiated nor warranted. Not only does it rely upon impaired and incomplete "evidence," but in a real sense his paper is not about "busing" at all, much less "mandatory busing." Three of the cities discussed—among them Boston, the subject of Armor's own research—had *voluntary*, not "mandatory busing." "Busing" was never cited as an independent variable, and many of the desegregation studies discussed involved some children who were not bused to reach their interracial schools. Indeed, in Armor's own investigation of METCO, some of the METCO children were not bused while many of the controls were.

Fourth, objections must be raised to the basic assumptions about racial change that undergird the entire article. Public school desegregation is regarded as largely a technical matter, a matter for social scientists more than for the courts. Emphasis is placed solely on the adaptive abilities of black children rather than on their constitutional rights. Moreover, the whole national context of individual and institutional racism is conveniently ignored, and interracial contact under any conditions is assumed to be "integration."

Now we wish to pursue these basic points in more detail.

UNREALISTIC STANDARDS FOR JUDGING THE EFFECTS OF "BUSING"

The article advances an "integration policy model" which it claims grew out of social science and guided "the integration movement." The model allegedly maintained that *all* school desegregation would result in improved black achievement, aspirations, self-esteem, racial attitudes, and educational and occupational opportunities (Armor, p. 96). This interpretation of "the integration policy model" is at sharp variance with what specialists in this field have been writing over the past generation.(1) The fundamental premise of social scientists over these years was that racial segregation as it is typically imposed in the United States leads directly to a multitude of negative effects not only for black America but for the nation at large. (The evidence for this premise is extensive, and Armor does not contest the premise.) But social scientists have not made the error of contending that because enforced racial segregation has negative effects, *all* racial desegregation will have positive effects. It requires little imagination to think of hostile conditions of school desegregation that would limit its benefits for both races.

At the heart of this misconception is a persistent misreading of Gordon Allport's (1954) theory of intergroup contact. Armor cites a quotation from Allport delineating the crucial conditions that he held to be essential before positive effects could be expected from intergroup contact: equal status, common goals, institutional supports, and a non-competitive atmosphere that is likely to lead to "the perception of common interests and common humanity." Yet Armor summarizes this quotation by stating: "The clear key to breaking the vicious circle, then, was contact." This is *not* what Allport wrote; the key, Allport argued, is contact *under particular conditions*.

Later in his article Armor adds a brief discussion of one of these condtions—equal status between the two groups. Allport and other contact theorists have maintained that this condition is met by equal status, dignity, and access to resources *within* the contact situation itself (e.g., Pettigrew, 1971). Armor reinterprets this condition so that it is met only if the two groups bring equal societal status *to* the situation, a rigorous test indeed in a society where racial discrimination has long been endemic. We know of no relevant contact research that supports this reinterpretation of the theory, and vague references to conflict in Northern Ireland and the Middle East hardly suffice as evidence. But armed with his own reinterpretation, Armor (p. 111) writes: "Therefore, we have to question whether integration programs for black and white children can ever fulfill the equal status condition as long as socio-economic and academic inequalities are not eliminated." Here the misreading of Allport's contact theory is fashioned into not only an explanation of presumed "negative" results from interracial schools but a not-so-subtle rationale for at best gradualism and at worst a return to racially segregated education throughout the nation.

The basic weakness, then, in this description of an "integration policy model" is that it assumes positive results for *all* interracial schools rather than for just those meeting the conditions for optimal contact. This erroneous assumption is best illustrated by reference to the chief policy document relied upon by Armor: *Racial Isolation in the Public Schools*, issued by the U.S. Commission on Civil Rights (1967). The quotation Armor cites from this report emphasizes the harmful effects of racially isolated schooling, and it does not specify all of the five hypotheses which he somehow deduces from it. That the Commission clearly understood that interracial schools in and of themselves are not necessarily effective schools is demonstrated by the following passage which was not quoted:

> Whether school desegregation is effective depends on a number of factors. These include the leadership given by State and local officials; the application of the plan to all schools in the community; the measures taken to minimize the possibility of racial friction in the newly desegregated schools; the maintenance or improvement of educational standards; the desegregation of classes within the schools as well as the schools themselves, and the availability of supportive services for individual students who lag in achievement.

The Commission Report discusses these factors in detail for over eight pages, factors neither mentioned nor measured by Armor. "The integration policy model," then, sets up unrealistic standards for judging the effects of "busing" by ignoring the conditions specified by the two principal sources cited. Its five criteria for success constitute a "straw man," far exceeding the standards applied for the evaluation of other educational programs.

The racial desegregation of schools is not a static but a complex, dynamic process. To evaluate it fairly, the critical conditions under which it takes place must be assessed. For this purpose, it is important to distinguish between desegregation and integration. Desegregation is achieved by simply ending segregation and bringing blacks and whites together; it implies nothing about the quality of the interracial interaction. Integration involves Allport's four conditions for positive intergroup contact, cross-racial acceptance, and equal dignity and access to resources for both racial groups.

The neglect of this distinction besets not only Armor's theoretical contentions but his empirical ones as well. No effort is made to look inside of the schools at the *process* of desegregation. The cursory descriptions of the "busing" investigations tell virtually nothing about the conditions of interracial contact that prevailed. (Indeed, a few of the initial reports of these studies failed to describe contact conditions.) For example, we should have been informed by Armor that transported black children in some Riverside schools arrive and leave earlier than the untransported white children and that they have separate reading classes—hardly practices likely to generate interracial contact and lead to integration (Singer, 1972). And we might have been told that minority students in Riverside who were most likely to be in interracial classrooms (high-ability students) performed far better after desegregation than before (Purl, 1971).

In fact, in his Detroit deposition for school segregation, Armor admitted that he had no measures or knowledge in his own study of the METCO schools of such crucial factors as teacher expectations and preparation, the racial composition of the faculties, ability tracking practices, and curriculum changes. A review of "the evidence on busing" is misleading at best without consideration of these indicators of the desegregation versus integration distinction.

A BIASED AND INCOMPLETE SELECTION OF STUDIES

Armor's article makes no attempt to review all of the available evidence on "busing," as its title implies. Instead, the reader is told about only a small number of studies, selected with an apparent bias toward those reporting few positive effects. One hint of this selection is found in Armor's footnote 1, where we learn that he arbitrarily excludes the entire southern United States from his purview, though this severe restriction is not indicated either in his title or his conclusions against "mandatory busing." This unexplained exclusion seems unwarranted, for the bulk of court-ordered "mandatory busing" has occurred in the South.

Armor omits at least *seven* key desegregation investigations—only one of which is from the South—that reach conclusions in conflict with those of his paper. All seven of these desegregation programs involved "busing," and all seven of the studies meet the paper's two stated criteria for inclusion—longitudinal data and an adequate control group. Table 1 summarizes these neglected research reports. Though five of them spanned only one school year, all seven reach *positive* conclusions concerning the effects of school desegregation upon the academic performance of black children. Moreover, none of them found that the process lowered white academic performance. No matter how Armor might wish to view these studies in retrospect, there was no reason for their omission in a paper than claimed to present "*the* evidence on busing."

Space limitations prevent a discussion here of these neglected investigations, but five points should be made about them. First, a number of them share methodological problems with the studies that Armor did choose to discuss. Indeed, reviewers of this research literature have uniformly found it methodologically weak (Matthai, 1968; O'Reilly, 1970; St. John, 1970; Weinberg, 1968). Second, these seven by no means exhaust the relevant research literature that meets the paper's dual criteria for inclusion. There are studies on desegregation without busing that reveal positive achievement effects (e.g., Anderson, 1966; Fortenberry, 1959; Frary and Goolsby, 1970). There are a few others that were also left out that found no significant achievement gains associated with desegregation (e.g., Fox, 1966, 1967, 1968). From the perspective of the desegregation versus integration distinction, this mixed picture is precisely what one would expect. Third, these seven studies are not obscure reports; all but the more recent Goldsboro and Sacramento studies are cited in one or more of the standard reviews available on the topic (Matthai, 1968; O'Reilly, 1970; St. John, 1970; Weinberg, 1968).

Fourth, the positive achievement effects revealed by these studies are often not just statistically significant (Armor's criterion) but, more important, are educationally significant as well. The study from Buffalo by Banks and DiPasquale (1969), for example, found a 2.5 month achievement advantage for the desegregated children. Over a 12-year school career, were such an advantage to be replicated each year, this would constitute 2.5 extra years of achievement—a critical addition that could mean the difference between functional illiteracy and marketable skills. Finally, these seven studies do not measure the "pure" effects of desegration any more than those cited by Armor. Probably there are no instances of school desegregation that are not confounded with curriculum changes, school quality, and other educational alterations. But our point is made: The few studies mentioned in Armor's article constitute an incomplete list and are selectively negative in results.

The cursory reviews of the few studies that Armor did select for attention allow only biased and incomplete descriptions. Since his article never probes the process going on inside the schools, it repeatedly omits mitigating circumstances surrounding black responses to desegregation. For example, no mention is made of the fact that educational services for the transported black students in Ann Arbor, Riverside, and Berkeley were actually *reduced* with the onset of desegregation (Carrigan, 1969; Frelow, 1971; and Purl, 1971). Nor is there any indication that Riverside initially placed many of its bused minority children in the same classrooms, and often with low-achieving white children (Henrick, 1968). No "integration model," not even the new one devised by Armor, is fairly tested under such conditions.

Moreover, the positive findings that favor desegregation in these studies are often obscured or simply ignored by Armor. In the case of Hartford, for instance, only Wechsler I.Q. data are cited, while extensive results from the

TABLE 1. *Seven Neglected Desegregation Investigations*

STUDY		DESIGN				ACHIEVEMENT RESULTS	
PLACE	AUTHOR(S)	GRADE LEVEL	TYPE OF COMPARISON	CONTROL VARIABLES	TIME OF DESEGREGATION	FOR BLACK CHILDREN	FOR WHITE CHILDREN (IF TESTED)
SOUTHERN DESEGREGATION							
Goldsboro, N.C.	King & Mayer (1971)[1] McCullough (1972)	7-11 cohort	White students and trend during segregation	Convergence curves for regression to mean effects and pre-desegregation trends	2 years	Statistically significant gains in reading closing part of black/white differential; gains in math scores do not close racial gap; gains greatest for initially high achievers	Both reading and math gains; gains greatest for high achievers
SUBURBAN BUSING PROGRAMS							
Newark-Verona, N.J.	Zdep & Joyce (1967)	1-2	Comparable non-transfers	—	1 year	Statistically significantly greater total achievement gains for desegrated in both grades	No negative effects (only difference favors the desegregated)
Rochester-West Iron-dequoit, N.Y.	Rock *et al.* (1968)	K-2	Comparable non-transfers	Teachers' ratings of ability	3 years	Statistically significantly greater verbal, reading, and math achievement gains on 13 of 27 comparisons for desegregated; no significant differences on remaining 14 comparisons	No negative effects (only differences favor the desegregated)

TABLE 1. *Continued*

	STUDY		DESIGN				ACHIEVEMENT RESULTS	
PLACE	AUTHOR(S)	GRADE LEVEL	TYPE OF COMPARISON	CONTROL VARIABLES	TIME OF DESEGRE-GATION		FOR BLACK CHILDREN	FOR WHITE CHILDREN (IF TESTED)
NORTHERN CENTRAL CITY DESEGREGATION								
Buffalo, N.Y.	Banks & DiPasquale (1969)	5-7	Comparable non-transfers	—	1 year		2½ months greater achieve-ment gain for the desegregated	No negative effects
New York, N.Y.	Slone (1968)	4	Comparable non-transfers	—	1 year		Statistically significantly greater math achievement gains, and somewhat greater reading gains (p<.10), for desegregated	No negative effects
Philadel-phia, Pa.	Laird & Weeks (1966)	4-6	Comparable non-transfers	I.Q., grade and sex	1 year		Statistically significantly greater reading, and some-what greater math, achieve-ment gains for desegregated in fourth and fifth grades	—
Sacramento, Cal.	Morrison & Stivers (1971)	2-6	Comparable non-transfers	—	1 year		Statistically significantly greater gains on three of ten comparisons (5 classes on 2 tests) and greater gains on 6 more, for desegregated	—

[1] Similar results for a cohort of second through fifth grade students have also been obtained in Goldsboro. After two years of desegregated education the *standardized* verbal and mathematical computation achievement scores of both the black and white students had risen. The verbal gains, though not the mathematical computation gains, closed the racial differential slightly. Robert R. Mayer, University of North Carolina at Chapel Hill, personal communication.

Primary Mental Abilities Test and measures of school achievement go undiscussed. When all three types of tests are considered together, a clear pattern of larger gains for the transported children emerges for all four grades from kindergarten through the third grade (Mahan, 1968). Likewise, black pupils in Ann Arbor attained a substantially higher mean I.Q. after one year of desegregation, but this fact is lost from sight by the use of a white comparison. A range of interesting results from Riverside is also omitted. Purl (1971) found that: (a) Bused students who were more dispersed in the classes of their receiving schools outperformed those who—through ability grouping or other means—were clustered in near-segregation style. (b) While the mean achievement of minority pupils with low initial ability scores declined relative to grade level, the achievement of minority pupils with high initial ability scores rose in the desegregated schools. (c) Minority children transported to schools characterized by higher achievement of the receiving white students gain significantly more than comparable minority children transported to schools characterized by low achievement, an effect not linked to the social class levels of the receiving students. (d) The one group of bused minority students who began their schooling in interracial schools achieved better than those who had first experienced segregated education.

The incomplete descriptions also fail to reveal major methodological weaknesses in these cited studies. The Berkeley (1971a) investigation, as a case in point, utilized different tests for comparison over time, precisely the same defect for which an investigation in Rochester (1971) showing a number of positive results is rejected without discussion. The White Plains (1967) investigation employs inadequate control groups drawn from earlier time periods, a faulty procedure that confounds the effects of events over time with those of desegregation.(2) Indeed, the negative conclusions of a follow-up study in Ann Arbor are given without recording the fact that it failed to meet either of the criteria purportedly used for inclusion, for it had no control group whatsoever nor did it gather longitudinal data on the same test (Aberdeen, 1969; Carrigan, 1969).

Finally, several newer reports on these same cities that present results favorable to desegregation are not utilized. Mahan and Mahan (1971), for example, provide more refined analyses on the Hartford achievement data. Pooling the first, third, and fifth grades,(3) they show that the desegregated children in Project Concern do significantly better after two years than their comparable segregated controls on the Wechsler I.Q. and on both the verbal and quantitative scores of the Primary Mental Abilities Test.

Though he cited a Master's thesis on New Haven desegregation, Armor failed to cite a better-known doctoral dissertaion on the same city.(4) Samuels (1971) studied 138 black students who had all attended inner-city kindergartens in 1969 and then were assigned *randomly* to one of three conditions: bused into suburban schools, received intensive compensatory education in New Haven schools, or attended regular New Haven schools. After two years, Samuels found that the bused children possessed significantly higher reading scores than the two control groups as well as higher word knowledge scores that approach statistical significance (p >.07). Their self-image scores were slightly higher, but not significantly different. Comparisons on word analysis and mathematics yielded no significant differences.

In Berkeley, Frelow (1971) studied the third and fourth grade achievement of poor children, most of them black, over a six-year period that witnessed rapid changes in the city's schools. Though this design, like that used in White Plains, lacks contemporaneous controls, he found that achievement scores rose significantly after the introduction of compensatory programs and went slightly higher still after desegregation despite a reduction in services. Frelow concludes that "when gains are measured against level of instructional services, desegregation produces the most prominent achievement results."

The contention that black children will learn more in integrated than in segregated schools is not tested when black data are compared with those of white control groups. Moreover, the use of a desegregated white control group ignores the possibility that *both* whites and blacks could benefit significantly from integration without "the racial gap" in achievement closing at all. As a matter of fact, precisely this possibility occurs in Riverside, Berkeley, and Ann Arbor—though this is not mentioned by Armor and is allowed to mask black gains in desegregated schools.

For Riverside, Armor reports that even for the fourth-grade group that had been desegregated since kindergarten "the minority/white gap had not diminished. . . ." But actually the white test scores being used for a comparison had improved after desegregation relative to national norms (Purl, 1971). Thus, the fact that the minority students held the "gap" constant represents improvement; this is indicated, too, by these minority students' relative gains in grade equivalents.

For Berkeley, Armor reports in a footnote that "black achievement is as far behind (or *further* behind) white achievement after two years of integration as before integration." But *both* white and black grade equivalents in grades one, two, and three went up across age cohorts after two years of desegregation; yet since they rose in virtually equal amounts, the "black/white gap" was not narrowed (Berkeley, 1971a, 1971b). The measure here is grade equivalents, not percentiles. Thus, keeping "the racial gap" from expanding is an accomplishment in itself for desegregation, since the typical result of segregated schools is an ever-widening "racial gap" in grade equivalents (Coleman *et al.*, 1966; Mosteller and Moynihan, 1972).

The most extreme case of this misleading use of white controls, however, occurs for Ann Arbor (Carrigan, 1969). Here the bused black students were "a multi-problem group" with a greater incidence of "general health problems" and behavioral "problems requiring special professional help." Yet they gained an average of 3.86 I.Q. points during their first year of desegregation. They were compared with generally high-status white children, many of whom came from academic families, who gained an average of 4.28 I.Q. points. "Busing" failed, in Armor's terms, because "the racial gap" did not close. But can a program which utilizes fewer services with a multi-problem group of youngsters, and yet is associated with a nearly four-point average increase in I.Q. during one school year, be unquestionably ruled a failure? We think not, even if these "bused" pupils did not gain more than high-achieving white youngsters from a university community.

This point represents a crucial difference between our perspective and Armor's. We believe it to be unrealistic to expect any type of educational innovation to close most of the racial differential in achievement while gross racial disparities, especially economic ones, remain in American society. Furthermore, we know of no social scientists who ever claimed school desegregation alone could close most of the differential. We are pleased to note the many instances where effective desegregation has apparently benefited the achievement of both black and white children, and where over a period of years it appears to close approximately a fourth of the differential.

But to insist that "mandatory busing" must close most of the achievement differential by itself in a short time or be abolished is, to understate the case, an extreme position. Indeed, Armor himself has wavered on this point. In *The Public Interest* he wrote: "The ideal control group, of course, would consist of black students who are identical to the integrated students in every way except for the integrated experience" (Armor, p. 97), though white students in the same school constituted an "adequate" control. Later, however, while testifying in support of anti-busing legislation before the Senate Subcommittee on Education, he used white pupils as the critical comparison. This stern criterion leads to some strange conclusions. A desegregation program that dramatically raises the achievement levels of both racial groups is judged a failure when it does not close most of the racial disparity, but another desegregation program that entirely closes the gap by raising the blacks' scores and *lowering* the whites' scores would have to be deemed a success!

SERIOUS WEAKNESSES IN THE METCO RESEARCH

Armor's article relies most heavily upon his own research on Boston's suburban program known as METCO. Far greater space—including a dozen graphs—is devoted to the METCO research than to all of the other research combined; and the METCO work is the only investigation that is relied upon for support of all five of the conclusions concerning the effects of "busing." Yet a careful reanalysis of these METCO data reveals a host of serious weaknesses that center on five concerns: (a) the unrepresentativeness of the METCO program, and problems regarding (b) the control group, (c) the sample, (d) test administration, and (e) the analysis.

a. *Unrepresentativeness of METCO program.* Not only is "busing" not "mandatory" in METCO, but the program is highly atypical of desegregation efforts with "busing" around the nation. METCO is a voluntary program, and it has disproportionately attracted middleclass black students. This class bias may help explain why METCO children in the first year of the program attained a higher average I.Q. than the white national average (Archibald, 1967) and why in Figures 1 and 2 of Armor's article all 10 grade levels show relatively high achievement scores. Moreover, METCO children comprise only a minute fraction of their student bodies, with less than four percent in any one school in 1969. Black faculty are rare in virtually all of the METCO schools. Indeed, some METCO schools have had all-white staffs, and until recently even all of the bus drivers were white. Thus, given METCO's "tokenism" in students and staff, as well as its social class bias, direct generalizations from this program to "busing" throughout the United States appear dubious at best.

b. *Control group problems.* The most serious weakness of the METCO research involves the students who were employed as "controls." The study's design obviously requires that none of these control students were either desegregated of "bused." But a careful review of the available records reveals that this essential condition is not met.(5) Among the 41 "control" youngsters at the elementary level, we obtained records on 17. Only seven of these 17 pupils were actually attending segregated schools during 1968-69, while 10 (59 percent) were attending desegregated schools. Similarly, among the 38 (out of a total of 41) "controls" at the junior and senior high levels whose records we obtained, only 14 were in segregated schools during the tested year, while 24 (63 percent) were attending desegregated schools.

All told, then, of the 55 students whose records were secured, 34 (62 percent) actually went to desegregated schools and many of them used buses and other means of transportation.(6) Even if we assume that all 27 students whose records were unavailable went to segregated schools (an unlikely possibility), these data still mean that at least 41 percent (34/82) of the "control" students were in fact experiencing a racially desegregated education. Indeed, these desegregated "controls" were generally in schools with a greater interracial mixture than those attended by the METCO children.

This failure of the METCO study to have an adequate control group cannot be overemphasized. It means that *all* of the METCO comparisons between the METCO and "control" children in Armor's article are not valid indications of any differences attributable to "busing" or school desegregation. For such comparisions may also reflect the different effects of suburban versus inner-city desegregation and token versus substantial desegregation. In short, we believe this weakness alone eliminates the METCO study from being relevant to "the evidence on busing," and makes our further criticisms of the study almost superfluous.

Other problems involve the use of siblings of METCO students as "controls." "This design feature by no means guarantees the equating of the groups," wrote Herbert Walberg (1969) in the initial write-up of this investigation, "since there may be bias in the family's choice of the child to be bused. . . ." Indeed, there is potential bias in the selection by families, but the direction is not clear. The academically superior child might be chosen more often by his parents; or, as

METCO officials suspect, the child having difficulties in Boston's schools might be chosen more often. Moreover, the use of siblings for controls tends to confound sex, grade level, and age with family climate and social class.

c. *Sample problems.* The METCO research suffers, too, from both small numbers and a severe loss of eligible subjects. Limited sample size makes finding statistically significant differences in achievement between the experimental and "control" groups less likely; or, put differently, small sample sizes aid in supporting the anti-desegregation thesis of the article. The extent of this problem is shown in Table 2, which provides the sample sizes by grade level. The question arises as to how large the METCO group differences in achievement would have had to be before the sample sizes employed could have detected a statistically significant difference even at the .05 level of confidence? By our calculation, the answer at the junior high level, for example, is that the METCO students would have had to gain at least 0.4 of a grade *more* in average achievement on the test norms than the "control" group.(7) This is an unrealistic expectation over a duration of only *seven* months, especially for comparisons among children who are close to grade level. An educationally meaningful average gain difference over such a short period would have been 0.2 of a grade more for the METCO students. But this would have required sample sizes of roughly 200 in each group to have reached statistical significance for a two-tailed test. Instead, only 125 METCO and 27 "control" junior high students

TABLE 2.   *METCO Sample Sizes by Grade Level and Type of School*

Grade Level	METCO[1]	"Control"	Segregated	Desegregated	Unavailable
			Type of School Attended By "Controls"		
3rd & 4th	88	14	2	3	9
5th & 6th	59	27	5	7	15
Elementary School Totals	**147**	**41**	**7**	**10**	**24**
7th	47	11	6	5	0
8th	31	10	4	5	1
9th	47	6	1	4	1
Junior High School Totals	**125**	**27**	**11**	**14**	**2**
10th	53	4	0	3	1
11th	18	8	3	5	0
12th	1	2	0	2	0
Senior High School Totals	**72**	**14**	**3**	**10**	**1**

[1] These data are taken from our reconstructed data tapes. Armor lists 123 junior high METCO students in his Figure 2, but he inadvertently dropped two cases.

were tested. The same point can be made about the other grade levels. We conclude, therefore, that the criterion of statistical significance was inappropriate for evaluating the METCO program when the sample sizes were so small.

The loss of subjects occurred in two stages. Among the elementary students, in the first test administration in October 1968, there was a 23 percent loss of eligible METCO students and a 35 percent loss of eligible "control" students.(8) In the second test administration in May 1969, 34 percent of the METCO and 56 percent of the "control" students who had taken the tests seven months earlier did not retake them. Combined, then, the achievement results on these students included only 51 percent of the eligible METCO and 28 percent of the eligible "control" participants. The situation was even worse for the junior and senior high students, whose achievement results were based on only 44 percent of the eligible METCO and only 20 percent of the eligible "control" participants. Furthermore, only eight percent of the "controls" took part in all three test administrations.

Contrast these percentages with Useem's (1971, 1972) response rate of 87 percent in her study of white students in METCO schools. Compare them, too, with the accepted survey research standard of at least a 70 to 80 percent response rate, and one can appreciate the high level of potential bias introduced by this loss of subjects from Armor's study. An attempt to compensate for these impaired data by utilizing cross-sectional results is not an adequate remedy for many reasons, some of which are provided by Armor himself when he condemns cross-sectional investigations. Besides, there was a considerable loss of eligible subjects, and thus potential bias, in the cross-sectional data as well.

d. *Test administration problems.* "The control group," Armor argued in his Detroit deposition for school segregation, "has to be measured in the same way that the treated group is." He further maintained that "we must measure them before the treatment, and put one through the treatment and one not, to assess the effect of a program." We agree, but his METCO research failed on both counts.

The third testing in May 1970, which involved attitudes but not achievement, took place under markedly contrasting conditions for the experimental and control groups. While the METCO children answered the questions in school, the control children answered them at home through a mailed questionnaire that explicitly requested the parents to serve as proctors. This procedure risks two related sources of bias. A wealth of research had demonstrated how different situations can lead to sharply different responses; and the home administration of the controls' testing opens the possibility for family members to influence the answers directly.

Armor expresses amazement that the METCO children revealed as a group more militant and ideological responses than the "control" children, but the differential testing administrations provide a possible explanation. Repeated surveys indicate that young black peers at school are far more likely to be militant and ideological than older parents at home (Campbell and Schuman, 1968; Goldman, 1970); and research in social psychology has shown that such different situational influences can have a sharp effect on group-linked attitudes (Charters and Newcomb, 1952).

On the second point, measuring the groups *before* the treatment, the METCO research also fails. The METCO pupils were measured initially in October 1968 *after* all of them had begun for a month or more their year in the METCO school. Moreover, 45 percent of the METCO children were not beginning "the treatment" of suburban eduation, for they had already been in the program for either one or two years.

Finally, studies utilizing achievement tests require well-motivated students who are trying to do their best. We learn from those in attendance at both the first and second test administrations, however, that motivation was apparently not high. And no wonder. The students, METCO and control, had no special incentive for taking the lengthy tests on a holiday in a Boston technical school described by Walberg (1969) as "an old, run-down, ill-cared-for building." This low level of motivation probably accounts for the small turnout for the second test.

e. *Analysis problems.* Even if there were no serious control group and sample problems, numerous data errors place Armor's analysis of the METCO results in serious question. One child was included who apparently did not take the verbal test initially at all; his post-test scores were then treated as a total gain from a base of zero. A sixth (25 of 151) of the junior high students initially scored virtually as high as the achievement test scoring allowed. Thus, this "ceiling effect" made it impossible for their post-test scores to advance, and their performance was treated as showing "no gain." Such problems, together with clerical errors, help explain why such talented children are shown to make such slight achievement gains in Armor's Figures 1 and 2. But given the irreparable control group and sampling problems, no purpose is served by a reanalysis of these data that corrects for these errors of analysis and data handling.

The reader is not told enough in Armor's article to evaluate the METCO research fully. Most of our critical comments are based on information gleaned from a reanalysis of the raw data, the examination of unpublished papers on the research (Archibald, 1967; Walberg, 1969; and Armor and Genova, 1970), and a review of Armor's court testimony concerning the research. The discussion of the METCO work is also inadequate in other ways: (a) Differential statistical standards are employed; (b) attitude differences between METCO schools are not shown; and (c) misleading claims of consistency with other research findings are advanced.

a. *Differential statistical standards.* Rigid standards of statistical significance are uniformly applied to findings that favor school desegregation. Findings of positive effects in other studies that approach statistical significance are summarily dismissed as "not significant." But these standards are relaxed considerably when findings interpreted as negative to school desegregation are discussed. For instance, Figure 3 is provided to show how the grades of METCO's junior and senior high school pupils declined slightly, and this finding in emphasized in the conclusions (Armor, p. 109). Yet there is no significant

FIGURE 1. *Attitudes of METCO and White Students Toward the METCO Program by High School*[1]

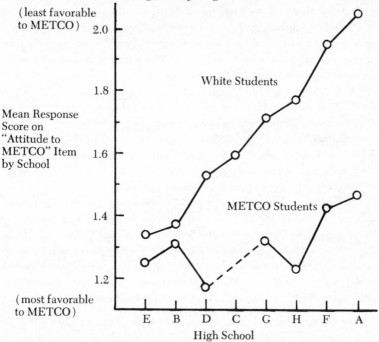

1 Data from METCO students in School C were not available. The Figure is taken from Useem (1971).

difference between the METCO and the control groups on changes in grades. Similarly, a slightly greater increase among METCO students in wanting a school with no more than half-white student bodies is emphasized (Armor, pp. 102-103). Though "... the differential change is not statistically significant," Figure 7 is devoted to it. And later in the conclusions, this finding is utilized without qualification as part of the evidence that "bused" black students have become more supportive of "black separatism."

b. *Attitude differences between METCO schools are not shown.* Armor's article assumes that the METCO program consisted of the same "treatment" for all of the children participating in it. Consequently, attitude differences across METCO schools were not shown; nor, as noted earlier, were any variables utilized to take into account what type of educational programs were actually occurring inside the various METCO schools.

Actually, of course, there are as many different METCO programs underway as there are separate METCO schools. But consider the contrasting policy implications of providing only the total results as opposed to school-by-school results. Suppose a particular school program aimed at improving racial attitudes were attempted in eight schools, and that the overall effect was minimal. The policy implication would be to regard the program a disappointment and to consider abandoning it. Suppose further that a meaningful effect had in fact been registered in all but two schools, but that attitudes in these two were so unfavorable that they virtually obscured the favorable attitudes of the other six in the total data. Now the policy implication *from the same data* would be to regard the program as encouraging and to find out how to change the deviant two to make them more like the successful six schools. In short, the variability across schools is a critical consideration in judging a program.

Our Figure 1, from Useem (1971), shows that a situation similar to this existed for the METCO program in 1969. Note that schools F and A evince by far the most anti-METCO sentiment among both white and black pupils. Note, too, that black attitudes toward METCO are consistently more favorable than those of whites, though there is a positive relationship across schools in the attitudes of the two groups. With such wide differences between METCO schools, how can a simple judgment of success or failure be passed upon the entire program?

c. *Misleading claims of consistency with other research findings are advanced.* Two studies are cited as providing supporting evidence for the METCO results; but their descriptions are so incomplete as to be highly misleading. Useem's (1971, 1972) METCO investigation is given as evidence for how interracial contact in METCO schools leads to worse race relations. Her complete findings, however, point to a different conclusion, and we shall return to these findings shortly. The other citation refers to Armor's earlier reanalysis of the Coleman report data:

> An extensive reanalysis of the Coleman data showed that even without controlling for social class factors, "naturally" integrated (i.e., nonbused) black sixth-grade groups were still one and one-half standard deviations behind white groups in the same schools, compared to a national gap of two standard deviations. This means that, assuming the Coleman data to be correct, the best that integration could do would be to move the average black group from the 2nd percentile to the 7th percentile (on the white scale, where the average white group is at the 50th percentile). (Armor, p. 100)

Such a statement is extremely misleading, and it requires clarification. It appears to assert that there is some upper limit on the possible achievement gains through "busing" of blacks relative to whites. No such assertion is possible. Moreover, the evidence for this claim is based on data from groups of children who are in general not bused and for whom there are only Coleman's cross-sectional data. The statement, then, implies a causal relation from cross-sectional data, a practice correctly condemned earlier by Armor. The statement further implies that there is some intrinsic, if unspecified, connection between the gains possible from "busing" and the inferred gains estimated from cross-sectional data.

More misleading still is the use of group percentiles. Technically, it may be correct that the average black group mean in desegregated sixth grades is only at the 7th percentile when compared with the means of white groups. But the obvious misinterpretation that can easily arise is that the average individual black student in a desegregated school is only at the 7th percentile compared with the individual white student norms. Such an interpretation is patently wrong. Though Armor can argue that his statement is technically accurate, we feel that he has an obligation to inform the lay reader fully so that such a misinterpretation could not occur.

The misleading statement utilizes standard deviations based on group means rather than on individual scores. Group standard deviations are invariably smaller than standard deviations based on the individuals within the groups. Instead of the average black group in desegregated sixth grades being at the 7th percentile of white group norms then, we estimate that the average black individual in desegregated sixth grades ranks between the 25th and 30th percentiles of white individual norms.(9) Indeed, Figure 2 of Armor's article shows that the black senior high students in the METCO research average between the 25th and 43rd percentiles in individual reading achievement.

Armor concludes that "busing" fails on four of the five standards he alone sets for it. One of these alleged failures concerns the academic achievement of black students. From the selected findings of selected studies, Armor concludes that desegregation research throughout the nation has typically found no statistically significant enhancement of black achievement. Further, he claims that the METCO results support this conclusion. But we have noted how this conclusion was reached through the omission of at least seven busing investigations with positive black achievement results and through serious weaknesses in the METCO research.

This is not the place for a complete review of the relevant research literature. But our evaluation of the available evidence points to a more encouraging, if more tentative and complex set of conclusions. First, the academic achievement of both white and black children is not lowered by the types of racial desegregation so far studied. Second, the achievement of white and especially of black children in desegregated schools is generally higher when some of the following critical conditions are met: equal racial access to the school's resources; classroom—not just school—desegregation (McPartland, 1968); the initiation of desegregation in the early grades; interracial staffs;(10) substantial rather than token student desegregation (Jencks and Brown, 1972); the maintenance of or increase in school services and remedial training; and the avoidance of strict ability grouping.

"Busing" also fails, according to Armor, because the grade average of the METCO students in junior and senior high schools declined. The average METCO grade decline is slight (-0.12 on a four-point scale), although he described it as "considerable" (Armor, p. 109). Nor is the difference in grade changes between the METCO and control groups statistically significant. Moreover, the greater drop in METCO grades than in control grades may be an artifact of the enormous non-response rate discussed earlier, for the full cross-sectional data show the controls' grades falling as much as those of the METCO children (-0.14 to -0.13).

Black grades also fell after desegregation in Evanston, we are informed in Armor's footnote 4. But we are not informed that the same study shows that white grades also fell and that there were no significant differences "in the frequencies of earned grades within each group" (Hsia, 1971). By contrast, when black pupils left a segregated junior high school in Sacramento in 1964, they soon received higher grades in the desegregated schools and maintained this improvement throughout their junior high years (Morrison and Stivers, 1971). However, none of these results are convincing, since differential grading practices are not controlled.

Armor further contends that "busing" fails because it lowers both the aspirations and academic self-concept of black children. Several qualifications are briefly discussed initially (Armor, pp. 101-102), but when the conclusions are drawn, this METCO "finding" has become unqualifiedly one of the four failures of "busing" (Armor, p. 109).

Actually, the METCO data on the subject are by no means clear. Two of Armor's three relevant Figures (5 and 6), those concerned with occupational aspirations and with "feeling more intelligent than classmates," show no significant change differences between the METCO and "control" groups. And the non-response bias may account for the one significant change difference—in regard to the desire to obtain a bachelor's degree (Figure 4)—since the full cross-sectional samples reveal a similar decline for both groups (−11 percent to −12 percent).

Two careful desegregation investigations from Pittsburgh and Evanston, however, have found lower black aspiratons combined with better academic performance. Black ninth graders in Pittsburgh had significantly higher arithmetic achievement and lower educational aspirations in desegregated schools (St. John and Smith, 1969). Similarly, both black and white pupils in Evanston's third, fourth, and fifth grades who had previously been in predominantly black schools reported somewhat lower academic self-concept scores after two years in predominantly white schools (Weber, Cook, and Campbell, 1971; Hsia, 1971). And we have noted that Evanston's black and white children made achievement gains during desegregation, though they were not statistically significant (Hsia, 1971). Since this effect occurred for both racial groups, these investigators inferred that this "social comparison effect" reflected adaptation to new norms and more realistic conceptions of academic performance.

The key to understanding the apparent paradox of reduced aspirations combined with increased achievement is the well-known psychological principle that achievement motivation and aspiration level are by no means identical. Researchers have repeatedly found that moderate motivational levels are best for learning and achievement (Atkinson, 1964). Some of this motivational research directly concerns black children. Katz (1967), for example, has demonstrated experimentally how unduly high aspirations can doom black students to serious learning difficulties. In his view, desegregation benefits learning among black children by lowering their aspirations to more effective and realistic levels. Veroff and Peele (1969) supported Katz's position in a study of desegregation in a small Michigan city. They found that achievement motivation, as measured by the choice of moderately difficult tasks, significantly increased for black boys after one year in a desegregated elementary school; black girls, however, did not evince the change.

If METCO had drastically curtained black ambitions to low levels, this would have been a negative result. But METCO reduced these ambitions only slightly, for they remained as high or higher than the ambitions of white students in METCO schools.(11) In short, when desegregation lowers rigidly high aspirations of black students to moderate, effective levels, it should be considered a positive, not a negative effect.

"Busing" fails again, in Armor's view, because he regards his METCO data as indicating that desegregation leads to negative effects for race relations. Once again, these METCO data are tenuous at best. Though much is made of it, the increase among METCO children in their desire to attend schools with at least half-black student bodies proves not to be significantly different from a similar increase among the "control" students (Figure 7). No control data are shown for black students' relations with white students (Figure 10), even though data without control comparisons are otherwise condemned by Armor and a large segment of the "control" group also attended interracial schools and had contact with white students. And as already noted, the differential administration of the third attitude questionnaire in 1970 is a critical factor which probably explains at least part of the difference between the two groups.

But if these supporting data are suspect, Armor's interpretations of them are even more suspect. "Militancy" and heightened "black consciousness and solidarity" are viewed as indicating "bad" race relations, though Armor adds, "It would be a mistake, of course, to view the increased racial solidarity of black students as a *completely* negative finding" (Armor, p. 113, italics added). Similarly, support for "black power" and a preference for a school with a student body that is evenly divided between the races are believed necessarily to involve "black separatism." Even sympathy for the Black Panthers is regarded as indicative of "anti-integration sentiments"; this despite the fact that the Panthers do not support racial segregation and removed Stokely Carmichael as a member because of his insistence on racial separatism.

These interpretations involve a logical contradiction in Armor's argument. He begins his article with the famous "hearts and minds" quotation of the 1954 Supreme Court ruling against *de jure* racial segregation of the public schools; and he employs it as evidence of the powerful influence of social science upon "the integration policy model." Yet the Supreme Court was maintaining that segregation led to black self-hate. Now when he interprets his data as showing that METCO "busing" leads to racial pride, militancy, and a desire to be among blacks as well as whites, Armor concludes that "the integration policy model" is proven wrong and that "busing" causes bad race relations.

The article admits that the METCO children are still supportive of the program, but emphasizes the trend toward "militancy." No consideration is given to the effects of the differential administration of the third-wave questionnaires; nor is any given to the possible effects of the study's having begun just after the 1968 assassinatin of Dr. Martin Luther King, Jr., a tragic event with wide repercussions for black/white interaction. Finally, the attitude results, like the achievement results, must be reinterpreted in the light of our discovery that much of the "control" group attends substantially desegregated schools. It could be, then, that the extreme tokenism of the METCO programs influenced these attitude results. They cannot be related to "busing" and desegregation, given the composition of the "control" group.

Nonetheless, Armor views these findings as a challenge to contact theory. To buttress this contention, he selectively cites a lone finding out of context from Useem's (1971, 1972) 1969 study of white racial attitudes in METCO schools.

> Nonetheless, although the evidence is not complete, what we have indicates that the white students themselves were negatively affected by the contact . . . [t]hose students who had direct classroom contact with bused black students showed *less* support for the busing program than those without direct contact. In fact, the kind of students who were generally the most supportive—the middle-class, high-achieving students—showed the largest decline in support as a result of contact with bused black students. This finding is based on cross-sectional data and does not indicate a change over time, but it is suggestive of the possibility that a general polarization has occurred for both racial groups. (Armor, pp. 103-104)

When drawing conclusions, however, he forgets his own caution against drawing causal inferences and flatly states that "white student attitudes in the receiving schools also tended to *become* less favorable to black students. . . ." (Armor, p. 112, italics added.)

The simple correlation between increased classroom contact and more negative feelings toward METCO among white students is statistically significant; but Armor fails to report that the relationship is no longer significant once such variables as sex, socio-economic status, and academic standing are taken into account. Moreover, this effect is limited to upper-status students of high ability who remain favorable to the program but who have their initially unrealistic expectations of blacks modified.

There is also a failure to report other relevant findings from Useem's work. For example, she found a statistically significant positive relationship between favorable white attitudes toward METCO and earlier equal status interracial contact in elementary school, summer camp, etc.; and this strong relationship remained significant after full controls were applied. Useem also found a relationship (p $<$ .08) between support for METCO and interracial contact in extracurricular activities. Moreover, she found that having a METCO friend is strongly linked to support of METCO, and is best predicted by equal status contact with blacks as a child and with METCO students in class and school activities.(12)

The one "success" of "busing," Armor admits, is that METCO appears to "channel" its students into colleges at higher rates than control students presumably from the same families. But this finding is couched with many qualifications that are conspicuously absent from his negative conclusions. Furthermore, his article actually understates METCO's success in this regard and fails to cite recent research that indicates that it may well be an important effect of interracial education in general.

Armor's article shows in its Figure 11 that 78 percent of the METCO graduating class of 1970 entered four-year colleges, compared to only 44 percent of the controls. By the fall of 1971, the percentages were 66 percent and 44 percent; and by the spring of 1971, 56 percent and 38 percent. (For universities, the spring 1971 figures were even more impressive, with 43 percent of the METCO graduates and only 12 percent of the controls enrolled.) Similarly, positive results are cited from another special program (Perry, 1972). But the article also implies that the METCO drop-out rate from college is excessively high, suggesting that the program pushes into college students who do not belong there. This point is answered as soon as one compares the METCO figures with other data on college attendance. For 1969 and 1970, the percentages of the *total* graduating classes of the METCO high schools going on to four-year colleges were 61 percent and 62 percent—all well below the 1969 and 1970 METCO figures of 77 percent and 78 percent (Useem, 1971).(13) Moreover, the 84 percent college retention rate of the 1970 METCO graduates who entered the second year of the four-year colleges is not abnormally low. In fact, it is slightly above the 78 percent national retention rate for white students in four-year colleges (Astin, 1972).

Nor was the 1970 METCO graduating class unusual. Robert Hayden, the director of METCO, kindly supplied us with data on the 32 METCO graduates of 1969. Twenty-eight (88 percent) entered college in the fall of 1969, while four began full-time employment. Three years later, attempts were made to contact the entire group, and 22 of the 28 college-attenders were reached. One was in the Army, and five had left college. Sixteen (73 percent), however, were still enrolled in college.

Yet Armor belittles such concrete results. He emphasizes that such findings are tentative, based on small samples, and may indicate that the future benefits of biracial schooling are limited to the collegebound. The importance of all three of these cautions is reduced, however, by a major research effort that goes unmentioned. Robert Crain (1970), using a 1966 survey of 1,624 adult blacks in the urban North, focused upon the occupational and income outcomes of desegregated education for high school graduates.(14) Crain concludes:

> American Negroes who attend integrated public schools have better jobs and higher incomes throughout at least the next three decades of their life. The differences in income cannot be accounted for by the higher educational attainment of alumni of integrated schools, or by the higher differences in social background. The most significant effect of integrated schools is probably not "educational." It is probably more important that

Negroes who attend integrated schools will have more contact with whites as adults, and tend to have more trust in whites than do Negroes from segregated schools. This in turn partially overcomes a crucial barrier to equal opportunity—the fact that information about employment opportunities is spread through types of informal social contacts to which few Negroes have access.

For the many reasons discussed above, the evidence does not justify Armor's unqualified conclusion: "The available evidence on busing, then, seems to lead to two clear policy conclusions. One is that mandatory busing for purposes of improving student achievement and interracial harmony is not effective and should not be adopted at this time" (Armor, p. 116). Interestingly, this conclusion was added to the final version after considerable publicity concerning Armor's paper had been generated by its repeated leaks to the mass media. An earlier draft had concluded only that "the data may fail to support mandatory busing as it is currently justified. . . ."

Armor also concludes that "voluntary busing" should continue for those who still believe in it and for the sake of social science research. Yet he never demonstrated, nor do we detect it when reviewing the evidence, that "mandatory" and "voluntary" desegregation lead to different effects. "Mandatory busing" is condemned out of hand even though his article rests most heavily on a voluntary program's effects, and rests entirely, except for Berkeley, upon token programs with small numbers and percentages of black children, while most "mandatory" programs involve larger numbers and percentages of black children in Southern cities excluded from consideration.

In a real sense, Armor's article does not concern itself with "busing" at all, save for its title and its conclusions. It does not provide us with direct evidence on the "busing" of school children for racial desegretion, for it never treats "busing" as an independent variable. Rather, his article is an attack upon the racial desegregation of public schools that often, but not always, involves "busing." Large numbers of the children in the few studies cited by Armor attend desegregated schools without "busing." And we have noted that in his own METCO study many of his so-called "controls," who were supposed to be "unbused" and segregated, were in fact, "bused" and desegregated. Furthermore, a check on his METCO sample finds that a substantial number were *not* bused. Armor was apparently aware of these problems, for he admitted in his court testimony for segregation in Detroit that "a more accurate title would be 'The Effects of Induced School Integration.' "

To our knowledge, there is actually no evidence whatsoever that "busing" for desegregation harms children. This is fortunate, since over 40 percent of all school children in the United States are "bused" daily (though only three percent are "bused" for purposes of achieving racial desegregation; Metropolitan Applied Research Center, 1972). Only one of the investigations mentioned in Armor's article actually utilized "busing" as an independent variable. It found, though this was also omitted, that black pupils in Evanston who were bused to desegregated schools attained significantly higher test score gains than those who either remained in or walked to desegregated schools (Hsia, 1971). This result may be an artifact of selection, but it at least indicates that "busing" *per se* did not impair achievement.

ASSUMPTIONS ABOUT RACIAL CHANGE ARE UNJUSTIFIED

To this point, our critique has answered Armor's argument within the narrow confines of his view of the process of racial desegregation of the public schools. But here we wish to break out of these confines and to challenge the basic assumptions about racial change that undergird his entire article. Armor's thesis is predicated on viewing school desegregation as a technical matter, an inconvenient intervention whose merit must be judged solely by how well black children manage to adapt to it. Blacks are once again the "object" whose reactions should determine "what is good for them." The conditions faced by black children go unmeasured and ignored, and the whole context of American race relations is conveniently forgotten. All interracial contact is assumed to constitute "integration." No mention whatsoever is made of white racism, individual and institutional, which the Kerner Commission maintained was at the root of the problem (National Advisory Commission on Civil Disorders, 1968). Nor is there any discussion of the strong argument that genuine integration is necessary primarily for its potential effects on white Americans and their racial attitudes.

Instead, the whole issue is portrayed as the creation of "liberal educators" who are "so intent on selling integration to reluctant white communities that they risk the danger of ignoring the opinion of the black community" (Armor, p. 115). Forgotten is the fact that the issue was the creation of black America, from Charles Hamilton Houston to Roy Wilkins, and that it has been continuously opposed by white America with every conceivable means.

Data from the limited METCO sample are generalized to the whole black community (Armor, p. 113). The anti-busing resolution of the National Black Political Convention held in Gary, Indiana, in March 1972 is emphasized, but the paradoxical fact that the same Convention also passed a strong "pro-busing" resolution is not cited. While it is achnowledged that "many black leaders favor school integration . . ." and that "the *majority* of blacks *may still* endorse the *concept* of integration . . ." (Armor, pp. 112, 115, italics added), the full range of support for school integration (not merely desegregation) in the black community is never revealed. "Would you like to see the children in your family go to school with white children or not?" When asked this question at the time of the METCO research in 1969, 78 percent of a national sample of black Americans (*up* from 70 percent three years before) chose "go with whites," as opposed to 9 percent "not with whites" and 14 percent "unsure" (Goldman, 1970).(15) Thus not just a majority but an overwhelming portion of black America still opts for school integration. If any further evidence were needed, the immediate and hostile public reactions of many blacks to the initial newspaper stories concerning Armor's paper should have supplied it. This is not to deny that there are strong doubts among blacks, especially the young, as to whether white America will ever allow genuine integration to become the national norm, doubts that are only reinforced by the assumptions upon which Armor's article is based.

Armor asserts that the burden must fall upon those who support school integration to prove that it works. Given America's unhappy racial history, we believe that the burden of proof rests with those who wish to maintain racial segregation. But actually such contentions miss the point. The courts' interpretation of the 14th Amendment of the United States Constitution, and not social scientists' opinions about black responses, ultimately governs the racial desegregation of the public schools and court-ordered transportation which may be needed to achieve it. This fundamental fact was dramatically demonstrated by the judicial reaction to Armor's deposition in the Detroit school case, a depoistion based on an earlier draft of "The Evidence on Busing." On June 12, 1972, U.S. District Court Judge Stephen H. Roth ruled the deposition inadmissible as evidence on the grounds of irrelevancy. The deposition, in Judge Roth's view, represented "a new rationale for a return to the discredited 'separate but equal' policy. . . ."

NOTES

(1) This is true from the early statements on the desegregation process by Clark (1953), Williams and Ryan (1954), Johnson (1954), and others (summarized in Coleman, 1960) to more recent statements by Katz (1964) and Pettigrew (1969, 1971).

(2) Matthai (1968) describes the White Plains (1967) research as follows: "The small numbers of Negro students tested (33 desegregated students; 36 from previous years); the lack of explicitness about comparability of the groups under study and the rationale of sample selection; the occasionally contradictory figures and tables; the lack of significance tests; the selection of only one grade level for study (plus a truncated comparison of another grade level); and the almost impenetrable prose of the research report make this study utterly equivocal."

(3) Grades two and four were excluded because of problems of sample drop-out. Earlier work showed somewhat greater gains for the desegregated youngsters in the second grade and for the segregated youngsters in the fourth grade (Mahan, 1968), so the omission of these two grades should not bias the results of this new analysis (Thomas Mahan, personal communication).

(4) More recently, a study has been released by the Center for Urban Education concerning 25 black first, second, and third graders bused under Project Concern from Bridgeport to Westport, Connecticut. Though the sample size renders its findings tentative, it found marked academic improvement for the "bused" children during one-and-a-half years when compared with similar unbused children remaining in the segregated sending school in Bridgeport. The

study also found no ill effects among the desegregated white children (Heller *et al.*, 1972).

(5) We wish to thank Robert Hayden of METCO, the Boston School System, and the families of the children contacted for their helpful cooperation in securing these data.

(6) We are here following the standard practice of defining a segregated school as one with a predominantly black student body. Had we employed a majority-white definition for a desegregated school, the "control" percentage attending desegregated would be 53 percent (29/55) instead of 62 percent (34/55). Small numbers of Chinese-American and Spanish-speaking students in a few of the schools explain the minor difference.

(7) Our projected sample sizes conservatively assume a standard deviation of the junior high gain scores of one grade level.

(8) Unfortunately for the discerning reader, Armor failed to mention these losses of elementary subjects in the one footnote he devotes to the subject. We obtained them from Walberg (1969).

(9) Using the Coleman report data, the standard deviation for groups of white students in desegregated schools in the Metropolitan North is only about 40 percent as large as the standard deviation of the white individual scores; or, on Coleman's verbal test, roughly four points where the standard deviation of the individual whites is 10 points (Coleman *et al.*, 1966). Since Armor finds that the mean for white groups in desegregated schools is roughly one-and-a-half group mean standard deviations larger than that for black groups in desegregated schools, we estimate that the average black child is roughly six points (1.5 x 4 points) behind the average white child. Translating this into individual percentiles and assuming that the average white in desegregated schools is at the 50th percentile, we arrive at our estimate that the average black pupil in desegregated schools is between the 25th and 30th percentiles.

(10) Bailey (1970) has also shown that high school "disruptions" and racial tensions are far less likely to occur when the black staff percentage is equal to or greater than the black student percentage.

(11) Useem (1971) studied white tenth graders' aspirations and attitudes in eight out of the nine secondary schools participating in the METCO program during 1968-69. She found white aspirations just equal to or below those reported for blacks in the same schools. Thus, 74 percent of the white students wanted to be above the middle of the class academically compared to about 80 percent of the black students; and 26 percent of the whites aspired to a professional or graduate school compared to 35 percent of the blacks.

(12) In his Detroit segregation testimony, Armor stated that he omitted these positive findings of contact because they were voluntary and therefore could have been caused by self-selection. But classrooms at the high school level often involve selection too. Besides, 72 percent of Useem's white students who had contact with METCO students in school activities had it in athletics. Armor's argument requires us to believe that tolerant white students would go out for football primarily to have contact with the few black players on the team.

(13) Data from one METCO high school was unobtainable for 1970, but the similarity of the percentages for the two years suggests that this does not introduce a serious bias.

(14) From these same data, Crain (1971) also finds "that those who attended integrated schools are more likely to have graduated from high schook, are more likely to have attended college, and score higher on a verbal test, than those who attended northern segregated schools. It seems likely that the higher achievement of Negroes in integrated schools can be attributed partly to differences in the character of their classmates, irrespective of race. In addition, however, there is evidence that attending integrated schools has an important impact in establishing social and psychological preconditions for achievement."

(15) Armor's data on black attitudes toward "busing" in his footnote 11 are outdated. By March 1972, black favored "busing" for integration by 54 percent to 34 percent (Harris, 1972).

REFERENCES:

Aberdeen, F.D., 1969. "Adjustment to Desegregation: A Description of Some Differences among Negro Elementary Pupils," unpublished Doctoral Dissertation, University of Michigan.

Allport, Gordon, W., 1954. The Nature of Prejudice. Cambridge, Massachusetts, Addison-Wesley.

Anderson, Louis V., 1966. "The Effects of Desegregation on the Achievement and Personality Patterns of Negro Children," unpublished Doctoral Dissertation, George Peabody College.

Archibald, David K., 1967. "Report on Change in Academic Achievement for a Sample of Elementary School Children: Progress Report on METCO," unpublished paper, Brookline, Massachusetts.

Armor, David J. The Evidence on Busing," The Public Interest, No. 28, Summer 1972, 90-126.

Armor, David J., 1972. "Deposition on Behalf of Defendants-Intervenor Allen Park Public Schools et al., Bradley et al. v. Miliken et al.," U.S. District Court Eastern District of Michigan, Southern Division, Civil Action No. 35257 (May 24, 1972).

Armor, David J. and William J. Genova, 1970. "METCO Student Attitudes and Aspirations: A Three-Year Evaluation," unpublished paper, Boston, Massachusetts.

Astin, A.W., 1972. "College Dropouts: A National Profile," American Council on Education Research Reports, Vol. 7, No. 1 (February).

Atkinson, J.W., 1964. An Introduction to Motivation, Princeton, N.J., Van Nostrand.

Bailey, S.K., 1970, Disruption in Urban Public Secondary Schools, Washington, D.C., National Association of Secondary School Principals.

Banks, Ronald and Mary E. DiPasquale, 1969. "A Study of the Educational Effectiveness of Integration," unpublished report, Buffalo Public Schools,

Buffalo, New York.

Berkeley Unified School District, 1971a. "Comparison of Achievement Test Scores Made by Berkeley Elementary Students Pre and Post Integration Eras, 1967-70," unpublished report, Berkeley, California.

Berkeley Unified School District, 1971b. "Preliminary Report of Group Achievement Test Results for 1970-71," unpublished report, Berkeley, California.

Campbell, A. and H. Schuman, 1968. "Racial Attitudes in Fifteen American Cities," in The National Advisory Commission on Civil Disorders, Supplemental Studies, Washington, D.C., U.S. Government Printing Office.

Carrigan, Patricia M., 1969. "School Desegregation Via Compulsory Pupil Transfer: Early Effects on Elementary School Children," Final Report for Project No. 6-1320, U.S. Office of Education.

Charters, W.W., Jr. and T.M. Newcomb, 1952. "Some Attitudinal Effects of Experimentally Increased Salience of a Membership Group," in G.E. Swanson, T.M. Newcomb, and E.L. Hartley (eds.), Readings in Social Psychology, revised edition, New York, Holt.

Clark, Kenneth, 1953. "Desegregation: An Appraisal of the Evidence," Journal of Social Issues, Vol. 9, Fall, 2-76.

Coleman, A.L., 1960. "Social Scientists' Predictions About Desegregation," Social Forces, Vol. 38, 258-262.

Coleman, James, et al., 1966. Equality of Educational Opportunity, Washington, D.C., U.S. Government Printing Office.

Crain, Robert L., 1970. "School Integration and Occupational Achievement of Negroes," American Journal of Sociology, Vol. 75, 593-606.

Crain, Robert L., 1971. "School Integration and Academic Achievement of Negroes," Sociology of Education, 1971, Vol. 44 (Winter), 1-26.

Fortenberry, James H., 1959, "The Achievement of Negro Pupils in Mixed and Non-Mixed Schools," unpublished Doctoral Dissertation, University of Oklahoma.

Fox, David, J., 1966. "Free Choice Open Enrollment—Elementary Schools," unpublished paper, Center for Urban Education, New York.

Fox, David J., 1967. "Evaluation of the New York City Title I Educational Projects 1966-1967. Expansion of the Free Choice Open Enrollment Program," unpublished paper, Center for Urban Education, New York.

Fox, David J., et al., 1968. "Services to Children in Open Enrollment Receiving Schools: Evaluation of ESEA Title I Projects in New York City, 1967-1968," unpublished paper, Center for Urban Education, New York.

Frary, Robert B. and Thomas M. Goolsby, Jr., 1970. "Achievement of Integrated and Segregated Negro and White First Graders in a Southern City," Integrated Education, Vol. 8, No. 4, 48-52.

Frelow, Robert D., 1971. "A Comparative Study of Resource Allocation: Compensatory Education and School Desegregation," unpublished Doctoral Dissertation, University of California, Berkeley.

Goldman, Peter, 1970. Report from Black America, New York, Simon and

Schuster.

Harris, Louis, 1972. "Antibusing Attitudes Harden," The Boston Globe, April 10, 1972.

Heller, Barbara, Carla Drije, Barry Kaufman, and Morton Inger, 1972. Project Concern: Westport, Connecticut, New York, Center for Urban Education.

Henrick, I.S., 1968. The Development of a School Integration Plan in Riverside, California: A History and Perspective," unpublished paper of the University of California, Riverside and the Riverside Unified School District.

Hsia, Jayjia, 1971. "Integration in Evanston, 1967-1971," Evanston, Illinois, Educational Testing Service.

Jencks, Christopher and Marsha Brown, 1972. "The Effects of Desegregation on Student Achievement: Some New Evidence from the Equality of Educational Opportunity Survey," unpublished paper, Harvard University.

Johnson, Guy, 1954. "A Sociologist Looks at Racial Desegregation in the South," Social Forces, Vol. 32, 1-10.

Katz, Irwin, 1964. "Review of Evidence Relating to Effects of Desegregation on the Intellectual Performance of Negroes," American Psychologist, Vol. 19, 381-399.

Katz, Irwin, 1967. "The Socialization of Academic Motivation in Minority Group Children," in D. Levine (ed.), Nebraska Symposium on Motivation, 1967, Lincoln, University of Nebraska Press.

King, Charles E. and Robert R. Mayer, 1971. "A Pilot Study of the Social and Educational Impact of School Desegregation," unpublished report, North Carolina Central University and University of North Carolina at Chapel Hill.

Laird, Mary Alice and Grace Weeks, 1966. "The Effect of Busing on Achievement in Reading and Arithmetic in Three Philadelphia Schools," unpublished paper, Division of Research, The School District of Philadelphia.

Mahan, Thomas W., 1968. Project Concern—1966-1968, Hartford, Connecticut, Hartford Public Schools.

Matthai, Robert A., 1968. "The Academic Performance of Negro Students: An Analysis of the Research Findings from Several Busing Programs," unpublished paper, Graduate School of Education, Harvard University.

McCullough, James S., 1972. "Academic Achievement Under School Desegregation in Southern City," unpublished paper, Department of City and Regional Planning, the University of North Carolina at Chapel Hill (January).

McPartland, James, 1968. "The Segregated Student in the Desegregated Schools: Sources of Influence on Negro Secondary Students," Report No. 21, Department of Social Relations, Johns Hopkins University.

Morrison, Edward B. and James A. Stivers, 1971. "A Summary of the Assessments of the District's Integration Programs, 1964-1971," Research Report No. 9 of Series 1971-72, Sacramento City Unified School District,

Sacramento, California.

Metropolitan Applied Research Center, 1972. Fact Book on Pupil Transportation, New York, M.A.R.C. Document No. 2.

Mosteller, Frederick and D.P. Moynihan (eds.), 1972. On Equality of Educational Opportunity, New York, Random House.

National Advisory Commission on Civil Disorder, 1968. Report, Washington, D.C., U.S. Government Printing Office.

O'Reilly, Robert P. (ed.), 1970. Racial and Social Class Isolation in the Schools, New York, Praeger.

Perry, George, 1972. "A Preliminary Evaluation of the Effects of ABC on College Attendance," unpublished paper, A Better Chance, Boston, Mass.

Pettigrew, Thomas F., 1969. "The Negro in Education: Problems and Proposals," in I. Katz and P. Gurin (eds.) Race and the Social Sciences, New York, Basic Books.

Pettigrew, Thomas F., 1971. Racially Separate or Together? New York, McGraw-Hill.

Purl, Mabel C., 1971. "The Achievement of Pupils in Desegregated Schools," unpublished paper. Riverside Unified School District, Riverside, California.

Rochester City School District, 1970. "Final Report: A Three-Year Longitudinal Study to Access a Fifteen Point Plan to Reduce Racial Isolation," Rochester, New York.

Rock, William C., Joanne E. Long, Herman R. Goldberg, and L. William Heinrich, 1968. "A Report on a Cooperative Program Between a City School District and a Suburban School District," unpublished paper, Rochester School District, Rochester, New York.

Roth, Stephen J., 1972. Bradley et al. v Milliken et al., U.S. District Court, Eastern District of Michigan, Southern Division, Civil Action No. 35257 (Opinion of June 12, 1972).

St. John, Nancy, 1970. "Desegregation and Minority Group Performance," Review of Educational Research, Vol. 40, 111-134.

St. John, Nancy and Marshall S. Smith, 1969. "School Racial Composition, Achievement, and Aspiration," unpublished paper, Graduate School of Education, Harvard University.

Samuels, Joseph M., 1971. "A Comparison of Projects Representative of Compensatory, Busing and Non-Compensatory Programs for Inner-City Students," unpublished Doctoral Dissertation, University of Connecticut.

Singer, Harry, 1972. "Effect of Integration on Achievement of Anglos, Blacks, and Mexican-Americans," unpublished paper, Department of Education, University of California, Riverside.

Slone, Irene, W., 1968. "The Effects of One School Pairing on Pupil Achievement, Anxieties, and Attitudes," unpublished Doctoral Dissertation, New York University.

United States Commission on Civil Rights, 1967. Racial Isolation in the Public Schools, Washington, D.C., U.S. Government Printing Office.

Useem, Elizabeth, 1971. "White Suburban Secondary Students in Schools with

Token Desegregation," unpublished Doctoral Dissertation, Graduate School of Education, Harvard University.

Useem, Elizabeth, 1972. "Correlates of Racial Attitudes Among White High School Students," unpublished paper read at the American Educational Research Association Meetings, Chicago.

Veroff, Joseph and S. Peele, 1969. "Initial Effects of Desegregation on the Achievement Motivation of Negro Elementary School Children," Journal of Social Issues, Vol. 25, No. 3, 71-91.

Walberg, Herbert J., 1969. "An Evaluation of an Urban-Suburban School Busing Program: Student Achievement and Perception of Class Learning Environments," unpublished paper, METCO, Boston, Massachusetts.

Weber, Stephen J., Thomas D. Cook, and Donald T. Campbell, 1971. "The Effect of School Integration on the Academic Self-Concept of Public School Students," unpublished paper read at the Midwestern Psychological Association meetings, Detroit.

Weinberg, Meyer, 1968. Desegretation Research: An Appriasal, Bloomington, Indiana, Phi Delta Kappa.

White Plains Public Schools, 1967. "A Three-Year Evaluation of the White Plains Racial Balance Plan," unpublished report, White Plains, New York.

Williams, Robin and Margaret Ryan, 1954. Schools in Transition: Community Experiences in Desegregation, Chapel Hill, University of North Carolina Press.

Zdep, Stanley M. and Diane Joyce, 1969. "The Newark-Verona Plan for Sharing Educational Opportunity," unpublished report PR-69-13, Educational Testing Service, Princeton, New Jersey.

MEXICAN-AMERICANS AND
THE DESEGREGATION OF SCHOOLS
IN THE SOUTHWEST

Guadalupe Salinas

On June 4, 1970, Federal District Judge Woodrow Seals, in *Cisneros v. Corpus Christi Independent School District*,(1) held that Mexican-Americans are an "identifiable ethnic minority group" for the purpose of public school desegregation.(2) Because Mexican-Americans are an identifiable group and have been subjected to discrimination in the Corpus Christi, Texas area, Judge Seals stated that Mexican-Americans are entitled to the same protection afforded Negroes under the landmark decision of *Brown v. Board of Education*.(3) The court found that the school district segregated Mexican-Americans, as well as Negroes, to such an extent that a dual school system resulted.(4) The parties were then asked to submit a desegregation plan which considered the three major ethnic groups: Negro, Mexican-American, and Anglo, that is, other whites besides Mexican-Americans.(5)

Cisneros is unique in that it is the first case in which a court officially recognized Mexican-Americans as an *identifiable ethnic minority group* for the purposes of public school desegregation. Before proceeding with a discussion of the significance of being an *identifiable ethnic minority group*, a definition of the phrase may be conducive to a better understanding of the court's holding. Mexican-Americans are considered by some to be a non-white racial group. However, the predominant view is that Mexican-Americans are white, even though many are *mestizos* (a hybrid of white and Indian). Nevertheless, like other white nationality groups who have been victims of discrimination, for example, the Jewish and Italian-Americans, Mexican-Americans have inherent characteristics which make them easily identifiable and susceptible to discrimination. Among these characteristics are brown skin color, a Spanish surname, and the Spanish language. The fact that this group is of Mexican descent and has certain inherent characteristics makes it an *identifiable ethnic group*.

Judge Seals characterized Mexican-Americans as an ethnic *minority* group. Mexican-Americans definitely are a numerical minority in the United States, representing about 2.5 percent of the population.(6) In Texas, this ethnic group comprises 14.5 percent of the population.(7) In Corpus Christi, where *Cisneros* arose, Mexican-Americans comprise 35.7 percent of the population.(8) However, Judge Seals does not rely on mere numbers to determine whether an ethnic group is a minority group. His principal test is whether the group is discriminated against in the schools through segregation, a discrimination facilitated by the group's economic and political impotence.(9) Thus, Mexican-Americans are an *identifiable ethnic minority group*, even in areas where they are the majority since many are economically and politically disadvantaged.

The court's holding, that Mexican-Americans are entitled to the protection given Negroes by *Brown*, is significant because it introduces a new group into the desegregation process. Federal courts should consider Mexican-American students in determining whether a unitary school system is in operation. More importantly, the court's recognition of Mexican-Americans should serve as a restraint on school districts which utilize the Mexican-American's classification of white by integrating them with Negroes to satisfy court desegregation orders. Further discussion about the mixing of Negroes and Mexican-Americans in minority schools is presented later.

This comment seeks to analyze whether Mexican-Americans should be considered an identifiable ethnic minority group for purposes of public school desegregation. After providing a brief history of the American of Mexican descent, the writer will discuss various civil rights problems encountered by Mexican-Americans and, more importantly the evolution of the desegregation doctrine as it pertains to Mexican-Americans.

HISTORICAL BACKGROUND OF THE MEXICAN-AMERICAN

Mexican-Americans are the second largest minority group in the United States.(10) In the Southwest (an area including Arizona, California, Colorado, New Mexico, and Texas), where 87 percent of this minority group resides, Mexican-Americans are the largest minority group.(11)

In the 1500's the Spanish began to settle this area, many years before the English established the first settlement at Jamestown in 1607. This early Spanish influence is evidenced in the number of States, cities, and rivers with Spanish names.(12) These Southwestern States came under Mexican rule after Mexico won her independence from Spain in 1821.

However, the vast Mexican nation encountered internal problems when Texas seceded in 1836 and again when the United States Congress voted in 1845 to allow Texas to enter the Union. Mexico had warned that admission into the Union would be equivalent to an act of war. In spite of Mexico's relative military weakness compared to the United States, the two countries engaged in armed conflict. The result was the defeat of Mexico and the signing of the Treaty of Guadalupe Hidalgo on February 2, 1848.(13) By the terms of the treaty, Mexico acknowledged the annexation of Texas and ceded the rest of the Southwest to the United States. In addition, the treaty guaranteed civil and property rights to those who became American citizens.(14)

Approximately 75,000 Mexicans decided to remain and receive American citizenship.(15) These Mexican-Americans were later supplemented by vast emigrations from Mexico. The first influx, precipitated by the social revolution in Mexico, began in 1910. A second wave of immigrants resulted in the increase of the Mexican-American population by nearly one million from 1910 to 1930. During and after World War II, attracted by the agricultural labor market, a third group of Mexicans came to the United States.(16) In addition, about 3500 Mexicans immigrate to this country each month, thus continuing the steady growth of the Mexican-American population.(17)

With the increase of the Mexican-American population, there was an increase in the prejudice of the predominant Anglo society. For example, Mexican-Americans, as well as Mexican nationals, were deported during the Great Depression to reduce the welfare rolls.(18) This prejudice resulted in the "largest mass trial for murder ever in the United States."(19) Such prejudice also led to the so-called "zoot suit" riots of 1943 in Los Angeles. The riots began when city police refused to intervene while over a hundred sailors roamed the streets for nearly a week beating and stripping Mexican-American youths in retaliation for the beating some sailors had received earlier from a gang of "zoot suiters."(20)

As a result of these and similar discriminatory practices, Mexican-American interest groups began to organize in order to defend *La Raza* (the race), as Mexican-Americans call themselves. In 1927 the League of United Latin American Citizens (LULAC) was formed in Texas. Shortly thereafter LULAC helped fund the first challenge against the segregation of Mexican-American school children.(21) In 1948, a Mexican-American war veteran, Dr. Hector P. Garcia, founded the American GI Forum for the purpose of protecting Mexican-American veterans from discriminatory practices which they "were being subjected to in the areas of education, employment, medical attention and housing. . . ."(22) The American GI Forum, which now has many chapters throughout the United States, has also helped support civil rights litigation.

In spite of the successes which LULAC and the GI Forum have accomplished, many Mexican-American youths have not been satisfied. Unlike their elders, Mexican-American youth activists, or *Chicanos* (the term is a derivation of *mejicano*, which is the Spanish term for Mexican), as they like to be called, refuse to be satisfied with justice on the installment plan, that is, gradual social progress. Instead, this new breed demands justice and equality for *La Raza* now.

In order to promote the advancement of Mexican-Americans, *Chicanos* throughout the Southwest have organized in recent years, mainly on college campuses.(23) For example, the Mexican-American Youth Organization (MAYO), which was founded in 1967 by San Antonio college students,(24) is currently organized at the two largest universities in Texas, The University of Texas and the University of Houston. In addition, MAYO chapters are active in the *barrios* (neighborhoods where the Mexican-American population is predominant).

The Mexican-American Legal Defense and Educational Fund (MALDEF), a *Chicano* (the term is not limited in its application to the youth activists) civil rights organization which was created in 1968,(25) is even more effective than these political groups. The previous lack of a legal defense organization perhaps best explains why Mexican-Americans have not been too active in civil rights litigation. In fact, the Supreme Court of the United States has decided a *Chicano* civil rights issue on only one occasion.(26) However, legal activities of MALDEF prompted a newspaper to note that "[m]ore legal attention has been focused on the problems of Texas' nearly two million Mexican-Americans during the past 11 months than during the entire history of *La Raza* in Texas."(27) This statement is applicable as well to the rest of the Southwest.(28)

MEXICAN-AMERICAN—AN IDENTIFIABLE ETHNIC MINORITY GROUP

Mexican-Americans, as a group, have been widely discriminated against. As a result, many Mexican-Americans have easily been able to identify with *La Raza*. On the other hand, there are many Mexican-Americans who have never personally experienced an act of discrimination and thus, find it difficult to empathize with the civil rights movement. Many of these adamantly assert that they are Americans and fail to identify with Mexican-Americans. In many cases, a light-skinned complexion has helped make life more "American" for them.(29) In addition, there are some who feel a stigma or a handicap if the term "Mexican" is used to describe them and who prefer a euphemistic label like Latin American or Spanish-speaking American. Finally, there is a group who, because of their ancestry of early Spanish colonists, call themselves Spanish-Americans and Hispanos. Nevertheless, in spite of what Spanish-surnamed Americans of the Southwest prefer to be called, the name Mexican-American is perhaps the best designation which can be applied objectively. Regardless of what they call themselves, one fact is clear—either they or their ancestors, including the Spanish colonists, came "north from Mexico."(30)

DISCRIMINATION IN EMPLOYMENT

Mexican-Americans, like Negroes, have encountered discriminatory practices by employers in hiring and promotion. What is worse, is that much of this discrimination is subtle. Employers often use the "high school diploma" or "we'll call you" tactics since they can no longer discriminate openly with impunity. As a result, it is often difficult to maintain a civil rights action. Since the Civil Rights Act of 1964(31) was passed, at least one Mexican-American has been successful, and many more cases have been filed. The one successful claim is the agreement reached in the case of *Urquidez v. General Telephone Co.*(32) The suit, a class action, resulted from the fact that Urquidez applied for employment, passed the tests, and had more job-related experience and education than several Anglo applicants who were subsequently hired. The settlement agreement acknowledged that Urquidez had a prima facie case of discrimination, awarded him $2,000, and provided that General Telephone would take definite steps to remedy past discriminatory practices.

In spite of the unusually small number of cases in the field of employment discrimination, the statistics and evidence indicate that discriminatory practices are very prevalent. For example, considering the Southwest alone, the unemployment rate among Mexican-Americans is double the Anglo rate—a statistic which understates the severity of the situation since farm workers are not included in unemployment statistics.(33) In addition, in 1960, 79 percent of all Mexican-American workers held unskilled and semi-skilled jobs.(34)

While some of the employment problems facing Mexican-Americans are attributable to their relatively low educational attainment,(35) there are indications of discrimination to offset much of that argument. For instance, in comparing the income of Mexican-Americans and Anglos who have completed the same number of school years, the income of Mexican-Americans is only 60 to 80 percent of the Anglo income.(36) Since passage of the Civil Rights Act of 1964, employers have resorted to more subtle practices, such as promoting Anglos before Mexican-Americans, even if the former are less educated and less skilled. Many employers, when questioned about such practices, rationalize that Anglo workers will not take orders from Mexican-Americans.(37) Consequently, the Mexican-American is denied the equal protection of the laws as guaranteed him by the Constitution of the United States(38) and by the Civil Rights Act of 1964.

As previously stated, many employment discrimination cases have been instituted, mostly by MALDEF-assisted plaintiffs. Two of these cases were delayed by motions to dismiss which have been denied,(39) and the cases are set for a hearing on the merits. MALDEF lists 15 additional pending cases.(40) Among the grounds urged for relief are: 1. refusal to hire because of national origin; 2. failure to promote over less-educated and less-experienced Anglos; 3. hiring Mexican-Americans only for low-paying positions; 4. paying different wages to Mexican-Americans and Anglos; and 5. underemployment while Anglos with less seniority are allowed more work time.(41)

One pending case, *Quiroz v. James H. Matthews & Co.*,(42) challenges some of the subtle, covert practices employers commonly use to deny Mexican-Americans equal opportunity. Quiroz alleges violation of his equal employment rights under Title VII of the Civil Rights Act of 1964.(43) The plaintiff, who had 16 years' experience, was replaced by an Anglo who had less job-related experience. Furthermore, Quiroz contends that the defendant pays

Mexican-American employees less than fellow Anglo employees receive for doing the same kind of work.(44)

SPANISH AND MEXICAN LAND GRANTS

Mexican-Americans have also suffered unjustly in the area of Spanish and Mexican land grants, an issue encountered generally in New Mexico and Colorado. The issue is whether Mexican-American land grantees or the heirs of these grantees, who by some means were defrauded of their land by various state officials, are entitled to compensation.

This issue was raised in *Vigil v. United States*,(45) a class action filed for those descendants of Spanish-surnamed Americans who lived in areas ceded to the United States by Mexico in 1848. The plaintiffs sought $1 million actual damages and $1 million punitive damages for each individual who was part of the class. However, the court held that the vague allegations in the complaint failed to satisfy the Federal Tort Claims Act and that there was no claim against the United States under the Civil Rights Acts for deprivation of property.

Although that complaint was vague, one *Chicano* writer has been more specific.(46) He claims Mexican-Americans have lost nearly four million acres of land.(47) This loss has occurred even though Article VIII of the Treaty of Guadalupe Hidalgo provides:

> The present owners, the heirs of these, and all Mexicans who may hereafter acquire said property by contract, shall enjoy with respect to it guaranties equally ample as if the same belonged to citizens of the United States.(48)

The writer argues that the shift from the Mexican legal system, where grand lands were immune from taxation and titles were unregistered, to the Anglo legal system of land taxation and title recordation was the major factor in the land losses which Mexican-Americans suffered.(49) Many landowners were divested of title by wealthy Anglo ranchers purchasing deeds at tax sales or by recording a claim to the property before the true owner.(50) Perhaps federal courts will grant relief to these aggrieved heirs of the land grantees when and if the complaints are clarified.

PUBLIC ACCOMMODATIONS

Mexican-Americans have been excluded from public accommodations. Fortunately the practice has subsided since the 1940's when Mexican-Americans were segregated from restaurants, theaters, and swimming pools.(51) Nevertheless, prejudice and overt acts of discrimination have contributed to making Mexican-Americans an identifiable ethnic minority group.

In 1944 Texas upheld the right of a proprietor to exclude any person for any reason whatsoever. including the fact that the person was of Mexican descent.(52) However, that same year a federal court in California held that Mexican-Americans *are* entitled to public accommodations such as other citizens enjoy.(53) In spite of this ruling and the Civil Rights Act of 1964, a federal court in 1968 found it necessary to enjoin the exclusion of Mexican-Americans from public swimming pool facilities.(54)

ADMINISTRATION OF JUSTICE

Mexican-Americans also face serious discrimination in the administration of justice. This discrimination, as well as the personal prejudice of police officers, often leads to physical and psychological injury to Mexican-Americans.(55) However, Mexican-Americans, like other minority groups, have encountered difficulty in getting grand juries to return indictments against police officers who use excessive force and insulting, derogatory language.(56) In one case a Mexican-American woman won a civil damages suit against a police officer.(57) The plaintiff claimed she had suffered physical and mental damages because of being forcefully undressed by two policewomen and two policemen to see if she had any concealed narcotics. Earlier, when the officers had entered the plaintiff's residence without a search warrant, the plaintiff demanded respect for her constitutional rights, but one officer told her to "go back to Mexico."(58)

Besides the treatment received from law enforcement officials,(59) Mexican-Americans are often inadequately represented on juries. Consequently, the juries hearing cases involving Mexican-American defendants are not "impartial"(60) juries since they fail to represent the community. These inequities still occur frequently, even though the United States Supreme Court held in *Hernandez v. Texas*(61) that "[t]he exclusion of otherwise eligible [Mexican-Americans] from jury service solely because of their ancestry or national origin is discrimination prohibited by the Fourteenth Amendment."(62) The Court stated that the absence of a Mexican-American juror for 25 years in a country where this ethnic group comprised 14 percent of the population "bespeaks discrimination, whether or not it was a conscious decision on the part of any individual jury commissioner."(63)

Prior to *Hernandez*, Texas courts refused to recognize the Mexican-American as a separate class—distinct from other whites—for purposes of determining whether there was an unconstitutional exclusion from juries.(64) The Texas courts limited the application of the equal protection clause to two classes, whites and Negroes. Since Mexican-Americans were legally considered white, the equal protection clause did not apply.

Nevertheless, this weak argument was overruled by the Supreme Court in *Hernandez* when it held that Mexican-Americans are a separate class, distinct from whites. The Court noted that historically "differences in race and color have defined *easily identifiable* groups which have at times required the aid of the courts in securing equal treatment under the laws."(65) Since *Hernandez*, courts have recognized Mexican-Americans as an identifiable ethnic group, although they have not always found discrimination.(66)

Recently, the Fifth Circuit overturned the 1942 rape conviction of a Mexican-American in El Paso County, Texas, because the juries that indicted and convicted him had excluded persons of his ethnic group.(67) Only 18 of the 600 grand jurors who served from 1936 to 1947 were Mexican-Americans, even though the county population was 15 to 20 percent Mexican-American.(68) The court stated that these figures "cry out 'discrimination' with unmistakable clarity."(69)

Although the discussion of discrimination toward Mexican-Americans dealt only with the issues of employment, land grants, public accommodations, and the administration of justice, this in no way limits the areas in which Mexican-Americans encounter injustices.(70) The issues discussed were selected to justify the holding in *Cisneros*, that Mexican-Americans are an identifiable ethnic minority group entitled to the protection of the 14th amendment in the area of school desegregation in the Southwest.

NON-JUDICIAL RECOGNITION

The Mexican-American has been recognized as a separate, identifiable group not only by the courts but also by other governmental institutions. For instance, the Civil Rights Act of 1964, by use of the term "national origin,"(71) impliedly includes Mexican-Americans and other "national origin" minority groups such as Puerto Ricans. Furthermore, recognizing the problems facing many Mexican-American school children, Congress passed the Bilingual Education Act(72) which seeks to facilitate the learning of English and at the same time allow the Spanish-speaking child to perfect his mother language and regain self-esteem through the encouraged learning of Spanish.(73) In addition, Congress created a cabinet committee whose purpose is to assure that federal programs are reaching Mexican-Americans and all other Spanish-speaking groups.(74) Also, through the creation of the United States Civil Rights Commission in 1957, Congress and the public have become better informed as to the injustices Mexican-Americans endure.(75) Other governmental agencies have researched the living conditions of the Mexican-American.(76) Finally, the Department of Health, Education, and Welfare (HEW) has issued regulations which prohibit the denial of equal educational opportunity on the basis of English language deficiency. The regulations apply to school districts accepting federally assisted programs and having at least 5 percent Mexican-American enrollment.(77)

THE CHICANO SCHOOL CASES

Since all three branches of government recognize Mexican-Americans as a minority group, the question which must be answered is whether *Chicano* students have been discriminated against by school districts to such an extent as to warrant their inclusions as a separate ethnic group in the desegregation plans for public schools in the Southwest. In other words, does the history of

Mexican-American school children in the predominantly Anglo school systems of the Southwest demand recognition of this educationally disadvantaged group as being separate and distinct from whites?

The practice of maintaining separate schools throughout the Southwest was never sanctioned by any State statute, although in California, a statute allowing separate schools for "Mongolians" and "Indians" was interpreted to include Mexican-Americans in the latter group.(78) Generally, the segregation of Mexican-Americans was enforced by the customs and regulations of school districts throughout the Southwest. Nevertheless, the segregation was de jure since sufficient State action was involved.

The struggle by Mexican-Americans against separate and unequal schools has been lengthy. In 1930 a Texas appelate court held in *Independent School District v. Salvatierra*(79) that school authorities in Del Rio, or anywhere else, have no power to segregate *Chicano* children "merely or solely because they are [Mexican-Americans]."(80) However, the school district successfully argued that the children's language deficiencies warranted their separate schooling, even though the superintendent conceded that "generally the best way to learn a language is to be associated with the people who speak that language."(81) The Attorney General of Texas later supported this holding by justifying education of the linguistically deficient in separate classrooms and even in separate buildings if necessary.(82)

The first federal district court decision in this area was *Mendez v. Westminister School District*(83) in 1946. The court held that the equal protection of the laws pertaining to the public school system in California is not met by providing "separate schools [with] the same technical facilities"(84) for Mexican-American children—words which are strikingly similar to the Supreme Court's holding in *Brown* 8 years later that "[s]eparate education facilities are inherently unequal."(85) The court observed that "[a] paramount requisite in the American system of public education is social equality. It must be open to all children by unified school association regardless of lineage."(86)

On appeal, the Ninth Circuit affirmed *Mendez*, finding that the school officials had acted "under color of State law" in segregating the Mexican-American students.(87) The appellate court reasoned that since the California segregation statute did not expressly include Mexican-Americans, their segregation denied due process and the equal protection of the laws.(88)

Following the landmark ruling in *Mendez*, a federal district court in Texas, in *Delgado v. Bastrop Independent School District*,(89) held that the segregation practices of the district were "arbitrary and discriminatory and in violation of [the 14th amendment]."(90) In addition, the court's instructions to Texas school districts stipulated that separate classes for those with language deficiences must be on the same campus with all other students,(91) thereby denying school officials the power to justify completely separate Mexican-Americans schools by use of the language deficiency argument.

Nevertheless, the *Delgado* requirement did not prevent the creation of evasive schemes in order to maintain segregated school facilities. For example, in

Driscoll, Texas, school authorities customarily required a majority of the Mexican-American children to spend 3 years in the first grade before promotion to the second.(92) After the *Delgado* case, Driscoll abandoned the maintenance of separate schools for Anglos and Mexican-Americans. However, the school district exploited the *Salvatierra* doctrine by drawing the line designating who must attend the language deficiency classes on a racial rather than a merit basis.(93) In *Hernandez v. Driscoll Consolidated Independent School District*(94) a Mexican-American child who could not speak Spanish was denied admission to the Anglo section until a lawyer was contacted. The court held that abusing the language deficiency of the Mexican-American children is "unreasonable race discrimination."(95) In a situation similar to *Driscoll*, Judge Seals, who later wrote the *Cisneros* opinion, enjoined the Odem Independent School District from operating and maintaining a separate school solely for Mexican-American children.(96)

After *Brown v. Board of Education*(97) the *Chicano* school cases began to assume a new dimension. Since Mexican-Americans were generally classified as whites, school districts began to integrate Negroes and Mexican-Americans while Anglos were assigned to all-Anglo schools. As a result, two educationally disadvantaged minority groups have been prevented from having maximum interaction with students of the predominant Anglo group. For example, in 1955 Negro and Mexican-Americans sued the El Centro School District in California for alleged "ethnic and racial discrimination and segregation by regulation, custom and usage.(98) In a rather narrow reading of *Brown*, the district court stated that *Brown*, which involved constitutional and statutory provisions, did not apply in situations where only customs and regulations were alleged. The court dismissed the complaint, claiming that where no specific regulation was set forth, plaintiffs must seek construction of the regulation in a State court.(99) On appeal, the Ninth Circuit reversed and remanded the case(100) holding that when the complaint alleged segregation of public school facilities on the basis of race or color, a federal constitutional issue had been raised, requiring the district court to exercise its jurisdiction. Instead of going to trial, the case apparently was settled out of court, but the segregation of Negroes and Mexican-Americans has continued in most of the Southwest.

Whether integrating Negroes and Mexican-Americans produce a unitary school system was the issue raised in *Keyes v. School District Number One*.(101) In *Keyes*, the court questioned the permissibility of adding the number of Negroes and Hispanos (as Mexican-Americans are referred to in Colorado) to reach a single minority category in order to classify the school as a segregated school.(102) Nevertheless, the court stated that "to the extent that Hispanos . . . are isolated in concentrated numbers, a school in which this has occurred is to be regarded as a segregated school, either *de facto* or *de jure*."(103) Failing to find de jure segregation, the court held that where the de facto segregated schools exist, they must provide equal educational opportunity, or a constitutional violation may exist.(104) As a result, the *Keyes* court revived the separate-but-equal doctrine(105) as to de facto segregated schools.

While *Keyes* did not answer whether mixing Blacks and *Chicanos* satisfies constitutional requirements, *Cisneros* did, holding that placing Negroes and Mexican-Americans in the same school did not achieve a unitary system.(106) However, *Keyes* involved de facto segregation, whereas *Cisneros* involved de jure segregation in the form of 1. locating schools in the Negro and Mexican-American neighborhoods; 2. bussing Anglo students to avoid the minority group schools; and 3. assigning Negro and Mexican-American teachers in disproportionate ratios to the segregated schools.(107)

In *Ross v. Eckels*(108) the Fifth Circuit appears to have disregarded the arguments advanced by Mexican-Americans and Negroes that mixing these minorities does not provide the equal educational opportunity of a unitary school system. In *Ross* the court implemented a pairing plan for the elementary schools of Houston, Texas, resulting in merging predominantly Negro schools with predominantly Mexican-American schools. Judge Clark, dissenting, relied on *Cisneros* in stating:

> I say it is a mock justice when we "force" the numbers by pairing disadvantaged Negro students into schools with members of this equally disadvantaged ethnic group [Mexican-Americans].(109)

Ross is an important case. First, *Ross* involves the sixth largest school district in the United States, having approximately 235,000 students.(110) Second, *Ross* involves a Southwestern city which, like Corpus Christi, has a tri-racial rather than a bi-racial student population. This tri-racial situation was recognized by the Houston school board when they voted unanimously to appeal the *Ross* case to the United States Supreme Court.(111)

Another case involving segregation of Mexican-Americans, *Perez v. Sonora Independent School District*,(112) held that the Sonora, Texas schools were operating in a "unitary, nondiscriminatory, fully desegregated school system."(113) MALDEF had offered evidence to show that in 1938 the Sonora school board passed a resolution enrolling Mexican-American children in the "Mexican School."(114) *Perez* is an important case for Mexican-Americans and the desegregation of schools in the Southwest in that it is the first desegregation case in which the Justice Department has intervened on behalf of Mexican-Americans.(115)

Since *Salvatierra* in 1930 the Mexican-American desegregation struggle has progressed slowly, considering the injustices which resulted first, from almost total segregation by the regulations of the various school districts, and second, from exploitation of the classification of Mexican-Americans as white. As *Brown* held, it is unconstitutional to segregate Blacks in the public school systems. Similarly, cases from *Mendez* in 1947 to *Perez* in 1970 have held that it is a violation of the equal protection clause of the 14th Amendment to maintain by "custom or regulation" segregated schools for Mexican-Americans. Consequently, assigning Negroes and Mexican-Americans to the same schools and excluding Anglos accomplishes an end that is exactly opposite to the goal desired by the educationally disadvantaged, that goal being the social encounters and interactions between the identifiable minority groups and Anglo-Americans. As a result, the desegregation or assignment plans, which school districts in the Southwest formulate in tri-racial situations, should include the three ethnic groups on a more or less proportionate basis. The necessity for this can perhaps be demonstrated by an analogy from criminal law:

1. If it is a crime to commit A, and
2. If it is a crime to commit B, then
3. One cannot commit A and B simultaneously and be absolved of the crimes.

The same applies to school districts which continue to segregate Negroes and Mexican-Americans from predominantly Anglo schools on the theory that a unitary school system is achieved by integrating the two minority groups, merely because one is technically classified as white. Actually the public school system remains a dual one with identifiable white schools and identifiable minority schools, thus justifying intervention of courts in situations where either identifiable minority group seeks relief.

Forty-one years have passed since Mexican-Americans first sought an equal educational opportunity by attendance at racially integrated schools. In many cases this goal has not been realized, even though Mexican-Americans have been successful in almost every case since *Mendez*.(116) Consequently, an affirmative answer is required for the question whether the history of the Mexican-American school children in the predominantly Anglo school systems of the Southwest demands recognition of them as an identifiable ethnic minority group.

THE SEGREGATION OF MEXICAN-AMERICAN CHILDREN

Residential segregation, whether resulting from economic necessity or discriminatory racial covenants, is a substantial factor in the de facto school segregation of Mexican-Americans. The residential segregation of Mexican-Americans ranges from a low of 30 percent in Sacramento, California to a high of 76 percent in Odessa, Texas.(117) The *Chicano* school cases can be compared to the amount of residential segregation in the areas where the cases arose, perhaps establishing a correlation between the residential segregation and allegations of unequal protection in the public school system:

Cases	Areas	Percentage of Mexican-American Residential Segregation(118)
Mendez (1946)	San Bernardino, California	67.9
Delgado (1948)	Austin, Texas	63.3
Gonzales (1951)	Phoenix, Arizona	57.8
Keyes (1970)	Denver, Colorado	60.0
Cisneros (1970)	Corpus Christi, Texas	72.2
Ross (1970)	Houston, Texas	65.2
Perez (1970)	San Angelo, Texas	65.7

This table reflects a positive correlation between de jure segregated schools and substantial racial segregation. This should be sufficient to shift the burden of proof to the defendant school districts in cases where de facto segregation is alleged.

Furthermore, *Dowell v. School Board*,(119) which holds that a neighborhood school policy is invalid when superimposed on residential segregation which was initiated by State enforcement of racial covenants, should be an aid to the Mexican-American's quest for an equal educational opportunity. There is support for the view that Mexican-Americans have been denied access to homes and apartments in predominantly Anglo areas.(120) These denials are aggravated by the economic reality that when one settles for a home in a residentially segregated neighborhood, the home is usually retained for some time.(121)

In 1948 *Shelley v. Kraemer*(122) held that State enforcement of private racial covenants is unconstitutional. As a result, State courts in California(123) and Texas(124) refused to enforce racial covenants which provided that "[n]o person or persons of the Mexican race or other than the Caucasian race shall use or occupy any buidings or any lot."(125) The patterns that developed prior to *Shelley* have not receded. School districts in the Southwest should not be allowed to allege that school segregation is merely de facto if there has been State action in pre-*Shelley* days. A plaintiff should not be required to prove any specific act of residential discrimination where a pattern of segregation appears. Requirements of actual proof allow unjustifiable delay in the immediate transformation to unitary school systems, an issue the Supreme Court considers to be of "paramount importance."(126)

ABILITY GROUPING

Like residential segregation, ability grouping (grouping students according to their talents and aptitudes) often leads to segregated education. However, unlike residential segregation, a factor external to the public school system, ability grouping is practiced within the school system. In schools that are to some extent desegregated, the tests and guides which are used indirectly lead to classes in which many Negroes, Mexican-Americans, or both are grouped into segregated classrooms. The results are by no means attributable to any inherent inadequacy on the part of minority group children. Instead, ability grouping which leads to ethnic and racial segregation can be traced to the nature of the social and environmental conditions which minority group children experience. When their aptitude is measured by a standardized national test, which is geared to represent the average white middle class student, the results are inherently biased against children who are culturally different from whites.(127)

In *Hobson v. Hansen*,(128) Judge Skelly Wright held that the school district's track system, a method of ability grouping, must be abolished because "[i]n practice, if not in concept, it discriminates against the disadvantaged child, particularly the Negro."(129) Judge Wright did not condemn all forms of ability grouping. However, he did question ability grouping when it unreasonably leads to or maintains continuous racial or socioeconomic segregation. In cases of such segregation, the effect is unreasonable and discriminatory because it fails to accomplish its aim—the grouping of pupils according to their capacities to learn. Because minority group children have had an educationally disadvantaged experience does not mean they msut be permanently restricted to low achievement.

Hobson may contribute much to the fall of the track systems employed in the Southwest. After all, when tests are given which result in highly disproportionate numbers of Mexican-Americans in the retarded or below average category, the classification is constitutionally suspect. The Supreme Court's language in *Hernandez* applies by analogy to the discriminatory effects of ability grouping in the Southwest: "The result [of an overrepresentation of Mexican-Americans in the below average category] bespeaks discrimination, whether or not it was a conscious decision on the part of any individual [school official]."(130)

Besides the language deficiency argument, other devices result in the segregation of Mexican-Americans, even in racially mixed schools. For example, standardized tests fail to judge accurately the Mexican-American's innate capacity to learn. The national tests may ask the *Chicano* child to match a picture with a word that is foreign to him but may be quite common to the middle class white child, who may have encountered its use within his environment. One must realize that these tests are geared to measure the average middle class white American. Consequently, *Chicano* children continue to score very low and to be placed in the lower intelligence sections, from which escape is practically impossible.(131)

An even more damaging practice is common in California. Mexican-American children, many of whom come from homes where Spanish is spoken daily, are given tests in English to determine their group level. Consequently, the language obstacle hinders the Spanish-speaking child and contributes to his lower score. As a result, many children score low enough to be classified as "Educable Mentally Retarded" (EMR). Once a child is placed in a special education class, his chance of escaping is minimal. In the San Diego, California school district, Mexican-Americans have challenged the unfair testing schemes which are employed and which result in disproportionate numbers of *Chicanos* in the EMR classes.(132)

In order to realize how examinations such as these deny equal protection to the Mexican-American student, one must perceive the discrepancy which results when the *Chicano* child is tested under varying condtions. Using the Wechsler Intelligence Scale for Children, 44 scored below 80 when tested in English. But when the test was administered to the same group in Spanish, only 20 scored below 80.(133) Consequently, when applied to children with a limited background in English, these tests are inadequate since they are unable to measure a child's capacity to learn and thus result in harmful discrimination to the Mexican-American child in the public schools of the Southwest.

Overall, there are many areas of the Southwest where segregated schools should be challenged as denying the equal protection of the laws. For example, Del Rio, Texas, the scene of the *Salvatierra* case in 1930, although it is a rather small town, has two school districts within the city limits: The Del Rio Independent School District, which is predominantly Anglo, and the San Felipe Independent School District, which is almost entirely Mexican-American.(134) Since the Del Rio schools are much better, the Anglo children from a nearby Air Force base are bussed at State expense to the Del Rio district schools, even though the base is located in the San Felipe district.(135) Although there are two technically separate school districts in Del Rio, they should be treated as one for purposes of school desegregation. The obvious reluctance of the Del Rio district to accept Mexican-Americans is evidenced by the fact that this school district's accreditation was questioned in 1949 for failure to integrage Mexican-American students.(136) This may support a claim of unconstitutional State action. However, assuming the Del Rio public school system is segregated on a de facto basis, the *Keyes*(137) separate-but-equal formula may play a decisive role in the desegregation of these schools. *Keyes* demands that segregated schools offer equal educational opportunity if they are to be constitutionally allowable. However, both physically and academically, the Del Rio district schools are superior. Besides being newer, Del Rio High School (mostly Anglo) offers 75 to 100 courses. On the other hand, San Felipe High School (Mexican-American) offers only 36 courses and cannot afford a vocational program.(138)

San Antonio, Texas, which is nearly 50 percent Mexican-American, employs a similar public school system. There are 13 school districts in and around the San Antonio area, of which five are predominantly Mexican-American and eight are predominantly Anglo-American.(139) Ninety percent of 82,000 of the Mexican-American students attend school in five predominantly Mexican-American districts. Because of the financial and educational inequities which result from having various independent school districts, residents of a nearly 100 percent Mexican-American school district have sued all the school districts in the San Antonio area.(140) The plaintiffs allege the Texas system of school financing, which allows each school district to collect taxes for use exclusively within that particular school system, violates the constitutional rights of children in the poorer districts to an equal educational opportunity. In a case of this type, *Hobson*, which also held that school boards cannot discriminate on the basis of poverty,(141) may be controlling, since the financing scheme does result, whether intentionally or not, in an unreasonable discrimination against the poor.

Ethnic isolation or concentration, as it exists in the Del Rio and San Antonio, Texas systems, is similar to that found throughout the Southwest, although it is least serious in California and most serious in Texas.(142) It is interesting to note that there is an inverse relationship between the educational level of Mexican-Americans in these two States.(143) In other words, where the ethnic segregation increases, the educational level decreases, and vice versa. This reaffirms the accepted view in desegregation cases that segregated educational facilities fail to offer an equal educational opportunity.(144)

ROSS V. ECKELS—THE HOUSTON SITUATION

As previously mentioned *Ross v. Eckels*(145) is a Fifth Circuit case in which a pairing order was issued for some Houston, Texas elementary schools. The result was the pairing of 27 predominantly Black and *Chicano* schools, whose segregated facilities resulted mostly from the de jure segregation of pre-1954 years and from the de facto segregation which developed as a result of the high rate of residential segregation in Houston. In many areas of the city, Negro neighborhoods are adjacent to Mexican-American *barrios*. Consequently, much of the neighborhood school "integration" which Houston does have is black-brown integration, lacking the white student population necessary in order to make the school system responsive both politically and educationally to the needs of the minority group population of Houston.

In the Southwest more than 50 percent of the Mexican-American students at the elementary school level attend predominantly Mexican-American schools.(146) For this reason, and since the *Ross* pairing order involved only elementary school children, this discussion will be limited to the elementary schools in Houston.

Judge Clark, in his dissenting opinion in *Ross*, denounced the pairing order as "mock justice" because it paired Negroes with another educationally disadvantaged group. An analysis of the school populations may prove Judge Clark's dissent to be more consistent with the prior development in the desegregation cases involving Blacks and *Chicanos*.(147)

The elementary grade level students in the Houston public schools number approximately 143,400.(148) Of these, 66,612 are Anglo; 53,875 are Negro; and 23,000 are Mexican-American. The respective percentages of each group in relation to the total student population in the elementary schools are 46.5 percent Anglo, 37.5 percent Negro, and 16 percent Mexican-American. Comparing the Anglo with the combined minority groups, Black and *Chicano* students comprise 53.5 percent of the student population. In addition, in 23 of the 170 elementary schools, the Mexican-American student population exceeds 50 percent, thus leading to ethnic imbalance. This does not include the many other schools where the combined minority group population greatly exceeds the 53.5 percent this combined group represents. In these 23 elementary schools, Mexican-Americans account for 74.9 percent of the total enrollment (13,300 out of a total of 17,750). In comparison to the entire Mexican-American school population, the 13,300 students in these ethnically concentrated schools account for 57.8 percent of the total *Chicano* population in elementary schools. As a result, Houston is typical of the elementary school segregation norm in the Southwest: Over 50 percent ethnic isolation.

Of the 27 schools involved in the *Ross* pairing order, only one was predominantly (50 percent or more) Anglo. It appears that the desegregation order excluded any meaningful integration of the Anglo student with the other identifiable groups in Houston. Overall, there were 2,368 Anglo, 6,233 Mexican-American, and 14,942 Negro students involved in the pairing plan. Consequently, 21,175 of the total 23,543 students, or 89.9 percent, were children of educationally disadvantaged backgrounds. The purpose of the desegregation cases, which is to establish unitary school systems and thereby provide meaningful social and educational encounters between students of all racial backgrounds, is not achieved by the *Ross* pairing order.(149)

CONCLUSION

Throughout the Southwest, the approximately 1.4 million Mexican-American students represent 17 percent of the total enrollment. Thus, *Chicanos* constitute the largest minority student group in this part of the United States.(150) These students have been neglected, both educationally(151) and legally. The low educational levels of Mexican-Americans imply that the school systems have failed to deal with this bilingual, bicultural group. Legally, the past failure of courts to require total disestablishment of dual school systems, such as in Del Rio, Texas after *Salvatierra*, has provided much support to the publicly-elected school boards in their attempt to maintain the segregation of Mexican-Americans.

As a result, Judge Seals' landmark ruling in *Cisneros* is cause for much optimism on the part of the Mexican-American population in the Southwest regarding the educational future of their children. In all respects, the holdings in *Brown* and its progeny apply to Mexican-Americans as well as to any other identifiable minority groups.

Cisneros is consistent with prior judicial development. Historically, Congress and the courts have granted Mexican-Americans protection from unreasonable discrimination in housing, employment, public accommodations, voting, the administration of justice, and in the field of equal educational opportunity. This protection has resulted from a recognition that Mexican-Americans are an identifiable ethnic minority group, whether because of physical characteristics, language, predominant religion, distinct culture, or Spanish surname(152) and are entitled to equal protection of the laws in the area of public school desegregation.

NOTES:

(1) Civil Action No. 68-C-95 (S.D. Tex., June 4, 1970) [hereinafter cited as *Cisneros*], noted, 49 TEX.L. REV. 337 (1971).

(2) Id. at 9-10.

(3) 347 U.S. 483 (1954). See also Swann v. Charlotte-Mecklenburg Bd. of Educ., 91 S.Ct. 1267 (1971).

(4) *Cisneros* at 13-14.

(5) Id. at 20-21.

(6) See THE NEW YORK TIMES ENCYCLOPEDIC ALMANAC 35, 288 (2d

ed. 1970).

(7) Id. at 245, 288.

(8) *Cisneros* at 10 n.34.

(9) Id. at 8 n.28.

(10) L. GREBLER, J. MOORE, & R. GUZMAN, THE MEXICAN-AMERICAN PEOPLE 14-15 (1970) [hereinafter cited as GREBLER, MOORE & GUZMAN]. The authors cite the Mexican-American population in 1960 as 3.8 million and estimate the 1970 count to be 5.6 million.

(11) Id. at 15.

(12) E.g., States: Arizona, California, Colorado, Texas; cities: San Antonio, Del Rio, San Francisco, Santa Fe, Pueblo; rivers: Rio Grande, Brazos, Guadalupe.

(13) 9 Stat. 922 (1848).

(14) Id. at 929-30, art. VIII.

(15) C. McWILLIAMS, NORTH FROM MEXICO 52 (1948) [hereinafter cited as McWILLIAMS].

(16) L.F. HERNANDEZ, A FORGOTTEN AMERICAN 8 (1969).

(17) U.S. BUREAU OF THE CENSUS, WE THE MEXICAN AMERICANS 2 (1970).

(18) McWILLIAMS 193.

(19) R. DANIELS & H.H.L. KITANO, AMERICAN RACISM 74 (1970). The authors refer to People v. Zammora, 66 Cal. App. 2d 166, 152 P.2d 180 (1944), in which 17 Mexican-American youths were indicted and convicted for murder, without any tangible evidence, in the death of another youth who was killed in a gang fight. The California appellate court reversed and remanded all the convictions.

(20) Id. at 77. The name "zoot suiters" was derived from the gaudy clothing worn by some of the *Chicano* youths.

(21) See Independent School Dist. v. Salvatierra, 33 S.W.2d 790 (Tex. Civ. App.—San Antonio 1930), cert. denied, 284 U.S. 580 (1931).

(22) AMERICAN GI FORUM, 21st ANNUAL CONVENTION, July 4, 1969. The incident leading to the creation of the GI Forum was the refusal in 1948 of Anglo citizens in Three Rivers, Texas to have a deceased Mexican-American veteran buried in the city's cemetery. The solider, Felix Longoria, was buried with honors in Arlington National Cemetery. San Angelo Standard-Times, July 6, 1969, § 1, at 1, col. 1.

(23) Judge Seals listed MAYO, LULAC, and the GI Forum as products of discriminatory practices. *Cisneros* 12.

(24) Steiner, Chicano Power, THE NEW REPUBLIC, June 20, 1970, at 17.

(25) The Texas Observer, April 11, 1969, at 6, col. 1 MALDEF is operating under an 8-year, $2.2 million Ford Foundation grant.

(26) See Hernandez v. Texas, 347 U.S. 475 (1954). The Supreme Court found that Mexican-Americans had been discriminated against in the selection of jurors in Jackson County, Texas, See also Tijerina v. Henry, 48 F.R.D. 274 (D.N.M.), appeal dismissed, 90 S. Ct. 1718 (1969) (Douglas, J., dissenting).

(27) The Texas Observer, April 11, 1969, at 6, col. 1.

(28) As of December 1969, MALDEF had filed civil rights suits against discrimination in hiring and promotion, the enforcement of the laws, voting rights, public accommodations, and education. See MALDEF Docket Report (Dec. 1969) [hereinafter cited as Docket Report].

(29) One author contends that the "brown skin color" of most Mexican-Americans makes them susceptible to Anglo prejudice against darker-skinned persons. See Forbes, Race and Color in Mexican-American Problems, 16 J. HUMAN REL, 55 (1968).

(30) McWILLIAMS.

(31) 42 U.S.C. § 200e-2 (1964).

(32) Civil Action No. 7680 (D.N.M., Sept. 24, 1969), discussed in 1 MALDEF Newsletter 1, Nov., 1969.

(33) H. ROWAN, THE MEXICAN AMERICAN 38, (Paper prepared for U.S. Comm'n on Civil Rights 1968).

(34) Id. at 39.

(35) The median school years completed by Mexican-Americans is 8.1, much lower than the 12.0 years achieved by Anglo students. GREBLER, MOORE & GUZMAN 143.

(36) W. FOGEL, MEXICAN AMERICANS IN SOUTHWEST LABOR MARKETS 191 (U.C.L.A. Mexican-American Study Project: Advance Report No. 10, 1967).

(37) H. ROWAN, THE MEXICAN AMERICAN 45, U.S. Comm'n on Civil Rights (1968).

(38) U.S. CONST. amend. XIV provides: "No State shall . . . deny to any person within its jurisdiction the equal protection of the laws." The Justice Department has sued an Arizona copper company for job opportunity discrimination against Mexican-Americans and Indians. Arizona Daily Star, Mar. 4, 1971. § B, at 1, col. 6.

(39) See Vigil v. American Tel. & Tel. Co., 305 F. Supp. 44 (D. Colo. 1969); Pena v. Hunt Tool Co., 296 F. Supp. 1003 (S.D. Tex. 1968). In another employment case, Moreno v. Henckel, 431 F.2d 1299 (5th Cir. 1970), the plaintiff was fired for circulating a petition of grievances concerning dissatisfaction with the rate of promotion for Mexican-American workers. The case was remanded since the district court incorrectly dismissed the case.

(40) See generally Docket Report, Tit. 2, Job Discrimination. The Justice Department has sued an Arizona firm and some unions for job opportunity discrimination against Mexican-Americans and Indians. Arizona Daily Star, Mar. 4, 1971, § B, at 1, col. 6.

(41) Id.

(42) Civil Action No. 69H-1082 (S.D. Tex., filed Nov. 4, 1969).

(43) 42 U.S.C. § 2000e-2 (1964) makes it unlawful for an employer to discriminate because of race, color, religion, sex, or national origin.

(44) Docket Report, Tit. 2, at 7.

(45) 293 F. Supp. 1176 (D. Colo. 1968).

(46) Valdez, Insurrection in New Mexico, 1 EL GRITO 14 (Fall, 1967).

(47) Id. at 19-20.

(48) 9 Stat. 922, 929-30 (1848).

(49) Valdez, Insurrection in New Mexico, 1 EL GRITO 14, 20-21 (Fall, 1967).

(50) See McWILLIAMS 76-78, supra note 15.

(51) For actual cases of ethnic discrimination in Texas see A. PERALES, ARE WE GOOD NEIGHBORS? 139-227 (1948) [hereinafter cited as PERALES].

(52) Terrell Wells Swimming Pool v. Rodriguez, 182 S.W.2d 824 (Tex. Civ. App.—San Antonio 1944, no writ); cf. Lueras v. Town of Lafayette, 100 Colo. 124, 65 P.2d 1431 (1937).

(53) Lopez v. Seccombe, 71 F. Supp. 769 (S.D. Cal. 1944).

(54) Beltran v. Patterson, Civil Action No. 68-59-W (W.D. Tex. 1968), cited in Brief for MALDEF as Amicus Curiae at 3, Ross v. Eckels, 434 F.2d 1140 (5th Cir. 1970).

(55) U.S. COMM'N ON CIVIL RIGHTS, MEXICAN AMERICANS AND THE ADMINISTRATION OF JUCTICE IN THE SOUTHWEST 2-6 (1970) [hereinafter cited as ADMINISTRATION OF JUSTICE].

(56) Id. at 4 n. 15.

(57) Lucero v. Donovan, 258 F. Supp. 979 (C.D. Cal. 1966).

(58) Lucero v. Donovan, 354 F.2d 16, 18 (9th Cir. 1965). Mrs. Lucero was a native-born citizen of the United States.

(59) For an insight into the distrust of the Texas Rangers by South Texas *Chicanos*, see ADMINISTRATION OF JUSTICE 16-17.

(60) See U.S. CONST. amend. VI.

(61) 347 U.S. 475 (1954).

(62) Id. at 479.

(63) Id. at 482.

(64) Hernandez v. State, 160 Tex. Crim. 72, 251 S.W.2d 531 (1952); Sanchez v. State, 156 Tex. Crim. 468, 243 S.W.2d 700 (1951); Salazar v. State, 149 Tex. Crim. 260, 193 S.W.2d 211 (1946); Sanchez v. State, 147 Tex. Crim. 436, 181 S.W.2d 87 (1944).

(65) 347 U.S. 475, 478 (1954) (emphasis added).

(66) See United States v. Hunt, 265 F. Supp. 178 (W.D. Tex. 1967); Gonzales v State, 414 S.W.2d 181 (Tex. Crim. App. 1967); Montoya v. People, 345 P.2d 1062 (Colo. 1959).

(67) Muniz v. Beto, 434 F.2d 697 (5th Cir. 1970).

(68) Id. at 703.

(69) Id. at 702.

(70) E.g., Voting rights: Mexican American Federation v. Naff, 299 F. Supp. 587 (E.D. Wash. 1969), rev'd, 39 U.S.L.W. 3296 (U.S. Jan. 12, 1971) (English literacy requirement upheld by the lower court); Castro v. State, 2 Cal. 3d 223, 466 P. 2d 244, 85 Cal. Rptr. 20 (1970) (English literacy requirement held unconstitutional). Housing: Valtierra v. Housing Authority, 313 F. Supp. 1

(N.D. Cal. 1970), rev'd sub nom. James v. Valtierra, 91 S.Ct. 1331 (1971). Judicial prejudice: Judge Gerald S. Chargin Speaks, 2 EL GRITO 4 (1969). In this juvenile court proceeding, Judge Chargin denounced a *Chicano* youth, who was charged with incest, and the "Mexican people" for acting "like an animal" and for being "miserable, lousy, rotten people." Chargin also stated that "[m]aybe Hitler was right" about having to destroy the animals in our society.

(71) 42 U.S.C. § 2000(a) (1964).

(72) 20 U.S.C. § 880b (Supp. V. 1970).

(73) The Mexican-American student has suffered serious emotional scars because of the "No Spanish" rule, whose violation by speaking Spanish on school grounds often has led to scolding and/or detention after school as punishment. The rule was probably derived from Tex. Laws 1933, ch. 125, § 1, at 325 (repealed 1969), which required all school business, except foreign language classes, to be conducted in English.

(74) 42 U.S.C. § 4301 (Supp. V, 1970).

(75) For example, the following reports have been published: U.S. COMM'N ON CIVIL RIGHTS, MEXICAN AMERICAN EDUCATION STUDY, REPORT 1: ETHNIC ISOLATION OF MEXICAN AMERICANS IN THE PUBLIC SCHOOLS OF THE SOUTHWEST (1970); U.S. COMM'N ON CIVIL RIGHTS, MEXICAN AMERICANS AND THE ADMINISTRATION OF JUSTICE IN THE SOUTHWEST (1970); H. ROWAN, THE MEXICAN AMERICAN, U.S. Comm'n on Civil Rights (1968); U.S. COMM'N ON CIVIL RIGHTS, HEARING HELD IN SAN ANTONIO, TEXAS, DECEMBER 9-14, 1968 (1968).

(76) U.S. BUREAU OF THE CENSUS, WE THE MEXICAN AMERICANS (1970); F.H. SCHMIDT, SPANISH SURNAMED AMERICAN EMPLOYMENT IN THE SOUTHWEST (1970) (A Study Prepared for the Colorado Civil Rights Comm'n under the auspices of the Equal Employment Opportunity Comm'n).

(77) Pottinger, Memorandum to School Districts with More Than Five Percent National Origin-Minority Group Children, May 25, 1970. Memorandum on file in Univ. of Houston Law Library. See also 35 Fed. Reg. 13442 (1970). The Department of Health, Education and Welfare suggested to the Houston school district that Mexican-Americans be appointed to the district's biracial committee. Houston Chronicle, Dec. 18, 1970, § 1, at 1, col. 8.

(78) T.I. EMERSON, 2 POLITICAL AND CIVIL RIGHTS IN THE UNITED STATES 1734 (3d ed. 1967) citing NATIONAL ASS'N OF INTERGROUP RELATIONS, Public School Segregation and Integration in the North, J. INTERGROUP REL. 1 (1963).

(79) 33 S.W.2d 790 (Tex. Civ. App.—San Antonio 1930), cert. denied, 284 U.S. 580 (1931).

(80) Id. at 795.

(81) Id. at 793.

(82) TEX. ATT'Y GEN. OP. No. V-128 (1947), reported in J.C. HINSLEY, TEXAS SCHOOL LAW 1109 (4th ed. 1968).

(83) 64 F. Supp. 544 (S.D. Cal. 1946), aff'd, 161 F.2d 774 (9th Cir. 1947).

(84) Id. at 549.

(85) Brown v. Board of Educ., 347 U.S.483, 495 (1954).

(86) 64 F. Supp. at 549.

(87) School Dist. v. Mendez, 161 F.2d 774, 779 (9th Cir. 1947), aff'g 64 F. Supp. 544 (S.D. Cal. 1946).

(88) Id. at 781.

(89) Civil Action No. 388 (W.D. Tex., June 15, 1948) (unreported); accord, Gonzales v. Sheely, 96 F. Supp. 1004 (D. Ariz. 1951).

(90) Id. at 1.

(91) Id. at 2.

(92) See Hernandez v. Driscoll Consol. Ind. School Dist., 2 RACE REL. L. REP. 329 (S.D. Tex. 1957).

(93) Id. at 331.

(94) 2 RACE REL. L. REP. 329 (S.D. Tex. 1957).

(95) Id. at 331-32.

(96) Chapa v. Odem Ind. School Dist., Civil Action No. 66-C-92 (S.D. Tex., July 27, 1967) (unreported).

(97) 347 U.S. 483 (1954).

(98) Romero v. Weakley, 131 F. Supp. 818, 820 (S.D. Cal.), rev'd, 226 F.2d 399 (9th Cir. 1955).

(99) Id. at 831.

(100) 226 F. 2d 399 (9th Cir. 1955).

(101) 313 F. Supp. 61 (D. Colo. 1970). (This opinion deals only with the issue of segregation in the school.)

(102) Id. at 69.

(103) Id. On the issue of the desegregation plan, the court expressed that apportionment of the three ethnic groups was desirable but not required. Id. at 98.

(104) Id. at 82-83. For another de facto case involving Chicanos and Blacks, see United States v. Lubbock Ind. School Dist., 316 F. Supp. 1310 (N.D. Tex. 1970).

(105) See Plessy v. Ferguson, 163 U.S. 537 (1896). The separate-but-equal doctrine was repudiated as to de jure school segregation by Brown v. Board of Educ., 347 U.S. 483 (1954).

(106) Cisneros at 13.

(107) Id. at 14-15.

(108) 434 F.2d 1140 (5th Cir. 1970).

(109) Id. at 1150 (dissenting opinion).

(110) Id. at 1141.

(111) Houston Chronicle, Sept. 15, 1970 § 1, at 1, col. 1.

(112) Civil Action No. 6-224 (N.D. Tex., Nov. 5, 1970). Sonora, Texas, had a "Mexican" elementary school which was 2 percent black and an all-Anglo elementary school.

(113) Id. at 2.

(114) Plaintiff's Motion for a Preliminary Injunction at 4, Perez v. Sonora Ind. School Dist., Civil Action No. 6-224 (N.D. Tex., Nov. 5, 1970).

(115) Houston Chronicle, Nov. 6, 1970, § 1, at 9, col. 7. The United States has also objected to the adoption of a desegregation plan in Austin, Texas whereby Blacks and Chicanos were integrated to the exclusin of Anglos, thus maintaining ethnically and racially identifiable schools. United States v. Texas Educ. Agency, Civil Action No. A-70-CA-80, (W.D. Tex., filed Aug. 7, 1970), cited in Brief for MALDEF as Amicus Curiae at 14, Ross v. Eckels, 434 F.2d 1140 (5th Cir. 1970).

(116) One case where Mexican-Americans and Negroes were denied relief is United States v. Lubbock Ind. School Dist., 316 F. Supp. 1310 (N.D. Tex. 1970), where the court found the segregation to be de facto.

(117) GREBLER, MOORE & GUZMAN 274, supra note 10. Zero percent segregation connotes a random scattering throughout the population; 100 percent represents total segregation.

(118) Id. at 275.

(119) 244 F. Supp. 971 (W.D. Okla.), aff'd sub nom. Board of Educ. v. Dowell, 375 F.2d 158 (10th Cir. 1965), cert. denied, 387 U.S. 931 (1967).

(120) PERALES 139-146, supra note 51.

(121) Kaplan, Segregation Litigation and the Schools—Part II: The General Northern Problem, 58 Nw. U.L. REV. 157, 212 (1964).

(122) 334 U.S. 1 (1948).

(123) Matthews v. Andrade, 87 Cal. App. 2d 906, 198 P.2d 66 (1948).

(124) Clifton v. Puente, 218 S.W.2d 272 (Tex. Civ. App.—San Antonio 1948,

(125) 87 Cal App. 2d 906, 198 P.2d 66 (1948). The language in Clifton was similar to that cited here.

(126) 396 U.S. 19, 20 (1969). See generally Wright, Public School Desegregation: Legal Remedies for De Facto Segregation, 16 W. RES. L. REV. 478 (1965).

(127) Hobson v. Hansen, 269 F. Supp. 401, 484-85 (D.D.C. 1967), appeal dismissed, 393 U.S. 801 (1968), aff'd sub nom., Smuck v. Hobson, 408 F.2d 175 (D.C. Cir. 1969).

(128) Id.

(129) Id. at 515; accord, Dove v. Parham, 282 F.2d 256, 261 (8th Cir. 1960).

(130) Hernandez v. Texas, 347 U.S. 475, 482 (1954).

(131) A suit has been filed in Texas against a district alleging segregation resulting both from design and from a rigid system of ability grouping. Zamora v. New Braunfels Ind. School Dist., Civil Action No. 68-205-SA (W.D. Tex., filed Aug. 28, 1968), cited in Docket Report, Tit. 3, Education, at 1.

(132) Covarrubias v. San Diego Unified School Dist., Civil Action No. 70-394-T (S.D. Cal., filed Dec. 1, 1970).

(133) M. WEINBERG, DESEGREGATION RESEARCH: AN APPRAISAL 265-66 (2d ed. 1970).

(134) U.S. COMM'N ON CIVIL RIGHTS, HEARING HELD IN SAN ANTONIO, TEXAS, December 9-14, 1968, at 295-304 (1968).

(135) Id. at 304.

(136) Id. at 305.

(137) 313 F. Supp. 61 (D. Colo. 1970).

(138) 2 Civil Rights Digest 16, 20 (1969).

(139) U.S. COMM'N ON CIVIL RIGHTS, MEXICAN AMERICAN EDUCATION STUDY, REPORT 1: ETHNIC ISOLATION OF MEXICAN AMERICANS IN THE PUBLIC SCHOOLS OF THE SOUTHWEST 26 (1970) [hereinafter cited as ETHNIC ISOLATION].

(140) Rodriguez v. San Antonio Ind. School Dist., 299 F. Supp. 476 (W.D. Tex. 1969) (issue here limited to whether a three-judge panel should hear the case).

(141) 269 F. Supp. at 513.

(142) ETHNIC ISOLATION 30.

(143) See GREBLER, MOORE & GUZMAN 144, supra note 10.

(144) A Connecticut Department of Education study shows that children bused to suburban classrooms from inner-city schools accelerate their reading ability as much as 18 months ahead of their urban counterparts who remain behind. Houston Chronicle, Nov. 8, 1970, § 1, at 2, col. 7.

(145) 434 F.2d 1140 (5th Cir. 1970).

(146) ETHNIC ISOLATION 35.

(147) E.g., Cisneros v. Corpus Christi Ind. School Dist., Civil Action No. 68-C-95 (S.D. Tex. June 4, 1970); Keyes v. School Dist. Number One, 313 F. Supp. 61 (D. Colo. 1970); Romero v. Weakley, 131 F. Supp. 818 (S.D. Cal.), rev'd, 226 F.2d 399 (9th Cir. 1955). These three cases involved segregation of Negroes and Mexican-Americans into minority schools.

(148) Houston Chronicle, Oct. 1, 1970, § 1, at 13, col. 1-2. All figures and percentages used in the analysis of the Houston elementary schools were derived from this article.

(149) Ross v. Eckels, 434 F.2d 1140 (5th Cir. 1970) was appealed to the Supreme Court of the United States by the Houston Independent School District because the court pairing order integrated two minority groups, Houston Chronicle, Sept. 15, 1970, § 1, at 1, col. 1. A motion to stay the pairing order was denied by the Supreme Court. Houston Chronicle, March 1, 1971, § 1, at 1, col. 1.

(150) ETHNIC ISOLATION 89.

(151) See T. P. CARTER, MEXICAN AMERICANS IN SCHOOL: A HISTORY OF EDUCATIONAL NEGLECT (1970).

(152) Cisneros v. Corpus Christi Ind. School Dist., Civil Action No. 68-C-95, at 10-11 (S.D. Tex. June 4, 1970).

MEXICAN-AMERICANS AND THE DESEGREGATION OF SCHOOLS IN THE SOUTHWEST—A SUPPLEMENT

Guadalupe Salinas

Since the original publication of this writer's article in the Houston Law Review, there have been additional cases of interest in the Chicano civil rights field. Also, there are some cases which the writer omitted but desires to discuss in this supplement.

One year after the Treaty of Guadalupe Hidalgo in 1848, those Mexicans who remained in the United States became American citizens. However, this did not clear up the citizenship problem for Chicanos. In the late 1890's Ricardo Rodriguez, a legal United States resident, filed an application to become a naturalized citizen. The United States denied it because *the law restricted naturalization to whites and persons of African descent.* The contention, therefore, was that Rodriguez was neither white nor black. In fact, the opposing lawyers described him as having "chocolate brown skin."(1) As a result, Rodriguez took his claim to court where the issue presented was, "Is Rodriguez ineligible for citizenship because he is not a 'white' person and apparently belongs to the Indian or red race?"(2)

In re Rodriguez(3) held that Rodriguez was entitled to citizenship, even though the court recognized that anthropoligically, Rodriguez "would probably not be classed as white."(4) Consequently, *this case verifies that historically the Chicano has been viewed as a separate group, distinct from whites, for generations.*(5)

DISCRIMINATION IN EMPLOYMENT

Of enormous importance to Chicanos, Blacks and Indians alike is the case of

Griggs v. Duke Power Company,(6) where the United States Supreme Court said:

> If an employment practice [e.g. aptitude test] which operates to exclude Negroes [Chicanos and Indians] cannot be shown to be related to job performance, the practice is prohibited.(7)

This case implies employers can no longer deny jobs because they fail a test, lack a high school diploma, or are unable to speak fluent English *unless* the employer can show the requirement is related to the job. For example, one does not have to pass an English vocabulary test to be qualified for a job as a telephone installer. Such a test merely serves to weed Chicanos out from many of these jobs. Therefore, Raza lawyers should study *Griggs* closely.

SPANISH AND MEXICAN LAND GRANTS

Of significant legal and historical value in the land grant area are the Supreme Court cases of *United States v. Rio Arriba Land and Cattle Company* (1897),(8) *United States v. Sandoval* (1897),(9) and *United States v. Santa Fe* (1897).(10) These cases are considered the "bulwark against the property rights of the impoverished Indo-Hispano (Chicano) of the Southwest."(11)

PUBLIC ACCOMMODATIONS

In the case of *In re Rodriguez* the Chicano was described as belonging to the Indian race. Apparently this view is still current in Arizona. In June, 1971, a Chicano friend of the writer, his family, and some friends went to the Grand Canyon on their vacation. On the way they stopped for breakfast at a restaurant in Cameron, Arizona. They sat down and waited . . . and waited. Meanwhile, the other customers were being served. After thirty minutes, they asked what they had to do to obtain service. The waitress, an Indian girl, told him that it was not the policy of the management to serve Indians! After a few demands, the Chicanos were served, but the rude manner in which the food was served amounted to a denial of services. The Department of Justice is currently investigating the incident.(12)

ADMINISTRATION OF JUSTICE

In *Tate v. Short*,(13) Peter Sanchez Navarro, a Chicano lawyer then with the Houston Legal Foundation, convinced the Supreme Court that one should not be confined to jail to work off a traffic fine. This case should serve as a basis for the release of a large number of Chicanos who remain jailed merely because they are too poor to pay the fine imposed.

SOCIAL WELFARE

In *Graham v. Richardson*(14) the Supreme Court ruled that State statutes which deny welfare benefits to resident aliens or to aliens who have not resided in the United States for a specified number of years violate the equal protection clause of the 14th Amendment. *Graham's* enforcement in Texas is currently being sought by a Mexican alien who has resided in the United States for 54 of her 60 years.(15)

VOTING

In *Garza v. Smith*(16) a federal district court ruled that the Texas Election Code denies illiterate voters equal protection because the Code allows assistance in the voting booth only to those that are physically handicapped and by implication, denies it to the "mentally" handicapped. The court said that the illiterate "is just as surely disabled as the blind or physically incapacitated voter, and therefore equally in need of assistance, yet the statutes forbid anyone to help him."(17)

MIGRANT WORKERS

In October, 1971 a federal district court in Michigan ruled that migrant workers are entitled to basic civil rights just as any other person. The facts were that a Chicano named Folgueras, representing a federal program designed for migrant workers, tried to enter Hassle's property to visit some migrants. However, Hassle beat Folgueras and got two deputy sheriffs to arrest him for criminal trespass. Folgueras recovered a money judgment against the three as well as a constitutional rule that property rights are subordinate to the farm workers' civil rights.(18)

CHICANO SCHOOL CASES IN CALIFORNIA AND COLORADO

Although Texas leads in the quantity of recent Chicano school cases, California leads in the quality of the legal reasoning. For example, in *People v. San Diego Unified School District*(19) a State appellate court held that the school district must take reasonably feasible steps to alleviate racial imbalance in the schools because it resulted from racially motivated State action perpetuating a previously existing imbalance whatever may have been its initial cause. The suit was brought by the attorney general on behalf of Mexican-American, Black, Oriental, and American Indian students.

Another important Chicano case is *Soria v. Oxnard School District*.(20) This federal district court case held that "separate education for the Mexican American and Negro American students in the Oxnard Elementary Schools is inferior to education in racially balanced schools within the district."(21)

Perhaps the most far-reaching case since *Brown* in 1954 is *Serrano v.*

Priest,(22) decided on August 30, 1971, by the California Supreme Court. *Serrano* held that the State's financing of the public school system, with its substantial dependence on local property taxes and resultant wide disparities in school revenue, violates the equal protection clause. The Court said:

> [T]his funding scheme invidiously discriminates against the poor because it makes the quality of a child's education a function of the wealth of his parents and neighbors.(23)

Unlike the vigorous duty required by California courts to overcome racial and ethnic imbalance, the Tenth Circuit, which includes Colorado, has reversed *Keyes* and ruled that in de facto cases, the school district is not required to develop a desegregation plan unless the imbalance resulted from racially motivated conduct.(24)

CHICANO SCHOOL CASES IN TEXAS

In Houston *Ross v. Eckels*, which calls for the pairing of Black and Chicano children, is still the law. On May 24, 1971, Judge Ben C. Connally threw La Raza out of court. The Mexican-American Education Council (MAEC) was seeking, through various Chicano parents, to intervene in the Houston school case.

Before the Houston school district was given serious orders to desegregate, Anglos went to white schools, Blacks went to black schools, and La Raza went to the brown schools. To some extent there has been white-brown integration. After the district received orders to desegregate the dual school system, the residentially segregated Blacks and Chicanos were paired into their neighborhood schools. As a result of being *used* as whites and not *treated* as whites, the Houston Chicanos boycotted the schools in September, 1970 and opened their own Huelga Schools. These Huelga Schools are presently operating with the assistance of volunteer teachers.

During the boycott, the school superintendent recognized Chicanos as an identifiable ethnic minority group. However, it was not binding unless Judge Connally could be convinced that Chicanos have been and are a separate ethnic group. The judge, in his opinion on the motion to intervene, displayed his ignorance of Chicano history and of the Texas Chicano school cases in saying:

> The Houston Independent School District (*as I believe has been true generally for school purposes throughout this state*) has always treated Latin-Americans as of the *Anglo* or White race.(25)

First, Judge Connally disregards reality when he claims Chicanos have always been treated as Whites in Texas schools. Generally, the documentation this writer has presented refutes that statement. More specifically, *Salvatierra, Delgado, Hernandez, Cisneros, Perez*, and many other cases are legal proof that Chicanos have been discriminated against because of their race and/or color.

Second, the Judge grossly exaggerates when he states that Latin-Americans have always been treated as of the *Anglo* race.

Judge Connally then implicitly accuses Chicanos of being racists:

> Content to be "White" for these many years, now, when the shoe begins to pinch, the would-be Intervenors wish to be treated not as Whites but as an "identifiable minority group." *In short they wish to be "integrated" with Whites, not Blacks.*(26)

What worries this writer is that Judge Connally never cited legal authority for his conclusions. Instead, his decision appears to reveal more of an individual personal opinion. The truth of the matter is that whenever MAEC presented official demands, one of them always called for a *tri-ethnic* desegregation plan, including Anglos, Chicanos, *and* Blacks. Nevertheless, the only relief Chicanos and Blacks can hope for is from the Fifth Circuit, the court which will soon rule on *Cisneros v. Corpus Christi Independent School District.*(27)

In *United States v. Austin Independent School District*(28) the central issue was whether Chicanos had been segregated by acts of the school district. Austin is 64.6% Anglo, 20.4% Chicano, and 15.1% Black. Judge Roberts conceded that even the most casual examination of Chicano culture discloses Chicanos are a separate ethnic group. Nevertheless, the court added:

> But the mere existence of an ethnic group, regardless of its racial origin, and standing alone, does not establish a case for integrating it with the remainder of the school population. Rather the plaintiff (HEW) must show that there had been some form of de jure (official) segregation against the ethnic minority.(29)

Judge Roberts held the Austin district had never segregated Chicanos, but he did note the inequity of integrating Blacks and Browns only:

> [T]here will be little educational value in a plan which merely integrates one socially and economically disadvantaged group, the blacks, with another, the Mexican-Americans.(30)

Tasby v. Estes,(31) the Dallas school case, is a class action filed by the Dallas Legal Services on behalf of Black and Chicano school children. The court held that Chicanos, although they constitute a clearly separate and identifiable ethnic group, failed to show official segregation by the Dallas school district. However, the court directed that any desegregation plan would take Chicanos into account. In addition, the court called for the creation of a tri-ethnic rather than a bi-racial committee and named five citizens from each of the three groups.

The plan in *Tasby* is unique in two ways. First, it encourages desegregation by providing a four-day week for students who volunteer to transfer from schools where they are the majority to schools where their race is the minority. Second, the plan substitutes physical contact among the different groups with a simultaneous two-way oral and visual communication on television.(32) The case is currently on appeal to the Fifth Circuit.

When the original school suit was filed in Bryan in 1961, it was filed by Blacks. This year the United States intervened, contending that Bryan operated 14 schools, three attended exclusively by Blacks and one attended predominantly by Chicanos. The district is 26.5% Black and 13.4% Chicano. The court found that 40% of the district's Chicano children attended a school where their race is in a large majority. Consequently, the court ordered Bryan to abstain from discriminating on the basis of race, color, *or ethnic origin*, thereby implying that Chicanos had been segregated officially by the district.(33)

Not all school desegregation requires court action. The Department of Health, Education and Welfare (HEW) can order the submission of a plan whenever it feels discriminatory conditions exist in a school district. This is what occurred in Victoria with regard to three elementary schools. The school board feels these schools are integrated, but as a MAYO member told the board, "All you have to do is to go to those schools to see that they are mostly Black and Chicano."(34) The status of the action in Victoria at the present time is unknown.

HEW also filed a civil rights "non-compliance" notice against the Weslaco school district. The district, whose student composition is 85.7% Chicano, has only 78 or 27.2% Chicano teachers. Another alleged violation is that four of the six elementary schools are nearly 100% Chicano.(35) To keep their federal funds, Weslaco adopted a single-grade campus, i.e., each elementary school has only one grade.

In *Rodriguez v. San Antonio Independent School District*,(36) the Chicano plaintiffs are seeking to invalidate the property tax system of school financing as California Chicanos did in *Serrano v. Priest*. However, Judge Spears has purposely delayed hearing the suit to wait for the Texas Legislature to remedy the situation.(37) Even though the legislature failed to act, the case has yet to be heard.

Another legal issue arising in San Antonio is the location of a new school. The NAACP claims that the construction of a new school in a particular location will result in the incorporation of two "handicapped groups"—Blacks and Chicanos—with only a small percentage of white students.(38)

This writer urged in his previous article that the Del Rio and San Felipe school districts should be treated as one for desegregation purposes.(39) In *United States v. State of Texas*(40) Judge Justice accomplished this by consolidating these two districts. The action arose after the Texas Education Agency refused to accept Anglo transfers to Del Rio from an Air Force base located within the San Felipe district. The refusal was based on the theory that allowing Anglo school children to escape attending an ethnically imbalanced school impedes the desegregation of the districts.(41) The district is now known as the San Felipe Del Rio Consolidated Independent School District.

In *Alvarado v. El Paso Independent School District*(42) the Fifth Circuit reversed a lower court's dismissal of a Chicano class action desegregation suit alleging racial and ethnic discrimination. The lower court judge said the plaintiffs had "failed to allege any specific act of discrimination which specifically affects any one of the Plaintiffs."(43) On the other hand, the Fifth Circuit held that "the complaint clearly states a cause of action," citing a few cases as authority *"and other cases too numerous to list."*(44)

Alvarado is important for the Texas school cases because it is the first time the Fifth Circuit has addressed itself *directly* to a Chicano school desegregation issue. The court did not rule on the legal questions involved, but it still recognized the identifiability of Mexican-Americans.

The Fifth Circuit first had occasion to deal with the Chicano issue in *Ross v. Eckels*, the Houston case. However, the reason the court allowed the pairing of Black and Chicano schools probably was because the issue was not ripe for decision. The court lacked the value of legal argument by an interest group like MALDEF (Mexican American Legal and Defense Education Fund). And more crucial, there were no Chicano plaintiffs (and there still are none) in *Ross*. This did not prevent Judge Clark from denouncing the Black-Brown integration as "mock justice." Any further developments in this field will be determined by the Fifth Circuit's decisions in the Corpus Christi, Austin, Dallas, El Paso, and Houston cases.

In *Morales v. Uvalde Independent School District*,(45) the district court dismissed a suit which is similar to the allegations made in *Alvarado*. The court said that any segregation in Uvalde schools was de facto, i.e., based on voluntary, residential patterns. In addition, the court claimed it could not allow "any and all groups of private individuals to institute suits to revamp and revise an entire school system which has been elected under the democratic process by the people."(46) Because of the similarity to *Alvarado*, the court has decided to delay the Uvalde case until *Alvarado* is finally decided by a higher court.

Cisneros v. Corpus Christi Independent School District is the landmark case that set off the current rash of Chicano school cases. Briefly, Judge Seals ruled that Chicanos are entitled to the protection of *Brown* and every other school case regarding Blacks since. Also, he held that integration of Blacks and Chicanos fails to produce a unitary school system.

Cisneros is tentatively set to be heard on November 16, 1971. It was originally decided in June, 1970. In October, 1970, Judge Seals allowed the Department of Justice and HEW to intervene,even though an anti-bussing group was denied. The reason for the differing treatment is that the national policy was then one favoring integration.

On July 2, 1971, Judge Seals issued his decision to bus 15,000 students in order to desegregate Corpus Christi, basing this remedy on *Swann v. Charlotte-Mecklenburg Board of Education*(48) This decision was appealed by the school district to the late Justice Black, who granted a stay. Justice Black said the Corpus Christi situation is "very anomalous, new and confusing."(49) Also, the Department of Justice said there was a "serious question" that there had been discrimination against Chicanos.(50)

On October 7, 1971, the Fifth Circuit voted against hearing *Cisneros* as a full court (16 judges), even though serious questions are involved.(51) Judge Bell, the only one in favor of having the entire court hear the case, stated that:

> [w]e have here a Mexican-American and Anglo segregation problem in a school district where school segregation between the two groups has never been required by law.(52)

Judge Bell fails to recognize that "law" includes not only State legislation and constitutions but also school board customs, regulations, and practices. It was school board practices that Judge Seals found had segregated Mexican-Americans from Anglo children. Nevertheless, it remains for the Fifth Circuit to rule on this question in *Cisneros*.

ABILITY GROUPING

In *Diana v. State Board of Education*(53) the plaintiff Chicano children contended that California's administration of intelligence tests resulted in a disproportionate number of Chicanos in Educable Mentally Retarded classes. The reason for this was that the tests 1) stress verbal skills and 2) are culturally biased since they are geared to measure the average middle class white child.

As a remedy, the court order and agreement requires, among other things, that all children whose primary home language is other than English from now on must be tested in both their primary language and in English with tests which put less stress on verbal skills.

MEXICAN-AMERICAN DESEGREGATION—THE FUTURE

As previously mentioned, the Del Rio, Texas school case is apparently settled with the consolidaiton of the Del Rio and San Felipe school districts.

In San Antonio, no decision has been rendered in *Rodriguez*, but *Serrano*, the California property tax case, is extremely relevant.

CONCLUSION

It is hoped that this supplement will offer the reader an insight into the ramifications *Cisneros* could have on the public schools of the Southwest. In addition, the supplement hopefully serves to inform the reader of other recent cases involving the civil rights of Mexican-Americans. The overall objective, however, is to convince the American judicial system that La Raza—Mexican-Americans, Chicanos, Hispanos, Latinos—has been treated unjustly educationally and legally, therefore requiring the intervention of the judiciary in areas of interest to La Raza. Otherwise, the constitutional rule of equal protection of the laws will be nothing more than an empty, unenforcible promise for Chicanos.

NOTES

(1) In re Rodriguez, 81 F. 337, 345 (W.D. Tex. 1897).

(2) Id. at 340.

(3) 81 F. 337 (W.D. Tex, 1897).

(4) Id. at 349.

(5) See also Sanchez, Pachucos in the Making, 4 COMMON GROUND 13 (1943), where De. George I. Sanchez of the University of Texas theorizes that discrimination has a causal relationship to the development of pachucos.

(6) 401 U.S. 424, 91 S. Ct. 849 (1971).

(7) 91 S. Ct. 849, 853 (1971).

(8) 167 U.S. 298 (1897).

(9) 167 U.S. 278 (1897).

(10) 165 U.S. 675 (1897).

(11) Letter from William L. Higgs to the United States Supreme Court, February 21, 1971.

(12) Interview with Jesse Cruz, July, 1971.

(13) 401 U.S. 395 (1971).

(14) Graham v. Richardson, 403 U.S. 365, 39 U.S.L.W. 4732 (U.S. June 14, 1971).

(15) Perez v. Hackney, Civil Action No. 70-H-1398 (S.D. Tex., filed July 16, 1971). See Comment, State Discrimination Against Mexican Aliens, 38 GEO. WASH. L. REV. 1091 (1970).

(16) 320 F. Supp. 131 (W.D. Tex. 1970).

(17) Id. at 137.

(18) Houston Chronicle, Oct. 4, 1971, § 1, at 11, col. 1. See also Gomez v. Florida State Employment Service, 417 F.2d 569 (5th Cir. 1969), where a migrant worker was allowed a civil rights action for damages.

(19) 96 Cal. Rptr. 658 (Cal. App. 1971).

(20) 328 F. Supp. 155 (C.D. Cal. 1971).

(21) Id. at 157.

(22) 96 Cal. Rptr. 601 (1971). See also Rodriguez v. San Antonio Ind. School Dist., 299 F. Supp. 476 (W.D. Tex. 1969).

(23) Id. at 604.

(24) Keyes v. School Dist. No. 1, 445 F.2d 990 (10th Cir. 1971), rev'g 313 F. Supp. 61, 313 F. Supp 90 (D. Colo. 1970).

(25) Ross v. Eckels, Civil Action No. 10444, at 6 (S.D. Tex. May 24, 1971) (emphasis added).

(26) Id. at 7 (emphasis added).

(27) *Cisneros* is scheduled for argument on November 16, 1971.

(28) Civil Action No. A-70-CA-80 (W.D. Tex. June 28, 1971).

(29) Corpus Christi Caller, June 29, 1971. § A, at 2, col. 3.

(30) Id. at col. 4. The Fifth Circuit Court of Appeals has decided to allow the NAACP and MALDEF to intervene. The groups felt the government would not adequately represent the Black and Chicano school children's needs. San Antonio

Express, Aug. 25, 1971, § A, at 16, col. 1.

(31) Civil Action No. 3-4211-C (N.D. Tex. Aug. 2, 1971).

(32) Id. at 7, 17.

(33) Thomas v. Bryan Ind. School Dist., Civil Action No. 13850, at 3-6 (S.D. Tex. July 23, 1971).

(34) Corpus Christi Caller, June 25, 1971, § D, at 16, col. 4.

(35) The McAllen Monitor, July 28, 1971, § A, at 1, col. 2.

(36) 299 F. Supp. 476 (W.D. Tex. 1969).

(37) San Antonio Express, Sept. 2, 1971. § A, at 1, col. 2.

(38) San Antonio Express, July 18, 1971, §D, at 2, col. 2.

(39) 8 HOUST. L. REV. 929, 948 (1971).

(40) Civil Action No. 5281 (E.D. Tex. Aug. 26, 1971).

(41) See United States v. State of Texas, 330 F. Supp. 235, 243 (E.D. Tex. 1971).

(42) 445 F.2d 1011 (5th Cir.) rev'g 326 F. Supp. 674 (W.D. Tex. 1971).

(43) 326 F. Supp. 674, 675 (W.D. Tex. 1971).

(44) Alvarado v. El Paso Ind. School Dist., 445 F.2d 1011 (5th Cir. 1971) (emphasis added).

(45) Civil Action No.   (W.D. Tex. June 1, 1971).

(46) San Antonio Express, June 25, 1971, § A, at 1, col. 2.

(47) 324 F. Supp. 599 (S.D. Tex. 1970).

(48) 402 U.S. 1 (1971). See generally Exelrod, Chicano Education: In Swann's Way? INEQUALITY IN EDUCATION 28 (1971).

(49) San Antonio Express, Aug. 20, 1971, § A, at 1, col. 3. Earlier, Judge Cox, a federal district court judge, issued a stay of Judge Seals' bussing mandate. The Fifth Circuit reversed.

(50) Id.

(51) No. 71-2397 (5th Cir. Oct. 7, 1971).

(52) Id. at 2.

(53) Civil Action No. C-70-37 RFP (N.D. Cal. Feb. 3, 1970).

MUTUAL PERCEPTIONS
OF RACIAL IMAGES:
WHITE, BLACK AND
JAPANESE AMERICAN

Minako Kurokawa

Stereotypes are not objectionable merely because they are generalizations about categories, since they are valuable when true. What is objectionable about them is their ethnocentrism and prejudice (Rose, 1964). Stereotypy is one of the most subtle yet powerful means of maintaining existing prejudices. At the core of the language of prejudice are *ethnophaulims* (*American Thesaurus of Slang*, 1953; *Dictionary of International Slurs*, 1944; Palmore, 1962), or derogatory terms used by the members of one ethnic group to describe the members of another. When openly expressed, they become a form of discrimination known as antilocution. The label attached to a person (or to a group) will determine the image of the person (group) to others as well as to himself, consequently affecting the behavior of the person and that of others toward him. Thus any derogatory epithet is detrimental to the self-esteem of the person and the esteem in which he is held by the rest of society.

All racial and ethnic groups use ethnophaulisms to refer to other groups. However, as Palmore (1962) observed, there is a close association between the amount of prejudice against an outgroup and the number of ethnophaulisms for it. The greater the hatred for a group, the more ethnophaulisms express and reinforce it, and vice versa. When the out-group is a different race, most ethnophaulisms express stereotyped physical differences or highly visible cultural differences involving such things as food, language, or common first names. The derivatives of most ethnophaulisms express some unfavorable stereotype.

In the white-dominant American society white ethnocentrism prevails, attributing a positive image to the whites and a negative one to other racial groups. Berlson and Salter's (1946) systematic study of characters in popular fiction between 1937 and 1943 indicated that the major parts were played by white Anglo-Saxon Protestants—tall, handsome, wealthy, intelligent, etc. In 1932 Katz and Braly (1933) asked 100 Princeton students to characterize various ethnic groups by selecting from a list of traits. Americans (whites) were described as industrious, intelligent, ambitious, and materialistic. Even Negroes, in 1935 and in 1942 (Meenes, 1943), described whites as intelligent, progressive, ambitious, and materialistic, although pleasure-loving and conceited. A 1950 sample (Gilbert, 1951) basically agreed with the previous samples on the image of whites, though indicating less unanimity among themselves than the 1932 sample.

In the 1932 study (Katz & Braly, 1933) Negroes were overwhelmingly described as superstitious (84%), lazy (75%), and happy-go-lucky (38%). Negroes themselves agreed in 1935 (Meenes, 1943) that they were superstitious (46%) but also gave less negative traits such as very religious (53%) and musical (54%). The 1950 students' views (Gilbert, 1951) of Negroes were more differentiated, yet they were not free from negative connotations. Such a negative racial image of Negroes reflected the white-black, master-slave relation of early days and the perpetuation of the inferior image of Negroes.

The Japanese, upon arrival in California, inherited the Chinese legacy of the "Yellow Peril" implying immorality, treachery, unscrupulous competition, and subversive intent (Hyde, 1955; Keim, 1941; Kurokawa, 1970; Mackie, 1857; Matthews, 1964; Prosser, 1908; tenBroek, 1968). In the initial stages Japanese and Chinese were lumped together under labels such as coolie, Asiatic, and yellow. The contraction "Jap," accentuated during World War II, first appeared consistently in the columns of the *Coast Seamen's Journal* during the 1890s (Matthews, 1964). However, except during World War II (Gundlach, 1944; Seago, 1947), the Japanese have generally been attributed positive qualities—such as intelligence, progressiveness, and industriousness (Gilbert, 1951; Katz & Braly, 1933; Meenes, 1943). In the thirties, as Katz and Braly (1933) observed, the people on the East Coast knew little about Asians except through California anti-Asian propaganda, but seemed to be aware of the rapid industrialization and modernization of Japan and viewed the Japanese in this framework.

Stereotypes provide categorical expections but the category may or may not confirm the expectancy. In short, minority members may accept the negative racial image and act accordingly, or they may rebel against the status of subordination Kurokawa, 1970).

There has been a great deal of literature (Bronfenbrenner, 1961; Simmons, 1961) implying that minority members accept the dominant image of themselves and reinforce it (the mirror image). This behavior is aptly called inauthenticity (Sartre, 1948; Seeman, 1966; Tiryakian, 1968). It is referred to by many people in portraying the behavior patterns of minority members. Observing the inauthentic Negro, Broyard (1950) defined authenticity as "stubborn adherence to one's essential self, in spite of the distorting pressures of one's situation." To Broyard, the Negro's essential self is his innate qualities and developed characteristics as an individual, as distinguished from his preponderantly defensive reactions as a member of an embattled minoirty. Avoiding a philosophical discussion of what is meant by essential self, Seeman (1966) analyzed three forms of inauthenticity (Goffman, 1963; Rinder & Campbell, 1952) in terms of social status and identity of categorical irrelevance, and of misconstruction and self-dection. In the first case the individual accepts an inappropriate identity which is defined by others. For instance, light Negro children are more acceptable to Negro children as friends than darker ones (Clark & Clark, 1947). Secondly, being convinced by the stereotype about his self-image, an individual is on guard in a way that leads to irrelevant imputations about the other's view of him. His behavior is guided by a misconstruction of the self. Thirdly, there is a subjective kind of inauthenticity, self-deception. Here a person has accepted the stereotype as his guide and does not allow himself to realize the falseness of his self-image. In short, the inauthentic person bases his behavior on a distorted view of reality and the distortion involves an overreference (Greenberg, 1950) to some status occupancy.

In recent years, however, assimilationism and conformity to white values have been challenged by those who advocate ethnic identity and, if necessary, a secessionist approach. The "Black is bautiful" movement seeks to create a new racial image of Negroes which is no longer subject to white racism. As a spin–off of "Black Power," there is an emergency of "Yellow Power" (Uyematsu, 1969) among the Asian Americans who have experienced a different type of discrimination. White conformity and racial identity advocates have supporters from different age brackets in each racial group, with the adults generally more conservative and the students more progressive.

The purpose of this paper is to compare the racial images of whites, blacks and certain yellows (Japanese Americans) as mutually perceived and differentially perceived by age groups.

METHODOLOGY

The research instrument used for college students and adults was the same as the one used by Katz and Braly (1933). A list of 84 adjectives was shown to the subjects who were instructed to choose 5 to describe each of the three groups: whites, blacks, and Japanese. Racial images held by children were determined by asking them to describe whites, blacks, and Japanese freely in their own words, rather than restricting them to the use of a difficult word list (Zeligs, 1941).

One hundred whites, 100 blacks and 100 Japanese American adults were selected by the quota sample method. This sample contained: (a) an equal number of males and females; (b) only adults in their forties; (c) a middle class vs. working class ratio of three to two for whites, and two to three for blacks and Japanese Americans, according to Hollingshead's (1957) two factor determinants of social class; and (d) only residents of Sacramento, California.

The college student sample consisted of 100 whites, 100 blacks, and 100 Japanese Americans at Sacramento State College. The test was given to several classes in order to select as a sample white and black students with equal numbers of both sexes and similar major subject composition for each group. Because the number of Japanese Americans in these classes was too small, the sample for this group was selected from the registration cards with the ratios of sex and major subject in mind. In addition to Sacramento students, who are considered to be relatively conservative, 50 Japanese American students were chosen from the Berkeley and the Los Angeles campuses of the University of California who were enrolled in the Asian American Study Programs and who were considered to be active in the civil rights movement. Here the sample was not intended to be random but was chosen to obtain a profile of politically active Japanese American students. They were predominantly social science majors of working-class origin.

For children, two white dominant schools and two racially mixed schools in Sacramento were selected, and the test was given to all the fourth and fifth graders in the classrooms. Later, 100 whites, 100 blacks, and 100 Japanese Americans were selected for analysis. Two-thirds of the whites were from the white dominant schools, while two-thirds of the blacks and the Japanese Americans were from the mixed schools.

It was hypothesized that positive traits will be attributed to whites by themselves, by blacks, and by Japanese Americans. The assimilation policy in American society has been a one-way flow toward the values and norms set by whites. The whites have considered themselves superior to people of other races. The blacks could not afford to attack the white supremacy (Abrahamas, 1970). The Japanese Americans, who were anxious to be accepted by the whites, accepted white values, although there is the interpretation that the whites and the Japanese Americans shared basically compatible values from the beginning (Caudill, 1952; Petersen, 1966).

Secondly, it was hypothesized that blacks, whites, and Japanese Americans are all likely to attribute negative traits to the blacks. The white derogation of blacks is the direct derivative of white supremacy. On the part of blacks, inauthenticity (acceptance of stereotype) might have been one of the few channels open to them to cope with frustration (Abrahamas, 1970; Broyard, 1950). Japanese Americans are likely to accept white values, including the latter's prejudice against blacks.

Thirdly, it was hypothesized that the general image of the Japanese perceived by Japanese Americans, by whites, and by blacks consists of positive attributes such as industriousness, intelligence, and ambition, but that there are some ambiguous feelings expressed by various groups about the status of the Japanese Americans. Traditionally Japanese Americans have been cited to blacks and other less successful minority groups as a model minority, being industrious and quiet. However, the image of the "quiet Americans" (Hosokawa, 1969) has been seriously criticized by Japanese American youths who feel that it has been used to perpetuate white racism.

It was hypothesized that middle-aged adults are more likely than college students or school children to accept stereotypical images of racial groups, including their own. This is based on the assumption that the adults have gone through a longer period of socialization involving conformity to the core values of the society and that they have established status in the society which they are afraid of losing.

In contrast, college students, who are encouraged to evaluate facts critically and who do not fear a loss of status in society, are likely to examine stereotypes with more open minds and to consider members of racial groups individually rather than categorically.

Prediction of child behavior is difficult because of the shortness of the socialization period and the variation in its contents. Children of ethnocentric parents are likely to accept stereotypes expressed by their parents. Because of lack of inhibition, children are more candid than adults about revealing prejudice and are more ready to make nasty remarks about children of other races. On the other hand, pre-adolescent children who have not started dating are relatively nondiscriminating in making friends. It is hypothesized that children in white dominant schools are likely to accept stereotyped images of racial groups and to be more explicit about expressing prejudice than are adults, but children in mixed schools are likely to have nonstereotypical ideas of children of different races (Fishman, 1961; Zeligs, 1941).

IMAGES OF WHITES

Adults. The hypothesis that whites are viewed with completely positive attributes by themselves and by others was only partially supported. It is true that none of the traits mentioned was entirely negative, but some of them were netural or connoted noncommendable qualities (see Table 1). In comparison with the picture of whites in 1932 as industrious, intelligent, and ambitious (Katz & Braly, 1933), the 1970 image of whites was predominantly that of being pleasure loving, materialistic, aggressive, and ambitious. The fact that the "pleasure loving" collected the greatest votes from whites (83%) seems to indicate that they do not consider it as a bad quality, although the reference to this behavior may reveal self-criticism. The white middle class value of instrumental activism, described by Parsons (1937), Merton (1957), and others, is accompanied by Veblen's (1934) "conspicuous consumption." White Americans in this study were significantly more likely to consider themselves to be progressive, industrious, and imaginative than did others who viewed the whites.

The Japanese American adults chosen in this sample were all nisei (the second generation). Based on previous literature (Caudill, 1952; Petersen, 1966) concerning the value compatibility between the Japanese and the Americans and their psychological make-up as quiet Americans (Hosokawa, 1969), it was expected that the discrepancy between the white and the nisei views would be very small. The data indicate major agreement between the two for the following traits: pleasure-loving, aggressive, ambitious, intelligent, individualistic, scientifically minded, alert and practical. There were, however, also disparities; whites described themselves significantly more frequently than the nisei to be progressive, industrious, conventional and imaginative. On the other hand, the nisei viewed whites as talkative, gregarious, and argumentative.

Students. The order of selection of traits by students was similiar to that of the adults (see Table 2). The whites were predominantly described by all the student samples as materialistic, aggressive, pleasure loving, and ambitious. However, as hypothesized in terms of age differentiation, the adults were significantly more stereotypical than the students (Significant at the .05 level by the Kolmogorov-Smirnov test of dispersion. The differences in dispersions of distributions are estimated by this test throughout the paper.) The responses of the latter were dispersed over a wide range of characteristics rather than clustered about a few traits. The degree of dispersion was measured by the number of traits which received 50% of the votes. If there had been no patterning in the picture that the respondents had of the whites, 42 (half of 84 characteristics listed) of the traits would have received 50% of the votes; if the respondents agreed perfectly on the 5 traits that were typical of a group, 2.5 traits would have received 50% of the votes. The degree of uniformity in attitudes among white adults was shown by the fact that only 3.9 traits were needed to include half of all selections referring to the whites, compared with 7.8 traits in the case of white students.

Furthermore, the differentiated and less stereotypical views of the students included negative traits for whites, imputation of which varied according to the race of the students. The black students were significantly more likely to describe whites as conceited and deceitful than were the white and the Sacramento sansei students. It should be recalled that few black adults portrayed whites negatively.

The areas of discrepancy and the degree of discrepancy between the white and Japanese American views did not differ greatly between adults and students. The whites often attributed to themselves a positive trait such as industriousness (30%), which was hardly marked by the Japanese American students. Instead, the latter tended to describe whites as talkative and straightforward, which might have been keenly felt by the "quiet Americans" (Hosokawa, 1969). The sensei, college-aged third generation Japanese Americans still seemed to have an image of whites similar to that of their parents. The main generational difference was that the students agreed upon significantly fewer traits than the adults; the sansei's ideas were more differentiated than the nisei's. Also the sansei seemed to be slightly more critical of whites than the nisei in that the former paid little attention to the positive attributes of the whites given by the latter.

Politically active Japanese American students in Berkeley and Los Angeles were more rigid and negative than others in describing whites; fifty percent of their votes clustered upon 5.5 traits: materialistic, pleasure loving, aggressive, deceitful, and conceited. Ambitiousness and industriousness were the expressions they used the least. This pattern seems to illustrate their politically

TABLE 1
ADULT IMAGES OF RACIAL GROUPS (IN PERCENTAGES)

	Image of Whites				Image of Blacks				Image of Japanese		
Trait	**W**	**B**	**JA**	**Trait**	**W**	**B**	**JA**	**Trait**	**W**	**B**	**JA**
Pleasure loving	83	71	75	Musical	69	81**	87	Loyal to family	77*	60	50
Materialistic	63**	45	50	Pleasure loving	42	54	50	Ambitious	50*	52**	33
Aggressive	50	40**	62	Loud	38*	21**	40	Courteous	50*	62***	32
Ambitious	50	42	50	Lazy	35		35	Industrious	50*	41	62
Progressive	42**	20	25	Happy-go-lucky	31	32		Efficient	42**		21
Industrious	29			Sensitive	31			Intelligent	42*	21	
Intelligent	29	23	21	Aggressive	19	23	19	Artistic	31		
Individualistic	29		21	Jovial	19*	35	33	Tradition loving	31	20	
Conventional	25			Materialistic	19	21		Conservative	27		48
Scientifically minded	25		25	Very religious	19*	33		Neat	27**	23	50
Alert	21		23	Quick tempered	27	23	22	Alert	23	35	23
Imaginative	21			Quarrelsome	23		17	Quiet	23		23
Practical	21	25	23	Revengeful	23			Reserved	23	23	52
Talkative			48	Talkative			38	Practical			32
Gregarious			21	Unreliable			27	Conventional			25
Argumentative			21	Ignorant		24	25	Honest			23
				Impulsive			27	Faithful			19
				Frivolous			25	Imitative			19
# of traits on which 50% of the sample are dispersed.	3.9	6.6	4.4		6.1	6.5	5.0		4.8	5.0	5.1

Note.—W: white adults, B: black adults, JA: Japanese American adults; N for each sample is 100.

$\llcorner \cdot \lrcorner$ $p < .05$
$\llcorner \cdot\cdot \lrcorner$ $p < .01$

TABLE 2

STUDENT IMAGES OF RACIAL GROUPS (PERCENTAGES)

Image of Whites					Image of Blacks					Image of Japanese				
Trait	W	B	JA₁	JA₂	Trait	W	B	JA₁	JA₂	Trait	W	B	JA₁	JA₂
Materialistic	67	43	50	70	Musical	38	61	50	40	Loyal to family	67	51	31	40
Aggressive	46	34	27	34	Aggressive	32	45	23	50	Ambitious	51	42	31	21
Pleasure loving	32	41	42	68	Impulsive	32	21	15	20	Intelligent	38	33		20
Ambitious	30	21	23		Persistent	24			36	Industrious	35	32	35	20
Industrious	30				Pleasure loving	22	15			Courteous	27	23	23	16
Impulsive	22		23	20	Straightforward	19	34	19	54	Conventional	24			22
Stubborn	16			18	Grasping	19				Efficient	19		15	
Conservative			23	18	Revengeful	16			38	Neat	16		15	
Talkative			23	26	Quick tempered		25	31	26	Tradition loving			38	30
Straightforward			15	26	Jovial		25	23	20	Reserved		25	31	38
Conceited		35		34	Materialistic		21	19		Conservative			27	54
Deceitful		37		40						Artistic			23	20
										Quiet		23	19	60
# of traits on which 50% of the sample are dispersed.	7.8	10.3	10.3	5.5		11.0	14.0	8.0	6.6		7.5	9.1	9.0	6.1

Note.—W: white students, B: black students, JA₁: Japanese American students, JA₂: Japanese American students at University of California; N for W, B, and JA₁ is 100 each; for JA₂, N is 50.

$p < .05$
$p < .01$

militant stance against "white racism" embodied in the materialism and pleasurism of capitalism.

Children. Since children were asked to describe racial groups freely in their own terms, the area covered by them was broad (see Table 3). The responses indicated that their frame of reference was their peers at school and their parents as representatives of racial groups.

The hypothesis that whites are described in positive terms alone was not supported among children, although the proportion of negative descriptions was small in general. Also, black and Japanese American children in white dominant schools were significantly more likely to refer to negative traits of whites than were their mixed-school counterparts.

As did the adults, children of all racial groups in both white dominant and racially mixed schools described whites repeatedly in economic terms. The whites have higher living standards, are rich, have big houses, and so on. The white children themselves pointed out that whites are materialistic and pleasure loving, while Japanese Americans and black children described whites as snobbish and conceited. Although white children are the product of the affluent society and enjoy it, they showed some difference in attitudes from their parental generation. The white adults described themselves as materialistic, pleasure loving, conventional, and practical, but very few emphasized the factors of being individualistic, religious, faithful, kind, democratic, and industrious. The white children, on the other hand, have not gone through the actual economic competition, nor have they been molded into conventions. Thus 48% of the children seemed to uphold idealistic images of the Americans—individualistic, industrious, ambitious—and 30% mentioned religiousness, faithfulness, and honesty. It is interesting to note that hardly any of the "Protestant ethic" traits were mentioned, directly or indirectly, by the blacks or by the Japanese Americans as attributes of whites.

For children of this age (fourth and fifth graders), the major concern was acceptance by peers, hence they emphasized sociability—popularity, leadership, and athletic prowess—rather than scholarship. As hypothesized, the majority of white children (65%) in white dominant schools described themselves as popular stars and leaders. They gave detailed reasons for whites' popularity—"they are nice, smart, tall, neat, pretty, handsome, dress well, and are good in sports"—which seems to be the reflection of heroes and heroines in fiction. In fact, many children indicated that these were desired rather than real images as they remarked wishfully that they would like to grow up to be tall, handsome, athletic, and attractive. The white popularity was recognized among black and Japanese American children, but significantly less frequently than among whites. Also, black and Japanese American children simply stated that whites are nice, kind, friendly, smart, fun to be with, or play well without elaborating on their physical attractiveness.

With reference to the age-specific hypothesis, note that the racial composition of schools had a different bearing on the dominant and the minority children in their perception of whites. White children in mixed schools were significantly

TABLE 3
CHILD IMAGES OF RACIAL GROUPS (PERCENTAGES)

Image of Whites

	W	B	JA
Economic features High living level, materialistic, snobbish	55 (64)	61 (50)	52 (50)
Protestant ethic Ambitious, industrious, practical, individualistic	48 (45)		
Religiosity Faithful, honest, kind, religious	(28)		
Popularity: Leadership Center of attraction, tall, handsome	65 (41)	32 (40)	28 (30)
Friendliness Outgoing, friendly	27 (26)	21 (40)	28 (62)
Negative traits Aggressive, mean, cheating	22 (20)	60 (33)	74 (30)
Physical differences Color of skin		50 (30)	30 (16)

Image of Blacks

	W	B	JA
Positive traits Good in sports, in music, in dancing	31 (50)	40 (57)	32 (46)
Friendliness Sensitive, jovial, happy, nice, outgoing	25 (30)	48 (65)	18 (30)
Neutrality Larger family, poor, different language	34 (40)	60 (30)	18 (20)
Negative traits Lazy, not smart, mean, fighting	82 (28)	20 (15)	36 (30)
Physical difference Curly hair, big nose, big lips		56 (25)	26 (20)

Image of Japanese

	W	B	JA
Quietness Shy, not speaking in classes	78 (38)	80 (39)	68 (40)
Tolerance "O.K.," nice, good	20 (50)	15 (45)	26 (68)
Intelligence Smart, good grades	65 (46)	60 (50)	82 (70)
Traditionalism Loyal to family	36 (38)	45 (49)	56 (58)
Negative traits	17	19	28
Physical difference	11	71 (20)	18

Note.—W: white, B: black, JA: Japanese American; N for each total sample is 100. Figures in parentheses refer to racially mixed school; upper figures refer to white dominant school.

* $p < .05$
** $p < .01$

less conscious of white popularity than their white-dominant school counterparts; while the school climate did not produce a significant difference in the perception of whites among the minority children.

Concerning interpersonal relations, whites were described as straightforward and friendly by a quarter of white children and a quarter of black and Japanese American children in the white dominant schools. Some Japanese American children in white dominant schools (28%) emphasized their friendship with white children but their descriptions were tainted with gratitude for patronage by the whites: "I have a good friend who is White. His folks treat me just like their family. They are like my own family." "My friend [white] is good to me. He draws me out of my shell." These statements were rarely found in the mixed schools, where friendship seemed to be based on more equal terms than at white dominant schools. Significantly greater percentages of blacks and Japanese in mixed schools than in white dominant schools claimed that whites were "friendly, nice, or good friends."

There was a significant difference in negative perception of whites in different school settings. As expected, white children gave few negative traits—aggressive, impulsive, conceited—which might even be interpreted as neutral. In contrast, in white dominant schools as many as 60% of black children and 74% of Japanese Americans attributed negative traits to the whites—mean, nasty, conceited, cheating, noisy, crazy, nutty. The Japanese American children complained particularly about the talkativeness of white children. The percentages of blacks and Japanese Americans reporting negative qualities in whites fell significantly in the racially mixed schools.

Another difference in perception of the white image was that while whites rarely refer to their physical differences, blacks (50% in white dominant schools and 30% in mixed schools) and Japanese Americans (30% in white dominant schools and 16% in the mixed schools)were more concerned with physical appearances, particularly the color of the skin.

IMAGES OF BLACKS

Adults. Although there were negative attributes given to blacks, such as loud, lazy, quarrelsome, the 1970 picture of blacks was entirely different from that of 1932 (Katz & Braly, 1933), which consisted of superstitiousness (84%), laziness (75%), ignorance (38%), or even physical dirtiness (17%). The predominant feature of the contemporary blacks depicted by themselves, by whites, and by Japanese Americans was their musicalness, which is a neutral epithet. The three groups agreed that blacks are pleasure loving, loud, aggressive, jovial, and quick tempered. The white view of blacks as sensitive (31%), revengeful (23%), and aggressive (19%) may reflect the former's apprehensiveness about contemporary militant blacks. The blacks described themselves as musical, pleasure loving, loud, happy-go-lucky, jovial, and quick tempered, but avoided distinctly negative attributes. It was the Japanese Americans who were most critical about blacks, depicting the latter in the classical stereotype of the Negro slave—lazy, ignorant, unreliable, impulsive, frivolous, musical, pleasure loving, and loud (see Table 1).

Students. Being musical was the dominant quality selected by all the racial groups, particularly frequently by blacks themselves (61%). Also consensus was found among the groups on the traits of aggressiveness, impulsiveness, and straightforwardness. The white description of blacks as persistent, revengeful, grasping, and aggressive seemed to convey white anxiety toward the rise of Black Power.

The black's self-image and the image perceived by the Sacramento Japanese American students agreed fairly well, although blacks accentuated certain traits more than the Japanese did. The Sacramento Japanese Americans' portrait of blacks reminds one of the black jazz band—musical, impulsive, quick tempered, jovial, and straightforward.

The politically active University of California Japanese American students emphasized black characteristics different from those of other groups. Although musicality, joviality, and impulsiveness were mentioned, a large percentage named such traits as aggressiveness, persistence, straightforwardness, and revenge seeking.

The age-specific hypothesis that students were significantly less stereotypical than adults in their description of racial images (see Table 2) was supported also for black imagery.

Children. As many as 82% of the white children in white dominant schools gave negative traits to blacks, the nature of which was somewhat different from those given by adults. Adults simply said that blacks are loud, grasping, aggressive, and revengeful; few mentioned such classical stereotypical traits as laziness and ignorance. On the other hand, school children were much more explicit in expressing their negative views about blacks. These views can be divided into three groups: (a) less intelligent, ignorant, stupid, lazy, smelling bad, physically dirty; (b) suspicious, stubborn, sly, unreliable, mean, having blood-shot eyes; (c) talkative, pugnacious, noisy, ostentatious, agitating, quarrelsome, tough, quick tempered, fighting, and aggressive (see Table 3).

However, the composition of the school had an impact upon the child's image of blacks. In racially mixed schools the percentage of negative responses by white children was only 28% in contrast to the 82% in the white dominant school. Also the percentage of positive responses about the black image was greater in the mixed school than in the white dominant school. The difference was particularly notable among white children.

Positive traits given by white children included two aspects: (a) attractiveness, consisting of sportsmanship, musical talent, and physical appearance; and (b) interpersonal relations, indicating their friendliness, sensitivity, joviality, aliveness—"fun to be with."

Over a third of the white children in white schools gave seemingly neutral factual descriptions, such as that blacks have different color of the skin, different language, go to different schools, are poor and hungry, are often absent from school, have large families, and their fathers are absent from home. These observations may indicate a lack of understanding of the underlying causes of the black's behavior. Also the fact is that these white children in white dominant schools did not have much personal contact with lower class black children; although they appeared knowledgeable about the black family and its social life, they often had only second-hand information from school textbooks and mass media, which are not free from biases (Marcus, 1961). Of the 40% of neutral responses of white children in mixed schools, 24% simply said that there is no difference whether the child is white or black.

A significantly larger percentage of black children in white dominant schools than others gave neutral descriptions. These children were not from the lower social class since the white-dominant school district usually coincides with the better residential quarters. It appears that they felt they should not give negative traits to the poorer blacks but seemed to be preoccupied with their distinctness from whites either in a sociological or a physiological context. Note that a significantly greater percentage of black children in white dominant schools than in mixed schools were conscious of the physical difference of blacks, such as bigger nose, bigger lips, curly hair, or dark skin.

A small percentage of self-descriptions by black children were negative, such as being stupid and quarrelsome. In comparison to white children, however, the list of negative traits cited by black children was far more restricted and of a much milder nature. Naturally they emphasized positive qualities. Nearly half of those in the white dominant school described blacks as being good in sports, music and dancing, and another half (some overlapping) reported that blacks are friendly and outgoing. The self-image of black children was still better in the mixed school.

Contrary to our hypothesis, Japanese American children, even in white dominant schools, were significantly less prejudiced toward blacks than the white children were. Only 36% of the former but 82% of the latter described blacks in negative terms. Japanese American children said that blacks are tough, mean, ugly, bad cheaters, make trouble, and talk too much, but nobody referred to the stereotypical image of blacks in the ghetto—having blood-shot eyes, smelling badly, or physically dirty.

A third of the Japanese American children mentioned the black's laziness, but few said that blacks were poor. On this matter, however, the white description is much more elaborate and detailed than that by Japanese American children. A quarter of the Japanese American children gave neutral descriptions, such as physical differences, mostly referring to the color of the skin.

A third of the Japanese American children in the white dominant school gave positive traits such as blacks' being good in sports and dancing. On a more personal level, Japanese Americans in the white dominant school said that "some" blacks are nice, while in the mixed school this qualification was seldom used. Another positive comment from Japanese American children was that blacks are strong because "they will stand up for you if someone is bad to you."

IMAGES OF JAPANESE

Adults. As hypothesized, the Japanese were described in positive terms as ambitious, industrious, efficient, and intelligent. In addition to such instrumental activism (Merton, 1957; Parsons, 1937), their traditionalism and familism were prevalent features. They were also described as courteous, reserved, and quiet. Although the expressions and emphases were slightly different, the traits chosen by the three racial groups were similar. The only negative quality, imitativeness, was pointed out by the nisei.

Students. As hypothesized, no negative traits were attributed the Japanese by any of the student samples studied. The Japanese were depicted as having a combination of instrumental activism and traditionalism.

With regard to the controversial label, "quietness," the radical sansei used it significantly more frequently than any other group. This in addition to the fact that the Japanese American characterized whites and blacks as talkative and aggressive, seems to expose a self-perception as quiet Americans. However, it should be noted that this was not a mirroring of the whites' image of them because whites did not think of the Japanese as quiet, at least not this student sample.

The second hypothesis—that students were less stereotypical than adults—was supported. The nisei were significantly more likely than the sansei to describe the Japanese as industrious and reserved. On the one hand, it might have been anticipated that the nisei would be more critical of the Japanese than the sansei since the former are anxious to become "Americanized" (accepted by the whites), while the sansei are reproachful of this type of conformity. On the other hand, the reserve hypothesis can be established: The nisei, who know more about Japan, are protective of the traditional cultural values, whereas the sansei do not appreciate the virtue of, say, quietness. In the sample studied, neither nisei nor sansei portrayed the Japanese in a negative image. The nisei's observation of the Japanese seemed to be slightly more detailed than the sansei's which might indicate the former's greater familiarity with the Japanese. For instance, while the nisei pointed out the traditional virtues of honesty and faithfulness, they did not fail to mention imitativeness. In case of the radical sansei, however, their use of quietness to describe the Japanese can be interpreted as their negative evaluation of docility.

Children. As hypothesized, children in general depicted the Japanese in positive or at least neutral terms, such as intelligent, quiet, traditional, and nice. The percentage of children giving negative views of the Japanese was small in the white dominant schools and almost nil in the mixed schools. Some said that "some" Japanese are sly, cruel, and warlike as often shown on TV. The more subtle and pervasive comments by white and black children were that the Japanese are stubborn, evasive, clannish, mask their feelings, and act strange to others. The Japanese American children were self-critical, referring to their clannishness.

In white dominant schools the Japanese were depicted by the majority of white (78%) and black (80%) children as quiet—bashful, shy, dainty, humorless, square, evasive, aren't bullies, not show-offs, don't say much in class although friendly once you get to know them. The Japanese American children themselves (67%) described Japanese as soft-spoken, quiet, polite, reserved, and nonaggressive. However, the percentage of those who reported quietness in the

Japanese fell significantly in the mixed schools. Here, over half of the children said that the Japanese are nice, kind, good, friendly, happy, and so on; the percentage of those reporting such favorable qualities was significantly smaller at white dominant schools. The children of all the sample groups agreed exceptionally well that the most outstanding feature of the Japanese is their intelligence. The Japanese were overwhelmingly described as smart, industrious, ambitious, intelligent, practical, alert and sophisticated. Some made the profound statement for children of this age that the Japanese have a strong inner desire to succeed.

Over a third of the white children and approximately half of the black and the Japanese American children noted the traditional culture aspects of the Japanese, describing them as loyal to their family ties, religious, courteous, neat, honest, artistic, good at hand work, and that they wear silk clothes. The white and the black children in white dominant schools more often offered superficial observations, such as "Japanese wear silk clothes," "they use chop-sticks," "they make pretty things," observations more likely formed through visits to ethnic areas than through personal contacts. Some of the Japanese American children who stressed traditional aspects indicated that their parents "are too strict, are old fashioned, have an accent, and sometimes are embarrassing."

The percentage of white and Japanese American children who pointed out the physical differences of the Japanese was small, but black children in white dominant schools seemed to be very aware (71%) of the physical differences (Arkoff & Herbert, 1966; Wagatsuma, 1968) of the Japanese black hair, funny eyes, slanted eyes, skinny, short—which may reflect their own concern with racial visibility.

SUMMARY AND DISCUSSION

In the 1932 Princeton study (Katz & Braly, 1933), whites were described as industrious, intelligent, ambitious, and materialistic; blacks were superstitious, lazy, ignorant, and happy-go-lucky; and the Japanese, intelligent, industrious, and progressive. In this 1970 Sacramento study, whites were portrayed as materialistic, straightforward, and pleasure loving; blacks were musical, impulsive, and aggressive; and the Japanese, loyal to family, ambitious and intelligent. However, the location and the composition of the samples as well as the time of these studies were so different that the concern of this paper is not with changes in stereotypes over time, but rather with the comparisons of (a) self- vs. other-perceptions of racial images, and (b) adults', students', and children's images of the three racial groups of whites, blacks and Japanese.

It was hypothesized that whites would in general receive attributions of positive traits from themselves, from blacks, and from Japanese Americans. Reciprocal hypotheses concerning the minority groups were that blacks are described in negative terms and that Japanese are portrayed as quiet and reserved, although industriousness and progressiveness are mentioned by themselves as well as by others. The age-specific hypotheses dealt with the degree of inauthenticity among adults, students, and children, stating (a) that adults were more likely than students to accept stereotypes even if acceptance involved a negative self-image (inauthenticity); and (b) that children from racially mixed schools held less stereotypical images than those from white dominant schools.

The images of whites to adults and students in the sample studied was predominantly pleasure loving and materialistic. Whether this is positive or negative depends on one's frame of reference. In the stoic, industrious Puritanism or Confucian view, materialism and love of pleasure are not virtues but should be restrained to attain higher spiritual goals. In the 1930 findings emphasis was placed on diligence and ambition to secure material success. In 1970 whites seem to be enjoying the fruits of the affluent society with pride, and other racial groups may have accepted it with envy—and possibly with cynicism.

The children's image of whites was also laden with economic features—"they are rich, have bigger houses, higher living standards." However, the children's main concern was popularity and leadership in the school context. The whites were considered by all three racial groups to be most popular and the center of attraction.

Contemporary blacks were no longer portrayed in negative or passive terms (such as lazy, ignorant, or physically dirty) but were considered to be (a) carefree, musical, pleasure loving, jovial, and (b) militant and aggressive. There was some variation of opinions in race- and age-specific groups. To whites, blacks seemed to be revengeful, sensitive, and aggressive, which might be interpreted as the anxiety of whites about the rising power of blacks. It was rather the Japanese American adult who was critical of blacks. The nisei, who may have been anxious to be accepted by whites and who may have overconformed (Prosser, 1908; Seago, 1947) to white values including the anti-black prejudice; seemed to be still revealing his old prejudice. Or it may be that the economically successful nisei is intolerant of the Negro, whom he sees as lazy and therefore unsuccessful (Caudill, 1952; Parsons, 1937; Petersen, 1966).

These hard-working, conforming, non-complaining, and economically successful nisei have been labelled as quiet Americans (Hosokawa, 1969) by politically radical sansei (the third-generation Japanese Americans). The latter are rebelling against the image of the quiet Americans and are inclined to adopt as a model the tactics of confrontation used by blacks. In this sense they have good reason to view blacks in the framework of militancy and aggression. They do not, or they refuse to, consider the blacks to be lazy or ignorant. If they feel blacks are lazy, the sensei might blame society for inducing them to laziness. Some sansei claim that the Japanese American success story of dilligence without complaint is nothing but the rationalization of an unfair social structure and helps to perpetuate institutionalized racism.

The majority of white and black children in white dominant schools expressed negative views of blacks. It is interesting to note that white children had negative images of blacks which were mainly derived from the latter's conduct rather than from the physical differences, while black children's negative self-image seemed to revolve around physical unattractiveness and economic deprivation. One might hazard a guess that both parties were defensive in different ways. The blacks claim that they are not considered attractive because of their physical appearance (Arkoff & Herbert, 1966; Wagatsuma, 1968), which results in low self-esteem and in undesirable behavior. The white children might assert that they are not concerned with physical differences, but that they cannot tolerate anybody being lazy or a troublemaker.

The image of the Japanese was a combination of traditionalism and modernity. They are perceived as loyal to their families, courteous, tradition loving, quiet, and reserved, and yet ambitious, industrious, intelligent, and efficient. While whites did not describe the Japanese as exceptionally quiet or reserved, the Japanese Americans seemed to be concerned with these traits. Furthermore, the latter tended to describe whites and blacks as talkative and straightforward. This may be the result of overconformity (Broyard, 1950; Prosser, 1908; Rinder & Campbell, 1952) and anticipatory socialization. Feeling that they are labelled as "quiet" implicitly or explicitly by the dominant group, they accept this image and act accordingly so as to avoid conflict. Additionally, the sansei college students of this study did not want to be docile and were frustrated by the average Japanese who they thought is too quiet. Finally, quietness does not necessarily imply a negative evaluation. The sansei may have been referring to the traditional Japanese value of disciplined strength under the surface of quietude (Nitobe, 1969).

The hypothesis of the minority member's inauthentic acceptance of a negative stereotype was not completely supported in this study. In the past several years the civil rights movements have changed their direction (Bell and Kristol, 1968). After a long period of struggle toward integration, some blacks are shifting their tactics toward secessionism, and some yellows are realizing the importance of self-realization instead of accommodation. Various antidefamation slogans such as "Black is beautiful," "Awakened Quiet Americans Are Speaking Up," are attempts to change negative images. Under these circumstances, the interpretation of the stereotypical racial images is very complex. When the politically-active socially-aware Japanese American students say that the Japanese are quiet, they are not meekly accepting the dominant white view of the Japanese. Instead, they are defying white soceity, which they believe has created and perpetuated the image of the quiet Japanese (tenBroek, 1968). The present study seems to indicate that, except among children, explicitly derogatory racial epithets are disappearing—perhaps to be replaced by more subtle ethnic humor. Whether it is white racism or reverse racism, it is hoped that the new stereotypes being created represent the categories more accurately than the classical ones have.

In the sample studied, white children in white dominant schools were significantly more likely than their mixed school counterparts to be impressed by their popularity and to view minorities in stereotypical frameworks. Black children in white dominant schools were more conscious of the physical differences among racial groups, found more fault with whites and were less likely to consider people, regardless of race, friendly than did black children in mixed schools. In the mixed schools the Japanese American children seemed to fare better than in white dominant schools, reporting whites to be friendly and the Japanese to be outgoing.

These findings imply positive effects of racial integration on school children. Minority children in white dominant schools seemed to be constantly aware of physical differences, felt intimidated by the dominant whites, and seemed unable to develop their potentialities. In racially mixed schools children of various racial groups held less stereotypical images of one another and reported more genuine and friendly interaction.

This seems to confirm the thesis that ignorance is a barrier to communication and that the more one knows about a person the less likely he is to feel hostility toward him (Allport, 1954; Blalock, 1967; Goodman, 1964). However, whether or not contact will decrease the amount of prejudice depends on the nature of the contact. While casual, superficial contact may reinforce prejudice, contacts that bring knowledge and acquaintance are likely to engender sounder beliefs concerning racial groups. School contact, if properly guided, may foster mutual understanding among children of various racial backgrounds.

REFERENCES

Abrahamas, D. Positively black. Engelwood Cliffs: Prentice-Hall, 1970.

Allport, G.W. The nature of prejudice. New York: Doubleday, 1965.

American thesaurus of slang. New York: Thomas Y. Crowell, 1953.

Arkoff, A., & Herbert, B. Body image and body dissatisfaction in Japanese Americans. Journal of Social Psychology, 1966, 68, 323-330.

Bell, D., & Kristol, I. (Eds.) Confrontation. New York: Basic Books, 1968.

Berlson, B., & Salter, P.J. Majority and minority Americans: An analysis of magazine fiction. Public Opinion Quarterly, 1946, 10, 168-190.

Blalock, H.M. Toward a theory of minority-group relations. New York: Wiley, 1967.

Bronfenbrenner, U. The mirror image in Soviet-American relations. Journal of Social Issues, 1961, 17 (3) 45-56.

Broyard, A. Portrait of the inauthentic Negro. Commentary, 1950, 10, 56—64.

Caudill, W. Japanese-American personality and acculturation. Genetic Psychology Monographs, 1952, 45, 3—102.

Clark, K., & Clark, M.P. Racial identification and preference in Negro children. In T.M. Newcomb and E.L. Hartley (Eds.), Readings in social psychology. New York: Holt, 1947.

Dictionary of International Slurs. Cambridge: Sci-Art Publishers, 1944.

Fishman, J.A. Childhood indoctrination for minority-group membership. Daedalus, 1961, 329-349.

Gilbert, G.M. Stereotype persistence and change among college students. Journal of Abnormal and Social Psychology, 1951, 46, 245-254.

Goffman, E. Stigma: Notes on the management of spoiled identity. Englewood Cliffs: Prentice-Hall, 1963.

Goodman, M.E. Race awareness among children. New York: Macmillan, 1964.

Greenberg, C. Self-hatred and Jewish chauvinism. Commentary, 1950, 10, 426-433.

Gundlach, R.H. The attitudes of enemy, allied, and domestic nationality groups as seen by college students of different regions. Journal of Social Psychology, 1944, 19, 249-258.

Hollingshead, A.H. Two factor index of social position. New Haven: Author, 1957.

Hosokawa, W. Nisei: The quiet Americans. New York: William Morrow, 1969.

Hyde, S.W. The Chinese stereotype in American melodrama. California Historical Society Quarterly, 1955, 357-367.

Katz, D., & Braly, K.W. Verbal stereotypes and racial prejudice. Journal of Abnormal and Social Psychology, 1933, 28, 280-290.

Keim, M.L. The Chinese as portrayed in the works of Bret Harte. Sociology and Social Research, 1941, 26, 441–450.

Kurokawa, M. Minority responses: Comparative views of reaction to subordination. New York: Random House, 1970.

Mackie, J.M. The Chinamen. Putnam's Monthly, 1857, 337-350.

Marcus. L. The Treatment of minorities in secondary school textbooks. (Pamphlet) New York: Anti-Defamation League of B'nai B'rith, 1961.

Matthews, F.H. White community and 'Yellow Peril.' Mississippi Valley Historical Review, 1964, 612-633.

Meenes, M. A comparison of racial stereotypes of 1935 and 1942. Journal of Social Psychology, 1943, 17, 327–336.

Merton, R.K. Social theory and social structure. Glencoe: Free Press, 1957.

Nitobe, I. Bushido: The soul of Japan. Rutland, Vermont: Charles E. Tuttle, 1969.

Palmore, E.B. Ethnophaulisms and ethnocentrism. American Journal of Sociology, 1962, 67, 442-445.

Parsons, T. The structure of social action. Glencoe: Free Press, 1937.

Petersen, W. Success story: Japanese American style. New York Times, January 9, 1966.

Prosser, W. T. The western view of the Japanese. World's Work, 1908, 10980–10991.

Rinder, I.D., & Campbell, D.T. Varieties of inauthenticity. Phylon, 1952, 13, 270–275.

Rose, P.I. They and we. New York: Random House, 1964.

Sartre, J. Portrait of the inauthentic Jew. Commentary, 1948, 389–397.

Seago, D.W. Stereotypes: Before Pearl Harbor and after. Journal of Psychology, 1947, 23, 55–63.

Seeman, M. Status and identity: The problem of inauthenticity. Pacific Sociological Review, 1966, 9, 67-73.

Simmons, O. G. The mutual images and expectations of Anglo-Americans and

Mexican-Americans, Daedalus, 1961, 286—299.

tenBroek, J., et al. Prejudice, war and the constitution. Berkeley: University of California Press, 1968.

Tiryakian, E.A. The existential self and the person. In C. Gordon and K.J. Gergen (Eds.) The self in social interaction. Vol. 1. New York: Wiley, 1968.

Uyematsu, A. The emergence of yellow power in America. Gidra, October 1969.

Veblen, T. The theory of the leisure class. New York: Modern Library, 1934.

Wagatsuma, H. The social perception of skin color in Japan. In J.H. Franklin (Ed.), Color and race. Boston: Beacon, 1968.

Zeligs, R. Influencing children's attitudes toward the Chinese. Sociology and Social Research, 1941, 26, 126-138.